CRUEL BUT NOT UNUSUAL

CRUEL BUT NOT UNUSUAL

Violence in Canadian Families
2nd edition

Ramona Alaggia & Cathy Vine, editors

WILFRID LAURIER
UNIVERSITY PRESS

Wilfrid Laurier University Press acknowledges the financial support of the Government of Canada through the Canada Book Fund for our publishing activities.

Library and Archives Canada Cataloguing in Publication

Cruel but not unusual : violence in Canadian families / Ramona Alaggia and Cathy Vine, editors. — 2nd ed.

Includes bibliographical references and index.
Also issued in electronic format.
ISBN 978-1-55458-827-5

1. Family violence—Canada. 2. Women—Violence against—Canada. 3. Children and violence—Canada. 4. Abused elderly—Canada. I. Alaggia, Ramona, 1957– II. Vine, Cathy, 1958–
HV6626.23.C3C79 2012   362.82'920971   C2012-904270-6

Electronic monograph issued in multiple formats.
Also issued in print format.
ISBN 978-1-55458-850-3 (PDF).—ISBN 978-1-55458-851-0 (EPUB)

1. Family violence—Canada. 2. Women—Violence against—Canada. 3. Children and violence—Canada. 4. Abused elderly—Canada. I. Alaggia, Ramona, 1957– II. Vine, Cathy, 1958–

HV6626.23.C3C79 2012   362.82'920971   C2012-904271-4

© 2012 Wilfrid Laurier University Press
Waterloo, Ontario N2L 3C5, Canada
www.wlupress.wlu.ca

Cover design by Blakeley Words+Pictures. Front-cover image: *i am here*, by Edwina Fernandes. Photo credit: Ryan Chynces. Text design by Daiva Villa, Chris Rowat Design.

This book is printed on FSC recycled paper and is certified Ecologo. It is made from 100% post-consumer fibre, processed chlorine free, and manufactured using biogas energy.

Printed in Canada

Every reasonable effort has been made to acquire permission for copyright material used in this text, and to acknowledge all such indebtedness accurately. Any errors and omissions called to the publisher's attention will be corrected in future printings.

RECYCLED
Paper made from recycled material
FSC
www.fsc.org   FSC® C103567

For my mother, who endured,
and my daughters, who have choices
Ramona Alaggia

For my children, family,
and friends who inspire and create change
Cathy Vine

CONTENTS

FOREWORD

Family violence is a very serious issue that has plagued society for centuries. However, it was only in the early 1980s that it began to emerge from the societal closet. Until that time, the abuse suffered by its victims had always taken place behind locked doors and, in most cases, it was considered a private family matter—nothing to do with anyone else.

When I became involved with the issue during that period, we naively thought that increasing public awareness would eliminate the problem. We were wrong. We very quickly recognized that the thick walls of secrecy surrounding family violence made discussion of the topic very difficult, if not impossible.

Many of its victims felt ashamed. They found it difficult to talk about their experiences and they worried about being judged by their neighbours and friends. There were many people in society who didn't want to discuss what they considered to be a private issue, too ugly for public discussion. There was also the problem of obtaining sound empirical evidence on family violence because little research work was being carried out.

Since that time, much has been learned. We can now say, without quali-fication, that family violence is the single biggest impediment to healthy human development.

It permeates all sectors of society, crossing all age, gender/sexual divers-ity, religious, cultural, ethno-racial, and social-economic boundaries. Personally, professionally, or vicariously through people we know, family violence touches everyone. It is an incredibly complex problem that does not exist in a vacuum. If a mother is abused, every child in the family is indirectly abused. This is especially damaging during a child's early years. There is a growing body of evidence about the profoundly harmful effects of violence on the developing brain. This evidence proves that between the period before birth and age three, prolonged exposure to negative experiences producing stress, fear, and anxiety can permanently affect a child's development in the areas of learning, health, and behaviour.

That is why, in recent years, economists have publicly acknowledged that family violence is a barrier to the social economic health of our nation.

Although much has been learned since the early 1980s, we have really only uncovered the tip of the iceberg. I am pleased to note, however, that research activity by both academics and practitioners across Canada has greatly increased over the past thirty years. Unquestionably, progress has been made in the creation and dissemination of knowledge and information.

In *Cruel but not unusual: Violence in Canadian families*, the researchers and authors cast light on the breadth, depth, pervasiveness, and magnitude of family violence in society. The first edition of this book appeared in 2006 and was well received and widely used in academic institutions and service agencies across Canada, so much so that a second edition was necessitated. The book tells a disturbing story. It reaches into the lower-profile areas of family violence. These are areas that, until now, have tended to fall between the cracks insofar as family violence is concerned. This book discusses, in depth, violence against people with disabilities; violence in same-sex partner relationships; violence in Aboriginal families and communities; violence in immigrant and refugee families; and violence against older adults. The authors also look extensively at issues of child maltreatment, incorporating data from the Canadian Incidence Study on Child Abuse and Neglect, and they reveal the effects on children exposed to family violence.

Together, the chapters shed light on the history, naming, and identification of specific characteristics of family violence in sectors that are less visible and about which less is known. The barriers in these areas are identified, as well as recommendations for practice and policy. This second edition includes a chapter dedicated to tracing the history and evolution of the women's movement in Canada, and the theoretical development that paralleled the movement's progress in addressing violence against women and children.

The book is comprehensive in its scope. It takes a life course perspective that covers family violence issues from the very early years of life, childhood, adulthood, and through to the elder years. Since the publication of the first edition in 2006, new knowledge has emerged, so all of the chapters have been updated and new ones added to reflect important new information. Trauma and the role of resilience are examined in light of neurobiological research and social-ecological considerations. We learn about the impact of violence on the brain and body and the great potential of the human spirit, along with the critical role of support and other diverse resources, when facing adversity. Another new chapter provides a thorough analysis of the "gender symmetry debate," which questions the gendered nature of intimate violence and signals the backlash that we continue to face and must confront head on and with scientific rigour.

The information in each chapter is based on sound empirical research conducted by qualified, accredited researchers and practitioners, each of whom is highly respected in his or her field. It provides invaluable information for those who are working directly with perpetrators and victims. Although much of the information in this book is distressing, there is hope in the knowledge that such comprehensive research activity is being carried out and that it will reach practitioners and the larger community.

It is also hoped that the information in this book will find its way into public policy and legislation.

If we are to truly eliminate the scourge of family violence and its devastating effects on the health and well-being of the people in our society, we must ensure that all preventative initiatives and remedial interventions are rooted in solid empirical evidence. Programs must be evidence-informed and constantly evaluated. We already know from past experience that we cannot deal effectively with this serious issue by setting up programs based on assumptions or anecdotal evidence. This has not worked in the past and it will not work in the future. More than that, it is a waste of our limited resources.

The conclusion of this book offers thought-provoking closing remarks that the editors believe can help direct work and action in family violence. These observations are offered with forthrightness and honesty because—despite the tremendous strides that have been made over the past three decades in bringing family violence to the public's attention; despite the increased number of treatment programs, safe houses, and community resources; despite stricter laws and restraining orders; despite better training for police forces and those working in the legal system—family violence continues to exist.

To all the researchers, contributors, and co-editors of this important book, I extend my heartfelt commendation for your invaluable work in creating and assembling this extensive information about your specific areas of expertise.

It is my sincere hope that the enormous amount of work you have put into the compilation of all this knowledge will benefit your colleagues, practitioners, and society at large.

The Honourable Margaret Norrie McCain

ACKNOWLEDGEMENTS

As with every worthwhile endeavour, the final product is, beyond doubt, the result of a collective effort. Many people supported the second edition of this book. First, we would like to thank Brian Henderson and Ryan Chynces at Wilfrid Laurier University Press for insisting that a second edition was needed and for supporting us to produce an even better book. The editorial review process was instrumental in helping us choose new topics to strengthen the book—we thank the reviewers for their insights. We are also excited to have new contributors on board; they join an incredibly committed group who welcomed the opportunity to update and expand their work. Once again, the voices of our contributors articulate this collection's vision most persuasively; we hope that our readers will learn as much from them as we have.

There is a whole cast of colleagues and friends from whom we drew ideas, assistance, encouragement, creative solutions, and critical feedback for the first edition and now others who assisted in this second edition— Sam Gardner, Jennifer Ma, Tiffany Regaudie, and Jennifer Root deserve special mention. Edwina Fernandes's cover art, entitled *I am here*, is greatly appreciated. She has captured the theme of erasure as a form of violence that manifests itself powerfully upon women's bodies, yet the work also conveys a strong message that violence transcends, and is not limited to, the physical. In her words, "Globally and locally violence is structured by erasure—mainstream denials of the continual violence of colonial conquest, and minimization of ways that violence differentially impacts marginalized bodies or communities. Most importantly, erasure continues to be met by strong opposition and resistance."

We especially want to thank Margaret McCain for her continued resolve to draw attention to the tragedy of family violence in every circle that she travels. We thank her again for writing the Foreword to this edition and drawing readers' awareness to significant new advances in the field.

Our partners, children, and close friends continue to inspire and support our work and distract us with the joys and minutiae of family life. We treasure it all.

Finally, we wish to acknowledge that the people who have been our greatest teachers are the littlest ones who told us repeatedly that it is not okay for people to hurt each other; the older ones, who have reflected quietly on lives that have been stolen from them; and all of the rest who say, over and over again, something must be done. This book is our response to all of you: it documents the harm, marks the advances, pinpoints the challenges, and intensifies our collective call for social justice.

INTRODUCTION
AND PERSPECTIVES ON VIOLENCE

INTRODUCTION

RAMONA ALAGGIA AND CATHY VINE

Violence in Canadian families is cruel and, regrettably, far from unusual. Affecting a wide range of people—from the very young to the very old—family violence is a social problem with far-reaching consequences. This field of study and practice is still relatively young despite the frequent occurrence and persistent and pervasive nature of violence in families. As we looked for materials to address these concerns—to help educators and students in the classroom and professionals in the field—we recognized there was no one text available that addressed the expansive range of issues within the Canadian context.

Over the years, distinctive fields of study and practice evolved to address particular forms of abuse, such as "woman abuse" and "child abuse," treating the issues as if they were mutually exclusive. In the 1980s, when we began working with children who had been sexually abused, we didn't consider what other forms of abuse might also be occurring in the family. Advocates and practitioners providing "specialized" services for abused women or children didn't work with each other. Children's mental health centres did not systematically explore abuse in their assessment procedures; hospitals didn't routinely screen for violence in a woman's relationship. Rarely did any of us turn our attention to the abuse of children and adults in institutions, let alone the abuse of older people in their families or in the settings responsible for their care. Academics and practitioners worked quite separately, unaware of one another's activities and potential contributions. For too long *all* these endeavours remained disconnected. Much has now changed.

This second edition of the book is the culmination of our desire to reflect these advances *and* stress the distance still to be travelled. The book is comprehensive in its coverage. We supply a current picture of the scope of the problem of violence in Canadian families. This picture reaches into the past to understand the legacies of history and looks closely at the present to reveal how the personal experiences of individuals, groups, and families are affected by broader social, structural, political, and legal influences. Together, the chapter authors offer extensive analyses of the range of problems and issues, and the legal, policy, and practice activity. The complexity of understanding and addressing violence becomes ever more apparent as the reader progresses from one chapter to the next.

"Family violence" is known by many names, and indeed naming and defining violence (or "abuse") is a challenge in and of itself. Early in our own work, we learned that using the term "family violence" (or "domestic violence," "woman abuse," "intimate partner violence," "gender-based violence," "corporal punishment," etc.) evokes a range of responses. Language is important: the naming of acts and problems communicates one's beliefs about cause and impact. All terms are limiting and limited by the very patriarchal structures that give rise to, and maintain, abuse against women, children, and the vulnerable. Thus, we did not ask our contributors to adopt set language and terms. Rather, the contributors used the words that best reflect their perspectives on how to name and describe the problem. Importantly, several of the contributors highlight the problems of naming when professionals define a person's experience; many people being victimized in their relationships do not identify themselves as being abused. While the first section sets the stage for highlighting the diversity of lenses, directed at different aspects of violence in families, the reader is encouraged to reflect on the range of perspectives throughout the book.

Across the life course, threats, humiliation, exploitation, and acts of physical and sexual abuse often produce emotional, psychological, and/or physical harm. For some, the consequences may be immediate and short term, while for others they may be much more enduring. The concept of the "cycle of violence" is popularly used to explain violence in relationships—that is, what is experienced and learned in childhood in the family, and further reinforced by cultural and societal factors, is destined to be repeated in adulthood. While these initial formulations were helpful as a starting point, the research, theory, and practice offered in this book will reveal the breadth and intricacy of these issues.

Over the years, debates flourished about issues such as the gendered nature of violence, victim blaming, medicalization of women's problems, false memory syndrome and false allegations, and the cultural relativism of child abuse, to name just a few. Unfortunately, some of these debates, and indeed some policy directives, have resulted in pitting women's rights against children's rights and best interests, a divisiveness of feminist paradigms giving rise to questions about a "right kind of feminist," and the formulation of explanations based on gender that excluded the views and experiences of women of colour and economically disadvantaged women, women with disabilities, and older women, men and women abused in their same-sex partner relationships, and men and women subjected to abuse as older adults.

The apparent dissension in the field initially seems perplexing and yet can also be understood to represent the diversity of orientations found in any established field. These differences ideally should generate enriching, productive debates resulting in an increased knowledge base and more effective practice. However, lay people and professionals alike have also had to work within a harsh fiscal climate in which funding for women's and children's services—let alone services for ethnocultural groups, older adults, lesbian, gay, bisexual, transgendered, and queer (LGBTQ) communities or people with disabilities—is relatively scarce, especially since the fiscal cutbacks began in the 1990s across much of Canada. Most recently, funding slashed in areas such as settlement services for newcomers to Canada has had serious implications for families affected by violence. And despite the advances in cross-discipline and inter-system collaborations, this hostile economic environment exacerbates fledgling partnerships and has even eliminated successful initiatives linking research, professional practice, activist, community, and grassroots groups.

THEORY

For the purposes of this book, we have used a feminist-informed approach as an overarching framework to assert that many forms of violence and abuse occur within the context of intimate and familial relationships, a manifestation of patriarchy, perpetuated by patriarchal structures. *Feminist theories* equip readers with a framework for examining causality and the societal structures that maintain violence in Canadian families, including the very structure of the family itself. *Feminist theories* are heterogeneous in nature and range from *liberal* to *Marxist* orientations, with differing emphases, and sometimes divergent views on issues such as equality, equity, self agency, and structural factors as targets for change in eradicating violence in families. Across *feminist theories*, patriarchal structures are understood to create and maintain imbalances because power in society is distributed based on gender, class, race, ability, age, and sexual orientation. Women and children are treated as property, women's work is devalued, and violence is a gendered issue where power is abused in intimate relationships. Naturally, abuse within LGBTQ communities tests this orientation because gender is no longer the primary focus for understanding when men abuse men and women abuse women in their intimate relationships.

More recently, feminist theorists have recognized there is no essential experience of gender oppression. Instead, a broader analysis brings into focus the ways in which women suffer multiple oppressions, where gender oppression frequently intersects with race, class, ability, age, and sexual orientation. Acknowledging these intersecting oppressions is critical to all analyses of violence. *Intersectionality theory* expands on *feminist theory* by offering a deeper understanding of these complex interrelationships.

While *feminist theories* have been helpful, no one theory alone explains the phenomenon of violence in families and intimate relationships. We provide a brief review of how theory has been used to explain such violence; contributing authors supply their own theoretical frameworks and together, we provide readers with a range of ways to understand and address violence. *Social learning theory* is used to explain the intergenerational transmission of intimate violence wherein children exposed to domestic violence, through inappropriate modelling, are at risk of becoming future victims or abusers, perpetuating the cycle of violence. *Social exchange theory* provides a framework for exploring how victimized people weigh up the consequences of confronting or fleeing their abusive situations based on perceived and actual risks and benefits of their actions. This theory is also used to understand how certain abuse is minimized, especially that against older people, who in North American society are perceived to have little to contribute in terms of productivity and are seen as taxing society's resources. In terms of understanding the influence of the family and environmental impact on the development of children, *developmental-ecological theory* has evolved to elucidate under what circumstances child abuse and neglect are more likely to occur and what stressors exist that limit optimal child development within an ecological context. The ecological context includes neighbourhood, community, and societal conditions that support, undermine, or mediate the family's abilities to promote healthy growth of children.

Previously, the "battered woman syndrome" advanced the notion that repetitive and predictable patterns of abuse in intimate relationships can be reliably discerned, suggesting that patterns of violence are universal, thus creating entry points for intervention. Notably, the "discovery" of the battered woman syndrome prompted the development of shelters, safe houses, and follow-up services for abused women across North America. While these supports represented significant early advances, *cycle of violence* theories have been challenged wherein cultural context, ethno-racial background, class, ability, and sexual orientation are seen to shape the experiences of abused people in unique and unpredictable ways. This has also raised issues about the accessibility of services for abused people who face structural barriers for a host of reasons. *Neurobiological trauma* and *resilience knowledge* and *theories* have also developed to enrich our awareness of the very real effects of violence on the body and brain and how children and adults are profoundly affected. While some struggle, others do well.

Structural theory brings into focus the conditions created through societal structures that marginalize groups of people and create barriers for redressing their situations and conditions. These societal structures maintain the group's minority and disempowered status, which is further reinforced by unjust policies, laws, and societal attitudes. Newcomers and immigrants who have not received landed status, for example, are particularly vulnerable and may be reluctant to be involved with authorities and social services for fear of jeopardizing their applying for status, an already onerous process. Often services are not offered in their language. Moreover, women with children may be reluctant to disclose domestic violence as this will trigger a child welfare investigation in most provinces today. In addition, structural theorists maintain that services have been developed in ways that reflect an ethnocentric, heterosexist orientation so that women of colour, gay, lesbian, bisexual, and transgendered people are excluded. Furthermore, *colonization theory* and other theories of oppression reveal the historical roots and structures that perpetuate oppression from one generation to the next. These theories explicate how groups of people have been "problematized" and labelled as pathological when in fact their problems are the result of two centuries of systematic subjugation. The consequences are evident in fractured communities and family life plagued by despair, self-abuse, and violence.

PERSPECTIVES ON VIOLENCE

As we have begun to establish, understanding violence really depends on how you look at it. Accordingly, we devote the first section of the book to five chapters, each one foregrounding one or more perspectives on particular aspects of violence. No picture of violence in Canada today is complete without providing the historical context for how we have arrived at this particular point in time. Deborah Sinclair's work in Chapter 1, "Voices of Women from the Margins: Re-examining Violence against Women," explores theoretical explanations of violence against women with a particular emphasis on feminist theories and the ways these perspectives have been applied in public discussion, research, and practice over time. She recognizes how the voices of particular groups of women have been excluded and marginalized in mainstream theory and practice and presents a more comprehensive model. This perspective takes us beyond the borders of patriarchy to examine the intersections of violence against women with other forms of inequality and oppression, including racism, colonialism, class privilege and exploitation, heterosexism, ableism, and ageism. The chapter concludes by challenging leaders in feminist social work activism and in the violence against women movement to bring the multiple voices of women from diverse social locations and world views to the centre of our theoretical analysis and everyday practice.

In Chapter 2, "Family Violence or Woman Abuse? Putting Gender Back into the Canadian Research Equation," Molly Dragiewicz brings yet another perspective into discussion when she challenges us to consider how "knowledge production" in Canada has shifted from an explicit focus on "violence against women" to one now couched in gender neutrality, called "family violence." She traces these changes, and discusses the current status of women in Canada and the differences in men's and women's experiences of violence in order to address the "gender symmetry debate." Dragiewicz talks about the cultural context giving rise to these discussions and examines the implications of neo-liberalism and anti-feminism on research, knowledge production, and practice.

In Chapter 3, "Is This Violence? Is This Sexual Violence? Recognizing and Defining Violence through Dialogue with French-Speaking Women," Ina Motoi explores the role of dialogue in recognizing and understanding violence and sexual violence. Dialogue is explored on multiple levels as a means to: recognize and define violence; create space for multiple perspectives; promote understanding within oneself or in conversation with another; and as a tool for intervention. Different contexts provide the backdrop: a *francophone minority context* in Ontario, where women from multiple cultures, races, and religions already live with "identity violence"; and the second, a *francophone majority context* in Quebec, where prostitution is debated on a political level and women grapple with experiences of sexual objectification on a personal level. For Motoi, dialogue is key to empowering women to create their own unique solutions to violence.

Thus far, the perspectives presented have highlighted violence against women as the focus of women's organizing over time to name and address the problem; how violence becomes "de-gendered" in knowledge production and public discussion when the term "family violence" is employed; and how violence is understood from the perspectives of individual women living with violence and sexual violence. From yet another vantage point, however, "family violence" is also used to include other members of the family victimized by violence. The abuse of children is the focus of Chapter 4,

"Child Corporal Punishment: Violence, Law, and Rights," in which Anne McGillivray and Joan E. Durrant demonstrate that "the road from Rome to the twenty-first century has been paved with justifications for violence against children." Here the authors examine the historical, legal, and current legislative contexts that support continued physical punishment of children in Canada. Is physical punishment violence? Is it an effective parenting technique? In Roman and common law, for example, both women and children lived under the "rule of the father." While women are no longer legally subject to "correction" by their husbands, the story is quite different for children. McGillivray and Durrant explore these questions as they assess the rights of children in the context of the Charter of Rights and Freedoms and the United Nations Convention on the Rights of the Child, and present the research on the short- and long-term effects of physical punishment. The authors demonstrate that the laws and views governing corporal punishment in Canada today represent "the untested assumptions of previous eras" and offer recommendations to professionals and policy-makers regarding the prevention of violence against children.

The last chapter in this introductory section brings two more perspectives to the fore. Thus far, we've begun to highlight some of the historical, legal, cultural, and feminist theoretical perspectives on violence in families. In Chapter 5, "Violence, Trauma, and Resilience," Michael Ungar and Bruce Perry use two approaches, *stress-response systems* and *social ecology*, to define, explain, and explore the interrelationships of violence, trauma, and resilience. How does violence affect our bodies and brains? What about subsequent development? How is it that some people are traumatized and others seem to be barely affected? Recent advances in neurobiology and resilience offer tremendous insights into some of the issues that have plagued researchers, practitioners, and individuals affected by violence themselves. This chapter completes the introductory section of the book where our goal has been to share some of the very different ways we examine and understand various aspects of violence. In the next section, in order to deepen understanding, we shift the focus to particular groups and some of the ways that violence is understood and experienced within marginalized communities.

MARGINALIZED COMMUNITIES AND VIOLENCE

In this section, the role of systemic oppression comes to the forefront as we examine violence in the lives of Aboriginal families, children and adults with disabilities, lesbian, gay, bisexual, transgendered, and queer (LGBTQ) communities, and immigrant and refugee families. Each of these chapters provides an in-depth examination of the historical and current experiences and issues faced by these diverse groups. Of note, while each of the groups is united by a common bond—be it culture, disability, or sexuality, for example—the authors are clear that each of these groups is made up of diverse members. Nevertheless, it is instructive to chronicle the oppression of a particular group and its experiences of violence. This focal point gives us a window into the issues that may cut across all marginalized groups and those that are unique to a group because of its particular characteristics and historical treatment through Canadian structures and policies.

In Chapter 6, "Systemic Oppression, Violence, and Healing in Aboriginal Families and Communities," Cyndy Baskin records the far-reaching and devastating consequences of colonization on First Nations communities and the systematic placement of Aboriginal children in residential schools. What does this have to do with violence in families? Baskin connects the past with the present, demonstrating that the legacy of colonization has had a profound impact on Aboriginal families, giving rise to soaring rates of violence in Aboriginal communities. Oppression is central to this analysis, and responses determined by Aboriginal traditions and values are critical to addressing violence and abuse.

While Baskin calls for a unique, culturally driven response to abuse in Aboriginal communities, in Chapter 7, "Violence, Protection, and Empowerment in the Lives of Children and Adults with Disabilities," Richard Sobsey and Sonia A. Sobon propose that anything short of fully involving people with disabilities in mainstream Canadian society will only perpetuate the high rates of abuse in their lives. Children with disabilities, for example, are 50 percent more likely than other children to be abused. Sobsey and Sobon also remind us that there is vast diversity among Canadians with disabilities, and emphasize the profound challenges in naming, counting, and understanding violence because of this. The authors challenge our very notion of "family" at the outset of the chapter by describing the abuse experienced by a young woman living in a group home. Should violence in institutions be included in our examination of violence in "families"? Further, they alert us that there may be several mechanisms at work in explaining the frequency of violence in the lives of people with disabilities: violence itself may cause disabilities; the presence of a disability may itself increase the risk for victimization; and other factors such as poverty, substance abuse, and isolation may increase the risk for both disability and victimization.

In Chapter 8, "Dynamics of Partner Abuse in Sexual and Gender Minority Communities," J. Roy Gillis and Shaindl Diamond shed light on yet another marginalized group's experiences of exclusion when they focus on intimate violence in LGBTQ communities. Along with challenging feminist conceptualizations of intimate violence, they chronicle the ways in which the needs of both victims and perpetrators continue to be ignored, if not exacerbated, by mainstream violence responses. Gillis and Diamond reveal the ways in which issues that are virtually uniquely experienced within LGBTQ communities play themselves out in perpetuating violence: fears that publicity about the incidence of abuse within LGBTQ communities will fuel homophobia, threats of outing or revealing HIV status, and heterosexism in police and counselling services, for example, all inevitably increase the dangers for those being victimized in their relationships.

In Chapter 9, "Domestic Violence and Child Abuse: Issues for Immigrant and Refugee Families," Ramona Alaggia and Sarah Maiter review the plight of women and children as immigrants, newcomers, and refugees in Canada. The systems central to intervening in child abuse and domestic violence have a unique impact on them, not only because of their immigrant status, but also the traditions and values of their home countries. Alaggia and Maiter explore the inherent problems with definitions, who gets counted, and the complexities involved with domestic violence and child welfare policy and practice responses when "private problems" require public action. They also provide an analysis of the service delivery system for immigrant families affected by abuse and violence and make recommendations for improved response.

By concentrating on the experiences of particular groups, this section of the book brings to light the multifaceted issues involved in identifying, naming, counting, understanding, and intervening in violence experienced by groups that are marginalized in Canadian society. In the next section, we take yet another approach to examining violence in families and intimate relationships—using a developmental perspective.

VIOLENCE ACROSS THE LIFE COURSE
Building on the work of the first two sections in applying a variety of perspectives to certain aspects of violence and to the experiences of particular groups, this section now approaches violence across the life course. From childhood through to adulthood and the elder years, we approach violence as it is experienced in families. We have already established that family takes many shapes and includes different members. For the purposes of this section, we ask you to think about the space that each of us calls home and the relationships with the people we are closest to—the people we call family. The chapters generally progress through family life stages, starting with children because of their developmental vulnerability, and proceeding through the life course.

In Chapter 10, "Children Abused, Neglected, and Living with Violence: An Overview," Cathy Vine, Nico Trocmé, Bruce McLaurin, and Barb Fallon provide an overview of the nature, scope, characteristics, and impact of child abuse, all the while recognizing that everything we know about how often children are abused, for example, is determined by how abuse is defined, investigated, verified, and then categorized. While an ever-expanding knowledge base regarding child development and the short- and long-term effects of child abuse and trauma inform the discussion, the authors highlight the challenges and issues that permeate the area. This overview chapter also introduces the reader to some of the issues—such as children's exposure to violence—that receive fuller examination in subsequent chapters. The authors interweave the voices of young people to keep them at the centre of the discussion.

In Chapter 11, "Children's Exposure to Domestic Violence: Integrating Policy, Research, and Practice to Address Children's Mental Health," Angélique Jenney and Ramona Alaggia delve into children's exposure to domestic violence, how the child welfare system responds, the kinds of programs available to address the effects and impact, and the ways in which research and clinical practice can usefully inform one another. Importantly, the authors spotlight how policy shapes system response and raise issues about how child welfare intervention to protect children can work against mothers coping with the impact of domestic violence.

In Chapter 12, "Whose Failure to Protect? Child Welfare Interventions When Men Abuse Mothers," Susan Strega further explores how policies and legislation shape system response and argues that "failure to protect" legislation maintains or even increases the dangers to mothers and children. Strega asserts that mothers are being held responsible for failing to protect their children from "witnessing" the violence being inflicted on them and asks why the system continues to focus on mothers while failing to even notice—let alone hold responsible—the men who are perpetrating the violence against them. "If we truly want to help children exposed to violence," stresses Strega, "we must engage purposefully with those who perpetrate it." She recommends policy and practice changes that would "enable child welfare to move from punishing and threatening mothers to more effectively working with them to protect both themselves and their children."

In Chapter 13, "Rendering Children Invisible: The Forces at Play during Separation and Divorce in the Context of Family Violence," Rachel Birnbaum provides yet another lens for examining and understanding the "the forces at play" when parents separate and/or divorce in the context of violence. She observes that even the language used to describe couples' relationships—"feuding," "high-conflict," "disputing families," "revenge seeking"—camouflages those instances when children are being used by one partner against another. The problems continue into disputes over custody and access. Birnbaum analyzes the evolution of the legislation that governs separation and divorce processes, arguing that children are invisible throughout, and concludes with a proposed framework for making children visible.

In Chapter 14, "Violence against Women: A Structural Perspective," Colleen Lundy reviews the prevalence and nature of gender-based violence in Canada. In 2001, for example, spousal violence accounted for one-quarter of all violent crimes reported to police services. Eighty-five percent of the victims were women and over two-thirds of those women were victimized by a current spouse. Lundy includes international comparisons and critically analyzes the violence surveys and measures used to produce this picture. A structural approach is used to explain the dynamics of male violence against women and affirms that it should guide analysis, policy, and practice responses. Lundy depicts the problem as deeply rooted in broad social, economic, and political conditions and institutions, and examines the organizing efforts of the anti-violence movement and the response of the state.

In Chapter 15, "Identifying, Assessing, and Treating Men Who Abuse and Women Abused by Intimate Partners," Leslie Tutty provides critical assessment and treatment principles for working with men who abuse and women who are abused by their intimate partners. Rather than waiting for individuals or couples to ask for help, Tutty asserts that the prevalence, along with the nature and risks inherent in all forms of violence, suggest that "every individual, couple (whether heterosexual or homosexual) and family seeking counselling be assessed for current or historical abuse." Tutty provides the necessary tools for sensitively raising the issue and describes a comprehensive approach for prioritizing safety and employing effective clinical interventions.

While many of the earlier chapters actively connect the lives and experiences of children and adults, the work presented in the last two chapters focuses almost exclusively on older adults. Importantly, the earlier material provides a foundation for highlighting the similarities and differences in how our understanding of abuse in the lives of older adults has evolved. While women are commonly credited with "breaking the silence" about sexual abuse and domestic violence, for example, the discovery of elder abuse as a social problem, in contrast, has been led by professionals. Add that dynamic to the ways in which we commonly depict older people as dependent, and we end up with the prospect of creating legislation aimed at protecting older adults akin to that developed for protecting children.

In Chapter 16, "Elder Abuse and Neglect in Canada: An Overview," Lynn McDonald, Julie Dergal, and April Collins provide an overview of the major developments in the field of elder abuse and neglect within Canada. They examine definitional problems, issues of reliability, and validity of data related to the incidence and prevalence of abuse, theoretical advances, and current challenges associated with identifying risk factors for abuse and neglect. Canadian legislative approaches, advances in protocols for detection and intervention, as well as innovations in programs are also discussed.

In Chapter 17, "Older People Are Subjects, Not Objects: Reconsidering Theory and Practice in Situations of Elder Abuse," Joan Harbison, Pam McKinley, and Donna Pettipas trace the development of elder abuse and neglect as a social problem. Their work reveals how older people become objects of our study and intervention as opposed to being subjects in their own lives. The authors review the structural factors and theoretical inadequacies responsible for this situation. They highlight the ethical questions involved in balancing autonomy, intervention, and protection. Case examples illuminate the issues involved in translating theory into practice, as well as how practice can inform theory.

In summary, this book brings together the work of practitioners and academics working in a range of settings across Canada. Our collective task is to identify, explore, and address experiences of violence in intimate relationships and families, profiling the range and variety of perspectives, highlighting the experiences of marginalized communities, and thoroughly examining violence throughout the family life course. We hope the information and chapter highlights provided thus far spark interest and spur the reader forward. It is also important to acknowledge that all of the material is understandably upsetting and at times overwhelming. We encourage you to approach the reading ahead with care and we hope that it increases your understanding and inspires action.

1

VOICES OF WOMEN FROM THE MARGINS
RE-EXAMINING VIOLENCE AGAINST WOMEN

DEBORAH SINCLAIR

INTRODUCTION

> It is currently accepted that violence against women is one of the most
> urgent human rights issues of our time, yet paradoxically, women do
> not benefit from a level of resources that would reflect this urgency.
> (Amnesty International, 2003)

This statement by Amnesty International reflects my experience as a feminist social work activist in the Violence against Women (VAW) movement
during the past four decades. Despite significant gains made in establishing a powerful voice in the public arena about the horrific nature of
violence against women globally, we have yet to reach consensus on how
to eliminate it. Multiple oppressions and systems interact to strengthen
conditions of discrimination and social injustice. These are sexist, heterosexist, racist, ageist, ableist, classist, and colonialist practices that we have
all inherited from our settler/invader ancestors in this country we call
Canada (known as Turtle Island by our Aboriginal sisters and brothers)
(Anderson, 2000), and that critical feminist scholars/activists within the
social work profession are committed to changing (Alaggia, Regehr & Rishchynski, 2009; Anderson, 2000; Baskin, 2006; Bograd, 1999; Bhuyan, 2008;
Mishna, 2012; Neysmith, 1999; Neysmith & Reitsma-Street, 2005; Sakamoto
& Pitner, 2005; Sakamoto, 2007; Sinclair, 2003; Williams, 2005).

Woman abuse has been linked to serious illness and poor health conditions such as substance use, mental health concerns (complex post-traumatic stress disorders—PTSD—depression, suicidal behaviours), gastrointestinal disorders, chronic pain syndrome, sexually transmitted diseases and HIV/AIDS, gynecological complications, including unwanted pregnancy, forced abortion, premature labour and birth, as well as injuries to women's unborn children (Krug, Dahlberg, Mercy, Zwi & Lozano, 2002). For women between the ages of fifteen and forty-four in particular, violence perpetrated by men accounts for greater injury, including death and permanent disability, than traffic accidents, illnesses such as cancer and malaria, and war combined (Krug et al., 2002).

Whether in times of peace or war, with rare exception, women are a primary target of men's violence because they are women. By examining intimate femicide statistics alone, we find alarming rates of this sobering fact. In the United States, one-third of women murdered each year are killed by intimate partners. In South Africa, a woman is killed every six hours by an intimate partner. In India, twenty-two women a day are murdered in dowry-related conflicts. In Guatemala, two women are murdered daily (Krug et al., 2002). Closer to home, a Canadian woman is murdered, on average, every six days by her intimate partner, and in Ontario every twelve days (Sinclair, 2003). The deaths of more than 520 missing and murdered Aboriginal women have been formally documented as part of the national Sisters in Spirit Campaign (Amnesty International, 2004).[1]

In Canada, researchers report that an estimated 653,000 women, representing 8 percent of all Canadian women, had experienced some form of spousal abuse in the previous five years (Statistics Canada, 2000, 2005). Shame, secrecy, and victim-blaming continue to silence women's experience of violence at the hands of their most intimate partner, resulting in statistics that reflect only a small portion of actual victims (Statistics Canada, 2008). The Canadian Violence against Women Survey (VAWS), internationally renowned for its methodology, reported that 29 percent of Canadian women ever married or living in a common-law relationship disclosed that they had been physically or sexually assaulted by their intimate partner (Rodgers, 1994). Forty percent of those same women in the VAWS study required medical attention and 45 percent of their assaults resulted in visible physical injuries, including cuts, bruises, burns, fractures, and broken bones. Ten percent of the women were forced to flee their own homes in fear for their lives and/or their children's lives (Johnson, 1996; Rodgers, 1994; Statistics Canada, 2002) (see Chapter 11 for detailed statistics).

Differential Impact on Women

Not all women, however, experience violence similarly as much will depend on their social location (class, race, nationality, immigration status, citizenship, ability, and sexual orientation) (Alaggia, Regehr & Rishchynski, 2009; Bhuyan, 2008; Crenshaw, 1989, 1995; Razack, 2002; Smith, 1987; Sokoloff & DuPont, 2005). Marginalized women suffer as much from the dangers of their social positions as they do from the dangers of intimate partner violence (IPV) (Richie, 2000). Similarly, men, too, will experience the consequences of their abusive behaviour in different ways, depending on their position in the hierarchy of organizing relations (their social location based on class, race, nationality, immigration status, citizenship, ability, and sexual orientation). This is an important factor to acknowledge and document as it has a significant impact on marginalized women's disclosure rates and help-seeking responses (Katz, 2006; Mederos, 2004; Richie, 2000). It is also a point that is most difficult for those of us who are mainstream Eurocentric VAW activists to grasp and is, in my experience, one of the greatest sources of tension between mainstream activists and those activists who work primarily with marginalized populations. For example, when a worker focuses solely on what is happening in the woman's intimate relationship with her partner and does not try to see the complexity of her life in its entirety, then the worker gets only a partial picture of her experience and is unlikely to engage with the woman in any meaningful way (see also Motoi's discussion in this volume).

The policy implications and meaning of such an international public health issue experienced by so many women across time, location, culture, and context are profound (Krug et al., 2002). VAW persists worldwide as a pervasive violation of human rights and a major impediment to achieving gender/race/class equity and access to resources. The unrelenting pressure on the United Nations from grassroots activists across the globe from 1976 to the present time resulted in a number of international declarations culminating most recently in the words of the UN secretary-general: "Such violence is unacceptable, whether perpetrated by the state and its agent or by family members or strangers, in the general public or private sphere, in peacetime or in times of conflict... [and] that as long as violence against women continues, we cannot claim to be making real progress towards equality, development and peace" (UN General Assembly, July 6, 2006, p. 9).

EXPLORING FEMINIST THEORIES

Having established the extent and severity of VAW, I now bring the reader's attention to theoretical explanations of VAW, with a particular emphasis on feminist theories and the ways these have been applied in research and practice. On the basis of this analysis, I will critique the extant theories and develop a more comprehensive model for understanding VAW. I will build upon the work of women who have been marginalized in mainstream theory and practice, especially Aboriginal women, women of colour, immigrant women, and poor women. I seek to make explicit the underlying reasons why certain groups of women have been excluded from the "culture of power" so as to avoid reproducing hierarchies based on gender, race, class, and other social categories (Ng, Staton & Scane, 1995).

Social justice is a life and death issue and one of primary concern to the social work profession. Anderson and her colleagues (2009) developed the notion of using a critical social justice lens to make explicit the power dynamics that lay beneath the increasing inequities that limit people's opportunities for health and wellness and their access to resources. Unmistakably, the issue of VAW falls into the broad category of women's health (physical, emotional, mental, and spiritual), both globally and locally. The particular material realities of women's lives—which include safety in private and public spaces, access to safe housing, access to nutritious food and safe drinking water, adequate income, access to meaningful education, safe and supportive work environments, affordable child-care arrangements, access to culturally relevant social services, and justice sector resources (criminal, family court, and child welfare)—are all critical social determinants of health and thus have a major impact on women's overall wellness and life satisfaction.

Historically and currently, mainstream VAW services and policies have been constructed to meet the needs of the dominant class of Canadian women—able-bodied, heterosexual, white, English-speaking, middle-class women. Research has been done primarily on white women's experience of IPV, allowing some scholars and activists to reach the erroneous generalization that all women suffer equally from IPV, thus giving rise to the notion of the "universal woman" (Richie, 2000). Taking this thinking further leads some activists and scholars to expect to "build an alliance on the foundation of shared victimization" without examining their different group position based on white privilege (Collins, 1998, p. 936). Despite the articulated social justice goals of the VAW movement to advance equity and access for *all* women, mainstream women have been the primary beneficiaries, leaving an ever-widening gap between the stated ideals and the actual practice of social justice. This is an unacceptable situation that needs to be remedied.

Historically, all of our institutions have told the same story—this discourse of white supremacy/dominance is transmitted through religion, education, literature, psychoanalysis, and other dominant institutions, and it is the story told through the eyes of elite, white European men (Foucault, 1980). Applying a critical feminist lens to address this problem will assist us to explore these dynamics in the service of making transparent what has been invisible to many in the VAW movement, including myself. Knowledge is power, and critical knowledge helps us reset our path in a more meaningful direction. During the past forty years in Ontario, I have been involved in the VAW movement as a feminist social work activist. The VAW movement operated within an analytical framework defined by white middle-class feminists like myself. Within that theoretical framework, gender was positioned as the primary form of oppression, which is now a highly contested site among contemporary feminist scholars (Sokoloff & Dupont, 2005; Richie, 2000; Todd & Lundy, 2006). It took the work of critical feminist scholars from a number of communities, traditions, and world views—black, indigenous, post-colonial, queer, disability, and critical white feminists—to challenge us to understand that by focusing *solely* on the experience of private violence of particular women in their homes, we may exclude the experience of public and structural forms of violence. It is often these experiences that shape the daily lives of Aboriginal women, women of colour, immigrant and refugee women, lesbian, bisexual, and transgender people, differently abled women, older women, and poor women.

Critical feminist scholars also teach us that when we focus solely on the "other" and do not include ourselves as a key actor in the relationship, we neglect to examine our own privilege and power, thus replicating the very hierarchical ruling relations we wish to dismantle. Our movement is per-fectly poised to take a leadership role in addressing these inequities that we witness daily on the front lines, but first we need to recognize that gender is but one form of oppression and that we must theoretically understand how systemic forms of violence intersect and interlock with VAW. If we do not collectively work to dismantle other equally oppressive systems, then we tacitly support them. Critical feminist scholars rightly suggest that an inter-sectionality approach that incorporates multiple forms of oppression and world views must be at the centre of the VAW movement theoretically and practically. However, the current theoretical base cannot be merely expanded to add on race, nationality, class, sexual orientation, and ability, but rather we must build a new model that will underpin our understanding of policies and practices that will guide our future work in the VAW movement, moving from a "single identity" movement to a "multiple identities" movement. In this introductory chapter, I will attempt to move us in this direction.

As a long-time feminist social work activist in the VAW movement, I have been challenged to theoretically reconsider the "primacy of gender" as the only explanatory "monolithic" model of violence against women (Bograd, 1999). Critical feminist scholars and anti-racist feminist activists have challenged the primacy of gender oppression, embedded in patriarchy, by opening up the discourse on domestic violence to include other forms of oppression and inequality such as ageism, heterosexism, class exploitation, racism, ethnocentrism, citizenship, colonialism, capitalism, and globalization, in order to deepen their understanding of how these intersect with gender oppression. No form of oppression is considered more critical than any other; rather, the impact of a particular disadvantage is understood within the interactions of all other forms of inequalities to which a woman is subjected (CRIAW, 2006; Jiwani, 2006). Expanding the discourse to include voices of battered women and their allies, from diverse social locations and cultural backgrounds—too often ignored, silenced, and rendered invisible in mainstream responses to domestic violence—strengthens and enriches the work of the VAW movement, theoretically and in practice (Ashcraft, 2000; Baines, 2007; Bannerji, 2000; Brah & Phoenix, 2004; Crenshaw, 1995; Emberley, 2001; Gelles & Loseke, 1993; McCann & Kim, 2003; Robinson, 2003; Sokoloff, 2008b).

In the past three decades, many theoretical explanations have emerged to help guide the social work field in its work with women who have been abused and their families, at both the micro and the macro level. These theories influence the policies and practices on the front line of social work agencies and grassroots women's services. They include, but are not limited to, the following: resource theory, social exchange theory, social learning theory, developmental-ecological theory, evolutionary psychological theory, socio-biological theory, general systems theory, and structural theory (Payne, 1997). However, for the purpose of this introductory chapter, I focus my attention on feminist standpoint theories—that is, theories that focus on women's lived experience of male violence and its impact on their *everyday* lives. These include, but are not limited to, learned helplessness theory and the cycle of violence (Walker, 1979), empowerment theory (Rose, 1990; Sinclair, 1985), survivor theory (Gondolf & Fisher, 1988), trauma theory (Herman, 1992), the notion of social entrapment (Ptacek, 1999), and, most recently, Evan Stark's (2007) theory of coercive control. These theories have contributed to increasing the field's understanding of woman abuse and its effects on the individual woman, as well as linking the underlying socio-economic and political context in which abusers use control tactics against their partners and the structural barriers that prevent many women from finding safety (Avis Myers, 2006; Bograd, 1999; Todd & Lundy, 2006).

In addition to these theories, there is an ever-expanding body of literature, captured under the umbrella of *intersectional feminist frameworks* (IFFs), that scholars and activists employ to theoretically untangle the ways in which the multiple identities that women inhabit in their daily lives affect their ability to manage/escape the violence in their lives (Bograd, 1999;

CRIAW, 2006). The current literature on the lived experience of abused women from diverse backgrounds appears to fall between two theoretical perspectives—"intersectionality" (Crenshaw, 1989) interchangeably referred to as the "the race, class, gender perspective" (Davis, 1981) and the "structural perspective" (Sokoloff & Dupont, 2005), which is frequently referred to as "interlocking oppressions" (Collins, 1990).

FROM WHERE I STAND

Feminist sociologist Dorothy Smith (1987) suggests that it is up to us as activists, social workers, and academics to take up the problems of individuals, to engage in an active process of defining issues, and to situate each within our organizational practices by bringing them into the light for critical examination so they can be made transparent. Walker (1990) goes on to suggest that:

> Concepts are not constructed randomly or accidentally, but are actual work processes in the production of knowledge. In themselves, concepts provide for particular courses of action, understood in this way, concepts can be seen to do more than name a phenomenon. They are part of a social relation (used here to signify an ongoing and concerted course of action) that organizes the particular phenomenon in specific ways and provides a response to what has been thus identified. (p. 11)

Naming the issue of VAW, therefore, depending on the particular perspective that one brings, will dictate the particular actions one engages in and is a clear reflection of one's particular epistemological and ontological position, whether named or not (Lather, 2006). In the 1970s, many white feminist activists and researchers had positioned themselves firmly in the epistemology that male violence against women is a direct result of patriarchal beliefs (Dobash & Dobash, 1979). Based on women's countless testimonies and heartbreaking disclosures of severe abuse, early second wave feminists sought to create legitimate alternative knowledge claims to the dominant discourse by "using the radical research tool of believing women and what they say" (Cole, 1995, p. 18) as their beginning point. Smith's (1987) advice, in her seminal work on institutional ethnography, suggests that we must situate the problem to be studied in the real world of practical, everyday activities, not from an abstract level, but from the entry point of particular people or a particular person.

In my case, my starting point was in the heady days of the 1970s, at the University of Toronto. (I was a fifth-generation European Canadian of Irish and Scottish heritage, raised in Prince Edward Island—English-speaking, white, middle-class, straight, able-bodied woman.) The first women's studies program was beginning at the University of Toronto and I was privileged to be part of those early class discussions (women's studies would become my minor). Women's Place had just opened its doors in 1971. This first women-only space provided safe haven for budding activists like myself and would provide the energy, focus, and planning years for the first women's shelter for battered women in the country, Interval House, which opened its doors in 1973. Later, in 1978, fresh out of a master's-level social work program, I was unaware that the arena I was entering would become my life's work. In those days, armed with a passion for social justice, a budding feminist awareness, and some personal experiences yet to be deconstructed, I had the good fortune to be mentored by feminist social workers committed to a high standard of practice and keen to make a difference. We developed a holistic community intervention model that provided a visual map of effective intervention aimed at both micro and macro levels (Sinclair & Harris, 1981). This document expressed a radical departure from the "pathology-based," "logical-positivist," "social worker as expert" view that was the dominant discourse in the social work profession at that time (Sewpaul, 2005).[2]

As a beginning point, I want to acknowledge that a major contribution of feminist pedagogies has been the challenge to "man-made" traditional conceptualizations of truth that can be described as oppressive, elitist, and exclusionary (Kaul, 2005). Feminist inquiry seeks to radically transform the values that determine how we view ourselves, others, our "herstory" and the world—that is, to ask "What is 'reality'?" from a feminist perspective. There is no question that there are multiple truths, depending on the participant/observer's perspective, and that each is value-laden and therefore political (Koro-Ljungberg, 2008; Mirchandani, 2005). To be part of the women's liberation movement is to be part of a radical movement that bases its politics on personal experience (Hawkesworth, 2006). There is no separation between personal experience and politics; they are intimately connected. The "personal is political" (Hanisch, 1969) and critical feminist theorists teach us that the "political is personal" (Richie, 2000). The emancipatory nature of feminism is such that what first feels like a private, personal problem, when made transparent, has a social cause, thus requiring a political solution from the collective (Rosewater & Walker, 1985). Since patriarchy began, at least five thousand years ago, according to Eisler and Loye (1990), there have always been diverse groups of women who have occupied themselves with this feminist task of demystifying that positivist, "objective reality," challenging its validity and replacing it with the lived experiences (subjectivities) of women who are constantly faced with the struggle of that "one down" position in the gender/race/class hierarchy

(Eisler & Loye, 1990; Guba & Lincoln, 1994). The particular issues that have preoccupied white, middle-class women scholars and activists are all problems that emerge out of "male-defined" versions of female experience, most particularly as they relate to our desire to own and control our bodies, sexuality, and reproductive health. These ideas have been most eloquently captured in the classic work of French philosopher Simone de Beauvoir (1953). Issues such as abortion and contraception, sexual harassment, pornography, prostitution, incest, and wife battering are all struggles with our "otherness," struggles born out of the condition of being "other" than male (Fawcett & Hearn, 2004; Razack, 1991). From this particular feminist standpoint, most experiences of women's oppression is caused by or is a result of a struggle against men's desire to define and control female sexuality, whether in the private sphere of an intimate relationship or in the public sphere of war. Intimidation, rape, and sexual humiliation are often the first tools of choice used by the perpetrators. However, this "gender as primary site of oppression" view has been widely criticized in the theoretical writings of women of colour scholars and activists.

> Taking issue with white feminists' generalizations about "women" and "men," feminist scholars of color have pointed out that gender is always mediated by race, class, ethnicity, sexual orientation, nationality, and a host of social vectors of power. Cautioning against overgeneralization, feminists of color have coined the term "intersectionality" to capture the intricate interplay of social forces that produce particular women and men as members of specific races, classes, ethnicities, and nationalities. (Crenshaw, 1989, as cited in Hawkesworth, 2006, p. 13)

ACTIVIST VOICES FROM THE FRONT

It is important to acknowledge that even prior to the naming of the term "intersectionality" in the scholarly literature, a number of feminist activists, particularly women of colour, had been working on the intersections of gender, race, and class since the 1970s. Most notably, members of the famous US Combahee River Collective (1982) first named their lived experience as black lesbians, thus differentiating themselves from the universal "we" of the mainstream women's movement, which too frequently reflected only white, middle-class women's experiences. Since that time, marginalized and racialized women have fought vigorously and painstakingly with few, if any, resources to name the disproportionate impact violence has upon racialized women, immigrant and refugee women, poor women, women with disabilities (both visible and invisible), lesbians, elderly women, and geographically isolated women (Sinclair, 2003). Audrey Lorde (1984) eloquently states in many of her writings, particularly *Sister Outsider*, that there is no hierarchy of oppression. However, she does clearly acknowledge that differences among women do exist. These terms of difference need not be mutually exclusive, suggesting that the complexity of women's lives is best understood using "both/and" language within a partnership model, rather than the "either/or" language of a dominator model (Eisler & Loye, 1990). Lorde, Eisler, and Loye's feminist world view is supported in the following postmodern perspective:

> To fall within the tracks of a bipolar reductionism and an either/or choice between the particular and the universal is to fall within the traps of modernism itself. The dangers of an over reliance on difference, on the one hand, or on essentialist notions of identity and experience, on the other, is that these may be used to justify stereotyping, exclusion of people, violation of human rights and a claim to the cultural superiority of the West. (Sewpaul, 2005, p. 217)

Currently, there are multiple strands of feminist thought and world views (i.e., conservative, liberal, socialist, radical, black, indigenous, eco-feminist, and postmodern, to name a few) that have challenged, resisted, reformed, and attempted to dismantle patriarchal systems and beliefs that hold men as essentially superior and dominant, and women as essentially inferior and subordinate (Hunnicutt, 2009; Kandiyoti, 1988; McCann & Kim, 2003). However, the dominant patriarchal argument held by many mainstream feminists has been rightly critiqued as an "essentialist" perspective that purports to view all women as having in common their gender as a primary bond—being born female, having the biological capacity to give birth, and sharing mothering and caretaking responsibilities. The same dangers for women of colour scholars can be noted when they have in common their race as their primary bond, to the neglect of class, ethnic and cultural differences, geographic location, immigration histories, sexual orientation, age, and ability (McCann & Kim, 2003). However, it is critical to note that there is one primary commonality among all white women, which is their experience of skin colour privilege and, conversely, that women of colour have in common their experience of racism (McIntosh, 1988). Eurocentric, able-bodied, straight, middle-class women had to learn that they did not speak for *all* women, especially poor working-class women, older women, women with disabilities, women of colour, and Aboriginal women (Anderson, 2000; Baskin, 2006; McCann & Kim, 2003; Sinclair, 2003). Even though many doors were opened for women as a result of the activist efforts of the mainstream women's movement, not *all* women's experiences were included in the dominant discourse. This is not to imply that the early feminist paradigm shift that occurred during the *second wave* of the women's movement was not far superior to previous approaches, which pathologized women's experience of abuse (Ashcraft, 2000; Bograd, 1999; Ferraro, 1996; hooks, 1981; Sinclair & Harris, 1981; Walker, 1990).

REMEMBERING THE HISTORICAL CONTEXT

Before I address the historical achievements of the *second wave* of the women's movement, where I locate my own beginning work, I will briefly provide an overview of what the terms "first wave," "second wave," and "third wave" feminisms refer to, in both the lived experiences or *everyday* activities of feminist activists (Smith, 1987) and in the scholarly literature particularly as it relates to Canada, though it is important to note that many voices have been left out of the official record of the history of the women's liberation movement.[3] To remedy that, I begin by opening up the space to hear what indigenous feminists have to say about the indigenous world view prior to contact with the patriarchal European world view.

INDIGENOUS WOMEN EMBODY WOMEN'S LIBERATION PRE-CONTACT

> The coming of the white man created chaos in all the old systems, which were for the most part superbly healthy, simultaneously cooperative and autonomous, peace-centered, and ritual-oriented. (Gunn Allen, 1992, p. 31)

These words reflect the views of many indigenous feminists who write about the role of women in their culture's pre-contact world (Anderson, 2000; Baskin, 2006; Channsoneuve, 2006, 2010; Emberley, 2001; Gunn Allen, 1992; Maracle, 1996; Smith, 2003; Yee, 2010). The indigenous world view held women in high regard and thus their women held a position of high status. The prevalent indigenous world view was an egalitarian, gynocentric/matriarchal model in which women's views were central to the well-being and survival of the community. Aboriginal women held positions of great leadership influence and were often the wise women/ Elders. Their child-bearing capacity was honoured and protected—they were held sacred as givers of life and thus creators of the next seven generations. This was diametrically in opposition to the world view promoted in the androcentric/patriarchal ideology of the "European white man." After contact, the colonizers/my ancestors, as an essential part of the civilizing mission/colonial project, had to systematically and intentionally dismantle Aboriginal women's power. Paula Gunn Allen (1992) provides guidance in how to reveal the colonial gaze and the subsequent political consequences in this transition from indigenous world views to hierarchical, patriarchal systems. She identifies four strategies used to dismantle the power of Aboriginal women. These included: (1) the belief in a female creator had to be replaced by a belief in a male creator; (2) the philosophies and the tribal governing institutions that form the foundation of indigenous culture had to be destroyed; (3) the people's sacred relationship with the land had to be disrupted—their land was stolen and they were dislocated to small contained spaces (reserves, reflecting substandard living conditions in many places across the country, particularly in the North), their cultural beliefs, ceremonies, and spiritual practices were denigrated, dehumanized, and named as pagan, primitive, and backward and ultimately outlawed; and lastly, (4) the clan structure that was collectivist and woman-centred was replaced by the dysfunctional patriarchal European nuclear family model. A movement to emancipate women was not a necessity in indigenous culture because it already existed. This indigenous respect for women was so evident that, as Mrs. Teall, a white woman in the late nineteenth century, wrote in an editorial in the *Syracuse Herald-Journal* reflecting on the high status of women in Iroquois society:

> They had one custom the white men are not ready, even yet, to accept. The women of the Iroquois had a public and influential position. They had a council of their own...which had the initiative in the discussion; subjects presented by them being settled in the councils of the chiefs and elders; in this latter council the women had an orator of their own (often of their own sex) to present and speak for them. There are sometimes female chiefs.... The wife owned all the property.... The family was hers; descent was counted through [the] mother. (Lopez, n.d., p. 101, as cited in Smith, 2003, p. 77)

In stark contrast, the patriarchal European world view held women and children in the British Empire and the colonies in low regard; they were commonly considered the property of the husband/father (the patriarch) to do with as he wished. This is our colonial legacy. Historically, women (particularly women in the role of wife) possessed no legal recognition or rights under the law. As such, they were without any legal remedy to challenge their husband's use of physical force and neglect. During the 1860s and thereafter in Canada, public condemnation of "wife assault" was noted in newspapers, local courts, and temperance literature. An Ontario property reform act of 1859 provided "Orders of Protection" for abused wives, giving them some financial protection and child custody rights. In 1909, for the first time in Canada, "wife abuse" was recognized as a crime separate from "common assault" (McLean, 2002). Gradually divorce laws were liberalized, allowing women to divorce on grounds of "extreme" cruelty, although it took until 1968 in Canada for the Federal Divorce Act to recognize this human right (Schechter, 1982; Sheehy, 2002; Sinclair, 2003).

The *first wave* of the women's movement began early in the nineteenth century and remained active until the First World War (Sheehy, 2002). The dominant voices tended to be white, middle-class women who were fighting to correct injustices they were experiencing themselves. They fought to achieve formal legal equality for equal status, rights, and obligations, meaning equality of treatment with white men. They were successful in their efforts to win the right to hold property, to vote (federal) and ultimately to achieve the status of "legal persons" with the decision in the Persons Case in 1929. They opened up their access to post-secondary education and increased the number of women in professions. However, French-speaking women in Quebec were excluded from voting until 1939, women (and men) of colour until 1947, and Aboriginal women (and men) until 1961, confirming the view that marginalized people's needs were not on the agenda for the first wave of the women's movement in Canada (Sinclair, 2003).

The *second wave* of the feminist movement, a term made popular by feminist activist Marsha Lear (Walker, 1995), spanned the period from the late 1960s to the 1980s and referred to the increased feminist consciousness developing within the civil rights movement, the anti-war movement, and the student political movement occurring across North American campuses (Schechter, 1982). In Canada, women fought for "substantive equality" as opposed to the "formal equality" of the *first wave* (Sheehy, 2002). Substantive equality acknowledges gender differences such as child-bearing, reproductive rights, and unpaid caring activities of women upon which the state, community, and family rely heavily (Neysmith & Reitsma-Street, 2005). As a result, substantive equality focuses on the end result of equal benefits and burdens for women and men. These may be achieved either by formal equality (equality of treatment) or by rules and practices specific to women. The goal was to acknowledge gender differences without being disadvantaged. Male violence against women was seen as a barrier to substantive equality and thus became one of the primary sites of feminist activity throughout the *second wave* of the movement, with women seeking the right to be free of male violence. The women's movement was successful in achieving many victories, including (but not limited to): the development of rape crisis services and women's shelters across the country; police directives to lay assault charges in cases of "wife assault"; prosecutor directives not to drop charges; the criminalization of marital rape of women in 1983; early intervention programs for men who wanted to change their abusive behaviour; support programs for children exposed to domestic violence with accompanying legislative reforms; and the development of violence prevention materials and training curricula for use by schools, social services, and the justice sector. Other related accomplishments included: equality guarantees in the Charter of Rights and Freedoms, 1982 (sections 15 and 28); reproductive freedom and access to abortion; equal pay for work of equal value legislation; and women's right to share in men's property, including pensions. The faces of feminism were varied, representing strands of feminist thinking drawn from the voices of black women, Aboriginal women, lesbians, poor women, and disabled women. Women from the margins were expanding the borders of feminist engagement beyond gender oppression to include race, class, sexual orientation, and ability, though their contributions often remained invisible or threatening to the mainstream women's movement (Davis, 1981; hooks, 2002; Lorde, 1984).

The *third wave* of the feminist movement was a term made famous by Rebecca Walker, the daughter of black feminist activist Alice Walker and goddaughter of white feminist icon, Gloria Steinem. She made headlines in 1992 when she wrote an article entitled "I Am the Third Wave" in a popular American feminist publication, *MS Magazine* (Walker, 1995). The *third wave* spanned the period from the 1990s to the present time, but its roots began in the *second wave*. Radical feminist leaders expressed dissatisfaction with the privileging of white, middle-class women's voices, particularly excluding issues of race and class (Davis, 1981; hooks, 2002; Lorde, 1984). Young women joined the struggle, insisting that equality for all women must acknowledge advantages of white supremacy, class privilege, the heterosexual presumption, and norms of ability, and must acknowledge the consequences for all marginalized and racialized women (Kinser, 2004; Sheehy, 2002; Sinclair; 2003; Walker, 1995). Feminist organizing in the *third wave* continues to focus on substantive equality, meaning all women's lived experience should be one of equity and access to resources, including the right to live a life free of violence. It aims to ensure that policies and practices reflect the diversity of women's lives. To this end, anti-racist and anti-oppression (ARAO) training are ongoing professional development expectations for those working in legal, health, education, social, and political institutions.

The goal of an independent women's movement in the *third wave* is to continue public debate and political pressure to effect social and legal change within a historical context that is culturally specific and collaborative. Legal—indeed, all—systems are to be held constantly accountable to women, grounded in the guiding principle that recognizes women live in *everyday* conditions that are fluid, particular, and specifically located rather than fixed and universal (Smith, 1987). Legislation, policy, and procedures are to be framed within an explicit analysis of power relationships, inequality of women's lives, and historical political relations. Laws and policies are to include internal mechanisms of ongoing monitoring and enforcement. Creative solutions are to be achieved by building coalitions and alliances with all equality-seeking groups and voices from multiple feminist movements and world views (Ashcraft, 2000; Bograd, 1999; Brah & Phoenix, 2004; Burman & Chantler, 2005; CRIAW, 2006; Crenshaw, 1995; hooks, 1994; Ritchie & Eby, 2007; Sheehy, 2002; Sinclair, 2003; Todd & Lundy, 2006; Walker, 1990; Walker, 1995).

Historical achievements of the *second and third waves* of the women's movement, as they relate to the achievements of the VAW sector in particular, were great. During this period, grassroots groups of women—many of them survivors of woman abuse themselves—and their allies began to speak out and identify the issue of VAW, particularly in heterosexual relationships, thus confirming Foucault's argument about the nature of power; that is, wherever there is oppression, there is also resistance. "Therefore, power is not something to be possessed; instead, it is a phenomenon that is exercised in social relations" (Wang, 1999, p. 192).

From a micro perspective, second wave feminists have agreed that underlying all abusive relationships there is a significant misuse of power and control dynamics directed at women, including psychological, sexual, humiliating, and demeaning tactics, which make it very difficult for women in these situations to leave, particularly if faced with life-threatening circumstances (Avis Myers, 2006; Davies, 1998; Dobash & Dobash, 1979; Essed, 1991). Historically, second wave feminists have addressed these issues by challenging political and legal institutions, and their efforts have moved this issue out of the private domain into the public sphere. However, it soon became evident that women would need urgent and immediate care if they were to escape violent situations, and thus the roots of the shelter movement were born (Schechter, 1982). Since that time, shelters have sprung up across the country to address the needs of women fleeing, most often with their children, to escape escalating violence from their intimate partners. Most of these early shelters were rooted in feminist standpoint thinking, which analyzed VAW as an outcome of socially constructed power imbalances inherent in gender relations (Fawcett & Hearn, 2004). Frequently, shelters became the hub of all VAW services in a particular community (Schecter, 1982).

Through the efforts of early second wave feminists from diverse perspectives, a wide range of programs and services expanded to include counselling services for abused women, their partners, and their children, legal advocacy, housing programs, peer-support programs, and advocacy. Feminist thinking has infiltrated mainstream institutions such as health, social services, child welfare, and criminal and family law arenas and, as a result, professionals in these areas have been challenged to adopt a gender-based understanding and approach of intervention in cases of domestic violence (Walker, 1990). A similar commitment to a culturally relevant approach to service delivery has yet to be achieved. However, despite the many gains second wave feminists have accomplished, most shelters continue to have waiting lists and, given the lack of political will and adequate resources, are barely able to meet the demands of their existing clientele, who tend to be young mothers with children. Despite ongoing strenuous efforts on the part of feminists, particularly given the political terrain of neo-liberal ideology within which most activists operate, it is not surprising that the specific needs of particular groups of abused women have remained largely unaddressed.

THEORETICAL FRAMEWORKS FOR UNDERSTANDING INTIMATE PARTNER VIOLENCE

While some feminist scholars think the analytic tool of "intersectionality" has been one of the greatest feminist contributions to women's studies in the past three decades (Hawkesworth, 2006), others suggest that the growing body of literature has not adequately addressed how this concept "subjectively" lives out in our everyday lives (Yuval-Davis, 2007). On an individual (micro) level, an *intersectional perspective* has been essential in giving voice to women from diverse cultural and religious backgrounds and social locations who have been abused. A monolithic model (i.e., *all* women who have been abused) has not been a useful tool to understand the complex forces that shape and constrain the *everyday* life of a woman inhabiting her multiple identities and the impact of those multiple identities on her experience of intimate partner violence. In academic women's studies, this *intersectional perspective* is also known by a number of other terms—integrated feminism, intersectionalities theory, women of colour perspectives, multiracial or multicultural feminism, to name but a few (McCann & Kim, 2003). The unifying theme in all of these approaches is the commitment to understanding the impact of multiple and interlocking experiences of oppression and its differential impact on the individual lives of women, their families, and their communities (Sokoloff & Dupont, 2005). However, some scholars are appropriately critical of the *intersectional perspective* when it remains focused solely on the unique differences and struggles of each group, entrapped in the non-productive approach of "identity politics" to the exclusion of making visible the underlying systemic oppressions upon which it rests (Collins, 2000). Sokoloff and Dupont (2005) cite the work of Anderson and Collins (2001) when they "distinguish

a structural approach as requiring 'analysis and criticism of existing systems of power and privilege; otherwise, *understanding diversity becomes just
one more privilege for those with the greatest access to' resources and power"*
(pp. 39–40; italics added).

Hulko (2009) takes this examination further as she tries to articulate
the difference between the theoretical concepts of *intersectional paradigm*
and *social location*. By *intersectional paradigm*, she refers to the interaction
of "identity categories (i.e., race/gender), processes (racializing/gendering),
and systems (racism/patriarchy)" (p. 47) and its use in the scholarly literature to explain the complex relationship between *intersectionality* and *interlocking oppressions* referred to earlier in this chapter. She then uses the term
"social location" to mean the result of this interaction of advantages and
disadvantages that play out in the *everyday* life of an abused woman and her
family. She uses the term "everyday" in the way Smith (1987) devised in her
early work on institutional ethnography. As a social worker like me, Hulko
(2009) struggles to bridge the theoretical world of the academy with the
everyday practice world of ARAO social work activism on the front line. She
encourages contemporary intersectionality theorists to acknowledge their
own privilege, analyze their own social location (including oppressions and
privileges), and name their own lived experience across time and place, in all
its complexity, as did her "intellectual ancestors" (Anderson, 2000; Collins,
1989; Crenshaw, 1989; hooks, 1994; Lorde, 1984; McCann & Kim, 2003).

PRACTICAL APPLICATION OF AN INTERSECTIONAL APPROACH

Sokoloff and Dupont (2005) outline the many strengths of applying an intersectional analysis to the work of understanding violence against women in an
intimate relationship. An intersectional and structural analysis permits us to:

1. *Challenge the monolithic nature of woman abuse that has been defined in
   the mainstream domestic violence literature:* This is a critical aim because
   it urges us to examine the differential impact of abuse on women and
   acknowledge that some women are at greater risk than others, depending
   on their social location.
2. *Acknowledge that the violence marginalized women experience from an
   individual abuser is only one form of violence they are exposed to in their
   daily lives:* Sexualized, racialized, and colonial violence are the backdrop
   to the *everyday* aspect of their lives (Smith, 1987).
3. *Expand the definition of woman abuse to include specific forms of domestic
   violence that allow us to connect the meaning of abuse to each woman's
   social, political, and historical context:* The experience of abuse must be
   understood within a culturally relevant framework that is meaningful

to her (for example, a Japanese woman might experience abuse when her partner overturns her dining room table as he attempts to challenge her legitimate role in her family) (Yoshioka & Choi, 2005).

4. *Expand the explanation of the structural causes of woman battering beyond the primacy of patriarchy as a monolithic pillar by including the interlocking oppressions of capitalism, imperialism, colonization, heterosexism, ableism, and ageism* (Razak, 1998): This allows us to examine how women's safety might be jeopardized, depending upon their social location. For instance, in terms of engaging with the criminal justice system, women of colour and Aboriginal women are often reluctant to call the police in case their partners may be further harmed because of racism, negative cultural stereotypes, and centuries of colonial thinking, which continues to underpin our current criminal justice system (Anderson, 2000; Baskin, 2006; Bograd, 1999; McGillivray, Comaskey & Marquis, 2001). Many immigrant women may fear risking deportation and thus also be reluctant to call the police (Alaggia, Regehr & Rischynsky, 2009; Kasturirangan, Krishnan & Riger, 2004). Lesbians may reject reaching out to police for fear of a homophobic response or because their partner may use the tactic of "outing" them in their private and public lives (Bornstein et al., 2006; Gillis & Diamond, 2006; Helfrich & Simpson, 2006). Disabled women, when considering their need to call the police, may be physically prevented from getting to a phone by their abuser, or their abuser may be an "intimate caregiver" rather than an "intimate partner" so they may believe they will not be eligible for police services (Powers et al., 2009). Lastly, older women may be so filled with shame and secrecy and be so unfamiliar with their rights that they may not believe they are entitled to police assistance (Straka & Montminy, 2006).

5. *Avoid the "essentializing" trap of misrepresenting women as one homogeneous group and running the risk of replicating disempowering images of women on the margins:* We need to address the question of how women are to be represented without blaming their race and culture, citizenship, sexual orientation, class, age, or ability. Too frequently, the result has been that we have unwittingly reinforced these negative stereotypes when we do not place their experience in a historical, socio-political context.

6. *Deepen our understanding of the complex nature of culture and the role it plays in our own lives and the lives of the women we serve:* We must avoid a simplistic view of culture that reinforces negative stereotypes and frequently takes the actions of an individual abuser and transfers them to the whole cultural group. It is possible to acknowledge differences among different groups of women, yet still examine the underlying structural

causes of oppression. All cultures can have both negative and positive traditions that can either reinforce the use of violence against women or have strengths that will help us eradicate it (Mederos, 2004). It is particularly important to unpack the notion that those of us who are white have no culture, or that white culture is associated with superiority and civilization (MacIntosh, 1988). This does not explain in the least why horrendous acts of violence are widespread occurrences in predominantly white communities across the Western world.

7. *Produce culturally relevant research that accurately represents the experience of abused women within a social, political, and historical context:* One of the greatest challenges for the field today is to think through how to address our colonial history and the differences of race and class in our research, particularly when we are examining prevalence rates. A promising practice guideline is to link any research findings specific to a particular group to their historical, socio-political context. For example, when speaking about the higher rates of domestic violence in Aboriginal communities in Canada, it is important to explain those statistical findings within the historical context of colonization, the Indian Act of 1868, the intergenerational trauma from the legacy of the residential schools and the "Sixties Scoop," which has resulted in extreme rates of poverty, unsafe drinking water, substandard housing, food insecurity, unemployment, isolation due to centuries of racism, and the continuing betrayal experienced as the dominant white culture refuses to negotiate on issues related to self-government, remains unwilling to settle more than twelve hundred outstanding land claims, and denies that as settlers/invaders, we all are living on stolen lands and thus benefit from the cultural genocide that has occurred historically and continues to this day (Anderson, 2000; Baskin, 2006; Razack, 1998; Sinclair, 2003).

IMPLICATIONS FOR PRACTICE

To ensure inclusivity within the VAW movement, all voices must be heard and every effort made to intentionally integrate anti-racist, anti-oppressive practices (ARAO) into all aspects of the work (Khosla, 2003). While cooperation and coalition-building are essential in the face of the current backlash, mainstream Eurocentric VAW workers must first develop a critical awareness and acknowledgement of white privilege, and take proactive steps to deconstruct it, realizing that with privilege comes responsibility. Smith's (1987) notion of the "necessity of deconstructing our social location" is useful here. Smith normalizes the human struggle and suggests that, depending on our social location, men will have to struggle harder than women to see sexism accurately, white people will have to struggle harder than people of colour to see racism accurately, and that people from the North will have to struggle harder than people from the South to understand the impact of (post) colonialism. Her work suggests that as a member of a dominant group, each of us has a vested interest in subjugating that knowledge, though perhaps not consciously, and that if and when each of us chooses to critically understand our privilege, we will have a harder or easier time, depending on where we sit in the power relations hierarchies. In each of our lives, moments of privilege and moments of oppression exist simultaneously at different points, in different contexts, and in relation to different people. Therefore, we all hold a partial view of power, depending upon where we sit at any given moment. This can still have value as there is no such thing as perfect knowledge for any of us (Yuval-Davis, 2006).

Applying this idea to our activist work means that in order for VAW workers to effectively advocate for women abuse survivors, in terms of both "batterer-generated" risks and "life-generated" risks, workers need to stretch across differences and develop expertise in ARAO practice (Baines, 2007; Davies, 1998; Elliot, 2002). Hence, training and education, as well as research, must also address how women, children, and men all face various oppressions, and must acknowledge that VAW is an issue involving the intersections of race, nationality, class, sexuality, ability, as well as gender. Sokoloff and Dupont (2005) suggest a number of things we can do to transform our practice, including the following: actively give voice to marginalized women; move women from the margins to the centre of our discussions; create cultural safety in our work spaces (not cultural competence); dispel stereotypical images of abused women and their partners; create new theoretical frameworks that are empowering and focus on success; and lastly, create alternative visions to seeing the mainstream criminal justice system as the primary and only form of intervention.

FUTURE DIRECTIONS

Theoretically, my task in this introductory chapter has been to challenge the "primacy of gender" as the only explanatory factor in the "monolithic" model of VAW, which has dominated the discourse, particularly in the *second wave* of the women's movement in most Western countries, including Canada. We must "move the critique beyond the borders of patriarchy and ethnocentrism" (Sokoloff & Pratt, 2005, p. 15) to examine the intersections of VAW with other forms of inequality and oppression, including racism, colonialism, class privilege and exploitation, heterosexism, ableism, and ageism, which are still too often ignored, silenced, and/ or made invisible. Our challenge as leaders in feminist social work activism and in the VAW movement is to ensure that the multiple voices of women who experience abuse, and who are from diverse social locations and world views, are at the centre of our theoretical analysis and everyday practice.

Future research, policy, and practice might consider how the VAW movement and the social work profession, both theoretically and in everyday practice, will benefit from extending the current ARAO feminist framework to include an anti-colonial lens (ACARAO) as an additional social work model. This conversation/curriculum would also include a close examination of the critical whiteness/critical race scholarly literature in an effort to assist, in particular, young white social work students (still the socially dominant group in social work schools) to develop a critical consciousness regarding their own privilege and oppression, as well as a familiarity with their colonizer legacies (Conwill, 2010; Delgado & Stafancic, 1997; Donnelly, Cook, van Ausdale & Foley, 2005). When we know ourselves well and acknowledge our own colonial and personal history, then we stand a better chance at being more effective allies. When we make equity and access to resources the priority in our political work and proactively reach out to marginalized women and their families in our communities, listening actively to their concerns, then together we can truly be authentic allies. When we can make our communities safe for the most vulnerable women, then and only then can we make them truly safe for *all* women.

The past, our stories, local and global, the present, our communities, cultures, languages and social practices—all may be spaces of marginalization, but they also have become spaces of resistance and hope. (Smith, 1999, p. 4)

NOTES

1 I credit my collaborations with my Aboriginal sisters and brothers for opening my mind to the devastating nature of historic trauma and the harmful effects of the legacy of colonization that they carry in their bodies, hearts, and memories on a daily basis. Through them, I have been introduced to indigenous research methodologies and healing practices that have assisted me in my own decolonizing journey. They are my inspiration for taking this journey. Over the years, I have had the honour to work with the staff from the Kabaeshiwim Shelter, Saugeen First Nation no. 29, Southampton, ON; the D'binooshnowin Crisis Centre of the Chippewas of Nawash Unceded First Nation in Orillia, ON; the Aboriginal Healing and Wellness Strategy; shelters and family violence programs from across Ontario and Na-Me-Res, an Aboriginal men's residence in Toronto. Since 2008, I have had the privilege of working closely with the staff of the Sisters in Spirit Campaign: Native Women's Association of Canada, and directly with the families of missing and murdered Aboriginal women from across Canada as their facilitator at the Third and Fourth National Family

Gatherings, held in Ottawa (September 2009) and Vancouver (November 2010). These women and men have been my teachers and allies. I am grateful to them. On a more personal note, my close relationship with indigenous scholar and activist Deborah Chansonneuve has been a source of invaluable mentoring, love, and support in my journey—*Miigwetch.*

2 Had this model (1981) been picked up by the federal government as the national demonstration pilot, it would have been a well-resourced pilot project for three years with a guaranteed funding base. Our team had been courted over the course of three years, and our mentor at the federal level left for personal reasons, unfortunately, during the negotiation period and her replacement turned out not to be an ally. She thought our work was too radical for the time; in particular, she did not like the political action component to the project and was clearly uncomfortable with our openly feminist approach. She sent us back to the drawing board with all kinds of new and quite unrealistic demands, and we decided, in consultation with our management, to no longer engage with this "political game." There were huge consequences for us as a team—we were disillusioned and the team eventually disbanded, each going our separate ways. I was chosen by the Ontario government to provide the first provincial one-day training on understanding and intervening in cases of wife assault. Eleven hundred workers, representing diverse sectors in forty-three communities across the province, were trained in a three-month period in the spring of 1984. Subsequent to the training, I was commissioned again by the province to write up my training notes. This became the first manual, *Understanding wife assault: A training manual for counselors and advocates,* on the topic and was released in 1985. This book proved to be a popular training tool because of its practical, how-to approach and became widely used by both social workers and counsellors in professional settings, as well as by activists in the grassroots (primarily shelter) movement.

3 The "waves" interpretation of understanding the history of feminist movements is a contested metaphor, particularly by critical feminist scholars and activists. Highlighting common themes that unify each wave implies a universal experience of women's struggles and minimizes the diversity of competing feminisms. Contributions by individuals, smaller collective actions, more radical factions, and marginalized groups of women in each of the waves are often not acknowledged or documented as part of the official history of the women's movement (Mann & Huffman, 2005).

REFERENCES

Alaggia, R., Regehr, C., & Rishchynski, G. (2009). Intimate partner violence and immigration laws in Canada: How far have we come? *International Journal of Law and Psychiatry, 32*(6), 335–41.

Amnesty International. (2003, November 25). Media release.

Amnesty International. (2004). *Stolen sisters: A human rights response to discrimination and violence against indigenous women in Canada.* AI Index: AMR 20/003/2004.

Anderson, J.M., Rodney, P., Reimer Kirkham, S., Browne, A.J., Khan, K.B., & Lynam, M.J. (2009). Inequities in health and health care viewed through the ethical lens of critical social justice: Contextual knowledge for the global priorities ahead. *Advances in Nursing Science, 32*(4), 282–94.

Anderson, K. (2000). *A recognition of being: Reconstructing native womanhood.* Toronto: Second Story Press.

Anderson, M., & Collins, P.H. (2001). Introduction. In M. Andersen & P.H. Collins (Eds.), *Race, class, and gender: An anthology* (4th ed., pp. 1–9). Belmont, CA: Wadsworth.

Ashcraft, C. (2000). Naming knowledge: A language for reconstructing domestic violence and systemic gender inequity. *Women and Language, 23*(1), 3.

Avis Myers, J. (2006). Escaping narratives of domination: Ideas for clinical practice with women oppressed by relationship violence. In R. Alaggia & C. Vine (Eds.), *Cruel but not unusual: Violence in Canadian families* (pp. 397–421). Waterloo: Wilfrid Laurier University Press.

Baines D. (Ed.). (2007). *Doing anti-oppressive practice: Building tranformative, politicized social work.* Halifax: Fernwood.

Bannerji, H. (2000). The paradox of diversity: The construction of a multicultural Canada and "women of color." *Women's Studies International Forum, 23*(5), 537–60.

Bannerji, H. (2005). Building from Marx: Reflections on class and race. *Social Justice, 32*(4), 144–60.

Baskin, C. (2006). Systemic oppression, violence, and healing in Aboriginal families and communities. In R. Alaggia & C. Vine (Eds.), *Cruel but not unusual: Violence in Canadian families* (pp. 15–48). Waterloo: Wilfrid Laurier University Press.

Bograd, M. (1999). Strengthening domestic violence theories: Intersections of race, class, sexual orientation, and gender. *Journal of Marital and Family Therapy, 25*(3), 275–89.

Bornstein, D.R., Fawcett, J., Sullivan, M., Senturia, K.D., & Shiu-Thornton, S. (2006). Understanding the experiences of lesbian, bisexual, and trans survivors of domestic violence: A qualitative study. *Journal of Homosexuality, 51*(1), 159–81.

Bhuyan, R. (2008). The production of the "battered immigrant" in public policy and domestic violence advocacy. *Journal of Interpersonal Violence, 23*(2), 153–70.

Brah, A., & Phoenix, A. (2004). Ain't I a woman? Revisiting intersectionality. *Journal of International Women's Studies, 5*(3), 75–86.

Burman, E., & Chantler, K. (2005). Domestic violence and minoritisation: Legal and policy barriers facing minoritized women leaving violent relationships. *International Journal of Law and Psychiatry, 28*(1), 59–74.

Channsonneuve, D. (2006). *Reclaiming connections: Understanding residential school trauma among Aboriginal people—a resource manual.* The Aboriginal Healing Foundation. Ottawa: Anishinabe Printing (Kitigan-Zibi).

Channsonneuve, D. (2010). *Culturally relevant gender based models of reconciliation.* Ottawa: Native Women's Association of Canada.

Cole, S.G. (1995). *Power surge: Sex, violence, and pornography.* Toronto: Second Story Press.

Collins, P.H. (1989). The social construction of black feminist thought. *Signs, 14*(4), 745–73.

Collins, P.H. (1998). The tie that binds: Race, gender, and US violence. *Ethnic and Racial Studies, 21*(5) 917–38.

Collins, P.H. (2000). *Black feminist thought: Knowledge, consciousness, and the politics of empowerment.* New York: Routledge.

Collins, P.H. (2001). Like one of the family: Race, ethnicity, and the paradox of US national identity. *Ethnic and Racial Studies,* 24(1), 3–28.

Combahee River Collective. (1982). A black feminist statement. In G.T. Hull, P. Bell Scott & B. Smith (Eds.), *All the men are black, all the women are white: But some of us are brave* (pp. 13–22). Old Westbury, NY: Feminist Press.

Conwill, W. (2010). Domestic violence among the black poor: Intersectionality and social justice. *International Journal for the Advancement of Counselling, 32*(1), 31–45.

Crenshaw, K.W. (1989). Demarginalizing the intersection of race and sex: A black feminist critique of antidiscrimination doctrine, feminist theory, and antiracist politics. *University of Chicago Legal Forum,* 138–67.

Crenshaw, K.W. (1995). *Critical race theory: The key writings that formed the movement.* New York: New Press.

CRIAW (Canadian Research Institute for the Advancement of Women). (2006). *Intersectional feminist frameworks: An emerging vision.* Ottawa: Canadian Research Institute for the Advancement of Women.

Davies, J. (1998). *Safety planning with battered women: Complex lives/difficult choice.* Thousand Oaks, CA: Sage.

Davis, A.Y. (1981). *Women, race, and class.* New York: Random House.

Delgado, R., & Stafancic, S. (Eds.). (1997). *Critical white studies: Looking behind the mirror.* Philadelphia: Temple University Press.

Dobash, R.E., & Dobash, R. (1979). *Violence against wives: A case against the patriarchy.* New York: Free Press.

Donnelly, D.A., Cook, K.J., van Ausdale, D.V., & Foley, L. (2005). White privilege, color blindness, and services to battered women. *Violence against Women, 11*(1), 6–37.

de Beauvoir, S. (1953). *The second sex.* London: Jonathan Cape.

Eisler, R., & Loye, D. (1990). *The partnership way.* San Francisco: Harper.

Elliot, A. (2002). Beck's sociology of risk: A critical assessment. *Sociology, 36*(2), 293–315.

Emberley, J.V. (2001). The bourgeois family, Aboriginal women, and colonial governance in Canada: A study in feminist historical and cultural materialism. *Signs, 27*(1), 59–85.

Essed, P. (1991). *Understanding everyday racism: An interdisciplinary theory.* Newbury Park, CA: Sage.

Fawcett, B., & Hearn, J. (2004). Researching others: Epistemology, experience, standpoints, and participation. *International Journal of Social Research Methodology, 7*(3), 201–18.

Ferraro, K.J. (1996). The dance of dependency: A genealogy of domestic violence discourse. *Hypatia, 11*(4), 77–92.

Foucault, M. (1980). *Power/knowledge: selected interviews and other writings, 1972–77.* Edited by Colin Gordon. New York: Pantheon.

Gelles, R.J., & Loseke, D.R. (Eds.). (1993). *Current controversies on family violence.* Newbury Park: Sage.

Gillis, J.R., & Diamond, S. (2006). Same-sex partner abuse: Challenges to the existing paradigms. In R. Alaggia & C. Vine (Eds.), *Cruel but not unusual: Violence in Canadian families* (pp. 127–46). Waterloo: Wilfrid Laurier University Press.

Gondolf, E.W., & Fisher, E.R. (1988). *Battered women as survivors.* New York: Lexington.

Guba, E., & Lincoln, Y. (1994). Competing paradigms in qualitative research. In N. Denzin & Y. Lincoln (Eds.), *Handbook of qualitative research* (pp. 105–17). Thousand Oaks, CA: Sage.

Gunn Allen, P. (1992). *The sacred hoop: Recovering the feminine in American Indian traditions.* Boston: Beacon Press.

Hanisch, C. (1969). The personal is political. In *Feminist revolution* (pp. 204–5). New York: Redstockings Collection.

Hawkesworth, M. (2006). *Feminist inquiry: From political conviction to methodological innovation.* London: Rutgers.

Helfrich, C.A., & Simpson, E.K. (2006). Improving services for lesbian clients: What do domestic violence agencies need to do? *Health Care for Women International, 27*(4), 344–61.

Herman, J. (1992). *Trauma and recovery: The aftermath of violence—from domestic abuse to political terror.* New York: Basic Books.

hooks, b. (1981). *Ain't I a woman.* Boston: South End Press.

hooks, b. (1994). *Teaching to transgress: Education as the practice of freedom.* New York: Routledge.

Hulko, W. (2009). The time- and context-contingent nature of intersectionality and interlocking oppressions. *Affilia, 24*(1), 44–55.

Hunnicutt, G. (2009). Varieties of patriarchy and violence against women. Resurrecting "patriarchy" as a theoretical tool. *Violence against Women, 15*(5), 553–73.

Jiwani, Y. (2006). *Discourse of denial: Mediations of race, gender, and violence.* Vancouver: UBC Press.

Johnson, H. (1996). *Dangerous domains: Violence against women in Canada.* Toronto: Nelson.

Kandiyoti, D. (1988). Bargaining with patriarchy. *Gender & Society, 2*(3), 274–89.

Kasturirangan, A., Krishnan, S., & Riger, S. (2004). The impact of culture and minority status on women's experience of domestic violence. *Trauma, Violence & Abuse, 5*(4), 318–32.

Katz, J. (2006). *The macho paradox: Why some men hurt women and how all men can help.* Naperville, IL: Sourcebooks.

Kaul, N. (2005). The anxious identities we inhabit: Post'isms and economic understandings. In D. Barker & E. Kuiper (Eds.), *Toward a feminist philosophy of economics* (pp. 194–210). London: Routledge.

Khosla, P. (2003). *If low-income women of color counted in Toronto.* Toronto: Community Social Planning Council of Toronto.

Kinser, A.E. (2004). Negotiating spaces for/through third-wave feminism. *NWSA Journal, 16*(3), 124–53.

Koro-Ljungberg, M. (2008). Validity and validation in the making in the context of qualitative research. *Qualitative Health Research, 18*(7), 983–89.

Krug, E.G., Dahlberg, L.L., Mercy, J.A., Zwi, A.B., & Lozano, R. (Eds.). (2002). *World report on violence and health.* Geneva: World Health Organization.

Lather, P. (2006). Paradigm proliferation as a good thing to think with: Teaching research in education as a wild profusion. *International Journal of Qualitative Studies in Education, 19*(1), 35–57.

Lorde, A. (1984). *Sister outsider.* New York: Crossing Press.

Loseke, D.R., Gelles, R.J., & Cavanaugh, M.M. (Eds.). (2005). *Current controversies on family violence* (2nd ed.). Thousand Oaks, CA: Sage.

Mann, S.A., & Huffman, D.J. (2005). The decentering of second wave feminism and the rise of the third wave. *Science and Society, 69*(1), 55–91.

Maracle, L. (1996). *I am woman.* Vancouver: Press Gang Publishers.

McCann, C.R., & Kim, S. (Eds.). (2003). *Feminist theory reader: Local and global perspectives.* London: Routledge.

McGillivray, A., Comaskey, B., & Marquis, G. (2001). Black eyes all of the time: Intimate violence, Aboriginal women & the justice system. *Journal of Canadian Studies, 36*(1), 166–79.

McIntosh, P. (1988). *White privilege and male privilege: A personal account of coming to see correspondences through work in women's studies.* Wellesley, MA: Wellesley College Center for Research on Women.

McLean, L. (2002). "Deserving" wives and "drunken" husbands: Wife beating, marital conduct, and the law in Ontario, 1850–1910. *Histoire Sociale/Social History, 35*(69), 59–61.

Mederos, F. (2004). *Accountability and connection with abusive men: A new child protection response to increasing family safety.* San Francisco: Family Violence Prevention Fund.

Mirchandani, R. (2005). Postmodernism and sociology: From the epistemological to the empirical. *Sociological Theory, 23*(1), 86–115.

Mishna, F. (2012). *Bullying: A guide to research, intervention, and prevention.* New York: Oxford University Press.

Montminy, L. (2005). Older women's experiences of psychological violence in their marital relationships. *Journal of Gerontological Social Work, 46*(2), 3–22.

Neysmith, S. (Ed.). (1999). *Critical issues for future social work practice with aging persons.* New York: Columbia University Press.

Neysmith, S., & Reitsma-Street, M. (2005). "Provisioning": Conceptulizing the work of women for the 21st century social policy. *Women's Studies International Forum, 28*(5), 381–91.

Ng, R., Staton, P.A., & Scane, J. (Eds.). (1995). *Anti-racism and critical approaches to education.* Westport, CT: Bergin & Garvy.

Payne, M. (1997). *Modern social work theory* (2nd ed.). Chicago: Lyceum Books.

Powers, L.E., Renker, P., Robinson-Welen, S., Oschwald, M., Hughes, R., Swank, P., & Curry, M.A. (2009). Interpersonal violence and women with disabilities: Analysis of safety promoting behaviors. *Violence against Women, 15*(9), 1040–69.

Ptacek, J. (1999). *Battered women in the courtroom: The power of judicial responses.* Boston: Northeastern University Press.

Razack, S. (1991). *Canadian feminism and the law: The women's Legal Education and Action Fund and the pursuit of equality.* Toronto: Second Story Press.

Razack, S. (1998). *Looking white people in the eye: Gender, race, and culture in courtrooms and classrooms.* Toronto: University of Toronto Press.

Razack, S. (2002). *Race, space, and the law: Unmapping a white settler society.* Toronto: Between the Lines Press.

Richie, B.E. (2000). A black feminist reflection on the antiviolence movement. *Signs, 25*(4), 1133–37.

Ritchie, D.J., & Eby, K.K. (2007). Transcending boundaries: An international, interdisciplinary community partnership to address domestic violence. *Journal of Community Practice, 15*(1–2), 121–45.

Rodgers, K. (1994). Wife assault: The findings of a national survey. *Juristat, 14*(9), 1–22. Canadian Centre for Justice Statistics, Statistics Canada.

Rose, S.M. (1990). Advocacy/empowerment: An approach to clinical practice for social work. *Journal of Sociology and Social Welfare, 17*(2), 41–52.

Rosewater, L.B., & Walker, L.E. (Eds.). (1985). *Handbook of feminist therapy: Women's issues in psychotherapy.* New York: Springer Publishing.

Sakamoto, I. (2007). A critical examination of immigrant acculturation: Toward an anti-oppressive social work with immigrant adults in a pluralistic society. *British Journal of Social Work, 37*(3), 515–35.

Sakamoto, I., & Pitner, R. (2005). Use of critical consciousness in anti-oppressive social work practice: Disentangling power dynamics at personal and structural levels. *British Journal of Social Work, 35*(4), 420–37.

Schechter, S. (1982). *Women and male violence: The visions and struggles of the battered women's movement.* Boston: South End Press.

Sewpaul, V. (2005). Global standards: Promise and pitfalls for re-inscribing social work into civil society. *International Journal of Social Welfare, 14*(3), 210–17.

Sheehy, E. (2002). Legal responses to violence against women in Canada. In K.M.J. McKenna & J. Larkin (Eds.), *Violence against women: New Canadian perspectives* (pp. 473–91). Toronto: Inanna Publications and Education.

Shirwadkar, S. (2004). Canadian domestic violence policy and Indian immigrant women. *Violence against Women, 10*(8), 860–79.

Sinclair, D. (1985). *Understanding wife assault: A training manual for counselors & advocates.* Toronto: Ontario Government Publications Services.

Sinclair, D. (2000). *In the center of the storm—Durham speaks out: A community response to custody and access issues affecting woman abuse survivors and their children.* Durham Region, ON: Violence Prevention Coordinating Council. Status of Women Canada.

Sinclair, D. (2003). *Overcoming the backlash: Telling the truth about power, privilege, and oppression. Exploring gender-based analysis in the context of violence against women—a resource kit for community agencies.* Durham Region, ON: Violence Prevention Coordinating Council. Status of Women Canada.

Sinclair, D., & Harris, S. (1981). *Domestic violence project: A comprehensive model for intervention into the issue of domestic violence.* Toronto: Family Service Association of Metropolitan Toronto.

Sokoloff, N. (2008a). Expanding the intersectional paradigm to better understand domestic violence in immigrant communities. *Critical Criminology, 16*(4), 229–55.

Sokoloff, N.J. (2008b). The intersectional paradigm and alternative visions to stopping domestic violence: What poor women, women of color, and immigrant women are teaching us about violence in the family. *International Journal of Sociology of the Family, 34*(2), 153–85.

Sokoloff, N.J., & Dupont, I. (2005). Domestic violence at the intersections of race, class, and gender: Challenges and contributions to understanding violence against marginalized women in diverse communities. *Violence against Women, 11*(1), 38–64.

Sokoloff, N.J., & Pratt, C. (Eds.). (2005). *Domestic violence at the margins: Readings on race, class, gender, and culture.* New Brunswick, NJ: Rutgers University Press.

Smith, A. (2003). Not an Indian tradition: The sexual colonization of Indian people. *Hypatia, 18*(2), 70–85.

Smith, D.E. (1987). *The everyday world as problematic: A feminist sociology.* Toronto: University of Toronto Press.

Smith, L.T. (1999). *Decolonizing methodologies: Research and indigenous peoples.* London: Zed Books.

Stark, E. (2007). *Coercive control: How men entrap women in personal life.* New York: Oxford University Press.

Statistics Canada. (2000). *Family violence in Canada: A statistical profile.* Ottawa: Minister of Industry.

Statistics Canada. (2002). *Family violence in Canada: A statistical profile.* Ottawa: Minister of Industry.

Statistics Canada. (2005). *Family violence in Canada: A statistical profile.* Ottawa: Minister of Industry.

Statistics Canada. (2008). *Family violence in Canada: A statistical profile.* Ottawa: Minister of Industry.

Straka, S.M., & Montminy, L. (2006). Responding to the needs of older women experiencing domestic violence. *Violence against Women, 12*(3), 251–52.

Todd, S., & Lundy, C. (2006). Framing woman abuse. In R. Alaggia & C. Vine (Eds.), *Cruel but not unusual: Violence in Canadian families* (pp. 327–69). Waterloo: Wilfrid Laurier University Press.

United Nations. (1993). *Declaration on the elimination of all forms of violence against women.* December paper presented at the United Nations General Assembly, New York.

United Nations Development Fund for Women. (2003). *Not a minute more: Ending violence against women.* New York: UNIFEM.

United Nations. (2006). *In-depth study on all forms of violence against women.* Report of the Secretary General to the General Assembly on July 6, New York.

Walker, G. (1990). *Family violence and the women's movement: The conceptual politics of struggle.* Toronto: University of Toronto Press.

Walker, L.E. (1979). *The battered woman.* New York: Harper & Row.

Walker, R. (1995). *To be real.* Toronto: Random House.

Wang, F. (1999). Resistance and old age: The subject behind the American seniors' movement. In A. Chambon, A. Irving & L. Epstein (Eds.), *Reading Foucault for social work* (pp. 189–218). New York: Columbia University Press.

Williams, C.C. (2005). Violence against women in the context of mental illness: Hidden costs of sisters' caregiving. *Canadian Woman's Studies/Les Cahiers de la Femme, 24*(1), 109–16.

Yee, J. (2010). I'm an indigenous feminist—and I'm angry. In T. Hennessy & E. Finn (Eds.), *Speaking truth to power: A reader on Canadian women's equality* (pp. 119–22). Ottawa: Canadian Centre for Policy Alternatives.

Yoshioka, M.R., & Choi, D.Y. (2005). Culture and interpersonal violence research paradigm shift to create a full continuum of domestic violence services. *Journal of Interpersonal Violence, 20*(4), 513–19.

Yuval-Davis, N. (2006). Intersectionality and feminist politics. *European Journal of Women's Studies, 13*(3), 193–209.

Yuval-Davis, N. (2007). Intersectionality, citizenship, and contemporary politics of belonging. *Critical Review of International Social and Political Philosophy, 10*(4), 561–74.

2

FAMILY VIOLENCE OR WOMAN ABUSE? PUTTING GENDER BACK INTO THE CANADIAN RESEARCH EQUATION

MOLLY DRAGIEWICZ

The trajectory of public response to feminist anti-violence work has moved from outright denial, to recognition, to backlash and re-privatization. (Gotell, 2007, p. 128)

INTRODUCTION

Research on violence against women has been among the most scrutinized areas in social science. From the beginning, efforts to empirically document the prevalence, incidence, and characteristics of violence against women have been hotly debated (DeKeseredy, 2011; Dragiewicz & DeKeseredy, forthcoming; Minaker & Snider, 2006). Objections that violence against women was rare have given way to acknowledgement that it is more common than once thought. Research on the outcomes of woman abuse has documented the serious ramifications of this type of violence for individual victims and the broader community. However, violence against women was not simply "discovered" by scholars in the 1960s, leading to a progressive growth of the literature. Knowledge production around violence against women has been fiercely contested, and feminist insights in particular have always been met with backlash (Gotell, 2007; Minaker & Snider, 2006; Randall, 1989; Sinclair, 2003).

Research on violence against women has been targeted with claims of politicization, as if other social science research is devoid of political implications. Although the act of delineating the boundaries of any crime is political by definition, violence against women seems to be disproportionately characterized as such. Indeed, the issue of violence against women has been raised in the service of numerous campaigns for social reform, feminist and otherwise, since the 1800s (Pleck, 1983).

This chapter first reviews the growth and changes in the Canadian research literature on violence against women over time. Then it describes key indicators of the current status of women in Canada. Next, it defines the terms "sex" and "gender" and the difference between them. In the following section, Canadian research on differences between women's and men's experiences of violence is discussed, including methodological issues and trends in the ways that violence is discussed by the Canadian government. This part of the chapter highlights key areas of the research that illustrate how different women's and men's experiences of violence are, including separation assault, homicide, injury, and other outcomes. Finally, the chapter addresses the cultural context in which Canadian discussions about violence and gender have unfolded, with special attention to neo-liberalism and anti-feminism and their implications for scholars and practitioners alike.

In Canada, as in other countries where violence against women has been recognized as a social problem, woman abuse was first brought to public attention by feminists working to secure women's rights to live free from violence. In the face of denial that violence against women was a problem worthy of collective concern, feminists first worked to document the harm that resulted from it. Drawing upon the first academic studies and information from hospitals, police, and coroners, feminists effectively argued that woman abuse was prevalent, harmful, and serious (Gotell, 2007; Sinclair, 2003). In addition, women's groups campaigned for years to achieve the social change that transformed violence against women from something that was condoned or ignored to something that was no longer socially acceptable (DeKeseredy, 2011; DeKeseredy & MacLeod, 1997; Johnson, 1996; Johnson & Dawson, 2011).

Although widespread disapproval of violence against women is often taken for granted in Canada, it required a major shift in the culture. It was a shift that women fought for every step of the way. Resistance to recognizing violence against women as a social problem is often left out of the story of the "discovery" of woman abuse, but it has been a part of the picture from the start. In 1977, the Canadian United Way sponsored a "family violence" conference in British Columbia. The National Clearinghouse on Family Violence was established in 1982. Health and Welfare Canada created the Family Violence Prevention Division in 1986. Each of these initiatives used gender-blind language that obscured the nature of the problem they were designed to address (Dragiewicz & DeKeseredy, forthcoming).

Even today, some scholars, activists, politicians, and commentators in Canada continue to actively resist efforts to address violence against women. To shine a light on this resistance, in 2003 the Violence Prevention Coordinating Council of Durham identified five significant areas of backlash against efforts to address violence against women: (1) cuts to services for survivors of violence; (2) increasing use of gender-blind language; (3) the push for presumptive joint custody in family law; (4) an increase in dual arrests; and (5) mainstream media repetition of anti-feminist rhetoric on violence and abuse (Sinclair, 2003, p. 4). Although it may not be evident at first glance, each of these areas is closely related. Campaigns to discredit feminist knowledge about woman abuse form the foundation of bolstering the other efforts. The promotion of a "gender-blind" approach to violence and abuse, and claims that the research supports this perspective, have been used as political tools to attack services for abused women, circumvent pro-arrest policies intended to rectify police non-response to violence against women, and undermine women and children's reports of abuse in custody cases (Boyd, 2003; Dragiewicz, 2011; Dragiewicz & DeKeseredy, forthcoming; Dragiewicz & Lindgren, 2009). All of these campaigns draw upon mass media, including mainstream and online outlets, to amplify and repeat claims that violence is not a gendered phenomenon (Dragiewicz & DeKeseredy, forthcoming).

HISTORICAL CONTEXT

Those opposed to woman abuse initially named the problem of wife battering. Subsequent discourses framed the issue as woman abuse or violence against women due to rapidly emerging recognition of the continuum of offences experienced by women throughout their lives and across marital status categories (DeKeseredy, 2011; DeKeseredy & MacLeod, 1997; Johnson, 1996; Johnson & Dawson, 2011; Minaker & Snider, 2006; Randall, 1989). As Melanie Randall explained:

> Some form of men's sexual intrusion or aggression touches virtually every woman's life. This can include the experience of being beaten in a marriage, sexually harassed on the street or at work, sexually abused as a child, raped while on a date with a male friend or boyfriend, or simply living in a society surrounded by pervasive images of sexual violence against women which are sold as entertainment in the media, in popular culture, and in pornography. (1989, p. 4)

Contrary to frequently repeated false claims, Canadian scholars who study woman abuse have never claimed that women are never violent or that only men abuse women (DeKeseredy & Dragiewicz, 2007). Indeed, MacLeod explicitly included same-sex abusers in her definition of wife battering in the first Canadian book published on the subject in 1980. While violence may be a pervasive and persistent part of the lives of both women and men, the nature of the experience is quantitatively and qualitatively different. Rather than somehow denying the existence of violence against men, feminist articulations of woman abuse highlight the particular causes, character, and dynamics of violence against women.

Feminists in Canada and other countries have called for social changes to prevent men's violence against women, and for structural changes that ameliorate women's risk of violence and entrapment in abusive relationships. While they have received a disproportionate amount of attention, interventions focused on the law and its application in the criminal justice system have always been only one part of calls for broad-based cultural, economic, and institutional changes to address violence against women. While there are multiple feminist theories that differ from one another substantially, feminist theories of violence share the unifying recognition that structural and cultural factors, including gender inequality, are central to the etiology of this type of violence. As Holly Johnson observed:

> The reason for studying violence against women lies in the context within which these events take place and the nature of these experiences for the women involved. The problem of violence against women is a problem of intimate violence. Few people would argue that women are uniquely vulnerable to sexual violence. Wife battering is also unique in that it occurs within a specific context that is different from violence that occurs in other arenas. Because of the social context of the husband-wife relationship that historically has awarded men higher social status and authority over their wives and children, domestic assaults on women take on a significantly different meaning than the same acts perpetrated by one man against another or by women against their husbands. Wife battering can have the effect of reinforcing the unequal status of the female partner, strengthening the husband's dominance and authority within the relationship, and more firmly entrenching her dependence on the abuser. The same acts by women don't have the same outcome. (internal citation omitted; Johnson, 1996, p. xviii)

In other words, the social location in which violence takes place shapes the qualities and the meaning of that violence. The meaning of violence cannot be understood without consideration of the gendered realities of life in contemporary and historical contexts.

All of the resources that are currently available to survivors of woman abuse—such as emergency shelters, rape crisis centres, hospital sexual assault and domestic violence programs, and transitional housing facilities—were developed to address the manifest need and disparate physical danger and socio-economic inequality faced by women leaving abusive male partners. Women's greater physical danger stems from men's disproportionate use of violence against female partners. It is also exacerbated by men's greater use of violence, including homicide and familicide, post-separation. Women's greater poverty stems from the persistent pay gap as well as women's disproportionate care of children. Women's ongoing greater participation in child care, combined with a lack of publicly supported child care, contributes to lifelong economic disadvantages relative to men. Emergency services for abused women were also designed to ameliorate the damage caused by the ongoing failures of the criminal justice system in protecting women from men's violence.

Prior to the feminist and battered women's movements, men who perpetrated violence against women who were their current or former intimate partners often did so with impunity (Goodmark, 2012; Schneider, 2000). While criminal laws were written in gender-neutral terms, they were applied in a deeply gendered fashion. This is not surprising given the degree to which our everyday lives are shaped by gender. The feminist and battered women's movements brought attention to the pervasive, systemic, and socially constructed nature of the gender-specific failure of formal and informal social controls at preventing violence and harm to women.

The results of feminist efforts to change the response to violence against women have been mixed. Status of Women Canada was established in 1976. When it published its first action plan on women's issues, *Towards equality for women*, violence against women was included as one of the key issues (Gotell, 1998, p. 42). However, the contextualizing term "violence against women," which recognized the continuum of violence in women's lives, was undermined by government division of the issue into separate, distinct, and de-gendered issues such as sexual assault and family violence (Gotell, 1998, p. 43).

By the mid-1980s, state funding for women's services, including shelters, was already being cut. Federal programs like the Secretary of State's Women's Program were also rearranged to decrease their political influence (Morrow, Hankivsky & Varcoe, 2004, p. 362). The 1989 Montreal massacre at the École Polytechnique de Montréal sparked partial respite efforts to address violence against women. In this incident, a man walked into a university classroom, systematically separated the women from the men, then shot fourteen women to death before turning the gun on himself. In his suicide note, the killer explicitly identified the murders as a political act targeting feminists, whom he blamed for his failure to attain the life to which he felt entitled.

Despite the perpetrator explicitly stating his anti-feminist motives, a heated public discussion of the meaning of the killings ensued. Some commentators complained bitterly that feminists were contextualizing the massacre within a larger patriarchal culture that engenders many forms of violence against women (Rosenberg, 2003; Rosenberg & Simon, 2000). Ironically, a major strand of response to this anti-feminist mass killing was to blame feminism for causing a man to kill feminists. Fierce cultural resistance to feminism in general and feminist understandings of violence and abuse in particular continues to this day. Indeed, the claim that feminism, rather than patriarchal structures and cultures, are the source of women's problems are a hallmark of backlash.

However, the high visibility of this horrific crime required a state response. The Canadian Panel on Violence against Women was convened in 1991, but neither its feminist, sociological approach to violence against women nor its structural recommendations for ending violence against women by promoting equality was implemented. The Canadian Panel on Violence against Women was superseded by the Family Violence Initiative, which has prioritized intervention rather than prevention, and shifted the focus from violence against women to family violence. Some Canadian feminists have argued that this signalled a shift from broad-based and political support for women's rights to a narrower focus on criminalizing violence against women, the ramifications of which continue to be debated (Morrow, Hankivsky & Varcoe, 2004, p. 363). As Morrow, Hankivsky, and Varcoe explain:

> As the issue of violence against women came increasingly on to the Canadian political agenda it was shaped by the aims and demands of the state in ways which de-politicized the original intent of the feminist anti-violence movement (to expose patriarchal systems of power and to establish women-specific supports) which meant governments were more likely to fund gender neutral systems of supports and professionalized responses. (internal citations omitted; 2004, p. 369)

The appropriation of research on violence against women into gender-blind family violence initiatives discredited the very sources that had been used to argue for the implementation of anti-violence efforts. Research with and from community organizations and shelters was increasingly dismissed in favour of government-designed studies, which relied on a narrow selection of quantitative methods (DeKeseredy & Dragiewicz, 2009).

In 1995, the Advisory Council on the Status of Women was eliminated, and the Family Violence Initiative had its funding slashed by $100 million. The minister responsible for the Status of Women was demoted from a Cabinet-level position to the secretary of state responsible for the Status of Women. In addition, the government cut public funding to feminist organizations like the National Action Committee on the Status of Women and other organizations working to promote women's rights (Morrow, Hankivsky & Varcoe, 2004, p. 362).

STATUS OF WOMEN IN CANADA

Although the popular assumption is that women in Canada are among the most liberated in the world, and either have achieved equality or are coming closer to it every year, the data present a different picture. The status of women in Canada has actually declined since 2006. As of 2010, Canada ranked 20th out of 134 countries (Hausman, Tyson & Zahidi, 2010, p. 8). While Canada ranks 8th in economic participation and opportunity, it ranks 35th in educational attainment, 47th in health and survival, and 36th in political empowerment for women (Hausman, Tyson & Zahidi, 2010, p. 10). Rather than an indication that we are living in a post-patriarchy that calls for de-gendered, post-feminist responses to social problems, contemporary social indicators point to ongoing structural and cultural inequality.

Complaints from anti-feminists that men are "the new women" and an "underclass" are undermined even by the sources they cite to support their own arguments. Indeed, an anti-feminist activist bitterly complained in a recent article in the *Toronto Star* that "a 2008 StatsCan study shows that, over the previous two decades, the gap in average hourly wages between men and women has been steadily shrinking. The 75.7 cents women earned on the male dollar in 1988 inflated to 83.3 cents by 2008—nearly a 12 per cent jump" (Cribb, 2011). The tortured logic that paints women's 17 percent lower wages as evidence of men's oppression aside, claims that gains for women or services for women are evidence of discrimination against men are the stock in trade of anti-feminist discourses. The *Star* article describes a "man-power backlash" in which the anti-feminist quoted in the article objects to battered women's shelters because "They are almost entirely set up for women victims but if you look at the statistics, there are a surprising percentage of cases where men are being victimized" (Cribb, 2011). Of course, these services exist because of men's disproportionate use of violence against female intimates, especially at separation. While they reference official Canadian sources, claims that women and men are equally violent seriously distort even the most conservative state-funded research.

KEY ISSUES IN UNDERSTANDING THE RESEARCH ON GENDER, SEX, AND VIOLENCE

Sex/Gender

Key to understanding the research on sex, gender, and violence is that the terms "sex" and "gender" are often misused and conflated. The distinction between these concepts has been widely taught to students in introductory sociology and psychology classes for more than forty years. Nonetheless, the terms are often used interchangeably in colloquial speech and writing. The terms continue to be frequently misused, even in scholarly writing. As a result, research findings may be unclear, un-interpretable, or misleading. In the simplest terms, sex refers to the ostensibly biological categories: male and female. Gender refers to the collection of social attributes associated with the sexes: masculine and feminine (Dragiewicz, 2009).

Many social scientists use sex category as a demographic variable in research, noting whether respondents are male or female. This variable may be useful in identifying similarities and differences between women and men. However, as public health researchers increasingly recognize, such findings are not as self-explanatory as they may seem on the surface (Fishman, Wick & Koenig, 1999; Phillips, 2005). Historically, differences between women and men were presumed to be based on essential biological differences. While it is true that there are biological differences between women and men, most differences identified by the sex variable are not of biological origin. For example, while men are more violent than women throughout the world, significant differences in the rates of woman abuse from country to country indicate that cultural factors engender or discourage this type of violence (Johnson, Ollus & Nevala, 2007). Accordingly, it is important to recognize that sex differences describe the characteristics of violence rather than its causes or contributing factors. Furthermore, the presence or absence of sex differences does not tell us about the importance of gendered factors in producing violence. In order to understand the role of gendered norms and institutions, it is necessary to investigate the gendered aspects of experience. For example, studies that use the sex categories female and male can tell us how many women and men have certain experiences. Still, the sex variable alone cannot tell us whether or not and similarities or differences across sex are caused by biological differences or socio-economic factors. This means that we can't directly learn about gender based on studies that measure only the sex category. However, even the conservative sources cited by anti-feminists in support of their claims that women are as violent as men indicate that women's and men's experiences of violence are very different.

CANADIAN RESEARCH ON SEX DIFFERENCES IN NON-FATAL VIOLENCE AGAINST INTIMATES

Efforts to promote the use of gender-blind language selectively cite research to incorrectly characterize violence as bi-directional, mutual, or "sex symmetrical." For example, *Family violence in Canada: A statistical profile 2000* notes that 8 percent of women and 7 percent of men "experienced some type of violence by a partner during the previous 5 years" (Pottie Bunge & Locke, 2000, p. 5). Some people cite this percentage as evidence that women's and men's violence is essentially the same. However, the same report finds marked differences in women's and men's experiences of violence. For example:

- Women were more likely than men to report "more severe" forms of violence.
- Women were more likely than men to report repeated victimization.
- Women were more likely than men to be injured by a partner.
- Women were more likely than men to report negative emotional consequences as a result of the violence.
- Women were more likely to experience forms of violence that came to the attention of the police.
- Women were much more likely to report fear that their lives were in danger. (Pottie Bunge & Locke, 2000, p. 5)

What this tells us is that looking at the percentage of women and men who have experienced some type of violence by a partner during the previous five years is not enough to understand the nature of that violence. Furthermore, looking at the prevalence of violence on its own is likely to produce extremely misleading results. In other words, counting people who have ever experienced any form of violence by a partner during a certain time period does not allow us to understand anything about violence well enough to help prevent it. Under crude prevalence counts, a man who has beaten his partner repeatedly and is pushed by her once are both victims of intimate partner violence. While both may have experienced aggression, this is not the full story. Such crude accounting obscures factors such as the context, meaning, and motives of violence, which are necessary to interpret the numbers accurately. For example, violence used to defend oneself—even lethal violence—means something very different in a court of law and in public opinion than offensive attacks. Counting these types of violence as equivalent is misleading.

Methodological Issues

In addition to selective citation of sources, it is important to note that methodological issues have a profound impact on statistics about violence. The reasons for underreporting of violence in survey research have been discussed extensively elsewhere (see, for example, DeKeseredy, 2011; DeKeseredy & Dragiewicz, 2007; Johnson & Dawson, 2011). StatsCan reports like the one cited above use data from the General Social Survey (GSS), which does not use state-of-the-art research methods for measuring violence and abuse. Instead, the GSS uses narrow definitions of violence based on the Criminal Code, omitting many of the types of violence and abuse frequently experienced by abused women (see DeKeseredy, 2011, for an in-depth discussion of state-of-the-art research methods and critiques of the GSS). In addition, its framing as a crime survey drives down reporting as respondents report only incidents they believe meet the threshold for being a crime. The person calling to introduce the GSS says: "We are calling you for a study on Canadians' safety. The purpose of the study is to better understand people's perceptions of crime and the justice system, and the extent of victimization in Canada" (GSS, cited in Brownridge, 2009, p. 16). As a result, the GSS yields only a fraction of actual cases of violence and abuse.

Comparing three often-cited sources of official data illustrates this point. Police, the GSS, and the Violence against Women Survey (VAWS) found very different rates of violence against women. Canada last sponsored a national study of violence against women in 1993. In that year, police reports yielded 46,800 physical assaults perpetrated by a spouse, the GSS found 107,500, and the VAWS reported 201,000. For sexual assaults by any perpetrator, police reported 15,200, the GSS reported 316,000, and the VAWS reported 572,000 (Johnson, 1996, pp. 41–42).

Not only do these numbers vary dramatically across sources, the under-reporting of sexual assaults to police was so extreme that police reports indicate a higher number of physical assaults against women than sexual assaults, while the other two sources indicate the opposite pattern—that sexual assault is more common than physical assault. This example shows how different research methods not only obscure a portion of the actual crimes, but distort even the picture of which types of violence are most common in women's lives.

Obfuscating Violence against Women

Recent government reports on family violence increasingly obscure the most elementary information about differences in women's and men's experiences of violence and abuse (DeKeseredy & Dragiewicz, 2009). *Family violence in Canada: A statistical profile 2011* is a case in point. The highlights on "self-reported spousal violence" combine victimization rates for women and men into an unintelligible and misleading aggregate figure. The report reads: "Of the 19 million Canadians who had a current or former spouse in 2009, 6% reported being physically or sexually victimized by their partner or spouse in the preceding five years" (Statistics Canada, 2011, p. 8). Choosing to report the percentage of victims in this fashion obscures much higher rates of sexual assault of women and much lower rates for men. Women aren't mentioned until page 6 of the report, in the discussion of violence against seniors.

However, even this report includes evidence that women and men experience very different forms of violence. The report indicates that: "females report more serious violence than males" (Statistics Canada, 2011, p. 10). For example: "Females who reported spousal violence were about three times more likely than males (34% versus 10%) to report that they had been sexually assaulted, beaten, choked or threatened with a gun or a knife by their partner or ex-partner in the previous 5 years" (Statistics Canada, 2011, p. 10). A chart is included in the report, which indicates what appear to be large sex differences in these types of violence, but the numbers are not reported for the different types of violence. Instead, the report indicates that the "proportion of victims who has reported the most severe form of spousal violence has remained stable since 2004" (Statistics Canada, 2011, p. 10). Brennan (2011) indicates that 42 percent of women and 18 percent of men victimized by intimates were physically injured (p. 13). Brennan also reports that 57 percent of female victims and 40 percent of male victims experience "multiple victimizations" (p. 9), and that 15 percent of women reported having obtained a restraining order against their abuser compared to 5 percent of men (p. 12). As DeKeseredy and Dragiewicz (2009) have argued elsewhere, "Even a cursory glance at these findings indicates that the violence experienced by women and men is neither similar nor equivalent."

However, the 2011 report obscures many other indicators of violence that have historically been reported and which show marked sex differences. For example, the data on victim hospitalization and fearing for their lives are unreported. The choice to omit or aggregate the numbers for types of violence showing marked sex differences in favour of an emphasis on similarities produces a misleading impression that violence is similar for women and men. A comparison with earlier reports illustrates this point well. *Family violence in Canada: A statistical profile 2000* reported that 8 percent of women and an "amount too small to be expressed" of men reported sexual assault by a current partner. Twenty-seven percent of women and 5 percent of men reported sexual assault by a former partner. In addition, 10 percent of women and an "amount too small to be expressed" of men reported being choked (Pottie Bunge & Locke, 2000, p. 13). The recent choice to omit reports of sexual assault and strangulation, which are common to female victims of intimate partner abuse, is just as political as stressing the importance of sex differences in understanding violence and abuse (DeKeseredy & Dragiewicz, 2009).

Separation Assault

The family violence reports also obscure other important aspects of violence against women. Although many police officers, judges, and child custody mediators mistakenly believe that men would stop using violence against women if they "just left," separation actually increases the risk of lethal and sub-lethal physical and sexual assault for many women. Marital status is not necessarily a reliable indicator of whether violence occurs pre- or post-separation. Indeed, scholars who study separation assault have utilized a range of definitions (see, for example, Brownridge, 2009, pp. 54–56).

Nonetheless, multiple Canadian studies have documented the increased risk to women from former husbands and boyfriends, with especially large differences in severe violence. Smith (1990, p. 50) found that 31 percent of divorced or separated women had been victimized by male partners compared to 13 percent of the women in intact relationships, based on women's reports of victimization. Brownridge noted that separated women reported the highest prevalence of violence, followed by divorced women, then married women (2009, p. 70). Brownridge, Chan, Hiebery-Murphy, Ristok, Tiwari, Leung, and Santos (2008) found that separated women reported nine times more violence than married women, and divorced women reported almost four times as much violence as married women (p. 117). Spiwak and Brownridge (2005) observed that 11 percent of separated women reported violence by a partner in the year prior to the survey (p. 110). For 57 percent of the women, violence began at separation, and was a continuation of previous violence for 29 percent (p. 110). In other words, for a significant portion of women, violence that began before separation continued after separation. In addition, violence begins at separation for many women.

The GSS findings indicate that risks for women and men are significantly different. Statistics Canada's 2000 *Family violence in Canada* report found that of women and men fifteen and older who had reported violence by a previous spouse in the five years preceding the survey, 27 percent of women (seventeen women) and 5 percent of men (twelve men) reported sexual assault. Twenty percent of women (eighty-six women) and 14 percent of men (thirty-five men) reported that their previous spouse used or threatened to use a gun or knife against them. Twenty-six percent of women (114 women) and 7 percent of men (eighteen men) reported they had been choked. Thirty-two percent of women (139 women) and 16 percent of men (forty-one men) reported having been beaten (p. 13). The 2011 report did not include any information on non-lethal separation assault that was disaggregated by sex. The choice to aggregate the numbers for women and men for this particular type of victimization hides significantly different rates for women and men. Readers may well assume that victimization is similar for women and men. Writing up the data in this fashion minimizes women's actual victimization while exaggerating men's.

Femicide

Perhaps the clearest illustration of the importance of context in understanding violence is intimate partner homicide. The most serious from of violence, homicide is profoundly gendered in Canada as elsewhere in the world. The 2011 report on *Family-related homicides, 2000 to 2009* notes that family homicides make up 35 percent of all solved homicides. Forty-seven percent of family homicides were spousal homicides. Spousal homicides were 16 percent of all solved homicides from 2000 to 2009 (Taylor-Butts & Porter, 2011, p. 32). Taylor-Butts and Porter noted that while men are the majority of homicide victims in general, women are the majority of victims in family and spousal homicides. The rate of spousal homicides of women is three to four times greater than the rate for men, and women are more than twice as likely (26 percent) as men (11 percent) to be killed by a partner from whom they are separated (p. 33).

In addition, significant sex differences were found in the type of relationship in which women and men were most at risk, with women most at risk from current husbands and men most at risk from common-law partners. In addition, significant differences emerged in the method of killing (Taylor-Butts & Porter, 2011). While stabbing was the most common method of killing, male victims were more likely to be stabbed (72 percent) than female victims (32 percent). Female victims were much more likely to be shot (26 percent) than men (11 percent). Women were also much more likely to be strangled, suffocated, or drowned (22 percent) than men (4 percent). Women were more than three times more likely (15 percent) to be beaten to death than men (5 percent) (p. 34). Although limited information on the context of spousal homicide is included in the 2011 family violence report, it does make certain facts clear. A much larger percentage of killings of women than men comprise spousal homicide. The relationship to the perpetrator is different, with women more likely to be killed post-separation, and the methods of killing differ substantially. These sex differences point to the need for different resources for women and men. However, more information is needed to understand the dynamics of spousal homicide in order to develop strategies for prevention.

Domestic violence death review committees provide a more complete picture. Although it is much easier to quantify fatal victimization than non-fatal victimization, even body counts are not as simple as they may seem at first glance. For example, The *Seventh annual report of the domestic violence death review committee—2009* indicates that between 2002 and 2008, there were 184 incidents of domestic homicide in Ontario, resulting in 253 deaths. Of these deaths, 159 were women, seventy-one were men, and twenty-three were children (Ontario Domestic Violence Death Review Committee, 2009, p. 9).

While these numbers are obviously different for women, men, and children, the disparity is even greater than it seems at first glance. Two of the 159 dead women (1 percent of cases) were perpetrators *and* fatalities in homicide-suicides. Fifty-five of the seventy-one dead men (77 percent of cases) were perpetrators *and* fatalities in homicide-suicides (Ontario Domestic Violence Death Review Committee, 2009, p. 9). In other words, even murder, the most easily quantifiable form of violence, requires some contextual details in order to make the numbers intelligible. Homicide-suicides comprised 23 percent of domestic homicides in Ontario between 2002 and 2008. Ninety-one percent of victims were female, and 92 percent of perpetrators were male (Ontario Domestic Violence Death Review Committee, 2009, p. 11). Relying on decontextualized body counts alone would provide an extremely misleading impression of the dynamics of this most serious form of abuse. These numbers also illustrate women's disproportionate need for emergency shelter relative to men. Many of these homicides were preceded by a history of violence and abuse, and many occurred at separation or divorce.

Outcomes of Violence

Help seeking is another area where the ongoing need for services for female victims of violence and abuse is evident. A recent Statistics Canada report on shelters for abused women found that "between April 1, 2009 and March 31, 2010 there were over 64,500 admissions of women to shelters across Canada, up 5% from 2007/2008. Almost one-third (31%) of these women had stayed at the shelter before, up from one-quarter (25%) in 2007/2008" (Burczycka & Cotter, 2011, p. 5). The large numbers of women seeking shelter from abusers, as well as the significant portion of women returning to shelter, reflect the repeated and serious nature of woman abuse in Canada. Despite this, only 40 percent of the women in shelter indicated they had reported the violence to police. Twenty-seven percent of the women reported that formal charges were laid against the abuser in the incident preceding entry into the shelter, and 26 percent reported there had been a restraining order against the abuser (Burczycka & Cotter, 2011, p. 15). These numbers indicate that the problem of violence against women is still a pressing one, and that many women require services targeted to woman abuse.

NEO-LIBERALISM, ANTI-FEMINISM, AND ATTACKS ON LAWS AND SERVICES THAT PROTECT WOMEN FROM ABUSE

Given the above evidence of persistent sex differences in violence against women and men by intimates, how can we understand claims that women are as violent as men? Like many other Western democracies, Canada has witnessed the ascendance of neo-liberal ideologies in recent years. These ideologies have contributed to retrenchment of social welfare programs that have specifically targeted women and other minorities (Morrow, Hankivsky & Varcoe, 2004). Cuts to social assistance, legal aid, and services for women have direct and serious implications for survivors of woman abuse.

Fiscal retrenchment has contributed to social policy trends wherein a focus on addressing crime and violence by promoting rights has been replaced with calls for individualized solutions to crime. Kelly Hannah-Moffat has described the "devolution of the state's responsibility for crime prevention and offender reform" (2000, p. 514) in which the language of social movements has been appropriated and turned against itself. In this way, the Canadian government has harnessed efforts to divest itself of responsibility for women's safety to calls for empowerment-based responses to social problems. By annexing the language of empowerment, which links political structures to personal struggles, and then focusing on the effects of disempowerment on individuals, the Canadian government has effectively returned the responsibility for avoiding violence to women themselves—for example, by calling the police and requesting that charges be laid or going to a shelter in response to violence rather than trying to prevent violence in the first place.

As Hannah-Moffat puts it, "The difficulty is that strategies of empowerment tend to resonate with multiple and conflicting objectives" (2000, p. 522). In the case of woman abuse, empowerment rhetoric can be focused on individual behaviours rather than structural factors. As a result, women are blamed for the failure to prevent violence done to them. In addition, the focus on individuals leads to the prioritization of responses to violence, which cannot address structural inequality. For example, funding job-training programs as a response to violence (so abused women can leave) may look empowering because women need incomes to be able to support themselves. However, funding job programs at the expense of child care services means that abused women will struggle to secure affordable child care so that they can actually go to work. In this context, where treating everyone the same is thought to demonstrate fairness, services designed to address women's socio-economic marginalization are attacked as discriminatory against men. Concomitant demands insist that these services, which are now funded at lower levels than in the past while facing greater demand, eliminate their focus on women's needs in order to serve everyone the same way. In some cases, services for women have been de-funded altogether, and the funding rerouted to generic crisis services (Morrow, Hankivsky, & Varcoe, 2004, p. 366).

We see this dynamic in the turn away from discussion of woman abuse toward gender-blind discourses on family violence and abuse. Even the conservative government statistics cited above point to profound differences between women's and men's experiences of violence, yet these data are framed in reports using the gender-neutral label of family violence. In order to claim that women are as violent as men, it would necessitate ignoring the majority of research on violence and the responses to it. Even the rudimentary measures of violence and abuse utilized in the GSS indicate that the dynamics of violence and abuse against women and men are very different. The fact that demand for emergency shelters for women is increasing rather than decreasing shows that woman abuse has not been eliminated.

It is essential that scholars and practitioners be aware of the political sources and implications of gender-blind rhetoric on violence and abuse. Complaints that violence against women is "hyped" by feminists for some sort of political traction, or that women and men experience violence by intimates in similar ways, are simply not supported by the data. Nonetheless, Canadian government publications increasingly adopt misleading and de-gendered discourses on violence. Clearly, this is a political choice. Unfortunately, it has negative ramifications for Canadians' understanding of the nature of violence and abuse against women and men. Anti-violence advocates and scholars need to hold the line and continue contextualizing violence against women as a continuum of harm, to write and speak accurately about who is doing what to whom and in what circumstances, and to defend the scholarship and services that we have fought hard to establish.

REFERENCES

Boyd, S.B. (2003). *Child custody, law, and women's work*. Toronto: Oxford University Press.

Brennan, S. (2011). *Self-reported spousal violence: 2009*. Ottawa: Statistics Canada, Canadian Centre for Justice Statistics.

Brownridge, D.A. (2009). *Violence against women: Vulnerable populations*. New York: Routledge. Retrieved from: http://www.routledge.com/books/details/9780415996082/.

Brownridge, D.A., Chan, K.L., Hiebery-Murphy, D., Ristok, J., Tiwari, A., Leung, W.C., & Santos, S.C. (2008). The elevated risk for non-lethal post-separation violence in Canada. *Journal of Interpersonal Violence, 23*(1), 117–35.

Burczycka, M., & Cotter, A. (2011). *Shelters for abused women in Canada, 2010*. Juristat. Ottawa: Statistics Canada, Canadian Centre for Justice Statistics.

Cribb, R. (2011, October 19). Cribb: Men are the new underclass. *Toronto Star.* Retrieved from: http://www.thestar.com/living/article/1071379--cribb-men -are-the-new-underclass.

DeKeseredy, W. (2011). *Violence against women: Myths, facts, controversies.* Toronto: University of Toronto Press.

DeKeseredy, W.S., & Dragiewicz, M. (2007). Understanding the complexities of feminist perspectives on woman abuse. *Violence against Women, 13*(8), 874–84.

DeKeseredy, W. S., & Dragiewicz, M. (2009). *Shifting public policy direction: Gen-der-focused versus bi-directional intimate partner violence.* Ottawa: Ontario Women's Directorate; Queen's Printer for Ontario. Retrieved from: http:// www.citizenship.gov.on.ca/owd/english/resources/publications/dvac/shifting _pp_direction.html.

DeKeseredy, W.S., & MacLeod, L. (1997). *Woman abuse: A sociological story.* Toronto: Harcourt Brace.

Dragiewicz, M. (2009). Why sex and gender matter in domestic violence research and advocacy. In E. Stark & E. Buzawa (Eds.), *Violence against women in fami-lies and relationships: Criminal justice and the law* (Vol. 3) (pp. 201–15). Santa Barbara, CA: Praeger.

Dragiewicz, M. (2011). *Equality with a vengeance: Men's rights groups, battered women, and antifeminist backlash.* Boston: Northeastern University Press.

Dragiewicz, M., & DeKeseredy, W.S. (forthcoming). Claims about women's use of non-fatal force in intimate relationships: A contextual review of the Cana-dian research. *Violence against Women.*

Dragiewicz, M., & Lindgren, Y. (2009). The gendered nature of domestic vio-lence: Statistical data for lawyers considering equal protection analysis. *American University Journal of Gender, Social Policy & the Law, 17*(2), 229–68.

Fishman, J.R., Wick, J.G., & Koenig, B.A. (1999). The use of "sex" and "gender" to define and characterize meaningful differences between men and women. *An agenda for research on women's health in the 21st century: The report of the task force.* Rockville, MD: Office of Research on Women's Health. Retrieved from: http://orwh.od.nih.gov/pubs/agenda_book_2.pdf.

Goodmark, L. (2012). *A troubled marriage: Domestic violence and the legal system.* New York: New York University Press.

Gotell, L. (1998). A critical look at state discourse on "violence against women": Some implications for feminist politics and women's citizenship. In M. Trem-blay & C. Andrew (Eds.), *Women and political representation in Canada* (pp. 39–84). Ottawa: University of Ottawa Press.

Gotell, L. (2007). The discursive disappearance of sexualized violence: Feminist law reform, judicial resistance, and neo-liberal sexual citizenship. In D.E. Chunn, S.B. Boyd & H. Lessard (Eds.), *Reaction and resistance: Feminism, law, and social change* (pp. 127–63). Vancouver: UBC Press.

Hannah-Moffat, K. (2000). Prisons that empower. *British Journal of Criminology, 40*(3), 510–31.

Hausman, R., Tyson, L.D., & Zahidi, S. (2010). *The global gender gap report*. Geneva: World Economic Forum.

Johnson, H. (1996). *Dangerous domains: Violence against women in Canada*. Toronto: Nelson.

Johnson, H., & Dawson, M. (2011). *Violence against women in Canada: Research and policy perspectives*. Toronto: Oxford University Press.

Johnson, H., Ollus, N., & Nevala, S. (2007). *Violence against women: An international perspective*. New York: Springer.

MacLeod, L. (1980). *Wife battering in Canada: The vicious circle*. Ottawa: Canadian Advisory Council on the Status of Women.

MacLeod, L. (1987). *Battered but not beaten: Preventing wife battering in Canada*. Ottawa: Canadian Advisory Council on the Status of Women.

Minaker, J.C., & Snider, L. (2006). Husband abuse: Equality with a vengeance? *Canadian Journal of Criminology and Criminal Justice/La Revue canadienne de criminologie et de justice pénale, 48*(5), 753–80.

Morrow, M., Hankivsky, O., & Varcoe, C. (2004). Women and violence: The effects of dismantling the welfare state. *Critical Social Policy, 24*(3), 358.

Ontario Domestic Violence Death Review Committee. (2009). *Seventh annual report of the Domestic Violence Death Review Committee—2009*. Toronto: Office of the Chief Coroner, Province of Ontario. Retrieved from: http://www.crvawc.ca/documents/DVDRC2010.pdf.

Phillips, S.P. (2005). Defining and measuring gender: A social determinant of health whose time has come. *International Journal for Equity in Health, 4*(11), 1–4.

Pleck, E. (1983). Feminist responses to "crimes against women," 1868–1896. *Signs, 8*(3), 451–70.

Pottie Bunge, V., & Locke, D. (2000). *Family violence in Canada: A statistical profile*. Ottawa: Statistics Canada, 2000.

Randall, M. (1989). *The politics of understanding wife abuse: Understanding the issues*. Toronto: Education Wife Assault.

Rosenberg, S. (2003). Neither forgotten nor fully remembered: Tracing an ambivalent public memory on the 10th anniversary of the Montréal Massacre. *Feminist Theory, 4*(1), 5–27.

Rosenberg, S., & Simon, R.I. (2000). Beyond the logic of emblemization: Remembering and learning from the Montreal massacre. *Educational Theory, 50*(2), 133–55.

Schneider, E. (2000). *Battered women and feminist lawmaking*. New Haven, CT: Yale University Press.

Sinclair, D. (2003). *Overcoming the backlash: Telling the truth about power, privilege, and oppression*. Oshawa: Gender Advisory Committee of the Violence Prevention Coordinating Council of Durham Region. Retrieved from: http://www.crvawc.ca/documents/overcomingthebacklash.pdf.

Smith, M.D. (1990). Sociodemographic risk factors in wife abuse: Results from a survey of Toronto women. *The Canadian Journal of Sociology/Cahiers canadiens de sociologie, 15*(1), 39–58.

Spiwak, R., & Brownridge, D.A. (2005). Separated women's risk for violence. *Journal of Divorce & Remarriage, 43*(3–4), 105–17.

Statistics Canada. (2011) *Family violence in Canada: A statistical profile.* Ottawa: Statistics Canada, Canadian Centre for Justice Statistics.

Taylor-Butts, A., & Porter, L. (2011). *Family-related homicides, 2000 to 2009.* Ottawa: Statistics Canada, Canadian Centre for Justice Statistics.

3

IS THIS VIOLENCE? IS THIS SEXUAL VIOLENCE? RECOGNIZING AND DEFINING VIOLENCE THROUGH DIALOGUE WITH FRENCH-SPEAKING WOMEN

INA MOTOI

> Re-question me, ask again your questions!
> Can you ask me more questions, please?[1]

"Is this violence?" was often the first question a woman asked when she contacted SOS-Femmes Line, a francophone emergency phone line operating in Ontario from 1988 to 2003. "Is this sexual violence?" is a question asked in Quebec in 2011, when we are trying to recognize and understand sexual objectification and its impact in the lives of women.

In this chapter, we will explore why these questions are asked and how using dialogue helps us understand the ways in which definitions of violence reveal diverse tensions and unfold through individual narratives. Through dialogue, whether it is by talking to oneself or to others, women define family violence and sexual violence. Their definitions influence their experiences of this violence. To illustrate this perspective, the two examples above will be developed. The first example involves exploring, recognizing, and defining family violence as counsellors working in a *francophone minority context* in which women from multiple cultures, races, and religions contacted SOS-Femmes Line for support. The second example takes place in a *francophone majority context* and involves group facilitators engaging in dialogue with women about their experiences of living with sexual objectification, feeling used "like a prostitute" (*rapport prostitutionnel*) in a couple, or in the context of prostitution.

First, in order to facilitate understanding, we will explore the notion of dialogue and its role in intervention. Second, we will use the two examples to illustrate how two methods of constructing dialogue define violence by bringing specific tensions into perspective:

- *contextual* method built through ongoing intervention in a francophone minority cultural context, facilitated by the development of an intercultural understanding and know-how (*savoir-faire*)
- *positional* method shaped by fierce feminist debate involving two distinctive, conflicting socio-political positions regarding prostitution and how their meta-narratives are contrasted by personal stories of women living with sexual objectification and prostitution, each position situating itself in comparison to the other positions

The common denominator of these two methods is dialogue. This dialogue, which recognizes and reveals an individual's knowledge about how and why she lives within a violent situation, fosters mutual understanding:

- between a woman searching for support and a woman offering it through the SOS-Femmes Line
- among women in a group discussing their own sexuality
- for a woman in dialogue with herself, constructing her own subjective theory about the distinction between sexuality, objectification, and prostitution, which she may or may not ever share in a dialogue with the group

As a final step toward understanding intervening with dialogue, we will discuss the existential, cultural, and ethical issues involved with this practice. But first, let's take a closer look at the notion of dialogue in intervention.

DIALOGUE IN INTERVENTION

The role of the counsellor or the group facilitator is to open up a space for dialogue. This exterior space enables a woman to externalize what has been a private, interior dialogue. For many of us involved in using this method, the result of dialogue is knowledge and this is a new experience. Yet, how did the notion of dialogue come to intervention?

The Notion of Dialogue

The following three perspectives address the concept of dialogue and help us capture the multiple facets of the interdependence that helps put experiences and thoughts into perspective.

Socrates[2] (fourth century BCE) sees "dialogue as thinking," which *accompanies* a person when dealing with his or her own problems and discovering the solutions—the answers are within the individual. Socrates sees himself as a midwife "delivering" dialectically (reasoning with arguments through contradictions) the spirit within, in a non-directive manner.

The circle of Bakhtin/Volochinov[3] (1929, 1930) understands the group as a space for dialogue outside oneself and dialogue as *groupalism*, "above all a human activity," made possible by humans grouping together to give importance and meaning to life in society. They are seeking a community of minds through significant proximity.

Markova (2007) refers to fundamental *exchange* through dialogue in which a story is linked with the story of another individual through *social representations*. This approach recognizes the human being as on the frontier between the interior and exterior spaces of dialogue.

"Talking Alone": An Internal Dialogue

According to Paveau (2010, p. 7), Bakhtin also recognizes that "any interior monologue has, in fact, a dialogical structure which takes the form of an interior debate with questions and answers, a dialogue with oneself made of statements followed by objections, clear separate replicas which are more or less developed." Paveau says that this interior dialogue happens without the other. We often witness in intervention "the annulment of the other in the narrative." By this stratagem, in order to find her own voice, a woman silences the other voices that are imposing themselves on her, offering other definitions of what she is living. To create her own meaning, the woman must make her interior dialogical space sovereign by not permitting any interpretation other than her own of what she lives as family or sexual violence. In this way, she can gather her own thoughts in freedom and continuity with herself, and consolidate herself as the subject of her own experience. This internal dialogue allows her to establish her own ability to give and to construct meaning in full subjectivity. "OK. This emotion is passing away. Now, I am able to say why it was there, I have the entire puzzle which is complete. At that time, I had just my emotions; I didn't have the entire puzzle."[4]

This internal dialogue is often the only intimate space in a life occupied by others. The woman develops, step by step, and by trial and error, her knowledge of who she is and how she faces the violence in her life. Then, as a second step, the will to dialogue with the other "manifests itself from her own subjectivity" (Paveau, 2010, p. 8) and the woman is strong enough to negotiate her own perspective of the violent experience in dialogue with another.

Narrating Her Own Thinking: An External Dialogue
Here are some concepts that allow us to create a space for external dialogue, in order to facilitate women's narrative of their own thinking:

- *Dialogue as relationship* (Racine, 2000) creates a particular context in which words can be defined by recognizing their nuances and mediating their understanding.
- *Narrative power* is active and critical, has its source in the woman's interior dialogue, and expresses itself in external dialogue. This power is lived as theoretical power, allowing a woman to construct her own meaning of what she lives as violent or not. In this way, the woman builds her own theory[5] of what she is living as knowledge, which is auto-verifying (Scott, 1989).
- *Experiential knowledge* ("*savoir expérientiel*"; Racine, 2000) is constructed by and in action as "intimate knowledge resulting from a direct relationship and reflected [from the woman as] subject to herself [or] to another subject . . ." (Taylor, cited in Racine, 2000, p. 54). To appropriate her own sexuality and family life, the woman has to enter into herself to contact her internal dialogical space and declare it sovereign since it is where she constructs her experiential knowledge. She can redefine the terms she is using in order to talk about what she lives, whenever necessary. The group or the counsellor recognizes a woman's *epistemological ownership* of her own narrative to construct the meaning she reveals. In this way, her knowledge of her experience is explained in her own words and allows her to orient herself on the territory of her own experience in order to act significantly for herself.
- *Life balance review* ("*bilan de vie*"; Hétu, 2000) is when the woman finds herself with the epistemological necessity to do so. This is the time and place of the narrative, where past experiences and life decisions are reinterpreted in order to reorganize them, to put them in balance, by creating new meanings.
- *Positional identity* (Chambon, 1993, p. 126) as a "rapport of the subject to the world and to others." This allows the woman to position herself in her own life history and, in this way, historicize and situate herself. The affirmation of self as subject of her own history or of her own sexuality facilitates a positional identity contrasting the available narratives in society.

Resistance: The Frontier between Internal Dialogue and External Dialogue

Can a woman living in a violent situation rebuild her identity of living as a subordinate object by resisting it? Can she assert a different interpretation of this situation by using her own internal dialogue and *position herself* as different, based on her gender or her culture? Is she using this resistance to affirm her own right to a different perspective, opinion, experience, or know-how? Can she question and transform domination through this resistance?

Do women from patriarchal cultures identify with the dominant narratives (Leonard & Leonard, 1999, p. 9) of their respective cultures or with the dominant feminist narrative in Ontario? Do women involved in prostitution identify with the dominant narrative of the sex industry or with feminist narratives and, if so, with which one—the radical one or the liberal one? Is this identification an act of docility (see Foucault, 1975, *"corps dociles"*) or a choice of affirming their gender identity as resistance in terms of "otherness" in a known territory?

A woman's resistance to a situation of sexual or family violence—in conjunction with patriarchal power, which objectifies her body (Leonard & Leonard, 1999, p. 8)—can be seen as the basis from which she will take control of her own life. Therefore, her resistance is an integral part of power, an element of its workings, as well as a source of its perpetual disorder. The woman's resistance comes with the *intention* to live differently (better): the emphasis is on how this person resists violence and wishes for change.

Family violence can be more than simply a problem to be identified—"I am living in a violent situation. We are all living the same violent situation." It is also a way of interacting, which often includes family and community. It is one spouse against another, a parent in opposition to her child, a child in opposition to her parent, etc. Further, a counsellor who insists or imposes her understanding on the "client's" problem can also initiate violence by silencing her voice and not taking into consideration her experiential knowledge. That's why we should talk about prostitution, for example, as a system: the woman prostitute, the client, the pimp, and the community in which prostitution exists. That's why even resistance has to be questioned. Who resists whom? For example, should a sixteen-year-old girl, running from her father and family who arranged for her to marry an older relative, be returned to them or protected from them? Whose resistance should have precedence over the other?

Through resistance as a frontier that severs interior dialogue from exterior dialogue, two definitions of violence were constructed: the first within the precise context of intervention (SOS-Femmes Line), and the second through the subjective (personal) positioning of women who were sexually objectified and who feel used "like a prostitute" in the context of a couple or in the context of prostitution.

IS THIS VIOLENCE? A CONTEXTUAL DEFINITION OF VIOLENCE

During a fifteen-year period, the counsellors on SOS-Femmes Line responded to more than fifty thousand calls. At first, these calls came almost exclusively from French Canadian-born women throughout Ontario. Over the years, however, the calls reflected the arrival of people from French-speaking regions around the world, such as Haiti, Congo, Burundi, Rwanda, Somalia, Ethiopia, Morocco, Tunisia, Egypt, and eastern Europe. Indeed, the historically rooted French Canadian linguistic minority living in an anglophone majority encountered newcomers willing to participate *in French* and position themselves in Ontario through this minority culture.

As director of the SOS Femmes Line from 1988 to 2003, intervention supervisor, and trainer, I quickly learned, at the risk of being hung up on, that how we wanted to help the women who were calling the emergency line and how they wanted to be helped were two very different things. Most of the time, we did not share the same understanding of violent situations as we followed a particular value-guided logic. For example, how could we distinguish a battered child from a disciplined one? Who should be making this decision? Whose values should be imposed upon whom? In both cases, we talk about goodwill, proven methods, children's welfare, but as the mother of four children living this dilemma told me clearly, "I am losing my children, they're becoming strangers, and this society punishes parents if we don't let children do what they want."[6]

It was clear that we had a choice to make: either we could continue to impose *our* interpretation on what these women lived, or we could enter fully into their situations *with* them through their narratives, and give them the space to define the problem and therefore the solution in dialogue with us. But often the exploration of what caused the problem was easier than identifying long-lasting solutions.

It was the very process of learning how to help women callers in a meaningful and enduring manner that provided the experiential knowledge and the intercultural know-how situated at the core of the counsellors' work. This ongoing context of apprenticeship, so to speak, meant that the counsellors learned, on a trial-by-fire basis, to dialogue with the women contacting the helpline. The process of dialoging with each woman, supporting her in making decisions consistent (or not) with her cultural positioning, formed the basis of intercultural feminist intervention.

In order to contextualize the very nature of intervening in family violence, the next section will put into perspective the francophone minority environment in Ontario and the cultural dialogue taking place: the construction of the notions of inferiority and identity violence, contradicting discourses on cultural identity, and specific issues that have an impact on family violence.

Inferiority and Identity Violence as Exclusion

In the 1980s, in feminist Franco-Ontarian[7] circles in southern Ontario, a francophone woman was said to experience a double inferiority, both as a woman and also as a francophone. In 2001, immigrant women coming from Africa and Asia were identified as a "visible ethno-cultural minority."[8] As francophones, they lived, by the same logic, a triple inferiority, which could also be described as intersectionality. In this perspective, this meant living identity violence because as a group or as individuals, they were kept in a subordinate social position through power dynamics that maintain their *exclusion* from the culturally dominant group. Table 3.1 illustrates the dynamics and identifies which actions were needed to counteract the violence.

Table 3.1   Triple Inferiority

Inferiority Dimension	Context	Forms of Violence	Required Action
As a woman	1980s feminism	• lack of equality within couple and in society • being treated like an object • lack of gender-specific services	• improve living conditions • make oneself heard, seen, and respected • establish gender-specific resources
As a francophone	historical francophone minority within an anglophone majority (linguistic and cultural dimensions)	• unable to speak a native language with historical rights • unable to receive services in French • assimilation and reduced cultural visibility and vitality	• struggle for recognition of historical linguistic rights • creation of accessible French services (1986 French Language Services Act)
As a visible ethnocultural minority (race, accent, lifestyle)	Canada's two official languages and politics of multiculturalism	• discrimination and racism • confined to a role limited to the status of service users • receiving interventions based only on a Western feminist perspective	• to be a user of services and to also have a role in decision-making, and a place in service management • funding and visible accountability of multicultural organizations • implementing multicultural intervention (diverse relational values and sensibilities)

Grimard (2004, p. 151) points to the "discourse which constructs the Francophone community through a system of inclusion and exclusion." This dynamic is marked by the tension between the *centre* of the community, occupied by the historical traditional elite[9] putting up a discourse of *homogeneity*, and the *periphery*, occupied, in our case, by women (1980s) and immigrants (2000s) organizing a discourse of contestation based on the notion of *diversity*.

Cultural identities, according to Grimard (2004), are strategically positioned. In order to exclude from one's own identity the definition of another, battles throughout history were waged to put the identity of the winner at the centre of society and to push the loser to the periphery. For years, the anglophone majority in Ontario excluded the language and culture of the Franco-Ontarian minority from the centre. So, is there a contradiction when, as a minority, Franco-Ontarians denounce assimilation through homogeneity—but as a majority, within their own culture, they promote it?

Cultural Dialogue in the Francophone Minority Context

In this multicultural context of a francophone community in a minority situation, in 2003, the Association canadienne-française de l'Ontario-Toronto (ACFO-Toronto), under the leadership of Marcel Grimard, changed its name, the only regional ACFO body to do so, and became l'Association des communautés francophones de l'Ontario-Toronto, thus keeping the same initials—ACFO). In this way, the Franco-Torontonians redefined through dialogue their own cultural identity as francophones, integrating the cultural presence of the French-speaking newcomers.

This change of perspective made integration, in theory, a two-way street. For some, this redefinition of identity was an act of social justice and of breathing new life into the cultural identity of a minority on its way to assimilation, and it was facilitated by the rules of a multicultural government ruling at the centre of the anglophone society. For others, this change was an insult as it once again questioned a cultural identity that took root historically in Ontario and was the fruit of a long and difficult struggle, a struggle that should be honoured by staying loyal to a "French Canadian" identity. The choice was clear: since 2003,[10] the term "French Canadian" (Association) was exchanged for "Francophony" (Assembly of) at the provincial level, but all the other regional ACFOs remained French Canadian, with the exception of ACFO-Toronto. Groups of individuals experienced the recognition of the right to give a different meaning to a same life situation in various different ways: living in French. Table 3.2 illustrates three discourses that contradict and overlap in this context (Grimard, 2004, pp. 149–51).

Table 3.2   Three Contradictory Discourses

Discourse	Values	Strategies
Traditional: Before 1960	• attachment to the land • survival of the French language • practice of Catholicism	• demonization of capitalism, syndicalism, and urban life • glorification of French Canadian culture
Modernizing: 1960 onward	• recognition of linguistic rights	• national differentiation of French Canadians from Québécois • separation of Québécois identity and regional identity (Franco-Ontarian, Franco-Manitoban, etc.) • adoption of the French Language Services Act (1986)
Globalizing: Mid-1980s onward	• French as a linguistic, cultural, commercial, and financial advantage • bilingualism as an asset for better employment • multiculturalism as the norm • social justice as rights equality	• redefining a francophone (for the national census) • denouncing discrimination and racism • adopting political correctness as the norm

Tensions Revealed by This Dialogue

An intercultural problematic as the Francophonie (a shared understanding through reciprocal interaction between different cultures that evolve as *common representations*) emerges—only at a *provincial level*—from the pressure to define the historical Franco-Ontarian identity as multicultural or plural (recognition of multiple parallel cultures in a society based on the principle of equality of individual rights). From this evident tension, some questions arise:

- Is the positional metaphor of "centre" and "periphery" part of the social representations that neutralize tensions or heighten them?
- Could Franco-Ontarians recognize the newcomers and assimilate them to maintain monoculturalism and the centrality of their own culture? How do we recognize and include multiple cultures? Is there a cultural saturation point on both sides as a shared impossibility to integrate what may be too different?
- Is there a tension between multiculturalism and monoculturalism, between multiculturalism and interculturalism, or between monoculturalism and interculturalism?
- Is the difference between adaptation, integration, and assimilation a question of degree of inclusion in a community or in a society? Is it

necessary to also have an intercultural dialogue between the diverse ghettoized cultures or only with the dominant culture?

Highly political, the power to define cultural identity was appropriated by Toronto francophones, in the spirit of equity, to fight against the branded, ongoing double or triple inferiority experienced in their lives. It is in this context that the intercultural was partially negotiated through cultural dialogue in Toronto in 2003. The newcomers' fight to ensure a minority francophone identity meant not accepting exclusion from a collective identity—even though this collective identity existed prior to their arrival—as it was deemed that this exclusion would be a form of identity violence. This identity violence, as a fight for legitimacy, becomes the background that fuels all other definitions of violence in the context of the intervention at SOS-Femmes Line. In this context of intervention, we are at an intersection between the following:

- *Great collective stories* historically forged for centuries as a foundation for a national culture in a nation-state, prescribed as a *unique collective identity*: stories specific to the bilingual and multinational country where the newcomers have settled and stories from the countries of origin of the newcomers.

and

- The great *story of a universal culture*, no longer originating from a nation's history, but instead from individual differences, with the notion of equality between cultures. Added to this phenomenon is the current globalization of the economy, which transforms culture into an object available for individual consumption through the mass production of *cultural products*.

Does this multi-polarization of cultural identity match personal experiences? The meaning of integration isn't clear anymore. Our intervention in family violence was through dialogue, revealing tensions, so it was political: the terms constructing the definition of violence could be used interchangeably according to how they were valued from person to person or from group to group.

Who Should Answer the Question "Is This Violence?"

If a *woman offering support* to another woman answers this question, it is critical that she recognizes she is in a position of power to define the other's

Table 3.3   Tensions in a Francophone Linguistic Minority Context in Ontario

Traditional Discourse: Before 1960	Modernizing Discourse: 1960 onward	Globalizing Discourse Mid-1980s onward
Centre		**Periphery**
For a long time the anglophone majority excluded the language and culture of the Franco-Ontarian minority.		As a minority, Franco-Ontarians retained a discourse of contestation to resist assimilation through homogenization of their own culture and language.
The majority of this linguistic minority is constructing a discourse of homogeneity when in the centre.		The minority of this linguistic minority is organizing a discourse of resistance based on the notion of diversity at the periphery.
Narrative of continuity and loyalty to its own history and cultural identity		Narrative of social justice
Nationalism as particularism		Multiculturalism as universalism (internationalization)
Interculturalism as universalism, allowing integration into one common culture		Multiculturalism as multiple parallel cultures in a society based on the principle of equality of individual rights

reality. This position is a contextual one. At SOS-Femmes Line, we found ourselves in this position: we chose to work as counsellors for a francophone feminist organization working with women.

But if it is the *woman asking for support* who answers this question, it required thinking *with* her and not *for* her, and recognizing her specific power to define for herself if her reality is violent or not. It also means understanding the emotional and cognitive resonance of a given cultural life or milieu.

Working alongside each woman, at the intersection of two or more cultures—at least those of the caller and of the counsellor—required continuous presence and innovation. By not denying the tensions, but, rather, by making them visible through this dialogue, the woman caller and the counsellor could understand the dynamics of tensions by building meaning together.

Further, in the context of the host society, specific causes of family violence may add themselves to identity violence and allow us to further contextualize family violence. A family is subject to strong cultural tensions that redefine the connections among its members and their own subjective cultural limits and boundaries. This ordeal can degenerate into violence. Yet we must ask again: What constitutes a violent situation? Who defines it

Table 3.4   Some Specific Causes and Consequences of Family Violence

Dimensions	Causes	Consequences
Absence of family and community connections	• interpersonal relationships in a *collectivist* society are valued differently than in an *individualistic* society • the inability to function and negotiate a problem as a family	• isolation • grief • shrinking of the personal world • family members can substitute for each other in their support
Different cultural values: • elders versus youth • male versus female • time • community • family unity • respect for authority, obedience, honour	• priority of interpersonal relationships (*relational culture*) over functional relationships (*functional* culture) • in a *patriarchal/matriarchal* society, elders are often at the top of the family social ladder and represent the family; this defines the relationships among the members of the family from an existential point of view, and is rooted in religious commandment, carrying the same weight as law • men and women are not equal: their roles are different, men are in command and women are subordinate • it is women's responsibility to teach spiritual and cultural values • the symbolic relations among the members of a family lead them to feel a sense of belonging to a cosmological order (spiritual approach); religion can be seen as culture	• search for community-based solutions • willingness to negotiate family and public space so that each individual affirms his or her position in the family hierarchy • relationship between the counsellor, viewed as the "representative of the government," and the newcomer could be expected to be one of dominant/dominated • confrontation between men and women, parents and children • choice between patriarchal and religious models and an egalitarian and secular approach
Inversion of traditional roles (man–woman, elder–youth, or parent–child)	• traditional sharing of tasks, depending on different competencies • traditional division of gender and age • more rapid cultural insertion of youth, especially through language, peer culture, and technology • inversion of "family provider" responsibilities (based on employment and stable income) • creation of a network of connections outside the home	• conflict of values • culture shock • feeling of the unfamiliar (*depaysement*) and loss of meaning: powerlessness • emotional upheaval • crisis threatening family unity • disqualification of the roles of father/parents and their defensive reactions, which could lead to resignation and withdrawal or violence
Failure in immigration would invalidate the entire immigration plan	• cutting off access to a better future • hopes resting on children, putting the weight of responsibility on their shoulders • strong Western competitiveness • necessity of parental sacrifice	• success is imperative • lack of access to positive role models • the child feels that he or she must become "more Canadian than the Canadians" • lack of continuity • loss of status • non-reunification of the family • linguistic isolation and ghettoization
Post-traumatic stress disorder	• war, genocide • torture, wartime rape • life in a refugee camp • loss of loved ones • cost of immigration is too great in losses and separations • to be in a continuous state of change	• emotional shock, which can resurface at any time and unbalance the individual • feeling shame and responsibility for the event • stigmatization • fear of deportation

as such? By what cultural perspective or societal ideology is the definition imposed, prescribed, or proposed? Table 3.4 illustrates these dimensions, causes, and consequences.

In some areas, defining family violence may be even more difficult. The existing social consensus with regard to a given definition of violence changed during the transitory period of immigration, and such is the case with genital mutilation. Then how do we situate ourselves when the legal definition of violence changes faster than some single individuals are able to integrate it into their own world view? This lack of synergy also creates tension.

IS THIS SEXUAL VIOLENCE? A POSITIONAL DEFINITION OF VIOLENCE

Let's now examine another definition of violence, this time constructed through the positioning of one meta-narrative (liberal feminism) in debate with another (radical feminism). We will also explore how individual women, met through intervention and research, living in situations of sexual objectification and prostitution, understand this violence.

Big Stories and Small Stories

In Quebec, since 2000, there have been two opposing feminist theories on the definition of prostitution.[11] *Liberal feminism* considers prostitution as "sex work" because it is a woman's human right to do what she wants with her body. This position maintains that violence is not the act of prostitution itself, but rather that violence occurs within the circumstances of doing "sex work," for example, in the context of human trafficking and child prostitution, where there is no consent or because of the social stigma surrounding prostitution. *Radical feminism* defines prostitution as violence against women. In this view, a woman's body cannot be bought because the act of purchasing it is a breach of her dignity and integrity—this is sexual exploitation. In this view, the society that accepts prostitution as a "profession" also accepts degradation and suffering (incest, sexual aggression, poverty) for the most vulnerable women and facilitates their transformation into sexual objects. The commodification and merchandising of the body and of sexual services is part of a consumer society that values profit at any price, at the expense of our humanity for both women and men.

In Abitibi, I searched for a way to advance this social debate on prostitution by revealing the *personal narratives* of women who were either involved in prostitution or were feeling used "like a prostitute" by a man or a woman within a couple. In this way, the focus shifted from individual-society to Self-Other, Ego-Alter, as Markova (2007) puts it.

Radical feminism denounces[12] patriarchal *power*, which subordinates women in order to make them *sexual objects*.[13] Postmodern feminism

Figure 3.1   Conceptual Framework

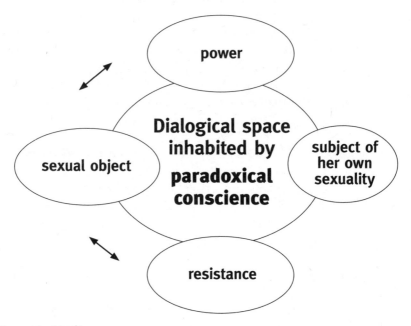

Source: Motoi (2008), p. 53.

asserts that women are not passive in response to this power and that they manifest their *résistance*[14] to different degrees. Along with these three concepts (power, sexual object, and resistance), I identified a fourth concept, the one of *sexual subject* or subject of her own sexuality, which allows us to understand sexual objectification not only as a fixed, unmoving dynamic, but as a process through and in which the person is acting and becoming, with the power to change it. My experience on the SOS-Femmes Line taught me that the woman who experiences herself as a sexual object also wants to construct or strengthen herself as a sexual subject. She lives, at the same time, through these two possibilities and also in connection between them as "paradoxical conscience."[15] These were the narratives that I wanted to research and understand further. Figure 3.1 shows the conceptual framework used for the subsequent research.

A Relational Definition of Sexual Violence
In 2004, women in Abitibi agreed to share with me how they construct knowledge from their own experiences of sexual violence. My goal was to give them a voice—their main objective was to help other isolated women

who also found themselves sexually objectified. To accomplish this, a narrative[16] research method was adapted for use with the group. The findings formed the foundation for a method of intervention with women living with sexual violence. This involves *accompanying* them to take possession (or "appropriation") of their own sexuality. An intervention guide was published in 2011 (Motoi & Dufour, 2011) and since then, sixty facilitators from several women's organizations have received training to implement the program or parts of it.

Initially, the research approach created a space for dialogue for nine women, a space in which they could share their knowledge. They examined *how* they distinguished between sexuality and prostitution. The purpose of this approach was not to identify "socially constructed" views of sexuality, but instead to validate each woman's own attribution of meaning to her sexual experience. The development of her sexual power stands on her theoretical power to build coherent and sustainable internal meanings.

A common denominator among the women I met was their desire to live their sexuality in the context of a relationship, to live a relational sexuality. Joos' notion of *relational violence*[17] clarifies this as "violence which is going against the relation itself": behaviours, attitudes, or actions that are not allowing for an interpersonal relationship. By this definition, sexual violence doesn't allow the subject to be in a relationship by placing her in the role of a sexual object. This is why internal dialogue is necessary for a woman to discern and define her own desire, limits, needs, and determine her own position as subject within her sexuality. Living this may or may not be accompanied by aggression or merchandising.

For the women I met, understanding themselves, through their internal dialogue, the concept of objectification was essential to recognizing the distinction between their own sexuality and feeling sexually objectified or used "like a prostitute." To them, by sharing their own thinking, they recognized prostitution as a *reference* point for their sexuality rather than defining it. This link with prostitution creates a tension through which these women need to navigate in their own sexual lives, and this will be explored in the next section.

Positioning Oneself as Subject of Her Own Sexuality

I wasn't myself anymore ... my woman's dignity. I ... was becoming an object. ... I really lost what was the foundation of a woman. It is that I am a human being. That I have values, feelings and needs like the other ... human beings. And this, it didn't matter anymore. It wasn't important anymore. What was important was first to satisfy the other and then to face...the shame and the humiliation...of what I did, to freeze those emotions. Because it was hurting too much.[18]

This internal strain between the woman as subject of her own sexuality and the woman as sexual object can be articulated around one principal tension.

But first, let's understand how the notion of "tension" is defined by this internal positioning of the woman as the subject of her sexuality, in her own space of dialogue. A tension is part of situations that are not defined, are inappropriately defined, or are still to be defined. For the woman living as a sexual object, this undefined sexual situation can be described by another as "normal." Nevertheless, for the women we met, who are isolated in their own internal worlds by a sexual-object situation, to live this tension is torture because they cannot sort it out. One term of the tension invalidates the other, and they are in a state of detachment.[19]

The women in the research group chose to look at the main *tension*[20]— not liking to be a sexual object, but putting themselves in the position of one. As one woman put it, "I don't like to be a sexual object, but I act as one. It's complicated." And another said: "So that he will leave me in peace, I was saying, 'Well, come, I will lay on my back, I will open my legs and empty yourself, and fast.'"[21]

Their first understanding of their sexual living is[22] *I don't like to be a sexual object*. The second understanding follows closely after the first one: *Nevertheless, I place myself as a sexual object*. These two contradictory living states can exist simultaneously—they can hide one behind the other, or oppose each other. It is then that women understand the tension between

Table 3.5   **Principal Tensions and Sub-tensions**

State of Living 1 I Don't Like to Be a Sexual Object	State of Living 2 Nevertheless, I Place Myself as a Sexual Object
I don't like to give pleasure only to the other.	On the other hand, I don't care about me.
I don't like to exceed my limits and to forget myself.	At the same time, I feel I place too many limits and I merchandise myself.
I realize that it is not valorizing for me to be a sexual object.	But I see that to be a sexual object gives me a few powers.
I have to say no a few times before the other will take it into consideration.	In this way, I give the message: Try again, I will finish by saying yes.
I feel that living as a sexual object is living my impotency (impuissance).	Yet I realize that in our society, we attach sexual power to women represented as sexual objects (socialization, publicity, pornography, etc.).

the two states of sexual living. These tensions can be further deconstructed, as Table 3.5 illustrates.

The merging of all these tensions creates a *grey zone* because the first state of living invalidates the second one and vice-versa. They cancel each other out. This is also the definition of a paradox.[23] That is why the term used is *parodoxical dynamics* of living as a sexual object. That's also why the meaning of what is lived is difficult to understand. The link of a woman living with sexual violence to her own sexuality is this grey zone.

THE PRACTICE OF DIALOGUE IN INTERVENTION

Describing feminist intervention that uses dialogue to recognize experiential knowledge and intercultural know-how involves developing a shared understanding of a violent situation that occurs in two steps:

1. The counsellor or facilitator and the woman caller or the women in a group recognize each other's right to provide different meanings to a similar life situation (Scott, 1989, p. 41).
2. Both parties together examine the existential, cultural, or ethical issues involved in this dialogue based on mutual understanding.

This is a process and not an intervention plan. This is a path that has not yet been constructed but will be created through the process.

Recognition of the Right to Provide Different Meanings to a Similar Life Situation

In French Ontario, establishing this right was not a simple task as different cultural identifications fought for recognition. Was the traditional tactic of inclusion/exclusion of "others who are not like us" still magically working to construct identities?

Within this host society, recognizing the counsellor's right to give a different meaning to a similar life situation can put the definitions of violence of the women asking for help into question. But in return, in this same situation, their definitions of violence as, for example, in the case of identity violence, can also cause us to question our own construction of what constitutes violence and our own dominant cultural or feminist identity. What are the limits of this mutual understanding?

Experiential knowledge (Racine, 2000, p. 169) is recognized through dialogue in intervention if connections are formed by communicating in ways that do not invalidate each other. Each person is responsible for her own understanding—this is the meaning of epistemological equality. From this perspective, attempting to understand another's cultural or sexual "world" and how she understands it may have an impact on how we see our own world. But to figure it out is not to accept it as right for ourselves because it may contradict our own values. Then there could be an entirely different choice to intervene with that understanding in mind.

In a group of women, expressing their own thoughts can happen only if the right to one's own perspective is acknowledged. They are not searching for approval from each other, but rather for coherence and pertinence within themselves. In this way the woman as subject of her own sexuality can work with herself to construct her own theory on what and how she is living sexual objectification.

As the counsellor or facilitator and the "helped" woman or women dialogue with this mutual understanding of their right to provide different meanings to a similar life situation, the second step of this dialogue in intervention can then take place. Both parties then together examine the issues chosen to safeguard the understanding of the "internal dialogue" of the "helped" woman. This gives her the power to create her own definitions of violence, and enables her to construct meaning in her own life.

Some Existential, Cultural, and Ethical Issues of Attributing Meaning to Violence

Existential Issues

Asking for help or participating in group discussion is taking action. This act alone can create a major shift in the subjective understanding of one's own life. The woman who asks for support can position her knowledge to be recognized through the dialogue with the counsellor or a group of women. This becomes an external point of reference for her. In this way, she can affirm that her tool of resistance is *her otherness as gender: being a woman subject of her own sexuality and life*. She affirms herself as different from the person who wants to dominate her, as other than a sexual object, other than the object of an intervention, other than from another culture. This woman constructs her identity and her perspective as a woman, and then she positions this identity and perspective in relation to someone other than herself.

How can we help women who have different definitions of violence? Experiential knowledge has taught me that it is through dialogue, when we walk through the issues together, that we can help the other, not necessarily to escape from the violent situation, but to manage her situation on her own terms. Once, one woman caller said of other services, "I hate it when they ask me, 'How do you feel?' and the counsellor responds with, 'Yes, I understand....' I like to call you because I can think with you, because you speak to me like an intelligent person...and I can say what I'm thinking."[24] Our role is to witness the woman's work to *construct her own thoughts with subjectivity* and *uniqueness,* offering her that precious time to *be herself* and *think by herself* to *construct meaning in her own sexual or family life.*

If we are not working through a dialogue, then we are taking for granted that the woman caller or participant in a group must share our view of her violent situation. If we assume this, without being certain through dialogue, we could face her silence—the shield obscuring her thoughts—so that she might better "hide" and avoid the counsellor's rejection.

There is not only the intervention situation to be kept in mind, there is also the outcome following the intervention where the woman finds herself alone, managing her emotional, economic, and cultural survival. This is why it is important *not to push her beyond her limits* as the abuser does. Outside the intervention context, she could feel lost without any point of reference, excluded and rejected from the familiar context in which she lives (family, community, street friends, etc.). Many women have told us this could be the worst violence to live. A woman's definition of violence and *her* limits are particular to her as a unique individual: "When I have the feeling or the thought, 'No, I don't like this,' I can stop or I can go on. But if I continue, why do I continue? If I know that I don't like this, it is because I already succeeded in passing over that limit."[25]

Cultural Issues

As seen in the contextual method, it is important to question the manner in which a particular culture and its values are positioned in our society. This questioning leads us to examine the possible uses of the Western feminist definition of violence as a tool that imposes a certain understanding that could silence some who have different definitions of violence. This could impose a hierarchy based on the *difference between "those who know" versus "those who do not know."*

Each woman comes from a specific cultural structure that can be described as individualistic or collectivistic; egalitarian or patriarchal/matriarchal; monogamous or polygamous; secular or religious. This structure provides her with the relational affective framework, a way of handling her daily life as well as the violent situation. Often, belonging to this cultural structure is more important for some than ending the violence in their family or sexual life. The intervention often forces the woman to confront the difficult choice between the two. It is a question of *inclusion or exclusion, as belonging or not, to a cultural community* with its own particular meaning of life and sexuality, which will exclude a woman if she does not follow the rules that define them.

Does the host society need to accept this multicultural diversity of definitions of violence? Would this acceptance promote cultural ghettoization without any other choice for women living with violence? Or should the host society ask the newcomers to accept their individualistic, egalitarian, monogamous, and secular values as a precondition for living in this country? Can there be a balance between the two perspectives, and where would it fall?

Intercultural feminist intervention is not multicultural intervention. It is not only an interaction between at least two different cultures—the culture of origin of the woman asking for support and the culture of the woman offering it—but it is also a shared construction through dialogue. It is more like laying all the cards on a table: knowing one's own cards, choosing to open up or close oneself to the other, and building bridges if necessary or possible.

In this complicated cultural context with all its tensions, the feminist culture of the women offering support may come up strongly against the patriarchal or polygamous or religious subordination of many women expressing a need for assistance. They may *not want to recognize or appreciate those values* since *their* (host) society has just fought to guarantee equality between men and women. And the response of the woman caller is not always a positive one! She doesn't necessarily want to talk about the violent situation or to identify herself as a victim. The comment: "How do you feel? Yes, I understand" will not naturally lessen the differences in values, priorities, and interests.

But when the answer is positive on both sides, then at first the emphasis should be on what the woman thinks about her situation, her feelings and thoughts, and what she wants to do about them. Can we give her the space to be herself without putting up "automated slogans"? She has the answer; we don't have the answer, only maybe some resources. And two of these resources are our solidarity and our intelligence as another thinking woman. And the woman offering support can ask: "What do you want to do with this situation? Do you want us to try to think together about it? Together can we find the limits of the situation?" Questioning each other is at the heart of the construction of meaning in intervention through dialogue.

The dynamic of intercultural intervention stands on communicating to negotiate common ground (James, 1999, pp. 65–95; Legault & Roy, 2000). Without this acknowledgement—that the construction of meaning is an individual act, to be recognized in dialogue with another—the two women could find the "helping situation" too existentially, culturally, and ethically frustrating, and may consequently give up on it.

The dynamics of violence carry varying weight and importance, depending on who is defining it and from which cultural standpoint. Often a woman in a precarious situation is so vulnerable that she does not feel ready to hear the "diagnosis": "Your family is experiencing family violence" or "You are living sexual violence." This may be like a blow to the face. A newly arrived woman often has priorities other than facing violence: economic survival and emotional continuity come first, and the rest comes after...maybe.

The definition of violence may also change, depending on which elements are at play. Is negotiating cultural identity, violence, and intercultural dialogue one of our strategies for putting an end to violence in our society? Is it built on clear values? Is the equality between men and women such a value?

Constructing meaning from a violent situation is the goal behind feminist intercultural intervention. But seen this way, everything can have a meaning of equal value. For example, we can defend the rights of an "abused" child as well as some parents' affirmation of their parental authority to discipline the child by inflicting corporal punishment. Or, we can defend the rights of a woman being battered, as well as some religious men's affirmation of their male authority to discipline a woman through physical or psychological acts. How and who should define what is the most important in our society if we don't create an intercultural space for dialogue in order to identify the issues at stake?

The Ethical Issues

In order to manage a violent situation on her own terms, each woman approaches a counsellor or a group to tell her own story (Riessman, 1991). As a result, she makes sense of her past experiences and constructs understanding (new meaning) by interpreting old meanings and also the dialogical intervention she experienced. This new meaning is not universal, nor is it fixed once and for all, but is fluid and contextual, produced internally, as in the case of sexual objectification. The woman can enact disapproval, liberation, oppression, etc. As a result, she affirms, through her narrative in dialogue with the other, a cultural or a subjective position in which she displays her "redefinition of her *rapport* (relationship) to the world to which she belongs" (Chambon, 1993, p. 126). It is up to her to negotiate her own belonging.

In dialogue, the woman is taking ownership of her own problems. This is a major issue for her: *being and staying the owner of what is private to her* and, in that way, keeping her life private to herself throughout the process of intervention. Nevertheless, the private is not political for most women from cultures or milieus where emotions are discussed only with a close friend. And what is private is occupied by others for women who feel used "as a prostitute" living in a couple or in living with prostitution. Is talking about privacy making it public? This tension between what is private and public is one of the tensions involved in the interventions we currently practise. This is not only a question of defining terms, but of defining the parameters of affective life, of the *private-public disjunction with its political issues*. This partly explains some women's silence when we ask them questions about their life experiences. Their position is clear: "I'm not calling you to talk about what I am living, experiencing, but to ask for help, for real resources."[26] Also, that may be why women in groups focused on sexuality don't like to graphically describe what they are experiencing, and instead prefer to explain their theories about what happened and exchange their knowledge. Women like epistemological work.

If we accept that we can construct knowledge individually, then we can also deconstruct "professional knowledge" in the field of intervention and no longer present it within the framework of feminist intercultural intervention as universal and objective, but as local and subjective. The woman, whether she is calling a helpline or sitting in a group, interprets her own narrative, and the counsellor or the facilitator interprets her own interpretation of the woman's narrative. This exchange of interpretations in dialogue creates an epistemological equality. This goes beyond ideology—one perspective for everyone that could control and quiet the others' voices and thoughts and keep them from affirming themselves beyond the definition of the problem and its solution. Truth and falseness could no longer be determined only by a binary logic[27] (good/bad, conformity/deviation, normal/pathologic, dominant/subordinate, etc.) organizing identity (aggressor/victim, those who know/those who don't know). Jointly, through dialogue in intervention, the counsellor or the facilitator and the woman, through the recognition of tensions, could manage a problematic situation on a community/co-operative[28] level. And here we must maintain proportionality: the "client" is not a client; she must be seen as the subject rather than the object of the intervention. She is a subject who is sovereign in her own internal dialogue with herself and in dialogue with others.

The redefinition of the situation comes as the result of a multi-voiced conversation about the situation (Laing, cited in Racine, 2000, p. 31). This dialogue, internal and external, is inhabited by "uncertainty and uniqueness" (Racine, 2000, p. 47) and allows the construction of specific knowledge (epistemology) for each subject. Consequently, we can see women as they are, "creators and interpreters of meaning." Knowledge can also be shared with others, depending on the various degrees of *proximity of meaning* (*proximité significative*) in action. This concept can be used in the realm of dialogical intervention as a basic concept in defining violence.

Narrative power can question the interests of all involved in a dialogue and can put into perspective all power relations, including the one with the counsellor or the facilitator. Using narrative power can become a necessary method for constructing one's own subjectivity (Self) and otherness (Other/ Alter), important dimensions of identity for women living with violence. Theoretical power orients the subject on the territory of her experience by building a theoretical map[29] (a plan, logical understanding, etc.) to find herself. "All social actors are social theorists" (Scott, 1989, p. 44). This is an ethical positioning and also one of the tensions in the definition of violence as the action to be taken is, above all, an ethical one. For example, Dufour in Motoi and Dufour (2011, p. 148), in analyzing "juvenile prostitution," uses the term "street abuse" because male clients, as adults, should protect children on the street instead of abusing them sexually by prostituting them.

Defining Violence Together through Dialogue

If the counsellor or the facilitator believes that the definition of violence must be made through joint thinking, it is important that she first question her privileges and assume them consciously in the sense that she has the choice to use them to her own advantage and to the advantage of the cultural or ideological group to which she belongs, or simply set them aside.

How do I position my culture(s) and my values within feminist intercultural intervention? Am I in the process of polarizing the intervention between "those who know" and "those who do not know"? What is my proximity of meaning to the person with whom I am carrying out this dialogue in intervention? In which relational or cultural context am I currently interfering? By what right? What sort of right of power is the woman seeking support proposing that I exert upon her and her family or milieu? In this intervention is there a symmetry to be constructed or must the asymmetry of power be maintained? What do I want from this relationship? Questioning and being questioned identifies the issues involved in attributing meaning to a given situation. Table 3.6 provides a synthesis of these issues.

Once we have recognized our reciprocal right to give a different meaning to a similar living situation and have identified for which existential, cultural, or ethical issues this is so, the "real" dialogue could begin. When we understand our choices and how we build our lives and sexualities, we can finally discuss a strategy for action. This allows both women—the one asking for support and the one offering it—to align their life contexts, with or without binding them together. Their choices belong to them individually.

Table 3.6   Issues of Attribution of Different Meanings to a Similar Living

Issues	Description
Existential issues	• surviving (economically, emotionally, cognitively, etc.) • ensuring one's otherness as gender—being a woman • constructing one's own subjectivity—being a subject of her own sexuality and life • taking the time and space to be and to think • knowing and assuming one's uniqueness • perceiving and constructing meaning in her own life • not pushing her beyond her limits
Cultural issues	• legitimizing cultural hierarchy based on the difference between those who know and those who do not know • experiencing the inclusion/exclusion of a culture/community • recognizing the power to affirm one's cultural identity by protecting the reference points constituting it (including the definition of violence) • belonging to one's own cultural (symbolic) "world"—being in a position to give meaning to a situation or negotiating meaning with oneself • expecting significant meaning proximity with the other
Ethical issues	• defining the parameters of personal affective life, including the private/ public disjunction and its political issues • finding and maintaining ownership of what is private • recognizing the other one's own ethical position as a political strength • living epistemological equality • taking the narrative power in the form of theoretical know-how • appropriating the power to define violent situations

CONCLUSION

The woman seeking support identifies her own needs, interests, and actions, and finds the solutions as she understands them. We, as counsellors or facilitators, are there to accompany her, through dialogue, to construct the necessary context that will allow her to appropriate her own power to define the violent situation and also to recognize her own theories and ethical know-how, which will allow her to act in a way that is meaningful for her. There are two important objectives: (1) creating the context in which the subject can learn what she needs in order to help herself in the best way possible, and (2) preserving her otherness as a woman.

For this, we have to take into consideration the fact that women's resistance to a violent situation, in accordance with the perspective used in this chapter, is the basis from which we can facilitate the visibility of her own knowledge of how to become empowered, to have control over her own life and sexuality, and to act or not, in her own problematic situation. Providing the woman with the recognition of her power through which she could make her know-how visible to herself is providing her with a place to construct her perspective to manage the situation on her own terms. In fact, we are there to support her, facilitating *her* work to find her own coherence. This is done through a process that is, above all, a narrative process in a dialogue. This is often the work of comparison, of building a real symmetry at the heart of the intervention, to find the limitations of the notion of family violence and of sexual violence and how tensions forge their definition.

Change, as much for the woman asking for support as for the counsellor or the facilitator, can be painful and difficult: defining and recognizing the violent situation are not givens—they must be constructed. And sometimes we do not know how to do it. While in full motion, we must, however, hang onto some points of reference. What are they? What do we want them to be?

We have moved above and beyond the discourse of charity and compassion, and even the discourse of empathy. Instead, we stand in solidarity, seeking continuities to create our own conceptual ingredients necessary for the intervention when there is the request for our support. The strength of women living with family violence or sexual violence makes us question the very notion of vulnerability. We need dialogue in intervention in order to understand together what violence and sexual violence are.

NOTES

1 Excerpt from research (Motoi & Dufour, 2011, p. 106).

2 Retrieved from: http://www.maxicours.com/se/fiche/4/0/13304.html.

3 Their work, made visible in the Western world in the 1980s by J. Kristeva and T. Todorov, is well known to linguists and theorists of the speech (AD, *analyse du discourse*), cited in Todorov (1981).

4 Excerpt from research (Motoi & Dufour, 2011, p. 117).

5 From the Greek *theôria*, "contemplation, observation, examination," a theory, in this intervention framework, is envisaged as an assemblage, in a body, of verifiable propositions that can predict sexual behaviour and development of specific sexual situations (Motoi & Dufour, 2011, p. 17).

6 Excerpt from SOS-Femmes Line intervention call.

7 According to two studies of women's needs led by the Réseau des femmes du sud de l'Ontario: Étude de Windsor (1988) and Étude de Hastings (1994).

8 "As of 2001, 41,598 Ontario Francophone belong to visible minorities. They make up 7.9% of the total Francophone population in Ontario [...]." Retrieved from: http://www.attorneygeneral.jus.gov.on.ca/english/justice-ont/french_language_services/statistics/francophone_minorities.asp.

9 I am building on Grimard's article, which is using the theoretical perspective of Giddens (1999).

10 Retrieved from: http://www.expressottawa.ca/Monde/2009-10-21/article -788412/ACFEO-ACFO-et-AFO-cent-ans-dhistoire-qui-seront-celebres-toute-lannee/1.

11 They were blocking each other through their arguments and counter-arguments since the fourth international conference on women, under the auspices of the UN, in Beijing in 1995.

12 From Marx to Kate Millett and from Barry to Bourdieu, the discourse on prostitution was one that demonstrated the patriarchal and capitalist dominance of women in our society. Greer, quoted in Motoi (2008, p. 20), said that "pornography is the theory and its practice is rape," that "pornography is hate propaganda against women," and that "the fear of rape for women is comparable to the fear of castration in men."

13 This concept has mobilized women since 1969 (see *Manifeste des bas rouges*, New York, 1969).

14 Leonard and Leonard (1999, pp. 8–9).

15 Ibid., p. 11: "contradictory consciousness" is living "internalization of contradictions as conflict."

16 I acknowledge that narrative therapy work done in the English community is different.

17 J.-E. Joos, *Clivage relationnel et violence: Éléments pour une théorie politique de la relation, à partir de la pensée de Frantz Fanon*, Collège Marie-de-France. Retrieved from: www.erudit.org/revue/tce/2000/v/n63/008184ar.pdf.

18 Research findings (Motoi, 2008).

19 For Barry (c.1995), distanciation is the first stage of the process of dehumanization in prostitution, followed by dissociation, disengagement, and disembodiment.

20 Motoi (2008, pp. 164–65).

21 Excerpt from research (Motoi & Dufour, 2011, p. 39).

22 Motoi (2008, pp. 164–65).

23 A paradox is a self-contradictory statement.

24 Excerpt from SOS-Femmes Line intervention call.

25 Excerpt from research (Motoi & Dufour, 2011, p. 74).

26 Excerpt from SOS-Femmes Line intervention call.

27 See postmodern feminism (Riessman, 1991; Scott, 1989; Leonard & Leonard, 1999) and Foucauldian scholarly criticism.

28 Aboriginal peoples' holistic and communitarian solutions share this tendency.

29 Bateson (1972, p. 449) discusses the importance of distinguishing between the map and the territory ("the map is not the territory"), as Alfred Korzybsky had indicated previously.

REFERENCES

Barry, K. (c.1995). *The prostitution of sexuality: The global exploitation of women.* New York: New York University Press.

Bateson, G. (1972). *Steps to an ecology of mind.* London: Granada.

Chambon, A. (1993). Les stratégies narratives du récit et de la parole. Comment progresse et s'échafaude une méthode d'analyse. *Sociologies et sociétés, 25*(2), 125–35.

Dufour, R. (2004). *Je vous salue Marion… Le point zéro de la prostitution.* Québec: MultiMondes.

Foucault, M. (1975). *Surveiller et punir.* Paris: Gallimard.

Giddens, A. (1999). *The consequences of modernity.* Stanford: Stanford University Press.

Grimard, M. (2004). L'Association des communautés francophones de l'Ontario de Toronto: de la chanson à l'action. *Francophonies d'Amérique, 18*(1), 149–55. Retrieved from: http:/muse.jhu/journals/francophonies_damerique/v18/18.1grimard.htlm.

Hétu, J.-L. (2000). *Bilan de vie* Montreal: Fides.

Hodgson, F.J. (1997). *Games pimps play: Pimps, players, and wives-in-law: A quantitative analysis of street prostitution.* Toronto: Canadian Scholars' Press.

Jaggar, A.M. (1994). Living with contradictions. *Controversies in feminist social ethics.* Boulder, CO: Westview Press.

James, C.E. (1999). Negotiating identity. *Seeing ourselves: Exploring race, ethnicity, and culture* (2nd ed.) (pp. 67–95). Toronto: Thomson.

Legault, G., & Roy, G. (2000). Les difficultés des intervenants sociaux auprès des clientèles d'immigration récente. In G. Legault (Ed.), *L'intervention culturelle* Montreal: Gaëtan Morin.

Leonard, L., & Leonard, P. (1999). Women on the margins, Ottawa. *Revue canadienne de service social, 16*(1), 5–17.

Lerbert-Sereni, F. (sous la direction). (2004). *L'intelligence des situations complexes et le paradoxe de la modélisation.* Paris: l'Harmattan.

Markova, I., Linell, P., & Grossen, M. (2007). *Dialogue in focus groups: Exploring socially shared knowledge.* London: Equinox.

Markova, I. (2007). *Dialogicité et représentations sociales.* Paris: PUF.

Motoi, I. (1988). *Étude de Windsor.* Toronto: Réseau des femmes du sud de l'Ontario.

Motoi, I. (1994). *Étude de Hastings.* Toronto: Réseau des femmes du sud de l'Ontario.

Motoi, I. (2008). Eurydice: Pouvoir définir son vécu comme sexualité ou comme prostitution, thèse de doctorat inédite. Montréal: Université de Montréal.

Motoi, I., & Dufour, R. (2011). *La femme, sa sexualité et son pouvoir sexuel, programme d'appropriation de sa sexualité.* Québec: PUQ.

Palombo, J. (Fall 1992). Narratives, self-cohesion, and the patient's search for meaning. *Clinical Social Work Journal, 20*(3), 249–70.

Paveau, M.-A. (2010). *La norme dialogique : Propositions critiques en philosophie du discours*, pp. 141–59. Retrieved from: http://semen.revues.org/8793. (cons. 22 mars).

Racine, G. (2000). *La production des savoirs d'expérience chez les intervenants sociaux.* Montréal: L'Harmattan, coll. Action and Savoir.

Riessman, C. (1991). When gender is not enough: Women interviewing women. In J. Lorber & S.A. Farrell (Eds.), *The social construction of gender* (pp. 217–36). London: Sage.

Scott, D. (1989 March). Meaning construction and social work practice. *Social Service Review, 63*, 39–51.

Todorov, T. (1981). *Mikhaïl Bakhtine et le principe dialogique.* Paris: Seuil.

Trinder, L. (2000). Reading the texts: Postmodernism feminism and the doing of research. In B. Fawcett, B. Featherstone, J. Fook, and A. Rossiter (Eds.), *Practice and Research in Social Work: Postmodern Feminist Perspectives* (pp. 39–61). London: Routledge.

4

CHILD CORPORAL PUNISHMENT
VIOLENCE, LAW, AND RIGHTS

ANNE MCGILLIVRAY AND JOAN E. DURRANT

INTRODUCTION

When a husband hits a wife, the act is a criminal assault and is strongly censured by Canadian society. But when a parent hits a child, our shared understanding of violence and illegitimate use of force is suspended. We debate the effectiveness of child physical punishment—"spanking"—in correcting children's behaviour. We may think of it as necessary and harmless. And we may refer to Section 43 of Canada's Criminal Code—the defence of "moderate correction"—to affirm its legitimacy. Why is it that our law has criminalized all forms of violence in the family, but offers a defence for that violence when it is directed at a child? The disjuncture between what Canadians understand to be an act of violence—an assault—and what some Canadians believe is a legitimate parental act of discipline is explored in this chapter.

Our understanding of childhood has undergone profound change over the last century. Once the legal property of their fathers (McGillivray, 2012a), children are now recognized as rights-bearers and legal subjects, entitled to all rights set out in the Canadian Charter of Rights and Freedoms ("the Charter") and in international law, notably the UN Convention on the Rights of the Child ("the Convention") (see Newell, 2011). How we view corporal punishment has also undergone profound change. It was once a routine power belonging to all those with magisterial status—masters of households, ships, armies, schools, prisons, apprentices, colonies, and courts—over those under their rule. Wives, children, servants, slaves, sailors, soldiers, pupils, prisoners, apprentices, indigenous peoples, and lawbreakers could, by law, be beaten. These laws are now gone, with one exception—the law permitting the corporal punishment of children.

It was once widely believed that corporal punishment was both necessary and good for children or, more recently, that it does not hurt children if used moderately. We now know, through extensive social science research, that none of this is true. Yet history, law, and belief continue to legitimate child assault. In this chapter we trace the historical roots of corporal punishment and its defence from Roman law to the Criminal Code. We compare "corrective" assault of children with that of wives. We consider the findings of social science research on physical punishment's outcomes for children. We summarize the limits placed on corrective assault under Section 43 by the Supreme Court of Canada in 2004. Finally, we offer recommendations regarding the prevention of violence against children in Canada.

HISTORICAL ROOTS

Historically, assaulting children was seen as central to their socialization. Corporal punishment—also called chastisement, castigation, physical punishment, and correction by force—was not only about punishing children for misdeeds. Like "breaking" horses, the child's will had to be broken to enable learning and spur obedience. "Spanking" is related to the German *spakkern, spenkern*, used in reference to horses in the 1700s (Webster, 1922).

Today, spanking is used to mean anything from taps, smacks, swats, and slaps to paddling, caning, beating, whipping, and belting. Under Canadian law, all are criminal assaults, yet all have been justified by Canadian courts if the assault was intended to correct the child, and committed by the child's parent or teacher. This justification or defence is codified as Section 43 of the Criminal Code.

The defence originates in the Roman law of *patria potestas*, a proprietary, magisterial, and arbitrary power belonging to the father as *pater familias*, head of the household. Incidental to *potestas* were the rights of: (1) custody of the child, including the child's labour and sale; (2) control of the child's education, religion, marriage, and emancipation; and (3) corporal punishment, including the infliction of death. Corporal punishment was seen as both necessary and virtuous: "Most of the ancient philosophers and lawmakers were in favour of flogging children, not only as a means of inducing them to conduct themselves well and tell the truth, but also as an aid to education itself" (Scott, 1938). In ancient Rome, children were ranked in legal and social status with slaves, whose sign was the lash.

Patria potestas was diminished in the late Roman Empire by a series of imperial edicts, first emancipating cruelly treated children from paternal control, and later treating child-killing as quasi-murder and finally as actual murder (McGillivray, 1997). In ad 365, the emperors Valentinian and Valens advised the Roman Senate "Concerning the Correction of Relatives":

> We grant the power of punishing minors to their elder relatives according to the nature of the offence which they have committed, in order that the remedy of such discipline may exert its influence over those whom a praiseworthy example at home has not induced to lead an honourable life.
>
> We, however, are not willing that the right to inflict extremely severe castigation for the faults of minors should be conferred, so that the exercise of paternal authority may correct the errors of youth and repress them by private chastisement. (Scott, 1939, Digest, Book 9, Title 15)

Punishment, discipline, correction, castigation, and chastisement refer to physical punishment. As an early comment states, "blows" are not punishable "when inflicted by a master or a parent; for the reason that they seem to be given rather for the purpose of correction than injury. They are punishable when anyone is beaten by a stranger in anger" (Scott, 1939, Digest, Book 48, Title 29, 16).

Roman law entered English common law through the *ius commune*, a university-taught mix of Roman and canon law studied by English lawyers. Thus, a thousand years later, the annotation on flogging reappears in the first major text on English law (Bracton, 1968, v. 2, p. 299): "Motive, as in whippings, which are not punishable if imposed by a master or parent (unless they are immoderate) since they are taken to be inflicted to correct not injure, but are punished when one is struck in anger by a stranger." Corporal punishment of children, slaves, malefactors, apprentices, servants, and others was justified by the desired outcome of degradation. Because of the loss of dignity inherent in corporal punishment, Bracton observes that "every corporal punishment, though of the slightest, is greater than any pecuniary one" (v. 2, p. 300).

The *familias* was resurrected in the Protestant Reformation to bolster the middle-class father (McGillivray, 2004; Stone, 1979). Manuals and broadsheets equated obedience to the father with obedience to God and king. Severe beating was a daily occurrence in homes, grammar schools, and colleges to enforce filial, state, and religious obedience. Although *pater potestas* would never fully return, the new father was similarly named temporal and spiritual head of the household, commanding the obedience of wife, children, and servants and inflicting corporal punishment. In his 1770 *Commentaries on the laws of England*, the influential jurist Blackstone (1962, Book i, chap. 16, paras. 452–53) states: "The ancient Roman laws gave the father a power of life and death over his children.... The power of a parent by our English laws is much more moderate; but still sufficient to keep the child in order and obedience." "Moderate chastisement" is the father's power to "lawfully correct his child being under age, in a reasonable manner for this is for the benefit of his education." It is a "right" derived from parental duties to maintain and educate children, "partly to enable the parent more effectually to perform his duty, and partly as a recompense for his care and trouble in the faithful discharge of it." It ends with the child's emancipation, "when the empire of the father ... gives place to the empire of reason."

By the late eighteenth century, criminal prosecution had become a more frequent response to severe child assault. Linda Pollock (1983) found 385 such cases from murder to assault to incest reported in *The Times* between 1785 and 1860. Physical assault cases involved severe beating and lasting injury, well beyond the scope of moderation even for the time. One defendant, for example, tortured and mutilated his child and claimed the right of physical correction. In sentencing the defendant, the court said that it would "demonstrate the error of that claim."

It was Hopley's case (1860), however, that defined moderate correction for the modern era. Hopley, a boarding school master, asked the father of a thirteen-year-old pupil for permission to "chastise" the boy "severely" and "that if necessary he should do it again and again" and "continue it at intervals even if he held out for hours." The father consented. Hopley administered his flogging for two and a half hours using a heavy brass-tipped stick. The boy died. The court convicted Hopley of manslaughter and sentenced him to four years of penal servitude, stating: "By the law of England, a parent or a schoolmaster ... may for the purpose of correcting what is evil in the child inflict moderate and reasonable corporal punishment, always, however, with this condition, that it is moderate and reasonable." Punishment in passion or rage, excessive in nature or degree, protracted beyond the child's endurance, or "with an instrument unfitted for the purpose" was excessive. Still, if the child died, it was manslaughter rather than murder. English law now restricts moderate correction to relatives having care of a child.

Before we turn to the Canadian defence of moderate correction of children, we consider the correction of wives to provide a context for understanding the assumptions underlying the notion of "lawful correction."

MODERATE CORRECTION OF WIVES

Today there is no legal defence for the assault of wives, however moderate, yet women, like children, were subject to corporal punishment under both Roman and common law. A wife was *sub virga viri*, under her husband's rod (Doggett, 1993). Her rights to security of the person, child custody, home and property, and freedom of movement and association were submerged under the rights of her husband. Under the legal doctrine of coverture, man and wife were one. That "one" was the man. A wife's sole protection from her husband's violence lay in a judicial writ obtained from a justice of the peace, binding him over to keep the peace. Violating the peace bond meant loss of the money put up as surety. This amounted to a minor tax on the rich wife beater, and was a protection unavailable to the poor.

Eirenarcha (Lambarde, 1581), a handbook used by justices of the peace throughout England for decades, stated that "some are allowed to have privately, a *natural*, and some a *civile* power (or authoritie) over others, so that they may be excused themselves if but (in reasonable manner) they correct and chastise them for their offenses" (Doggett, 1993, p. 281). Chastisement of wives and children was a "natural" power.

Almost two centuries later, Blackstone (1769/1962: Book i, chap. 15, para. 432) called this "the old law":

> The husband also (by the old law) might give his wife moderate correction. For, as he is to answer for her misbehaviour, the law thought it reasonable to entrust him with this power of restraining her, by domestic chastisement, in the same moderation that a man is allowed to correct his apprentice or his children... [but] the lower rank of people, who were always fond of the old common law, still claim and exert their ancient privilege.

For Blackstone, the power over wives was ebbing, but the power over children was unquestionable. The influence of Blackstone's *Commentaries* on the development of the law was profound, going far to explain the differential treatment of women and children under the assault law.

In *Jackson's case* (1891), a husband claimed custody of his estranged wife and, with it, the power to chastise her. He did not claim the more general right of chastisement (conceding that this was not now law), but the right to use necessary violence to imprison her in his house. The English Court of Appeal dismissed the claim as based on "quaint and absurd dicta" that did not now represent the law of England, if it ever did. English wives were not "abject slaves." That decision contradicts centuries of English law and may be due to the huge feminist and public support for Mrs. Jackson.

Campaigns were mounted throughout the nineteenth century to reform the morals of the poor by, among other things, discouraging cruelty to children and wives. By the closing decades of that century, child welfare agencies were established in Canada, as elsewhere, with the power to apprehend cruelly treated children. Even so, the power of moderate correction of children remained intact. The power over wives was gone.

THE CANADIAN CRIMINAL CODE

The question for nineteenth-century judges and educators was not whether child corporal punishment should be legal or whether it was needed, but rather how moderate it should be (McGillivray & Milne, 2011). Reflecting Hopley's case, the annotation to the 1869 Canadian Criminal Law Consolidation Act states: "Moderate and reasonable correction may properly be given by parents, masters and other persons, having authority in *foro domestico* [the domestic sphere], to those who are under their care, but if the correction be immoderate or unreasonable, either in the measure of it, or in the instrument made use of for that purpose, it will be either murder or manslaughter, according to the circumstances of the case."

The defence of moderate correction of children was drafted in 1879 by Lord Blackburn, chair of the English Imperial Draft Code Commission. Based on Hopley's case and James Fitzjames Stephen's (1887) formulation of the judgment, the defence was codified as Section 55: "It is lawful for every parent, or person in the place of a parent, schoolmaster or master, to use force by way of correction towards any child, pupil or apprentice under his care, provided that such force is reasonable under the circumstances." In the 1955 clean-up of the Code, "lawful" became "justified," masters and apprentices were removed, and the section was renumbered Section 43. It now states: "Every schoolteacher, parent or person standing in the place of a parent is justified in using force by way of correction toward a pupil or child, as the case may be, who is under his care, if the force does not exceed what is reasonable under the circumstances." What began as a prohibition on child killing under Roman law became an excuse, a power, a virtue, a right, a prerogative, a defence, and a justification. While the language has been updated, there has been no substantive change from the Roman edict issued over sixteen hundred years ago. The defence preserves the belief that assaulting children is a necessary and virtuous tutorial duty.

The Supreme Court of Canada first considered Section 43 in 1984, in *Ogg-Moss v. R.* Ogg-Moss, in which a mental retardation counsellor repeatedly hit an adult patient with a large metal spoon for spilling milk. Assaulting an adult patient is not protected by Section 43. The court cited Blackstone in terming Section 43 a "disciplinary prerogative" and a "justification" as "it considers such an action not a wrongful, but a *rightful* one." The court noted "that unless the force is 'by way of correction,' that is, for the benefit of the education of the child, the use of force will not be justified." This poses an important question. "Education" here means more than schooling. It includes all aspects of child-rearing and socialization. If it can be shown that corporal punishment offers no benefit to children, would this end its legal justification? Social science evidence is key to answering this question. In the years since *Ogg-Moss*, we have learned much about the effects of corrective assault on children.

THE FINDINGS OF SOCIAL SCIENCE RESEARCH

In justifying corporal punishment when the motive is to correct the child, the law assumes that corporal punishment works. But the law arose sixteen hundred years before developmental psychology and systematic research methods existed, and long before violence against children was identified as a social problem. It represents the untested assumptions of previous eras.

With advances in theory (see Durrant, 2011; Smith, 2011) and research methodology, these assumptions can now be tested empirically, and they have been. Over the past six decades, more than 185 studies have been conducted on the impact of corporal punishment. Early in this decade, a landmark meta-analysis of the findings of eighty-eight of these studies was conducted (Gershoff, 2002). Studies that defined corporal punishment as acts that would cause severe injury were excluded from the analysis (beating, punching, kicking, leaving a mark on the body). Corporal punishment was defined as its "everyday" forms (spanking, slapping, pinching, smacking, or hitting with a hand or object). The findings demonstrate that even these acts are consistently associated with negative outcomes for children and the adults they will become.

Physical Injury

Much of the controversy surrounding corporal punishment hinges on the belief that "punishment" and "abuse" are two separate entities, differently motivated and executed, and easily distinguished. In fact, most abuse *is* physical punishment, carried out by a caregiver with disciplinary intent (Gil, 1970; Kadushin & Martin, 1981). Gershoff found that physical punishment was a risk factor for physical harm in all of the ten studies of this relationship that she examined. The Canadian Incidence Study of Reported Child Abuse and Neglect (CIS: Trocmé et al., 2001) revealed that three-fourths of child physical abuse cases substantiated in 1998 occurred in the context of punishment (Trocmé & Durrant, 2003). This finding was replicated in the 2003 cycle of the CIS (Trocmé et al., 2005), accounting for more than eighteen thousand cases of substantiated child maltreatment in that year (Durrant et al., 2006). When parents physically punish, they may not intend to harm the child. Most perpetrators of physical abuse believe that they have a right to physically punish the child and that their behaviour was justified by the circumstances (Dietrich, Berkowitz, Kadushin & McGloin, 1990; Gil, 1970; Peltoniemi, 1983). But their heightened emotional arousal increases the intensity of the force to a dangerous or injurious level (Vasta, 1982).

The more often caregivers use even mild physical punishment, the more likely they are to inflict severe violence. In a large Quebec study (Clément, Bouchard, Jetté & Laferrière, 2000), children who were pinched, shaken, or spanked by their parents were seven times more likely to also be punched, kicked, or hit with an object by their parents than those who had not been subjected to minor physical violence.

Child Mental Health

Injury is the most commonly used criterion for determining whether a child has been "abused." But this criterion creates a false dichotomy between "abusive" and "disciplinary" acts. Why? First, most acts that we define as abuse are the same as those that we define as punishment. Injury is often a matter of chance. The shaking that distresses a six-year-old can injure the brain of a two-year-old and kill an infant. The slap that bruises a three-year-old may leave no mark on a seven-year-old and drive a thirteen-year-old into a retaliatory rage.

Second, acts that do not result in physical injury may result in significant psychological harm. In her meta-analysis, Gershoff (2002) found that physical punishment was related to poorer child mental health in all of the twelve studies examining this relationship. It is a predictor of depression, unhappiness, anxiety, feelings of hopelessness, alcohol and drug use, and general psychological maladjustment (Afifi, Brownridge, Cox & Sareen, 2006; Csorba et al., 2001; DuRant, Cadenhead, Pendergrast, Slavens & Linder, 1994; Eamon, 2001; Lansford et al., 2005; Lau, Liu, Cheung, Yu & Wong, 1999; Rodriguez, 2003; Steely & Rohner, 2006). Turner and Finkelhor (1996) found that even low frequencies of physical punishment (spanking, slapping, hitting without objects) predicted psychological distress among youth (e.g., sadness, low self-esteem), even when the supportive quality of the parent–child relationship was taken into account.

The relationship between physical punishment and poorer mental health persists into adulthood (Turner & Muller, 2004). Gershoff (2002) found that childhood experience of physical punishment was associated with poorer adult mental health (e.g., depression, substance abuse) in all eight of the studies examining this relationship. In a large Ontario study, those adults who reported having been slapped or spanked as children, but not physic-ally or sexually abused, had an increased lifetime rate of anxiety disorders and alcohol use or dependence (MacMillan et al., 1999).

What explains these relationships? Parent–child attachment may be disrupted when the parent becomes a source of pain to the child (Coyl, Roggman & Newland, 2002), increasing the child's susceptibility to psycho-logical stressors. It also may be the case that the stress induced by physical punishment interferes with the brain's hormonal regulation system, increas-ing children's vulnerability to the effects of challenging life events (Bugental, Martorell & Barraza, 2003). Indeed, evidence is growing of the impact of childhood maltreatment on the response of the hypothalamic-pituitary-adrenal axis, which regulates stress responses (McGowan et al., 2009), and on the dopaminergic regions associated with vulnerability to the abuse of drugs and alcohol (Sheu et al., 2010).

Family and Social Relationships
Punishment is the application of an aversive stimulus to decrease an unwanted behaviour. *Physical* punishment is the deliberate infliction of pain or discomfort with the intent to decrease a behaviour. In some instances, it may have its desired effect, temporarily stopping a child from performing an unwanted behaviour. However, what is likely not desired is the damage it can cause to the child's social relationships.

Erosion of the Parent–Child Relationship
As humans, we learn to avoid sources of pain. When a parent deliberately inflicts pain on a child, the child's lesson may be that the parent is a source of pain to be avoided (Azrin & Holz, 1966; Bugental & Goodnow, 1998; Parke, 1977; Saarni, Mumme & Campos, 1998), leading to fear, anxiety, insecurity, and anger (Coyl, Roggman & Newland, 2002; Graziano, Hamblen & Plante, 1996) and eroding the parent–child relationship. Indeed, all of the thirteen studies in Gershoff's (2002) analysis that addressed this question revealed that physical punishment predicts weaker parent–child relationships. Even at two years of age, children who are physically punished are more likely to distance themselves from their mothers than those who are not physically punished (Crockenberg, 1987).

Impaired Moral Internalization
Another side effect of punishment is that it motivates extrinsically rather than intrinsically; that is, the child may stop performing a punished behav-iour in order to avoid the punishment, not because the wrongfulness of the behaviour is understood and internalized. Children who are physically

punished are less likely to internalize moral values than children who are not physically punished. This relationship was found in thirteen of fifteen studies examined by Gershoff (2002). Physical punishment predicts lower levels of: resistance to temptation, altruistic behaviour, empathy, and moral judgment (Kerr, Lopez, Olson & Sameroff, 2004; Lopez, Bonenberger & Schneider, 2001). By relying on external rather than internal controls, physical punishment focuses one's attention on the hurt suffered by oneself rather than on how one's behaviour hurts others (Hoffman, 1994).

Increased Aggression
Punishment provides not only a consequence for past behaviour, but also a model for future behaviour. In the case of physical punishment, the model is social problem-solving through aggression. Modelling is a powerful means of teaching and learning, particularly when the role model has both power and prestige (Bandura, 1971). When this modelling effect is added to the decreased moral internalization and empathy linked to physical punishment, a recipe is created for increasing aggression in the child. It is therefore not surprising that physical punishment has been found consistently to predict increased levels of aggression in children and youth. In her analysis of twenty-seven studies of this relationship, Gershoff (2002) found that physical punishment was associated with increased child aggression in all twenty-seven. Since her meta-analysis was published, evidence of this relationship has continued to accumulate.

The forms of aggression linked to physical punishment suggest that the modelling effect generalizes widely, includes disruptive behaviour and aggressive conduct problems (Aucoin, Frick & Bodin, 2006; Javo, Rønning, Heyerdahl & Rudmin, 2004; Kerr, Lopez, Olson & Sameroff, 2004; McLoyd & Smith, 2002; Olsen, Ceballo & Park, 2002; Stormshak, Bierman, McMahon & Lengua, 2000), physical fighting and bullying (Ohene, Ireland, McNelly & Borowsky, 2006), hitting and attacking siblings (Larzelere, 1986; Straus, 1990), hitting parents (Brezina, 1999; Larzelere, 1986; Ulman & Straus, 2003), verbal aggression (Pagani et al., 2004), retaliatory aggression against peers (Strassberg, Dodge, Pettit & Bates, 1994), and dating violence (Douglas & Straus, 2006; Simons, Lin & Gordon, 1998).

Some studies in this area address the question of causality: Is children's aggression eliciting or elicited by physical punishment? A growing number of longitudinal studies follow large groups of children to explore whether their aggression increases or decreases over time in response to physical punishment. These studies show that physical punishment does indeed contribute to increases in aggression (Grogan-Kaylor, 2005; Lansford et al., 2011; Mulvaney & Mebert, 2007; Slade & Wissow, 2004; Taylor, Manganello,

Lee & Rice, 2010). In a full examination of this issue, Gershoff and Bitensky (2007) conclude that, after initial child behaviour is accounted for, physical punishment predicts increased child behaviour problems.

Family Violence

Gershoff (2002) found a link between physical punishment and aggression in adulthood in all four studies that examined this relationship. Each time physical punishment is used, the parent has lost another opportunity to give the child a constructive model of conflict resolution, and the likelihood increases that the child will view physical aggression as a legitimate means of responding to conflict and frustration (Buntain-Ricklefs, Kemper, Bell & Babonis, 1994). The effects are seen when the child becomes a spouse and a parent. Physically punished children, when adults, were more likely to abuse a spouse or child in all five studies that addressed this relationship (Gershoff, 2002).

Physical punishment also establishes the child's norms for violence. The strongest predictor of adult approval of a particular form of punishment is the experience of that form of punishment as a child. The rate of approval of common forms of punishment, such as shaking or hitting with a belt, and severe forms, such as burning or tying up, is two to three times greater among those who have experienced them than among those who have not (Buntain-Ricklefs et al., 1994).

Children who experience severe physical punishment tend to believe, as adults, that such punishment is normal and non-abusive (Anderson & Payne, 1994; Bower & Knutson, 1996; Bower-Russa, Knutson & Winebarger, 2001; Buntain-Ricklefs et al., 1994; Kelder, McNamara, Carlson & Lynn, 1991; Miller & Knutson, 1997; Rohner, Kean & Cournoyer, 1991; Straus, 1994). For example, in a study of more than eleven thousand adults, 74 percent of those who were severely physically punished as children (punched, kicked, choked) did not think that they had been abused (Knutson & Selner, 1994). Of those who were hit with more than five different types of objects, 49 percent did not think this was abuse; 44 percent of those who had sustained more than two types of injuries from the punishment, and 38 percent of those who had required two different types of medical services for these injuries did not think they had been abused (Knutson & Selner, 1994).

Experiences of violence in childhood, particularly when inflicted by a parent, can raise the adult's threshold for defining an act as violent (Coontz & Martin, 1988; Rorty, Yager & Rossotto, 1995). A form of punishment considered to be severe and abusive by someone who was never hit as a child may be considered trivial and normal by someone who was severely punished. This personal definition or model is then carried into intimate relationships with spouses and children, contributing to the cycle of mal-treatment (Graziano & Namaste, 1990; Straus & Smith, 1992).

Anti-Social Behaviour

Given its links with reduced empathy, impaired moral internalization, and lowered thresholds for tolerance of violence, it is not surprising that physical punishment is associated with bullying, lying, lack of remorse, and other anti-social behaviours in childhood and adolescence. This relationship has been demonstrated in eleven of twelve studies examining it (Gershoff, 2002). While parents may believe that physical punishment will keep their children out of trouble, it actually predicts delinquency and anti-social behaviour over the long term (Grogan-Kaylor, 2004; Gunnoe & Mariner, 1997; Loeber et al., 2000; Straus, Sugarman & Giles-Sims, 1997) and this tendency is maintained into adulthood. Physical punishment was associated with higher levels of adult criminal and anti-social behaviour in four of the five studies that examined this relationship (Gershoff, 2002).

Cognitive Development

Physical punishment is implicated not only in children's emotional and behavioural difficulties, but also in impaired intellectual development. For example, the more frequently children are physically punished, the lower their IQs (Aucoin, Frick & Bodin, 2006; Smith & Brooks-Gunn, 1997), the poorer their school achievement (Parkinson, Wallis, Prince & Harvey, 1982), and the poorer their language comprehension (Gest, Freeman, Domitrovich & Welsh, 2004). To examine the causal relationship between physical punishment and cognitive development, researchers have begun to study it over time. In a study of more than five thousand children from birth to age thirteen, physical punishment was found to predict lower levels of receptive vocabulary and reading recognition (Bradley, Corwyn, Burchinal, McAdoo & García Coll, 2001). More recently, Straus and Paschall (2009) found that in two age cohorts of children (two- to four-year-olds and five- to nine-year-olds), those who were rarely or never physically punished gained on cognitive ability relative to those who were physically punished. In this study, the more children were physically punished, the more they fell behind those who were not. Recent neuro-imaging studies suggest that physical punishment may actually reduce the volume of grey matter in the brain's prefrontal cortex (Tomoda et al., 2009).

These findings may be rooted in the connection between children's learning and their social relationships (Rogoff, 1990; Vygotsky, 1978). Adults engage children in learning when they communicate sensitively and meaningfully with them. Through this process, children become increasingly competent and confident, willing to take initiative in solving problems. Physical punishment is coercive and aversive, rather than supportive and engaging. Therefore, it might interfere with the parent–child learning relationship. Indeed, Straus and Paschall (2009) found that the less mothers physically punished their children, the more cognitive stimulation they provided, such as reading; talking about colours, shapes, and letters; and providing books.

Research on Short-Term Outcomes
The only "beneficial" effect of physical punishment that has been identified is immediate compliance, in three out of five studies (Gershoff, 2002). Parents commonly believe that physical punishment works because the child, when hit, stops the unwanted behaviour. But this belief needs to be analyzed. First, immediate compliance is not a developmental outcome, but a short-term effect. Over time, compliance may turn into resistance and resentment, leading in turn to erosion of the parent–child relationship, increased aggression within and outside the family, mental health problems, and other effects discussed above. Short-term compliance, then, may be achieved at the expense of healthy development.

Second, even if immediate compliance were considered an important parenting outcome, physical punishment is no more effective than other methods in achieving it (Day & Roberts, 1983; Roberts & Powers, 1990). Constructive methods for eliciting child compliance include modelling, systematic reinforcement, environmental restructuring, and reasoning and explaining. Effective methods for reducing unwanted behaviour include preventive strategies, systematic non-reinforcement, logical consequences, distraction, and reasoning and explaining.

Third, the effectiveness of physical punishment in eliciting compliance is questionable. In an experimental study in which parents were trained to spank their children in a systematic way, an average of eight spankings in a single experimental session was required to make the child comply (Bean & Roberts, 1981). This finding suggests that the effectiveness of physical punishment in inducing compliance is quite limited. It also indicates that the risk of escalation of physical punishment to increasingly severe levels is high because over time, the child can habituate to the parent's use of force. To compensate for reduced compliance and greater resistance, the frequency and degree of the parent's force can escalate.

Fourth, compliance elicited by fear is qualitatively different than compliance arising from an internal motivation to do what is right. Compliance induced by force or duress is not true compliance.

Fifth, even if physical punishment reliably elicited compliance, this does not justify its use. A person who assaults a spouse may achieve compliance, but this effect does not justify the use of force, morally or legally. The results of spousal violence are seen in damaged relationships, fear, anxiety, and growing hostility. Justifying physical punishment on the basis of its ability to elicit compliance merely preserves the power imbalance between children and adults. When children themselves are asked for their views on physical punishment, their responses often reveal insight into the power dynamic inherent in this practice and cast a different light on the notion of compliance. For example, a recent qualitative study (Saunders & Goddard, 2010) yielded the following statements from children about physical punishment:

It's what keeps us apart, adults are more important than children (ten-year-old, p. 136).

Adults have basically more power. They have a greater say.... It really frustrates me when...I will have an opinion but I can't do much with it (thirteen-year-old, p. 137).

If adults [have] physical contact with someone, like punching 'em, it's against the law...they could go to jail, they could be charged with assault. And that's exact same for smacking. But...if you're a kid, and it's in the house, it's okay because they're your kids. If you are a kid, it doesn't really matter...you barely have any say (ten-year-old, p. 138).

[Physical punishment is like] being squashed.... I reckon animals are more well treated. In some cases...it just makes you feel like you're a nothing, you're a cockroach (eleven-year-old, p. 153).

Being smacked is like being treated like something very little and not important to the rest of the world (twelve-year-old, p. 153).

Section 43 of the Criminal Code justifies physical punishment on the assumption that it induces social compliance and is necessary for children's socialization. Neither argument is supported by the empirical evidence. Instead, the evidence shows that physical punishment puts children at risk for injury, poorer mental health, impaired parent–child relationships, weaker moral internalization, increased aggression and anti-social behaviour, impaired learning, and future violence against a spouse or child. Therefore, physical punishment cannot be justified on the basis that it benefits children.

There is a second problem with Section 43. By justifying the assault of children, it denies their rights as human beings. These rights are set out in the *Charter* and made explicit in the landmark *Convention on the Rights of the Child*.

CHILDREN'S RIGHTS AND CONSTITUTIONALITY

The Convention on the Rights of the Child

Adopted by the UN General Assembly 1989, the Convention was ratified more quickly and by more states than any other international treaty. Canada ratified the Convention in 1991, which means that: (1) our laws must comply with its standards; (2) we must report every five years to the UN Committee on the Rights of the Child ("the UN Committee"), which monitors state compliance; and (3) we must act in good faith on the UN Committee's recommendations. Four sections of the Convention are relevant to corporal punishment:

- Article 3 requires that the child's best interests be a primary consideration in all legal and administrative actions concerning the child.
- Article 19 requires that all appropriate measures are taken to protect children from all forms of physical or mental violence, injury or abuse, and to provide violence prevention programs.
- Article 28 requires that the administration of school discipline respects the child's dignity.
- Article 37 requires that children are not subjected to degrading treatment.

The UN Committee "has stressed that corporal punishment of children is incompatible with the Convention" (Committee on the Rights of the Child, 1994) and has recommended to Canada "that the physical punishment of children in families be prohibited" (Committee on the Rights of the Child, 1995). In 1999, Canada responded:

> The government has been seeking to reinforce and clarify protection under the Criminal Code. A non-government organization, the Canadian Foundation for Children, Youth and the Law, has received funding from the government-funded Court Challenges program to apply to a Canadian court for a determination as to whether s. 43 of the Criminal Code infringes children's constitutional rights under the Canadian Charter of Rights and Freedoms.

In other words, law reform was left to the private sector and the courts, rather than the parliamentary reform process called for by the UN Committee. Moreover, the government itself opposed this challenge every step of the way. This story is summarized in the following section.

Canadian Foundation for Children, Youth, and the Law vs. Canada (Attorney General)

In 1999, the Canadian Foundation for Children, Youth, and the Law ("the Foundation") launched a constitutional challenge to Section 43, arguing that it violates the Charter and the Convention. The Charter is part of the Constitution of Canada, meaning that the courts have the power to strike down a law, government program, or policy that unreasonably restricts or denies a right or freedom protected by the Charter. The Foundation's challenge was first heard by the Ontario Superior Court of Justice. The court ruled in 2000 that Section 43 does not deny children's equality rights under Section 15 of the Charter, their right to security of the person under Section 7, or their right to be free of cruel and unusual treatment or punishment under Section 12.

The Foundation appealed to the Ontario Court of Appeal. That court ruled in 2001 that, while Section 43 denies children's equality rights, the law is justified under Section 1 of the Charter (Canadian Foundation for Children, Youth, and the Law, 2002; McGillivray, 2004). The Foundation then appealed to the Supreme Court of Canada.

In 2003, in the midst of the court challenge, the UN Committee called for the repeal of Section 43 and a legislative ban on "all forms of violence against children, however light" (paras. 32–33). In 2004, in a six-to-three decision, the Supreme Court of Canada upheld Section 43. Chief Justice Beverley McLachlin, writing for the majority, found no violation of children's rights under either the Charter or the Convention. Justice McLachlin did not refer to the Committee's 2003 comments, noting instead that "mild" violence does not infringe the Convention. Section 43, she wrote, includes only "the mildest forms of assault." She set out limits on the protection to adults provided by Section 43. The punishment: (1) must not be used on children under two or over twelve, or on any child who suffers from a disability or other factor making the child incapable of learning from the correction; (2) must not involve "degrading, inhuman or harmful conduct" or "the use of objects or blows or slaps to the head"; (3) must not stem from "frustration, loss of temper or abusive personality"; and (4) may only be carried out by parents (teachers can no longer assault children to punish them but only to restrain them). On the questions of dignity and vulnerability that are central to equality, Justice McLachlin wrote:

> Children often feel a sense of disempowerment and vulnerability; this reality must be considered when assessing the impact of s. 43 on a child's sense of dignity. Yet, as emphasized, the force permitted is limited and must be set against the reality of a child's mother or father being charged and pulled into the criminal justice system.

Three judges wrote dissenting judgments, accusing the majority of exceeding the limits of judicial interpretation. By setting out new limits on the use of force, they argued, the decision makes new law, and this is beyond the power of the court. All three found that Section 43 violates children's rights under the Charter. Two would strike down Section 43, while the third would "save" Section 43 under Section 1 of the Charter as a reasonable limit on the rights of children, but would strike teachers from Section 43. (For further details on the court challenge and the Supreme Court's decision, see Carter, 2005; Durrant, 2007; Grover, 2003; McGillivray, 2012a, 2012b; McGillivray & Milne, 2011; Turner, 2002; Watkinson, 2006.)

Implications of the Supreme Court Decision (Canadian Foundation)
While the Supreme Court guidelines in *Canadian Foundation* offer some clarity, they fail to protect the majority of Canada's children. They are also not grounded in the realities of child maltreatment. Of the 25,257 incidents of child physical abuse that were substantiated in Canada in 2003, 91 percent were carried out by parents, 77 percent were intended as punishment, and 69 percent involved children between the ages of two and twelve (Durrant et al., 2009). In 71 percent of cases, no injury was observed (Durrant et al., 2009), yet these acts carried such risk that they were substantiated as maltreatment. Therefore, it is no longer useful to differentiate physical punishment from physical abuse in terms of the perpetrator, the adult's intent, the child's age, or whether injury was sustained, yet this is precisely what the Supreme Court did in its list of limits.

Third, the court put the burden of proof on the one claiming violation of rights and not on the government under Section 1. This violates the structure of the Charter. If assault can be justified on the basis of vulnerability, then this decision makes it far more difficult for vulnerable people to achieve equality in future cases.

Fourth, the decision ignores Canada's commitment to the Convention. Canada's leadership in human rights and childhood standards is now in question.

Last, and most important, the decision is disrespectful of the dignity of children. The Criminal Code has not been amended to reflect the decision. The status of children as the only sentient beings who can be assaulted at will in Canada is unchanged.

CONCLUSION AND RECOMMENDATIONS
Corporal punishment is the intentional infliction of pain for the purpose of correction, an act that would be considered a criminal assault if directed at an adult. But the Canadian Criminal Code provides a defence to assault for parents, teachers, and people standing in the place of parents if the act was intended to correct a child's behaviour.

In the fifteen years preceding the Supreme Court's decision, courts excused assaults causing bodily harm and assaults with rulers, sticks, belts, and other objects (Durrant, 2007, p. 101). Raising welts did not amount to bodily harm (1999) and hitting a child with a belt was a legally accepted form of punishment (2001).

Has the Supreme Court of Canada's list of limits on the use of corrective force made a difference? In 2009, a father who pushed his son in the face, causing him to stumble and bruise his head, was acquitted; "minor corrective force of a transitory and trifling nature" is not corporal punishment and anger is "part and parcel of correcting a child." A bus driver who taped a six-year-old learning-impaired boy to his seat and taped a sock in his mouth was given the benefit of s. 43 (2009). A father who threw his fifteen-year-old daughter into his truck was acquitted on appeal (2008); the force used was not for correction but for restraint and it was reasonable "in light of the offence calling for correction." A teacher charged with fourteen counts of common assault and four of assault with a weapon for hitting learning-impaired first- and second-graders with books and rulers, pushing their faces into desks, and shoving them to the floor was acquitted (2007); while the force was "beyond the absolute minimum required," *Canadian Foundation* permits touching and the children were not hurt. A father who burned his seven-year-old son with a cigarette lighter to teach him not to set fires was acquitted at trial (2006); the court found the assault to be both unintentional and educational in intent. On appeal, the father was convicted of assault with a weapon. A mother who hit her thirteen-year-old daughter on the face for refusing to turn off the television was acquitted (2004); *Canadian Foundation* permits "minor corrective force of a transitory and trifling nature." Only slaps to the head that can be characterized as corporal punishment are unreasonable. Because this slap was not corporal punishment, it was not unreasonable.

In each of these cases at least one of the Supreme Court's limits was violated, demonstrating the futility of redefining the indefinable (McGillivray, 2012b). The failure of Canadian courts to establish a coherent and defensible standard in well over a century is not resolved.

In a growing number of other countries, the situation is very different. The governments of thirty-two countries have repealed their legal defences to corrective assault and have affirmed children's rights to full legal protection in explicit prohibitions of physical punishment. These countries are South Sudan (2011); Kenya, Tunisia, Congo, and Poland (2010); Liechtenstein, Luxembourg, Moldova, and Costa Rica (2008); Spain, Venezuela, Uruguay, Portugal, New Zealand, Togo, and Netherlands (2007); Greece (2006); Hungary (2005); Romania and Ukraine (2004); Iceland (2003); Germany, Israel, and Bulgaria (2000); Croatia (1999); Latvia (1998); Denmark (1997); Cyprus (1994); Austria (1989); Norway (1987); Finland (1983); and Sweden (1979) (Global Initiative to End All Corporal Punishment of Children, 2011). The primary purpose of these countries' explicit prohibitions is to affirm children's rights to physical integrity and dignity. (For details on the history and outcomes of Sweden's groundbreaking prohibition, see Durrant, 1999, 2000, 2003; Durrant & Olsen, 1997; Durrant, Rose-Krasnor & Broberg, 2003. For information on reform efforts in Canada and eighteen other states, see Durrant & Smith, 2011.)

In 2004, the Parliamentary Assembly of the Council of Europe recommended a Europe-wide ban on corporal punishment. In 1996, the Supreme Court of Italy ruled that "the use of violence for educational purposes can no longer be considered lawful." In 2005, the Supreme Court of Nepal ruled that the Child Act provision permitting "minor beating" is unlawful. On the international stage, Canada's failure to ban corporal punishment is viewed as a glaring human rights violation.

In Canada's efforts to prevent violence against children, preventing physical punishment must become a central and explicit focus (Straus, 2000). We recommend three key components of a primary prevention initiative:

1. a clear and consistent message in law and from all levels of government that hitting children is neither socially acceptable nor legally defensible
2. a universal public education campaign aimed at altering attitudes toward physical punishment
3. a collaboration among response systems (child protection, law enforcement, health) to develop protocols and programs that respect children's rights to protection, as well as their developmental needs; enlightened policy and law in this area can become instruments of education and support for families, rather than instruments of punishment and coercion (McGillivray, 2003)

The road from Rome to the twenty-first century has been paved with justifications for violence against children. The Supreme Court of Canada lost its opportunity to pave a new road to the future, one that respects children's rights and dignity. Its decision denies children's rights and ignores Canada's obligations under the Convention; sets a bad precedent for vulnerable groups seeking equality under the Charter; leaves most Canadian children without the full protection of the criminal law; and sends the message that hitting children is still acceptable (Durrant, Sigvaldason & Bednar, 2008). Change will require continuous and consistent messages from those who work with children and families; policies and guidelines and statutory reform at every level; a sustained education campaign; taking seriously the views of children on how they should be treated; and full recognition of children as rights-bearers. As criminal law is the most powerful legal statement on right conduct, it will require abolishing Section 43. Abolition will signal real commitment to children's rights here and on the world stage.

REFERENCES

Afifi, T.O., Brownridge, D.A., Cox, B.J., & Sareen, J. (2006). Physical punishment, childhood abuse, and psychiatric disorders. *Child Abuse & Neglect, 30*, 1093–1103.

Anderson, S., & Payne, M.A. (1994). Corporal punishment in elementary education: Views of Barbadian schoolchildren. *Child Abuse & Neglect, 18*, 377–86.

Aucoin, K.J., Frick, P.J., & Bodin, S.D. (2006). Corporal punishment and child adjustment. *Journal of Applied Developmental Psychology, 27*, 527–41.

Azrin, N.H., & Holz, W.C. (1966). Punishment. In W.K. Honig (Ed.), *Operant behavior* (pp. 380–447). New York: Appleton-Century-Crofts.

Bandura, A. (1971). *Social learning theory.* New York: General Learning Press.

Bean, A.W., & Roberts, M.W. (1981). The effect of time-out release contingencies on changes in child noncompliance. *Journal of Abnormal Child Psychology, 9*, 95–105.

Bernstein, M. (2004). The decision of the Supreme Court of Canada upholding the constitutionality of Section 43 of the Criminal Code of Canada: What this decision means to the child welfare sector. *Journal of the Ontario Association of Children's Aid Societies, 48*(2), 2–14.

Blackstone, W., (1962). *Commentaries on the Laws of England,* 4 vols. (orig. pub. Oxford 1765–69). Boston: Beacon.

Bower, M.E., & Knutson, J.F. (1996). Attitudes toward physical discipline as a function of disciplinary history and self-labelling as physically abused. *Child Abuse & Neglect, 20*, 689–99.

Bower-Russa, M.E., Knutson, J.F., & Winebarger, A. (2001). Disciplinary history, adult disciplinary attitudes, and risk for abusive parenting. *Journal of Community Psychology, 29*, 219–40.

Boyson, R. (2002). *Equal protection for children: An overview of the experience of countries that accord children full legal protection from physical punishment.* London: National Society for the Prevention of Cruelty to Children.

Bracton, Henry de. (1968). *Bracton on the laws and customs of England.* Cambridge, MA: Harvard University Press. (Original work published c.1250.)

Bradley, R.H., Corwyn, R.F., Burchinal, M., McAdoo, H.P., & García Coll, C. (2001). The home environments of children in the United States, Part II: Relations with behavioral development through age thirteen. *Child Development, 72*, 1868–86.

Brezina, R. (1999). Teenage violence toward parents as an adaptation to family strain: Evidence from a national survey of male adolescents. *Youth & Society, 416*, 424–25.

Buckland, W.W. (1963). *A text-book of Roman law from Augustus to Justinian* (3rd ed., rev.). Cambridge: Cambridge University Press.

Bugental, D.B., & Goodnow, J.J. (1998). Socialization processes. In W. Damon & N. Eisenberg (Eds.), *Social, emotional, and personality development* (pp. 389–462). New York: Wiley.

Bugental, D.B., Martorell, G.A., & Barraza, V. (2003). The hormonal costs of subtle forms of infant maltreatment. *Hormones and Behavior, 43*, 237–44.

Buntain-Ricklefs, J.J., Kemper, K.J., Bell, M., & Babonis, T. (1994). Punishments: What predicts adult approval? *Child Abuse & Neglect, 18*, 945–55.

Canada. Criminal Code, R.S.C. 1985, c. C-45.

Canadian Foundation for Children, Youth, and the Law v. Canada (Attorney General). 2002: Ontario Court of Appeal.

Canadian Foundation for Children, Youth and the Law v. Canada (Attorney General), (2002) 207 D.L.R. (4th) 632 (Ont. CA) (January 15, 2002)

Canadian Foundation for Children, Youth, and the Law v. Canada (Attorney General), [2004] 1 S.C.R. 76. Appeal from the Ontario Court of Appeal (2002), 57 O.R. (3d) 511, 207 D.L.R. (4th) 632, 161 C.C.C. (3d) 178, 154 O.A.C. 144, 48 C.R. (5th) 218, 23 R.F.L. (5th) 101, 90 C.R.R. (2d) 223, [2002] O.J. No. 61 (QL), affirming Superior Court of Justice (2000), 49 O.R. (3d) 662, 188 D.L.R. (4th) 718, 146 C.C.C. (3d) 362, 36 C.R. (5th) 334, 76 C.R.R. (2d) 251, [2000] O.J. No. 2535 (QL). Appeal dismissed, Binnie J. dissenting in part and Arbour and Deschamps JJ. dissenting.

Carter, M. (2005). The constitutional validity of the corporal punishment defence in Canada: A critical analysis of Canadian foundation for children, youth, and the law versus Canada. *International Review of Victimology, 12*(2), 189–211.

Clément, M.E., Bouchard, C., Jetté, M., & Laferrière, S. (2000). *La violence familiale dans la vie des enfants du Québec.* Québec: Institut de la Statistique du Québec.

Committee on the Rights of the Child (CRC) (1994). UN Doc. CRC/C/34.

Committee on the Rights of the Child. (1995, June). Consideration of reports, concluding observations, Canada. Report adopted by the Committee at its 233rd meeting on June 9, 1995. crc/c/43. 9 June 1996. ge 95-18144.

Committee on the Rights of the Child. (2003a). Consideration of reports submitted by states parties under article 40 of the Convention, thirty-fourth session, crc/c.15/Add. 215 (2003).

Committee on the Rights of the Child. (2003b). Consideration of reports submitted by state parties under article 44 of the Convention, thirty-fourth session, crc/c/15/Add. 215.

Coontz, P.D., & Martin, J.A. (1988). Understanding violent mothers and fathers: Assessing explanations offered by mothers and fathers of their use of control punishment. In G.T. Hotaling, D. Finkelhor, J.T. Kirkpatrick & M.A. Straus (Eds.), *Family abuse and its consequences: New directions in research* (pp. 77–90). Newbury Park, CA: Sage.

Coyl, D.D., Roggman, L.A., & Newland, L.A. (2002). Stress, maternal depression, and negative mother–infant interactions in relation to infant attachment. *Infant Mental Health Journal, 23,* 145–63.

Crockenberg, S. (1987). Predictors and correlates of anger toward and punitive control of toddlers by adolescent mothers. *Child Development, 58,* 964–75.

Csorba, J., Rozsa, S., Vetro, A., Gadoros, J., Makra, J., Somogyi, E., et al. (2001). Family and school-related stresses in depressed Hungarian children. *European Psychiatry, 16,* 18–26.

Day, D.E., & Roberts, M.W. (1983). An analysis of the physical punishment component of a parent training program. *Journal of Abnormal Child Psychology, 11,* 141–52.

Dietrich, D., Berkowitz, L., Kadushin, A., & McGloin, J. (1990). Some factors influencing abusers' justification of their child abuse. *Child Abuse & Neglect, 14,* 337–45.

Doggett, M. (1993). *Marriage, wife-beating, and the law in Victorian England.* Columbia: University of South Carolina Press.

Douglas, E.M., & Straus, M.A. (2006). Assault and injury of dating partners by university students in 19 countries and its relation to corporal punishment experienced as a child. *European Journal of Criminology, 3,* 293–318.

DuRant, R.H., Cadenhead, C., Pendergrast, R.A., Slavens, G., & Linder, C.W. (1994). Factors associated with the use of violence among urban Black adolescents. *American Journal of Public Health, 84,* 612–17.

Durrant, J.E. (1999). Evaluating the success of Sweden's corporal punishment ban. *Child Abuse & Neglect, 23,* 435–48.

Durrant, J.E. (2000). Trends in youth crime and well-being in Sweden since the abolition of corporal punishment. *Youth & Society, 31,* 437–55.

Durrant, J.E. (2003). Legal reform and attitudes toward physical punishment in Sweden. *International Journal of Children's Rights, 11,* 147–74.

Durrant, J.E. (2007). Corporal punishment: A violation of the rights of the child. In R.B. Howe & K. Covell (Eds.), *Children's rights in Canada: A question of commitment* (pp. 99–125). Waterloo, ON: Wilfrid Laurier University Press.

Durrant, J.E. (2011). The empirical rationale for eliminating physical punishment. In J.E. Durrant & A.B. Smith (eds.), *Global pathways to abolishing corporal punishment: Realizing children's rights* (pp. 42–63). New York: Routledge.

Durrant, J.E., & Olsen, G.M. (1997). Parenting and public policy: Contextualizing the Swedish corporal punishment ban. *Journal of Social Welfare and Family Law, 19,* 443–61.

Durrant, J.E., Rose-Krasnor, L., & Broberg, A.G. (2003). Maternal beliefs about physical punishment in Sweden and Canada. *Journal of Comparative Family Studies, 34,* 586–604.

Durrant, J.E., Sigvaldason, N., & Bednar, L. (2008). What did the Canadian public learn from the 2004 Supreme Court decision on physical punishment? *International Journal of Children's Rights, 16,* 229–47.

Durrant, J.E., & Smith, A.B. (2011). *Global pathways to abolishing physical punishment: Realizing children's rights.* New York: Routledge.

Durrant, J.E., Trocmé, N., Fallon, B., Milne, C., & Black, T. (2009). Protection of children from physical maltreatment in Canada: An evaluation of the Supreme Court's definition of reasonable force. *Journal of Aggression, Maltreatment, and Trauma, 18*, 64–87.

Durrant, J.E., Trocmé, N., Fallon, B., Milne, C., Black, T., & Knoke, D. (2006). *Punitive violence against children in Canada.* Technical Paper Series HT091-02001/001/SS, Task no. 16. Ottawa: Public Health Agency of Canada.

Eamon, M.K. (2001). Antecedents and socioemotional consequences of physical punishment on children in two-parent families. *Child Abuse & Neglect, 25*, 787–802.

Gershoff, E.T. (2002). Corporal punishment by parents and associated child behaviors and experiences: A meta-analytic and theoretical review. *Psychological Bulletin, 128*, 539–79.

Gershoff, E.T., & Bitensky, S.H. (2007). The case against corporal punishment of children: Converging evidence from social science research and international human rights law and implications for US public policy. *Psychology, Public Policy, and Law, 13*, 231–72.

Gest, S.D., Freeman, N.R., Domitrovich, C.E., & Welsh, J.A. (2004). Shared book reading and children's language comprehensive skills: The moderating role of parental discipline practices. *Early Childhood Research Quarterly, 19*, 319–36.

Gil, D.G. (1970). *Violence against children: Physical child abuse in the United States.* Cambridge, MA: Harvard University Press.

Global Initiative to End All Corporal Punishment of Children. (2011). Retrieved from: http://www.endcorporalpunishment.org/pages/progress/prohib_states.html.

Graziano, A.M., Hamblen, J.L., & Plante, W.A. (1996). Subabusive violence in childrearing in middle-class American families. *Pediatrics, 98*(4) (Suppl.), 845–51.

Graziano, A.M., & Namaste, K.A. (1990). Parental use of physical force in child discipline. *Journal of Interpersonal Violence, 5*, 449–63.

Grogan-Kaylor, A. (2004). The effect of corporal punishment on antisocial behavior in children. *Social Work Research, 28*, 153–61.

Grogan-Kaylor, A. (2005). Corporal punishment and the growth trajectory of children's antisocial behavior. *Child Maltreatment, 10*, 283–92.

Grover, S.C. (2003). Negating the child's inclusive right to security of the person: A charter analysis of the s.43 Canadian Criminal Code defense to corporal punishment of a minor. *Murdoch University Electronic Journal of Law, 10*(4). Retrieved from: www.murdoch.edu.au/elaw/indices/issue/v10n4.html.

Gunnoe, M.L., & Mariner, C.L. (1997). Toward a developmental-contextual model of the effects of parental spanking on children's aggression. *Archives of Pediatric Adolescent Medicine, 151*, 768–75.

Heale, W. (1978). *An apologie for women.* New York: Garland. (Original work published 1609.)

Hirschi, T. (1969). *Causes of delinquency.* Berkeley: University of California Press.

Hoffman, M.L. (1994). Discipline and internalization. *Developmental Psychology, 30,* 26–28.

Javo, C., Rønning, J.A., Heyerdahl, S., & Rudmin, F.W. (2004). Parenting correlates of child behavior problems in a multiethnic community sample of preschool children in northern Norway. *European Child and Adolescent Psychiatry, 13,* 8–18.

Kadushin, A., & Martin, J.A. (1981). *Child abuse: An interactional event.* New York: Columbia University Press.

Kelder, L.R., McNamara, J.R., Carlson, B., & Lynn, S.J. (1991). Perceptions of physical punishment: The relations to childhood and adolescent experiences. *Journal of Interpersonal Violence, 6,* 432–45.

Kerr, D.C., Lopez, N.L., Olson, S.L., & Sameroff, A.J. (2004). Parental discipline and externalizing behaviour problems in early childhood: The roles of moral regulation and child gender. *Journal of Abnormal Child Psychology, 32,* 369–83.

Knutson, J.F., & Selner, M.B. (1994). Punitive childhood experiences reported by young adults over a 10-year period. *Child Abuse & Neglect, 18,* 155–66.

Lansford, J.E., Chang, L., Dodge, K.A., Malone, P.S., Oburu, P., Palmérus, K., Bacchini, D., Pastorelli, C., Bombi, A.S., Zelli, A., Tapanya, S., Chaudhary, N., Deater-Deckard, K., Manke, B., & Quinn, N. (2005). Physical discipline and children's adjustment: Cultural normativeness as a moderator. *Child Development, 76,* 1234–46.

Lansford, J.E., Criss, M.M., Laird, R.D., Shaw, D.S., Pettit, G.S., Bates, J.E., & Dodge, K.A. (2011). Reciprocal relations between parents' physical discipline and children's externalizing behavior during middle childhood and adolescence. *Developmental Psychopathology, 23,* 225–38.

Larzelere, R.E. (1986). Moderate spanking: Model or deterrent of children's aggression in the family? *Journal of Family Violence, 1,* 27–36.

Lau, J.T.F., Liu, J.L.Y., Cheung, J.C.K., Yu, A., & Wong, C.K. (1999). Prevalence and correlates of physical abuse in Hong Kong Chinese adolescents: A population-based approach. *Child Abuse & Neglect, 23,* 549–57.

Loeber, R., Drinkwater, M., Yin, Y., Anderson, S.J., Schmidt, L.C., & Crawford, A. (2000). Stability of family interaction from ages 6 to 18. *Journal of Abnormal Child Psychology, 28,* 353–69.

Lopez, N.L., Bonenberger, J.L., & Schneider, H.G. (2001). Parental disciplinary history, current levels of empathy, and moral reasoning in young adults. *North American Journal of Psychology, 3,* 193–204.

MacMillan, H.L., Boyle, M.H., Wong, M.Y.Y., Duku, E.K., Fleming, J.E., & Walsh, C.A. (1999). Slapping and spanking in childhood and its association with lifetime prevalence of psychiatric disorders in a general population sample. *Canadian Medical Association Journal, 161,* 805–9.

McGillivray, A. (1997). He'll learn it on his body: Disciplining childhood in Canadian law. *International Journal of Children's Rights, 5,* 193–242.

McGillivray, A. (2003). Child physical assault: Law, equality, and intervention. *Manitoba Law Journal, 30,* 133–66.

McGillivray, A. (2004). Childhood in the shadow of *parens patriae.* In S. Ross, H. Goelman & S. Marshall (Eds.), *Multiple lenses, multiple images: Perspectives on the child across time, space, and disciplines* (pp. 38–72). Toronto: University of Toronto Press.

McGillivray, A. (2012a). Children's rights, paternal power, and fiduciary duty: From Roman law to the Supreme Court of Canada. *International Journal of Children's Rights, 18,* 21–54.

McGillivray, A. (2012b). Nowhere to stand: Correction by force in the Supreme Court of Canada. In S. Anand (Ed.), *Children and the law: Essays in honor of Nicholas Bala* (pp. 57–76). Toronto: Irwin Law.

McGillivray, A., & Milne, C. (2011). Canada: The rocky road of repeal. In J.E. Durrant & A.B. Smith (Eds.), *Global pathways to abolishing physical punishment: Realizing children's rights* (pp. 98–111). New York: Routledge.

McGowan, P.O., Sasaki, A., D'Alessio, A.C., Dymov, S., Labonté, B., Szyf, M., Turecki, G., & Meaney, M.J. (2009). Epigenetic regulation of the glucocorticoid receptor in human brain associates with childhood abuse. *Nature Neuroscience, 12,* 342–48.

McLoyd, V.C., & Smith, J. (2002). Physical discipline and behavior problems in African American, European American, and Hispanic children: Emotional support as a moderator. *Journal of Marriage and the Family, 64,* 40–53.

Miller, K.S., & Knutson, J.F. (1997). Reports of severe physical punishment and exposure to animal cruelty by inmates convicted of felonies and by university students. *Child Abuse & Neglect, 21,* 59–82.

Mulvaney, MK., & Mebert, C.J. (2007). Parental corporal punishment predicts behavior problems in early childhood. *Journal of Family Psychology, 21,* 381–97.

Newell, P. (2011). The human rights imperative to eliminate physical punishment. In J.E. Durrant & A.B. Smith (Eds.), *Global pathways to abolishing corporal punishment: Realizing children's rights* (pp. 7–26). New York: Routledge.

Ogg-Moss v. R. [1984] 2S.C.R. 173.

Ohene, S.A., Ireland, M., McNeely, C., & Borowsky, I. W. (2006). Parental expectations, physical punishment, and violence among adolescents who score positive on a psychosocial screening test in primary care. *Pediatrics, 117,* 441–47.

Olson, S.L., Ceballo, R., & Park, C. (2002). Early problem behavior among children from low-income mother-headed families: A multiple risk perspective. *Journal of Clinical Child and Adolescent Psychology, 31,* 419–30.

Pagani, L.S., Tremblay, R.E., Nagin, D., Zoccolillo, M., Vitaro, F., & McDuff, P. (2004). Risk factor models for adolescent verbal and physical aggression toward mothers. *International Journal of Behavioral Development, 28,* 528–37.

Parke, R.D. (1977). Some effects of punishment on children's behavior—revisited. In E.M. Hetherington & R.D. Parke (Eds.), *Contemporary readings in child psychology* (pp. 176–88). New York: McGraw-Hill.

Parkinson, C.E., Wallis, S.M., Prince, J., & Harvey, D. (1982). Research note: Rating the home environment of school-age children: A comparison with general cognitive index and school progress. *Journal of Child Psychology and Psychiatry, 23,* 329–33.

Peltoniemi, T. (1983). Child abuse and physical punishment of children in Finland. *Child Abuse & Neglect, 7,* 33–36.

Pollock, L.A. (1983). *Forgotten children: Parent–child relations from 1500 to 1900.* Cambridge: Cambridge University Press.

Roberts, M.W., & Powers, S.W. (1990). Adjusting chair timeout enforcement procedures for oppositional children. *Behavior Therapy, 21,* 257–71.

Rodriguez, C.M. (2003). Parental discipline and abuse potential affects on child depression, anxiety, and attributions. *Journal of Marriage and Family, 65,* 809–17.

Rogoff, B. (1990). *Apprenticeship in thinking: Cognitive development in social context.* New York: Oxford University Press.

Rohner, R.P., Kean, K.J., & Cournoyer, D.E. (1991). Effects of corporal punishment, perceived caretaker warmth, and cultural beliefs on the psychological adjustment of children in St. Kitts, West Indies. *Journal of Marriage and the Family, 53,* 681–93.

Rorty, M., Yager, J., & Rossotto, E. (1995). Aspects of childhood physical punishment and family environment correlates in bulimia nervosa. *Child Abuse & Neglect, 19,* 659–67.

Saarni, C., Mumme, D.L., & Campos, J.J. (1998). Emotional development: Action, communication, and understanding. In W. Damon & N. Eisenberg (Eds.), *Social, emotional, and personality development* (pp. 237–309). New York: Wiley.

Saunders, B.J., & Goddard, C. (2010). *Physical punishment in childhood: The rights of the child.* Chichester, UK: Wiley-Blackwell.

Scott, G.R. (1938). *The history of corporal punishment: A survey of flagellation in its historical, anthropological, and sociological aspects.* London: T. Werner Laurie.

Scott, S.P. (Ed.). (1939). *The civil law code of Justinian.* Cincinnati: Central Trust.

Sheu, Y.-S., Polcari, A., Anderson, C.M., & Teicher, M.H. (2010). Harsh corporal punishment is associated with increased T2 relaxation time in dopamine-rich regions. *Neuroimage, 53,* 412–19.

Simons, R.L., Lin, K.H., & Gordon, L.C., (1998). Socialization in the family of origin and male dating violence: A prospective study. *Journal of Marriage and the Family, 60,* 467–78.

Slade, E.P., & Wissow, L.S. (2004). Spanking in early childhood and later behaviour problems: A prospective study of infants and young toddlers. *Pediatrics, 113,* 1321–30.

Smith, A.B. (2011). The theoretical rationale for eliminating physical punishment. In J.E. Durrant & A.B. Smith (Eds.), *Global pathways to abolishing corporal punishment: Realizing children's rights* (pp. 27–41). New York: Routledge.

Smith, J.R., & Brooks-Gunn, J. (1997). Correlates and consequences of harsh discipline for young children. *Archives of Pediatric and Adolescent Medicine, 151*, 777–86.

Steely, A.C., & Rohner, R.P. (2006). Relations among corporal punishment, perceived parental acceptance, and psychological adjustment in Jamaican youths. *Cross-Cultural Research, 40*, 268–86.

Stephen, J.F. (1887). *A digest of the criminal law (crimes and punishments)* (4th ed.). London: Macmillan.

Stone, L. (1979). *The family, sex, and marriage in England 1500–1800.* Harmondsworth, UK: Penguin.

Stormshak, E.A., Bierman, K.L., McMahon, R.J., & Lengua, L.J. (2000). Parenting practices and child disruptive behavior problems in early elementary school. *Journal of Clinical Child Psychology, 29*, 17–29.

Strassberg, Z., Dodge, K.A., Pettit, G.S., & Bates, J.E. (1994). Spanking in the home and children's subsequent aggression toward kindergarten peers. *Development and Psychopathology, 6*, 445–61.

Straus, M.A. (1990). Ordinary violence, child abuse, and wife beating: What do they have in common? In M.A. Straus & R.J. Gelles (Eds.), *Physical violence in American families: Risk factors and adaptations to violence in 8,145 families* (pp. 403–24). New Brunswick, NJ: Transaction.

Straus, M.A. (1994). *Beating the devil out of them: Corporal punishment in American families.* New York: Lexington.

Straus, M.A. (2000). Corporal punishment and the primary prevention of child abuse. *Child Abuse & Neglect, 24*(9), 1109–1114.

Straus, M.A., & Paschall, M.J. (2009). Corporal punishment by mothers and development of children's cognitive ability: A longitudinal study of two nationally representative age cohorts. *Journal of Aggression, Maltreatment, and Trauma, 19*, 459–83.

Straus, M.A., & Smith, C. (1992). Family patterns and child abuse. In M.A. Straus & R.J. Gelles (Eds.), *Physical violence in American families: Risk factors and adaptations to violence in 8,145 families* (pp. 245–61). New Brunswick, NJ: Transaction.

Straus, M.A., Sugarman, D.B., & Giles-Sims, J. (1997). Spanking by parents and subsequent antisocial behavior of children. *Archives of Pediatrics & Adolescent Medicine, 151*, 761–67.

Taylor, C.A., Manganello, J.A., Lee, S.J., & Rice, J.C. (2010). Mothers' spanking of 3-year-old children and subsequent risk of children's aggressive behavior. *Pediatrics, 125*, 1057–1065.

Tomoda, A., Suzuki, H., Rabi, K., Sheu, Y.-S., Polcari, A., & Teicher, M.H. (2009). Reduced prefrontal cortical gray matter volume in young adults exposed to harsh corporal punishment. *Neuroimage, 47*(Supp. 2), T66–T71.

Trocmé, N., & Durrant, J. (2003). Physical punishment and the response of the Canadian child welfare system: Implications for legislative reform. *Journal of Social Welfare and Family Law, 25*, 39–56.

Trocmé, N., Fallon, B., MacLaurin, B., Daciuk, J., Felstiner, C., Black, T., Tonmyr, L., Blackstock, C., Barter, K., Turcotte, D., & Cloutier, R. (2005). *Canadian Incidence Study of Reported Child Abuse and Neglect—2003: Major findings.* Ottawa: Minister of Public Works and Government Services Canada.

Trocmé, N., MacLaurin, B., Fallon, B., Daciuk, J., Billingsley, D., Tourigny, M., et al. (2001). *Canadian Incidence Study of Reported Child Abuse and Neglect.* Ottawa: National Clearinghouse on Family Violence.

Turner, H.A., & Finkelhor, D. (1996). Corporal punishment as a stressor among youth. *Journal of Marriage and the Family, 58*, 155–66.

Turner, H.A., & Muller, P.A. (2004). Long-term effects of child corporal punishment on depressive symptoms in young adults: Potential moderators and mediators. *Journal of Family Issues, 25*, 761–82.

Turner, S.M. (2002). *Something to cry about: An argument against corporal punishment of children in Canada.* Waterloo, ON: Wilfrid Laurier University Press.

Ulman, A., & Straus, M.A. (2003). Violence by children against mothers in relation to violence between parents and corporal punishment by parents. *Journal of Comparative Family Studies, 34*, 41–60.

United Nations. (1992). Draft declaration on the elimination of violence against women, adopted by the United Nations General Assembly, December 20, 1993.

United Nations Committee on the Rights of the Child. (1995). UN Committee on the Rights of the Child, ninth session, consideration of reports submitted by state parties under article 44 of the convention: Canada (UN/CRC/C/15 Add,37, June 20, 1995).

Vasta, R. (1982). Physical child abuse: A dual-component analysis. *Developmental Review, 2*, 125–49.

Vygotsky, L.S. (1978). *Mind in society: The development of higher psychological processes.* London: Harvard University Press.

Watkinson, A.M. (2006). Supreme Court of Canada stands behind corporal punishment—sort of. *International Social Work, 49*(4), 531–35.

Webster, N. (1922). *Webster's new international dictionary of the English language.* W.T. Harris (Ed.). Springfield, MA: G. & C. Merriam.

5

VIOLENCE, TRAUMA, AND RESILIENCE

MICHAEL UNGAR AND BRUCE D. PERRY

INTRODUCTION

When it comes to violence in families, one of the persistent challenges has been to better understand *exactly how* abuse and violence affect the individual child or adult. How does a physical or verbal act, or even a threat, for example, get under someone's "skin" and affect brains and bodies? How is it that particular acts or threats are traumatizing to some, but appear to have little effect on others? In recent years, "resilience" has become a popular concept to explain how some people avoid the negative effects that follow exposure to violence. Is it actually "resilience" that mediates the experience? If the effects of abuse and violence change the body and brain, how do relationship-based interventions support recovery?

While we recognize that there are multiple perspectives we can use to understand and address the effects of violence and abuse, for the purposes of this chapter, we decided to bring two complementing viewpoints into a dialogue. Using two lenses, *developmental neurobiology* and *social ecology*, we will review and discuss some of the biopsychosocial factors that influence whether an individual is likely to demonstrate vulnerability or resilience in the face of extreme adverse experiences such as those associated with domestic and family violence. We will then show that while it might be appealing to think of resilience as simply the lack of problems and normal functioning (going to school or work, avoiding drugs or risky sexual activity, etc.) following adversity, a social ecological understanding of resilience explains *how* individuals can be supported to resist, recover from, and sometimes even grow from such experiences. Three different stories (Cassandra, Steven, and Deanne) will help illustrate how individuals are affected by violence and some of the factors that may minimize harm and promote recovery.

Cassandra, now five, was born with a difficult-to-sooth temperament, but was provided with attentive, attuned, and responsive caregiving by experienced and well-regulated parents. She was provided many opportunities for exploration and novelty-seeking in safe, predictable, and controllable ways during early childhood. She and her family are connected to community and culture with many stable and enduring relationships. However, after her grandmother died, her grandfather came to live with the family. He began to threaten and torment Cassandra whenever her parents were out of the house. She withdrew, avoided contact, and her teacher observed that in a very short time she had changed from a bright, social child into a nervous and isolated one. Her parents' repeated questions and obvious worry that something was wrong heightened Cassandra's fears that something bad was going to happen to her, just like her grandfather predicted.

Steven, now sixteen, was born with the genetic gifts that, under typical circumstances, could have led to a very well-regulated, flexibly responsive, and "hardy" stress-response capacity. He was born to a single mother who is a member of an isolated, marginalized indigenous group that was the target of cultural genocide in previous generations. Steven's grandmother was taken to residential school 1,500 kilometres away from family, community, and culture. Physically and emotionally abused there, she returned to her community, hoping to reconnect with family. She became pregnant with Steven's mother soon after. By the age of three, due to chronic neglect, Steven's mother was taken into care and raised in a series of foster homes away from her community. At twenty, she too returned to her community and attempted to reconnect with her mother and several siblings. She drank to excess, became pregnant, and kept drinking. Steven developed with the epigenetic and intrauterine effects that profoundly compromised the capacity of his stress-response systems to develop normally. Maternal–child interactions were inconsistent, chaotic, and episodically disrupted by domestic violence.

Deanne, now forty-seven, and was born to a middle-class family in the suburbs of a major urban centre. During infancy and the first two years of life, she benefited from an attentive and loving mother. After the birth of her younger sister, however, her mother suffered from severe depression. Her father worked long hours to avoid being at home. When he was at home, he was verbally and physically abusive to Deanne and her three younger siblings. An older cousin sexually abused her from age six to eight; a "boyfriend" sexually assaulted her on multiple occasions when she was a teen. Despite all of this, she did well in school, went to university, and is a successful professional. She sees herself as a "tough cookie" who has persevered through a tough life. Recently her sister's husband groped her while they were doing the dishes in the kitchen together. This seemingly mild incident triggered a complete breakdown. Deanne went on extended sick leave and began to take medication to calm her nerves.

These individual narratives illustrate key factors involved in vulnerability and resilience. We will use these throughout the chapter to highlight the multiple and interactive elements that appear to protect and heal individuals following extreme adversity. Moreover, we will examine those factors that increase vulnerability and, as we will see, vulnerability can stem not just from overwhelming stressors, but, as in the case of Deanne, seemingly mild ones as well.

STRESS-RESPONSE SYSTEMS

Life is transition: waking from sleep, moving from place to place, engaging new and familiar people, satiating hunger, quenching thirst, learning a new concept, mastering a new motor skill. Every day, each person experiences thousands of transitions. Negotiating these continuous mini-challenges requires a complex array of interconnected physiological systems and neural networks to monitor, process, and act on the inner and outer environments. This array constitutes our "stress-response" systems, collectively influencing every part of our bodies and brains. In any given situation, the stress-response systems can change the way we think, feel, behave, digest food, pump blood, mobilize white blood cells, release insulin, lift weights, and hundreds of other body and brain-mediated functions. Thought, behaviour, and emotion are all influenced by the activity of our stress-response systems. When these systems are flexible and well regulated, there can be a parallel flexibility and regulation in our thought, feelings, and behaviour—a person can adapt and cope when facing novelty, transitions, stress, and distress. Yet when these systems are dysregulated, an individual may be easily overwhelmed by the minor challenges of everyday life and, in response to unpredictable or prolonged stress, experience profound deterioration in both mental and physical health.

This conceptualization of stress response emphasizes that human development results from an individual's interactions with the social ecologies that mediate or accentuate risk exposure. A child who is particularly vulnerable to stress, but who experiences little or none, may appear to cope better than the child who has more capacity to cope, but is overwhelmed by the compounding effect of multiple chronic and acute stressors. Viewed over time, the irony of the situation is that the overprotected child who experiences few challenges during development may not be properly inoculated against future stress. The child who is challenged or even overwhelmed early, but is supported during recovery, may develop coping strategies and a neurobiological flexibility in her or his stress-response systems that will be functional for a lifetime. Under optimal conditions, the environment provides manageable amounts of stress to maximize a child's development, but not so unpredictable, severe, or prolonged that these experiences traumatize the child or hinder a child's development.

The factors that predict an individual's capacity to cope, and whether the nature of the coping is adaptive or maladaptive, range from the biological to the psychological, interpersonal, and socio-cultural. A facilitative environment, including the constellation of social services provided to mitigate risk and promote well-being (child welfare, mental health and addictions, special education, and community-based models of care, etc.), also plays an important role in whether individuals who are exposed to extreme adverse experiences follow negative patterns of development, maintain normal functioning, or exceed expectations and grow from their experience, exhibiting what is sometimes referred to as post-traumatic growth (Tedeschi & Calhoun, 1996). Resilience, in turn, is associated with maintaining normal functioning or exceeding expectations after an adverse experience.

Individual-Level Stress-Response Systems
The stress-response systems are widely distributed through the brain and rest of the body. Though the complex neurobiology of these interrelated systems is beyond the scope of this chapter, the general neural architecture of these systems is important to understand if we are to predict which processes help individuals adapt following extreme adverse experiences. The core components of these stress-response networks are neurotransmitter systems with receptive dendritic nets and cell bodies in the lower areas of the brain (brain stem and diencephalon), which then send direct connections to every other part of the brain (and indirectly to the body). This distribution allows these systems to influence or even control a remarkable array of functions mediated by every other part of the brain (e.g., cognitive, social, emotional, behavioural, neuroendocrine, and autonomic functioning).

These stress-response networks are receiving input from the external and internal environments—sensing, processing, storing, perceiving, and acting on this information. This monitoring is sensitive to novelty, transitions, and, especially, perceived threat. The stress-response systems control a continuous process of modulation, regulation, and compensation to maintain a state of equilibrium or homeostasis. Whenever the input alters this homeostasis or is associated with a previously stored threat, these networks initiate compensatory, adaptive responses to re-establish homeostasis or take the necessary actions to survive (Perry & Pollard, 1998).

Individual Responses to Threat
Individual responses to threat can vary tremendously. This is not surprising considering the vast distribution of neural functions that are available to the

stress-response network. The specific adaptive changes taken by the brain to respond to the incoming threat-related signals will vary, depending upon many factors; different elements of the widely distributed neural system will be recruited and others will be shut down to conserve energy and focus the body's response to threat. Under normal circumstances (i.e., a normal stress-response capability), the responses are graded, proportional to the level of the perceived threat; when the threat is mild, a moderate activation of key systems takes place; when extreme, intense and prolonged activation will occur. The adaptive responses are specific to the nature of the threat, either preparing to flee or fight or preparing to be overwhelmed and injured. In cases of abnormal development or sensitivity of the stress-response systems (see later sections), the responses to potential threat are inappropriate and out of proportion; trauma can make these systems overactive and overly reactive (see Perry, 2008).

Whatever the adaptive response during an extreme experience, the key issue for the development of subsequent pathology is how long these systems are activated. The brain changes in a "use-dependent" fashion. The longer and more intense the activation during the actual event and subsequent exposure, the more likely there will be molecular changes in the stress-response systems, which will lead to long-term functional changes. These extreme adverse experiences can cause alterations that lead to sensitized, dysfunctional neural networks; essentially the state of fear can become the persisting trait of anxiety, for example. What were once adaptive neurobiological states can become, over time, maladaptive traits (Perry et al., 1995). In turn, anything that can prevent or modulate the prolonged activation of these systems can minimize long-term negative functional consequences of an extreme experience.

Determinants of Stress-Response System Capability

Genetic: All complex neurophysiological systems comprise thousands of proteins. This means that there will necessarily be a range of genetic variations that can be seen in the full expression of individual stress-response neurobiology observed in the population. Further, it is not unreasonable to assume that this variation in composition will be paralleled by variation in flexibility and functional capability. Certainly in animal models, this is the case (e.g., Perry et al., 1983). In preliminary human studies, genetic variations in key neural proteins associated with the stress-response networks appear to increase risk for the development of neuropsychiatric symptoms following maltreatment (Caspi et al., 2002, 2003).

Epigenetic: Recent studies are showing that genetic *expression*—or whether or not a gene within a person's DNA gets turned on or off—can be directly affected by environmental influences present in the life of the biological parents (and grandparents). This preconception impact on development has yet to be fully characterized—particularly in humans—but there is clear evidence that epigenetics can affect stress-response neural networks development and alter reactivity and flexibility of these systems (e.g., Harshaw, 2008).

Intrauterine: There is an abundance of research on the impact of intrauterine stress, alcohol exposure, and drug use on the development of the fetal brain. The neural networks that will ultimately be responsible for mediating the stress response are profoundly influenced by prenatal factors (see Perry, 1988, 2002). Alcohol, nicotine, extreme maternal distress, drug exposure, infection, and hypoxia are a few of the intrauterine insults that can alter the development of stress-response networks in the fetus.

Early childhood experiences: Early in life the brain is organizing at a remarkable rate, with more than 80 percent of the major structural changes taking place during the first four years. The key neural networks involved in the stress response develop early in life (see Perry, 2001a, 2008). Experiences during early childhood have a greater potential to influence functional organization of these systems in either positive or negative ways; therefore, early developmental trauma and neglect have a "disproportionate influence on brain organization and later brain functioning" (see Perry, 2002, 2008). Children exposed to threat and who have minimal buffering from caregivers, develop overactive and overly reactive stress-response systems.

Primary caregivers are the external stress regulators for the infant. With attentive, attuned, and responsive caregiving, the pattern of stressors (hunger, thirst, cold, fear) will be moderate, predictable, and, to some degree, controllable. It is these patterns of postnatal stressors that can lead to the development of a more flexible and "resilient" stress-response capacity (Tronick, 2006). In contrast, a depressed, distressed, inconsistent, or absent caregiver will contribute to abnormal organization and functional development of two crucial and interrelated neural systems (the stress response and relational). The result is a child more vulnerable to future stressors and less capable of benefiting from nurturing interactions that might help buffer stress, distress, and trauma later in life. The "protective" and regulating presence of a predictable, nurturing caregiver can attenuate the increased risk.

Adverse experiences: The impact of traumatic stress on the developing child has been well documented. Many studies have documented trauma-related psychopathology such as post-traumatic stress disorder (PTSD) (for review, see: Bremner, 2003; De Bellis & Thomas, 2003; Glaser, 2000; Perry, 1994, 2001b; Teicher et al., 2002). Table 5.1 summarizes the key fac-

Table 5.1   Risk Factors That Increase and Decrease the Impact of Trauma on Biopsychosocial Development

	Event-Related Factors	Individual Characteristics	Family and Social Factors
Increase Risk *(Prolong the intensity or duration of the acute stress response)*	• Multiple or repeated event (in this case, ongoing threat) • Physical injury to child • Involves physical injury or death to loved one, particularly the mother • Perpetrator is a family member • Dismembered or disfigured bodies seen • Destroys home, school, or community • Disrupts community infrastructure (e.g., Hurricane Katrina) • Long duration, difficult recovery (e.g., 2004 tsunami)	• Female • Age (younger more vulnerable) • Subjective perception of physical harm • History of previous exposure to trauma • No cultural or religious anchors • No shared experience with peers (experiential isolation) • Low IQ • Pre-existing neuropsychiatric disorder (especially anxiety related)	• Trauma has direct impact on caregivers • Anxiety in primary caregivers • Continuing threat and disruption to family • Chaotic, overwhelmed family • Physical isolation • Distant caregiving • Absent caregivers
Decrease Risk *(Decrease intensity or duration of the acute stress response)*	• Single event • Perpetrator is stranger • No disruption of family or community structure • Short duration (e.g., tornado)	• Cognitively capable of understanding abstract concepts • Healthy coping skills • Educated about normative post-traumatic responses • Immediate post-traumatic interventions • Strong ties to cultural or religious belief systems	• Intact, nurturing family supports • Non-traumatized caregivers • Caregivers educated about normative post-traumatic responses • Strong family beliefs • Mature and attuned parenting skills

tors that appear to be related to subsequent development of trauma-related psychopathology. The development of this psychopathology appears to be due to alterations in key stress-response neural networks (Danese et al., 2009; Perry et al., 1995).

DEFINING TRAUMA

Trauma is one of the most overused, poorly defined concepts in neuropsychiatry. Popular use of the term "trauma" or "traumatic" has further confounded a physiologically meaningful or psychologically useful definition. People refer to an event as a trauma or as "traumatic." Yet we know that there are multiple individually specific outcomes from any group experiencing the same event. Indeed, most events labelled "traumatic" (e.g., school shooting, car accident, combat) don't appear to result in enduring negative mental health effects for the majority of individuals experiencing the "trauma." With this said, overt mental health problems such as post-traumatic stress disorder are not the only negative outcomes following an adverse experience. Many studies have documented long-term compromise in multiple domains of functioning following "traumatic" experiences. The Adverse Childhood Experience (ACE) studies, for example, have documented increased risk for a host of emotional, social, behavioural, and physical health problems following abuse and related traumatic experiences in childhood (Anda et al., 2006; Felliti et al., 1998). These epidemiological studies examined the relationship between adverse childhood experiences, including child abuse and a wide range of functional indicators in adult life. Among the ACE findings are a graded increase in risk (i.e., more abuse = more risk) for affective symptoms and panic attacks, memory problems, hallucinations, poor anger control, perpetrating partner violence, unhealthy sexual behaviour (early intercourse, promiscuity, sexual dissatisfaction), suicide, substance abuse, alcohol use and abuse, and smoking. In addition there is a significant increased risk for a range of physical health problems following child abuse. Risk for the major causes of death in adult life is increased following adverse childhood experiences (Felitti et al., 1998).

So what is trauma? From a neurodevelopmental perspective, trauma is not the event—it is the individual's response to the event. Traumatic stress occurs when an extreme experience overwhelms and alters the individual's stress-related physiological systems in a way that results in functional compromise in *any* of the widely distributed stress-response systems (e.g., neuroimmune, neuroendocrine, autonomic, and central nervous system networks). For example, if there are two children witnessing a violent act and one has a very reactive stress-response system, this child can experience a prolonged stress-response activation that results in a long-term change in neural networks related to attention, sleep, cognition, and affect regulation. He was traumatized; for him the act was a "traumatic event." The other child has a well-regulated stress-response system; after the event there are supportive and nurturing caregivers to help him make cognitive sense and receive relational and somatosensory (e.g., holding, hugging, rocking) regulation. Within weeks he is sleeping, eating, concentrating, and, while the experience was negative, his stress response (and other functioning) has returned to a normal baseline. The event was not traumatizing; he demonstrated resilience. Indeed, he may have actually strengthened his stress response and emotional and cognitive capacities in ways that result in "post-traumatic" growth. Again, this term, while common, is not neurodevelopmentally accurate. It is more accurate to

Figure 5.1   Variable Life Trajectories of "Resilience" and
"Vulnerability"

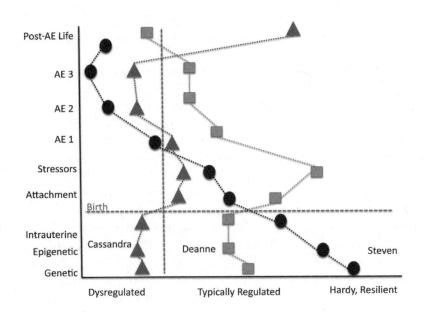

label this as "resilience-recruitment" growth; the growth occurred because of the presence of factors that recruited and reinforced his strengths—a belief system, a relational network, the somatosensory regulatory impact of loving caregivers, friends, and family.

On a neurophysiological level, it is impossible for an extreme experience not to change a person. The key questions are *whether* experience-related changes result in functional compromise and, if so, how this will manifest (e.g., physical, emotional, social, cognitive health). Furthermore, we know that activation of the stress response in predictable, moderate ways leads to a more flexible and functional stress-response capacity, i.e., stress in the right doses, patterns, and timing makes the stress-response systems stronger and more capable (Tronick, 2006).

Cassandra, Steven, and Deanne illustrate the primary and essential point that multiple factors contribute to "vulnerability" and "resilience" over the lifespan and will result in a lifelong *process* determining at any given point what an individual's stress-response capacities will be. Indeed, as seen with Deanne, at one point in life an individual may demonstrate remarkable "resilience," yet at another point, a moderate stressor can overwhelm the individual and result in significant dysfunction.

Figure 5.1 illustrates the three trajectories of variability in stress-response capacity for our three examples. At conception there are likely a range of genetic contributors to the development and optimal functionality of the stress response. At various points in development, factors known to influence the development and functionality of the stress-response networks influence the individual's specific capacity.

Cassandra (triangles) has genetic vulnerability, but experiences a good prenatal environment with a supported, healthy mother. At birth, she is born with a difficult-to-sooth temperament, but is provided with attentive, attuned, and responsive caregiving by experienced and well-regulated parents. Cassandra and her family are connected to their community and culture with many stable and enduring relationships. When the grandfather's abusive behaviours increase (see Figure 5.1; AE = Adverse Event), there is a transient deterioration of stress-response capacity and expression of various emotional, social, cognitive, and physical problems associated with this dysregulation—she crosses the red line from marginally regulated to dysregulated. Over time, however, Cassandra benefits from the continuing investment of family, community, and therapeutic efforts and she begins to heal, restores her regulated stress-response capacity, and shows improvement in all of the areas of previous dysfunction. Indeed, over time she develops significant regulatory strengths and is able to use her history of adversity to enrich and reinforce her belief system, capacity for empathy, and sense of competence—"Look what I've overcome." Posttraumatic growth is an important but understudied area where concepts of trauma and resilience merge.

Deanne (squares) had an average and typical genetic potential and optimal prenatal environment. At birth, she also had a very attentive, attuned, and responsive mother attending to her first-born. The household was not yet chaotic or threatening, and as a toddler Deanne had multiple opportunities in early childhood for moderate, predictable, and controllable stress, essentially creating an "inoculation" against future stressors. In contrast to Cassandra, her genetic potential allows her to develop a more flexible and "hardy" stress-response capability with very similar high-quality bonding and developmental opportunities (i.e., she moves further to the right than Cassandra with the similar developmental experiences). Anchored internally by a strong set of beliefs, buffered by strong, enduring relational connections and with more "hardy" stress-response systems, she is able to cope with the increasing dysfunction, threat, and chaos of her home as more children are born, her mother suffers severe depression, and she experiences sexual abuse at several points in her development. Despite all of this, she remains to the right of the "dysregulation" red line and is able to function at a high level in school, work, and the community. Yet the long history of adversity has had a cost. Her stress-response systems are more vulnerable despite her success, and the experience of fondling by her brother-in-law triggers cue-associated stress-response activation from her previous abuse. This overwhelms her adequate but strained stress-response capacities and she becomes dysregulated and dysfunctional. Despite this, with therapeutic, family, and community supports, she will likely be capable of returning to a more functional state. In this case, the fondling was "traumatic." It overwhelmed her stress response's capacity to regulate. While a more extreme experience (when judged by any observer), such as being the victim of her father's physical abuse while a child, resulted in less "trauma"—she was able to continue functioning at school and with friends—her stress-response systems were more flexible and capable at that point in her life. Yet the assaults by her father did contribute to the long-term deterioration and "wearing out" of the early inoculation to stressors she received from her genetic, epigenetic, intrauterine, and attachment-related experiences.

Steven (circles) was born with the genetic gifts that, under typical circumstances, could lead to a very well-regulated, flexibly responsive, and hardy stress-response capacity. Yet, as described in the introduction, Steven developed with the epigenetic and intrauterine vulnerabilities that profoundly compromised the capacity of his stress-response systems to develop normally. Maternal–child interactions were inconsistent, chaotic, and episodically disrupted by domestic violence. By the time Steven was exposed to the chaos and violence in his community and home, he had a poorly organized, sensitized stress-response system and was living in a transient, disconnected relational milieu. With no social supports beyond his family or community to anchor, buffer, or heal Steven from these extreme experiences, he was highly vulnerable and reactive to almost any challenging experience, including novelty, transition, and the typical challenges of school. The inability to self-regulate—such as seen with Steven—means that he will be highly likely to seek forms of regulation from external and often unhealthy sources, such as alcohol, huffing, various drugs of abuse, cutting, and sexual activity. Conventional Western mental health interventions are likely to fail; once, twice, even daily contact with a therapist is inadequate to meet Steven's profound relational and regulatory needs. In contrast, reconnection to culture and community, relational permanence with stable and nurturing adults capable of patience, persistence, and predictability, are necessary for Steven to begin to regulate and recover his functional potential. Only then would conventional therapeutic interventions be likely to contribute to his long-term healthy development.

DEFINING RESILIENCE

Resilience is a process that engages the biological, psychological, and social resources individuals require to resist the negative impact of adversity, recover from exposure and the temporary decline in functioning that follows, or grow as a consequence of the experience. While one could argue that "resilience" refers to the individual qualities (intellectual capacity, executive functioning skills, positive self-regard, etc.) that make it more likely individuals will succeed, it is more useful to focus on "resilience" as process. This latter view highlights the mechanisms by which individuals and their environments interact to optimize human development in contexts where there is significant exposure to risk (Masten, 1994, 2010; Luthar, Cicchetti & Becker, 2000). In this regard, resilience is not something one has or doesn't have. Instead, resilience is a dynamic phenomenon, facilitated at multiple levels, from early interventions that help neglected children develop the neurophysiological capacity to form healthy attachments, to social service interventions that ensure abused children are empowered in their case planning and given a voice in decisions concerning their programs of care (Ungar, 2011). Therefore, rather than thinking of resilience as a quality of the individual alone, it is better defined as the capacity of individuals to *navigate* their way to the resources they need, and *negotiate* for those resources to be provided in ways that are meaningful (Ungar, 2005). A definition such as this highlights resilience as a process. Individuals may need motivation and the biological capacity to seek change in threatening contexts and establish homeostasis in a way that supports well-being, but that can be achieved only when the individual's social and physical ecology—their environment—provides the relationships and opportunities required to succeed. When supportive resources are provided in ways that are consistent with the individual's values, they are much more likely to be appreciated and used.

Key Principles

Because of the complexity of the interrelated factors that predict resilience after extreme adversity, resilience is best understood as reflecting these key principles: *dynamic process, equifinality and multifinality, and differential impact.*

Dynamic process: For individuals who have experienced trauma, their capacity to cope afterwards is the result of individual qualities facilitated or constrained by their environments. Resilience is not a state, but a description of the dynamic processes individuals engage in with others. As Luthar et al. (2000) explained, depending on the level of risk and the degree of competence shown to cope with risk, resilience-promoting processes may be protective (helping individuals avoid further decline in functioning), stabilizing (maintaining normal levels of functioning), enhancing (increasing functioning beyond normal expectations), or reactive (there is progressively more decline in functioning over time as exposure to stress continues). The processes most likely to occur are always the result of the individuals' resources interacting with the resources available and accessible to them in their environments.

Equifinality and multifinality: From psychology, the concept of equifinality—different causal factors leading to similar outcomes—can also be applied to resilience. For example, different early experiences, such as sexual abuse and divorce, can lead to the same negative outcome, such as a particular psychological disorder like depression. The concept of multifinality—similar or identical causes leading to different outcomes—can also be applied to resilience-related processes. For example, children from marginalized communities who are removed from their families and placed with families from the dominant culture report widely divergent experiences with many deeply distressed by their placements, while others view their placements outside their culture as advantageous (Blackstock & Trocmé, 2005). The processes that lead to a set of outcomes (such as gainful employment or a caring, committed relationship with a peer) may be widely divergent and dependent upon the resources available and accessible to an individual. On a related note, it is important to consider how we *perceive* or *understand* "desirable outcomes." It is not enough to try to influence a child's navigations to successful coping; we must also look at whether the outcomes *the child* perceives as positive are also those that are valued by others around him or her.

Differential impact: People react very differently to similar adversities. Likewise, the protective quality of a particular individual capacity (like an optimistic attitude) or environmental resource (a good school or progressive parental leave policy) will vary, depending on the amount and nature of stress an individual experiences. In low-stress environments, a particular strength may have little or no effect on overall development, while for a child in a very difficult and dangerous home or community, a protective factor like persistence, a mentor, or a safe school may provide an immense advantage to the child's psychosocial well-being. Therefore, a protective process that may be helpful to an individual exposed to catastrophic stressors may exert little influence, or a negative influence, on another individual who is exposed to the same degree of stress. For example, neglected children whose parents have a mental illness may experience their role as caregivers for their parents (adultification) as a source of self-esteem and the means to compensate for a lack of caring from others (Godsall, Jukovic, Emshoff, Gerson & Stanwyck, 2004). This same process of engaging a child in the care of a parent is likely to have a negative impact on the child when the parent is not perceived by the child (or the community) as requiring the child's help. In these cases, the emotional dependency of the parent on the child is experienced as a threat to the child's development (Hooper, Marotta & Lanthier, 2008). In other words, the process of demonstrating caring for someone else can contribute to a child's resilience under some circumstances, but may harm a child's psychosocial development in contexts where the same process of adultification is perceived as exploitive (Ungar, Theron & Didkowsky, 2011).

RESILIENCE AND TRAUMA—EXTREME ENDS OF THE SAME CONTINUUM?

Are trauma and resilience extreme ends of the continuum of the capacity of the body's stress-response systems? Popular understanding would suggest *yes*, but in fact the story is much more complex. A key challenge to studying the impact of developmental trauma is that it is almost impossible to study all of the meaningful outcomes following adversity. Do we label as resilient the boy who does not meet clinical criteria for active psychiatric disorder (e.g., post-traumatic stress disorder) following physical abuse? Did these adverse experiences result in altered immune function or increased autonomic reactivity that will lead to increased risk for heart disease, asthma, and diabetes later in life? When adversity alters his development in ways that greatly diminish his potential, but do not cause overt failure or pathology, is that resilience? Are there processes at play that mitigate the impact of risk on the boy's functioning, maintaining adaptive behavioural outcomes, behaviours that are not overtly problematic (i.e., the boy still goes to school but does not excel)? Understood this way, extreme adversity produces both immediate and long-term changes in adaptation, meaning that resilience must be understood as *processes over time* that help individuals cope in the best way possible with adversity and trauma (Schoon, 2006; Werner & Smith, 2001). In other words, even with trauma can come resilience.

We do not use the term "resilient" or invoke resilience other than in the context of stress, adversity, or trauma. Why is this? First, from a neurophysiological perspective, then, it is the *individual's response* to the event that defines the degree of trauma. While trauma and resilience may be intertwined, in neurobiological terms, they are not extreme ends of the continuum of the capacity of the body's stress-response systems. Likewise, when understood sociologically, trauma and resilience are both interactional processes where one thwarts human development after exposure to dangerous situations, while the other supports recovery and adaptation. Second, the processes that create resilience are related to the nature and amount of adverse circumstances that surround the developing child. To illustrate, a supportive grandparent is helpful to every child's development, but if there is no threat to the child's development, then the influence of the grandparent is relatively small, diluted by the sheer number of other supports a child has and the lack of need for a close attachment with a parent substitute. However, in a context where development is threatened, that same grandparent may exert a potentially large influence on the child's developmental trajectory, ensuring later success through his or her encouragement and support. A grandparent, for example, may provide an abused child with a safe place to stay away from the offending parent, a source of validation, as well as cultural resources that enhance identity.

DIALOGUE: THE INTERSECTING CONCEPTS OF TRAUMA AND RESILIENCE

Returning to the three earlier case studies—Cassandra, Steven, and Deanne—we can speculate which protective factors might mitigate the impact of extreme adversity (reducing vulnerability) and promote resilience. Given that each has been exposed to significant levels of violence, and all are showing the impact of that violence on their functioning, there are a number of protective processes that might benefit them and that reflect what we know about resilience. Two of the most important are those related to relationships and context.

The Power of Relationships

A major determinant of stress-response activation is the relational milieu. This powerful relationally mediated effect is due to mirroring qualities of the human brain. We tend to mirror the affect and physiological states of the people around us. When an anxious child is with loving and supportive adults, she will feel calm. When another child is in the immediate aftermath of an extreme experience and he is alone, there can be no relationally mediated calming effect, or if the adults who are with the child are equally overwhelmed and anxious, their fear will be contagious. In very powerful ways, then, people who are present in a person's life will modulate the activity and reactivity of the stress response (see Ludy-Dobson & Perry, 2010). Many of the documented factors associated with resilience can be viewed as working through the relational mediated modulation of the stress-response networks. Social connectedness, for example, is viewed as a protective factor against many forms of child maltreatment, including physical abuse, neglect, and non-organic failure to thrive (e.g., Belsky et. al., 2005; Caliso & Milner, 1992; Chan, 1994; Coohey, 1996; Egeland, Jacobvitz & Sroufe, 1988; Gaudin et al., 1993; Hashima & Amato, 1994; Rak & Patterson, 1996; Travis & Combs-Orme, 2007).

Therefore, for young people like Cassandra and Steven, a change in the relational milieu can be expected to change the nature of their stress response.

The removal from the home of an abusive adult (in Cassandra's case, the grandfather), or placement in a stable, nurturing, and culturally appropriate foster placement (a possible benefit for Steven) would be expected to create the optimal environment to change troubling patterns of reactivity following exposure to stressors. In a context where abuse is severe enough to require the involvement of child protection services, these same protective processes are evident in models of effective practice that emphasize systems of care that increase the stability of placement for children who must be removed from their families. Optimizing the potential for bonding with a primary caregiver is of critical importance to the child who has experienced prolonged neglect or abuse (Newton, Litrownik & Landsverk, 2000).

In the case of an adult like Deanne, the same principles apply. Relational quality, density, and permanence are key elements in creating a safe and regulating environment in which to heal. Often if these are present, psychoeducation and supportive therapeutic processes take hold quickly and can restore previous regulatory capacities. Without these, conventional therapeutic efforts are often ineffective.

Contextual Factors

Despite the multiple physical and psychological effects of adverse experiences, interactions among family, school, and other community subsystems, as well as cultural and political factors, can create the conditions for children to experience the resilience associated with recovery from trauma. These systems, alone and in interaction with one another, provide a milieu in which abused children find the resources that match their needs and are perceived as meaningful to them (Ungar, 2005). The contextual processes required for resilience among children who have been traumatized by neglect and abuse are experiences of social justice, access to material resources such as housing and safety, a sense of belonging in their community (and a sense of life purpose that is acknowledged by others), and cultural adherence (Kirmayer, Dandeneau, Marshall, Phillips & Williamson, 2012; Ungar et al., 2007). These factors, like the individual and relational factors mentioned earlier, are interactive; as one changes, others will change as well. For example, a child like Cassandra from a more advantaged community, or Steven from a marginalized community, who receives child protection services may be further harmed unless the manner in which those services are delivered is sensitive to the child's, and the child's family's, unique culture and context. Likewise, since more children from lower SES homes are brought under protection orders than children from higher SES homes, socio-political factors—such as access to affordable housing, safe streets, income support, employment programs, and other indirect factors that increase the capacity of the child's environment to care for the child—are important aspects of promoting resilience. Furthermore, the chances of healing from trauma will be better in contexts where there are functioning primary caregivers who themselves are treated fairly in their communities and for whom there are opportunities to gain access to the resources required to provide care for their child (Armstrong, Birnie-Lefcovich & Ungar, 2005; Yoshikawa & Kalil, 2011).

In this regard, a wealthy nation like Canada should be able to provide the resources that make children and adults more resilient. It is unfortunate that some marginalized communities, including Aboriginal peoples, rural Canadians, and Canadians with mental illnesses or living in poverty, are all at greater risk of having children who are both traumatized and likely to suffer the secondary trauma of apprehension (Trocmé, Phaneuf, Scarth, Fallon & MacLaurin, 2003). For adults like Deanne who have a mental health problem, strategies that optimize access to services are likely to help increase their resilience, especially when these services are also responsive to the person's context and culture.

TRANSLATING UNDERSTANDING INTO PRACTICE

There are practical implications that follow from an understanding of trauma and resilience when working with children who have been exposed to severe, prolonged threats to their development, such as domestic violence (Perry, 2009). There is a desperate need to infuse developmentally sensitive and trauma-informed concepts into our efforts to serve maltreated children and their families. Neurophysiological adaptability, relational aspects of resilience associated with epigenetics, as well as the social determinants of biopsychosocial growth should all inform policies and programming that mitigate the negative impact of stressors and promote positive development. Among the processes that are most likely to bolster resilience are early intervention, promoting relational density, maintaining relational permanence, creating congruence between child and resources, and multi-systemic integration of services.

Early intervention: Results from longitudinal studies of children living in poverty suggest that while earlier is always better, it is never too late to intervene (Garmezy, 1991; Sroufe, Egeland, Carlson & Collins, 2005). Early interventions tend to have the most impact when the original threat to the child's development is removed and changes in living conditions and supports are sustained. Head Start programs, for example, are most likely to show positive results when children are adequately resourced for learning throughout their childhoods (Webster-Stratton, 2001).

Relational density: Relational density refers to the amount or dose of attachments that contribute to children's positive development. With the principle of differential impact in mind, children who need the most secure attachments are those who have experienced the greatest number of stressors. In this regard, more connections are better for the children most exposed to violence (Combrinck-Graham, 1995; Wekerle, Waechter & Chung, 2012).

Relational permanence: The impact of relational density, or the proximity and number of close relationships a child experiences, is balanced by the need for relational permanence. For child welfare systems, permanence may be difficult to achieve when foster placements break down and primary workers, tasked with supervising a child, change jobs. The more services support children's secure attachments to individual foster parents or caseworkers, the more likely children are to experience a social ecology that facilitates optimal development under stress (Barter, 2000).

Congruence between the child's needs and services: A growing trend toward both child-centred practice and a postmodern appreciation for competing discourses regarding children's experiences of health and well-being is changing services for trauma-affected children (Bottrell, 2009; Ungar, 2004). Increasingly, congruence is sought between the individual needs of the child and the interventions that are offered. In practice this means that service providers are striving to appreciate the meaning that children attach to the processes associated with resilience. Across cultures and contexts, a child's meta-cognitions and culturally embedded value systems make some interventions less relevant than others. When service providers negotiate with children for the right constellation of services that meet a child's needs in ways meaningful to the child, it is more likely that the negative sequelae from exposure to traumatic events will be prevented (Eggerman & Panter-Brick, 2010).

Multi-systemic integration: Moving up one more ecological level to the domain of multiple systems that are tasked with providing services to children who experience trauma, there is abundant evidence that the more systems integrate their responses to children, the better children will cope (Madsen, 2009; Santisteban & Mena, 2009). Multi-systemic integration congruent with the child's perception of need has the potential to optimize services and create coherent service models that avoid disjointed or conflicting programming. For example, the mental health needs of a child may contribute to a plan of care that involves a period of time away from school, while educational providers may want to maintain the child in school. The same child is often a client of the child welfare service whose mandate to place the child in a foster placement to secure the child's safety may conflict with the expressed desire of an older child, for example, to remain at home or to continue at the same school, assuming foster placement would result in the child changing schools (Ungar, 2007). The better coordinated the goals of each system, the more likely children will be to have their resilience facilitated.

In combination, these principles of effective practice provide the resources to sustain children's capacities to cope and facilitate biopsychosocial development by matching the child's needs with social service programming and infrastructure. There are many examples of successful initiatives that reflect these principles. Mental health interventions that are coordinated between a child's school, social workers, parents, and other supports have the potential to address patterns of problem behaviour among children (e.g., Barfield et al., 2011). Likewise, coordinated child abuse treatment centres provide safe spaces to investigate child abuse (Jones, Cross, Walsh & Simone, 2007). These centres are a particularly good example of these principles in practice, providing a density of relationships, continuity in care, and service coordination that match the needs of children for efficient assessment and treatment after abuse. Services for older youth may also reflect these best-practice principles. For example, well-integrated multi-service centres for homeless youth that meet their needs for housing, employment counselling, educational support, and psychological services that address the stigma associated with homelessness provide a service structure that reflects best practices with regard to youth who have experienced trauma (Kennedy, Agbenyiga, Kasiborski & Gladden, 2010). While most of these interventions have not been examined for their impact on trauma specifically, the changes in behaviour and engagement in positive relationships that result are likely to predict positive developmental gains that counter the effects of past victimization.

LOOKING TO THE FUTURE

Though the effects of trauma are now known to cause long-term threats to normative biopsychosocial development, there is abundant evidence that the deleterious effects of extreme adverse experience during childhood can be mitigated and vulnerability prevented. As we now know, resilience only partly reflects the individual's capacity to recover; it also depends on how well the environment facilitates recovery and growth at neurological and interactional levels. Social policy and the services that it informs can change the odds stacked against children who have experienced trauma. Whether there is the motivation to make resources available and accessible, however, remains the question. What we know is that early and developmentally targeted interventions that address the functional vulnerabilities caused by extreme adversity can repair much of the damage done by adverse life events. Contextual and cultural sensitivity can help guide interventions so they are more likely to be effective for populations that experience the marginalization associated with the problems that cause trauma and the resulting subsequent behaviours. To the extent that we use the emerging concepts of traumatology and development to further our understanding of the processes that contribute to recovery and growth, the more likely we are to respond to children coping with stress with interventions well suited to nurturing resilience.

REFERENCES

Anda, R.F., Felitti, R.F., Walker, J., Whitfield, C., Bremner, D.J., Perry, B.D., et al. (2006). The enduring effects of childhood abuse and related experiences: A convergence of evidence from neurobiology and epidemiology. *European Archives of Psychiatric and Clinical Neuroscience, 256*, 174–86.

Armstrong, M., Birnie-Lefcovich, S., & Ungar, M. (2005). Pathways between social support, quality of parenting, and child resilience: A transactional model. *Journal of Family and Child Studies, 14*(2), 269–81.

Barfield, S., Gaskill, R., Dobson, C., & Perry, B.D. (2011, October 31) Neurosequential model of therapeutics in a therapeutic preschool: Implications for work with children with complex neuropsychiatric problems. *International Journal of Play Therapy.* doi:10.1037/a0025955.

Barke, E.J. (2006). Do the effects of early severe deprivation on cognition persist into early adolescence? Findings from the English and Romanian Adoptees Study. *Child Development, 77*(3), 696–711.

Barter, K. (2000). Services for vulnerable children: A conceptualization. In J. Turner & F. Turner (Eds.), *Canadian social welfare: IV* (pp. 250–65). Toronto: Pearson Education.

Belsky, J., Jaffee, S.R., Sligo, J., Woodward, L., & Silva, P.A. (2005). Intergenerational transmission of warm-sensitive-stimulating parenting: A prospective study of mothers and fathers of 3 year olds. *Child Development, 76*, 384–96.

Blackstock, C., & Trocmé, N. (2005). Community-based child welfare for Aboriginal children: Supporting resilience through structural change. In M. Ungar (Ed.), *Handbook for working with children and youth: Pathways to resilience across cultures and contexts* (pp. 105–20). Thousand Oaks, CA: Sage.

Bottrell, D. (2009). Understanding "marginal" perspectives: Towards a social theory of resilience. *Qualitative Social Work, 8*(3), 321–40.

Bremner, J.D. (2003). Long-term effects of childhood abuse on brain and neurobiology. *Child and Adolescent Psychiatric Clinics of North America, 12*, 271–92.

Bronfenbrenner, U., & Morris, P.A. (2006). The bioecological model of human development. In R.M. Lerner & W. Damon (Eds.), *Handbook of child psychology* (6th ed., pp. 793–828). Hoboken, NJ: John Wiley & Sons.

Caliso, J.A., & Milner, J.S. (1992). Childhood history of abuse and child abuse screening. *Child Abuse and Neglect, 16*, 647–59.

Caspi, A., McClay, J., Moffitt, T.E., Mill, J., Martin, J., Craig, I.W., et al. (2002) Role of genotype in the cycle of violence in maltreated children. Science, 297, 851–54.

Caspi, A., Sugden, K., Moffitt, T.E., Taylor, A., Craig, I.W., Harrington, H., et al. (2003). Influence of life stress on depression: Moderation by a polymorphism in the 5-HTT gene. Science, 301, 386–89.

Chan, Y. (1994). Parenting stress and social support of mothers who physically abuse their children in Hong Kong. Child Abuse & Neglect, 18(3), 261–69.

Combrinck-Graham, L. (Ed.). (1995). Children in families at risk: Maintaining the connections. New York: Guilford.

Coohey, C. (1996). Child maltreatment: Testing the social isolation hypothesis. Child Abuse & Neglect, 20, 241–51.

Danese, A., Moffitt, T.E., Harrington, H., Milne, B.J., Polanczyk, G., et al. (2009). Adverse childhood experiences and adult risk factors for age-related disease: Depression, inflammation, and clustering of metabolic risk markers. Archives of Pediatrics and Adolescent Medicine, 163, 1135–43.

De Bellis, M., & Thomas, L. (2003). Biologic findings of post-traumatic stress disorder and child maltreatment. Current Psychiatry Reports, 5, 108–17.

Edmiston, E.E., Wang, F., Mazure, C.M., Guiney, J., Sinha, R., Mayes, L.C., Blumberg, H.P. (2011). Corticostriatal-limbic gray matter morphology in adolescents with self-reported exposure to childhood maltreatment. Archives of Pediatrics and Adolescent Medicine, 165, 1069–77.

Egeland, B., Jacobvitz, D., & Sroufe, L.A. (1988). Breaking the cycle of abuse. Child Development, 59, 1080–88.

Eggerman, M., & Panter-Brick, C. (2010). Suffering, hope, and entrapment: Resilience and cultural values in Afghanistan. Social Science & Medicine, 71, 71–83.

Evans, S.E., Davies, C., & DiLillo, D. (2008). Exposure to domestic violence: A meta-analysis of child and adolescent outcomes. Aggression and Violent Behaviour, 13, 131–40.

Felitti, V.J., Anda, R.F., Nordenberg, D., Williamson, D.F., Spitz, A.M., Edwards, V., et al. (1998). Relationship of childhood abuse and household dysfunction to many of the leading causes of death in adults. The Adverse Childhood Experiences Study. American Journal of Preventive Medicine, 14, 245–58.

Foley, D.L., Eaves, L.J., Wormley, B., Silberg, J.L., Maes, H.H., Kuhn, J., et al. (2004). Childhood adversity, monoamine oxidase A genotype, and risk for conduct disorder. Archives of General Psychiatry, 61, 738–44.

Garmezy, N. (1991). Resiliency and vulnerability to adverse developmental outcomes associated with poverty. American Behavioural Scientist, 34(4), 416–30.

Gaudin, J., Polansky, N., Kilpatrick, N., & Shilton, P. (1993). Loneliness, depression, stress, and social support in neglectful homes. American Journal of Orthopsychiatry, 63, 597–605.

Glaser, D. (2000). Child abuse and neglect and the brain: A review. Journal of Child Psychology and Psychiatry, 41, 97–116.

Godsall, R.E., Jurkovic, G.J., Emshoff, J., Anderson, L., & Stanwyck, D. (2004). Why some kids do well in bad situations: Relation of parental alcohol misuse and parentification to children's self-concept. *Substance Use & Misuse, 39*(5), 789–809.

Harshaw, C. (2008). Alimentary epigenetics: A developmental psychobiological systems view of perception of hunger, thirst, and satiety. *Developmental Reviews, 28*(4), 541–69.

Hashima, P., & Amato, P. (1994). Poverty, social support, and parental behaviour. *Child Development, 65*, 394–403.

Hooper, L.M., Marotta, S.A., & Lanthier, R.P. (2008). Predictors of growth and distress following childhood parentification: A retrospective exploratory study. *Journal of Child and Family Studies, 17*, 693–705.

Johnson, L.R., Hou, M., Prager, E.M., & LeDoux, J.E. (2011). Regulation of the fear network by mediators of stress: Norepinephrine alters the balance between cortical and subcortical afferent excitation of the lateral amygdala. *Frontiers in Behavioral Neuroscience, 5*(23), 1–7.

Jones, L.M., Cross, T.P., Walsh, W.A., & Simone, M. (2007). Do Children's Advocacy Centers improve families' experiences of child sexual abuse investigations? *Child Abuse & Neglect, 31*(10), 1069–85.

Kennedy, A.C., Agbenyiga, D.L., Kasiborski, N., & Gladden, J. (2010). Risk chains over the life course among homeless urban adolescent mothers: Altering their trajectories through formal support. *Children and Youth Services Review, 32*, 1740–49.

Kirmayer, L.J., Dandeneau, S., Marshall, E., Phillips, K., & Williamson, K.J. (2012). Toward an ecology of stories: Indigenous perspectives on resilience. In M. Ungar (Ed.), *The social ecology of resilience: A handbook of theory and practice* (pp. 399–414). New York: Springer.

Ludy-Dobson, C., & Perry, B.D. (2010). The role of healthy relational interactions in buffering the impact of childhood trauma. In E. Gil (Ed.), *Working with children to heal interpersonal trauma* (pp. 26–44). New York: Guilford Press.

Luthar, S., Cicchetti, D., & Becker, B. (2000). The construct of resilience: A critical evaluation and guidelines for future work. *Child Development, 71*, 543–62. Retrieved from: http://www.ncbi.nlm.nih.gov/pmc/articles/PMC1885202/.

Madsen, W.C. (2009). Collaborative helping: A practice framework for family-centered services. *Family Process, 48*(1), 103–16.

Masten, A.S. (1994). Resilience in individual development: Successful adaptation despite risk and adversity. In M. Wang (Ed.), *Educational resilience in inner-city America: Challenges and prospects* (pp. 3–25). Hillsdale, NJ: Lawrence Erlbaum Associates.

Masten, A.S. (2010). Ordinary magic: Lessons from research on human development. *Education Canada, 49*(3). Retrieved from: http://www.cea-ace.ca/sites/cea-ace.ca/files/EdCan-2009-v49-n3-Masten.pdf.

McCrory, E.J., DeBrito, S.A., Sebastian, C.L., Mechelli, A., Bird, G., Kelly, P.A., & Viding, E. (2011) Heightened neural reactivity to threat in child victims of family violence. *Current Biology, 21*(23), R947–R948.

Newton, R.R., Litrownik, A.J., & Landsverk, J.A. (2000) Children and youth in foster care: Disentangling the relationship between problem behaviours and number of placements. *Child Abuse and Neglect, 24*(10), 1363–74.

Perry, B.D. (1988). Placental and blood element neurotransmitter receptor regulation in humans: Potential models for studying neurochemical mechanisms underlying behavioural teratology. *Progress in Brain Research, 73*, 189–206.

Perry, B.D. (1994). Neurobiological sequelae of childhood trauma: Post-traumatic stress disorders in children. In M. Murberg (Ed.), *Catecholamines in post-traumatic stress disorder: Emerging concepts* (pp. 253–76). Washington, DC: American Psychiatric Press.

Perry, B.D. (2001a). The neuroarcheology of childhood maltreatment: The neurodevelopmental costs of adverse childhood events. In K. Franey, R. Geffner & R. Falconer (Eds.), *The cost of maltreatment: Who pays? We all do* (pp. 15–37). San Diego: Family Violence and Sexual Assault Institute.

Perry, B.D. (2001b). The neurodevelopmental impact of violence in childhood. In D. Schetky & E.P. Benedek (Eds.), *Textbook of child and adolescent forensic psychiatry* (pp. 221–38). Washington, DC: American Psychiatric Press.

Perry, B.D. (2002). Childhood experience and the expression of genetic potential: What childhood neglect tells us about nature and nurture. *Brain and Mind, 3*, 79–100.

Perry, B.D. (2008). Child maltreatment: The role of abuse and neglect in developmental psychopathology. In T.P. Beauchaine & S.P. Hinshaw (Eds.), *Textbook of child and adolescent psychopathology* (pp. 93–128). New York: Wiley.

Perry, B.D. (2009). Examining child maltreatment through a neurodevelopmental lens: Clinical application of the neurosequential model of therapeutics. *Journal of Loss and Trauma, 14*, 240–55.

Perry, B.D., & Pollard, R. (1998). Homeostasis, stress, trauma, and adaptation: A neurodevelopmental view of childhood trauma. *Child and Adolescent Psychiatric Clinics of North America, 7*, 33–51.

Perry, B.D., Pollard, R., Blakely, T., Baker, W., & Vigilante, D. (1995). Childhood trauma, the neurobiology of adaptation and "use-dependent" development of the brain: How "states" become "traits." *Infant Mental Health Journal, 16*(4), 271–91.

Perry, B.D., Stolk, J.M., Vantini, G., Guchhait, R.B., & U'Prichard, D.C. (1983). Strain differences in rat brain epinephrine synthesis and alpha-adrenergic receptor number: Apparent in vivo regulation of brain alpha-adrenergic receptors by epinephrine. *Science, 221*, 1297–99.

Rak, C.F., & Patterson, L.E. (1996). Promoting resilience in at-risk children. *Journal of Counseling & Development, 74*, 368–73.

Santisteban, D.A., & Mena, M.P. (2009). Culturally informed and flexible family-based treatment for adolescents: A tailored and integrative treatment for Hispanic youth. *Family Process, 48*(2), 253–68.

Schoon, I. (2006). *Risk and resilience: Adaptations in changing times.* Cambridge, UK: Cambridge University Press.

Sroufe, L.A., Egeland, B., Carlson, E.A., & Collins, W.A. (2005). *The development of the person: The Minnesota study of risk and adaptation from birth to adulthood.* New York: Guilford.

Tedeschi, R.G., & Calhoun, L.G. (1996). The posttraumatic growth inventory: Measuring the positive legacy of trauma. *Journal of Traumatic Stress, 9,* 455–71.

Teicher, M.H, Andersen, S.L., Polcari, A., Anderson, C.M., & Navalta, C.P. (2002). Developmental neurobiology of childhood stress and trauma. *Psychiatric Clinics of North America, 25*(2), 397–426.

Travis, W.J., & Combs-Orme, T. (2007). Resilient parenting: Overcoming poor parental bonding. *Social Work Research, 31*(3), 135–49.

Trocmé, N., Phaneuf, G., Scarth, S., Fallon, B., & MacLaurin, B. (2003). The Canadian Incidence Study of Reported Child Abuse and Neglect: Methodology and major findings. In K. Kufeldt & B. McKenzie (Eds.), *Child welfare: Connecting research, policy, and practice* (pp. 13–26). Waterloo, ON: Wilfrid Laurier University Press.

Tronick, E. (2006). The stress of normal development and interaction leads to the development of resilience and variation. In B. Lester, A. Masten & B. McEwen (Eds.), *Resilience in children. Annals New York Academy of Science, 1094,* 83–104.

Ungar, M. (2004). A constructionist discourse on resilience: Multiple contexts, multiple realities among at-risk children and youth. *Youth and Society, 35*(3), 341–65.

Ungar, M. (2005). Pathways to resilience among children in child welfare, corrections, mental health, and educational settings: Navigation and negotiation. *Child and Youth Care Forum, 34*(6), 423–44.

Ungar, M. (2007). Contextual and cultural aspects of resilience in child welfare settings. In I. Brown, F. Chaze, D. Fuchs, J. Lafrance, S. McKay & S. Thomas-Prokop (Eds.), *Putting a human face on child welfare* (pp. 1–24). Toronto: Centre of Excellence for Child Welfare.

Ungar, M. (2011). The social ecology of resilience: Addressing contextual and cultural ambiguity of a nascent construct. *American Journal of Orthopsychiatry, 81,* 1–17.

Ungar, M., Brown, M., Liebenberg, L., Othman, R., Kwong, W.M., Armstrong, M., & Gilgun, J. (2007). Unique pathways to resilience across cultures. *Adolescence, 42*(166), 287–310.

Ungar, M., Theron, L., & Didkowsky, N. (2011). Adolescents' precocious and developmentally appropriate contributions to their families' well-being and resilience in five countries. *Family Relations, 60*(2), 231–46.

Webster-Stratton, C. (2001). Preventing conduct problems, promoting social competence: A parent and teacher training partnership in Head Start. *Journal of Clinical Child Psychology, 30*(3), 283–302.

Wekerle, C., Waechter, R., & Chung, R. (2012). Contexts of vulnerability and resilience: Child maltreatment, cognitive functioning, and close relationships. In M. Ungar (Ed.), *The social ecology of resilience: A handbook of theory and practice* (pp. 187–98). New York: Springer.

Werner, E.E., & Smith, R.S. (2001). Journeys from childhood to midlife: Risk, resilience, and recovery. Ithaca, NY: Cornell University Press.

Yoshikawa, H., & Kalil, A. (2011). The effects of parental undocumented status on the developmental contexts of young children in immigrant families. *Child Development Perspectives, 5*(4), 291–97.

MARGINALIZED COMMUNITIES AND VIOLENCE

6

SYSTEMIC OPPRESSION, VIOLENCE, AND HEALING IN ABORIGINAL FAMILIES AND COMMUNITIES

CYNDY BASKIN

Family violence within Canada's Aboriginal communities, both on and off reserve, is more prevalent than in the rest of society. Even so, comparatively little has been written and published about this topic. Aboriginal peoples assert that this is a direct result of the colonization process, which continues to have a horrific hold on many families and communities (Brownridge, 2003; Bruce, 1998; Chapin, 1994; Durst, MacDonald & Parsons, 1999; Fiddler, 1991; Frank, 1992; LaRocque, 1994; Maracle, 1993; Ontario Native Women's Association, 1989; Ontario Native Women's Association & Ontario Federation of Indian Friendship Centres, 2007). For the most part, the criminalization of family violence and Western methods of intervention and treatment have not helped to ease the situation. In fact, often Aboriginal peoples report being revictimized by these processes. In addition, the professions of law enforcement and social work continue to be viewed as an extension of colonization by many communities because they are seen as agents of social control rather than of social change (Baskin, 2002; Bruce, 1998; Frank, 1992; Hamilton & Sinclair, 1991; Health Canada, 1996; O'Donnell, 2000).

Interventions in the area of family violence within Aboriginal communities must take an approach that is community controlled and culture based. Such an approach must be holistic in nature and, therefore, needs to include interventions that centre on community awareness, healing processes for the entire family, and an alternative to the present criminal justice system.

This chapter will explore issues related to family violence within Canada's Aboriginal population. It will examine the history of colonization and its impact upon Aboriginal peoples, including its direct connection to family violence today. Some Aboriginal perspectives will be explained, as understood and implemented by the author, along with their relevance to family violence interventions and healing. Services for women, children, and men will be addressed, with brief references to programs that operate from a culture-based approach. Furthermore, a specific urban culture-based program will be examined at length.

LOCATING MYSELF

Aboriginal peoples tend to introduce themselves and begin relationships before they move into any task. I am of Mi'kmaq and Irish descent. My spirit name translates as "The Woman Who Passes on the Teachings," and I belong to the Fish Clan. Originally from New Brunswick, I have lived in Toronto, Ontario, for several years. As a social worker, I have developed, implemented, and trained other Aboriginal service providers in family violence healing programs for the past twenty years. Currently, I am an associate professor in the School of Social Work at Ryerson University. I am straight, able-bodied, lower middle class, a survivor of family violence and the mental health system, a partner, and a mother.

I am choosing to consistently use the term "Aboriginal" throughout this chapter. It is my understanding that this term includes all of us— status and non-status First Nations, Métis, those of mixed blood, Inuit, and Innu.

DEFINING FAMILY VIOLENCE

In mainstream literature, the closest definition of violence in intimate relationships that fits with an Aboriginal perspective is a feminist definition of violence against women. The fit exists because both feminist and Aboriginal definitions of this form of violence go beyond individualizing it to linking it to wider society and the systems under which we live. From a feminist analysis, "violence against women is a multifaceted problem which encompasses physical, sexual, psychological, and economic violations of women and which is integrally linked to the social/economic/political structures, values, and policies that silence women in our society, support gender-based discrimination and maintain women's inequality" (Canadian Advisory Council on the Status of Women, 1991, p. 5).

In taking this analysis one step further to examine inequality based on race as well as gender, an ethic of domination on which authority and power in our society is based is relevant. This ethic of domination

> has allowed men to dominate women, parents to spank children, one class or race to devalue and control another... we have come to believe that this is morally right because the "other" is of inferior rank in our hierarchy of values—due to gender, age, race, physical, mental or economic difference.... The right to use violence, if necessary, to maintain that domination is based on our belief that it is morally right to do so for the sake of preserving order and is made easier by the belief that the other is of inferior ability, responsibility or status. (Health Canada, 1989, p. 21)

In defining family violence, Aboriginal peoples have applied this general ethic of domination to our specific history. Thus, Aboriginal peoples define family violence as

> a consequence of colonization, forced assimilation, and cultural geno-cide; the learned negative, cumulative, multi-generational actions, values, beliefs, attitudes, and behavioural patterns practiced by one or more peoples that weaken or destroy the harmony and well-being of an Aboriginal individual, family, extended family, community or Nation. (Aboriginal Family Healing Joint Steering Committee, 1993, p. 6)

This definition has remained strong and operational for many years. Aboriginal peoples choose to refer to abusive behaviour in intimate relation-ships as family violence because of the value placed on the family and our holistic world view. For Aboriginal peoples, an emphasis on the well-being of the family and community is valued above that of the individual. The individual is seen in the context of the family, which is seen in the context of the community. Thus, from this holistic perspective, when an individual is harmed, it is believed that this affects all others in that person's family and community.

This perspective means that interventions in family violence must focus on both victims and offenders—women, children, and men. It does not negate the fact that, as in wider society, it is usually women and children who are the victims of violence and men who are the perpetrators. How-ever, it does mean that family violence is viewed as a community problem that requires healing of all members of the family. The abuser in the family does not need to be sacrificed. Since family violence is learned behaviour, it can be unlearned. Communities need to take responsibility for the healing process of all family members, which includes those who have perpetrated violence. Even though offenders of family violence have committed some-times horrific acts upon their partners and children and caused long-lasting harm, we—members of Aboriginal communities and of larger Canadian society—have created them. Thus, we must assist them in the process of ending their violence and implementing healthy ways of dealing with life's difficulties and relating to others.

An Aboriginal holistic approach to healing involves each family member recovering from the confusion, powerlessness, shame, and inferiority that are a part of violence in Aboriginal families. It means learning non-violent ways of relating to other family members based on Aboriginal values. It includes the use of traditional teachings, ceremonies, and a way of life to guide Aboriginal family members to health and well-being. Healing for families does not mean family therapy. It usually means healing circles and ceremonies with community members in similar situations. Eventually, family circles can take place, but not until all those involved are ready and wanting to participate.

A holistic approach avoids isolating family members—for which main-stream services providers, including feminist ones, have been criticized—because they often have a polarized understanding of violence against women:

> Women are seen as pure and blameless victims and men are seen as brutal, cruel victimizers who have never been tender. This approach not only tends to isolate battered women, but to fragment the servi-ces created to reach them.... Battered women may be isolated from the batterers and may be encouraged to view them as unreachable, hopeless and unchangeable. These stereotypes encourage polarized thinking and labeling, rather than more holistic solutions which take many variables into consideration. (MacLeod, 1989, p. 10)

PREVALENCE OF VIOLENCE

The results of the most recent Statistics Canada report titled *Family violence in Canada: A statistical profile* (2011), which contains statistics gathered in 2009, indicates that those who self-identified as Aboriginal peoples were almost twice as likely as those who did not to report being the victim of spousal violence (10 percent versus 6 percent). However, in 2010, if a woman was Inuit living in Nunavut, she was 6.5 times more likely to report spousal abuse than anyone else (National Collaborating Centre for Aboriginal Health, 2010). In 2004, Statistics Canada reported that Aboriginal peoples were three times more likely than non-Aboriginal ones to face spousal abuse (21 percent versus 7 percent). The Native Women's Association of Canada had further information to add in 2007, stating that Aboriginal women faced more severe and life-threatening acts of domestic violence—such as being beaten, choked, assaulted with a gun or knife, and being sexually assaulted—than non-Aboriginal women at 54 percent compared to 37 percent. According to Statistics Canada, in 2001, approximately 20 percent of Aboriginal peoples reported being assaulted by a spouse compared to 7 percent of the non-Aboriginal population, with Aboriginal women being at higher risk of spousal violence (Brennan, 2011). Twenty-five percent of Aboriginal women were assaulted by a current or former spouse between 1997 and 2001—twice the rate for Aboriginal men and three times the rate for non-Aboriginal women and men (Brennan, 2011). Rates of spousal homicide among Aboriginal women were more than eight times higher than for non-Aboriginal women—47.2 per million compared to 5.8 per million (Brennan, 2011).

Further, the Ontario Native Women's Association (ONWA, 1989; Ontario Native Women's Association & Ontario Federation of Indian Friendship Centres, 2007) reports the incidence of family violence in Aboriginal communities as eight times higher than the average for Canadian society as a whole. In surveys on family violence conducted by ONWA in 1989 and by ONWA and the Ontario Federation of Indian Friendship Centres in 2007, 84 percent of respondents indicated that family violence occurs in their communities. Respondents indicated that women were most frequently abused in a family context (88 percent), followed by children (51 percent), and the abuser was identified as the woman's partner with an incidence of 84 percent. With regard to specific forms of abuse, 89 percent indicated that psychological and emotional abuse was a feature, and 57 percent indicated that sexual abuse was a feature. In addition, 78 percent of the people surveyed believed that Aboriginal family violence affects all members of the family and community.

In a London, Ontario, area study, "71 percent of the urban sample and 48 percent of the reserve sample of Oneida women had experienced assault at the hands of current or past partners" (Chartrand & McKay, 2006, p. 57). For a study in Lethbridge, Alberta, sixty-one Aboriginal women were recruited. Of this non-random sample, "91 percent of the respondents said they had personal experience with family violence" (ONWA, 1989, p. 57). Eighty-two percent of these women identified psychological and verbal abuse; 77 percent reported slapping; 64 percent reported hitting; 54 percent reported punching; and 16 percent said they had been forced into sex with partners (Royal Commission on Aboriginal Peoples, 1996). The findings of a study conducted in Toronto by the Canadian Panel on Violence against Women indicated that "54 percent of women had experienced some form of unwanted or intrusive sexual experience before reaching the age of sixteen; 51 percent of women had experienced rape or attempted rape; and 27 percent of women had experienced physical assault in an intimate relationship" (Royal Commission on Aboriginal Peoples, 1996, p. 58).

Although Aboriginal peoples only make up about 4 percent of the Canadian population, 22,500 children in the care of child welfare, or 30 percent of the total children in the care population in Canada, are Aboriginal (Bennett & Blackstock, 2003; Fleras & Elliott, 1999; Fournier & Crey, 1997). The reason behind this high statistic is grounded in ongoing racist and colonialist policies that exist even in Aboriginal child welfare agencies. According to researchers Bennett and Blackstock (2003):

> Up to this day, provisions in both federal and provincial legislation dictate how child welfare will be governed, administered, and, often delivered by the over 120+ Aboriginal Child and Family Service Agencies in Canada. This would not be so controversial if the provincial and federal systems were meeting the needs of Aboriginal children and youth but the evidence overwhelmingly indicates that the current legislation, policy and practice of child welfare are not making meaningful differences in supporting the well-being of Aboriginal children and youth. (p. 57)

Trocmé's (2001) was the first nationwide study to examine the incidence of reported child abuse cases. Aboriginal children and families were identified as a major group to examine because of concerns about overrepresentation of these children in the child welfare system. Ten years later, this study reported that 29 percent of Aboriginal children are in the care of child welfare compared to 11 percent of non-Aboriginal children. The major reason for Aboriginal children being in the care of the state is neglect at 56 percent compared to non-Aboriginal children at 25 percent (MacLaurin et al, 2003). Since neglect continues to be the primary type of child maltreatment when it comes to Aboriginal families and communities, clearly a greater emphasis on structural factors, specifically poverty, needs to be addressed (Baskin, 2007a, 2007b; Blackstock, Bennett & Trocme, 2004; Trocmé, 2001; MacLaurin et al., 2003).

Despite the inherent right to care for our children, Aboriginal authority has still not been fully recognized in practice by the federal or provincial/territorial governments in Canada. Hence, child welfare services delivered to Aboriginal peoples by aboriginally controlled child welfare agencies continue to be mandated through federal and provincial legislation (Association of Native Child and Family Services Agencies of Ontario, 2001).

A review of the literature revealed no statistics on the abuse of elderly people in Aboriginal families and communities. This certainly does not mean that it does not exist. Some Aboriginal Elders, traditional teachers, and service providers are speaking up about senior abuse in workshops and conferences based on what they have personally heard and witnessed from family and community members.

HISTORICAL CONTEXT

In order to understand a definition of family violence from many Aboriginal perspectives and the higher levels of violence experienced by Aboriginal peoples, one needs to have a thorough knowledge of the history and treatment of Aboriginal peoples. This history has been deliberately left out of Canadian consciousness. A number of factors are linked to violence in Aboriginal communities, including economic and social deprivation, substance abuse, the intergenerational cycle of violence, the breakdown of healthy family life, and the loss of traditional values. It is important to emphasize, however, that all of these factors are the result of colonization and ongoing systemic oppression.

It is widely believed by Aboriginal peoples across the globe that family violence rarely existed prior to the breakdown of traditional societies caused by colonization. We know this because it has been passed down from generation to generation via oral teachings by our Elders. Family violence did not exist because of the values connected to women and children and because of the strong collective set-up of communities.

In the original teachings the Creator gave to Aboriginal peoples at the time of creation, women were valued as sacred because of their ability to give life and thereby bring new spirits onto the Earth. Women were viewed as equal to men, although the roles and responsibilities of each were different. Women were the first teachers of children; they were responsible for all that occurred in their lodges; they were medicine people, healers, and spiritual leaders; and they participated in all decision-making political processes. Men were the protectors and providers for all the people; they ensured all life's necessities for the elderly; they worked at spirituality and healing abilities; and they carried out political leadership at the direction of the women. Such roles and responsibilities held equal power and both were necessary to ensure balance within communities.

In these original teachings, children were seen as gifts from the Creator. They were believed to be more spirit than human for the first seven years of life. They were both blessings to and the responsibility of parents and all members of the community. Everyone participated in the raising of children through role modelling and oral storytelling. Children and old people were believed to be the most sacred because children had recently come from the spirit world and the old ones would soon be returning there.

Within these original teachings is also an emphasis on the importance of the collective over the individual. The people needed each other for survival and to keep balance and harmony among themselves. Thus, they lived in close quarters, shared what they had, and watched out for each other. Clans were established and passed from one generation to the next. These clans had specific responsibilities such as mediation, healing, or protection. When problems arose, clan representatives were responsible for leading resolution processes between people.

Hence, with these values about women, children, and collective responsibility embedded in the world views and the practicalities of living close together where everyone knew what was going on with everyone else, family violence was not likely to occur. If it did, it was dealt with by the collective in ways that held an offender accountable to the victim and the community.

Prior to contact with Europeans, Aboriginal peoples had their own governments, laws, means of resolving disputes, and values based on their cultures and spirituality. Elders were responsible for collectively teaching the people their history, traditions, customs, values, and beliefs, and in assisting them to maintain their well-being and good health. Aboriginal peoples believed that all life was interconnected with the individual, who was connected to the family, which was connected to the community, which was connected to the nation. The nation was connected to the Earth and everything on it, which was connected to the spirit world.

This holistic world view was also applied at the individual level. A person was viewed as being made up of four aspects: psychological, physical, emotional, and spiritual. The focus was on keeping all four aspects of the person strong. In Aboriginal belief systems, if the body weakened and was the only part that was treated, then healing could not effectively take place. If the body became ill, then the spirit, mind, and emotions were also affected and had to be treated as well.

European peoples came to this continent with a different world view, one based on Christianity and capitalism. The process of colonization grew in large part out of a belief that humankind was to "fill the earth and subdue it, rule over the fish in the sea, the birds of heaven, and every living thing that moves upon the earth" (Hamilton & Sinclair, 1991, p. 21).

Historical events of systemic violence toward Aboriginal peoples include:

- the brutality perpetrated upon Aboriginal peoples by the French and English in securing pelts during the fur trade
- abuse against Aboriginal peoples during the period of their slavery (early 1600s to 1833) in New France
- the use of women for the purpose of breeding as the direct result of a law passed in 1770, which sought to address the shortage of English and Scottish labourers
- the extermination of the entire Beothuk nation on the East Coast of Canada
- the wars waged against the original peoples of the Plains as a result of the British government's desire to settle the West
- the hanging of seven Aboriginal men, including Louis Riel, in 1885 in western Canada
- the banning of political activity in Aboriginal communities from the 1800s to the 1960s, which eliminated any challenges to colonial rule (Adams, 1999)

The Indian Act of 1876 was the vehicle by which the goal of assimilating Aboriginal peoples was to be implemented, and it governed every facet of Aboriginal life. This Act, along with the creation of the reserve system, imposed a capitalist, patriarchal governance structure on Aboriginal communities. Through the Indian Act, the Canadian government sought to make Aboriginal peoples into imitation Europeans, to eradicate Aboriginal values through education and religion, and to establish new economic and political systems, and new concepts of property. This all led to the disempowerment and devaluation of Aboriginal women and their roles within families and communities.

Specific practices of assimilation were the outlawing of traditional Aboriginal ceremonies, the enforced training of men to become farmers and women to become domestics, and a systematic indoctrination of Christian theory and practice through the residential school system. The establishment of residential schools was rationalized by the assertion that these institutions would make Aboriginal children competitive with white people, moral, industrious, and self-supporting. These schools equated Euro-Canadian socio-economic standards and materialism with success, progress, and civilization. They taught Aboriginal children to aspire to be like Euro-Canadians rather than who they were, and yet they never accepted them as equals in Canadian society.

Residential schooling is a direct cause of family violence in Aboriginal communities because, in addition to the widespread abuse of the children who attended these institutions, it led to the decline of parenting skills in children who were denied their appropriate parental role models. This removal of Aboriginal children from their parents, extended families, and communities continued with the child welfare system, which consistently placed children in non-Aboriginal families and communities. Hence, generations of Aboriginal children did not learn about the central role of family in their cultures (Fournier & Crey, 1997; Knockwood, 1992).

An oppressive, bureaucratic system of government has been imposed upon Aboriginal peoples at the cost of many of our traditional governing practices and spiritual beliefs. A colonizing government, through the Indian Act, which continues to control the lives of Aboriginal peoples today, created the reserve system, outlawed many spiritual practices, eliminated an egalitarian economic system, and ignored our inherent right to self-government. This, in turn, has created great social confusion within Aboriginal communities. Canadian–Aboriginal relations have provided the environment from which the profound social and economic problems, such as family violence, have taken root. The issue of family violence cannot be separated from the larger issues in Aboriginal-Canadian relations because it has arisen from, and in response to, these larger issues.

From an Aboriginal analysis, family violence in our communities is the result of, and a reaction to, a system of domination, disrespect, and bureaucratic control. It stems from the consequences and devastation of forced white colonial policies of assimilation and cultural genocide over the past several centuries. Aboriginal peoples have internalized this oppression and thus its impact is felt in the family. The treatment of women and children within the family is a reflection of the treatment of Aboriginal peoples in a broader context.

GLOBAL CONTEXT

The colonization of Aboriginal peoples occurred around the world in strikingly similar ways to those implemented in Canada such as residential schools, child welfare, the outlawing of spirituality and governance, and the removal of power from women. Statistics on the prevalence of family violence in countries such as Australia, New Zealand, and the United States are also remarkably similar to those in Canada. In Australia, indigenous women are thirty-five times more likely to face domestic violence and ten times more likely to die as a result of it than non-indigenous women (Council of Australia Governments, 2011). Indigenous women in New Zealand are assaulted at three times the national average (Kruger et al., 2004; Minority Rights Group International, 2011), which is the same for those in the United States (Department of Justice, 2011). Across all of these countries, in 30–60 percent of domestic violence situations, the children face neglect and witness the violence done to their mothers (Bangar-White & Larrington, 2005).

Indigenous communities in Canada, Australia, New Zealand, and the United States also agree on how to eliminate family violence. All highlight the necessity of community-led approaches, including a return to indigenous forms of governance, holistic perspectives, spirituality, values, cultural norms, and the training of committed staff and mentors (Bangar-White & Larrington, 2005; Council of Australia Governments, 2011; Department of Justice, 2011; Kruger et al., 2004; Minority Rights Group International, 2011).

COMPARISON WITH FEMINIST ANALYSIS

The Aboriginal analysis of family violence as viewed from a historical context, which examines broader society's role in the problem, has much in common with a feminist analysis of woman abuse. A feminist analysis of woman abuse extends its view of violence to include the relationship between the family and the broader social, economic, and political environment. By including social factors, a feminist analysis does not reduce the causes of woman abuse exclusively to intra-familial factors. Thus, although the individual family may be the setting of violent behaviour, it may not be its source. Such an analysis deals with the larger question of why men abuse women.

A feminist analysis stresses that society cannot alleviate woman abuse without addressing the underlying social causes of it. The problem of woman abuse will not be eliminated until society radically alters the social conditions that allow for it in the first place. This involves identifying the attitudes, practices, and values that socialize men to be "masculine"—to be aggressive, dominating, and violent. It means challenging sexist society's belief that masculinity is infused with aggression and dominance in relation to women, as evidenced by the clear overall higher status of men in Canadian society. It also involves acknowledging that women are economically, socially, and politically devalued and discriminated against throughout society and eradicating these structural inequalities (Randall, 1989).

However, structural inequalities are not based only on gender. They are also based on race, as well as many other factors. Aboriginal peoples are especially vulnerable to oppression because of the historical racist attitudes and actions of, for example, the criminal justice system, which does little more than send Aboriginal peoples to jail, and mainstream social services, which continue to alienate Aboriginal peoples through their exclusively Eurocentric perspectives. Aboriginal women who are abused by their partners are often reluctant to call the police for help because they know that their partners will be unfairly dealt with by the police and the courts. In addition, many Aboriginal women have seen the Canadian legal process and social services agencies—for example, through child welfare legislation—work against their interests because of racism, which makes them even more unlikely to turn to these services for help. Fear, then, is often the reason why many Aboriginal women do not contact the police—fear of further violence, of their children being taken away, and of their partners going to jail. Furthermore, women often feel at risk not only from their partners but also from police inaction, racism, and victim-blaming (McGillivray & Comaskey, 1999) In addition, the current policy of zero tolerance regarding domestic violence may, in fact, deny women any choices:

> Already disempowered by abuse, women are further disempowered when the justice system "takes over" the criminal prosecution of a partner.... Women who take the stand against a partner find... that their interests are subordinated to broader justice goals, and their role is simply as witness for the crown.... The victim is "essentialized," and her subjectivity is important only as it fits within the confines of the system. Her own voice, her experience, and her damage may be lost. (McGillivray & Comaskey, 1999, p. 112)

Many Aboriginal women living in abusive relationships who have children feel further disempowered and fearful of the very systems that are supposed to protect children. These systems include mandated Aboriginal child welfare agencies, which must abide by the same legislation as all other child welfare organizations. This is because many Aboriginal women share a

> frustration with the "children who witness violence" policy. They see it as driving them into deeper silence because of the threat of apprehension. This policy prevents them from getting therapy for their children or for themselves. Over and over again, women stressed the need for services for their children and youth, without having the threat of this information being used against them in a harmful way. (Stewart, Huntley & Blaney, 2001, p. 51)

Another major distinction between a feminist analysis and an Aboriginal one is that Aboriginal male dominance is distinct from non-Aboriginal patterns of dominance as Aboriginal males do not have access to equitable opportunities and positions in Canadian society (Dickson, 1989). Thus, although Aboriginal men have power and control over their partners and children, once again due to racism, they have very little of it within Canadian society.

Furthermore, there is the issue of Aboriginal peoples' inherent right to self-government. When Aboriginal peoples refer to structural changes, they mean that "changes for First Nations are linked to structural changes in which First Nations are empowered to determine their own future" (Frank, 1992, p. 8). Every Aboriginal woman's concern is framed in the context of concerns that are important to Aboriginal peoples, which include self-government.

Clearly, there are interlocking oppressions between Aboriginal women and all women. This helps to explain why women are overwhelmingly the victims of abuse in all families and intimate relationships. However, the issues of race and sovereignty are never to be underestimated within this comparison. From a feminist analysis, then, men's violence against women will not end until economic, political, and social equality is achieved for all women. From an Aboriginal analysis, family violence in our communities will not end until racial equality in the form of self-government for Aboriginal peoples is restored.

According to Ladner (2009), the literature on Aboriginal self-governance and people's health shows that "there is a definitive correlation between self-determination and community well-being, and that self-determination may be a determining factor in enabling/disabling communities in crisis and in understanding resiliency" (p. 93). Indeed, some authors have indicated that youth suicide rates are much lower in Aboriginal communities that are self-governing (Chandler & Lalonde, 2008; Hallett, Chandler & Lalonde, 2007). It follows, then, that there would be lower rates of family violence in such communities, but this has yet to be explored.

An atmosphere of secrecy accompanies family violence. Although Aboriginal peoples are well aware of the high rates of family violence within their communities, they may live in a situation where everybody knows, but no one talks about it or deals openly with it. Hence, living with family violence becomes an accepted part of life that many people simply endure. Turning to alcohol and drugs, for example, often becomes the tool of survival.

Another layer of silence can be related to power dynamics within communities. If, for example, an abuser is in a position of power, the victim or other community members may not disclose the abuse for fear of repercussions or because they will not be believed. Thus, in such situations, sometimes even unknowingly, community members protect abusers rather than victims.

A fog of learned helplessness settles in upon some families and communities. People become resigned and feel that nothing can be done about family violence. Their sense of hopelessness is reflected in the lack of services in communities to assist people with issues related to family violence. For some, the only solution is to leave their home communities, but, of course, this may not be helpful because violence exists in urban centres as well.

Breaking the silence and educating *all* Canadians about one of the greatest sources of family violence in Aboriginal communities is a major focus of the Truth and Reconciliation Commission of Canada (TRC). According to the chairperson of the commission, the Honourable Justice Murray Sinclair of the Cree Nation (Sinclair, 2010), "Broken families, addiction, estrangement, violence, suicide—this is the corrosive legacy of the residential schools" (p. 6).

Unresolved trauma has been passed on from one generation to the next since the period of the residential school system. This often expresses itself through violence within families. The TRC supports strategies to facilitate reconciliation, hope, and healing for families through, for example, an endowment to the Aboriginal Healing Foundation (Sinclair, 2010). Well known in many parts of the world, the TRC is an inspiration for other countries, such as Australia and the United States, in their endeavours to address the legacy of residential school systems.

CULTURE-BASED INTERVENTIONS

Given the historical context of family violence in Aboriginal communities, it is understandable that many Aboriginal peoples do not use mainstream services to help them with their situations. Specific reasons for this have been cited as:

- racism within agencies
- fear of losing one's children
- fear of being revictimized
- inability of services to meet their needs (services not being family focused or relevant in other cultural ways)
- fragmentation of services (isolation of various needs) (Baskin, 2002; Frank, 1992; Health Canada, 1996)

In addition, Aboriginal peoples have been portrayed in white North American culture in negative and stereotypical ways. These often promote and condone violence against Aboriginal women, thereby making it difficult for them to reach out to white people for help. Racism by both individuals and mainstream systems promote violence through a differential response and treatment of Aboriginal peoples (Bruce, 1998).

Programs that are based upon the cultures and traditions of Aboriginal peoples and that involve Aboriginal methods of healing have a much greater chance of succeeding than do programs developed and managed by non-Aboriginal agencies. In keeping with the principle of Aboriginal self-government, it is the right and responsibility of Aboriginal communities to take control of family violence interventions. The movement toward Aboriginal self-determination, rooted in community-based responsibility, action, ownership, and empowerment, needs to be respected and supported. Aboriginal communities must have the jurisdiction, legal responsibility, and financial resources to determine their own local priorities, standards, and organizational capacities to address all aspects of family violence interventions. This includes community-based healing for all of its members.

For Aboriginal peoples, the concept of healing—rather than merely responding to incidents of violence—and the focus on wellness demand a strategy that is different from the current responses to family violence. There is a contradiction between the Aboriginal solution, which seeks harmony and balance among individuals, the family, and community, and the mainstream one, which is crisis-oriented, punishes the abuser, and separates the family and community (Maracle, 1993).

Recovering positive Aboriginal identities will contribute to healing within Aboriginal communities. Aboriginal peoples cannot look outside their cultures for their self-image. Aboriginal traditional values, especially in the area of relationships, carry the instructions for healing. Aboriginal traditional healing works for Aboriginal peoples because dealing with family violence involves more than the cessation of harmful behaviours. It involves building healthy relationships within families and communities by:

- focusing on self-esteem and self-worth as Aboriginal peoples
- offering support
- using symbols that engage the senses and the gifts of the Earth, rather than only words, to heal
- teaching respect for the self, family, community, and the Earth
- taking the focus away from an individualistic approach to the situation
- balancing the four aspects (psychological, physical, emotional, and spiritual) of the person, so that she or he can use all of her or his resources
- promoting ways of achieving harmony and integration within (Vancouver Native Education Centre, 1991)

In the studies conducted on family violence in Aboriginal communities, the related problem that respondents most often identified is substance abuse. Generally, for all populations, the literature indicates that alcohol abuse is a common feature of domestic violence cases, with estimates ranging from 40 percent to 50 percent (Brant, 1998; Brownridge, 2002, 2003; Brownridge & Halli, 2001; Rosenbaum & Maiuro, 1990). Conclusions tend to agree that there is much alcohol abuse among spouse abusers and much wife abuse among alcohol abusers. However, it is also true that the large majority of spouse abusers do not drink prior to their violent episodes and that a large percentage of alcoholics are not violent towards their wives. Alcohol use is associated with an increased probability of wife abuse, even though the linkage is neither necessary nor sufficient. (Rosenbaum & Mairuo, 1990, p. 285)

This may be the case in the non-Aboriginal population, but not so in the Aboriginal one. The combination of substance abuse and family violence is far higher in the Aboriginal population, estimated from 85 percent to 95 percent (Frank, 1992). Thus, an Aboriginal holistic approach cannot ignore these important connections, but rather would address substance misuse in its family violence intervention programs.

WOMEN

As with all women who are living in violent situations, safety is the first concern. Shelters for women and children—if available—are one option. However, the issue of whether or not women want to leave their homes, even if appropriate shelters are available, remains. For those who would prefer to stay in their homes without the offender present, the solution may be to remove him. This could be achieved by providing a residence for abusive men that offers both protection for women and healing for men.

Another area of concern is whether or not women are being heard in terms of what they need from services. If they are not heard, they may "perceive the intervention as controlling and disempowering, and some-times create barriers to this intervention in order to maintain some control over their lives, even though they may want help" (MacLeod, 1989, p. 25). Aboriginal women must be provided with opportunities at the community level—whether that is in their First Nation, urban centres, or in shelters—to discuss issues of importance to them, including a course for resolutions relating to family violence and their empowerment.

One of the greatest concerns that abused women identify as a barrier to seeking assistance is that when they do reach out for help to escape the abuse, their parenting is scrutinized. Their continuing fear of seeking help is "escalated by the risk of losing custody of their children through their admission of family 'problems.' The solution is put on the woman who is 'guilty' of 'providing a poor home environment' for her child" (MacLeod, 1989, p. 13). This is most apparent in the Aboriginal population given the relationship that Aboriginal peoples have with the child welfare system.

Another barrier to women seeking help is service providers' attitudes toward men who are abusive. Women who suffer through violence rarely feel long-term anger, hate, or the need for revenge toward their abusers (MacLeod, 1989). Yet, according to women who have sought help, "it seems like everybody I talk to, who says they want to help me, wants me to fight back...the last thing I want is more fighting" (MacLeod, 1989, p. 23).

This response is made clear by many Aboriginal women who would like to see arbitration and support systems for all family members in their communities. They do not see the solution to family violence in the criminal justice system. Their criticism is that when Aboriginal offenders are charged, they are incarcerated. They return home after serving their sentences. They do not receive treatment while incarcerated, thereby putting women at risk once again when the offenders are released. For many Aboriginal women, this type of intervention is useless because the causes of abuse are not dealt with (Hamilton & Sinclair, 1991; Proulx & Perrault, 2000; Wallace, 2002; Weinrath, 2000).

Aboriginal women are also clear on what they do want. Many want help either to keep their families together or eventually reunite them. They emphasize that aboriginally designed and directed programs are what they want to assist them, and they believe that only such services will emphasize healing for the whole family. They are not comfortable with counselling that excludes the abuser from a healing process and stresses the necessity of the woman leaving her partner (Hamilton & Sinclair, 1991). Women want choices and alternatives, rather than being told what to do, whether by mainstream society or by Aboriginal communities.

Of equal importance is the healing process for Aboriginal women who have experienced family violence. This process needs to include cultural empowerment for women who traditionally played a central role within the family, community, government, and in spiritual ceremonies. Women need to hear the traditional teachings that were passed on through the oral histories of Aboriginal peoples from generation to generation that focus on men and women as being equal in power and having autonomy within their personal lives. In this way, they will come to understand that they were never considered inferior in Aboriginal communities until European expansion undermined their value as equal partners in these communities. A major key to putting an end to female mistreatment is Aboriginal women's resumption of their traditional roles.

CHILDREN

As a result of the high rates of alcohol abuse and family violence in Aboriginal communities, Aboriginal children are more likely than their non-Aboriginal counterparts to experience the loss of parents and other family members (Fiddler, 1991). Loss takes the form of family breakups, desertions, suicides, and death caused by violence. Research into the experience of repeated and traumatic loss among Aboriginal children indicates that they carry symptoms of underlying depression, low self-esteem, and feelings of worthlessness, which are manifested in substance abuse, developmental delays, anxiety, and self-destructive behaviours such as suicide attempts (Fiddler, 1991).

In addition, many young Aboriginal people do not fully understand their heritage and cultures, which often results in identity conflict. Furthermore, Aboriginal children may grow up with the perception that being Aboriginal is equated with poverty, powerlessness, substance abuse, and violence.

A healing process for children needs to include both immediate assistance and long-term education. Aboriginal children need to learn about the nature and responsibility of violence as well as appropriate social problem-solving skills. Such a healing process holds promise for preventing family violence for future generations of Aboriginal peoples.

MEN

Over the centuries, due to the colonization process, some Aboriginal men have adopted the same attitudes toward women and children as many of their non-Aboriginal counterparts. They have not escaped the imposition of a social order that debases women and condones the sexual and physical violation of women and children. The colonization process explains family violence in Aboriginal families and communities—it does not justify it. Violent Aboriginal men are accountable for their violence and must take responsibility for it.

Although there is widespread societal support for a strong message that woman assault is a crime, those working to prevent it are asking whether the use of criminal justice sanctions as a major social response to stop violence and to change public attitudes is too punitive an approach to the problem. For Aboriginal communities, solutions are required that will enhance overall healing, while ensuring accountability for violent behaviour. Aspects of the criminalization of violent behaviour are not conducive to healing. Although some progress has been made, the continuing focus of the current justice system on the offender alone restricts the system's ability to promote a healing approach.

A major issue that must be addressed in the intervention of healing for offenders is the protection of women and children. This is particularly important for those Aboriginal families who wish to remain living together while undergoing a healing process. The ultimate goal of intervening in family violence is to end the violence inflicted by offenders, but, in the meantime, victims must be protected. The safety of women and children must be weighed as heavily as the interests of offenders in healing. Thus, to ensure that the interests of victims of violence are properly addressed in a healing program, all procedures and practices must be evaluated from the perspective of whether they advance or endanger the safety of women and children. Warning victims that an offender represents a danger does not suffice in achieving the balance between victim protection and offender healing.

Aboriginal communities emphasize healing for offenders that will focus on:

- accountability for behaviour
- an exploration for the reasons for violence
- ways to cope appropriately with anger and other powerful emotions
- a chance to learn new coping and problem-solving skills
- addressing substance abuse (Ontario Native Women's Association, 1989)

Furthermore, healing programs for offenders must utilize Aboriginal values, traditions, and practices, and must be designed and staffed by Aboriginal facilitators who draw on the wisdom and guidance of healthy Elders and traditional teachers. They must also stress the need for Aboriginal men to participate in the restoration of women and children to their rightful place.

CRIMINAL JUSTICE SYSTEM

Proportionate to other Canadians, Aboriginal peoples are overrepresented in Canada's jails and prisons. Since the 1970s, Aboriginal peoples have found themselves increasingly engaged with the criminal justice system (Adelburg, 1993; Hamilton & Sinclair, 1991; LaPrairie, 1994; McGillivray & Comaskey, 1999; McIvor, 1992). Many Aboriginal peoples do not see the Canadian justice system as beneficial to them and they want this addressed within self-government initiatives.

There is a fundamental difference in the understanding of justice from the dominant society's view and from the Aboriginal perspectives. The dominant society emphasizes punishing the "deviant" to make that person conform and to protect other members of society. The purpose of a justice system, from the Aboriginal world view, is to restore the peace and equilibrium within the community and to reconcile the accused with his or her conscience and with the individual and family who have been wronged (Hamilton & Sinclair, 1991).

In the traditional way, wrongdoing is a collective responsibility and the process involves all parties acknowledging the wrong, allowing for atonement, and installing a system of reparation or compensation in order to restore harmony. This could involve an expression of regret for the injury done by the offender or the presentation of gifts or payment of some kind (Green, 1998; Hamilton & Sinclair, 1991; McGillivray & Comaskey, 1999; McIvor & Nahanee, 1998). To Aboriginal peoples, sentencing the offender to incarceration or placing him on probation means relieving the offender of any responsibility for a just restitution of the wrong. It is viewed as a total vindication of the wrongdoer and an abdication of the duty of justice.

Many Aboriginal communities are implementing their traditional way of justice without incarcerating the offender. In order for this process to be fully implemented in addition to the process described, perpetrators of woman assault must participate in culture-based family violence healing programs. The notion of implementing traditional ways of justice is supported by McGillivray and Comaskey's (1999) study under specific conditions. In this study, nineteen of the twenty-six women interviewed thought that culture-based justice was "worth a try but set out conditions that were to be met if it were to be acceptable to them. These included ensuring the safety of women and children, taking into account the nature and severity of the offence, the supervision, nature, and length of the disposition, deciding who should be present at the meeting or circle, and protection from the offender's manipulation of results" (p. 128). In other words, Aboriginal women clearly want choices and ways to have their voices heard in this process, which are absent in the judicial system. If not carefully watched, the voices of Aboriginal women can be lost in community-based justice alternatives as well.

Interestingly enough, twenty of the twenty-six women in the study nevertheless favoured jail sentences because they saw this as offering them safety and abusers punishment. This finding of the study conflicts with others (Alberta Law Reform Institute, 1995; Baskin, 1996, 1997; Hamilton & Sinclair, 1991; MacLeod, 1987) on this topic in which women respondents desired healing for abusers rather than punishment. This ambiguity comes as no surprise, nor should the fact that not all Aboriginal women think the same way about this issue or any other, for that matter. It is apparent that those communities that wish to return to a culture-based system of justice must listen and take heed of women's voices of disagreement.

CULTURE-BASED HEALING INITIATIVES

Much work is now being put into culture-based family violence intervention programs across Canada. In Ontario, several provincial ministries and Aboriginal organizations launched the Aboriginal Healing and Wellness Strategy (AHWS) in 1994 to address family violence and health issues. As of 2009, this initiative funds the following services throughout Ontario:

- 125 community prevention and health promotion workers in family violence education and prevention programs in 105 communities

- crisis intervention teams in forty-seven remote northern communities that respond to immediate incidents of family violence
- community crisis workers in twenty-six urban communities
- ten healing lodges for treatment of sexual and physical abuse and addictions
- ten shelters for women and children (Aboriginal Healing and Wellness Strategy, 2009)

In addition, by 2009, when the provincial government renewed its continued support of AHWS, the strategy had funded 360 projects, which served 450,000 community members and trained a thousand staff per year in health and social services across Ontario.

The Aboriginal Healing Foundation (AHF) is a federally funded, aboriginally run, non-profit organization that began in 1998 to support community-based healing initiatives for Aboriginal peoples on and off reserves who have been affected by the abuses in residential schools and by intergenerational impacts, including family violence. Presently, the AHF (2011) funds twelve healing lodges across the country. In 2002, the AHF reported that many "individuals and communities were clearly motivated to break the cycle of physical and sexual abuse." In fact, "some community teams claim that the silence around sexual abuse and family violence has finally been broken" (pp. 4–5). Evaluations cited best practices as family circles, group-focused healing, traditional healing, use of Aboriginal languages, involvement of Elders, storytelling, and camps on the land (Aboriginal Healing Foundation, 2002, 2003, 2006). Unfortunately, the Canadian government has indicated that there will be no further funding for the AHF after the fall of 2012 (AHF, 2011).

MINO-YAA-DAA

All of the analysis and Aboriginal perspectives provided in this chapter went into the development and implementation of a family violence intervention program for an urban Aboriginal community of about three hundred people. I was involved in all aspects of the program, which ran from 1995 to 2000. Early in the service implementation, women and children attended a circle together to give the program an Aboriginal name. As most of the community members who attended were Anishnawbe, a name was chosen in this language—Mino-Yaa-Daa—which means "healing together."

The Mino-Yaa-Daa program offered services to children on a rotating basis according to age, which included activities such as learning the responsibilities of caring for sacred objects, lighting the fire, and smudging, which helped them feel good about themselves as Aboriginal peoples.

The relationship between children and facilitators is critical, so developing trust, security, and a safe environment were major principles of the program. Children also require firm but caring and consistent guidelines in order to feel safe and be able to set appropriate boundaries with others, so this, too, was emphasized. Respect for the needs of children and their ownership of the circle was another major principle of the Mino-Yaa-Daa program. Thus, the children themselves, rather than the facilitators, set most of the boundaries or rules for the circle and the consequences for breaking them.

All of these factors created an accepting, non-judgmental atmosphere in which children could share their stories and feelings about their experiences of family violence, knowing that what was said in the circle stayed in the circle (with the exception of child protection issues). In doing so, they learned that they were not alone, that they were not the cause of their parents' actions, and that breaking the silence helped to change how they felt about themselves.

Activities for the children's circles were developed around the goals and objectives of the program, which included:

- development of self-esteem and positive Aboriginal identity
- appropriate expression of feelings
- safety in the home and community
- letting go of self-blaming attitudes about issues related to family violence
- healthy ways of coping with problematic situations
- resolving conflicts without violence
- incorporating traditional teachings, values, and practices in their lives
- effective communication

Other components of the services for children included:

- Elders' teachings
- spiritual ceremonies such as the sweat lodge and full moon
- cultural responsibilities such as fire-keeping and preparing medicines
- case conferencing with other agencies and service providers
- contact with parents

A major purpose of the Mino-Yaa-Daa program's services for women was to bring the community's women together. Only through women joining together can the disempowering silence around issues related to family violence be broken. By coming together in a circle, women learned that they were not alone and that their situations and feelings were similar to those of others. They learned how to trust, take risks, and both give and receive support, thereby building relationships and a community of empowered women.

As with children, women, too, need a safe place of their own in order to express their needs and concerns and begin the healing process. Therefore, the women negotiated their own boundaries for the circle to suit their needs for safety and comfort. The circle implemented both culture-based and some Western healing practices (as long as they were compatible with the values of Aboriginal world views). Medicines for smudging, sacred objects for holding, and traditional teachings on the topics raised in the circle were always available, but never imposed on anyone.

Within the circles, participants and facilitators addressed the following topics:

- self-esteem and positive identity as Aboriginal women
- healthy relationships with children, partners, and community members based on non-victimization
- identification, expression, and appropriate release of feelings
- healthy, empowering coping behaviours
- self-care
- removal of stigmas and labels
- letting go of past experiences that interfere with the present
- conflict resolution
- values, beliefs, and healing practices of Aboriginal cultures
- decision-making and planning for the future
- role modelling

Two important elements were emphasized in the women's circles. The first was a focus on tools that women learned in the circles and then used to help them in their daily lives. This was important because what was learned in the circles needed to have value to women in practical ways. The other was the need for women to support each other and develop relationships outside of the program. This was important to create the Aboriginal cultural value of interdependency, which emphasizes how everyone has gifts and resources inside them and the natural ability to help others. Incorporated into all program services for women was the Aboriginal belief in the healing powers of laughter. We had fun! Other services offered to women by the Mino-Yaa-Daa program included sweat-lodge ceremonies, Elders' teaching circles, full-moon ceremonies, and individual crisis intervention sessions as requested.

Eradicating violence toward women cannot be done without men changing their abusive behaviours and attitudes. In addition to the circles offered to men, all of the other services that were offered to children and women were available to them as well (except full-moon ceremonies).

The facilitators of the men's circles were a man and a woman who symbolized equality and respect between men and women, along with a strong recognition of the roles and responsibilities of both, according to Aboriginal world views. Participants often asked the female facilitator to discuss circle topics from the perspective of an Aboriginal woman. In addition, participants valued building a relationship with a strong woman who usually took the lead in circle facilitation and in challenging the men on abusive attitudes. Both facilitators participated in the men's sweats and Elders' teaching circles. For the men's component of the program, the Elders were also a man and a woman, again stressing equality between the two and the valuable learning that comes from female teachers.

Two principles lay at the foundation of the program's services for men: non-judgment and accountability. In order for men to understand and change abusive behaviours, they must feel safe enough to open up about them. Although abusive actions were seen as wrong, men were never viewed as "bad people." The second principle stressed that circle participants were responsible for their actions and accountable to those they had hurt in keeping with Aboriginal world views of justice.

Within the men's circles, facilitators and participants addressed the areas that were covered in the women's circles as well as the following:

- identification of physical, psychological, spiritual, and emotional abuse
- attitudes about controlling and abusive behaviours
- power and control
- breaking the cycle of violence
- origins of family violence
- making amends to their partners, families, and community
- roles and responsibilities of men according to Aboriginal world views
- substance misuse
- appropriate ways of dealing with anger and other powerful emotions

The men's component of the Mino-Yaa-Daa program was also one of the ten recognized Partner Assault Response Strategy programs (PARS) in Toronto, supervised by the Woman Abuse Council of Toronto. During the six years of its operation, it was the only aboriginally focused program on the roster, meaning that it could accept men who went through the specialized domestic violence courts.

In addition to these services, the Mino-Yaa-Daa program also included community healing. This involved community members' participation in the following ways:

- Elders'/traditional teachers' teaching circles
- educational workshops on issues related to family violence, community responsibility, and community healing
- feasts and socials
- sweat-lodge and full-moon ceremonies
- workshops on drum making, singing, and dancing
- cultural events focused on children and youth
- development and implementation of a community watch safety program
- participation in demonstrations
- facilitation of a four-day community healing conference, which included a special ceremony to commit to ending family violence

In order to assess the impact of the Mino-Yaa-Daa program on its participants, an evaluation process built into the development of the program was conducted at the end of each year. Evaluation goals included assessment of attitudes about issues related to family violence, responses to services and activities, cognitive and behavioural changes in relating to others and coping with problem situations, safety, and recommendations for changes in future services. The methodologies of the evaluation included pre- and post-program questionnaires on attitudes about issues of family violence, weekly reports completed by program facilitators, evaluation forms on the degree of satisfaction with services, and interviews.

Evaluations consistently indicated that children learned how to solve problems and keep themselves safer from attending the circles. They discussed that they "learned what to do when a person approached [them] to try to take [them] away" and "what to do when parents were fighting" (Mino-Yaa-Daa Program Evaluation, 1995–2001). Children explained in the interviews that when a violent incident occurs, "even though some people tell [them] not to call the police, [they] know it is best to call them." They also explained that they knew to leave the violent situation and go to another adult's place, where they would be safe. Some children recommended that "it helps to stay calm [in such situations] and to get someone that can help" (Mino-Yaa-Daa Program Evaluation, 1995–2001).

Parents reported positive changes in their children from attending the circles, including how their children related to them and dealt with problem situations. They described their children as "being more mature," "able to teach others about the medicines," "more confident," "feeling special," "more outgoing," "able to talk more," "having a greater interest in the culture and traditions," and "proud of who they are" (Mino-Yaa-Daa Program Evaluation, 1995–2001). Some parents noted specific changes in how their children were relating and dealing with feelings and problems. These changes were described as "closer relationships" with parents, "expressing their feelings honestly," "suggesting ways to work out situations at home," and "speaking up about what [they] want." Parents added that they were receptive to these changes in their children because they had a positive effect on family relationships. Some commented that they were "able to correct unfair responsibilities placed on children," that they had begun to "smudge together as a family," they saw their children "speaking to [them] and other adults with respect," and that they "participated in solving problems at home as a family" (Mino-Yaa-Daa Program Evaluation, 1995–2001).

In the women's programming, a participant expressed that attending an Elders' teaching circle provided by the program helped her to relate the traditional teachings to her life and thereby understand a difficult situation she was going through. Another woman explained how the program helped her to clarify her values and beliefs so that she was better able to provide direction to her children. A third woman spoke about how she had grown much closer to family members and had been able to "deal with a lot of hard issues" with them because of what she had learned in the circles.

Other comments made by participants of the women's circle included that the program helped them to work through issues with their partners, to talk more openly, to set clear boundaries with others, to unlock issues connected to their past, to be more assertive, and to deal with confrontation in healthy ways. Most discussed how they came to understand that they did not cause the violence toward them, that they gained the confidence to leave abusive relationships, and that they had begun to implement self-care in their lives.

All participants of the men's program indicated that they were able to give and receive support within the circle, and some noted that they were able to support participants outside the circle as well. When asked to address how they were dealing with anger rather than becoming violent, all provided examples of "expressing it in a healing way, so I won't hurt someone or myself." Examples included "loud screams in a pillow," "hitting a pillow or punching bag," "talking to someone I can trust," "going for a walk," "exercising," "smudging," "deep breathing," and "crying because sometimes after the anger, there's sadness" (Mino-Yaa-Daa Program Evaluation, 1995–2001).

Men's circle participants stated that they used what they learned in the circles in their everyday lives. One participant related that he incorporated the techniques and teachings from the circle "all the time and it works daily." Another reported that if he did not use what he had learned, "I wouldn't even be able to handle getting to the bus stop." A third related that he was "making a punching bag" similar to the one used in the circles.

Another indicated that he thought over issues carefully, incorporating what he had learned from the circle and then he talked to his partner. A fifth participant indicated that "I'm a very angry person, so I have to use what I learned quite frequently. To heal, you have to apply it, work on it all the time" (Mino-Yaa-Daa Program Evaluation, 1995–2001).

Most participants in the men's circle commented that attendance in the Mino-Yaa-Daa program helped them in their relationships with partners. For some, this meant eventually accepting that the relationships were not going to continue, but that they needed to carry on with their responsibilities as fathers. Others stated that they worked more with their partners in recognizing exactly what the problems were and in dealing with them, they talked more with their partners, and they spent more time at home with their families. They generally described their relationships with their families as "improved," "better," and "more healthy." Some indicated that family members had begun to tell them they saw positive changes in them.

In the six years of the Mino-Yaa-Daa program's existence, to the best of my knowledge, only one participant reoffended by assaulting his partner. No mechanisms were built into the program evaluation to track ex-participants over the long term. However, as Aboriginal peoples tend to develop relationships that last beyond formal programs, I know from personal, ongoing contact with past participants that many of them have moved on to good lives. As far as I know, all of the women and their children stayed together. A few women are now attending university, some are working at Aboriginal agencies to help other women, a couple have returned to their reserve communities to work on family violence interventions, and others are singing in women's hand-drum groups and dancing at powwows. Some left their abusive partners and never returned, while others reunited with their partners who had made true changes. The men who were involved went on in similar ways as the women. Two of these men are now my friends, they are in healthy relationships, one has his own business, the other has a child, and both have been to my home and hung out with my son.

These friendships speak to what I wrote earlier about not sacrificing men who have been perpetrators of family violence and about how violence is learned behaviour that can be unlearned. This also speaks to Aboriginal values related to community responsibility and inclusiveness. Regardless of what Aboriginal peoples may or may not do, they are all a part of our community. Each person has value and gifts to share with everyone else. Each person has inherent worth. The healing process brings all of this out of people so that we may engage with them as their true selves. Obviously, I know this to be true or I would never allow these men to be around my precious (and highly protected) child.

CONCLUSION

It is impossible to understand the context of family violence in Aboriginal families and communities without an awareness of the history of colonization and present-day systemic racism. With this understanding comes a deeper appreciation of why dominant society's solutions to these social problems usually do not help, and how programs based on Aboriginal world views have a far greater chance of success. A culture-based and community-controlled approach that focuses on holistic services is the choice of most communities today. We must be mindful, however, that this approach includes listening to all voices and addressing the concerns and safety issues of those voices.

Aboriginal service providers, educators, and researchers need to document, evaluate, and publish our good work on culture-based family violence healing programs. We have so much to offer each other about the struggles and the successes. Those of us who are privileged have a responsibility to mentor others in carrying out the work, and we have ways of knowing and healing that are valuable to all humankind. It is time for us to share our knowledge and experiences.

DEDICATION

For Brandy Buswa, who, at the young age of eleven years, inspired me to begin my healing work with offenders of family violence.

REFERENCES

Aboriginal Family Healing Joint Steering Committee. (1993). *For generations to* come: The time is now: A strategy for Aboriginal family healing—Final report of the Aboriginal Family Healing Joint Steering Committee. Toronto: The Committee. Retrieved from: openlibrary.org/books/OL17273552M/For_generations_to_come.

Aboriginal Healing and Wellness Strategy. (2009). *Supporting Aboriginal people: Aboriginal Healing and Wellness Strategy.* Ottawa: Ontario Ministry of Community and Social Services. Retrieved from: http://www.mcss.gov.on.ca/en/mcss/programs/community/programsforaboriginalpeople.aspx.

Aboriginal Healing Foundation. (2001). *An interim evaluation report of Aboriginal Healing Foundation program activity.* Retrieved from: http://www. ahf.ca/.

Aboriginal Healing Foundation. (2002). *Aboriginal Healing Foundation evaluation update.* Retrieved from: http://www.ahf.ca/.

Aboriginal Healing Foundation. (2003). *Third interim evaluation report of the Aboriginal Healing Foundation program activity.* Ottawa: AHF. Retrieved from: http://www.ahf.ca/publications/evaluation-series.

Aboriginal Healing Foundation. (2006). *AHF final report.* Ottawa: AHF. Retrieved from: http://www.ahf.ca/publications/research-series.

Aboriginal Healing Foundation. (2011). *Funded projects.* Ottawa: AHF. Retrieved from: http://www.ahf.ca/funded-projects.

Adams, H. (1999). *Tortured people: The politics of colonization.* Penticton, BC: Theytus.

Adelburg, E. (1993). Aboriginal women and prison reform. In E. Adelburg & C. Currie (Eds.), *In conflict with the law: Women and the Canadian justice system* (pp. 76–92). Vancouver: Press Gang.

Alberta Law Reform Institute. (1995). *Domestic abuse: Toward an effective legal response.* Discussion report no. 15. Edmonton: Alberta Law Reform Institute.

Association of Native Child and Family Services Agencies of Ontario. (2001). Annual report 2000–2001. Thunder Bay: Association of Native Child and Family Services Agencies of Ontario. Retrieved from: www.nativecfs.org/familyservices/index. php.

Bangar-White, H., & Larrington, J. (2005). *Intersection of domestic violence and child victimization in Indian country.* Retrieved from: http://www.swclap.org/pdfs/INTERSECTIONDVANDKIDS.

Baskin, C. (1996). *Gabriel Dumont community information manual.* Toronto: Gabriel Dumont Non-profit Homes (Metro Toronto).

Baskin, C. (1997). Mino-Yaa-Daa: An urban community-based approach. *Native Social Work Journal, 1*(1), 55–67.

Baskin, C. (2002a). *Mino-Yaa-Daa Program Evaluation, 1995–2001.* Toronto: Gabriel Dumont Non-Profit Homes.

Baskin, C. (2002b). Holistic healing and accountability: Indigenous restorative justice. *Child Care in Practice, 8*(2), 133–36.

Baskin, C. (2007a). Aboriginal youth talk about structural determinants as the causes of their homelessness. First Peoples Child and Family Review, 3(3), 31–42.

Baskin, C. (2007b). Structural determinants as the cause of homelessness for Aboriginal youth. *Critical Social Work, 8*(1). Retrieved from: www.critical socialwork.com.

Bennett, M., & Blackstock, C. (2003). *A literature review and annotated bibliography focusing on aspects of Aboriginal child welfare in Canada.* Ottawa: First Nations Research Site of the Centre of Excellence for Child Welfare. Retrieved from: www.fncfcs.com.

Blackstock, C., Trocmé, N., & Bennett, M. (2004). Child maltreatment investigations among Aboriginal and non-Aboriginal families in Canada. *Violence against Women, 10*(8), 901–16. doi:10.1177/1077801204266312.

Brant, C.C. (1998). *A collection of chapters, lectures, workshops, and thoughts.* Ottawa: Native Mental Health Association of Canada.

Brennan, S. (2011). *Violent victimization of Aboriginal women in the Canadian provinces, 2009.* Ottawa: Statistics Canada. Retrieved from: http://www.statcan.gc/pub/85-002-x/2011001/article/11439-eng.pdf.

Brownridge, D.A. (2002). Cultural variation in male partner violence against women: A comparison of Quebec with the rest of Canada. *Violence against Women, 8*(1), 87–115.

Brownridge, D.A. (2003). Male partner violence against Aboriginal women in Canada: An empirical analysis. *Journal of Interpersonal Violence, 18*(1), 65–83.

Brownridge, D.A., & Halli, S.S. (2001). *Explaining violence against women in Canada.* Lanham: Lexington.

Bruce, L. (1998). A culturally sensitive approach to working with Aboriginal women. *Manitoba Social Worker, 30*(2), 1, 8–10.

Canadian Advisory Council on the Status of Women. (2001). *Male violence against women: The brutal face of inequality.* Ottawa: Canadian Centre for Justice Statistics.

Chandler, M.J., & Lalonde, C.E. (2008). Cultural continuity as a protective factor against suicide in First Nations youth. *Horizons—A Special Issue on Aboriginal Youth, Hope or Heartbreak: Aboriginal Youth and Canada's Future 10*(1), 68–72.

Chapin, D. (1994). *Peace on earth begins in the home.* Duluth, MN: Mending the Sacred Hoop.

Chartrand, L., & McKay, C. (2006). *A review of research on criminal victimization and First Nations, Métis and Inuit peoples, 1990 to 2001.* Policy Centre for Victim Issues, Research and Statistics Division. Ottawa: Department of Justice.

Council of Australia Governments. (2011). *National plan to reduce violence against women and their children, including the first three-year action plan.* Retrieved from: http://www.fahcsia.gov.au/sa/women/progserv/violence/nationalplan/Documents/national_plan.

Department of Justice. (2011). *Attorney General Holder announces violence against women tribal prosecution task force in Indian country.* Retrieved from: http://www.justice.gov/opa/pr/2011/January/11-ag-086.html.

Dickson, G. (1989). *Iskew: Empowering victims of wife abuse in Native studies review.* Saskatoon: University of Saskatchewan.

Durst, D., MacDonald, J., & Parsons, D. (1999). Finding our way: A community needs assessment on violence in Native families in Canada. *Journal of Community Practice, 6*(1), 45–59.

Fiddler, S. (1991). *Genesis of family violence in Native society.* Unpublished manuscript, University of Toronto.

Fleras, A., & Elliott, J.L. (1999). *Unequal relations: An introduction to race, ethnic, and Aboriginal dynamics in Canada.* Toronto: Pearson Education Canada.

Fournier, S., & Crey, E. (1997). *Stolen from our embrace: The abduction of First Nations children and the restoration of Aboriginal communities.* Vancouver: Douglas and McIntyre.

Frank, S. (1992). *Family violence in Aboriginal communities.* Unpublished manuscript, University of Toronto.

Green, R.G. (1998). *Justice in Aboriginal communities: Sentencing alternatives.* Saskatoon: Purich.

Hallett, D., Chandler, M.J., & Lalonde, C.E. (2007). Aboriginal language knowledge and youth suicide. *Cognitive Development, 22*(3), 392–99.

Hamilton, A.C., & Sinclair, C.M. (1991). *Report of the Aboriginal Justice Inquiry of Manitoba.* Winnipeg: Province of Manitoba.

Health Canada. (1989). *Working together: 1989 national forum on family violence—Proceedings.* Ottawa: Health Canada.

Health Canada. (1996). *Family violence in Aboriginal communities: An Aboriginal perspective.* Ottawa: Health Canada.

Knockwood, I. (1992). *Out of the depths.* Lockeport, NS: Roseway.

Kruger, T., Pitman, M., Grennell, D., McDonald, T., Mariu, D., Pomare, A., Mita, T., Maihi, M., & Lawson-Te, A. (2004). *Transforming* whanau *violence: A conceptual framework: An updated former second Maori taskforce on* whanau *violence* (2nd ed.). Retrieved from: http://www.nzfvc.org.nz/goodpracticedocument.aspx?doc=4.

Ladner, K. (2009). Understanding the impact of self-determination on communities in crisis. *Journal of Aboriginal Health, 5*(2), 88–101.

LaPrairie, C. (1994). *Seen but not heard: Native people in the inner city.* Ottawa: Department of Justice.

LaRoque, E. (1994). *Violence in Aboriginal communities.* Ottawa: Health Canada.

MacLaurin, B., Trocmé, N., Fallon, B., Blackstock, C., Pitman, L., & McCormak, M. (2003). *A comparison of First Nations and non-Aboriginal children investigated for maltreatment in Canada in 2003.* Ottawa: Canadian Child Welfare Research Portal. Retrieved from: http://www.cecw-cepb.ca/infosheets/comparison-first-nations-and-non-aboriginal-2003.

MacLeod, L. (1987). *Battered but not beaten: Preventing wife abuse in Canada.* Ottawa: Canadian Advisory Council on the Status of Women.

MacLeod, L. (1989). *Preventing wife battering: Towards a new understanding.* Ottawa: Canadian Council on Social Development.

Maracle, S. (1993). Family violence: An Aboriginal perspective. *Vis-à-vis, 10*(4), 1, 4.

McGillivray, A., & Comaskey, B. (1999). *Black eyes all the time: Intimate violence, Aboriginal women, and the justice system.* Toronto: University of Toronto Press.

McIvor, S. (1992). *Aboriginal justice, women, and violence.* Ottawa: Native Women's Association of Canada.

McIvor, S., & Nahanee, T. (1998). Aboriginal women: Invisible victims of violence. In K. Bonneycastle & G. Rigakos (Eds.), *Unsettling truths: Battered women, policy, politics, and contemporary research in Canada* (pp. 63–70). Vancouver: Collective Press.

Minority Rights Group International. (2011). *State of the world's minorities and indigenous peoples 2011—New Zealand.* Retrieved from: http://www.unhcr.org/refworld/docid/4e16d366c.htm.

National Collaborating Centre for Aboriginal Health. (2010). *Family violence as a social determinant of First Nations, Inuit, and Metis health.* Retrieved from: http://www.nccah-ccnsa.ca/docs/fact%20sheets/social%20determinates/NCCAH_fs_familyviolence_EN.

Native Women's Association of Canada. (2007). *Social determinants of health and Canada's Aboriginal women.* Ottawa: NWAC. Retrieved from: http://www.nwac.ca/sites/default/files/reports/NWAC_WHO-CSDH_Submission 2007-06-04.

O'Donnell, T. (2000). *Family violence project: Workshop report.* Toronto: Centre for Indigenous Sovereignty.

Ontario Native Women's Association. (1989). *Breaking free—a proposal for change to Aboriginal family violence.* Thunder Bay, ON: Ontario Native Women's Association.

Ontario Native Women's Association & Ontario Federation of Indian Friendship Centres. (2007). *A strategic framework to end violence against Aboriginal women.* Retrieved from: onwa-tbay.ca/PDF%20Files/Forms/Final%20Draft-20End%20 Violence%20A.

Proulx, J., & Perrault, S. (2000). *No place for violence: Canadian Aboriginal alternatives.* Halifax: Fernwood Publishing Company.

Randall, M. (1989). *The politics of woman abuse: Understanding the issues.* Toronto: Ontario Women's Directorate.

Rosenbaum, A., & Maiuro, R. (1990). Perpetrators of spouse abuse. In R.T. Ammerman & M. Hersen (Eds.), *Treatment of family violence* (pp. 280–309). Toronto: John Wiley and Sons.

Royal Commission on Aboriginal Peoples. (1996). *People to people, nation to nation: Highlights from the report of the Royal Commission on Aboriginal Peoples.* Ottawa. Retrieved from: http://www.aadnc-aandc.gc.ca/eng/1100100014597#chp1.

Sinclair, M. (2010). *Presentation to the Senate Committee on Aboriginal peoples. Truth and Reconciliation Commission of Canada.* Retrieved from: http://www .trc.ca/websites/trcinstitution/File/pdfs/senate%20speech_handout_copy _E_Final.

Statistics Canada. (2004). *Violence against Aboriginal women.* Ottawa: Statistics Canada. Retrieved from: http://www.statcan.gc.ca/pub/85-570-x/2006001/ findings-resultats/4054081-eng.htm.

Statistics Canada. (2011). *Family violence in Canada: A statistical profile.* Ottawa: Statistics Canada. Retrieved from: http://www.phac-aspc.gc.ca/ncfv-cnivf/ pdfs/fv-85-224-XWE-eng.

Stewart, W., Huntley, A., & Blaney, F. (2001). *The implications of restorative justice for Aboriginal women and children survivors of violence: A comparative overview of five communities in British Columbia.* Ottawa: Law Commission of Canada.

Trainor, C., & Mihorean, K. (Eds.). (2001). *Family violence in Canada: A statistical profile.* Ottawa: Statistics Canada.

Trocmé, N. (2001). *Canadian Incidence Study of Reported Child Abuse and Neglect Final Report.* Ottawa: Public Health Agency of Canada. Retrieved from: http://www.phac-aspc.gc.on/publicat/cisfr-ecirf/index-eng.php.

Vancouver Native Education Centre. (1991). *Training family violence workers.* Vancouver: Vancouver Native Education Centre.

Wallace, H. (2002). *Family violence: Legal, medical, and social perspectives.* Toronto: Allyn and Bacon.

Weinrath, M. (2000). Violent victimization and fear of crime among Canadian Aboriginals. In N.J. Pallone (Ed.), *Race, ethnicity, sexual orientation, and violent crime: The realities and the myths* (pp. 107–20). New York: Haworth Press.

7

VIOLENCE, PROTECTION, AND EMPOWERMENT IN THE LIVES OF CHILDREN AND ADULTS WITH DISABILITIES

RICHARD SOBSEY AND SONIA A. SOBON

Mary lives in a group home in Canada. For the last eight years, she has shared her home with three other women and four men who have both psychiatric disorders and intellectual disabilities. These eight individuals spend a lot more time together than most Canadian families. They eat breakfast and supper together seven days a week and, with rare exceptions, have all three meals together on Saturday and Sunday. They spend most evenings at home, and when they do attend recreational activities, they always go with at least one other group home resident. All the adults in the home sleep in one of four bedrooms and there is never a locked door between them. Mary shares a bedroom with one of the other women. Mary has had some consensual sexual intimacy with one of the men in her group home, but another man who lives there has violently sexually assaulted her on five different occasions. In addition, Mary is frequently bullied by Barbara, one of the other women who live with her. Mary fears Barbara and most of the time she tries to avoid physical violence by just giving Barbara whatever she wants. Nevertheless, Barbara often slaps or pinches Mary and has beaten her up on almost two dozen occasions.

Her group home staff members are aware of the problem. The residents who assaulted Mary were counselled, punished through fines and loss of privileges, and threatened that unless their behaviour improves, they may be returned to the large psychiatric institution where they lived before being moved to the group home. The doctor increased Barbara's antipsychotic medications in an attempt to reduce her aggressive behaviour. He also sent Mary for sexual assault counselling after one of the assaults. The counsellor felt that the first and most important goal was establishing a sense of boundaries and personal safety for Mary, but no one knew how to achieve that while Mary continued to sleep in an unlocked bedroom in the same house with a man who repeatedly raped her and a woman who had done her best to crush Mary's skull. Mary asked about moving out of the group home, but was told that the only option for her now was to move back to the institution she left years earlier, a place where Mary had experienced even more extreme violence.

INTRODUCTION

Clearly, Mary is a victim of violence, but should we consider this to be family violence? Although the group of people who live in Mary's group home would not meet some of the narrowest definitions of family, they certainly meet many of the broader definitions. There is a long-term relationship, with a high degree of intimacy and interdependency, and there is an implicit set of rules for interacting with family members that differs from rules for interacting with outsiders. Equally importantly, there is a perception of and response to violence within the "family" that differs from the perception of and response to similar acts of violence committed against outsiders.

This chapter reviews contemporary research on the relationship between violence and disability and describes some current approaches to prevention and intervention services. It also discusses some of the issues related to prevention and intervention services and makes some recommendations for design and implementation of appropriate services. The same broad spectrum of family violence that affects other people also affects Canadians with disabilities. In two essential ways, however, family violence differs for children and adults with disabilities. First, while many Canadians with disabilities live in more traditional families, many others live in group homes, foster care, and other social units that share many characteristics of more traditional families, but stretch the boundaries of our definition of family. Second, both the frequency and the characteristics of the violence that occurs in their families differ. Before exploring these differences, however, it seems appropriate to clearly describe Canadians with disabilities and how many Canadians have disabilities.

CONSTRUCTING DISABILITY

There is no universally accepted definition of disability and no universal agreement on which or how many Canadians have disabilities. Both formal and informal definitions of disability change over time. Winzer (1993) points out the problems created by circular, exclusive, and inconsistent definitions used by a variety of disciplines to identify disabilities in children and goes on to suggest that:

Special Education itself uses many vague and inconsistent definitions and, lacking clear definitions, it is almost impossible to estimate prevalence. Because school systems tend to interpret a child's condition according to the services provided, a child may be called learning disabled in one school system and counted as a low achiever in another. (p. 15)

Differences in how various disabilities are defined are often huge. For example, in England, the term "*learning disabilities*" refers to children and adults with general intellectual disabilities. In the United States and Canada, however, most definitions of *learning disabilities* specifically exclude children and adults with general intellectual disabilities and are restricted only to individuals who have very specific deficits in only one or two areas of academic performance. Adding to the confusion about this condition is the fact that American-Canadian-style learning disabilities were unknown until described by Kirk in 1963 and now have become the most frequently diagnosed disabilities in children, although there remains considerable disagreement on diagnostic criteria (Winzer, 1993). Sleeter (1986) is one of many who have suggested that learning disabilities are socially constructed and function to provide a rationale that creates "protective areas for white middle-class, failing children [or] remedial classes for students previously classified as retarded or slow" (p. 46). The view that learning disabilities and other categories of disability are socially constructed does not necessarily imply that there is no objective basis for classifying at least some children and adults in these categories. It does imply, however, that our understanding of learning disabilities (and other categories of disability) must consider pragmatic social forces, and that all definitions of disability are at least partially invented rather than discovered within some objectively verifiable reality.

Much has been written about the social construction of other categories of disabilities and of disability in general among children and adults. Foucault's (1965) work on the social construction of mental illness, psychiatric disorders, and madness was instrumental in initiating much of that discussion. Today, most experts recognize that while many disabilities have some objectively verifiable basis, others may not, and that even when some objectively verifiable component is present, social construction plays a major part in our conceptualization of disability. Most modern conceptual definitions of disability recognize this essential social component, while most legal and administrative definitions attempt to ignore social constructions and establish objective criteria.

Older definitions of disability focused more on specific medical diagnoses or physical limitations and were based on the notion that disability exists as an objective reality, and differences in definitions and diagnoses only reflected the limitations of our accuracy in describing or recognizing disability. Disabilities were conceptualized as an outcome of disease or injury (De Kleijn-De Vrankrijker, 2003). These kinds of definitions continue to be used frequently for the determination of legal status or program eligibility. For example, mobility impairment may be defined as the inability to walk 200 metres for the purpose of eligibility for special parking privileges. Blindness may be defined as being able to see at a distance of only six metres what a person with typical vision can see at sixty metres. Intellectual disability may be defined as a score of sixty-nine or less on an IQ test. While these kinds of definitions are objective in the sense that they are uniform, they are problematic because they fail to consider the complexity of human experience and conditions. For example, if two people have difficulty walking and one can walk only 195 metres, while the other can walk 205 metres under the same standard conditions, the definition presented above suggests that the first person has mobility impairment and the second does not, even though the difference in walking distance is small. Learning more about the two individuals, we might discover that while the first person can walk only 195 metres, he can do it under almost any condition and rarely falls. The second person, however, who can walk 205 metres down the hall of the hospital when tested, cannot walk up or down steps or even negotiate a curb, has great difficulty with hills or uneven pavement, and falls frequently, resulting in fractures of her brittle bones. Comparing these two individuals, an objective definition that rigidly excludes the second individual from eligibility for special parking privileges seems unfair and arbitrary.

Today's definitions address these issues by considering disability to exist as a complex interaction between physical or mental status, other personal attributes, and social and physical environmental factors. In these models, disability is not a stable condition; it changes depending on contextual factors. For example, intellectual disabilities are no longer diagnosed simply on the basis of an intelligence test score. The same level of intellectual ability that causes significant disadvantages during school, with its heavy requirement for performance of cognitive tasks, may cause no significant disability before or after school years. Not surprisingly, the number of people diagnosed with intellectual disabilities rises sharply as children enter school and declines significantly when they finish school (e.g., Larsen et al., 2001). In this model of disability, a disability can be said to exist only when a mental or physical limitation results in a significant social disadvantage, and the severity of the disability is evaluated on the basis of the extent of this social disadvantage. This kind of definition has been shown to have advantages both from conceptual and practical perspectives, but creates some difficulties in quantifying the frequency of disabilities. Since disabilities appear and disappear at various ages and in various environmental contexts, small differences in the way that disabilities are identified or that data are collected can produce huge variations in the number of people with disabilities identified.

Compounding the definitional problem is the fact that many common definitions of disability are circular. Saloviita (2003), for example, points out that many texts on special education define children with disabilities, exceptional students, or special needs students as those who require special education and define special education as the learning programs required by exceptional students, special needs students, or students with disabilities.

As a result of all the concerns discussed here, there is no stable and precise definition of disability. Conceptual definitions, which incorporate environmental and social factors, have advantages for understanding disability. They better reflect the inherent instability of disability and continuum of abilities and disabilities that exist, rather than artificially constructing exclusive categories like *normal* and *disabled*. Nevertheless, these conceptual definitions are not very useful for establishing precise criteria to determine exactly who has a disability and who does not, or for reliably determining the number of individuals who have disabilities.

For the purpose of this chapter, the concept of disability is defined as an impairment of a physical or mental structure or function that is associated with a significant social disadvantage within family, community, or vocational environments. However, in discussing research on violence against people with disabilities or even in estimating how many Canadians have disabilities, it is important to recognize that almost every study uses a different definition and set of criteria. As a result, it is impossible to make a meaningful comparison of results from different studies.

DIVERSITY AMONG CANADIANS WITH DISABILITIES

Regardless of how we define or categorize disabilities, it is important to recognize that there is vast diversity among Canadians with disabilities. Individuals included in this group can be men or women, children or adults. They come from all ethnic and religious backgrounds. The nature and the extent of their physical and mental impairments are equally diverse. An individual with a major psychiatric disorder, such as schizophrenia, has no more or less in common with an individual with major mobility impairment than either of them does with a person who has no disability. Similarly, in many ways, an individual with a mild intellectual disability is much more like an individual without an intellectual disability than an individual with a severe or profound intellectual disability.

In spite of this diversity, there are some important social realities that affect many people with disabilities. Social and economic marginalization is an important one. Canadians with disabilities are 50 percent less likely to finish high school and are 50 percent more likely to be out of the labour force (Statistics Canada, 2003). In 2006, 53.5 percent of Canadians with disabilities were employed compared to 75.1 percent of other Canadians (Statistics Canada, 2007a). In 2001, the median household income from all sources for Canadians with disabilities was $14,094, which was 38.5 percent less than the median for other Canadians (Statistics Canada, 2003). This means that the majority of Canadians with disabilities live in households well below the poverty line.

COUNTING CANADIANS WITH DISABILITIES

In spite of the previously described definitional problems, it may be useful to consider how many Canadians have disabilities. Statistics Canada's (2007) Participation and Activity Limitation Survey (PALS) found that 14.6 percent of the population reported limitations in their daily activities due to disabilities in 2006. The number of Canadians reporting disabilities increased 21.2 percent from the previous survey five years earlier. This estimate of 4,400,000 Canadians with disabilities is high compared to some other estimates because the question asked did not specify the degree of limitation of activities. However, there is also some reason to believe that this may be a low estimate in some respects. First, the survey was based on a telephone survey of residences. Canadians living in nursing homes, institutions, and other extended care facilities were completely excluded from the estimate. Second, the estimates of the numbers of children with disabilities appear much lower than school-based estimates. For example, about 8 percent of all children attending school in Canada receive special programming because of diagnosed disabilities (e.g., Crealock & Bachor, 1995), but Statistics Canada reported that only 4 percent of children aged five to fourteen had disabilities. According to this survey, 35.4 percent of Canadians with disabilities experience mild limitations, such as chronic backache, which limits vigorous exercise, but about 39.8 percent of Canadians with disabilities have severe to very severe impairments such as arthritis, which has made them completely unable to walk.

PEOPLE WITH DISABILITIES AS FAMILY MEMBERS

With the growing recognition of "non-traditional families," it may be difficult to label any family typical or atypical. Fish (2000) points out that about half of first marriages end in divorce, about half of divorces involve children, and about 35 percent of children live with a step-parent before they reach age eighteen. In addition, large numbers of children live with adoptive parents, foster parents, or other unrelated caregivers. Interracial and cross-cultural marriages, which were considered controversial by some Canadians a generation or two ago, now appear to be well accepted by mainstream society. While gay and lesbian families remain the target of controversy, there can be little doubt that contemporary Canadian society has progressed toward greater acceptance of them (Krauss, 2003) and that millions of children in North America grow up with gay and lesbian parents (Fish, 2000). In addition, significant numbers of Canadians live with roommates, in various forms of intentional communities, or other family alternatives. While current trends leave little doubt that families are changing, our comparison with "traditional families" of the past may be misleading. McDaniel and Tepperman (2004), for example, suggest that the so-called traditional Canadian family never existed, that family structure has always been in flux, and that each generation has viewed their contemporary families as non-traditional departures from previous generations.

Families defy precise definition, making it necessary for sociologists to refer more generally to terms like "families and family-like relationships" (McDaniel & Tepperman, 2004, p. 1). Nevertheless, some common elements can be seen among families. These typically include: (1) interdependency (e.g., psychological, social, economic); (2) intimacy (often, but not necessarily including sexual intimacy); (3) protection (particularly of vulnerable family members); (4) caregiving; (5) interpersonal control; and (6) intrafamilial rules and expectations that are distinct from those outside the family. Family relationships may be formalized through religious or legal recognition, as in marriage or adoption, or remain informal. While there is no specific time specified, family relationships are inherently enduring since some significant amount of time may be required to establish intimacy and interdependency.

Considering the diversity in contemporary Canadian families and family alternatives, it is difficult to clearly identify or quantify exactly how families differ for children and adults with disabilities. Nevertheless, there can be little doubt that both formal structures and informal characteristics of families are different for many Canadians who have disabilities. For example, young children with disabilities are much more likely to live in foster care or with other unrelated caregivers than children without disabilities (Borthwick-Duffy, Widaman, Little & Eyman, 1992). Adults with significant disabilities are much more likely to live with their parents, relatives, or paid caregivers, and much less likely to live independently as compared to other adults.

It is also difficult to state a precise number of Canadian children living in foster care because a number of different programs exist, such as government-supported foster placements with extended family members and various forms of group care, that blur the line between foster care, natural families, and other living alternatives, and these alternatives are categorized differently in different provinces. However, a 2003 estimate of seventy-six thousand would be reasonable (Farris-Manning & Zandstra, 2003). Alberta, for example, reported nine thousand children in government care, including forty-six hundred in foster care in 2008 (Government of Alberta, 2008). The majority of children who live in foster care have at least one significant disability (Fish, 2000). About half have significant developmental delays, and about one-third have severe emotional problems (Fish, 2000). Many others have physical or sensory disabilities. The reasons for the large number of children with disabilities in foster care are numerous. First, some children are placed in foster care because their natural parents cannot meet the intensive needs resulting from their children's disabilities. Second, some rural Canadians place their children in urban foster care because they require advanced medical support or educational services unavailable in their home communities (Children from the Far North, 1994). Third, many children are placed in foster care because they are abused or neglected and have disabilities that result from harm done in their natural families. For example, most children who are hospitalized for child abuse by shaking and who survive have long-term or permanent neurological disabilities (Bonnier et al., 2003). Fourth, children with disabilities are less likely to be adopted so they remain in the foster care system for longer periods of time. Fifth, some children with disabilities are more likely to be orphaned or have parents whose own disabilities interfere with caring for their children. For example, mothers infected with HIV and mothers with chronic substance abuse problems are much more likely to have children with disabilities, but are less likely to be able to care for them than other mothers. Sixth, as discussed later in this chapter, children with disabilities are more likely to be abused and neglected within natural families, resulting in a greater likelihood of child-welfare intervention. Other mechanisms are also thought to contribute to the concentration of children with disabilities in foster care.

Some adults with disabilities also live in foster families, which can be distinguished from group homes because the caregivers live in the home rather than working shifts. In addition, many others live in supported residential care. These individuals live in their own homes with the support of full-time or part-time caregivers. Many individuals depend on paid caregivers for assistance with toileting, bathing, eating, dressing, and other activities of daily living that require a close personal contact that other Canadians experience only in their most intimate relationships.

Fish (2000) points out that adopted children with disabilities are more likely than other children to be placed with gay or lesbian couples, single parents, and other non-traditional parents. This occurs because so-called traditional families are often given priority by adoption agencies and typically given a choice between children with and without disabilities, leaving the children with disabilities for families who are given lower priorities. It may also be true that adoptive parents from non-traditional families, who have often experienced discrimination and marginalization in their own lives, show a greater willingness to accept a child with special needs.

Of course, many Canadians with disabilities live in so-called traditional families, but the large number living in a wide spectrum of family alternatives makes it important to consider the nature of family for people with disabilities before considering family violence.

The association between violence and disability has been explored much more thoroughly in research on child abuse than in research on other forms of family violence (e.g., Sobsey, 2002). Nevertheless, many aspects of the relationship between violence and disability remain unexplored among children, and enough research has been completed on violence against adults with disabilities to yield some preliminary conclusions.

VIOLENCE AGAINST CHILDREN WITH DISABILITIES

Although there is clear evidence of increased rates of violence against both children and adults with disabilities, studies linking child maltreatment with disability are more numerous and, in some cases, more scientific than studies of violence against adults with disabilities. High rates of violence have been reported among various groups of children with disabilities since the 1960s. For example, Elmer and Gregg (1967), in a follow-up study of abused children, found that half of the children had intellectual disabilities, many times more than would be expected by chance. While this and other similar findings suggested a strong relationship between child maltreatment and disability, it was not the central focus of the study, and this finding was given limited attention at the time. In addition, the methods used in this and other studies were not ideal for accurately determining the relative risk or prevalence among children with and without disabilities. Among those who noticed Elmer and Gregg's finding and other similar findings at the time, it was generally assumed that the high rate of intellectual disabilities resulted from damaged nervous systems resulting from physical trauma. However, the results of other studies raised concern about this interpretation. Davies (1978–79) conducted studies of brainwaves of incest survivors during the

1970s. A high rate of epilepsy had been reported among incest survivors, even when sexual abuse was not accompanied by physical abuse. Davies set out to show that their seizures were psychogenic (resulting from emotional factors) rather than neurogenic (resulting from damage to the central nervous system). Therefore, he hypothesized that brainwave patterns would be normal among incest survivors who exhibited seizures. Davies found that 27 percent (six) of the twenty-two incest survivors studied had a history of seizures, much more than the 1 or 2 percent that might be expected by chance. Electroencephalographs (EEGs), however, revealed brainwave patterns consistent with epilepsy. In addition to epileptic-like EEGs recorded for the six incest survivors with seizures, eleven of the other incest survivors had atypical EEGs. In all, seventeen (77 percent) of the incest survivors had EEGs with abnormalities consistent with epilepsy, a finding that was difficult to explain at the time. More recent studies confirm that severe psychological trauma can result in lasting changes in neural conductivity (e.g., Cook, Ciorciari, Varker & Devilly, 2009).

Numerous small and often methodologically weak studies continued to show a relationship between child abuse and disability. By 1987, a Canadian review of studies on child maltreatment and disability concluded that, in spite of differences in effect size, and methodological weaknesses in individual studies considered together, there was convincing evidence that children with a wide range of disabilities were 50 percent more likely to have been abused than other children.

Small-scale studies continue to be published confirming the link between child maltreatment and disability. For example, Ebeling and Nurkkala (2002) studied the histories of Finnish children with developmental, behavioural, and emotional disabilities admitted to a psychiatric facility. Of forty-one patients, 88 percent had been confirmed victims of some form of significant violence. When suspected violence was included, the number affected rose even higher. Active physical violence was known or highly suspected in the lives of 90 percent of the patients with developmental disorders, 78 percent of patients with behaviour disorders, 67 percent of the patients with psychosis, and 37 percent of patients with affective disorders.

In the early 1990s, a large-scale study was undertaken in the United States based on a nationally representative sample of child abuse reports and designed specifically to overcome some of the methodological weaknesses of small-scale studies. This study (Crosse, Kaye & Ratnofsky, 1993) confirmed that a much higher proportion of abused children had disabilities than would be expected based on their proportion in the general population. It appeared to show an incidence of disability 70 percent higher among abused children than among the general population. It also found that

14.1 percent of all abused children (slightly more than one in seven) had identified disabilities while pointing out that this was likely a low estimate since children living in foster care, group homes, and other such settings were largely excluded from the sample. While this study may have seemed to provide the definitive answer to the problem, closer examination results in puzzling findings and methodological concerns. For example, intellectual disabilities, the category of childhood disability that had been most frequently linked to child abuse in the past, was not significantly more frequent among children who had been abused than other children. Perhaps even more surprisingly, specific learning disabilities were significantly less frequent among abused children than other children, giving the impression that learning disabilities acted somehow as a protective factor or that abuse somehow cured or prevented learning disabilities. A closer examination of the study, however, also reveals a major weakness of the design. Rather than including a control group of children who were not abused in the study, comparison figures were taken from a separate and independent epidemiological study of childhood disabilities conducted by the US Department of Education. The two studies used different categories of disability and, more importantly, had very different age ranges. The Department of Education study was restricted to children ages six to seventeen, while the sample of abused children included ages zero to seventeen. Forty percent of the abused children were younger than the youngest child in the comparison group, and many disabilities, including intellectual disabilities, do not occur equally frequently among preschool- and school-aged children. To make a comparison between the two studies, one would have to assume that math and reading difficulties are diagnosed at the same rate among six-month-old babies as among grade-school children.

Sullivan and Knutson (2000) overcame this problem using a different approach. Starting with a cohort of about fifty thousand children in Omaha, they checked all the children's school records to see if they had been diagnosed as having disabilities. They also checked all their names with child protection, police, and foster care review records to determine if they had any substantiated history of abuse. This study had greater internal validity because the same diagnostic criteria and age range were applied to all the children. Because it was not a nationally representative sample and did not include all young children, its generalization beyond Omaha or to younger children remains questionable. Nevertheless, it provides the most scientific estimate currently available. Sullivan and Knutson concluded that children with disabilities were 3.4 times as likely as other children to have a history of maltreatment, and that 31 percent of all children with disabilities had a substantiated history of maltreatment. Children with disabilities were

3.9 times as likely to be emotionally abused, 3.8 times as likely to be physically abused, 3.8 times as likely to be neglected, and 3.1 times as likely to be sexually abused as children without disabilities.

As pointed out by Kendall-Tackett (2002), this study not only provides the clearest and most convincing evidence to date, it is also the first to present a large enough sample of abused children with disabilities to meaningfully consider the relationship between child maltreatment and various specific disabilities. Children with diagnosed disabilities made up 22 percent of all abused children, but some specific disabilities were more strongly associated with abuse than others. More than half of children with behaviour disorders, more than a third of children with speech and language disorders, and more than a quarter of children with mental retardation and of children with health impairments had confirmed histories of maltreatment. Children with behaviour disorders, for example, were about seven times as likely to be neglected, emotionally abused, and physically abused as children without disabilities and were 5.5 times as likely to be sexually abused as children without disabilities. Children with communication disorders experienced five times the rate of physical abuse and neglect and three times the rate of sexual abuse as children without disabilities. Children with intellectual disabilities were between 3.8 and 4.0 times as likely to experience all four categories of maltreatment as children without disabilities, and children with mobility or orthopedic disabilities had approximately twice the rate as children without disabilities for all four categories of maltreatment.

Similar results have been found in the United Kingdom. Spencer and colleagues (2005) studied 119,729 children born between 1983 and 2001 in West Sussex. They compared the rates of maltreatment among children with various categories of disability (e.g., physical disability, intellectual disability, autism) with the rates among children without disabilities. Compared to children without diagnosed disabilities, children with conduct disorders were 11.5 times more likely to be registered as abused, those with moderate or severe intellectual disabilities were 6.5 times more likely to be registered as abused, and those with non-conduct psychological disorders were 5.24 times more likely to be registered as abused.

Prior to 2001, no large-scale, controlled study of child abuse in Canada reported on the relative frequency of children with disabilities among maltreated children. Nevertheless, based on the American and international evidence, along with consistent Canadian data from small-scale research that suggested similar findings, Canadian researchers had concluded that Canadian children with disabilities faced a similar situation (Sobsey & Varnhagen, 1989; Frazee & Seeley, 2000). In 2001 with the release of the landmark *Canadian Incidence Study of Reported Child Abuse and Neglect*, a nationally representative sample of Canadian child abuse reports was collected and analyzed in a manner that addressed disability. Although disability status was not the major focus of the study, the study did collect and present useful information on a number of "physical, emotional, and cognitive...child functioning issues" (Trocmé et al., 2001, p. 70) that were roughly equivalent to the disability categories in the Sullivan and Knutson (2000) study. The results also appear similar with the study reporting 26 percent of all abused children exhibited one or more child functioning issues. Because the categories and criteria were different, it would be hard to say that this was higher or lower than the 22 percent with disabilities reported by Sullivan and Knutson (2000), but it appears to be generally consistent with it. Like the first American study, the lack of incidence data from a non-abused, age-controlled comparison group makes it difficult to determine exactly how much more frequent these findings were among abused children than the general population. While the rate of 26 percent in the Canadian study is marginally higher than the 22 percent in the Omaha study and much higher then the 14 percent found in the Crosse, Kaye, and Ratnofsky (1993) study, potential differences in Canadian and American methods make it difficult to draw comparisons between countries. However, using the Canadian PALS data for children described earlier in the chapter, the expected number of children in the population with disabilities is not more than 7 percent, making the 26 percent estimate among abused children more than 3.7 times the expected number. This might be considered a working estimate of relative prevalence of disabilities among abused children, but it must be considered a very tentative estimate because of the lack of common criteria and procedures for identification. Taken together with the data from the American studies, it is reasonable to consider the relative prevalence of disabilities among abused children somewhere between two and four times that in the general population.

From the research to date, we can conclude several things with great certainty. First, there is a significant association between childhood disability and child maltreatment. Children with disabilities are probably two to four times more common among maltreated children than among other children. Second, large numbers (about one-fourth) of abused children have diagnosed disabilities. Clearly, services for abused children must be equipped to meet the needs of children with disabilities before we can consider them equipped to meet the needs of abused children as a whole. Third, the association between child maltreatment and childhood disability affects all categories of maltreatment. Fourth, some specific disabilities are associated with higher rates of abuse, and the strongest association exists between behaviour disorders and abuse.

Nevertheless, many important aspects of the connection between abuse and disability remain unknown. Several very different mechanisms could link violence to disability. The results of the studies previously discussed could be explained by violence causing disabilities. No doubt, this mechanism plays some role, but to explain the large numbers of abused children with disabilities found in this study, the role of violence in causing disability would have to be radically revised upward from current estimates (Sobsey, 2002). Second, the results of these studies could be explained by disability or the social perception of disability leading to victimization. One particular form of this mechanism, the dependency-stress hypothesis, was commonly assumed to explain this relationship for many years. This hypothesis assumes that children with disabilities require more care, and the demand of this care results in increased stress on caregivers. Abuse by caregivers is then assumed to be a response to stress. This hypothesis may seem easier to apply to emotional or physical abuse than to sexual abuse. However, several studies designed to test this hypothesis failed to provide evidence to support the hypothesis (Sobsey, 2002). Nevertheless, there may be other mechanisms that increase risk for children with disabilities. These are discussed later in this chapter. A third link between child abuse and disability may be through mutual risk factors. For example, serious substance abuse problems in prospective parents increase the risk of a child being born with a disability and also increase the risk for family violence. Similarly, there is growing evidence that abuse of women during pregnancy increases the risk that the child will be born with a disability and also increases the risk for child abuse after the child is born. These and other shared risk factors may account for a significant portion of the association between disability and child abuse (Sobsey, 2002).

VIOLENCE AGAINST ADULTS WITH DISABILITIES

Until recently, scientific evidence connecting violence and disability for adults was much less complete. While there is still much work to be done, the last decade has greatly added to our scientific knowledge of violence against adults with disabilities. Rand and Harrell (2009) published data from the 2007 US National Crime Victimization Study. They concluded that in 2007, American adults (i.e., age twelve or older) experienced 716,320 non-fatal violent crimes, including 240,070 serious violent crimes (aggravated assaults, robberies, sexual assaults). Overall, people with disabilities experienced violence 1.5 times as frequently as people without disabilities, and individuals with disabilities were twice as likely to be sexually assaulted. Women with disabilities experienced violence more frequently than men. People with cognitive disabilities experienced more violence than people with other categories of disability, and people with multiple disabilities experienced the highest rate of victimization. Among crime victims with disabilities, 19 percent believed that they had been targeted for victimization because of their disability.

Perrault (2009) published a similar study based on data collected by Statistics Canada in 2004. This study compared rates of violent crimes against Canadian adults (fifteen years old or older) with activity limitations to the rates of those without activity limitations. He reported that the "rate of violent victimization, including sexual assault, robbery and physical assault, was 2 times higher for persons with activity limitations than for persons without limitations" (p. 6), and "the personal victimization rate, which is violent victimization or theft of personal property, for persons with mental or behavioural disorder, was 4 times higher than the rate for persons with no mental disorder" (p. 6). Most (65 percent) of the crimes against people with disabilities were committed by people they knew.

These large-scale epidemiological studies provide powerful evidence of elevated rates of violence against adults with disabilities, but large-scale epidemiological studies also tend to obscure important details. For example, they group a very wide variety of categories and severities of disabilities together, which tends to obscure the relationship between more specific groups and the risk for violence.

Wilson and Brewer (1992) provide a good example of a study of violence against adults with intellectual disabilities. They adapted a crime victimization study used with other Australian adults and used it with a group of adults with intellectual developmental disabilities. They found that violent crime occurred 4.2 times as frequently for adults with disabilities than for other adults. For women with intellectual disabilities, sexual assaults occurred 10.7 times as frequently as for other Australian women.

Hassouneh-Phillips and Curry (2002) critiqued research conducted from 1990 to 2001 that focused primarily on women with disabilities who had experienced abuse. Five of the studies utilized quantitative methodology and five used qualitative methods. Like women in the general population, many women with disabilities experience violence with intimate partners (Hassouneh-Phillips & Curry, 2002). Hassouneh-Phillips and Curry concluded that the findings from these ten studies converged on several points. Common patterns of abuse found among people who had been abused in the general population were identified in many of the studies as being prevalent among women with disabilities. Most assailants of women with disabilities were men, and most assaults happened in the woman's home or place of residence. In addition, many of the studies found that women with disabilities were also at risk of abuse from other contacts, such as family members, friends, personal care workers, transportation providers, and health care employees. Some of the findings suggested that women with disabilities had to contend with some additional difficulties that women without disabilities are not likely to encounter. Besides being at risk for the physical, emotional, and sexual abuse experienced by women without disabilities, women with disabilities were also subjected to some forms of abuse specific to their disability. For example, abuse took the form of unwanted sexual comments from people who were assisting them during bathing or dressing, removal or destruction of an assistive device, or withholding or theft of essential medications (Hassouneh-Phillips & Curry, 2002). Women with disabilities indicated that their experience of the abuse was further complicated by disability-related challenges, such as lowered self-esteem, negative self-image, and societal attitudes that devalue women with disabilities.

Young, Nosek, Howland, Chanpong, and Rintala (1997) suggest that women with disabilities may be subjected to violence at rates similar to those experienced by other women, but they are at a greater risk of being abused for a longer period of time than women without disabilities. In many cases, this may be a result of a higher level of physical, social, and economic dependency than other women. For example, women with disabilities living with men without disabilities may be more likely to lose custody of their children in divorce or separation because they are viewed as less able to care for their children. As a result, women with disabilities may feel that it is better to tolerate mistreatment than to lose their children.

One study focused on the experiences that abused women with disabilities had as a result of their personal assistance services (PAS). PAS abuse is a form of violence unique to individuals with disabilities who require these services, and is probably best understood as a form of family violence because it typically takes place in the home and because of the intimate nature of the care typically provided. For many women, physical assistance or home care is essential to living in their own homes or apartments rather than nursing homes or other institutional care. The PAS can include one or more people who will help with daily tasks that the person would otherwise do herself if she did not have a disability (Powers, Curry, Oschwald & Maley, 2002). The PAS abuse that was reported by the women in this study included: "physical, sexual, verbal, and financial abuse, threat of physical abuse, neglect, withholding or destruction of equipment, inappropriate administration of medications, providing PAS while intoxicated, and inappropriate exertion of physical or verbal control" (Powers et al., 2002, p. 10). The results from this study challenged the belief that women with particular disabilities, such as cognitive disabilities, are more vulnerable and require a different set of PAS prevention strategies from women with other types of disabilities. Some of the barriers to abuse management identified by the women who experienced PAS abuse were: "low provider wages, don't know whom to call, shortage of qualified providers and lack of back-up providers; embarrassment, and fear of provider backlash" (Powers et al., 2002, p. 10). In short, a high level of dependency on care providers, combined with difficulty replacing care providers and fear that the replacements may be even more abusive, left many women feeling powerless to escape from caregiver abuse.

Curry, Hassouneh-Phillips, and Johnston-Silverberg (2001) report that 75 percent of the forty-seven women with disabilities whom they surveyed reported experiencing one or more types of abuse within the past year from someone they knew. Furthermore, the vast majority experienced two or more types, which included: (1) being yelled at over and over again (36 percent); (2) theft or financial abuse (30 percent); (3) feeling unsafe with someone (23 percent); (4) refusal to assist with an important physical need (19 percent); (5) damage or disabling of equipment (11 percent); (6) threats of or actual physical abuse (4 percent); (7) medication abuse, such as being overdosed with medication to induce sleep and reduce demands on the care provider or theft of needed medication (2 percent); and (8) sexual abuse (2 percent). Of particular concern is the fact that 71 percent of the women who indicated that they had been abused did not have a backup personal assistance provider.

While abuse of women with disabilities by caregivers has been given specific attention in research, PAS abuse is not unique to women. Ulicny, White, Bradford, and Mathews (1990) studied PAS abuse among ninety-one men and women using independent living centre attendant services programs. They reported that 40 percent of the respondents had experienced theft and 10 percent had experienced physical abuse from their caregivers. Men and women experienced similar rates of abuse.

Often people with disabilities have little control over who provides personal care. In many cases, PAS services are provided through agencies that hire and train staff. Unfortunately, agencies sometimes fail to exercise care in selecting and training staff. For example, the family of one quadriplegic man who went to one of the oldest and most trusted agencies to contract for PAS services, was surprised to find out the caregiver sent into their home was a six-time felon. Unfortunately, they did not find out until after the caregiver murdered the man he was to care for and another family member (Ellement, 1998). Equally disturbing, there is evidence that people with disabilities who have complained about PAS abuse have been branded as troublemakers and denied services by PAS agencies (Sobsey, 1994).

INTIMATE PARTNER VIOLENCE

Violence against intimate partners, including spouses, affects many Canadians. Prototypically, males commit violence against their female partners, but in some cases the gender roles are reversed and in others violence occurs in the context of a same-sex relationship. In addition, gender roles may play out somewhat differently when they interact with disability issues. Male violence has often been tied to male physical, social, and economic power along with the cultural attitudes and beliefs that perpetuate them. However, disability can shift the power differential in relationships. Because women are typically younger than their partners and because men are at greater risk of some kinds of disabilities, disability may play a major role in altering the stereotypical power relationship. In some cases, spouses who have been abused by their partners find themselves in a more dominant role as their aging partners become weakened or disabled.

Brownridge, Ristock, and Hiebert-Murphy (2008) used data from several Statistics Canada studies to determine the relative risk for intimate partner violence among Canadian women with disabilities compared to other Canadian women. They found that women with disabilities were twice as likely to experience some form of intimate partner violence and three times as likely to experience the most severe forms of intimate partner violence. In addition, they found that partners of women with disabilities were more likely to exhibit patriarchal domination over their partners, which included jealousy and possessive behaviours. This behaviour pattern among the male partners was the factor that appeared to best explain the elevated rates of abuse.

Casteel, Martin, Smith, Gurka, and Kupper (2008) conducted a national retrospective longitudinal study of over six thousand non-institutionalized women in the United States and found that women with severe disability were four times more likely to experience sexual assault than women without disabilities. A study conducted by Alriksson-Schmidt, Armour, and Thibadeau (2010) found that adolescent girls in the United States were at increased risk of experiencing sexual violence if they had a long-term health problem or a physical disability. Barrett, O'Day, Roche, and Carlson (2009) explored the relationship among disability, intimate partner violence, health status, and access to care. In their study, 33.2 percent of women with disabilities reported having experienced intimate partner violence compared to 21.2 percent of women without disabilities. Women with disabilities who experienced intimate partner violence were 35 percent less likely to report good to excellent health, compared to women with disabilities who had not experienced intimate partner violence, and 58 percent more likely to indicate having unmet health care needs due to their cost.

It is important to remember studies that compare reported rates of inter-personal violence can reflect relative risk accurately only if the reporting rates are similar in both groups of women. There is some reason to suspect that women with disabilities who experience intimate partner violence may be less likely to report their abuse than women without disabilities. If this hypothesis is correct, the actual relative risk for women with disabilities experiencing violence would be higher than the relative risk of reporting violence.

MECHANISMS

We can be certain that some part of the association between violence and disability is due to each of three potential linking mechanisms: (1) violence causes disabilities; (2) the presence of a disability acts directly or indirectly to increase risk for victimization; and (3) other factors (e.g., poverty, oppression, substance abuse, isolation) increase the risk for both disability and victimization. There are specific cases in which each of these mechanisms of association can be identified, but the relative contribution of each mechanism remains unknown.

Currently, the ecological or multi-factorial model is frequently used as an aid to understanding the ways in which disability may lead to increased risk for violence or abuse. In a thorough review of this model, Petersilia (2001) points out that it is the most comprehensive model available and appears to be useful, but that many of the mechanisms incorporated in the model remain untested. Embry (2000) conducted some research, however, that provides a global test with the model and generally found results consist-ent with the model.

This multi-factorial model is based largely on Belsky's (1980) ecological model of child maltreatment with some additional elements integrated into the original model and modifications that make it applicable to adults as well as children. Violence and abuse are seen as occurring in the context of interactions between individuals who are characterized by power differen-tials. Impairments can contribute to power inequities in several ways. There may be direct effects. Many people with disabilities are less able to physic-ally defend themselves, escape a dangerous situation, or recruit help. Some people with disabilities have more difficulty recognizing a situation in which they are at risk of being abused. Indirect effects, social consequences of dis-abilities, can contribute additional risk. People with disabilities are often isolated and taught to be compliant, which makes them more vulnerable. Power differentials, in turn are influenced by relationships, environments, and cultures and moderated by social control agencies (e.g., police, child welfare agencies, informal social networks) that potentially compensate for or exaggerate power imbalances. Cultural attitudes and beliefs are seen as having a strong role in influencing risk. For example, people with disabilities may be seen as having such poor quality of life that additional suffering is of lesser consequence.

SERVICES

Services for children and adults with disabilities that address issues of violence can be divided conceptually into prevention and intervention services. In practice, the boundaries between prevention and intervention services often blur. Prevention services typically attempt to teach or empower the individual to minimize risk, but can also be aimed toward systemic change. Intervention services may include counselling, health care, legal, and a variety of other services. Traditionally, many of the prevention and intervention programs that serve other children and adults have excluded or inappropriately served people with disabilities. In some cases, making services accessible to individuals with disabilities is as simple as changing a policy that excludes them. In other cases, programs must eliminate physical barriers or alter programs to make them accessible. Attempts to expand these services to better meet the needs of people with disabilities have sometimes focused on better inclusion of people with disabilities within generic services and sometimes developed special, parallel services for individuals with disabilities. Both of these approaches have strengths and weaknesses, but inclusive services that can meet everyone's needs are ideal. More interorganizational staff training among interpersonal violence service providers and organizations providing services to people with disabilities would likely help facilitate more inclusive and enhanced intervention and prevention services for people with disabilities (Lund, 2011).

Individual and group counselling has been used effectively with a wide range of people with significant language impairments, who were previously considered to be unable to benefit from this type of intervention (e.g., Razza, Tomasulo & Sobsey, 2011). Face-to-face behavioural, cognitive, and less verbal interventions have been found to be effective for some people with intellectual disabilities (Lund, 2011). There is some indication that computer-assisted programs can be effective for screening and educational purposes among people with disabilities, especially if they have experienced abuse (Oshwald, Renker, Hughes, Arthur, Powers & Curry, 2009; Robinson-Whelen, Hughes, Powers, Oschwald, Renker, Swank & Curry, 2010), with the exception of deaf or hard-of-hearing women who did not express a preference for interacting with a computer-assisted program (Oshwald, Renker, Hughes, Arthur, Powers & Curry, 2009).

The historical isolation of people with disabilities from the mainstream and the frequent occurrence of violence in segregated services suggest that environmental factors associated with separate services are likely to per-petuate risk for abuse and violence. Victims of violence with disabilities generally need the same support services as others, and have been found to use both formal and informal ways of seeking help (Barrett & St. Pierre, 2011). In many cases, violence is a pervasive theme in the lives of people with disabilities rather than a brief episode. Counselling often requires consideration of a much broader array of events and feelings than just the specific experiences of victimization that led to referral (Mansell & Sobsey, 2001).

ISSUES

There are many specific issues associated with violence against people with disabilities. For example, institutional abuse has been widely discussed, and because people with disabilities are much more likely to live in institutional settings, institutional violence is particularly relevant to them. A discussion of two distinctive and less often examined issues—disability paraphilias and mercy killings—follows.

Disability Paraphilias

One unusual issue in the discussion of sexual violence against women with disabilities is related to various disabilities as sexual fetishes. Although this issue has received the most attention with regard to men attracted to women who have one or more limb amputated, it can also apply to other forms of disabilities. Acrotomophilia—sexual attraction to amputees—is surprisingly common. It has been the focus of at least two regularly pub-lished "men's magazines" and numerous websites for "devotees" (the term commonly used for men who are attracted to amputees). Other disability paraphilias focus on women or, less commonly, men with leg braces or other orthotic devices. Elman (1997) is among those who see this kind of fetishizing disability as a particularly brutal form of objectification that puts women with disabilities at particular risk for violence and abuse.

Perhaps unexpectedly, some of the strongest defence for devotees comes from women who are amputees. In fact, at least several of the magazines, pay-per-view websites, and other major outlets for amputee photos and related materials are run by women with disabilities (Kafer, 2000; Waxman-Fiduccia, 1999). Some of these women suggest that women with disabilities are commonly desexualized by society and that sexualizing disability is a refreshing change. Others point out that few potential sex partners are neu-tral about amputation or other disabilities, so it is better to have a partner who finds one's disability attractive than one who may be repulsed by it. Kim Barreda (2003) points out that because a man is initially attracted to women with a particular eye or hair colour or some other physical attribute, we do not automatically assume this to be a mental illness or that this precludes the development of a healthy relationship. As an amputee woman, Barreda suggests that good, caring, and empowering relationships can develop between amputee women and men who are attracted to them. She also recognizes, however, that some devotees are dangerous stalkers who violate women's privacy and never see a human being beyond the single trait that initially attracts them.

Filicides and Mercy Killings

Mercy killings of spouses and children and other filicides of children with disabilities are particularly troubling issues. The killing of spouses and children is often portrayed as acts of empowerment, free will, and compassion, but often troubling questions remain regarding other interpretations.

Canetto and Hollenshead (2000) analyzed patterns in mercy killings. Most cases involved older women with varying degrees of disability who were killed by their husbands. Methods varied, but the most frequent method was shooting. The degree of illness or disability varied from none to very severe. A ten-year project by the US Federal Bureau of Investigation's National Center for the Analysis of Violent Crime developed a classification of homicide based on analysis of cases and includes the category "mercy-homicides." They conclude that "most often, the real motivation for mercy killing has little to do with the offenders' feelings of compassion or pity for the victim. The sense of power and control that the offender derives from killing is usually the real motive" (Douglass, Burgess, Burgess & Ressler, 1992, p. 111). Often illness or disability raises or exacerbates control issues in the lives of families. A sense of inadequacy arises from the inability to cure a condition or to stem its progress. Uncertainty about when death will occur or the rate of debilitation also threatens family members' sense of being in control. In some cases, frustration arises from the inability to control pain. The spouse or parent, who views his or her role as protector, may be particularly troubled by the sense that life is slipping beyond control. An illusion of reasserting control may be created by mercy killing. In some cases, other factors may enter into the equation. Family members who exercised high levels of control over their wives or children may resent the control of physicians, which often emerges during major health challenges. Some may see the family wealth being depleted by a lingering condition and feel that the depletion would be halted by a quicker death. Others may already be planning a new family or other life changes after an anticipated death that is repeatedly delayed.

In their classic book on euthanasia, *The right to die*, husband and wife authors Derek Humphrey and Ann Wickett (1990) also acknowledge that one of the most frequent forms of mercy killing is husbands killing their wives. Among the examples they discuss is the case of Cynthia Koestler, who was "fifty-five and in good health," but who apparently committed suicide along with her husband Arthur Koestler, who was seventy-seven and had Parkinson's disease and leukemia. In what Humphrey and Wickett refer to as a footnote to her husband's suicide note, Cynthia reported that she felt she "cannot live without Arthur" (p. 143). In a bizarre parallel, the previous day, she had also euthanized their pet dog, David, who also in good health, but presumed it would be better for him to die rather than live without his master. Like the Indian custom of suttee, in which the wife is burned on the husband's funeral pyre, the occasional cases of euthanasia described by Humphrey and Wickett in which women die simply because their husbands choose to do so raise serious issues of male domination and questions of voluntary choice. A study of 225 murder-suicides among older husband–wife dyads (Solari, 2007) found that popular media often report murder suicides among older couples as mercy killings, but concluded that "Rather than a consensual suicide pact or a hopeless situation of mercy killing, the evidence suggested a dominant and controlling perpetrator made the uni-lateral decision without the consent (or knowledge) of the victim" (p. 449).

Humphrey and Wickett (1990) pointed out that psychiatrists blame such suicides of wives who want to die with their husbands on "male dominance of the weaker partner" (p. 142) and that in this specific case "such a strong personality as Koestler's must have been an overpowering influence" (p. 144). They also indicate that feminists were "quick to say it was a part of patriarchal bias in our culture" (p. 144). However, Humphrey and Wickett suggest, "every-one who knew them well could see the inevitable logic of her act" (p. 144).

Ironically, Wickett had married co-author Humphrey after he had assisted his first wife in committing suicide. Later, after Wickett was also diagnosed with cancer, Humphrey walked out on the marriage three weeks after Wickett's lumpectomy. She and Humphrey divorced, and she claimed that he was pressuring her to commit suicide (Fadiman, 1994). Wickett, who had been an eloquent advocate for assisted suicide and euthanasia, clearly had changed sides, allying herself with anti-euthanasia advocate Rita Marker before her death. Although she had successful surgery for her cancer, Wickett did die as a result of suicide, blaming Humphrey for driving her to it and claiming he had murdered his first wife rather than assisting her suicide. Humphrey dismissed her claims as the result of mental health problems and anger because he left her after she was diagnosed with cancer (Fadiman, 1994; Grogan, 2000).

Similar issues arose in the case of Terri Schindler Schiavo. After Terri entered a coma in 1990, her husband was awarded $300,000 and another $700,000 was awarded for her care in a medical malpractice case. Since Terri was no longer able to speak for herself, her husband was empowered to make decisions for her. In 1998, he petitioned the court to have her feeding tube removed so that his wife would die. Terri's husband said that she had no chance of recovery, was in an unresponsive "vegetative" state, and previously told him that she would want to die if such a situation ever arose. Her parents argued that Terri was responsive at times, that some experts did not believe she was in a persistent vegetative state, and that as a Catholic, their daughter would never choose to bring about her own death. They pointed out that Michael Schiavo had a conflict of interest because of financial considerations and his stated plans to marry his current love interest whom he lived with and who was mother to his two children (Terri's right to die, 2003). The legal battles extended until 2005, when Terri Schiavo's feeding tube was removed by court order and she died.

Questions of empowerment or domination arise in Canadian cases. Sue Rodriguez became a symbol of an empowered woman making her own choices when she gave her powerful videotaped testimony before the Canadian Parliament, asking for medical assistance with suicide because she had amyotrophic lateral sclerosis, a degenerative neurological disease: "I want to ask you gentlemen, if I cannot give consent to my own death, then whose body is this? Who owns my life?" Nevertheless, when Rodriguez's biographer asked her if her death wish was due to her disability or due to her feelings of being rejected by her husband and possibly her son, Rodriguez could only indicate that she did not know (Birnie & Rodriguez, 1994). It is even more disturbing that after statements from a letter attributed to Rodriguez denouncing the Amyotrophic Lateral Sclerosis Society of BC for opposing her campaign to allow assisted suicide, signed with the large shaky initials SR, were published in the *Vancouver Sun* (Mullens, 1993a), Rodriguez angrily denied any knowledge of the letter, and John Hofsess, head of the Right to Die Society, "acknowledged that he had penned the Rodriguez signature" (Mullens, 1993b, p. A3).

In defending his actions, Hofsess and the Right to Die Society indicated that they had acted in good faith because they routinely spoke for her and did not need her approval to issue statements in her name. In fact, according to them, Hofsess authored all of Rodriguez's public statements, including the script for her famous words before Parliament. In addition, they argued that Rodriguez had promised "never to grant an interview with any journalist without his (Hofsess's) prior knowledge and approval" (Right to Die Society, 1995). Thus, in his view, Hofsess had not done anything wrong in speaking for Rodriguez or signing her initials to the note, and it was Rodriguez who violated her contract by attempting to speak for herself (Right to Die Society, 1995). They suggest that it was difficult to enforce their contract with Rodriguez because "Who could publicly complain against or sue a terminally ill person for breach of contract?" (Right to Die Society, 1995).

Eventually, Rodriguez broke away from the Right to Die Society, but, according to Hofsess and the Right to Die Society, this was not an act of independence. In an open letter to the CBS television show *60 Minutes*, complaining that the show had unfairly portrayed Hofsess as manipulating Rodriguez, they suggest that she had come under the powerful influence of another man, MP Svend Robinson, who had his own agenda for Rodriguez. They suggest Robinson became "the central architect of her plans...her closest friend...[and eventually he] virtually became her surrogate husband" (Right to Die Society, 1995). According to Hofsess and the Right to Die Society, Robinson influenced Rodriguez to break off her relationship with the Right to Die Society because "with Hofsess in the picture, Svend Robinson could not gain control of the scenario as he ultimately wanted it to unfold" (Right to Die Society, 1995).

There is no doubt that Sue Rodriguez thought of ending her life before she met either Hofsess or Robinson. That never changed. Although Rodriguez broke off her relationship with Hofsess and the Right to Die Society, she was unwavering in her commitment to bring about her own death. Nevertheless, her confusion about whether it was her disability or marital difficulties that drove this wish was disturbing. Her close relationship with two powerful personalities who had pre-existing interests in advancing the cause of assisted suicide raises further questions.

The killing of children with disabilities is perhaps even more troubling. Canadian mothers and fathers have killed or attempted to kill children with disabilities with some regularity, while investigation of other suspicious deaths leaves unanswered questions about cases that go unidentified as homicides or unprosecuted.

In Canada, about 80 percent of murdered children under the age of fourteen are killed by one or both parents. Children with disabilities appear frequently among these children. In our review of thirty-six Canadian filicides and attempted filicides (excluding another eight cases in which parents also killed themselves) of children with developmental disabilities, only nine parents served time in jail. Of these parents, only one father received a life sentence without parole, and he killed two children, one without a disability. Of the remaining parents, only one received life without parole for ten years, and of the remaining seven, typical sentences ranged from one to four years. Some cases that did not lead to convictions were simply not prosecuted, although police recommended prosecution or inquests ruled the deaths as homicides. In most cases, parents who simply said that the stress of raising a child with a disability was too much for them were allowed to plead guilty to manslaughter and given conditional sentences or community service assignments. While raising a child with a disability can be stressful, there is no reason to believe that the stresses involved are more severe than those associated with poverty, single parenting, marital discord, social isolation, discrimination, or a number of other common situations that parents face. Why, as a society, are we more willing to excuse parents facing this particular kind of stress and not all the others?

TOWARD PREVENTION

Considering the large number and complex interaction of factors that contribute to violence against people with disabilities, it is necessary for prevention to address many different issues. One group of prevention strategies is aimed at the individuals at risk for victimization. Sex education and personal safety skill training are commonly presented as important parts of prevention (Sobsey, 1994). Training to improve decision-making skills (Khemka & Hickson, 2000) and intervention to enhance overall communication skills are also useful for some individuals. A review of the literature related to teaching abuse-prevention skills to people with intellectual disabilities found some progress has been made, although further development in this area is needed (Barger, Wacker, Macy & Parish, 2009; Doughty & Kane, 2010). Too much reliance on training the individual to be "violence resistant," while ignoring the powerful social realities that contribute to the vulnerability of people with disabilities, however, is unlikely to produce meaningful protection, may divert attention from more productive efforts, and validates the notion that the problem lies with the victim.

The second group of prevention strategies addresses the environmental and societal conditions that contribute to the vulnerability of people with disabilities. As long as most people with disabilities are impoverished, isolated, and marginalized, they are unlikely to avoid the high rates of violence and abuse that others in similar social circumstances experience. As long as people with disabilities are devalued and isolated, potential offenders will view them as ideal victims. Historically, inclusion has played a powerful role in controlling violence against people with disabilities. Although periodic exposés of institutional abuse have shocked the public for centuries, most of the violence associated with institutional care was hidden from society, and occasional revelations of horrors seemed too distant for practical responses (Helander, 2004). For example, when actress Frances Farmer's autobiography, *Will there really be a morning?* was published in 1972, alleging horrific abuses she experienced in a Washington mental hospital, including being forced to eat feces and repeatedly being held down by orderlies while she was raped by dozens of soldiers from a neighbouring military base, there was great public interest. A decade later, the book was made into a popular movie with graphic portrayals of her abuse, Jessica Lange was nominated for an Academy Award for her portrayal of Farmer, and there was more discussion of the validity of Farmer's allegations. While the public read, watched, and generally accepted the violence as real, there was no public interest generated to address violence in institutions.

As more people with disabilities live in the community and fewer are hidden in institutions, institutional violence threatens smaller numbers of people with disabilities. Violence against people with disabilities in the community appears to be a smaller but more visible problem. With less isolation, people with disabilities become less vulnerable, though inclusion has been far from a total solution to violence for two reasons. While community living is an important first step in normalizing risks, many people with disabilities remain isolated in the community. Simply moving them from large rural institutions to socially isolated group homes in the middle of towns or cities does little to reduce risks. In one study of paid caregivers of adults with developmental disabilities, 14 percent of caregivers admitted that they engaged in violence toward residents in their care, and 35 percent admitted to witnessing or being implicated in violence (Strand, Benzein & Saveman, 2004). The prevention strategies identified by some women with disabilities who had reported having been abused during PAS included "choosing one's provider, having access to abuse resources (e.g., crisis line, support groups, emergency transportation), and having information and support necessary for clarifying and managing the PAS relationship" (Powers et al., 2002, p. 10). They also wanted easier accessibility to women's shelters, collaboration with shelters to provide PAS and to replace medications and aids left behind in the home they were fleeing from, and collaboration with law enforcement for removal of the abuser from the home (Powers et al., 2002). Researchers recommend that universal screening for abuse among women with disabilities should be conducted at the time of contact with rehabilitation centres, health care facilities, and other related professional settings (Hassouneh-Phillips & Curry, 2002), and that assessment should be conducted of men in treatment who have perpetrated violence against women with disabilities to identify their attitudes about disabilities and how these attitudes may have contributed to their violent behaviour (Brownridge et al., 2008).

To more meaningfully reduce risk, people with disabilities must become part of the social fabric. In addition, while inclusion can help normalize risk for people with disabilities, normalization at best only reduces excessive risk to the rate experienced by other members of the community. As this goal is approached, reducing risks for people with disabilities typically means reducing the risks for all people and the community as a whole. This suggests that much of our effort toward protecting people with disabilities from violence should be directed toward efforts that reduce risks for all members of society. For example, seeking to reduce patriarchal dominance, and jealous and possessive behaviours, which one study (Brownridge et al., 2008) found prevalent among male abusers of women with disabilities, would likely benefit society as a whole. When we think of violence against people with disabilities as a violence problem and not a disability problem, it seems obvious that including people with disabilities in our general violence prevention strategies makes sense. This suggests that we need to look for more ways to include people with disabilities in generic prevention programs and focus less on special programs. An added benefit is that people with disabilities can be useful assets to their community crime prevention programs. For example, depending on staffing needs, group homes may be the only houses in a community where people are home during the day or awake late at night. As such, they can be important assets to neighbourhood watch programs. Thus, people with disabilities can become active partners and assets to their community's violence prevention initiatives.

Some organizations of Canadians with disabilities have engaged in research, advocacy, law reform, and empowerment of people with disabilities to effect both individual and social change that will help to reduce the risk of violence for people with disabilities. DisAbled Women's Network (DAWN) Canada has maintained a focus on this issue since its inception in 1985. Other organizations, such as People First and the Council of Canadians with Disabilities, have also made efforts to address the issue of violence against people with disabilities. The roles of individuals with disabilities and the organizations that represent them are essential to prevention efforts since empowerment of people with disabilities is critical to mitigating the power imbalances that often contribute to violence.

CONCLUSION
This chapter discusses violence against people with disabilities. Child abuse studies clearly show a strong association between disability status and child maltreatment. Evidence from studies of adults is much less complete, but the available evidence suggests a similar association between violence and disability for adults. It is important to remember that this association can result from several different mechanisms, and there is little research to tell us how much to attribute to violence as a cause of disability, disability as a

risk factor for violence, and other linking mechanisms. The effects of violence on children and adults with disabilities are similar to the effects on other victims of violence. Programs for prevention and intervention need to provide appropriate services to people with disabilities.

REFERENCES

Alriksson-Schmidt, A., Armour, B., & Thibadeau, J. (2010). Are adolescent girls with a physical disability at increased risk for sexual violence? *Journal of School Health, 80*(7), 361–67.

Barger, E., Wacker, J., Macy, R., & Parish, S. (2009). Sexual assault prevention for women with intellectual disabilities: A critical review of the evidence. *Intellectual and Developmental Disabilities, 47*(4), 249–62.

Barreda, K. (2003, January/February). Devotee phenomenon. *Active Living Magazine, 11*, 16–19.

Barrett, K., O'Day, B., Roche, A., & Carlson, B.L. (2009). Intimate partner violence, health status, and health care access among women with disabilities. *Women's Health Issues, 19*, 94–100.

Barrett, B., & St. Pierre, M. (2011). Variations in women's help seeking in response to intimate partner violence: Findings from a Canadian population-based study. *Violence against Women, 17*(1), 47–70.

Belsky, J. (1980). Child maltreatment: An ecological integration. *American Psychologist, 35*(4), 320–35.

Birnie, L.H., & Rodriguez, S. (1994). *Uncommon will: The death and life of Sue Rodriguez.* Toronto: Macmillan.

Bonnier, C., et al. (2003). Neuroimaging of intraparenchymal lesions predicts outcome in shaken baby syndrome. *Pediatrics, 112*(4), 808–14.

Borthwick-Duffy, S.A., Widaman, K.F., Little, T.D., & Eyman, R.K. (1992). *Foster family care for persons with mental retardation.* Washington, DC: American Association on Mental Retardation.

Brownridge, D.A., Ristock, J., & Hiebert-Murphy, D. (2008). The high risk of IPV against Canadian women with disabilities. *Medical Science Monitor, 14*(5), PH27–32.

Canetto, S.S., & Hollenshead, J.D. (2000). Older women and mercy killing. *Omega, 42*(1), 83–89.

Casteel, C., Martin, S.L., Smith, J.B., Gurka, K.K., & Kupper, L.L. (2008). National study of physical and sexual assault among women with disabilities. *Injury Prevention, 14*, 87–90.

Children from Far North need short-term care in city. (1994, March 14). *Gazette,* p. C7.

Cook, F., Ciorciari, J., Varker, T., & Devilly, G.J. (2009). Changes in long-term neural connectivity following psychological trauma. *Clinical Neurophysiology, 120*(2), 309–14.

Crealock, C., & Bachor, D.G. (1995). *Instructional strategies for students with special needs* (2nd ed.). Scarborough, ON: Allyn and Bacon.

Crosse, S.B., Kaye, E., & Ratnofsky, A.C. (1993). *A report on the maltreatment of children with disabilities.* Contract no: 105-89-1630. Washington, DC: National Center on Child Abuse and Neglect.

Curry, M.A., Hassouneh-Phillips, D., Johnston-Silverberg, A. (2001). Abuse of women with disabilities: An ecological model and review. *Violence against Women, 7*(1), 60–79.

Davies, R.K. (1978–79). Incest: Some neuropsychiatric findings. *International Journal of Psychiatry in Medicine, 9*(2), 117–21.

De Kleijn-De Vrankrijker, M.W. (2003). The long way from the International Classification of Impairments, Disabilities, and Handicaps (ICIDH) to the International Classification of Functioning, Disability, and Health (ICF). *Disability & Rehabilitation, 25*, 561–64.

Doughty, A., & Kane, L. (2010). Teaching abuse-protection skills to people with intellectual disabilities: A review of the literature. *Research in Developmental Disabilities, 31*, 331–37.

Douglass, J.E., Burgess, A.W., Burgess, A.G., & Ressler, R.K. (1992). *Crime classification manual: A standard system for investigating and classifying violent crimes.* San Francisco: Jossey-Bass.

Ebeling, H., & Nurkkala, H. (2002). Children and adolescents with developmental disorders and violence. *International Journal of Circumpolar Health, 61*(Suppl. 2), 51–60.

Ellement, J. (1998, February 28). Family of slain patients settles. *Boston Globe*, p. B3.

Elman, R.A. (1997). Disability pornography: The fetishization of women's vulnerabilities. *Violence against Women, 3*(3), 257–70.

Elmer, E., & Gregg, G.S. (1967). Developmental characteristics of abused children. *Pediatrics, 40*(4, Part I), 596–602.

Embry, R.A. (2000). An examination of risk factors for the maltreatment of deaf children. *Dissertation Abstracts International, 67*(07), 2919A (umi no. 9979609).

Fadiman, A. (1994, April 1). Death news: requiem for the Hemlock Quarterly. *Harper's Magazine, 288*, 74.

Farmer, F. (1972). *Will there really be a morning? An autobiography.* New York: Putnam.

Farris-Manning, C., & Zandstra, M. (2003). *Children in care in Canada.* Child Welfare League of Canada. Retrieved from: http://www.nationalchildrensalliance.com/nca/pubs/2003/Children_in_Care_March_2003.pdf.

Fish, M.C. (2000). Children with special needs in nontraditional families. In M.J. Fine & R.L. Simpson (Eds.), *Collaboration with parents and families of children and youth with exceptionalities* (2nd ed., pp. 49–68). Austin: PRO-ED.

Foucault, M. (1965). *Madness and civilization.* R. Howard (Trans.). New York: Random House. (Original work published 1961.)

Frazee, C., & Seeley, P. (2000). *Abuse of children with disabilities: Information from the National Clearinghouse on Family Violence.* Ottawa: National Clearinghouse on Family Violence.

Government of Alberta: Human Services, Children, and Youth. (2008). *Statis-tics.* Retrieved from: http://www.child.alberta.ca/home/584.cfm.

Grogan, D. (2000, March 12). The founder of a "right to die" group walks out on his wife when cancer threatens her life. *People Weekly, 33*(10), 76.

Hassouneh-Phillips, D., & Curry, M.A. (2002). Abuse of women with disabili-ties: State of the science. *Rehabilitation Counseling Bulletin, 45,* 96–104.

Helander, E. (2004). *The world of the defenseless.* Iaşi, Romania: Asrom.

Humphrey, D., & Wickett, A. (1990). *The right to die: An historical and legal per-spective on euthanasia.* Eugene, OR: Hemlock Society.

Kafer, A. (2000, June–July). Women: Amputated desire, resistant desire: Female amputees in the devotee community. *Disability World.* Retrieved from: http://www.disabilityworld.org/June-July2000/Women/SDS.htm.

Kendall-Tackett, K. (2002). Abuse and neglect of children with disabilities. *Rehabilitation Psychology News, 29,* 12–13.

Khemka, I., & Hickson, L. (2000). Decision-making by adults with mental retar-dation in simulated situations of abuse. *Mental Retardation, 38*(1), 15–26.

Krauss, C. (2003, June 15). Gay Canadians' quest for marriage seems near vic-tory. *New York Times,* p. 3.

Larson, S.A., Lakin, K.C., Anderson, L., Kwak, N., Lee, J.H., & Anderson, D. (2001). Prevalence of mental retardation and developmental disabilities: Estimates from the 1994/1995 National Health Interview Survey Disability Supplements. *American Journal of Mental Retardation, 106,* 231–52.

Lund, E.M. (2011). Community-based services and interventions for adults with disabilities who have experienced interpersonal violence: A review of the lit-erature. *Trauma, Violence, & Abuse, 12*(4), 171–82.

Mansell, S., & Sobsey, R. (2001). *Counseling victims of sexual abuse with develop-mental disabilities.* Kingston, NY: NADD.

McDaniel, S.A., & Tepperman, L. (2004). *Close relations: An introduction to soci-ology of families* (2nd ed.). Toronto: Pearson Prentice-Hall.

Mullens, A. (1993a, January 29). Rodriguez says ALS duo adding to "misery." *Vancouver Sun,* p. A3.

Mullens, A. (1993b, January 30). Rodriguez angry over letter to Sun penned in her name. *Vancouver Sun,* p. A3.

Oschwald, M., Renker, P., Hughes, R.B., Arthur, A., Powers, L.E., & Curry, M.A. (2009). Development of an accessible audio computer-assisted self-interview (A-CASI) to screen for abuse and provide safety strategies for women with disabilities. *Journal of Interpersonal Violence, 24*(5), 795–818.

Perrault, S. (2009). *Criminal victimization and health: A profile of victimization among persons with activity limitations or other health problems.* Ottawa: Sta-tistics Canada, Canadian Centre for Justice Statistics.

Petersilia, J. (2001). Crime victims with developmental disabilities—A review essay. *Criminal Justice and Behaviour, 28*(6), 655–94.

Powers, L.E., Curry, M.A., Oschwald, M., & Maley, S. (2002). Barriers and strat-egies in addressing abuse: A survey of disabled women's experiences. *Journal of Rehabilitation, 68*(1), 4–13.

Rand, M.R., & Harrel, E. (2009). *National crime victimization survey: Crime against people with disabilities, 2007.* Washington, DC: US Department of Justice, Office of Justice Programs, Bureau of Justice Statistics.

Razza, N.J., Tomasulo, D.J., & Sobsey, D. (2011). Group psychotherapy for trauma-related disorders in people with intellectual disabilities. *Advances in Mental Health and Intellectual Disabilities, 5*(5), 40–45.

Right to Die Society. (1995, March 14). Whose life is it, anyway? [Open letter to CBS News.] Retrieved from: http://www.rights.org /60_min.html.

Robinson-Whelen, S., Hughes, R.B., Powers, L.E., Oschwald, M., Renker, P., Swank, P.R., & Curry, M.A. (2010). Efficacy of computerized abuse and safety assessment intervention for women with disabilities: A randomized controlled trial. *Rehabilitation Psychology, 55*(2), 97–107.

Saloviita, T. (2003, September). *Special education as an ideology: Constructions of domination in the professional language.* Paper presented at the seventh annual Research Conference of the Nordic Network of Disability Research, Jyväskylä, Finland.

Secretariat to the Federal/Provincial/Territorial Working Group on Child and Family Services Information. (2002, March). *Child welfare in Canada 2000. The role of provincial and territorial authorities in the provision of child protection services: CFS Information Child and Family Services.* Ottawa: Human Resources Development Canada.

Sleeter, C.E. (1986). Learning disabilities: The social construction of special education category. *Exceptional Children, 53*, 46–54.

Sobsey, R. (1994). *Violence and abuse in the lives of people with disabilities: The end of silent acceptance?* Baltimore: Paul H. Brookes.

Sobsey, R. (2002). Exceptionality, education, and maltreatment, *Exceptionality, 10*(1), 29–48.

Sobsey, R., & Varnhagen, C. (1989). Sexual abuse of people with disabilities. In M. Csapo & L. Gougen (Eds.), *Special education across Canada: Challenges for the 90's* (pp. 199–218). Vancouver: Centre for Human Development & Research.

Solari, S. (2007). Patterns of intimate partner homicide suicide in later life: Strategies for prevention. *Clinical Interventions in Aging, 2*(3), 441–52.

Spencer, N., Devereux, E., Wallace, A., Sundrum, R., Shenoy, M., Bacchus, C., et al. (2005). Disabling conditions and registration for child abuse and neglect: A population-based study. *Pediatrics, 116*(3), 609–13.

Statistics Canada. (2003). *Education, employment, and income of adults with and without disabilities—Tables: Participation and limitation survey, 2001.* Catalogue no. 89-587-xe. Ottawa: Statistics Canada.

Statistics Canada. (2007a). *Participation and activity limitation survey 2006: Labour force experience of people with disabilities in Canada.* Retrieved from: http://www.statcan.gc.ca/pub/89-628-x/89-628-x2008007-eng.pdf.

Statistics Canada. (2007b, December 3). Participation and activity limitation survey: A profile of disability in Canada. *The Daily*, pp. 2–5.

Strand, M., Benzein, E., & Saveman, B.I. (2004). Violence in the care of adult persons with intellectual disabilities. *Journal of Clinical Nursing, 13*(4), 506–14.

Sullivan, P.M., & Knutson, J.F. (2000). Maltreatment and disabilities: A population-based epidemiological study. *Child Abuse & Neglect, 24*(10), 1257–73.

Terri's right to die. (2003, October 19). *Toronto Star*, p. A14.

Trocmé, N., Maclaurin, B., Fallon, B., Daciuk, J., Billingsley, D., Tourigny, M., et al. (2001). *Canadian incidence study of reported child abuse*. Ottawa: Health Canada.

Ulicny, G.R., White, G.W., Bradford, B., & Mathews, R.M. (1990). Consumer exploitation by attendants: How often does it happen and can anything be done about it? *Rehabilitation Counseling Bulletin, 33*, 240–46.

Waxman-Fiduccia, B.F. (1999). Sexual imagery of physically disabled women: Erotic? Perverse? Sexist? *Sexuality and Disability, 17*, 280–82.

Wilson, C., & Brewer, N. (1992). The incidence of criminal victimization of individuals with an intellectual disability. *Australian Psychologist, 27*(2), 114–17.

Winzer, M. (1993). *Children with exceptionalities in Canadian classrooms*. Scarborough, ON: Prentice-Hall Allyn and Bacon.

Young, M.E., Nosek, M.A., Howland, C.A., Chanpong, G., & Rintala, D.H. (1997). Prevalence of abuse of women with physical disabilities. *Archives of Physical Medicine and Rehabilitation Supplement, 78*(12) (Suppl. 5), S34–S38.

8

DYNAMICS OF PARTNER ABUSE IN SEXUAL AND GENDER MINORITY COMMUNITIES

J. ROY GILLIS AND SHAINDL DIAMOND

INTRODUCTION

Partner abuse in lesbian, gay, bisexual, transgender, and queer (LGBTQ) relationships is a relatively new area of focus in theory and research about intimate partner violence, an area traditionally dominated by discussion about male violence against women. The topic is also a relatively new concern for members of LGBTQ communities whose energies have been focused on the legalization of sex acts, civil rights for LGBTQ peoples, and, since the 1980s, the HIV epidemic. It has only been since the early 1980s that lesbians have begun to write and speak about partner abuse (Lobel, 1986; Ristock, 2002), then gay men began discussing the topic (Island & Letellier, 1991) and, more recently, theorizing and research on partner abuse have begun in the trans communities (Brown, 2011; Goldberg & White, 2011) and about two-spirited individuals (Taylor & Ristock, 2011). This chapter provides an overview of some of the theoretical, research, and clinical service issues in the area of partner abuse in LGBTQ relationships focusing on the Canadian context and research wherever possible. It begins with an examination of the current research, which estimates the prevalence and correlates of partner abuse in LGBTQ relationships. Feminist theories of intimate partner abuse are then examined in the context of partner abuse in LGBTQ relationships, and difficulties with the essentialization of gender inherent in some of these analyses are highlighted (Davis & Glass, 2011). Factors specific to LGBTQ relationships—such as homophobia, heterosexism, outing, and HIV status—are also discussed, and their unique contribution to the problem is acknowledged. The emerging recognition that *intersectionality*, the complex social contexts created by the intersections of various systems of power, is an important framework to consider when analyzing same-sex partner abuse (Hiebert-Murphy, Ristock & Brownridge, 2011) is discussed. Within this context, a discussion of some of the cultural influences on abuse and coercive behaviour in LGBTQ relationships occurs. Considerations of this intersectionality, in turn, lead us to a deeper exploration and recognition of the social contexts within which same-sex partner violence occurs. Quotes from LGBTQ survivors of abuse are included to illustrate various points throughout the chapter. The chapter concludes with a discussion of the problematic police response to same-sex partner abuse, the lack of appropriate services and "safe spaces" for LGBTQ survivors of partner abuse, and recent developments in clinical services for same-sex batterers.

A COMMUNITY IN DENIAL?

Since the basis for understanding any concept is sharing the same definition, the working definition of partner abuse for this chapter is one proposed by the Violence in Same-Sex Relationship Information Project (1997): "Abuse in relationships is any behaviour or pattern of behaviour used to coerce, dominate, or isolate the other partner. It is the use of any form of power that is imposed by one partner over the other to maintain control within the relationship" (p. 2). The existence of a current definition of partner abuse, however, does not negate the fact that public recognition of partner abuse in LGBTQ relationships has occurred relatively recently (Lobel, 1986; Renzetti, 1988). As Island and Letellier (1991) state in their groundbreaking book on gay and bisexual male partner abuse, "gay [and bisexual] men's domestic violence is not a new problem, just a newly recognized problem" (p. 1). In part, this delay in the acknowledgement of LGBTQ partner abuse is a consequence of the heterosexism inherent in woman abuse and domestic violence theory and practice (Brown, 2008; Davis & Glass, 2011; Girshick, 2002; Letellier, 1994; Ristock, 2001; Russo, 1999). This heterosexism is apparent in the use of such terms as "domestic violence," "wife abuse," or "spousal abuse," which tend to define the abuse as occurring only in the context of marriage to the exclusion of other types of relationships and living arrangements. Thus, the term "partner abuse" is used in this chapter.

Heterosexist definitions in and of themselves, however, do not explain the lack of services or the invisibility of partner abuse in LGBTQ relationships in books on domestic violence. It is also a function of LGBTQ communities that are reluctant to acknowledge the existence of partner abuse in their midst (Brown, 2008; Russo, 1999) and respond with the appropriate educational programs and clinical services. Some leaders of queer communities have expressed private discomfort and concern at the thought of LGBTQ individuals being responsible for violence committed against members of their own communities. They prefer to conceptualize violence solely as something done to our communities by unfriendly external sources, such as perpetrators of hate crimes. This "hiding of our dirty linen" may foster a more favourable and sympathetic media portrayal of our communities, but it denies the real suffering of individuals abused by their partners (Island & Letellier, 1991). There is also a well-grounded fear that the public acknowledgement of partner abuse in LGBTQ relationships will lead to further pathologizing and stigmatizing of LGBTQ communities. Unfortunately, this fear of damage is being realized, as some authors are already using research about partner abuse to pathologize LGBTQ people (see, for example, Cameron, 2003).

In spite of these obstacles, a considerable number of journal articles and books have begun to address some of the theoretical and clinical issues related to partner abuse in LGBTQ relationships (Burke & Follingstad, 1999; Island & Letellier, 1991; Leventhal & Lundy, 1999; Renzetti, 1992, 1996; Ristock, 2001, 2003). While the role of many early articles and books in the field was to alert readers to the existence of same-sex partner abuse (Island & Letellier, 1991; Lobel, 1986; Renzetti, 1988), later authors have gone on to challenge the existing paradigms surrounding interventions for intimate abuse (Brown, 2008; Davis & Glass, 2011; Girshick, 2002; Island & Letellier, 1991; McClennen, 2005; Merrill, 1996; Ristock, 2001). Some authors have attempted to develop models for treating partner abuse (Leventhal & Lundy, 1999; Mendoza & Dolan-Soto, 2011; Ristock, 2003), and current research gives us better empirical evidence concerning the prevalence and correlates of this problem (Burke, Jordan & Owen, 2002; Greenwood et al., 2002; McClennen, 2005; McClennen, Summers & Daley, 2002; Murray & Mobley, 2009; Stanley, Taylor, Bartholomew, Oram & Landolt, 1999). In fact, this emerging body of theory and research in the area of same-sex partner abuse is posing questions and developing new models of treatment delivery that challenge existing paradigms and orthodoxies in the larger field of partner abuse, hopefully contributing to breakthroughs in the field in general.

ESTIMATES OF PREVALENCE

Research and speculation on the prevalence of partner abuse in LGBTQ relationships has yielded widely varying estimates of prevalence for both gay men and lesbians (Murray & Mobley, 2009; Turell, 2000). There are many reasons for these divergent estimates and most are associated with a general lack of attention to rigorous experimental methodology (McClennen, 2005;

Murray & Mobley, 2009). Early research on prevalence, for example, used differing and non-standardized definitions of abuse, convenience samples that were not representative of the LGBTQ population, failed to specify the gender of the perpetrator, and relied on unreliable measures. Similar difficulties occur when researchers attempt to estimate the prevalence of partner abuse in heterosexual relationships (Intimate Partner Abuse and Relationship Violence Working Group, 2001). However, a recent methodological review of prevalence research on same-sex partner abuse suggests that the situation is improving (Murray & Mobley, 2009).

Turell (2000), using a sample of 499 gay, lesbian, bisexual, and transgendered individuals, found that approximately 32 percent of gay men and lesbians report physical violence in current or past relationships, and approximately 9 percent report physical violence in current relationships. Analysis of the US National Violence against Women Survey found that women in lesbian relationships experience lifetime prevalence rates of 35.4 percent for physical assault by intimates and 11.4 percent for sexual assault by intimates (Intimate Partner Abuse and Relationship Violence Working Group, 2001). The corresponding rates for men who live with men were 21.5 percent for physical assault and 0 percent for sexual assault (Intimate Partner Abuse and Relationship Violence Working Group, 2001). While reporting bias was a problem in many areas, the study authors were particularly dubious about the complete absence of sexual assault reported by men living with men. In another important investigation of prevalence, Greenwood et al. (2002), using a probability sample of 2,881 men who had sex with men, found a prevalence rate of 22 percent for physical abuse and 5 percent for sexual assault. Likewise, in a randomized telephone survey of gay and bisexual men in the West End of Vancouver, BC, Bartholomew, Regan, Oram, and White (2008) found that participants reported a lifetime prevalence of 44 percent for "ever having been physically abused by a partner." This same sample also reported a 38 percent lifetime prevalence for "ever physically abusing an intimate partner." In addition, nearly all participants reported that they had psychologically abused an intimate partner and had been psychologically abused by an intimate partner at some time in the past.

Overall, the research on prevalence has found inconsistent gender differences in same-sex partner abuse (Murray & Mobley, 2009). However, the findings also suggest that men living in intimate relationships with other men face a significantly increased risk of physical violence when compared to men living in intimate relationships with women (Murray & Mobley, 2009), while the rate for women living with women is probably lower (Murray & Mobley, 2009). Statistics indicating the prevalence of abuse experienced by trans people in the context of intimate relationships are not yet available, although the Intimate Partner Abuse and Relationship Violence Working Group (2001) and others (Brown, 2007) report evidence that it does occur. Even without precise estimates of what the actual prevalence rates of same-sex partner abuse is, the research to date indicates that the problem of abuse in LGBTQ communities is considerable (McClennen, 2005; Murray & Mobley, 2009).

FEMINIST THEORIES OF PARTNER ABUSE

Feminist theories of partner abuse have offered many important insights into the dynamics experienced in LGBTQ relationships as research has shown that there are many similar trends in how power is abused in hetero-sexual and LGBTQ relationships alike. For example, as found in abuse in heterosexual relationships, the achievement of control and domination over one's partner is often the goal in such LGBTQ relationships (McClennen, 2005). Similarly, it is difficult for many abuse survivors to leave a relation-ship. Survivors are made to feel responsible for their own abuse and may even assist in covering up the abusive behaviour. Although survivors in both heterosexual and LGBTQ relationships often hope that their partner's abuse will stop, the abuse regularly recurs and the severity often increases (Pitt & Dolan-Soto, 2001; Walker, 1979). Clinicians working with LGBTQ partner abuse survivors (Peterman & Dixon, 2003) have also noted the existence of the well-known "cycle of violence" phenomenon first described by Walker (1979) for partner abuse survivors in heterosexual relationships. Furthermore, physical injury, emotional impairment, and psychological distress are common to those abused in heterosexual and LGBTQ rela-tionships. This suggests a great deal of similarity between the two groups that might be used by some to justify treating the groups in the same way. However, the contextual factors that distinguish the experience of partner abuse in LGBTQ relations from abuse in heterosexual relationships can alter the nature and the expression of the abuse experienced. Therefore, it is important to make note of these differences and pay attention to the specificities affecting LGBTQ relationships, which, in turn, pose challenges to some feminist theorizing about violence.

    With their focus on heterosexual relationships, some feminist theories have conceptualized abuse as something that a man does to a woman. Bat-tering is due to differences in perceived power, physical size, and economic resources that flow from gender and gender roles. Within this frame-work, men abusing men in intimate relationships is conceivable, but of minor importance. The possibility of a woman abusing another woman in an intimate relationship is inconceivable because gender differences are absent (Langhinrichsen-Rohling, 2005). Thus, "women-only spaces," such as shelters, are considered "safe spaces" for all women, including lesbians. From this standpoint, the acknowledgement of women abusing other women is threatening, as this could lend credibility to critics who suggest that women are as likely to batter as men.

> When I was first coming out people were constructing safe space as women space where [it turned out] there were more perpetrators in the room than there were in any other kind of group I went to. So, it's about the way that safe space had been constructed by the fact that women do feel comfortable with other women 'cause we've been socialized differently for the most part than men. And there's a shared something there. You need to trust somebody...it completely cracks apart the belief in lesbian utopia. (Girshick, 2002, p. 49)

Some feminist theorists have conceptualized partner abuse as violence perpetrated by heterosexual men against women within the context of patriarchy or as "the manifestation and institutionalization of male dominance over women and children in the family, and the extension of male dominance over women in society in general" (Lerner, 1986, p. 239). This conceptualization of male violence against women offers an important and useful analysis as patriarchy plays a key role in perpetuating social, economic, political, and cultural inequalities between men and women in our society. However, the conceptual tools used by some feminists for detecting and analyzing gender-based hierarchies are not always sufficient for understanding hierarchies based on sexuality, race, class, and other social location factors. In response, some theorists have pointed out the limitations of such feminist approaches. For example, Girshick (2002) has stated that: "this system of male dominance is built on aspects that have little relevance to the lives of non-heterosexuals—the institution of marriage, women as the property of men, women's economic dependence on men, and the home as a private sphere" (p. 16). Other theorists have expanded on existing feminist theories by introducing analyses that consider how intersecting structures of domination enter into the institution of family and shape power dynamics in intimate relationships (Martindale, 1995; McClennen, 2005). These authors are building on the work of racialized women who first articulated that their experiences could not be captured by theories of gender or racial oppression alone, but rather needed to be understood as the result of interacting systems of oppression (capitalism, patriarchy, and white supremacy, for example) (Krane, Oxman-Martinez & Ducey, 2000; Davis & Glass, 2011). Likewise, the authors of this chapter propose that any theories developed about partner abuse in LGBTQ relationships need to address power dynamics defined by many intersecting forms of systemic oppression, including sexism, heterosexism, transphobia, racism, classism, and ableism.

Partner abuse in lesbian relationships poses another more obvious challenge to some feminist theorizing about lesbianism. Historically, lesbianism has been romanticized in some parts of the feminist movement as a woman-identified bond that resists the powerful patriarchal institution of heterosexuality, while normalizing a specific lesbian feminist identity that fits well into the already existing concept of the universal woman (Martindale, 1995; Rich, 1980). For example, Rich's "Compulsory heterosexuality and lesbian existence" (1980) is a classic feminist text that emphasizes commonalities between lesbian and heterosexual women, using radical feminist theory to stress gender as the primary form of social difference. Rich paints an image of the lesbian as an ideal woman who is not bound to sex or historical impurities—she is, rather, a representation of a resistance to gender oppression in a form that is respectable and seductive to the mainstream heterosexual audience (Martindale, 1995). Rich's lesbian is easily co-opted into the mainstream feminist movement as she is stripped of all other oppressions and identities—forms other than those traditionally accepted by liberal feminists. Within this idealized, egalitarian construct of lesbianism, there is no place for the lesbian abuser or any other woman who does not fit the mould of a good feminist, and other factors shaped by power dynamics are ignored.

Trans women also pose a challenge to parts of the feminist movement that rely on essentialist notions of womanhood (Brown, 2007; Goldberg & White, 2011). Such tensions among feminists have been particularly apparent in the last decade regarding issues of women-only spaces secured for survivors of abuse. While most feminists challenge biology as the basis for gender roles, some others argue that trans women cannot be women because they have been socialized as men (Darke & Cope, 2002). Organizing around the concept of identity politics, these feminists claim that trans women simply cannot understand women's experiences of gender oppression and, therefore, should be barred from women-only spaces. This simplistic analysis assumes that all women experience the same oppressed position in society, with sexism as the primary cause, and ignores all other power imbalances stemming from oppressive forces other than patriarchy. Many feminists and trans advocates have countered these arguments by pointing out that women do not represent a universal group who share the same experience, but rather a group that is oppressed under patriarchy in many different ways that are shaped by processes of gender, race, disability, sexuality, and other factors (Goldberg & White, 2011). The transphobic attitudes of some women should not be used to justify the exclusion of trans women from women's spaces or services. In recent years, due to the hard work of trans activists and many feminists, organizations offering services to women survivors of violence have begun to open their doors to trans people (Brown, 2007; Darke & Cope, 2002, Goldberg & White, 2011).

In developing theories of intimate partner abuse, it is important to acknowledge the misleading portrayal of women's common experience of oppression and look to other theorists who are developing much-needed theories and movements intended to address how intersecting systems of oppression play out in the lives of differently situated people. Our theorizing of violence must evolve and move away from conceptualizations of universal experiences of being a woman or a man. Such universal understandings of sex are built on false and essentialist assumptions that ignore the diversity among people based on gender, sexuality, class, race, and ability, and fail to account for the power dynamics among different marginalized groups (Bent-Goodley, 2005; Davis & Glass, 2011; Hiebert-Murphy et al., 2011; Sokoloff & Dupont, 2005). For example, Collins (2000) used the term "matrix of domination" to describe how systems of power and oppression that are inseparable work together to create diverse effects in the lives of differently situated people. Her writing has emphasized the interconnected oppressions of race, ethnicity, gender, class, ability, and sexual orientation, and has highlighted how women can be marginalized for many aspects of their identity (Collins, 2000). Following this lead, we must take up the challenge of theorizing the impact of other power differentials to develop models of partner abuse and methods of service delivery that address the specific needs of those who suffer compound forms of marginalization (Bent-Goodley, 2005; Sokoloff & Dupont, 2005).

> They *talk* about challenging their classism...And they *talk* about challenging sexism, misogyny, and lesbophobia...But they don't *do* it at the personal level. Despite that they say that "the personal is political"...they've actually separated their personal and political lives. And they don't do their personal work. (Davis & Glass, 2011, p. 29)

THE IMPACT OF HOMOPHOBIA, HETEROSEXISM, AND OTHER OPPRESSIONS

Voices within LGBTQ communities are challenging the gender-focused lens traditionally used to view intimate partner violence and are striving to create a broader vision of how power differentials can manifest in intimate relationships (Davis & Glass, 2011; Letellier, 1994; Ristock, 2001, 2003). No longer do we insist that the abusive lesbian is taking on the "butch" role in the relationship or that the abused partner is the traditional feminine partner. While some of the tools that abusers use against their partners to maintain control—physical, sexual, and emotional abuse, intimidation, threats—are common to both heterosexual and LGBTQ relationships, the specific oppressions that people experience based on sexuality, gender, race, class, and other factors influence how perpetrators of abuse take advantage of the victims' specific vulnerabilities (Allen & Leventhal, 1999). In particular, recent research on same-sex partner abuse has focused on the concept of minority stress identified by Meyer (1995) as the combined effects of internalized homophobia, perceived stigma, and discrimination on the well-being of LGBTQ individuals. Examining samples of gays, lesbians, and bisexual men, several researchers have shown associations between the perpetration of same-sex partner abuse in men and measures of minority stress (Bartholomew et al., 2008, Mendoza, 2011), as well as for women (Carvalho, Lewis, Derlega, Winstead & Viggiano, 2011).

Looking at these minority stress factors at a societal rather than an individual level, it is important to recognize how cultural heterosexism and homophobia inevitably influence LGBTQ people and their relationships. Heterosexism is defined as "an ideological system that denies, denigrates, and stigmatizes any non-heterosexual form of behaviour, identity, relationship, or community" (Herek, 1990, p. 89). As expressed as cultural heterosexism (Gillis, 1998; Herek, 1990), it permeates our laws, religions, media, literature, professions, education, language, services, and any other imaginable human institution to reinforce heteronormativity (Gillis, 1998). Similarly, transphobia, defined as "emotional disgust toward individuals who do not conform to society's gender expectations" (Hill & Willoughby, 2005, p. 533), affects many trans people in both blatant and subtle ways. Patriarchy, heterosexism, transphobia, and other forms of structural oppression reinforce oppressive gender role expectations that inhibit the societal recognition of partner abuse in LGBTQ relationships. According to the prescribed gender roles, men should be able to defend themselves against other men and women, and those who cannot or choose not to defend themselves are deemed "weak," "effeminate," or "less than a man." Women are denied the right to feel anger and are expected to internalize negativity rather than express it externally toward others. In this way, gay men are made to feel responsible for their own abuse, and women abusers are made invisible by these gender stereotypes.

> We don't talk about…[same-sex partner abuse]…as gay men and lesbians, perhaps out of fear that we'll be viewed as "wimps" for not being able to stand up for ourselves. (Kennedy, 1998)

Women don't have skills to deal with [violence].... We are not trained to. We are trained to be submissive. We're trained to be "pacifiers," and "pleasers." (Davis & Glass, 2011, p. 30)

Understandably, LGBTQ people are vulnerable to feelings of isolation when existing in heterosexist and homophobic contexts, especially when they are disconnected from the larger LGBTQ community. Some LGBTQ people lack support from their families of origin when family members are not prepared to accept an LGBTQ family member for familial, ethnic, or cultural norms and/or religious beliefs or negative stereotype. "I was in my early 20s and caught up in the excitement and wonder of 'coming out' as a lesbian.... At first the relationship was wonderful.... I did finally leave the day she almost killed me.... I tried to go to my relatives, but they told me, 'You make your bed, you lie in it'" (Leventhal & Lundy, 1999, pp. 3–5). Ristock (2003) describes in her research a desperation that manifests when an isolated individual finds community through an abusive partner. Many LGBTQ people, "in the absence of socially sanctioned supports for their relationships, lesbian, gay, and bisexual people create their own relationship models and support systems" (Division 44/Committee on Lesbian, Gay, Bisexual, and Transgender Concerns Guidelines Revision Task Force, 2011, para 7), and leaving an abusive partner can mean losing this critical support network (Ristock, 2003). In this way, the need to be part of a non-heterosexist discourse can increase one's vulnerability in abusive relationships. "It was my first experience with a woman; I didn't care which woman it was... I was too young and insecure about the whole relationship—gay relationships, whatever. Anybody could have walked all over me" (Ristock, 2003, p. 335). In order for LGBTQ people to develop empowered sexual and gender identities, they must critically examine and unlearn internalized heterosexist, homophobic, and sexist roles that reinforce hegemonic definitions of reality. Some theorists assert that same-sex violence stems from internalized and institutionalized misogyny, homophobia, and heterosexism as LGBTQ people also learn to use violence and hatred against those who do not fit the hegemonic ideal (Faulkner, 1998). "Fear and rage can be misdirected at partners who can come to represent the things we have learned to hate in ourselves and who may symbolize all that we have been taught to fear in our heterosexist and misogynist culture" (Canadian Panel on Violence against Women, 1993, p. 74). This is how the consideration of an intersectional analysis leads us to consider more complex models of partner abuse, a task that still requires more research and theory-building.

POWER AND CONTROL IN LESBIAN, GAY, TRANSGENDER, AND BISEXUAL RELATIONSHIPS

Perpetrators of intimate violence use certain tactics to achieve control over their partners, including physical, sexual, psychological, and emotional abuse. The Power and Control Wheel, developed by the Domestic Abuse Intervention Project in Duluth, Minnesota (Pence, 1993), is used by service providers to demonstrate the dynamics of power and control in abusive relationships. Dynamics specific to LGBTQ relationships have been added to the traditional Duluth Model Power and Control Wheel (Pence, 1993) to create the Gay, Lesbian, Bisexual, and Trans Power and Control Wheel (Texas Council on Family Violence, 2012) (see Figure 8.1). This instrument serves as a more useful tool for understanding and discussing partner abuse in LGBTQ relationships.

"Outing" represents one control strategy specific to LGBTQ abuse, as is reflected in the "homo/biphobia" and "transphobia" sections of the Power and Control Wheel (see Figure 8.1). For those who are "in the closet," the abuser can threaten to reveal the victim's sexual and/or gender identity as a means of control, thereby endangering the victim's relationships with family members, friends, co-workers, or employers (National Coalition of Anti-Violence Programs, 2004). Similarly, HIV status can be used as a basis of power and control and is included in Figure 8.1 under the category of HIV-Related Abuse. In cases where the victim is HIV-positive, the abuser may threaten to tell others about the partner's HIV status, withhold access to medications or medical care, limit the partner's contact with other individuals, foster economic dependency, or threaten violence in ways that might cause HIV-related complications. An abuser who is HIV-positive might infect or threaten to infect the victim or use guilt to force the partner to remain in the relationship.

> [My partner] told me that he was going to file criminal charges against me and that he was going to tell everyone I had given him HIV. Soon after, he called my sister and my brother and outed me as gay and HIV positive. He knows that I am not out at work and to my family. I continued receiving harassing phone calls from him and started receiving emails from the "Department of Health" which I suspect are really from my ex, who says that if I "stick" with him, he'll protect me from the health department. (National Coalition of Anti-Violence Programs, 2003, p. 18)

Survivors of violence might also fear that even if they reach out for help, they will not be taken seriously by the police, domestic violence services, or their

Table 8.1   Power and Control in Lesbian, Gay, Transgender, and Bisexual Relationships

Homo/Biphobia
A part of heterosexism. Using awareness of fear and hatred of lesbians, gay men, and bisexuals to convince partner of danger in reaching out to others. Controlling expression of sexual identity and connections to community. Outing sexual identity. Shaming. Questioning status as a "real" lesbian, gay man, bisexual.

Transphobia
Using fear and hatred of anyone who challenges traditional gender expression, and/or who is transsexual, to convince partner of danger in reaching out to others. Controlling expression of gender identity and connections to community. Outing gender identity. Shaming. Questioning validity of one's gender.

Psychological & Emotional Abuse
Criticizing constantly. Using verbal abuse, in-sults and ridicule. Undermining self-esteem. Trying to humiliate or degrade in private or public. Manipulating with lies and false promises. Denying partner's reality.

Threats
Making physical, emotional, economic or sexual threats. Threatening to harm family or friends. Threatening to make a report to city, state, or federal authorities that would jeopardize custody, economic situation, immigration or legal status. Threatening suicide.

Heterosexism
Perpetuating and utilizing invisibility of LGB relationships to define relationship norms. Using heterosexual roles to normalize abuse and shame partner for same sex and bisexual desires. Using cultural invisibility to isolate partner and reinforce control. Limiting connection to community.

Isolation
Restricting freedom. Controlling personal social contacts, access to information, and participation in groups or organizations. Limiting the who, what, where, and when of daily life. Restraining movement, locking partner in or out.

Intimidation
Creating fear by using looks, actions, gestures, and destroying personal items, mementos, or photos. Breaking windows or furniture. Throwing or smashing objects. Trashing clothes, hurting or killing pets.

Power & Control
in Lesbian, Gay, Transgender & Bisexual Relationships

Physical Abuse
Slapping, hitting, shoving, biting, choking, pushing, punching, beating, kicking, stabbing, shooting, or killing. Using weapons.

Entitlement
Treating partner as inferior; race, education, wealth, politics, class privilege or lack of, physical ability, and anti-Semitism. Demanding that needs always come first. Interfering with partner's job, personal needs, and family obligations.

Using Children
Threats or actions to take children away or have them removed. Using children to relay messages. Threats to or actual harm to children. Threats to, or revealing of, sexual or gender orientation to children or others to jeopardize parent–child relationships, custody or relationships with family, friends, school, or others.

HIV-Related Abuse
Threatening to reveal HIV status to others. Blaming partner for having HIV. Withholding medical or social services. Telling partner she or he is "dirty." Using illness to justify abuse status to others.

Sexual Abuse
Forcing sex. Forcing specific sex acts or sex with others. Physial assaults to "sexual" body areas. Refusing to practice safer sex. In S&M refusing to negotiate or not respecting contract/scene limits or safe words.

Economic Abuse
Controlling economic resources and how they are used. Stealing money, credit cards, or checks. Running up debt. Fostering total economic dependency. Using economic status to determine relationship roles/norms, including controlling purchase of clothes, food, etc.

Adapted from *Lesbian, gay, bisexual & transgender domestic violence in 2002: A report of the National Coalition of Anti-Violence Programs* (p. 59). New York: New York City Gay & Lesbian Anti-Violence Project (July 2003).

friends and family. Abusers often play on these fears by reiterating that no one will help LGBTQ victims, and the wider societal context of heterosexism and transphobia reinforces these messages (Allen & Leventhal, 1999; National Coalition of Anti-Violence Projects, 2003): "I was afraid I would be told I deserved it because of my lifestyle or that it [the violence] would be minimized. Being shut out of some people's lives due to my lifestyle made it even harder to know who would support me" (Girshick, 2002, p. 31). LGBTQ individuals experiencing partner abuse often have difficulty in recognizing that they are being abused. This is, in part, due to the abuser, who encourages the abused partner to believe that the abuse is justified because of the victim's own personal shortcomings (Mendoza & Dolan-Soto, 2011), and, in part, due to internalized homophobia and transphobia, which encourages LGBTQ individuals to believe that they have no right to expect better treatment in society (Mendoza, 2011). However, when these tactics are explained and identified and the underlying goals of maintaining power and control over the individual are also explained, individuals are more readily able to identify that they have been abused. Program coordinators of LGBTQ partner abuse survivor and perpetrator groups report that the Power and Control Wheel for Lesbian, Gay, Transgender, and Bisexual Relationships has been a useful tool for LGBTQ people to identify the forms of oppression and abuse they are experiencing or perpetrating in their relationships (Durish, 2011; Mendoza & Dolan-Soto, 2011).

POLICE RESPONSE AND COUNSELLING SERVICES FOR SURVIVORS AND PERPETRATORS

The first point of system contact for both survivors and perpetrators of partner abuse in LGBTQ relationships is often the police. Police officers are often perplexed when arriving at domestic violence situations involving two men or two women because the familiar and typical gender dynamic of the man abusing the woman is absent. Without this heteronormative context to apply their simple rubric, police officers are often at a loss to know which person to charge. Too often, as a result, the police response is to charge both partners or dismiss the abusive situation as a "fair fight" between two men or two women. In addition, police officers sometimes express blatant homophobia themselves or "act as its instruments in other contexts" (National Coalition of Anti-Violence Programs, 2003, p. 14). Understandably, many LGBTQ people are wary of seeking police intervention, fearing a biased response or violence "based in long histories of entrenched racism, sexism, homo- and transphobia" within the criminal justice system" (National Coalition of Anti-Violence Programs, 2003, p. 15). When police respond to same-sex partner abuse with these kinds of biases inherent in their actions, a process of secondary victimization occurs. The quote below describes one individual's experience of a police response to a call involving same-sex partner abuse: "Police were dispatched to our home at least half a dozen times either in response to my frantic 911 calls or the calls of concerned neighbours. Each time officers arrived they seemed to chalk it up to a couple of fags having it out and left without doing anything more than warning us to settle down" (Kennedy, 1998). Community police liaison committees have been formed in many Canadian and US cities in response, in part, to deal with concerns about how police have responded to calls involving same-sex partner abuse (see, for example, in Toronto: http://www.torontopolice.on.ca/communitymobilization/ccc.php and in Ottawa: http://glbt.ottawapolice.ca/viewFile.asp?content_id=353). While these developments promise hope for change, many members of the LGBTQ communities have a historic deep distrust for police based on their experiences of being singled out by the police for selective prosecution, experiences of criminal entrapment, homophobic comments and assaults, and a general perception that LGBTQ people cannot turn to the police when they have experienced a crime and expect to be treated the way heterosexual citizens would be (Bruner, 1981; Intimate Partner Abuse and Relationship Violence Working Group, 2001; Kuehnle & Sullivan, 2003). Education and monitoring of police response in this area clearly needs to continue.

Problems also exist with the availability and quality of counselling and victim support services available to survivors. Sometimes these programs can be based on problematic assumptions. Some counsellors working in the field of partner abuse in LGBTQ relationships continue to uncritically endorse several key assumptions stemming from the traditional feminist analysis of intimate violence. For example, many service providers believe that it is always possible to discern which partner is the perpetrator of the abuse and which partner is the abused (Leventhal & Lundy, 1999; Mendoza & Dolan-Soto, 2011; Pitt & Dolan-Soto, 2001) based on intense questioning and clinical intuition. A set of related assumptions is that mutual battering can never occur, and that perpetrators can never switch roles to become the abused in subsequent relationships (Fray-Witzer, 1999; Mendoza & Dolan-Soto, 2011; Peterman & Dixon, 2003). Although current theory and research are challenging some of these deeply held beliefs (Bartholomew et al., 2008; Carvalho et al., 2011; McClennen, 2005; Ristock, 2002; Stanley et al., 1999), these tenets continue to influence service delivery models.

[A shelter I worked at] was really invested in the whole analysis about the patriarchy, and really into "We're all women here, therefore we're all safe" routine. Lesbians are going to start a utopia because we're all women.... I think that their analysis of battering not only didn't include lesbian battering but made lesbian battering impossible. (Girshick, 2002, p. 149)

The inability of LGBTQ abuse survivors to access existing domestic violence services has been a constant complaint of counsellors in the area (Pitt & Dolan-Soto, 2001), and formal programs for LGBTQ survivors exist only in the major cities (National Coalition of Anti-Violence Programs, 2003; Ristock, 2002). Many agencies and programs offering services for partner abuse in LGBTQ relationships offer services only to survivors and not perpetrators (Ristock, 2002). Those with the economic resources often seek private counselling to avoid contending with heterosexist assumptions in existing services (Ristock, 2002). Personal safety is a paramount concern voiced by all survivors, but often nothing is done to assist them (Ristock, 2002). While "out" lesbians, bisexual, queer, or trans women may be welcome in some shelters for battered women, many more gain access to services by pretending to be heterosexual or cisgendered (Ristock, 2002). Many lesbian survivors report problems with mainstream agencies when service providers and other survivors fail to understand their desires and needs or respond in heterosexist ways (Girshick, 2002; Ristock, 2002).

I want... an agency... to be a lesbian group... probably... an s/m specific group, because my experience has been that people who don't participate or haven't participated really don't have an understanding of what's going on.... They tend to say things that they think are comforting but really you end up explaining your sexual desire, which doesn't really help. It's kind of [like] being in a heterosexual group and you end up explaining your lesbianism, which isn't really the issue... [this] complicates how you can process the actual act of violence or abuse. (Girshick, 2002, p. 154)

The situation is more desperate for gay and bisexual male survivors of partner abuse since they are excluded from women's shelters (Durish, 2011). This is also often the case for transgendered people, although over the past few years, many women's organizations are coming to realize the importance of developing trans-inclusive policies (Brown, 2007; Darke & Cope, 2002). Currently, there is no shelter devoted to LGBTQ abuse survivors in Canada: "I... discovered that no shelters were available to me. Because I was a gay male victim of domestic violence I was left to fend for myself.... So there I was: no shelter, no mental health support.... I was on my own at a point of extreme anxiety and crisis" (Levanthal & Lundy, 1999, p. 11).

Other services, such as phone counselling lines for domestic violence, often refuse to take calls from abused gay or bisexual men or relegate them to the lowest priority. When LGBTQ people do access crisis lines, phone workers often lack the training to understand and deal appropriately with the situation at hand. "The hot line worker didn't know how to react because it was a woman who attacked me.... She didn't seem to understand and she didn't seem concerned. It took so much for me to dial that phone number, and it just made me feel worse" (Girshick, 2002, p. 31). This is not to suggest that mainstream domestic violence services should bear all the responsibility for providing services to same-sex abuse survivors, nor should the already inadequate financial resources available to these programs be diverted to abuse programs for LGBTQ people (Renzetti, 1996). Ideally, LGBTQ communities could secure enough funding to develop services and education programs dealing with the specific needs of survivors and perpetrators of partner abuse (Durish, 2011; Mendoza & Dolan-Soto, 2011).

Some successful attempts at community-level education have already occurred (Durish, 2011; Violence in Same-Sex Relationship Information Project, 1997). At this time, however, the funding priorities of most governments create a situation in which LGBTQ people must rely, in part, on existing partner abuse services geared mainly toward heterosexual women. Despite these barriers, various LGBTQ community agencies and individuals have worked to create resources (see Appendix 1) and programs specific to partner abuse in LGBTQ relationships. Another example of a community agency-based educational and intervention program effort was the Gay Partner Abuse Project (GPAP) (http://www.gaypartnerabuseproject .org/), located in Toronto, Canada. Gathering funds from various community, private, and government sources, GPAP and the Coalition against Same-Sex Partner Abuse (CASPA) (http://www.familyservicetoronto.org/programs/ dks/casspa.pdf) were able to fund the distribution and publication of education pamphlets on partner abuse in LGBTQ relationships on an existing website of a community-based agency (see http://www. woman abuseprevention.com/html/same-sex_partner_abuse.html). This initiative was followed by a three-year educational and research project, the Same-Sex Partner Abuse Project (Durish, 2011), based out of the David Kelley Lesbian, Gay, Bisexual, Trans, Queer (LGBTQ) Counselling Program of the Family Service Association in Toronto (see http://www.familyservicetoronto.org/ programs/dks/abusebrochures.html). This project produced a series of educational brochures targeted at different groups within LGBTQ communities, as well as conducting some preliminary research about preparedness of community-based agencies to deal with same-sex partner abuse. These various community initiatives have come to an end after the initial periods of grant funding were completed.

In contrast, the treatment of batterers, typically funded by the court system, has survived and, to some extent, flourished. The Partner Assault Response (PAR) program of the David Kelley Lesbian, Gay, Bisexual, Trans, Queer (LGBTQ) Counselling Program in Toronto (Mendoza & Dolan-Soto, 2011), founded in 2001, is an excellent example of such a treatment program. With funding from the Ministry of the Attorney General of Ontario and following the best practice guidelines of the Woman Abuse Council of Toronto (http://www.womanabuse.ca), PAR hired three staff to run the program. They developed a sixteen-week-long group intervention program that combined male and female LGBTQ participants mandated for treatment for partner abuse by the court system. This program, derived largely from the Duluth Model (see http://www.theduluthmodel.org) (Pence, 1993), also includes elements of cognitive therapy and art therapy. The PAR project also found that the exclusive use of a gender-based lens did not serve their clients and programming needs well (Mendoza & Dolan-Soto, 2011), and have moved to a more intersectional approach where contexts such as race, class, disability, sexual orientation, and gender identity are more explicitly incorporated into the curriculum of the program. Mendoza and Dolan-Soto (2011) also provide some observations and recommendations worth reviewing for those interested in creating programming for the treatment of same-sex batterers.

FUTURE DIRECTIONS

Ending partner abuse in LGBTQ relationships and violent behaviour in general requires us to consider new analyses of the problem and shift some of our energies from victim and perpetrator services to a type of community education that results in attitude and behaviour change. In our culture, where movies glorify violence and leaders choose war over negotiation to solve global conflict, it is not surprising that individuals adopt similar tactics in their interpersonal relationships. We are all products of a society that is infused with sexist, racist, heterosexist, ableist, and classist values. The use of an intersectionality approach in examining such oppressions will assist in developing more complex theoretical models and will guide us in designing better intervention programs. We must reject coercion and violence as a means of solving problems and model egalitarian and peaceful models of conflict resolution in all our activities. Simultaneously, we must confront our oppressive attitudes and behaviours that legitimize the control and humiliation of others. Efforts at educating and changing the views of politicians, funding agencies, and the general public through media campaigns and lobbying represent a community-level response to partner abuse. The extent to which we are successful in this will determine, in part, how successful we will be in ending the problem of partner abuse in LGBTQ relationships. The goal of creating a less violent and coercive society is one we can all share.

REFERENCES

Allen, C., & Leventhal, B. (1999). History, culture, and identity: What makes GLBTQ battering different. In B. Leventhal & S.E. Lundy (Eds.), *Same-sex domestic violence: Strategies for change* (pp. 43–55). Thousand Oaks, CA: Sage.

Bartholomew, K., Regan, K.V., Oram, D., & White, M.A. (2008). Correlates of partner abuse in male same-sex relationships. *Violence and Victims, 23*, 344–60.

Bent-Goodley, T.B. (2005). Culture and domestic violence: Transforming knowledge development. *Journal of Interpersonal Violence, 20*, 195–203.

Brown, C. (2008). Gender-role implications of same-sex intimate partner abuse. *Journal of Family Violence, 23*, 457–62.

Brown, N. (2007). Stories from outside the frame: Intimate partner abuse in sexual-minority women's relationships with transsexual men. *Feminism & Psychology, 17*, 373–93.

Brown, N. (2011). Holding tensions of victimization and perpetration: Partner abuse in trans communities. In J.L. Ristock (Ed.), *Intimate partner violence in LGBTQ lives* (pp. 153–68). New York: Routledge.

Bruner, A. (1981). *Study of relations between the homosexual community and the police: Report to Mayor Arthur Eggleton and the Council of the City of Toronto.* Toronto: Author.

Burke, L.K., & Follingstad, D.R. (1999). Violence in lesbian and gay relationships: Theory, prevalence, and correlational factors. *Clinical Psychology Review, 19*, 487–512.

Burke, T.W, Jordan, M.L, & Owen, S.S. (2002). Cross-national comparison of gay and lesbian domestic violence. *Journal of Contemporary Criminal Justice, 18*, 231–57.

Cameron, P. (2003). Domestic violence among homosexual partners. *Psychological Reports, 93*, 410–16.

Canadian Panel on Violence against Women. (1993). *Changing the landscape: Ending violence—achieving equality.* Ottawa: Minister of Supply and Services Canada.

Carvalho, A.F., Lewis, R.J., Derlega, V.J., Winstead, B.A, & Viggiano, C. (2011). Internalized sexual minority stressors and same-sex intimate partner violence. *Journal of Family Violence, 26*, 501–9.

Collins, P.H. (2000). *Black feminist thought: Knowledge, consciousness, and the politics of empowerment.* New York: Routledge.

Darke, J., & Cope, A. (2002). *Trans inclusion policy manual for women's organizations.* Vancouver: Trans Alliance Society.

Davis, K., & Glass, N. (2011). Reframing the heteronormative constructions of lesbian partner violence: An Australian case study. In J.L. Ristock (Ed.), *Intimate partner violence in LGBTQ lives* (pp. 13–36). New York: Routledge.

Division 44/Committee on Lesbian, Gay, Bisexual, and Transgender Concerns Guidelines Revision Task Force. (2011). *Guidelines for psychological practice with lesbian, gay, and bisexual clients.* Retrieved from: http://www.apa.org/pi/lgbt/resources/guidelines.aspx?item=4.

Durish, P. (2011). Documenting the Same-Sex Abuse Project, Toronto, Canada. In J.L. Ristock (Ed.), *Intimate partner violence in LGBTQ lives* (pp. 232–57). New York: Routledge.

Faulkner, E. (1998). Woman-to-woman abuse: Analyzing extant accounts of lesbian battering. In E.D. Bonnycastle & G.S. Rigakos (Eds.), *Unsettling truths: Battered women, policy, politics, and contemporary research in Canada* (pp. 52–62). Vancouver: Collective Press.

Fray-Witzer, E. (1999). Twice abused: Same-sex domestic violence and the law. In B. Leventhal & S.E. Lundy (Eds.), *Same-sex domestic violence: Strategies for change* (pp. 19–42). Thousand Oaks, CA: Sage.

Gillis, J.R. (1998). Cultural heterosexism and the family. In A.R. D'Augelli & C.J. Patterson (Eds.), *Lesbian, gay, and bisexual identities in families: Psychological perspectives* (pp. 249–69). New York: Oxford University Press.

Girshick, L.B. (2002). *Woman-to-woman sexual violence: Does she call it rape?* Ann Arbor, MI: Northeastern University Press.

Goldberg, J.M., & White, C. (2011). Reflections on approaches to trans anti-violence education. In J.L. Ristock (Ed.), *Intimate partner violence in LGBTQ lives* (pp. 56–80). New York: Routledge.

Greenwood, G.L., Relf, M.V., Huang, B., Pollack, L.M., Canchola, J.A., & Catania, J.A. (2002). Battering victimization among a probability-based sample of men who have sex with men. *American Journal of Public Health, 92,* 1964–69.

Herek, G.M. (1990). The context of anti-gay violence: Notes on cultural and psychological heterosexism. *Journal of Interpersonal Violence, 5*(3), 316–33.

Hiebert-Murphy, D., Ristock, J.L., & Brownridge, D.A. (2011). The meaning of "risk" for intimate partner violence among women in same-sex relationships. In J.L. Ristock (Ed.), *Intimate partner violence in LGBTQ lives* (pp. 38–55). New York: Routledge.

Hill, D.B, & Willoughby, B.L.B. (2005). The development and validation of the genderism and transphobia scale. *Sex Roles, 53,* 531–44.

Intimate Partner Abuse and Relationship Violence Working Group. (2001). *Intimate partner abuse and relationship violence.* Retrieved March 27, 2012, from: http://www.apa.org/about/division/activities/partner-abuse.pdf.

Island, D., & Letellier, P. (1991). *Men who beat the men who love them.* New York: Harrington Park Press.

Kennedy, J. (1998). *My own story.* Retrieved March 27, 2012, from: http://www.gaypartnerabuseproject.org/.

Krane, J., & Oxman-Martinez, J., & Ducey, K. (2000). Violence against women and ethnoracial minority women: Examining assumptions about ethnicity and "race." *Canadian Ethnic Studies, 32,* 1–18.

Kuehnle, K., & Sullivan, A. (2003). Gay and lesbian victimization: Reporting factors in domestic violence and bias incidents. *Criminal Justice and Behavior, 30,* 85–96.

Langhinrichsen-Rohling, J. (2005). Top 10 greatest "hits": Important findings and future directions for intimate partner violence research. *Journal of Interpersonal Violence, 20*, 108–18.

Leifer, R. (1990). Introduction: The medical model as the ideology of the therapeutic state. *The Journal of Mind and Behaviour, 11*, 247–58.

Lerner, G. (1986). *The creation of patriarchy.* London: Oxford University Press.

Letellier, P. (1994). Gay and bisexual domestic violence victimization: Challenges to feminist theory and responses to violence. *Violence & Victims, 9*, 95–106.

Leventhal, B., & Lundy, S.E. (Eds.). (1999). *Same-sex domestic violence: Strategies for change.* Thousand Oaks, CA: Sage.

Lobel, K. (1986). *Naming the violence.* Seattle: Seal Press.

Martindale, K. (1995). What makes lesbianism thinkable? Theorizing lesbianism from Adrienne Rich to queer theory. In N. Mandell (Ed.), *Feminist issues: Race, class, and sexuality* (pp. 67–94). Scarborough: Prentice-Hall.

McClennen, J.C. (2005). Domestic violence between same-gender partners: Recent findings and future research. *Journal of Interpersonal Violence, 20*, 149–54.

McClennen, J.C., Summers, A.B., & Daley, J.G. (2002). The Lesbian Partner Abuse Scale. *Research on Social Work Practice, 12*, 277–92.

Mendoza, J. (2011). The impact of minority stress on gay male partner abuse. In J.L. Ristock (Ed.), *Intimate partner violence in LGBTQ lives* (pp. 169–81). New York: Routledge.

Mendoza, J., & Dolan-Soto, D.R. (2011). Running same-sex batterer groups: Critical reflections on the New York City Gay and Lesbian Anti-Violence Project and the Toronto David Kelley Services' Partner Assault Response Program. In J.L. Ristock (Ed.), *Intimate partner violence in LGBTQ lives* (pp. 274–300). New York: Routledge.

Merrill, G.S. (1996). Ruling the exceptions: Same-sex battering and domestic violence theory. In M.C. Renzetti & C.H. Miley (Eds.), *Violence in gay and lesbian domestic partnerships* (pp. 9–22). New York: Harrington Park Press/ Haworth Press.

Meyer, I.H. (1995). Minority stress and mental health in gay men. *Journal of Health and Social Behavior, 36*, 38–56.

Murray, C.E., & Mobley, A.E. (2009). Empirical research about same-sex partner violence: A methodological review. *Journal of Homosexuality, 56*, 361–86.

National Coalition of Anti-Violence Programs. (2004). Lesbian, gay, bisexual and transgender domestic violence, 2003 supplement: An update from the National Coalition of Anti-Violence Programs. Retrieved June 15, 2012, from: http://www.avp.org/publications/reports/2003NCAVPdvrpt.pdf.

New York City Gay & Lesbian Anti-Violence Project. (2003, July). *Lesbian, gay, bisexual & transgender domestic violence in 2002: A report of the National Coalition of Anti-violence Programs.* New York: Author.

Pence, E. (1993). *Education groups for men who batter: The Duluth model.* New York: Springer.

Peterman, L., & Dixon, C.G. (2003). Domestic violence between same-sex partners: Implications for counseling. *Journal of Counseling and Development, 81,* 40–47.

Pitt, E., & Dolan-Soto, D. (2001). Clinical considerations in working with victims of same-sex domestic violence. *Journal of the Gay and Lesbian Medical Association, 5,* 163–69.

Renzetti, C.M. (1988). Violence in lesbian relationships: A preliminary analysis of causal factors. *Journal of Interpersonal Violence, 3,* 381–99.

Renzetti, C.M. (1992). *Violent betrayal: Partner abuse in lesbian relationships.* Thousand Oaks, CA: Sage.

Renzetti, C.M. (1996). The poverty of services for battered lesbians. In C.M. Renzetti & C.H. Miley (Eds.), *Violence in gay and lesbian domestic partnerships* (pp. 61–68). New York: Harrington Park Press/Haworth Press.

Rich, A. (1980). Compulsory heterosexuality and lesbian existence. *Signs, 5,* 631–60.

Ristock, J.L. (2001). Decentering heterosexuality: Responses of feminist counsellor's to abuse in lesbian relationships. *Women & Therapy, 23,* 59–72.

Ristock, J.L. (2002). *No more secrets: Violence in lesbian relationships.* New York: Routledge.

Ristock, J.L. (2003). Exploring dynamics of abusive lesbian relationships: Preliminary analysis of a multi-site, qualitative study. *American Journal of Community Psychology, 31,* 329–41.

Russo, A. (1999). Lesbians organizing lesbians against battering. In B. Leventhal & S.E. Lundy (Eds.), *Same-sex domestic violence: Strategies for change* (pp. 83–96). Thousand Oaks, CA: Sage.

Sokoloff, N.J., & Dupont, I. (2005). Domestic violence at the intersections of race, class, and gender: Challenges and contributions to understanding violence against marginalized women in diverse communities. *Journal of Interpersonal Violence, 20,* 38–64.

Stanley, J.L., Taylor, T., Bartholomew, K., Oram, D., & Landolt, M. (1999, August). *An exploration of partner violence in male same-sex relationships.* Paper presented at the annual meeting of the American Psychological Association, Boston.

Taylor, C.G., & Ristock, J.L. (2011). "We are all treaty people": An anti-oppressive research ethics of solidarity with indigenous LGBTQ people living with partner violence. In J.L. Ristock (Ed.), *Intimate partner violence in LGBTQ lives* (pp. 301–20). New York: Routledge.

Texas Council on Family Violence. (2012). Retrieved from: http://www.tcfv.org.

Turell, S.C. (2000). A descriptive analysis of same-sex relationship violence for a diverse sample. *Journal of Family Violence, 15,* 281–93.

Violence in Same-Sex Relationship Information Project. (1997). *Abuse in same-sex relationships.* Retrieved from: http://www. womanabuseprevention.com/html/same-sex_partner_abuse.html.

Walker, L.E. (1979). *The battered woman.* New York: Harper & Row.

RESOURCES
Selected Canadian and US web-based resources for same-sex partner abuse:

Canadian Resources
Coalition against Same-Sex Partner Abuse
http://www.womanabuseprevention.com/html/same-sex_part ner_abuse.html

Education Wife Assault
http://www.womanabuseprevention.com/html/same-sex_partner _abuse.html

Family Service Toronto-David Kelley Services
http://www.familyservicetoronto.org/programs/dks/res_samesex.html

519 Church Street Community Center Anti-Violence Program
http://www.the519.org/public_html/programs/avp/index.shtml

Gay on Gay Violence
http://www.web.apc.org/~jharnick/violence.html

Gay Partner Abuse Project
http://www.gaypartnerabuseproject.org/

2 Spirited People of the 1st Nations
http://www.2spirits.com/

United States Resources
Community United against Violence
http://www.cuav.org/dv.htm

FORGE (For Ourselves: Reworking Gender Expression)
http://forge-forward.org/

Gay, Lesbian, Bisexual, and Transgender Domestic Violence
http://www.rainbowdomesticviolence.itgo.com/

Gay Men's Domestic Abuse Project
http://gmdvp.org/

The Network
http://www.thenetworklared.org/

The New York City Gay & Lesbian Anti-Violence Project
http://www.avp.org/

9

DOMESTIC VIOLENCE AND CHILD ABUSE ISSUES FOR IMMIGRANT AND REFUGEE FAMILIES

RAMONA ALAGGIA AND SARAH MAITER

INTRODUCTION

Immigrant families have been migrating to Canada in steadily increasing numbers over the past several decades. Changes in Canada's immigration policy over the last forty years, together with international events, have resulted in increased movement of people and a rise in Canada's immigrant population. The 2006 Census of Canada, for example, estimated that immigrants represented virtually one in five (19.8 percent) of the total population. Between 2001 and 2006, Canada's foreign-born population increased by 13.6 percent, representing two-thirds of the growth in population. The Canadian-born population grew by only 3.3 percent during the same period (Statistics Canada, 2006). This trend is expected to continue for at least the immediate future. The vast majority of newcomers to Canada settle in one of three large urban areas: Toronto (40.4 percent), Montreal (14.9 percent), and Vancouver (13.7 percent) (Chui, Tran & Meheux, 2007).

Extrapolating the numbers of immigrant and refugee women affected by domestic violence from these census data is difficult, however, because few efforts have focused on determining the prevalence of domestic violence in immigrant communities (McDonald, 1999). Partly, there is reluctance to track social problems in immigrant communities for fear of perpetuating negative stereotyping. As well, women in these communities may not speak either of Canada's official languages (English or French), making it difficult to collect survey information, or they may not be accessible through regular recruitment channels since they may not have access to a phone or make use of mainstream services used by women with longer histories in Canada.

These immigration trends and dynamics have implications for the helping professions. According to the 2001 census (Statistics Canada, 2001), the Canadian population born outside of Canada reflected over two hundred ethnicities, many of whom experience linguistic barriers daily since they often do not speak either of Canada's official languages proficiently or well enough to understand legal or technical language. It is important to bear in mind that it is mostly immigrant and refugee women who do not speak either of the official languages fluently and are clearly disadvantaged in dealing with French and English systems (Kamateros, 2004; MacLeod & Shin, 1994). Furthermore, of the 1.8 million immigrants who arrived during the 1990s, 17 percent were children aged between five and sixteen. Most of these immigrant children (69 percent) lived in Toronto, Vancouver, and Montreal. In fact, nearly one in five (17 percent) school-age children living in Toronto and Vancouver had immigrated within the past ten years, as did about 7 percent of Montreal's school-age children. In Toronto, one-half of the school-age children who came in the 1990s spoke a language other than English or French most often at home in 2001, compared with 61 percent in Vancouver, and 43 percent in Montreal (Statistics Canada, 2001). In addition, due to changes in Canadian immigration policies (Ralston, 1999), the largest numbers of immigrants are now from the Southeast Asian and South Asian regions. These statistics suggest that both adult services and child welfare systems are increasingly involved with families from diverse ethno-racial backgrounds, made up of many different cultural groups— many of whom are from visible minority groups—reflecting a wide range of beliefs and values, and for whom English or French may not be the primary language spoken by either the parents or children.

Given this diversity, we would like to note that we do not view the "immigrant experience" as a homogeneous phenomenon as if all immigrants are similar and have the same reactions and experiences within the Canadian system. Rather, we are identifying and conveying major trends and recurring themes, all of which need to be cautiously integrated into any understanding of professional work with immigrant clients while still respecting the uniqueness of each client's experience. We also make reference to newcomers as the people who are new to Canada (usually under three years) and in the process of seeking permanent citizenship status.

THE MIGRATION EXPERIENCE: FOR BETTER OR FOR WORSE?

Once they arrive in Canada, immigrants face a host of challenges related to the stress of acculturation, language acquisition, isolation, discrimination, financial hardship, and mourning the loss of their country. They also confront new and unfamiliar systems, beginning with a complex Canadian immigration system, but also including school systems, health care systems, and social services. Some immigrants suffer the additional stress of traumatic loss having left their country of origin during wartime or political upheaval. Regardless of their reasons for migrating, they bring with them deeply embedded cultural and familial values, religious beliefs, and societal expectations regarding sexual and gender roles acquired in their country of origin. All of these factors shape beliefs and attitudes regarding familial relations, including marital arrangements, assigned gender roles, child-rearing practices, and the role of extended family. When abuse or violence is a reality in the family life of immigrants, how it is understood and addressed is influenced by all of these factors. Seeking help and making use of Canadian social services can become yet another stress, presenting additional dilemmas to each woman (see Motoi in this volume for further discussion).

Feminist scholars and practitioners have recently focused on the role of culture in perpetuating beliefs regarding sex roles that contribute to men's gender oppression of women. Further, the social location of children, wherein the rights of children are marginalized, is culturally bound, and some parenting practices that are deemed abusive by child welfare systems, such as the use of corporal punishment, may be regarded by parents as necessary for socialization and character building. While Canadian society is not free from cultural beliefs and institutional arrangements that contribute to and maintain gender inequality, Canadian domestic violence policies, child welfare legislation, and support services are acknowledged to be some of the most advanced in the world (Shirwadkar, 2004). Crisis lines for women and children, specialized domestic violence units, screening and reporting practices, shelters for abused women and street youth, domestic violence and child abuse awareness campaigns, and treatment programs have evolved as our knowledge base has developed. However, for immigrant and refugee families, structural obstacles, ethnocultural prohibitions, language barriers, and fears about being deported or losing their children complicate their ability to make use of such services. In some cases they may not even be aware of services available to them.

Research on the lived experiences of immigrant women as they encounter policies and programs intended to reduce domestic violence and child abuse is identifying some of the obstacles to bringing a family's private pain into the public domain: isolation, lack of social supports (such as housing and financial aid), language barriers, suspicion of state intervention, fear of discriminatory treatment, fear of racism, and being cut off from extended family and their cultural community (Alaggia, Regehr & Rishchynski, 2009; Lee, 2000; Shirwadkar, 2004). The first section of this chapter provides a context for the experiences of newcomer, immigrant, and refugee women who are victims and survivors of domestic violence. Policies related to immigration and service provision will be examined in terms of their impact on immigrant women's disclosure and help-seeking behaviours. The second section of the chapter focuses on issues of child abuse and neglect in immigrant families. The impact of child welfare policies that drive child protection practices will be explored in relation to the treatment of immigrant families. The third section of the chapter will provide an analysis of the service delivery system for immigrant families affected by domestic violence and child abuse and makes recommendations for improved response. In addition, the authors have conducted two recent studies with newcomer and immigrant participants, aimed at learning more about their experiences. One study documents the disclosure and help-seeking actions of women who have experienced domestic violence, and the other documents the perceptions of immigrant parents regarding child abuse and neglect. Quotes from participants are provided to illustrate themes that represent their struggles with domestic violence and the Canadian system of policies and services.

DOMESTIC VIOLENCE AND IMMIGRANT AND REFUGEE WOMEN

How Big Is the Problem of Intimate Partner Violence?

Despite increased public awareness in recent years, domestic violence continues to persist as a social phenomenon with serious consequences. Statistics Canada (2005) estimates that 653,000 Canadian women have experienced some form of domestic abuse, and when incidences of abuse in previous relationships are included, 21 percent of Canadian women reported violence. This is clearly a gendered issue (see Dragiewicz in this volume for further discussion). Other estimates suggest that one in every six women in Canada is abused by her partner each year, and over 60 percent of female homicides in Canada are due to family violence (Woman Abuse Council of Toronto, 1998). As well, Statistics Canada (2005) cites that "women continue to suffer more serious and repeated spousal violence than do men and incur more serious consequences as a result of this violence" (p. 13). Furthermore, in the most recent Transition Home Survey, between April 1, 2003, and March 31, 2004, more than 95,000 women and children were admitted to 473 shelters across Canada, the majority of whom were escaping abuse (Taylor-Butts, 2005).

Given the way in which data are collected, it is difficult to discern how immigrant and refugee women are represented in these numbers. To begin with, when we refer to immigrant and refugee women, we must define these groups. The term "immigrant women" in this chapter refers to women who have come voluntarily to Canada, as well as those who have been forced to leave their own countries as refugees and undocumented immigrants (McDonald, 1999; Ng, 1996). Ng also points out that these women, regardless of their immigration status or length of time in the country, will remain "immigrant women." Furthermore, it is important to acknowledge the existence of women who are undocumented immigrants and who have arrived in Canada outside of the formal legal channels of the immigration application process. Their numbers remain largely unknown since undocumented immigrant women will not disclose their lack of status as this will almost certainly result in detention and deportation.

Clearly, there is reluctance to track social problems in immigrant communities for fear of perpetuating negative stereotyping, but there is also a danger in the avoidance of documenting numbers of domestic violence cases affecting immigrant and refugee women as this inaction can potentially render these serious problems invisible.

In McDonald's (1999) review of the literature regarding domestic violence in the lives of immigrant women in Canada, she found "a notable absence of studies and statistics on the prevalence of domestic violence in immigrant communities" (p. 164). Not even the 1993 Violence against Women Survey (VAWS) produced numbers pertaining to immigrant and refugee women. As well, methodological problems plague prevalence studies since most surveys are done by telephone and only in English or French. Thus, we are left with little data to help us know more precisely how many, and in what ways, immigrant women are affected by domestic violence in Canada.

LINKING THEORY AND THE EXPERIENCES OF IMMIGRANT WOMEN

Using an overarching feminist theoretical framework for understanding woman abuse in intimate relationships, we conclude that this social problem is deeply rooted in the patriarchal structures that support men's abuse of power over their intimate partners (Bograd, 1999; Duffy & Momirov, 1997; McPhail, Busch, Kulkarni & Rice, 2007). While there is evidence to indicate that some women abuse their male partners, research shows that the vast majority of violence occurs against women (Avis, 1992; Dragiewicz, 2009). From this feminist perspective, woman abuse is explained by males' privileged position in patriarchal societies. Historically, there have been few

tangible consequences for violent male behaviour, which has contributed to
the perpetuation of woman abuse (DeKeseredy & Dragiewicz, 2007; Duffy
& Momirov, 1997). In Canada, lawmakers and legislators have been predominantly male. Thus, laws and society's larger structures have favoured
men and kept women (and children) in marginalized positions. Women
have been further subordinated by their role in the labour market, which
devalues child care and domestic labour. Many women are financially
dependent on their partners and vulnerable to men's misuse and abuse of
power. Women who work outside of the home are often underpaid, and
if they separate from their partners, they are frequently disadvantaged
in terms of securing good legal counsel. If the marriage/partnership dis-
solves permanently and they have children, they are further financially
disadvantaged as lone mothers and often end up homeless for periods of
time (Sev'er, 2002; Zorza, 1996).

Intersectionality theory (Crenshaw, 1991; Nixon & Humphreys, 2010)
aids us in gaining a deeper understanding of the complexities of domestic
violence beyond gender and sexism as the primary focus or only source of
violence. Feminist theorists recognize that women suffer multiple oppressions and that gender oppression intersects with race, class, ability, age, and
sexual orientation. These intersecting oppressions should be included in
all analyses involving immigrant women and violence. Immigrant women
experience patriarchal structures in the same ways as Canadian-born
women, but may also be subjected to additional sources of violence, such
as racism, class oppression, and ableism.

Of note, their precarious position in the legal system as they try to secure
Canadian citizenship makes them vulnerable to structural violence. When
confronted with violence in their intimate relationships, disclosing and/or
reporting abuse by their husbands is a formidable and often unthinkable
act for immigrant women, whether they are newcomers or more established
Canadian residents. Research indicates that they are less likely to call the
police, seek help, or use the shelter system and related services because of
fears of deportation, lack of economic resources, isolation, and language
barriers (Alaggia, Regehr & Jenney, 2012; Bhola & Nelson, 1990).

Further, women sponsored by their partners are in an even more vulnerable position if they consider reporting abuse because of their precarious
status when being sponsored. This is a significant concern since 62 percent
of those entering Canada under sponsorship from family members in 2006
were women (Citizenship & Immigration Canada, 2007). Newcomer women
fear jeopardizing their application for Canadian citizenship if they report
their partners for abuse. Immigrant women cite numerous reasons for these
apprehensions, such as lacking information about the Canadian legal sys-

tem, distrusting government and authorities, facing language barriers, and fearing disapproval and isolation from their communities if they disclose relationship violence (Alaggia, Regehr & Rishchynski, 2009; Coutinho, 1986; Law Courts Education Society of British Columbia, 1995).

Women also fear losing their children to their husbands if a separation occurs. While custody and access cases that come before the courts are presumably being treated in more fair and equitable ways when woman abuse has been identified, some decisions are still being made on the assumption that abused women are not victims and that the perpetrator no longer poses a threat against her or the children (Jaffe & Crooks, 2004; Shaffer & Bala, 2004). Research is also documenting fears about child welfare intervention because of recent legislation that children exposed to domestic violence are now deemed as cases for investigation (Alaggia, Jenney, Mazzuca & Redmond, 2007; Sev'er, 2002).

Additionally, because migration typically involves leaving friends, families, and communities behind, immigrant women tend to be isolated and have few social supports to reach out to. There are often strong cultural and religious taboos against challenging male authority, undergoing separation and divorce, and being a single woman with children. In one of our studies, this woman explained: "For the recently arrived women, everything is new. If you don't know the language, it is difficult to adjust to everything. Many of the women, like me, are in closed apartments. Isolated, trapped, locked.... I couldn't speak in the language, so I kept quiet" (Alaggia, Regehr & Rishchynski, 2009, p. 338).

While feminist theories help to explain the external forces that precipitate and perpetuate woman abuse in intimate relationships, interpersonal factors can also account for the maintenance of violence in intimate relationships. For example, it is important to take into consideration trauma theory in elucidating how women make decisions about remaining in or leaving an abusive relationship. Unfortunately, the effects of other traumas may be present in women's lives, so that repeated traumatic experiences (historic and/or current) can set off a complex set of psychological reactions such as hyper-arousal, numbing of emotions, dissociation, anxiety, and various phobias (Jones, Hughes & Ulrike, 2001). Regardless of the circumstances under which women are abused, many are traumatized in ways that make their responses to their abusive partners and children appear irrational or indifferent. Trauma theory further explains these reactions in terms of the persistent re-experiencing of the trauma and avoidance of traumatic stimuli (Herman, 1992, 1997). Traumatic bonding can also develop wherein women become "frozen" in the abusive relationship and cannot leave. In these cases women may appear to be willing participants in the violent aspects of the relationship by accepting the abuser's world view that they deserve to be abused (Graham, Rawlings & Rimmi, 1988; Herman, 1997).

For immigrant and refugee women, there may be a myriad of other reasons that inhibit them from leaving, or encourage their return to, these dangerous relationships, especially when the violence in their intimate relationships is compounded by historic trauma experienced in their country of origin. Childhood trauma, events such as war, use of rape as a weapon, and other oppressive practices they experienced can alter their psychological reactions in ways that impede their ability to flee from the current abusive relationship. Coupled with cultural taboos and anticipated ostracism from their ethnic communities, abused immigrant women may be left with very few options.

LINKING THE SOCIO-LEGAL-POLITICAL CONTEXT WITH THE EXPERIENCES OF IMMIGRANT WOMEN

As well as developing an understanding of the interpersonal and intrapersonal factors involved in domestic violence, examining the socio-legal-political context is important to understand how self-agency is facilitated or impeded by laws, policies, and programs. In the area of violence against women, Canada has developed among the most advanced policies and programs to redress problems of domestic violence (Shirwadkar, 2004). For example, the federal government implemented the Family Violence Initiative to reduce violence against women, of which the Multiculturalism Program of Canada is a part. The Criminal Justice Program is another initiative that precipitated amendments to the Criminal Code of Canada, offering better protection to all women facing violence in their intimate relationships. However, these policies and programs do not adequately acknowledge and address the unique issues faced by immigrant and refugee women in domestic violence situations. While judges, police, and prosecutors are offered in-depth programs to increase awareness of issues of domestic violence since the Canadian Judicial Council passed new resolutions, these programs do not necessarily respond to the unique and specific needs of immigrant women. Furthermore, immigrant and refugee women may fear and/or distrust the Canadian legal system based on experiences with the legal systems in their home countries. Often the legal systems in their countries of origin are extensions of a repressive government and sexist policies (McDonald, 1999). Thus, interactions with legal systems in the host country may evoke anxieties about experiences in the past.

In addition, women fear deportation because of their immigration status, which becomes even more unstable if their sponsor becomes involved in the criminal justice system. Many do not know or do not have available to them information regarding their rights in "sponsorship breakdown" due to family violence. In their study, Alaggia and colleagues (2009) include one woman's description of another's situation: "She is waiting for papers. That man knows she cannot go. That is why he always tortures her. She is afraid of everything" (p. 339).

Indeed, immigration policies originating from within Citizenship and Immigration Canada (CIC) have direct, significant impacts on immigrant women who are victims and survivors of domestic violence. CIC policies currently include provisions for women sponsored by their husbands (including fiancés and common-law partners) who identify as victims of domestic violence, wherein they may apply for permanent residence on humanitarian and compassionate (H&C) grounds. When domestic violence is occurring in the relationship, situations can be classified as "sponsorship breakdown," which requires an abused woman to make an H&C application so that she can seek legal status as an independent applicant. However, these applications take a long time to process, are costly, and may result in women remaining in abusive relationships until their application is granted (Community Legal Education Ontario, 2004; Rachin, 1997). The process of applying is taxing and women in these situations are strongly encouraged to seek legal advice—which they may not be able to afford—especially if they are not married but engaged to be married or are in a common-law union (Community Legal Education Ontario, 2004). For example, the H&C application requires the applicant to demonstrate how established she is in Canada based on such criteria as employment history in Canada, job references, volunteer work done in Canada, skills upgrading and training done in Canada, her ability to speak French or English, what types of assets and savings she has in Canada, and her level of integration into the community (Citizenship and Immigration Canada, 2008). The woman also shoulders the burden of responsibility for proving that abuse has occurred through formal documentation, which may be unavailable since she may have been reluctant to disclose the abuse to professionals or call the police (Alaggia, Regehr & Rishchynski, 2009). Once immigrant women review the list, they often feel they will not be able to meet the conditions of the application, especially if they are newcomers, poorly educated, and financially dependent on their sponsor, therefore causing them to give up before they start. One may question the very essence of this as a "humanitarian" provision given that as an independent applicant, she is now assessed on the criteria established for independent applicants while her position as caregiver in the home has disadvantaged her in achieving these criteria. Furthermore, research shows that they are often misinformed about immigration policies and rules, and fear their own deportation and that of their spouse

(Alaggia, Regehr & Rishschynski, 2009; Landau, 2001; Pratt, 1995), suggesting that often they are unaware of the H&C policy in the first place. Women mentioned additional fears about any involvement with immigration authorities as illustrated by the following comment: "Yes, if you get divorced they will send you back to your country. If this happens before the three-year mark then there is that fear, so you have to keep it [the abuse] hidden in fear that they may send you back" (Alaggia, Regehr & Rischynski, 2009, p. 339).

IMPACT OF SERVICE RESPONSE AND SERVICE BARRIERS FOR ABUSED IMMIGRANT WOMEN

Police and Criminal Justice Response to Intimate Partner Violence

In the wake of initiatives designed to raise awareness of domestic violence among police (Baker, Jaffe, Berkowitz & Berkman, 2002), a growing number of police forces have adopted mandatory charging policies in cases where they are dispatched to investigate domestic violence incidents. These often result in criminal charges laid against a husband where abuse has been determined, even if his wife does not want to press charges. Some women are not aware of what actions will ensue as a result of making a 911 call. In these cases, women are often surprised and fear further repercussions by the abusive spouse after he is charged and released on bail. The criminal justice system is further bound by "no-drop" policies wherein the victim is not able to drop charges against the perpetrator at a later date.

Martin and Mosher (1995) point out that the potential harm for any women resulting from criminal justice intervention includes the loss of economic security, increased institutional surveillance, breakup of the family unit, and isolation from communities. Moreover, women lose control of their situations and advocacy efforts for victims of violence inadvertently "backfire" (McDermott & Garofalo, 2004). However, these issues are exacerbated for immigrant women. Financial hardship is a reality, especially for immigrant women since they are often sponsored by their husbands to be in Canada (Pratt, 1995) and may not be readily employable. Responsibilities for children and lack of child care resources further hamper their attempts to become financially independent if their relationship breaks down. Given that many women are highly financially dependent on their husbands, they are further thrust into a situation where they have to seek court intervention to receive support if they take action to dissolve the relationship due to abuse (Anderson, 1993). A chain reaction of events is potentially set off when police are involved and charges are laid over which they have little control. Some immigrant women have expressed fear of losing their children as a result of calling the police. As one mother said, "Call the police and then they take the children from the home. This happened to a friend" (Alaggia, Regehr & Rischynski, 2009, p. 338).)p. 338)

In the aftermath of reporting domestic violence to the police, whereby the decision of charging is out of their hands, immigrant women are more vulnerable because they may not speak English or French, are intimidated by the bureaucratic and legal processes they inevitably encounter, and often lack the financial resources for legal representation they will need, especially if they have to make an H&C application (Landau, 2001; Rachin, 1997). Most people whose first language is one of Canada's official languages and who have had to deal with legal processes can attest to the difficulties with legalese (the language used in legal documents) and technical terms. As well as facing pending court proceedings, if immigrant women fear for their safety, they may also need to secure a restraining order. Finally, they may encounter criticism and stigmatization from their extended family and ethnic community. In cultures where separation or divorce is prohibited or scorned, immigrant women are further confronted by isolation from communities that were once a source of support (Coutinho, 1986; Lee, 2000; Shirwadkar, 2004). As one study respondent explained, "Call the police. I can see how it is helpful, but what about after? The police take the man and then what? Separate? Or divorce? No" (Alaggia, Regehr & Jenney, 2012, p. 306).

Women are concerned about the implications of police intervention and may not call in emergency situations, thus increasing their risk. Although intended to be helpful, mandatory charging and "no-drop" policies can deter abused women from seeking intervention because of their fear of deportation, anticipated disapproval by their cultural communities, communication barriers, lack of education, economic barriers, and host country perception (Alaggia, Regehr & Rishchynsky, 2009; McDermott & Garofalo, 2004). They may also anticipate negative consequences of such actions on immigration status, precipitating deportation of the husband, or delaying the conferral of citizenship because of a criminal record. Women also fear that their husbands will be disproportionately punished in the criminal justice system because of ethno-racial prejudices (Pratt, 1995).

Health Care Response to Intimate Partner Violence

Many medical organizations recommend that physicians make efforts to identify and refer patients who have experienced intimate partner violence (Rhodes & Levinson, 2003). This has resulted in domestic violence screening tools being utilized in numerous health care settings and physician offices in an effort to encourage disclosure and decrease violence against women. However, health care researchers concede that it is unclear whether these tools are effective or whether identification of domestic violence improves outcomes for women in the short or the long term (Rhodes & Levinson,

2003; Wathen & MacMillan, 2003). A systematic review of the screening literature shows little evidence (based on rigorously designed studies) that these tools are effective in decreasing violence against women (Wathen & MacMillan, 2003), and that the experiences of immigrant women are not represented clearly in these studies.

However, we can speculate that newcomer and established immigrant women may face specific barriers in disclosing intimate partner violence to health care providers. First, they may not have access to the health care system when they initially arrive in Canada because they are not immediately eligible for most provincial health insurance coverage. Many provinces have a three-month waiting period from the time that an individual establishes residency in the province. This raises a fundamental question as to whether newcomer women are even being seen in the health care system during that time. Second, when accessing emergency care, domestic violence screening may not be done in the woman's language or in a culturally responsive manner. Third, many established immigrant women are patients of physicians who are members of their cultural group and they may withhold disclosure for fear of being disbelieved, dismissed, or counselled into accepting their situation. They may also worry about having subsequent contact with their physician in their cultural community, or that confidentiality oaths will be broken and information passed on to partners or other family members, which would put them at further risk.

THE INTERSECTION OF CHILD WELFARE POLICIES AND INTIMATE PARTNER VIOLENCE

Child welfare legislation and policies across Canada have recently evolved to include children exposed to domestic violence as being potentially in need of protection. Cases where children are suspected of being in such situations are now routinely investigated. While there are growing concerns among helping professionals who are legislated to report cases of domestic violence in homes where children are known to reside about this practice, referrals to child protection agencies have increased significantly (Trocmé, 2003). This has affected not only child welfare practices but also how other professional services deal with children and families. For example, as mentioned in the previous section, numerous police forces have adopted mandatory reporting procedures for any domestic dispute calls they respond to.

These concerns include questioning whether such reporting policies have a negative impact on abused women. Women may, for example, choose not to disclose domestic violence because they fear contact with child welfare authorities. While this legislation has been constructed to protect the well-being of children, unintended negative consequences on mothers have been documented (Jaffe, Crooks & Wolfe, 2003). Provisions under "failure to protect" makes mothers accountable in certain situations: hypothetically, mothers are viewed as failing to protect their children from witnessing and being exposed to domestic violence if they are unable to leave the abusive relationship. Children can be apprehended under these circumstances (Edleson, 1998; Magen, 1999). (For in-depth discussion, see Jenney and Alaggia, and Strega in this volume.)

Therefore, immigrant women may be even more reluctant to disclose domestic violence as they already fear any negative involvement with authorities, especially child welfare involvement, which could result in losing their children. Immigrant women have expressed fears of child welfare involvement, as women commented through the following observation: "But when you go with a child as soon as the family shelter—automatically Children's Aid is involved. And as a mother, I don't need to have to get Children's Aid involved. They might take her away. I don't like it so I'm not going there" (Alaggia, Regehr & Jenney, 2012, p. 308).

It is quite conceivable that the services designed to help women and children living with domestic violence are being avoided altogether by women, including immigrant women. For example, many shelters for abused women and their children are now under directives to report to child protection services if a woman chooses to return to her partner. At the same time, research has indicated that women often go through a series of separations and reconciliations with abusive partners before actually making a final decision to leave, so that returning to the abusive partner is highly likely (Johnson, 1992; Mehrotra, 1999; Metraux & Culhane, 1999; Poorman, 2002). Immigrant women may be even more vulnerable to this pattern because once they leave, they lack the social supports to sustain themselves apart from the relationship, and return as a result of this lack (Dasgupta, 2000). Clearly, for an immigrant woman, the decision to leave a marriage is a complicated one, given that she may already be ambivalent about fleeing to a shelter with her children due to cultural disapproval and systemic barriers. In addition, being aware of child welfare policies that can possibly disrupt her relationship with her children can cause a woman to completely retreat from such action. Thus, it is not surprising to find that immigrant women are less likely to use shelters and other domestic violence services, given that both perceived and real deterrents exist.

Having reviewed contextual issues related to intimate partner violence in the lives of immigrant women, policy impacts, and service response, the chapter now turns its focus to child abuse issues in immigrant families. Frameworks for understanding child abuse and child protection risks and issues in diverse ethno-racial families will be provided. The context of immigrant family life in relation to child welfare, along with service needs and barriers, will be presented as well.

CHILD ABUSE AND NEGLECT AND IMMIGRANT AND REFUGEE FAMILIES IN CANADA

Despite the current high rates of immigration to Canada mentioned earlier in the chapter, there is a dearth of research-based knowledge about immigrant groups and the child welfare system. The term "immigrant families" in this section refers to couples with children where one or both spouses have come voluntarily to Canada, as well as those who have been forced to leave their own countries as refugees and undocumented immigrants. As with immigrant women, immigrant families continue to be seen as "immigrants" regardless of their length of stay in Canada, meaning that although the term "immigrant" has specific meaning denoting someone who has moved to Canada, it is also socially constructed to differentiate between people who are seen to have an inherent right to be a part of the Canadian fabric by having been born in Canada versus those who have migrated to Canada. Typically, racialized people, even if born in Canada, are viewed as immigrants as opposed to their white counterparts who are not, while white immigrants are more quickly accepted into the Canadian fabric than are racialized immigrants. Pon, Gosine, and Phillips (2011) note that earlier racist immigration policies in Canada were replaced by a point system (which had its own racist undercurrents), but that by the time the point system was implemented, white supremacist narratives resulted in the popular discourse of non-whites as "newcomers" or "immigrants" in Canada, despite the long-standing presence of blacks and Asians in Canada. Indeed, the literature on child welfare services for culturally and ethnically diverse families often relates to services for immigrant families, conflating this diversity with being an immigrant. The emergence of this literature is also acknowledgement that child welfare systems come from a Eurocentric base and may not be uniformly applicable to diverse populations. Authors such as Abney (1996), Este (2003), and McPhatter (1997) address cultural/ethnic/racial diversity and the child welfare system, providing much useful insight into this diversity, but some of the unique needs of immigrant families in the child welfare system still need further extrapolation.

LINKING THEORETICAL FRAMEWORKS FOR UNDERSTANDING CHILD ABUSE AND NEGLECT TO THE EXPERIENCES OF IMMIGRANT FAMILIES

The ecological perspective is widely accepted as a means for understanding the etiology of child maltreatment (Belsky, 1993; Browne, 1988). Belsky proposes four "predisposing" risk factors: (1) parent factors (e.g., history of abuse, personality, psychological resources); (2) child factors (e.g., age, physical health, behaviour, temperament); (3) community and social support networks; and (4) environmental factors that can create contexts for families where child maltreatment can occur. This perspective provides some parameters for exploring the aforementioned factors for families and for understanding both the strengths and struggles of families. While there is no way to predict that any one of these factors could lead to child maltreatment, these factors can combine in ways that leave children vulnerable in families. For immigrant families, these so-called risk factors may be exacerbated by the process of migration and the associated psychological distress and settlement struggles that may arise. In effect, migration adds another layer of stress that has an influence on each of these factors and should be included in our analysis of immigrant families and child maltreatment.

Browne (1988) also proposes four factors that need exploration in understanding child maltreatment within families: individual (e.g., mental health), familial (e.g., family structure), social (e.g., degree and type of connections with informal networks), and cultural (e.g., attitudes toward obedience and corporal punishment). Browne's framework adds to Belsky's in that it brings attention to family structure and cultural factors. Both these frameworks can help us better understand child maltreatment in immigrant families. Their value lies in the ecological focus, which helps us to resist blaming a culture or a cultural group for abuse, but rather looks at the interactions of various elements that can result in family violence. Different families from a particular ethnocultural group or from an immigrant group will exhibit differential behaviours, depending on their niche within this ecological framework.

THE CONTEXT OF IMMIGRANT FAMILY LIFE IN RELATION TO CHILD WELFARE

Today immigrants move to Canada for reasons similar to those of immigrants in previous years. Immigrants may have experienced considerable hardships in their lives because of a number of factors, including lack of development and resources, lack of freedoms, violence, persecution, lack of a future for children, overcrowding, hopes for career advancement, and an overall hope for a better quality of life. These immigrants would have engaged in extensive planning prior to their moves. Refugees, on the other hand, are forced to flee their country at minimal notice, often arriving in Canada after experiencing war, terror, and trauma and spending time in refugee camps. Both refugees and immigrants will feel displaced and unsettled as they try to integrate into their new country. In moving to a new country, immigrants leave behind familiar social support networks, which Williams (1998) calls "plausibility structures." These structures "provide a foundation for knowledge, customs, morals, leadership styles and commitments, supporting civic order and personal health" (Williams, 1998, p. 186). In the migration process, individuals and families suffer from a loss of meaning systems, which are embedded in one's culture and which influence relationships with others. Migration results in the disruption of both external and internal meaning systems. External meaning systems include language, social networks, institutions, and values, while internal meaning systems include separations and reunions, trauma and crisis, grief and mourning, disorienting anxieties, and cultural identity (Falicov, 1996).

Immigrants come to their new country with considerable hope for an improved life for themselves and for their children. However, once they are here, they often find the settlement and adjustment phase to be particularly challenging. These challenges arise at both the internal psychological and external environmental levels. At the internal level, individuals can experience psychological distress, including: culture shock; a sense of marginalization, isolation and alienation; psychosomatic symptoms such as palpitations, dizziness, insomnia; anxiety and depression; and posttraumatic stress (Doyle & Visano, 1987; Garza-Guerro, 1974; Grinberg & Grinberg, 1989; Herberg, 1993; Naidoo & Edwards, 1991; Steiner & Bansil, 1989). Environmental challenges for immigrant families arise in the community in terms of ethnicity, religion, race, and social networks in the areas of the living environment (housing, neighbourhood, and their safety), work (income, schedule, stability, satisfaction, and discrimination), school (achievement, discipline, parent involvement, race, and ethnicity), and other institutions (legal, medical, mental health) (Falicov, 1995).

A recent study (Maiter, Stalker & Alaggia, 2009) of immigrant families involved with the child welfare system highlights their immigration-related experiences. Themes from this qualitative study noted the following: loneliness, financial struggles, language struggles, struggles to provide for the family, and a sense of betrayal and hopelessness. Participants discussed the extreme hardships they were experiencing in meeting the needs of their families and in obtaining the resources to care for themselves personally. Clearly, not all immigrants will have such extreme struggles or overwhelming sense of loss. However, some immigrants, as noted by the participants in this study, do experience stressors that can be devastating, such as isolation, loss of social support and identity, as exemplified in the following statement: "Life is dramatically changed because everyone here is very busy and don't have time to spare for you...but back in Bangladesh we have a lot of friends, relatives, parents. We are parents. We are children. We are nieces. We are in-laws" (Maiter, Stalker & Alaggia, 2009, p. 32). Previous research (Coohey, 1996; Gracia & Musitu, 2003) has also identified the factors noted above in the lives of families involved with the child welfare system, and the importance of community and formal and informal social supports for families both for prevention and intervention are also well known (Korbin, 2003; Manji, Maiter & Palmer, 2005). The struggles of many families who come into contact with child welfare services in relation to poverty and finances are further exacerbated for the immigrant families in this sample because of low English proficiency, which then impacts their ability to secure employment. These stressors are, however, additive because foreign credentials and experience are not recognized by the host country. Thus, a clear path to ending poverty is not so easily available to immigrants, as noted by this mother:

> I was working Saturday and Sunday, and 12-hour shifts, too. There was nothing much to do but work 7 days in a row. I worked as a sewing machine operator 5 days, and in the evening I worked in the bakery. I was working 12-hour shifts, and at that time I was paid 5 dollars an hour. My husband also worked driving a taxi. (Maiter, Stalker & Alaggia, 2009, p. 33)

Not clearly identified in the literature, but discussed by participants, are their feelings of betrayal and hopelessness, and a questioning of whether their decision to migrate was the correct one. For example, a father in his forties noted:

> I did my 4 years master's degree, and my 6 years another master's degree. I got my visa as a computer system programmer. I proudly got a visa, I proudly came over here, and now I'm getting social assistance. My children are growing up on social assistance. Me, I'm an educated person, but I'm living on social assistance. Me, my education, my everything is gone. (Maiter, Stalker & Alaggia, 2009, pp. 33–34)

Inevitably, family members can experience depression and other mental health problems when confronted with these situations (Segal & Mayadas, 2005).

The lived experiences of immigrants often prove to be quite different from their expectations. Furthermore, families may have considered the challenges of finding work, housing, and friends, but not thought about how legislation in their new country, for example, would have an impact on them. For example, child welfare legislation in all provinces has advanced considerably to intervene in situations where child abuse and neglect are known to be or are suspected to be occurring. Immigrant parents may be completely unaware of these laws and may parent in ways contradictory to the legislation in Canada. Thus, for example, in their home country they may have used physical force to discipline children. If this force became excessive, the extended family would have intervened, or it may have gone unstopped. However, in their new country, they will find that their parenting actions are scrutinized by many professionals and that child welfare will intervene.

CHILD PROTECTION ISSUES FOR DIVERSE ETHNO-RACIAL FAMILIES

Considerable literature highlights the increasing diversity of Western nations and the need for culturally competent child welfare services (Abney, 1996; Este, 2003; Fontes, 2005; Leung, Cheung & Stevenson, 1997; Maiter, 2001, 2004; McPhatter, 1997). Korbin (1991), one of the earliest writers attempting to explicate factors in child maltreatment and ethnic diversity, suggests three areas for consideration: (1) parenting practices that may be acceptable in one culture but not another; (2) limits within a culture suggesting that the practice is out of the range of acceptability and is considered abuse; and (3) societal factors such as poverty, poor health care, lack of housing, and similar issues that are beyond the control of parents.

These areas provide some guidelines for understanding that different cultures might hold varying beliefs about child-rearing practices, especially in relation to discipline and the use of corporal punishment, while also recognizing the impact of societal factors that can contribute to child maltreatment. The research on cultural minority groups and child maltreatment is often conflicting and sparse (Fontes, 2005). Literature from the United States suggests that the rates of child abuse in community samples of diverse ethnic groups are fairly similar across groups (Charlow 2001–2, cited in Fontes, 2005). While the rates of child maltreatment may be similar, African American, Native American, and Latin American children are overrepresented in reported rates of child maltreatment compared to white and Asian American children, who are underrepresented (Chipungu & Bent-Goodley, 2003; Roberts, 2002). Causes for the differential rates of representation are not clear, but possibly include: differences in actual rates due to differences in rates of poverty, cultural differences, and quality of neighbourhoods (Coulton, Korbin & Su, 1999); biases in reporting, substantiating, and managing suspected child abuse cases (Ards, Chung & Myers, 1998); lack of social services and supports for some communities (Abney, 1996); and more adversarial approaches being used with minority families, resulting in increased numbers of court proceedings (Tjaden & Thoennes, 1992).

Given that we do not have specific data on immigrant families in the child welfare system, we share data on racialized families in the child welfare system. Like other authors in this area, we are conflating immigrants with racialized families. We do this recognizing that there are some similarities of issues experienced, and indeed many researchers are examining issues relating to migration when exploring issues of race. Still, the needs of non-racialized immigrant families and child welfare services must also be considered. Many of the issues discussed, such as loss of supports and networks, also apply to these families. Research on racialized and immigrant families in the child welfare system in Canada is sparse. However, two recent studies provide some information. Researchers note that racial minority children and families are overrepresented in the Canadian child protection system compared to their proportion in the general census (Blackstock, Trocmé & Bennett, 2004; Lavergne, Dufour, Trocmé & Larrivee, 2008). Blackstock et al. (2004) conducted an analysis of data from a 1998 Canadian Incidence Study of Child Abuse and Neglect and reported that Aboriginals (50 percent) and visible minorities (41 percent) had higher rates of *substantiation* of maltreatment compared to non-Aboriginals (38 percent). When differentiating by type of maltreatment, punishment-related physical abuse was highest for the visible minority group (35 percent), followed by non-Aboriginal (22 percent) and Aboriginal groups (8 percent). Lavergne et al. (2008) analyzed data from a later maltreatment incidence study and found similar trends. Asian children reported for physical abuse accounted for 14 percent of the sample, a proportion that is 1.6 times greater than their proportion in census data. Asian children also had the highest substantiation rate for physical abuse. The authors note that risk factors for the parents of Asian children (personal issues and difficult housing), however, were lower than in other groups. Factors leading to these higher rates are thus unclear, raising questions of worker perception and racial bias in identification, reporting, and decision-making or cultural differences in the use of physical discipline.

Researchers who have attempted to understand cultural differences in definitions of child maltreatment, differences in parenting values and practices, and help-seeking patterns report mixed findings. Similar to some researchers (Giovannoni & Beccerra, 1979; Rose & Meezan, 1996), Maiter, Alaggia, and Trocmé (2004) found in their study that South Asian immigrant parents identified inappropriate parenting practices and abuse in vignettes presented to them. They further note that the parents in their sample did not differ from the general population in their concerns about appropriate parenting approaches. They found, for example, that persistent and excessive use of physical discipline was considered inappropriate; parental practices that may have negative emotional consequences for children were recognized as inappropriate; and concerns were noted about lack of proper supervision of children. In this same study, although the use of corporal punishment was not condoned, there was also no major opposition to it. In contrast, Payne (1989) did find a greater tolerance for, and practice of, corporal punishment from a sample of adults in Barbados, but also noted an attitude shift in the younger respondents, who were less likely to support corporal punishment of children. Indeed, it is now being recognized that there is significant commonality and consensus among various groups on definitions of maltreatment (Dubowitz, Klockner, Starr & Black, 1998; Portwood, 1999).

Although Hong and Hong (1991) and Shor (1998, 1999) discovered that parents' cultural values influenced their approaches to child-rearing, findings regarding parents' actions were inconclusive. For example, Hong and Hong found that the Chinese respondents in their study rated physical discipline as "less severe" than did the Hispanic and white respondents. The researchers, however, were unable to distinguish whether physical discipline was the preferred method of discipline for the Chinese parents. As well, they could not account for differences within groups. Similarities in the responses of participants from all three ethnic groups were noted for neglect of a child's physical health, uncommon sleeping habits, and encouragement of children to commit crimes. Essentially, participants from all three ethnic groups in this study described vignettes depicting these elements as inappropriate. These findings suggest that there may be considerable commonalities in what different ethnic groups consider to be inappropriate parental actions. Still, Hong and Hong (1991), Maiter (2004), and Shor (1998, 1999) identified values important to Chinese American families, South Asian Canadian families, Orthodox Jewish families, and Jewish families from the former Soviet Union that guide parental practices and could result in conflicts in families and increased intervention by the child welfare system. Collectivist values of respect and acceptance of the decisions of elders, obedience to them, and preference for relationships within family and kinship networks were values important to these families.

IMMIGRANT FAMILIES FACING CHILD WELFARE INTERVENTION AND SERVICE NEEDS AND BARRIERS

Immigrant families who come to the attention of child welfare are often isolated, lack family and community supports, are poor, are unemployed or underemployed, may not speak English or French, and are often unfamiliar with the resources available to them (Maiter & Stalker, 2011; Maiter, Stalker & Alaggia, 2009). Along with this, they may be completely baffled by the intervention of the child welfare system. They struggle to understand the mandate and role of child welfare agencies and are further confused by the current child-centred approach adopted by the child welfare system. This approach may lead immigrant parents to think that social service agencies are not there to provide help and support for families, but to protect children in isolation from their parents. When the child welfare system intervenes in immigrant families, their child-centred approach can feel particularly threatening to families from collectivist cultural backgrounds, especially when they do not know Canadian legislation. Because of this, child welfare workers will need to be especially careful in their work with immigrant families. They need to make extra efforts to build relationships with parents, be more persistent in sharing information with them, and let parents know that they are cognizant of the hardships they are experiencing. Along with this, immigrant parents will need to be educated about the child welfare mandate, be guided to resources, and their workers will need to advocate for them to obtain counselling and therapeutic services.

Fear of government agencies, concerns that their religion or ethnicity might be stigmatized because of the family problems they are experiencing, and a sense of shame for being investigated by child welfare are further barriers to services. Since the role of child welfare may not be understood, negotiating peaceful settlements in child welfare disputes could also be a challenge. Families may not wish to acknowledge that their behaviour is inappropriate because of concerns that they themselves will subsequently be treated harshly by authorities. This can be further aggravated when family members do not speak English or French and there is a delay in the availability of interpreters to assist.

Studies show that linguistic barriers are an obstacle to accessing services (Chand, 2005; Maiter, 2003; Thoburn et al., 2005); that poor interpreting and translation services can prevent full access to social services (Chand, 2005; Humphreys, Atkar & Baldwin, 1999); that many social service organizations lack specific policies on the provision of services to minorities (Pugh & Williams, 2006); and that these organizations are poorly prepared to meet the needs of these communities (Pugh & Williams, 2006). An examination of case files and attendance at case conferences of Asian families led Humphreys and colleagues to note that workers did not have the intention to discriminate against Asian children and families, but *the effects* of their work—interpreter services falling short, placement needs not being met, the context of families not being addressed—provided an experience of oppression for these families and contributed to negative outcomes for children and families. More recently, a comparative study (Kriz & Skivenes, 2009) of Norway and England of services to families not proficient in the national language showed that social workers in both countries faced many challenges when using interpreters, including the loss of information, time, and trust, which then prevented the building of positive relationships. The authors raise the concern that their findings suggest that these families may be losing out on accurate assessments and access to services.

Researchers have also explored the perspectives of ethno-racial parents within the system about their daily struggles and their experiences of service from the child protection system. In a qualitative investigation with minority immigrant parents who were involved with the child protection system, Maiter and colleagues (2009) identified issues—such as the loss of resources, the threat to a sense of mastery, and the challenge to self-esteem experienced by the immigrant families interviewed—to be critical factors affecting family life and parenting practices. A sense of competence and mastery was threatened by unfamiliar culture and norms and mores, and low proficiency in the dominant language led to difficult communication.

While visible minority families investigated by child protection workers experience a host of struggles, they may also be overrepresented in the system because these children are more likely than other children to come to the attention of child protection professionals in crises (Chand, 2005; Chand & Thoburn, 2005; Qureshi, Berridge & Wenman, 2000; Thoburn, Chand & Proctor, 2005). Waiting until a crisis develops before children come to the attention of child welfare professionals can spell additional difficulties for families. Parents may lose the chance to give input that might have helped had intervention come at an earlier stage. This is particularly problematic as adversarial dealings between professionals and parents are more likely at later stages (Qureshi et al., 2000). In some cases, a lack of knowledge that support services even exist precludes access to them (Gilligan & Akhtar, 2005). This obstacle may be due, in part, to linguistic barriers (Chand, 2005; Maiter, 2003; Thoburn et al., 2005). Familiarity with the child care system and the role of professionals can result in fear of these systems, subsequently inhibiting full access (Deepak, 2005; Maiter, 2003; Qureshi et al., 2000), as can poor interpreting and translation services (Chand, 2005; Humphreys, Atkar & Baldwin, 1999).

Furthermore, social services, for the most part, have been designed for the white population (Qureshi et al., 2000). Consequently, many barriers discussed in the literature are in relation to the dominance of Western standards and practices and individualistic bias in child protection services (Imam, 1994; Mullender et al., 2002; Thoburn et al., 2005). Inadequate strategies for recruiting minority staff are frequently mentioned as barriers (O'Neale, 2000; Qureshi et al., 2000; Thoburn et al., 2005). Significantly, even when minority staff members are recruited by mainstream agencies, Western perceptions prevail (Thoburn et al., 2005). Some visible minority community members' willingness to access services are influenced by fears of not having their cultural needs understood or met and fears of being treated more harshly (Maiter et al., 2004; Maiter et al., 2009; Thoburn et al., 2005). Research conducted on child sexual abuse revealed concerns over the effects of disclosing abuse. Participants were worried that problems would intensify rather than get better and they were also concerned that they would be blamed or they would not be believed (Gilligan & Akhtar, 2005, 2006).

Interviews with parents involved with the child protection system (Maiter & Stalker, 2011) show that they have had both positive and negative experiences with their workers and the system. Although many reported negative experiences, others also reported being satisfied with the intervention as it brought about positive changes for the family. For example, one participant noted that "the services that I got, it gave me energy to keep my whole family together because it could have been unfortunate. I could have left my wife, lost my kids, if I'm fighting with her, my kids would have been affected but somehow I managed" (Maiter & Stalker, 2011, p. 143). Many of the parents were receptive to intervention, and indeed expressed a desire to improve their family situations. These situations, however, are complex. On the one hand they hope to get help with family struggles with the intervention of the child welfare system, but, on the other hand, they were disappointed as they did not get the help they needed. Ultimately they felt scrutinized by the system. Like other parents involved with child protection (Trotter, 2002), this study revealed that parents wanted to be clearly informed about the reasons for intervention and the agencies' subsequent involvement, feeling that in their experience, this clarity and transparency was lacking. Parents in this study provided good insights into their experiences with the child welfare system. In addition to being better informed about the role of the child protection worker and agency, they wanted both instrumental and therapeutic help with the problems they were experiencing, together with guidance in parenting, referrals to parenting and support groups, a focus on the family as a whole, and consideration of their unique cultural and contextual situations (Maiter & Stalker, 2011).

CONCLUSION AND RECOMMENDATIONS

Cultural constraints, program limitations and structural barriers all play a critical role in preventing immigrant families from accessing or receiving services in situations of domestic violence and child abuse. With regard to cultural constraints, immigrant families may have very mixed feelings about seeking out and receiving social services. In their country of origin, they are perceived as competent and successful because they have negotiated the challenges of migrating to a Western country. Once here, they may not be willing to share their struggles with family members back home, they may not yet have networks available here to seek help from. Moreover, they may not have a clear understanding of social services and legislation in the host country. In fact, they may be unaware of the availability of services altogether. This leaves them in vulnerable situations where problems can escalate. If services are being provided and are not experienced as helpful, immigrant clients may be unwilling to give this critical feedback to service providers for a number of reasons. These include a sense of gratitude for any help they are receiving and an unwillingness to disrupt the helping relationship, or concern that if they "complain," they may risk losing or compromising the service they are receiving.

Furthermore, seeking help for private family matters may not be cultur-ally sanctioned, especially if it threatens the integrity of the family unit. As well, some immigrant families have reason to fear authorities because of pre-vious experiences in their countries of origin, so that police and child wel-fare intervention may be viewed as potentially dangerous with unpredictable outcomes (McDonald, 1999). Racial discrimination and punitive treatment by authorities are also deterrents for immigrant families. Some women are reluctant to involve police in domestic disputes because they anticipate harsh, unfair treatment of their partner due to perceived and real racial discrimination (Pratt, 1995). While they want the abuse to stop, they do not want to subject their husbands to harmful situations.

In terms of programmatic limitations, immigrant families may not per-ceive mainstream social service agencies as meeting their needs. Lack of language facility, concern that their needs will not be valued, and appre-hension about being judged for their cultural values and norms could all contribute to family members feeling unwelcome in mainstream social ser-vice agencies. Studies have shown that race and ethnicity are not adequately addressed in practice. Sue and Sue (1990) found that 50 percent of people of colour terminated counselling after one session compared to 30 per-cent of white people. The reasons cited for termination were a lack of non-white staff, the traditional approach to service provision, poor responses to the educational and vocational needs of these clients, and an antagonistic response to culture, class, and language. Specifically, for immigrant women who are experiencing violence, the shelter system may appear just as harsh as remaining in their situation (Sev'er, 2002). Some immigrant women may want to leave their spouses, but are concerned that shelters will not welcome them because of their race or ethnic background. Furthermore, they may experience a sense of isolation and exclusion if they do not have a command of English or French. While they may have left their spouses because of violence, their connections to their culture may continue to be important to them (Coutinho, 1986). If there is any sense of their culture being judged for the abuse they are experiencing, they might resist obtaining help because of a sense of shame about their culture.

Ethno-specific agencies and settlement services have been found to be useful for some immigrant families experiencing social problems (Tator, 1996). In such agencies, families can establish lifelong and sustaining networks with other members participating in groups that other social service agencies are unable to provide. However, some immigrant families may wish to avoid ethno-specific agencies because they do not want individuals with similar backgrounds to know they are experiencing family problems. A sense of shame for what they perceive as failure on their part can prevent families from accessing these services. Families may also be concerned about issues of confidentiality or being known to the counsellors at the agency. For these families, it is essential to link them with relevant social supports or they will fall through the cracks in obtaining services as their needs may not be adequately met in mainstream agencies.

Regardless of these aforementioned challenges, mainstream agencies should make efforts to hire staff who are representative of the community served by the agency and/or have interpreters whenever needed, and recognize that immigrant clients are often isolated and without social support or networks to help them with instrumental needs. While, on the one hand, religion and culture may seem to be the root cause of the problems for immigrant clients, on the other hand, they are also sources of support in a country where families do not have many networks. Thus, exploration of the impact of these supports should be addressed cautiously and tentatively, especially if the family is dealing with a mainstream agency.

Getting the word out to immigrant families in their language is central to enabling them to seek help. One such innovative program, the Ethnic Media Outreach Project, was piloted in Montreal (Kamateros, 2004). This domestic violence awareness campaign was aimed at women who would not otherwise be reached through English or French language campaigns. The campaign was launched through ethnic newspapers, radio, and television stations servicing twelve ethnic communities. Offering services in a client's preferred language is another crucial aspect to effective service delivery. In Ontario, Here to Help group treatment programs have been implemented for abused mothers and their children. In Toronto, the program is offered in several languages specific to the communities they serve (see Jenney and Alaggia in this volume). Head Start, Better Babies Better Beginnings, and public health services can be valuable for newcomer families, but because of concerns about being reported to child welfare, immigrant families underutilize these services. Also, because of complex problems, immigrant families often need sustained services, but time-limited programs and waiting lists sometimes deter families from receiving needed services. Services located directly in the ethnic communities help to ensure that they reach the people they are intended to serve.

Structural barriers, policies, and related practices can prevent immigrant families from identifying concerns or seeking/receiving help (Alaggia, Regehr & Rishchynski, 2009). Fear is a central concern for both immigrant families and refugees. When their immigration status is unresolved, there is often a sense that seeking help or even identifying the need for help can put them in jeopardy. If they anticipate that certain policies, such as reporting policies, will infringe on their immigration status, their help-seeking options become limited. They will withhold disclosing abuse, for example, if they believe that their status and relationships in their cultural community or with extended family could be jeopardized by a professional's subsequent actions. While most policies are set in place to protect people's well-being and rights, unintended consequences may play a major role in shaping people's actions, especially if they are already disempowered in their personal relationships. Immigration procedures that are costly and difficult to understand and act on (such as humanitarian and compassionate provisions) should be reviewed and amended accordingly. Child welfare legislation needs to be evaluated and amended in ways that promote, not inhibit, disclosure of acts of family violence.

Finally, models of culturally and ethnically sensitive practice should be identified and adhered to and should follow two basic principles: (1) respect for cultural differences between client and worker is essential; and (2) ongoing self-examination for prejudicial beliefs and behaviours is required of all professionals. Cross-cultural work must include knowledge and awareness of systemic discrimination, structural barriers, and social inequities. Global forms of oppression are imbedded in the prejudices of individual social workers and within the profession as a whole (Alaggia & Marziali, 2003). All practitioners share responsibility for increasing awareness and eradicating systemic discrimination. We need to incorporate specific approaches in our methods of intervention that recognize and address the needs of immigrant populations and we need to work to redress pervasive societal discriminatory policies and practices.

REFERENCES

Abney, V.D. (1996). Cultural competency in the field of child maltreatment. In J.E.B. Myers, L. Berliner, J. Brier, C. Terry Hendrix, C. Jenny & T.A. Reid (Eds.), The *apsac* handbook on child maltreatment (2nd ed., pp. 477–86). Thousand Oaks, CA: Sage.

Alaggia, R., Jenney, A., Mazzuca, J., & Redmond, M. (2007). In whose best interest? A Canadian case study of the impact of child welfare policies in cases of domestic violence, *Journal of Brief Therapy and Crisis Intervention, 7*(4), 275–90.

Alaggia, R., & Marziali, E. (2003). Social work with Canadians of Italian background: Applying cultural concepts to bicultural and intergenerational issues in clinical practice. In A. Al-Krenawi & J. Graham (Eds.), *Multicultural social work in Canada* (pp. 150–73). Toronto: Oxford University Press.

Alaggia, R., Regehr, C., & Jenney, A. (2012). Risky business: An ecological analysis of intimate partner violence disclosure. *Research on Social Work Practice*, *22*(3), 301–12.

Alaggia, R., Regehr, C., & Rishchynski, G. (2009). Intimate partner violence and immigration laws in Canada: How far have we come? *International Journal of Psychiatry and the Law, 32*(6), 335–41.

Anderson, M. (1993). A license to abuse: The impact of conditional status on female immigrants. *Yale Law Journal, 102*, 1401–30.

Ards, S., Chung, C., & Myers, S.L. (1998). The effects of sample selection bias on racial differences in child abuse reporting. *Child Abuse and Neglect, 22*(2), 103–15.

Avis, J.M. (1992). Current trends in feminist thought and therapy: Perspectives on sexual abuse and violence within families in North America. *Journal of Feminist Family Therapy, 3–4*, 87–99.

Baker, L.B., Jaffe, P.G., Berkowitz, S.J., & Berkman, M. (2002). *A handbook for police responding to domestic violence: Promoting safer communities by integrating research and practice.* London, ON: Department of Justice Canada.

Belsky, J. (1993). Etiology of child maltreatment: A developmental-ecological analysis. *Psychological Bulletin, 114*(3), 413–34.

Bhola, S., & Nelson, T. (1990). *Cross-cultural training manual: Service providers training manual.* Calgary: Calgary Immigrant Woman's Centre.

Blackstock, C., Trocmé, N., & Bennett, M. (2004). Child maltreatment investigations among Aboriginal and non-Aboriginal families in Canada. *Violence against Women, 10*(8), 901.

Bograd, M. (1999). Strengthening domestic violence theories: Intersections of race, class, sexual orientation, and gender. *Journal of Marital and Family Therapy, 25*(3), 275–89.

Browne, D.W. (1988). High-risk infants and child maltreatment: Conceptual and research model for determining factors predictive of child maltreatment. *Early Child Development and Care, 31*, 43–53.

Chand, A. (2005). Do you speak English? Language barriers in child protection social work with minority ethnic families. *British Journal of Social Work, 35*(6), 807–21.

Chand, A., & Thoburn, J. (2005). Research review: Child and family support services with minority ethnic families: What can we learn from research? *Child and Family Social Work, 10*, 169.

Chipungu, S.S., & Bent-Goodley, T.B. (2003). Race, poverty, and child maltreatment. *APSAC Advisor, 15*(2), 9–10.

Chui, T., Tran, K., & Meheux, H. (2007). *Immigration in Canada: A portrait of the foreign-born population, 2006 Census: Findings.* Statistics Canada.

Retrieved from: http://www12.statcan.ca/english/census06/analysis/immcit/index.cfm.

Citizenship and Immigration Canada. (2007). Sponsoring your family. Immigration Canada. Retrieved from: http://www.cic.gc.ca/english/immigrate/sponsor/index.asp.

Citizenship and Immigration Canada. (2008). *Immigration applications in Canada made on humanitarian or compassionate grounds.* Immigration Canada. Retrieved from: http://www.cic.gc.ca/English/resources/manuals/ip/ip05e.pdf.

Community Legal Education Ontario. (2004). *Immigration and refugee fact sheet.* London, ON: Department of Justice Canada.

Coohey, C. (1996). Child maltreatment: Testing the social isolation hypothesis. *Child Abuse and Neglect, 20*(3), 241–54.

Coulton, C.J., Korbin, J.E., & Su, M. (1999). Neighborhoods and child maltreatment: A multilevel study. *Child Abuse and Neglect, 23*, 1019–40.

Coutinho, T. (1986). *The specific problems of battered immigrant women: A review of the literature.* Toronto: Education Wife Assault.

Crenshaw, K. (1991). Mapping the margins: Intersectionality, identity politics, and violence against women of color. *Stanford Law Review, 43*, 1241–99.

Dasgupta, S.D. (2000). Charting the course: An overview of domestic violence in the South Asian community. *US Journal of Social Distress and the Homeless, 9*(3), 173–85.

DeKeseredy, W.S., & Dragiewicz, M. (2007). Understanding the complexities of feminist perspectives on woman abuse. *Violence against Women, 13*(8), 874–84.

Doyle, R., & Visano, L. (1987). *A time for action! Access to health and social services for members of diverse racial and cultural groups.* Toronto: Social Planning Council of Metropolitan Toronto.

Dragiewicz, M. (2009). Why sex and gender matter in domestic violence research and advocacy. In E. Stark & E. Buzawa (Eds.), *Violence against women in families and relationships: Criminal justice and the law* (Vol. 3) (pp. 201–15). Santa Barbara: Praeger.

Dubowitz, H., Klockner, A., Starr, A., Jr., & Black, M.M. (1998). Community and professional definitions of child neglect. Child Maltreatment, 3(3), 235–43.

Duffy, A., & Momirov, J. (1997). *Family violence: A Canadian introduction.* Toronto: James Lorimer.

Edleson, J.L. (1998). Responsible mothers and invisible men. *Journal of Interpersonal Violence, 13*(2), 294–98.

Este, D. (2003). Cultural diversity in child welfare. In K. Kufeldt & B. McKenzie (Eds.), *Child welfare: Connecting research, policy, and practice* (pp. 405–10). Waterloo, ON: Wilfrid Laurier University Press.

Falicov, C.J. (1995). Training to think culturally: A multidimensional comparative framework. *Family Process, 34*, 373–88.

Falicov, C.J. (1996). Mexican families. In M. McGoldrick, J. Pearce & J. Giordano (Eds.), *Ethnicity and family therapy* (pp. 169–82). New York: Guildford.

Fontes, L.A. (2005). *Child abuse and culture: Working with diverse families.* New York: Guildford.

Garza-Guerro, A.C. (1974). Culture shock: Its mourning, and the vicissitudes of identity. *Journal of the American Psychoanalytic Association, 22,* 408–29.

Gilligan, P., & Akhtar, S. (2005). Child sexual abuse among Asian communities: Developing materials to raise awareness in Bradford. *Practice, 17*(4), 267–84. Retrieved from: EBSCO database.

Gilligan, P., & Akhtar, S. (2006). Cultural barriers to the disclosure of child sexual abuse in Asian communities: Listening to what women say. *British Journal of Social Work, 36*(8), 1361–77.

Giovannoni, J.M., & Becerra, R.M. (1979). *Defining child abuse.* New York: Free Press.

Gracia, E., & Musitu, G. (2003). Social isolation from communities and child maltreatment: A cross-cultural comparison. *Child Abuse and Neglect, 27,* 153–68.

Graham, D., Rawlings, E., & Rimmi, N. (1988). Survivors of terror: Battered women, hostages, and the Stockholm syndrome. In K. Yllo & M. Bograd (Eds.), *Feminist perspectives on wife abuse* (pp. 217–33). Newbury Park, CA: Sage.

Grinberg, L., & Grinberg, R. (1989). *Psychoanalytic perspectives on migration and exile.* New Haven, CT: Yale University Press.

Herberg, D.C. (1993). *Frameworks for racial and cultural diversity: Teaching and learning for practitioners.* Toronto: Canadian Scholars' Press.

Herman, J.L. (1992). Complex PTSD: A syndrome in survivors of prolonged and repeated trauma. *Journal of Traumatic Stress, 5,* 377–91.

Herman, J.L. (1997). *Trauma and recovery.* New York: Basic Books.

Hong, G.H., & Hong, L.K. (1991). Comparative perspectives on child abuse and neglect: Chinese versus Hispanics and Whites. *Child Welfare, 70*(4), 463–75.

Humphreys, C., Atkar, S., & Baldwin, N. (1999). Discrimination in child protection work: Recurring themes in work with Asian families. *Child and Family Social Work, 4*(4), 283–91.

Imam, U.F. (1994). Asian children and domestic violence. In A. Mullender & R. Morley (Eds.), *Putting men's abuse of women on the child care agenda* (pp. 188–99). London: Whiting & Birch.

Jaffe, P., & Crooks, C. (2004). Partner violence and child custody cases. *Violence against Women, 10*(8), 917–34.

Jaffe, P.G., Crooks, C.V., & Wolfe, D.A. (2003). Legal and policy responses to children exposed to domestic violence: The need to evaluate intended and unintended consequences. *Clinical Child and Family Psychology Review, 6*(3), 205–13.

Johnson, I.M. (1992). Economic, situational, and psychological correlates of the decision-making process of battered women. *Families in Society, 73,* 168–76.

Jones, L., Hughes, M., & Ulrike, U. (2001, April). Post-traumatic stress disorder in victims of domestic violence. *Trauma, Violence & Abuse, 2*(2), 99–119.

Kamateros, M. (2004). The ethnic media outreach project: "Canada is a country for women." In P. Jaffe, L. Baker & A. Cunningham (Eds.), *Protecting children from domestic violence: Strategies for community intervention* (pp. 141–52). New York: Guilford.

Korbin, J.E. (1991). Cross-cultural perspectives and research directions for the 21st century. *Child Abuse and Neglect: The International Journal, 15*(1), 67–77.

Korbin, J.E. (2003). Neighborhood and community connectedness in child maltreatment research. *Child Abuse and Neglect, 27,* 137–40.

Kriz, K., & Skivens, M. (2009). Lost in translation: How child welfare workers in Norway and England experience language difficulties when working with minority ethnic families. *British Journal of Social Work,* 1–15. Advance Access, published online March 27, 2009.

Landau, T. (2001). Women's experiences with mandatory charging for wife assault in Ontario, Canada: A case against the prosecution. *International Review of Victimology (Special Issue on Domestic Violence), 7*(1), 141–57.

Lavergne, C., Dufour, S., Trocmé, N., & Larrivee, M. (2008). Visible minority, Aboriginal, and Caucasian children investigated by Canadian protective services. *Child Protection, 87*(2), 59–76.

Law Courts Education Society of British Columbia. (1995). *Domestic violence and the courts: Immigrants and visible minority perceptions.* Vancouver: Law Courts Education Society of British Columbia.

Lee, M. (2000). Understanding Chinese battered women in North America: A review of literature and practice implications. In D. DeAnda (Ed.), *Violence: Diverse populations and communities* (pp. 215–41). New York: Haworth Press.

Leung, P., Cheung, K., & Stevenson, K.M. (1997). A strengths approach to ethnically sensitive practice for child protective service workers. *Child Welfare, 73*(6), 707–21.

MacLeod, L., & Shin, M. (1994). *Like a wingless bird: A tribute to the survival and courage of women who are abused and who speak neither English nor French.* Ottawa: National Clearinghouse on Family Violence.

Magen, R. (1999). In the best interests of battered women: Reconceptualizing allegations of failure to protect. *Child Maltreatment, 4*(2), 127–35.

Maiter, S. (2001). *Child welfare in a multicultural context: Definitions, values, and service issues* (Unpublished doctoral dissertation). University of Toronto, Toronto.

Maiter, S. (2003). The context of culture: Social work practice with Canadians of South Asian background. In A. Al-Krenawi & J.R. Graham (Eds.), *Multicultural social work in Canada* (pp. 365–87). Toronto: Oxford University Press.

Maiter, S. (2004). Considering context and culture in child protection services to ethnically diverse families: An example from research with parents from the Indian sub continent (South Asians). *Journal of Social Work Research and Evaluation, 5*(1), 63–80.

Maiter, S., Alaggia, R., & Trocmé, N. (2004). Perceptions of child maltreatment by parents from the Indian sub continent: Challenging myths about culturally based abusive parenting practices. *Child Maltreatment, 9*(3), 309–24.

Maiter, S., & Stalker, C. (2011). South Asian immigrants' experience of child protection services: Are we recognizing strengths and resilience? Child and Family Social Work, 16, 138–48.

Maiter, S., Stalker, C., & Alaggia, R. (2005). *Enhancing functioning of newcomer families with young children: Expanding horizons for the early years.* Paper presented at the Joint Conference of the Infant Mental Health Promotion Project and the Ontario Association for Infant Development, Toronto.

Maiter, S., Stalker, C., & Alaggia, R. (2009). The experiences of minority immigrant families receiving child welfare services: Understanding how to reduce risk and increase protective factors. *Families in Society, 90*(1), 28–36.

Manji, S., Maiter, S., & Palmer, S. (2005). Community and informal support for recipients of child protective services. *Child and Youth Services Review, 27*(3), 291–308.

Martin, D., & Mosher, J. (1995). Unkept promises: Experiences of immigrant women with the neo-criminalization of wife abuse. *Canadian Journal of Women and the Law, 8*, 3–44.

McDermott, J.M., & Garofalo, J. (2004). When advocacy for domestic violence victims backfires. *Violence against Women, 10*(11), 1245–66.

McDonald, S. (1999). Not in the numbers: Immigrant women and domestic abuse. *Canadian Woman Studies, 19*(3), 163–67.

McPhail, B.A., Busch, N.B., Kulkarni, S., & Rice, G. (2007). An integrative feminist model: The evolving feminist perspective on intimate partner violence. *Violence against Women, 13*(8), 817–41.

McPhatter, A.R. (1997). Cultural competence in child welfare: What is it? How do we achieve it? What happens without it? *Child Welfare, 76*(1), 255–78.

Mehrotra, T. (1999). The social construction of wife abuse: Experiences of Asian Indian women in the United States. *Violence against Women, 5*(6), 619–40.

Metraux, S., & Culhane, D. (1999). Family dynamics, housing, and recurring homelessness among women in New York City. *Journal of Family Issues, 20*(3), 371–96.

Mullender, A., Hague, G., Imam, U., Kelly, L., Malos, E., & Regan, L. (2002). Barriers of racism, ethnicity, and culture. In A. Mullender (Ed.), *Children's perspectives on domestic violence* (pp. 132–55). London: Sage.

Naidoo, J.C., & Edwards, R.G. (1991). Combating racism involving visible minorities: A review of relevant research and policy development. *Canadian Social Work Review, 8*(2), 211–35.

Ng, R. (1996). *The politics of community services.* Halifax: Fernwood.

Nixon, J., & Humphreys, C. (2010). Marshalling the evidence: Using intersectionality in the domestic violence frame. *Social Politics, 17*(2), 137–58.

O'Neale, V. (2000). *Excellence not excuses: Inspection of services for ethnic minority children and families.* London: Social Services Inspectorate/Department of Health. Retrieved June 21, 2007 from: www.dh.gov.uk/prod_consum_dh/idcplg?IdcService=GET_FILE&dID=25415&Rendition=Web.

Payne, M.A. (1989). Use and abuse of corporal punishment: A Caribbean view. *Child Abuse and Neglect, 13*, 389–401.

Pratt, A. (1995). New immigrant and refugee battered women: The intersection of immigration and criminal justice policy. In M. Valverde, L. MacLeod &

H. Johnson (Eds.), *Wife assault and the criminal justice system: Issues and policies* (pp. 84–104). Toronto: Centre for Criminology, University of Toronto.

Pon, G., Gosine, K., & Phillips, D. (2011). Immediate response: Addressing anti-Native and anti-black racism in child welfare. *International Journal of Child, Youth, and Family Studies, 3 & 4*, 385–409.

Poorman, P.B. (2002). Perceptions of thriving by women who have experienced abuse or status-related oppression. *Psychology of Women Quarterly, 26*, 51–62.

Portwood, S.G. (1999). Coming to terms with a consensual definition of child maltreatment. *Child Maltreatment, 4*(1), 56–68.

Pugh, R., & Williams, D. (2006). Language policy and provision in social service organizations. *British Journal of Social Work, 36*, 1227–44.

Qureshi, T., Berridge, D., & Wenman, H. (2000). *Where to turn? Family support for South Asian communities—a case study.* London: National Children's Bureau.

Rachin, L. (1997). The spousal assault policy: A critical analysis. *Osgoode Hall Law Journal, 35*(4), 785–804.

Ralston, H. (1999). Canadian immigration policy in the twentieth century: Its impact on South Asian women. *Canadian Woman Studies, 19*(3), 33–37.

Rhodes, K.V., & Levinson, W. (2003). Interventions for intimate partner violence against women: Clinical applications. *JAMA, 289*(5), 601–5.

Roberts, D. (2002). *Shattered bonds: The color of child welfare.* New York: Basic Books.

Rose, S.J., & Meezan, W. (1996). Variations in perceptions of child neglect. *Child Welfare, 75*(2), 139–60.

Segal, U.A., & Mayadas, N.S. (2005). Assessment of issues facing immigrant and refugee families. *Child Welfare, 84*(5), 563–84.

Sev'er, A. (2002). A feminist analysis of flight of abused women, plight of Canadian shelters: Another road to homelessness. *Journal of Social Distress and Homelessness, 11*(4), 307–24.

Shaffer, M., & Bala, N. (2004). The role of family courts in domestic violence: The Canadian experience. In P. Jaffe, L. Baker & A. Cunningham (Eds.), *Protecting children from domestic violence: Strategies for community intervention* (pp. 171–87). New York: Guilford.

Shirwadkar, S. (2004). Canadian domestic violence policy and Indian immigrant women. *Violence against Women, 10*(8), 860–79.

Shor, R. (1998, July–August). The significance of religion in advancing a culturally sensitive approach towards child maltreatment. *Families in Society: The Journal of Contemporary Human Services, 79*(4), 400–9.

Shor, R. (1999). Inappropriate child rearing practices as perceived by Jewish immigrant parents from the former Soviet Union. *Child Abuse and Neglect, 23*(5), 487–99.

Statistics Canada. (2001). *Canadian crime statistics 2000.* Catalogue no. 85–205. Ottawa: Canadian Centre for Justice Statistics, Statistics Canada.

Statistics Canada. (2005). *Family violence in Canada: A statistical profile 2005.* Catalogue no. 85-224-xie. Ottawa: Canadian Centre for Justice Statistics.

Statistics Canada. (2006). *Immigration in Canada: A portrait of the foreign-born population, 2006 Census.* Catalogue no. 97-557-XIE.

Steiner, G., & Bansil, R. (1989). Cultural patterns and the family system in Asian Indians: Implications for psychotherapy. *Journal of Comparative Family Studies, 20*(3), 371–75.

Sue, D.W., & Sue, D. (1990). *Counseling the culturally different: Theory and practice.* New York: Wiley.

Tator, C. (1996). Anti-racism and the human service delivery system. In C.E. James (Ed.), *Perspectives on racism and the human services sector* (pp. 152–70). Toronto: University of Toronto Press.

Taylor-Butts, A. (2005). Shelters for abused women. *Juristat, 25*(3). Catalogue no. 85002. Ottawa: Canadian Centre for Justice Statistics.

Thoburn, J., Chand, A., & Proctor, J. (2005). *Child welfare services for minority and ethnic families.* London: Jessica Kingsley Publishers. Retrieved from: http://site.ebrary.com.proxy.ucfv.ca:2048/lib/ucfv/Doc?id=10082296.

Tjaden, P.G., & Thoennes, N. (1992). Predictors of legal intervention in child maltreatment cases. *Child Abuse and Neglect, 16*, 807–21.

Trocmé, N. (2003). *Differential response to changes in reported child maltreatment: Federal program and policy implications (OIS 1993/1998).* Centre of Excellence in Child Welfare Report. Toronto: Faculty of Social Work, University of Toronto.

Trotter, C. (2002). Worker skill and client outcome in child protection. *Child Abuse Review, 11*, 38–50.

Wathen, C.N., & MacMillan, H.L. (2003). Interventions for violence against women. *JAMA, 289*(5), 589–600.

Williams, R.B. (1998, July). Asian American and Pakistani religions in the United States. *Annals, AAPSS, 558*, 178–95.

Woman Abuse Council of Toronto. (1998). *Taking action against woman abuse.* Toronto City Council, unpublished report, Toronto, Ontario.

Yoshihama, M. (2000). Reinterpreting strength and safety in a socio-cultural context: Dynamics of domestic violence and experiences of women of Japanese descent. *Children and Youth Services Review, 22*(3/4), 207–29.

Zorza, J. (1996). Woman battering: A major cause of homelessness. *National Clearinghouse Review, 25*, 420–29.

VIOLENCE ACROSS THE LIFE COURSE

10

CHILDREN ABUSED, NEGLECTED, AND LIVING WITH VIOLENCE
AN OVERVIEW

CATHY VINE, NICO TROCMÉ, BRUCE MACLAURIN, AND BARBARA FALLON

> Violence has pretty much been my life since the day I was born.
> —Youth participant, *Just listen to me:*
> *Youth voices on violence* (Ma, 2004)

INTRODUCTION

As Canadians, we would agree that children need to be fed, sheltered, and nurtured, and that we want them to grow up to be happy, healthy, and successful. Many of us would also agree that children should not be physically assaulted, held captive, or humiliated.

And yet as soon as we examine any of these assertions more closely, we arrive at some of the dilemmas central to addressing child abuse. Definitions vary as one person's view of what constitutes abuse—"hitting"—is another person's method for discipline—"spanking." Some of us express doubt about whether certain behaviours actually do harm—"It was just a little slap...it happened when she was four." Some wonder whether "children's rights" now override "parents' rights" and certainly, some question who ultimately holds the authority for raising children—the family or the state?

Clearly, how we view, care for, and protect children is influenced by legal, social, political, economic, cultural, and religious traditions along with an ever-expanding knowledge base regarding child development and the short- and long-term effects of child abuse and trauma.

Using a question-and-answer format and drawing on the findings of the 2008 Canadian Incidence Study of Reported Child Abuse and Neglect (CIS-2008), along with other major studies, this chapter will wade into the heart of these matters by addressing key questions and issues concerning child abuse and neglect—also referred to as child maltreatment—in Canada. Our goal is to provide readers with an overview of the nature, scope, characteristics, and impact of child maltreatment as it can be understood from the experience of the child and within the contexts and limitations of research and the systems involved in responding. Throughout, we feature quotes from young people who shared their views through two very different forums. The first involved eighty youth participating in round-table discussions on violence in Ontario in 2004, which resulted in the report *Just listen to me: Youth voices on violence*. The second, more recent, process involved youth holding their own hearings at Queen's Park, home of the Ontario Legislature. Their views are reflected in, *My REAL life book: Report from the Youth Leaving Care Hearings*, published in 2012.[1] We will also highlight and profile a variety of issues and concerns worthy of closer examination. It is important to assert from the outset, nevertheless, that "the study of child maltreatment is in its infancy in Canada" (Ward & Bennett, 2003, p. 919).

Focusing on the abuse that children experience within their families allows us to sharpen our understanding of children's experiences in the place they call home. However, it is important to recognize that children are also abused within a variety of settings (e.g., schools, recreation centres, places of worship, etc.) and through relationships formed outside of their families (e.g., coaches, neighbours, tutors, peers, online, etc.). Furthermore, children abused in their families may also be subsequently taken into the care of child welfare and placed in foster homes, group homes, residential treatment facilities, and other institutional settings, and it is important to include some discussion about the experience of abuse in these "substitute" family settings as well.

Issue profile   **Abuse in Substitute Families and Institutions**

In addition to the typical challenges of securing money for rent, food, tuition and books, I had to find a way to pay for treatment for debilitating depression that stemmed from the loss of my parents and the subsequent abuse that followed while I was in care.

—Ken, thirty-one, former youth in care,
My REAL life book (Youth Leaving Care Hearings, 2012)

Similar to the women who spoke out publicly in the 1960s and 1970s about the incest they had experienced in their families, in more recent decades there has been a groundswell of adults coming forward to disclose their experiences of physical, sexual, and emotional abuse in residential schools, reformatories, group homes, and foster care. (See also Baskin in this volume regarding Aboriginal experiences in residential schools; and Sobsey and Sobon in this volume regarding children with disabilities living in substitute family settings and institutions.) These disclosures continue to have an impact on how governments and institutions address child abuse. The Law Commission of Canada's report *Restoring dignity—responding to child abuse in Canadian institutions* (2000), examined a range of possible processes to address the human consequences of child physical and sexual abuse that took place in institutions run or funded by governments. Better understanding of the long-term occurrence and impact of institutional child abuse will provide direction as to how we can more effectively address child abuse both *within* institutions and *through* institutions like schools, where children spend so much of their daily lives. Wolfe and colleagues (2001) summarize the challenges: "Dealing with institutional abuse becomes problematic because it often involves individuals in positions of trust, power and authority, the very individuals we rely on to protect our children from harm, and the same individuals who run the institution" (p. 21).

It is important to note that while the Canadian Incidence Study (CIS) was the first national study in Canada to document rates of child abuse and neglect, its focus was confined to maltreatment brought to the attention of child welfare services whose mandate is to attend to the welfare of children living with their families. At the Youth Leaving Care Hearings held in Toronto in November 2011, some of the participants spoke about experiencing abuse in the care system. Being isolated and vulnerable were two of several key themes identified through the hearings and serve as a fresh reminder that children being cared for within substitute family settings continue to be at risk for abuse (Report from the Youth Leaving Care Hearings, 2012).

HOW BIG IS THE PROBLEM OF CHILD ABUSE IN CANADA?

Unfortunately, there is no simple or definitive answer to this question for some of the reasons outlined above: no single, agreed-upon definition; hesitation to identify some behaviours as abusive; exclusion of potential sources of abuse (many surveys ask about acts committed by adults, but don't include acts committed by siblings, for example); inconsistent methods of collecting statistics; children's reluctance to tell, for many reasons, including fear of retribution, and so on. Even with these limitations, we can say that for physical and sexual abuse—the forms of abuse that people most often associate with "child abuse"—the incidence is disquieting:

- Approximately 31 percent of adult men and 21 percent of adult women report a history of physical abuse—this figure actually *excludes* slapping and spanking experienced in childhood (MacMillan et al., 1997).
- Approximately 12 percent to 20 percent of adult women and 3 percent to 11 percent of adult men report a history of child sexual abuse (MacMillan et al., 1997; Gilbert, Widom, Browne, et al., 2009).

This leads researchers to conclude that child abuse is a common occurrence for girls and boys in Canada. "It is hard to envision a serious condition in childhood that affects as many children as maltreatment" (MacMillan, 2000, p. 703).

The issue of child abuse has been of concern to Canadians dating back to the late 1800s, when early child welfare measures were established to address public alarm about cruelty to children and neglect (Jones & Rutman, 1981). Its evolution as a social problem in and of itself is worthy of extensive analysis; suffice it to say, Canadians have been most comfortable viewing child abuse as a problem that affects others, most notably, the poor, and to those cultures that are popularly (but erroneously) believed to condone its use. (See McGillivray and Durrant in this volume regarding how understanding about corporal punishment has evolved; see Birnbaum in this volume regarding the consistently secondary status of children and their rights when compared to their parents.)

Child abuse began receiving nationally focused attention in the 1980s and 1990s. Two key reports on child sexual abuse—the first prepared by the Committee on Sexual Offences against Children and Youth and commonly referred to as the Badgley Report (1984), and the second, *Reaching for solutions*, prepared by Rix Rogers (1990)—had a significant impact on establishing sexual abuse as a form of child abuse and influenced policy and practice accordingly. These and other developments culminated in the mounting of the CIS-1998, the first national study to examine the incidence of reported maltreatment and the characteristics of families investigated by child welfare. The ways in which the data were gathered for this study illuminate the issue of how much we can know about the incidence of child abuse and neglect through research findings derived from reports of child welfare investigations.

THE CANADIAN INCIDENCE STUDY OF REPORTED CHILD ABUSE AND NEGLECT (CIS-2008)

The CIS-2008 is the third nationwide study of the incidence and characteristics of child abuse and neglect investigated across Canada (Trocmé et al., 2010). The study was previously conducted in 1998 (Trocmé et al.,

2001) and 2003 (Trocmé, Fallon, MacLaurin, Daciuk, Felstiner, Black et al., 2005) and provides an updated profile of investigations in Canada as well as a comparison of rates of investigated maltreatment across the three cycles. The 2008 cycle tracked 15,980 investigations conducted in 112 child welfare service areas sampled from every province and territory in Canada in 2008. Information about the outcomes of the investigations and key child and family characteristics was collected directly from the investigating child welfare workers. The study did not include cases that were not reported to authorities, nor did it include cases only investigated by the police. National annual estimates were then derived from the CIS-2008 sample using weights reflecting annual case activity in the selected service areas and the child population in the selected areas relative to the whole country.

> **ISSUE PROFILE**   Reporting Suspected Child Abuse and Neglect
>
> In Canada, provincial and territorial laws govern the reporting of suspected child abuse and neglect. In most jurisdictions, community members and professionals alike are required to report any suspicious cases to the appropriate authority. Child welfare is authorized to investigate suspected abuse within families, whereas the police almost exclusively investigate abuse suspected to have been committed by someone outside the family. In many communities, investigations are conducted jointly by police and child welfare, following well-established community protocols. Reports are investigated to determine if abuse has occurred or if a child is at risk for abuse. While most professional schools provide training regarding the obligations of "mandated reporters" (such as social workers, educators, physicians), there is no concerted effort to educate members of the general public about their obligations. Instead, community members often learn about their responsibility when particular cases receive media coverage.

An estimated 235,842 child maltreatment investigations were conducted in Canada in 2008, a rate of 39.16 investigations per thousand children. Thirty-six percent of investigations were substantiated (14.19 per thousand) and an additional 8 percent of investigations of maltreatment remained suspected. A third of all investigations were unsubstantiated while approximately a quarter of all investigations focused on concerns about possible risk of future maltreatment. The incidence rate of investigated maltreatment was 21.47 per one thousand children for the CIS-1998 and increased to 38.33 per thousand for the CIS-2003. The dramatic increase between 1998 and 2003 may be explained by changes in how cases are substantiated; more systematic identification of victimized siblings; and greater awareness of emotional maltreatment and exposure to domestic violence (Trocmé, Fallon & MacLaurin, 2011; Trocmé, Fallon, MacLaurin et al., 2011).

ISSUE PROFILE   Understanding "False Allegations"

Reports of suspected abuse are investigated and a determination is made. This involves classifying the allegation as substantiated, suspected, or unsubstantiated. These distinctions have been developed to aid child welfare workers in their critical role of determining what has occurred or is at risk of occurring and deciding how best to ensure the safety of the child. A child's experience, developmental capacity, and situation-specific factors such as fear would all influence her or his ability to provide the kind of evidence necessary for child welfare to formally draw conclusions about risk and harm. In all cycles of the CIS, the majority of all reports were made in good faith, but between 4 percent and 5 percent of investigations were judged to be unsubstantiated and intentionally false. In most cases a report is made in good faith; for example, a recreation leader notices bruising on a child's leg and becomes concerned when the child doesn't want to talk about how it happened. Upon investigation, the source of the bruising is found to be from an accidental injury sustained in a fall rather than evidence of a more suspicious injury. In this case, the recreation leader has fulfilled her or his obligation, reported in "good faith," and the authorities have carried out their role. It is critical for professionals and community members to know that most reports that turn out to be unsubstantiated are made in good faith and are by far more common than false allegations (Knott, Trocmé & Bala, 2004). Given the public and media tension about the issue of "false allegations," it is quite surprising to learn that they occur relatively infrequently. Even more surprising, perhaps, is that while false allegations do occur most often in the context of custody or access disputes, most of the fabricated reports concern neglect rather than sexual abuse (Knott, Trocmé & Bala, 2004). There is no question that intentional false allegations create serious problems for the accused, their families, and the system. However, it is also concerning that the heightened attention to the issue of "false allegations" has fuelled "no touch" and "no staff alone" policies in a range of settings. These policies were designed and instituted expressly to protect staff from "false allegations," regardless of whether physical contact or privacy between adults and children is considered to be positive or negative. Contrast this with the concerning number of children who commonly experience abuse. These children spend most days in schools and in after school care and recreation programs, and there are no legislative or organizational policies in place to promote disclosures that may deliver them from abuse.

How the CIS Findings Compare to Other Research

The rate of substantiated victimization reported in the United States by the National Child Abuse and Neglect Data System (NCANDS) for 2008 was 9.5 per one thousand children, a decrease from 10.9 per one thousand children in 2005. Of these cases, 71.1 percent were classified as neglect, 16.1 percent as physical abuse, 9.1 percent as sexual abuse, 7.5 percent as psychological maltreatment, and 2.2 percent as medical neglect. In addition, 9.0 percent of victims experienced other types of maltreatment, including abandonment, threats of harm, or congenital drug addiction (US Department of Health and Human Services, 2009). By comparison, the rate of substanti-

Table 10.1   Estimated* Rate and Incidence of Child Maltreatment Investigations by Level of Substantiation in Canada in 2008 (CIS-2008)

	Maltreatment Investigations			Risk Investigations			
				Future Maltreatment			
	Sub-stantiated	*Suspected*	*Unsub-stantiated*	*Risk*	*Unknown Risk*	*No Risk*	*Total*
Maltreatment Investigations							
Child investigations	85,440	17,918	71,053	12,018	10,124	39,289	235,842
Incidence per 1,000 children	14.19	2.98	11.8	2.00	1.67	6.52	39.16
Row percentage	36%	8%	30%	5%	4%	17%	100%

Note: * Weighted estimates are based on a sample of 15,980 investigations

ated maltreatment reported by the CIS-2008 is 14.19 per one thousand children (Trocmé et al., 2010). The primary category of maltreatment included neglect (34 percent), exposure to intimate partner violence (34 percent), physical abuse (20 percent), emotional maltreatment (9 percent), and sexual abuse (3 percent)—see Table 10.2. The higher rate of victimization reported in Canada can be explained to a large extent by broader mandates in Canada, especially with respect to the inclusion of many more cases of exposure to intimate partner violence.[2]

The National Incidence Studies (NIS) in the United States provide a broader picture of the scope of the problem by including cases reported to child protection authorities as well as cases identified by professionals—in health, education, social service, and justice—who work with children. The NIS-4 reported an overall victimization rate of 17.1 per one thousand under the harm standard classification, which counts only children who have experienced demonstrable harm as a result of the maltreatment (Sedlak et al., 2010). This study also collects data under the endangerment standard classification, which expands definitions to include children who were not yet harmed by maltreatment, but who experienced maltreatment that placed them in danger of being harmed. The incidence rate for the endangerment standard is 39.5 per one thousand, 11.3 per one thousand for forms of abuse, and 30.6 per one thousand for forms of neglect.

Another point of comparison is childhood prevalence rates. Prevalence studies report rates of victimization during childhood, as opposed to incidence statistics that measure rates of victimization during a specific year. The most extensive child maltreatment prevalence data available in Canada are from an adult population health survey conducted in Ontario in 1990. Despite the time that has passed since it was conducted, it is still the most recent population study in Canada. As mentioned above, 31 percent of men and 21.1 percent of women reported that they had been physically abused during their childhood, and 12.8 percent of women and 4.3 percent of men reported a history of sexual abuse (MacMillan et al., 1997).

Secrets one girl is desperate to tell. This is my private childhood hell.
—Sophie, twenty-two, former youth in care,
My REAL life book (Youth Leaving Care Hearings, 2012)

Figure 10.1   Scope of the CIS-2008: CIS Iceberg

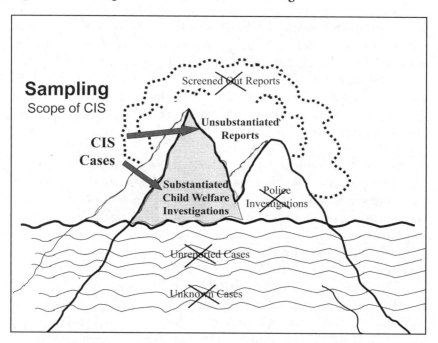

Source: Adapted from N. Trocmé, D. McPhee, K.K. Tam, & T. Hay, *Ontario incidence study of reported child abuse and neglect* (Toronto: Institute for the Prevention of Child Abuse, 1994).

The CIS-2008 data presented in this chapter are limited to cases that have been reported to and investigated by child welfare authorities. On the basis of findings from adult recall surveys of childhood victimization and findings from the NIS studies of professionals working with children, one must assume that the CIS-2008 cases represent the "tip of the iceberg." Pictured in Figure 10.1, this concept is quite useful in showing the dichotomy between the experiences of abuse that become known to child welfare and police officials ("the tip") and the larger yet unknown number of those experiences that stay hidden ("below the surface") until well into adulthood, if indeed they are ever disclosed at all. This also means that police, child welfare, and other community-based mental health responses to child abuse only ever address the needs of children whose abuse comes to their attention. For the broader numbers of children who struggle with behavioural problems, negative peer relationships, or depression—just some of the symptoms commonly linked with maltreatment—abuse, which may be at the root of these difficulties, may not be uncovered or ever reach the attention of authorities. Unfortunately, more accurate data on childhood victimization are not available in Canada.

WHAT CONSTITUTES CHILD ABUSE?

When you're two years old, you don't care. You're a hellion. I would
go around and hit my mom, because I didn't know better. I grew
up with my dad hitting my mom, trying to kill me, holding a gun to
my head or my mom's. He killed my dog in my hands. So I grew
up around violence and so I thought it was okay to hit my mom.
I hit my mom.
—Youth participant, *Just listen to me: Youth
voices on violence* (Ma, 2004)

We tend to think of child abuse as *acts inflicted on children* such as physical abuse (hitting, kicking, biting) and sexual abuse (touching, exposing, inviting/involving a child in a sexual activity). These are actions that result or may result in causing harm to a child. We think less often about other forms such as *verbal acts* (belittling, screaming, and threatening) or *acts of omission* (failure to supervise or provide necessities of life), which might fall under emotional and psychological abuse or neglect. It was only recently that a child's exposure to intimate partner violence, for example, was recognized as a form of emotional maltreatment requiring child welfare involvement.

Issue Profile   Language and Naming

Examining terms like "exposure to spousal violence," "exposure to domestic violence," or "intimate partner violence," for example, brings into focus some of the problems with naming the forms of child abuse. Even terms such as "physical" and "sexual" abuse, which have been in use for decades, tend to inadvertently emphasize the "physical" act of the abuse, overshadowing the emotional and psychological aspects, and masking any sense of the longer-term impact. When it comes to sexual abuse, for example, *fondling* is commonly considered "less traumatic" and *sexual intercourse* is commonly considered the "worst" form of assault. (The legal process further contributes to this concept of "ranking" the seriousness of certain forms of abuse.) This obscures the betrayal and shame experienced by many children when there is any violation of the body and psychic boundary. This perception also diminishes recognition of the impact of "grooming" on normal developmental processes. Adults and children alike grimace when someone (often with kind intentions) reminds them that they were "just" fondled or abused "only" once. Now, the term "exposure" is used more often to label a child's experience of her or his mother being abused by her partner. Previously, "witnessing" was used, and as we learned more about the child's experience, the inadequacies of the term became more apparent. For example, witnessing connotes the temporary, passive experience of a bystander—"Children are not 'witnesses' to events in their homes" (Cunningham & Baker, 2007, p. 6). Children who live with domestic violence endure many of the anxieties and tensions that accompany the dynamics of intimate violence as if they were directly involved. Indeed, in many situations, children are equally at risk when they try to intervene to protect a parent. In other situations, children may not directly "see" the violence but instead "hear" it taking place as they lie in their beds at night. Reducing their experiences to "witnessing" minimizes the dangers and negates their sometimes very active efforts to manage and/ or stop the violence (see Jenney and Alaggia in this volume for more in-depth discussion).

Examining the specific forms of abuse allows us to break down child abuse or child maltreatment into distinct components so that we can look more closely at the behaviours that are associated with each form and the frequency it takes place. Knowing more about the forms also offers some direction for intervention. However, the problems with separating one form of child maltreatment from another require comment: "Tendencies among professionals to compartmentalize aspects of the problem and place them in watertight compartments create their own problems, as there are more similarities than differences in the various characteristics and manifestations of abuse" (Iwaniec, 1995, p. 189).

Forms of Maltreatment

I think verbal violence is more lasting. It's more lasting because with the physical stuff, scars can heal and stuff. And sometimes I'll

> remember my dad beating me, but I won't remember the intensity
> or the pain, but I'll remember my dad saying "you piece of shit"
> or something and that, that'll stick with me.
> —Youth participant, *Just listen to me:*
> *Youth voices on violence* (Ma, 2004)

Drawing again on the findings of the CIS-2008, this section focuses on the subsample of substantiated investigations (N = 6,163) and the five major forms of maltreatment: physical abuse, sexual abuse, neglect, emotional maltreatment, and exposure to intimate partner violence.

Each substantiated investigation was classified by the investigating worker under up to three forms of maltreatment from a list of thirty-two possible categories, subsumed in Table 10.2 under five major forms of maltreatment. Neglect was the primary category of maltreatment in 34 percent of substantiated cases, followed by exposure to intimate partner violence (34 percent), physical abuse (20 percent), emotional maltreatment (9 percent), and sexual abuse (3 percent).

Once again, the picture provided by the research (see Figure 10.2) does not fit with the images that come to mind about which form of abuse occurs most often. For example, given the degree of media attention to child sexual abuse, one would expect it to have the highest incidence. As it turns out, all other forms of child maltreatment are reported and substantiated at a higher rate than sexual abuse. It should be noted, however, that these estimates do not include later reports of sexual abuse or reports that are investigated only by the police, where the perpetrator is living outside the family home and there is no concern about parental responsibility.

Table 10.2   **Primary Categories of Substantiated Maltreatment, Estimated Rates for Canada in 2008 (CIS-2008)**

	Substantiated Investigations	Proportion of All Substantiated Investigations
Physical abuse	17,212	20%
Sexual abuse	2,607	3%
Neglect	28,939	34%
Emotional maltreatment	7,423	9%
Exposure to intimate partner violence	29,259	34%
Total	85,440	100%

Note: Weighted estimates are based on a sample of 6,163 substantiated investigations.

Figure 10.2   Primary Category of Substantiated Maltreatment in Canada in 2008 (CIS-2008)

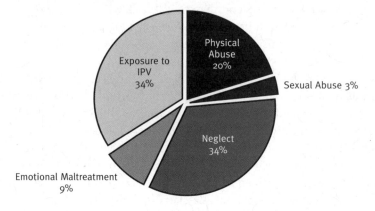

I'm pretty sure I would have died without the CAS.
So, I would not be living.
—Anonymous, *My REAL life book*
(Youth Leaving Care Hearings, 2012)

Physical Abuse

Cases of investigated maltreatment were classified as physical abuse if the child was suspected to have suffered or to be at substantial risk of suffering physical harm at the hands of his or her caregiver. In Canada in 2008, there were an estimated 17,212 substantiated investigations where physical abuse was the primary concern. Primary forms of substantiated physical abuse reported most frequently include hitting with a hand (46 percent); shaking, pushing, grabbing, or throwing (23 percent); hitting with an object (18 percent); punching, kicking, or biting (6 percent); and choking, poisoning, or stabbing (1 percent). In addition, other types of unspecified physical abuse were noted for 6 percent of substantiated cases. Notably, a high proportion of substantiated cases involving physical abuse occur in the context of punishment. This is consistent with previous studies of physical abuse that have found that most of these cases arise out of a context of punishment (Gil, 1970; Kadushin & Martin, 1981; Margolin, 1990; see Trocmé & Durrant, 2003, for a review; see McGillivray and Durrant's discussion in this volume tracing the corporal punishment of children, its effects, and the role of Section 43 in legitimating the use of physical force).

Table 10.3   Forms of Substantiated Physical Abuse, Estimated Rates for Canada in 2008 (CIS-2008)

	Substantiated Investigations	Proportion of All Substantiated Physical Abuse
Shake, push, grab, or throw	4,031	23%
Hit with hand	7,942	46%
Punch, kick, or bite	985	6%
Hit with object	3,066	18%
Choking, poisoning, stabbing	139	1%
Other physical abuse	1,049	6%
Total	17,212	100%

Note: Weighted estimates are based on a sample of 6,163 investigations. Rows add up to more than the total because some cases involve several forms of maltreatment.

Sexual Abuse

Sexual abuse was identified as the primary category of maltreatment in an estimated 5,870 of the substantiated cases in CIS-2008. Most forms of substantiated sexual abuse involve sexual contact, including fondling (48 percent) and intercourse (20 percent). Acts of exposure or voyeurism were rarely documented; however, it should be noted again that in most jurisdictions, these cases would be investigated solely by the police unless the alleged perpetrator was a parent or other family member. The incidence rate of substantiated child sexual abuse has been decreasing over the three cycles of the CIS and it is difficult to know for certain if this change actually reflects a decline in the rate—perhaps as a result of greater public awareness and strong coordination among the systems—or an increased reluctance to report for the very same reasons. Recent work is beginning to examine this trend in the United States as well as in Canada (Jones & Finkelhor, 2003; Finkelhor & Jones, 2004; Collin-Vezina et al., 2010).

Exposure to Intimate Partner Violence

Exposure to intimate partner violence was the primary substantiated form of maltreatment in over 29,000 investigations across Canada in 2008. This accounts for 34 percent of all substantiated cases. As noted in the first two cycles of the CIS, the estimated number of substantiated cases involving intimate partner violence increased dramatically between 1998 and 2003.

Table 10.4   Forms of Substantiated Sexual Abuse, Estimated Rates for Canada in 2008 (CIS-2008)

	Substantiated Investigations	Proportion of All Substantiated Sexual Abuse
Penetration	524	20%
Attempted penetration	—	3%
Oral sex	129	5%
Fondling	1,258	48%
Sex talk or images	145	6%
Voyeurism	—	1%
Exhibitionism	—	3%
Exploitation	—	2%
Other sexual abuse	331	13%
Total	2,607	100%

Note: Weighted estimates are based on a sample of 6,163 investigations.
(—) estimates are too low to report reliably.
Column adds up to more than 100 percent because some cases involve several forms of maltreatment.

However, it levelled between 2003 and 2008. With growing awareness of the negative impact of exposure to intimate partner violence on children, more provinces and territories have added exposure to intimate partner violence as a category of maltreatment requiring child welfare involvement. Legislative and policy changes were instituted in response to research evidence and public concerns.

The CIS-2008 documented exposure to intimate partner violence in three ways. *Direct witness to physical violence* included situations where the child was present and witnessed the violence between the intimate partners. *Indirect exposure to physical violence* included situations where the child over-

ISSUE PROFILE   Should Exposure to Intimate Partner Violence Be Considered a Form of Child Maltreatment?

There is some debate about the classification of exposure to intimate partner violence as a form of child maltreatment. While there is general consensus about the negative impact of exposure on children, there is concern that mothers who are victimized by their partners are being unfairly held accountable for failing to protect their children from the same violence that is being inflicted on them (for further discussion, see Jenney and Alaggia, and Strega in this volume).

Table 10.5   Forms of Substantiated Exposure to Intimate Partner
Violence, Estimated Rates for Canada in 2008 (CIS-2008)

	Substantiated Investigations	Proportion of All Substantiated Exposure to IPV
Direct witness to physical violence	13,901	48%
Indirect exposure to physical violence	7,070	24%
Exposure to emotional violence	8,288	28%
Total	29,259	100%

Note: Weighted estimates are based on a sample of 6,163 investigations. Column adds up to more than 100 percent because some cases involve several forms of maltreatment.

heard the violence or saw the immediate consequences of the assault or was told or overheard conversations about the violence. The final type is where the child is *exposed directly or indirectly to emotional violence* between the two partners. Direct witness to physical violence was noted in 48 percent of the 29,259 cases of intimate partner violence, followed by exposure to emotional violence (28 percent) and indirect exposure to physical violence (24 percent).

Neglect
Child neglect occurs when a child's parents or caregivers do not provide the requisite attention to his or her emotional, psychological, or physical development. Unlike abuse, which usually occurs in the form of an incident, neglect more often involves chronic situations that are not as easily identified. Substantiated neglect was the primary category of maltreatment for an estimated 28,939 investigations in 2008 or 34 percent of all substantiated maltreatment investigations. Forms of substantiated neglect include failure to supervise, leading to physical harm (44 percent of all neglect cases). This is followed by physical neglect (32 percent), abandonment (8 percent), educational neglect (6 percent), medical neglect (5 percent), failure to provide psychiatric treatment (3 percent), failure to supervise leading to sexual abuse (2 percent), and permitting criminal behaviour (1 percent).

Emotional Maltreatment
Emotional maltreatment involves acts or omissions by parents or caregivers that cause or could cause serious behavioural, cognitive, emotional, or mental disorders (Trocmé, Fallon, MacLaurin et al., 2011). It can include verbal threats, socially isolating a child, intimidation, exploitation, terrorizing, or routinely making unreasonable demands on a child. In Canada in 2008, emotional maltreatment was the primary substantiated category

of maltreatment for an estimated 7,423 child investigations or 9 percent of all substantiated investigations. This form of maltreatment had one of the higher substantiation rates (48 percent) second only to exposure to intimate partner violence. The CIS-2008 tracked five forms of emotional maltreatment. The most common form was verbal abuse or belittling (32 percent of all substantiated emotional maltreatment investigations), followed by non-partner physical violence (27 percent), inadequate nurturing or affection (19 percent), terrorizing or threat of violence (16 percent), exploiting or corrupting behaviour (5 percent), and isolation or confinement (2 percent).

WHICH CHILDREN ARE MOST AT RISK FOR CHILD MALTREATMENT?

Should we be concerned about one group of children over another? Are some children more at risk for particular types of abuse? Are disabled children the most vulnerable? Maltreatment rates in children with developmental delays, for example, are indeed higher: children with delays are overrepresented in all four categories of maltreatment (i.e., physical abuse, sexual abuse, emotional maltreatment, and neglect). However, the relationship between violence and disability is complex (see Sobsey and Sobon in this volume for in-depth discussion of these issues). Furthermore, although 5 percent of children in Canada are Aboriginal, they make up 19 percent of reports to child welfare and 22 percent of all substantiated investigations in the CIS-2008. We profile some of the characteristics of Aboriginal families below and refer the reader to Baskin in this volume for further discussion of the history and context of child welfare intervention in the lives of Aboriginal families.[3]

Figure 10.3   **Aboriginal Heritage of Children, in Substantiated Maltreatment Investigations in Canada in 2008 (CIS-2008)**

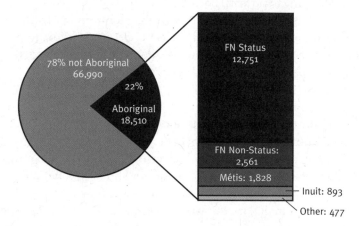

ISSUE PROFILE   First Nations Children and Risk for
Maltreatment

First Nations children are four times more likely to be investigated by child welfare services in Canada and First Nations and twelve times more likely to be placed in out-of-home care during these investigations. Furthermore, when they come into contact with child welfare authorities, First Nations families present a higher risk profile compared to investigated non-Aboriginal families: they were larger, led by younger parents, who were more often single, dependent on social assistance, living in overcrowded housing, and more likely to have moved multiple times in the last year. These cases were significantly more likely to have been previously open for service and to involve neglect. Investigating child welfare workers were more likely to note concerns about intimate partner violence, alcohol abuse, lack of social supports, drug/solvent abuse, and a history of living in foster care/ group homes for First Nations parents compared to non-Aboriginal parents. The children themselves, however, did not differ significantly on many child functioning variables. First Nations and non-Aboriginal children were equally likely to have academic difficulties, and display aggressive, depression/anxiety, and self-harming behaviours. Differences were noted in the rate of alcohol abuse, drug/solvent abuse, substance abuse-related birth defects, and running away. Many First Nations families involved in child welfare investigations may require programs offering longer term, comprehensive services designed to help them address the multiple factors—such as poverty, substance abuse, domestic violence, and social isolation—which pose chronic challenges to their abilities to ensure the well-being of First Nations children. (Sinha, Trocmé, Fallon et al., 2011)

While we provided examples of the rates of maltreatment for two particular groups of children, at the same time, it is difficult and potentially misguided to pinpoint precise factors that identify some children as more vulnerable to maltreatment. Our ever-expanding knowledge base continually introduces new factors for consideration. For example, abuse is substantiated at a much higher rate in investigations involving Aboriginal children and children from visible minority families when compared to non-Aboriginal families. Why is this? See Alaggia and Maiter in this volume for more in-depth discussion. We also run the risk of overlooking the most obvious factor: the dependency and vulnerability of all children by virtue of their developmental stage. Furthermore, research has tended to examine single forms of abuse and associated risk factors. However, many children experience multiple forms of abuse and neglect. Children exposed to domestic violence, for example, experience emotional abuse and are more likely to be sexually abused (Hiebert-Murphy, 2001; Kellogg & Menard, 2003). It is therefore evident that clusters of factors and the contexts of children's lived experience need to be taken into account.

Household Characteristics

> We were also so poor and had to move multiple times and mainly
> survived on dry cereal, tomato sandwiches and a mixture of mashed
> potatoes, tomatoes and noodles, because that was all we could afford.
> —Nate, nineteen, youth in care, *My REAL life book*
> (Youth Leaving Care Hearings, 2012)

Family violence is often perceived to occur in a context of poverty and
isolation. While families living in such circumstances are overrepresented
in the child welfare system, one should also be careful to not ignore family
violence in higher income groups or stigmatize poor families.

The figures in Table 10.6 illustrate the environmental risk factors most
commonly associated with the different forms of child abuse. For example,
24 percent of the children experiencing physical abuse had experienced a
move in the previous twelve months, and 30 percent lived with parents who
appeared to lack social support. Children who experience sexual abuse are
typically understood to live in isolated families and yet, according to the
data presented above, only 21 percent of these families were described as
lacking social support. As expected, the children experiencing neglect lived
in situations with higher risk factors: 34 percent of the families had moved
recently, 45 percent were dependent on social assistance, and 49 percent
lacked social support, while only 51 percent lived in a two-parent family
and only 20 percent lived in a purchased home.

Table 10.6   Household Characteristics by Substantiated Categories of
Maltreatment, Estimated Rates for Canada in 2008
(CIS-2008)

	Physical Abuse	Sexual Abuse	Neglect	Emotional Maltreatment	Exposure to Intimate Partner Violence
Substantiated maltreatment	17,212	2,607	28,939	7,423	29,259
Household characteristics Recent move	24%	27%	34%	30%	32%
Dependent on benefits such as social assistance	18%	25%	45%	37%	29%
Live in purchased home	48%	45%	20%	29%	33%
Two-parent family	68%	54%	51%	54%	71%
Lack of social support	30%	21%	49%	39%	35%

Parental Characteristics

> I came from an alcoholic father who was very abusive. And I
> don't go around drinking and beating up people.... It doesn't always
> happen, but I have seen it happen.... But it is a choice of will and
> if you have a higher willpower.... My goal is not to become my father.
> —Youth participant, *Just listen to me: Youth
> voices on violence* (Ma, 2004)

The CIS-2008 collected data on parental functioning and family stressors. The characteristics most commonly associated with child maltreatment are displayed in Table 10.7. Of note, the strong presence of substance abuse, mental health concerns, domestic violence, and childhood history of out-of-home placement speaks to the need to provide interventions that specifically address these issues for parents.

Child Characteristics

There were almost an equal number of boys and girls investigated because of maltreatment-related concerns: 51 percent of investigations involved boys, 49 percent involved girls. The proportion of males to females in substantiated maltreatment was an even 50 percent. The variation was noted in the age distribution in which males aged eight to eleven were more likely to be investigated for maltreatment than their female peers (39.79 versus 34.50

Table 10.7 **Primary Parental Characteristics by Substantiated Categories of Maltreatment, Estimated Rates for Canada in 2008 (CIS-2008)**

	Physical Abuse	Sexual Abuse	Neglect	Emotional Maltreatment	Exposure to Intimate Partner Violence
Substantiated maltreatment	17,212	2,607	28,939	7,4232	9,259
Parental risk factors					
Alcohol abuse	9%	6%	33%	24%	18%
Drug abuse	7%	5%	29%	17%	12%
Mental health issues	20%	5%	34%	6%	23%
Victim of domestic violence	23%	16%	29%	39%	82%
History of foster care/ group home	3%	7%	10%	10%	8%

Table 10.8   Number of Substantiated Sexual Abuse Investigations for Canada in 2008 (CIS-2008)

Gender		% of Substantiated Sexual Abuse Investigations
0–3 male	—	2%
0–3 female	—	3%
4–7 male	135	5%
4–7 female	505	19%
8–11 male	140	5%
8–11 female	440	17%
12–15 male	106	4%
12–15 female	1,132	43%
All males	446	17%
All females	2,161	83%
Total	2,607	100%

Note: (—) Estimates are too low to report reliably.

per one thousand children), while girls aged twelve to fifteen were more likely to be investigated for maltreatment than their male peers (38.68 versus 30.09 per one thousand children). The incidence rates for boys (51.63 per one thousand boys) and girls (50.00 per one thousand girls) under the age of a year were the highest for all age groups.

Concerning physical abuse, 55 percent of investigations involved boys and 45 percent involved girls. There was a higher proportion of boys for physical abuse investigations in the zero-to-three age group (59 percent for boys), the four to seven age group (60 percent for boys), and the eight-to-eleven age group (61 percent for boys). This was reversed for physical abuse investigations for the twelve-to-fifteen age group as girls make up 56 percent of the investigations compared to 44 percent for boys. The older the child, the more likely that the allegation of physical abuse was substantiated: when boys and girls were under age four, only 21 percent and 35 percent respectively were substantiated. When the investigations involved adolescent females and males, 49 percent and 44 percent respectively were substantiated.

Concerning sexual abuse, 68 percent of investigations involved girls compared to 32 percent for boys. The percentage of girls in substantiated sexual abuse investigations was higher as 83 percent of the investigations involved girls compared to 17 percent involving boys. The substantiation rate ranged for sexual abuse involving girls ranged from 14 percent for those aged zero to three years old to 39 percent for those aged twelve to fifteen years old.

For child sexual abuse investigations involving boys, the substantiation rate ranged between a low of 12 percent for those four to seven years old to a high of 15 percent for those twelve to fifteen years old. Over three-quarters (83 percent) of victims of sexual abuse were girls.

A review of investigated neglect cases suggests there is a more even distribution across age and gender; however, there is a higher proportion of males in each age group for substantiated cases of neglect. For emotional maltreatment investigations, there is a higher proportion of boys for the zero-to-three, four-to-seven, and eight-to-eleven age groups, while for the twelve-to-fifteen age group, girls make up almost 61 percent of the emotional maltreatment investigations. For substantiated cases of emotional maltreatment, girls make up 65 percent of investigations for the adolescent group.

Child Functioning Concerns
Investigating workers were also asked to complete a checklist concerning the child's functioning, shown in Table 10.9. In cases where physical abuse

Table 10.9   Child Characteristics by Substantiated Categories of Maltreatment, Estimated Rates for Canada in 2008 (CIS-2008)

	Physical Abuse	Sexual Abuse	Neglect	Emotional Maltreatment	Exposure to Intimate Partner Violence
Substantiated maltreatment	17,212	2,607	28,939	7,423	29,259
Child Characteristics					
Depression/anxiety/ withdrawal	25%	32%	20%	25%	12%
Self-harming behaviours	9%	13%	7%	7%	2%
ADD/ADHD	17%	5%	13%	12%	5%
Attachment issues	16%	14%	18%	18%	7%
Aggression	26%	10%	17%	17%	8%
Inappropriate sexual behaviours	5%	24%	6%	2%	1%
Intellectual/ develop disability	13%	14%	15%	14%	6%
Failure to meet develop milestones	8%	11%	13%	8%	5%
Academic difficulties	33%	26%	30%	25%	10%
Physical disability	2%	2%	2%	2%	1%
Alcohol use	4%	5%	5%	5%	1%
Drug/solvent use	6%	5%	6%	6%	1%

was the primary form of substantiated maltreatment, the following concerns were noted most often: substance abuse, academic difficulties, aggression, and depression.

Perpetrator Characteristics

No examination of risk factors would be complete without considering the data concerning who is actually abusing the child. Child abuse requires an act to be committed, whereas neglect involves *not* taking required action, such as supervising a child or protecting a child from harm.

Unlike sexual abuse, in 94 percent of substantiated physical abuse investigations, the perpetrator is a biological caregiver. Perpetrators were parents (biological or step-parent) in 38 percent of substantiated sexual abuse investigations, whereas in an estimated 39 percent of substantiated sexual abuse investigations, the perpetrator was a relative (an aunt, uncle, cousin, grandparent, or sibling). Over a quarter of perpetrators were non-relatives (28 percent), although most were known to the family, including babysitters, family friends, and children's friends. This highlights the importance of helping children, youth, and parents to understand that child maltreatment overwhelmingly occurs in the context of a relationship with the child; rarely is it committed by strangers. Ironically, "stranger danger" and "don't talk to strangers" policies are practised in many households, adding to the fears associated with community-based crime and detracting from the risks inherent in children's most familiar relationships.

HOW HARMFUL IS CHILD ABUSE?

> From my experience growing up, I always felt like the adults were not
> going to do anything for me. Like if I told them that someone was
> hurting me, or doing something, or saying something, they
> didn't protect me.
> —Youth participant, *Just listen to me: Youth*
> *voices on violence* (Ma, 2004)

Children exhibit a range of reactions to their experiences of abuse and the symptoms may or may not be evident before, during, or after discovery of the abuse (National Clearinghouse on Family Violence, 2006). Accurately assessing the impact of child maltreatment is yet another challenge associated with addressing child abuse. For example, while it is generally agreed that there are commonly experienced effects, there are effects that are also uniquely experienced (Chaffin et al., 1996). No two children experience abuse in exactly the same way. An experience can be traumatic for one child, but not so for another. MacMillan (2000) makes an analogous assertion regarding sexual abuse: "Most psychiatric treatment focuses on a disorder or syndrome; sexual abuse is an experience" (p. 708). Generally, however, "maltreated children are likely to display major behavior problems and marked emotional difficulties" (Ethier et al., 2004, p. 1266).

Many people—professionals, parents, and young people themselves—believe that abuse is harmful and that damaging effects are inevitable; others may minimize the impact. Some may presume that any form of sexual abuse is far more damaging than chronic physical abuse, or may overlook the impact of hunger on a child's growing body that compromises being able to concentrate at school. In any of these examples, conclusions are being drawn without conducting a thorough assessment of the precise ways children understand and are affected by their experiences. As well, we need to assess *all of the domains* potentially affected by abuse and neglect: physical, emotional, cognitive, and social development (MacMillan, 2000).

The challenges go even beyond this. As many as 40 percent of children who experience sexual abuse, for example, appear to exhibit no symptoms at the time of disclosure (Kendall-Tackett, Williams & Finkelhor, 1993). Symptoms can then surface soon after or emerge over the long term. On the one hand, symptoms may be quite evident in very young children because they are still developing their capacity to regulate their feelings and behaviours. On the other hand, the onset of adolescence, the birth of a child, or simply a smell may trigger the emergence of long-dormant memories and the concomitant symptomology. As a field, we have tended to focus on specific effects and symptoms rather than thinking about how they interact with one another and combine cumulatively over time to influence critical development (MacKenzie, Kotch & Lee, 2011).

We will review the effects documented in the CIS-2008 and provide a summary of the effects commonly associated with child maltreatment, starting with physical injury.

Injury

> You can get a spanking and everything…but people crush down
> your self-esteem also, you know? Making you not want to do anything
> with your life, making you throw away your life and you wanna
> kill yourself.
> —Youth participant, *Just listen to me: Youth
> voices on violence* (Ma, 2004)

Most injuries documented in the CIS-2008 arose out of a context of physical abuse. These typically involve minor bruises, cuts, or scrapes that were not severe enough to require medical attention. As shown in Table 10.10, severe injuries were relatively rarely noted, although over one thousand children were nevertheless injured severely enough to require medical attention.

While injuries were often documented in cases of physical abuse, in over half of all substantiated cases, no injury had been documented. The relatively large number of uninjured cases documented across Canada reflects current standards for intervention, which include situations where children have been harmed as well as those where children are at substantial risk of harm.

Referring to the findings of a large Quebec study (Clément et al., 2000), Durrant, Ensom, and the Coalition on Physical Punishment of Children and Youth (2004) report that: "the children who experienced minor physical violence (e.g., pinching, shaking, spanking) were seven times more likely to experience severe violence (e.g., punching, kicking, hitting with an object). Therefore, physical punishment is likely to escalate into injurious violence in the lives of many children" (p. 7).

It is also important to note that physical harm is not the only concern in cases of physical abuse. Physical abuse leaves emotional scars that do not

Table 10.10   Type and Severity of Physical Harm in Cases of Substantiated Physical Abuse, Estimated Rates for Canada 2008 (CIS-2008)

Type of Harm	Maltreated Children	% of Maltreated Children	No Medical Treatment	Medical Treatment Required
No physical injury noted	12,710	74%	N/A	N/A
Bruises, cuts, or scrapes	3,968	23%	3,408	560
Burns or scalds	—	‹1%	—	—
Broken bones	110	‹1%	—	110
Head trauma	308	2%	—	296
Other health condition	237	1%	185	—
Total	17,212	100%	3,635	1,062

Note: Total is less than the sum of the specific types of harm because some cases involve multiple types of harm. (—) Estimates are too low to report reliably.
Moderate harm means that an injury or health condition due to maltreatment was noted during the investigation, and severe means that medical attention was required.

heal as quickly as most physical injuries. The work undertaken to prepare the *Joint statement on physical punishment of children and youth* concludes that "deliberately inflicted pain can lead to fear, anxiety, insecurity and anger in a child, eroding the parent–child relationship as he learns to avoid his parent" (Durrant, Ensom & the Coalition on Physical Punishment of Children and Youth, 2004, p. 7). The *Joint statement* summarizes the findings of an extensive literature review as follows: physical punishment is associated with depression, unhappiness, anxiety, and feelings of hopelessness in children and youth, and is linked to an increased likelihood of delinquent behaviour, impaired parent–child relationships, and impaired social relationships. There is an increased tendency to act out, bully, lie, attack their siblings, hit their parents, retaliate aggressively against peers, and not show remorse. Later in adulthood, physical punishment in childhood has been linked to the development of adult aggression, criminal and anti-social behaviour, and the abuse of one's own child or spouse, along with poorer adult mental health, including depression, anxiety disorders, dependence, and alcoholism. Physical punishment in childhood has been linked to a greater tolerance of violence in adulthood (Coalition on the Physical Punishment of Children and Youth, 2003). (See McGillivray and Durrant in this volume for further discussion of short- and longer-term consequences.)

The following summarizes the emotional, cognitive, and behavioural symptomology noted most frequently by investigating workers in the CIS-2008 according to maltreatment type. It should be noted that these child functioning concerns are identified by workers at the time of the initial assessment period and that further concerns would become apparent over an extended time frame.

- *Physical abuse:* Academic difficulties, aggression, attachment issues, ADD/ADHD, and depression/anxiety or withdrawal
- *Sexual abuse:* Depression/anxiety or withdrawal, inappropriate sexual behaviour, and academic difficulties
- *Neglect:* Academic difficulties, depression/anxiety or withdrawal, aggression, and failure to meet developmental milestones
- *Emotional maltreatment:* Aggression, attachment issues, and academic difficulties
- *Exposure to intimate partner violence:* Depression/anxiety or withdrawal and academic difficulties

As noted, children who "look good," "seem fine," or appear to be "asymptomatic" may be overlooked. It may be that they are internalizing rather than externalizing their symptoms (Hall, 1993). As mentioned, symptoms may be delayed, situation specific, or intermittent. "Most trauma signs are unlikely to be observed in clinical settings during an assessment. Most occur at night or early morning and are a part of the child's response to daily living: eating, sleeping, bathing and toileting" (Hall, 1993, p. 3).

Commonly occurring problems include fear, anxiety, post-traumatic stress symptoms, depression, sexual difficulties, poor self-esteem, stigmatization, difficulty with trust, cognitive distortions, difficulty with affective processing, aggression, peer socialization deficits, and other problems (Saunders, Berliner & Hanson, 2004). In their review of the literature, Saunders, Berliner, and Hanson (2004) determined that "about half of sexually abused and one third of physically abused children will meet diagnostic criteria for post-traumatic stress disorder (PTSD) (p. 25)." *Exposure* to family violence can be as traumatic as the *experience* of abuse itself in terms of short-term and long-term impacts (Jaffe, 1995).

Monahon (1993) notes additional signs that a child may have been traumatized: specific fears, sudden panic or distress, separation anxiety, startle responses and nervousness, fear denial, behavioural regression, toileting accidents, unwanted images and thoughts, loss of pleasure in previously enjoyable activities, retelling and replaying of trauma, post-traumatic play, withdrawal and constriction, sleep-related difficulties, personality changes, complaints of aches and pains, misinterpretation of cause and meaning of trauma, accident-proneness and recklessness, and anniversary reactions.

Jaffe (1995) offers the following understanding regarding the link between childhood experience of maltreatment and later life impact:

> Abuse experiences in one's family of origin create vulnerability for further victimization by others as well as a propensity to use power and control as a means of resolving conflict. In addition to prior abuse experiences, the risk of becoming a victim or perpetrator of violence increases as a result of negative influences from peers (condoning violence), the absence of compensatory factors (e.g., success at school; healthy relationships with siblings and friends), and the relative lack of alternative sources of information, all of which serve to counteract existing biased attitudes, and beliefs.

In this volume, Anne McGillivray and Joan Durrant offer the most recent research findings and understanding regarding the impact of physical punishment. As well, recent advances in the study of how our brains and bodies work help us to better understand the effects of abuse on stress-response systems. Quite simply, extreme experiences change the person. Fortunately, evolving work in this field and other related areas such as resilience have much to offer in terms of understanding the impact of abuse and facilitating recovery (Reaching IN...Reaching OUT, 2010). In this volume, Bruce Perry and Michael Ungar provide an in-depth examination and discussion of trauma and resilience.

Finally, we noted at the beginning of the chapter that a number of children and youth may be removed from their families as a result of abuse and placed in foster care and other group care settings and institutions. Judy Finlay, Ontario's child advocate from 1991 to 2007, drew attention to the multiple burdens carried by these young people—their abuse and the impact of separation from their families, all culminating in "critical life point" (Finlay, 2003b), which then predisposes them to "poor adjustment in institutional cultures." These circumstances set them on a trajectory, where some cross over from the children's service system into the criminal justice system. We heard this message again from youth at the Youth Leaving Care Hearings, supported by Irwin Elman, the provincial advocate for children and youth, appointed in 2008, where one stated: "Growing up in this type of environment is going to set youth up for trouble in the future. All their lives they learn to relate through power and consequences and when they leave care, the structures aren't there anymore. Many are lucky and learn to adapt...but others do not know how to cope and end up re-institutionalized" (Youth Leaving Care Hearings, 2012, p. 17). The hearings and companion report are expected to be a catalyst for much-needed policy and practice changes in this area.

CONCLUSION

> Well, the thing is that you have a voice...children have a voice,
> and no one wants to hear them. People say "Oh, let them talk, and
> let them do this and that." And then you have these things, and
> we sit down and talk about it, but our voices are not heard.
> —Youth participant, *Just listen to me:*
> *Youth voices on violence* (Ma, 2004)

The problem of child maltreatment in Canada is common, complex, and enduring. The more we continue to uncover about its incidence and impact, the better equipped we will be to implement urgently needed changes to policy and practice. The distance we have come in how we view, care for, and protect children as a society is undeniably influenced by enduring legal, social, cultural, and religious traditions. To this we add an ever-expanding knowledge base regarding child development and the short- and long-term effects of child abuse and trauma. The journey is clearly influenced by key tensions arising in defining and understanding the nature, scope, characteristics, and impact of child maltreatment. While our goal is to understand more about the lived experience from children themselves, our efforts are curtailed by the very nature of abuse, the contexts and limitations of research, and the systems involved in responding. There is no question of the "burden of suffering" associated with children's abuse in Canada. The challenge is to shift the burden more fully onto the shoulders of legislators, policy-makers, researchers, practitioners, and members of the Canadian public, in order to give it the urgent and rigorous attention it requires.

> I'm here today because I want to tell you that I want a future…
> I haven't been getting the help that I need and I want, and
> I feel very isolated.
> —Name withheld, sixteen, youth in care,
> *My REAL life book* (Youth Leaving Care Hearings, 2012)

NOTES

1 To learn more about the Youth Leaving Care Hearings and their impact, see: http://provincialadvocate.on.ca/main/en/about/aboutus.cfm.

2 It should also be noted that the NCANDS estimates are unduplicated, whereas the CIS estimates count each new investigation within the same year as separate incidents. The duplicate NCANDS victim rate for 2008 was 10.3 per one thousand.

3 From the glossary of Kiskisik Awasisak (Sinha et al., 2011). *Aboriginal peoples*: The descendants of the original inhabitants of North America. The Canadian Constitution of 1982 recognizes three groups of Aboriginal peoples: Indians, Métis, and Inuit. These are three separate peoples with unique heritages, languages, cultural practices, and spiritual beliefs (Indian and Northern Affairs Canada [INAC], 2009). *First Nations*: A term that came into common usage in the 1970s to replace the word "Indian." Although the term "First Nation" is widely used, no legal definition of it exists. Among its uses, the term "First Nations peoples" refers to the Indian peoples in Canada, both Status and non-Status. Some have also adopted the term "First Nation" to replace the word "band" in the name of their community (INAC, 2009).

REFERENCES

Belsky, J. (1993). Etiology of child maltreatment: A developmental-ecological analysis. *Psychological Bulletin, 114*(3), 413–34.

Blackstock, C., Trocmé, N., & Bennett, M. (2004). Child welfare response to Aboriginal and non-Aboriginal children in Canada: A comparative analysis. *Violence against Women, 10*(8), 901–16.

Chaffin, M., Bonner, B.L., Worley, K.B., & Lawson, L. (1996). Treating abused adolescents. In L. Berliner, J.A. Bulkley, C. Jenny & T. Reid (Eds.), *APSAC handbook on child maltreatment* (pp. 119–39). Thousand Oaks, CA: Sage.

Clément, M.E., Bouchard, C., Jetté, M., Laferrière, S. (2000). *La violence familiale dans la vie des enfants du Québec.* Québec: Institut de la Statistique du Québec.

Coalition on the Physical Punishment of Children and Youth. (2003, April 25). *Joint statement on physical punishment of children and youth.* Ottawa: Children's Hospital of Eastern Ontario.

Collin-Vezina, D., Helie, S., & Trocmé, N. (2010). Is child sexual abuse declining in Canada? An analysis of child welfare data. *Child Abuse and Neglect, 34*(11), 807–12.

Committee on the Rights of the Child. (2003). Consideration of reports submitted by States Parties under Article 40 of the Convention. Thirty-fourth session, crc/c.15/Add.215 (2003).

Committee on Sexual Offences against Children and Youth. (1984). *Sexual Offences against Children: Report of the Committee on Sexual Offences against Children and Youth* (the Badgely Report). Vols. 1 and 2. Ottawa: Department of Supply and Services.

Cunningham, A., & Baker, L. (2007). *Little eyes, little ears: How violence against a mother shapes children as they grow.* Centre for Children & Families in the Justice System. Retrieved from: National Clearinghouse on Family Violence.

Durrant, J.E., Ensom, R., & the Coalition on Physical Punishment of Children and Youth. (2004). *Joint statement on physical punishment of children and youth.* Ottawa: Coalition on Physical Punishment of Children and Youth.

Ethier, L.S., Lemellin, J.-P., & Lacharite, C. (2004). A longitudinal study of the effects of chronic maltreatment on children's behavioral and emotional problems. *Child Abuse & Neglect 28*(2004), 1265–78.

Finkelhor, D. (1994). Current information on the scope and nature of child sexual abuse. *The Future of Children, 4*(2), 31–53.

Finkelhor, D., & Jones, L.M. (2004). *Explanations for the decline in child sexual abuse cases.* Washington, DC: Office of Juvenile Justice and Delinquency Prevention.

Finlay, J. (2003a). Child advocacy: Drawing the line in the sand. In *Mental health and patients' rights in Ontario: Yesterday, today, and tomorrow* (Twentieth Anniversary Special Report, pp. 95–97). Toronto: Psychiatric Patient Advocate Office, Government of Ontario.

Finlay, J. (2003b). *Crossover kids: Care to custody.* Toronto: Office of Child and Family Service Advocacy.

Finlay, J. (2004). *The dynamics of peer violence in youth custody.* Toronto: Voices for Children.

Gil, D.G. (1970). *Violence against children: Physical abuse in the United States.* Cambridge, MA: Harvard University Press.

Gilbert, R., Widom, C.S., Browne, K., Fergusson, D., Webb, E., & Janson, S. (2009). Burden and consequences of child maltreatment in high-income countries. *The Lancet, 373*(9658), 68–81.

Hall, D.K. (1993). *Assessing child trauma*. Toronto: Institute for the Prevention of Child Abuse. (For copies, contact the author at Child Development Institute, 197 Euclid Avenue, Toronto, Ontario, M6J 2J8, Canada.)

Hiebert-Murphy, D. (2001). Partner abuse among women whose children have been sexually abused: An exploratory study. *Journal of Child Sexual Abuse, 10*(1), 109–18.

Indian and Northern Affairs Canada. (2009). Terminology. Available from Aboriginal Affairs and Northern Development Canada. Retrieved from: http://www.aadnc-aandc.gc.ca/eng/1100100014642.

Iwaniec, D. (1995). *The emotionally abused and neglected child*. Chichester, UK: Wiley.

Jaffe, P. (1995). Children of domestic violence: Special challenges in custody and visitation dispute resolution. In J. Carter, B. Hart & C. Deisler (Eds.), *Domestic violence and children: Resolving custody and visitation disputes* (pp. 19–30). San Francisco: Family Violence Prevention Fund.

Jones, A., & Rutman, L. (1981). *In the children's aid: J.J. Kelso and child welfare in Ontario*. Toronto: University of Toronto Press.

Jones, L.M., & Finkelhor, D. (2003). Putting together evidence on declining trends in sexual abuse: A complex puzzle. *Child Abuse and Neglect, 27*, 133–35.

Kadushin, A., & Martin, J.A. (1981). *Child abuse: An interactional event*. New York: Columbia University.

Kellogg, N.D., & Menard, S.W. (2003). Violence among family members of children and adolescents evaluated for sexual abuse. *Child Abuse and Neglect, 27*, 1367–76.

Kendall-Tackett, K.A., Williams, L.M., Finkelhor, D. (1993). Impact of sexual abuse on children: A review and synthesis of recent empirical studies. *Psychological Bulletin, 113*, 164–80.

Knott, T., Trocmé, N., & Bala, N. (2004). *False allegations of abuse and neglect*. CECW Information Sheet no. 13e. Toronto: Faculty of Social Work, University of Toronto.

Law Commission of Canada. (2000). *Restoring dignity: Responding to child abuse in Canadian institutions*. Ottawa: Ministry of Public Works and Government Services.

Ma, S.J. (2004). *Just listen to me: Youth voices on violence*. Toronto: Voices for Children and Office of Child and Family Service Advocacy.

MacKenzie, M.J., Kotch, J.B., & Lee, L.-C. (2011). Toward a cumulative ecological risk model for the etiology of child maltreatment. *Children and Youth Services Review, 33*(9), 1638–47. doi: 10.1016/j.childyouth.2011.04.018.

MacMillan, H.L. (2000). Child maltreatment: What we know in the year 2000. *Canadian Journal of Psychiatry, 45*(8): 702–10.

MacMillan, H., Fleming, J., Trocmé, N., Boyle, M., Wong, M., Racine, Y., et al. (1997). Prevalence of child physical and sexual abuse in a community sample: Results from the Ontario Health Supplement. *Journal of the American Academy of Medicine, 278*(2), 131–35.

MacMillan, H.L., Wathen, C.N., Barlow, J., Fergusson, D.M., Leventhal, J.M., & Taussig, H.N. (2009). Interventions to prevent child maltreatment and associated impairment. *The Lancet, 373*(9659), 250–66.

Margolin, L. (1990). Fatal child neglect. *Child Welfare, 69*(4), 309–19.

Monahon, C. (1993). *Children and trauma.* New York: Lexington.

National Clearinghouse on Family Violence. (2006). *Child maltreatment: A "what to do" guide for professionals who work with children.* Prepared by Chiachen Cheng et al. Ottawa: Public Health Agency of Canada.

Pleck, J.H. (1997). Paternal involvement: Levels, sources, and consequences. In M.E. Lamb (Ed.), *The role of the father in child development* (pp. 104–20). New York: Wiley.

Reaching IN...Reaching OUT. (2010). *Resilience: Successful navigation through significant threat.* Report prepared for the Ontario Ministry of Children and Youth Services. Toronto: Child & Family Partnership. Retrieved from: http://www.reachinginreachingout.com/documents/MCYS%20Resilience%20Report%2011-16-10%20Dissemination.pdf.

Rogers, R. (1990). *Reaching for solutions: The summary report of the special advisor to the minister of National Health and Welfare on child sexual abuse in Canada/À la recherche de solutions: Résumé du rapport du conseiller spécial du ministre de la Santé nationale et du Bien-être social en matière d'agressions sexuelles contre les enfants au Canada.* Ottawa: Health and Welfare Canada.

Saunders, B.E., Berliner, L., & Hanson, R.F. (2004). *Guidelines for the psychosocial treatment of intrafamilial child physical and sexual abuse.* Charleston: Authors. Retrieved from: http://www .musc.edu /cvc/.

Sedlak, A.J., & Broadhurst, D.D. (1996). *Third national incidence study of child abuse and neglect.* Washington, DC: US Department of Health and Human Services.

Sedlak, A.J., Mettenburg, J., Basena, M., Petta, I., McPherson, K., Greene, A., & Li, S. (2010). *Fourth National Incidence Study of Child Abuse and Neglect (NIS_4): Report to Congress.* Washington, DC: US Department of Health and Human Services, Administration for Children and Families

Sinha, V., Trocmé, N., Fallon, B., MacLaurin, B., Fast, E., Thomas Prokop, S., et al. (2011). *Kiskisik Awasisak: Remember the children: Understanding the over-representation of First Nations children in the child welfare system.* Ottawa: Assembly of First Nations.

Trocmé, N., (2005). *Introduction to CIS Cycle II presentation.* Centre of Excellence for Child Welfare. Montreal: McGill University, School of Social Work. Retrieved from: http://www.cecw-cepb .ca/DocsEng/cis2Training.pdf.

Trocmé, N., & Durrant, J. (2003). Physical punishment and the response of the Canadian child welfare system: Implications for legislative reform. *Journal of Social Welfare and Family Law, 25,* 39–56.

Trocmé, N., Fallon, B., MacLaurin, B., Chamberland, C., Chabot, M., & Esposito, T. (2011). Shifting definitions of emotional maltreatment: An analysis child welfare investigation laws and practices in Canada. *Child Abuse & Neglect, 35,* 831–40.

Trocmé, N., Fallon, B., MacLaurin, B., Daciuk, J., Felstiner, C., Black, T., et al. (2005). *Canadian Incidence Study of Reported Child Abuse and Neglect 2003: Major findings*. Ottawa: Minister of Public Works and Government Services Canada.

Trocmé, N., Fallon, B., MacLaurin, B., Sinha, V., Black, T., Fast, E., et al. (2010). Rates of maltreatment-related investigations in the CIS-1998, CIS-2003, and CIS-2008. In Public Health Agency of Canada (Ed.), *Canadian Incidence Study of Reported Child Abuse and Neglect-2008: Major findings*. Ottawa: Public Health Agency of Canada.

Trocmé, N., Fallon, B., MacLaurin, B., Sinha, V., Black, T., Fast, E., Felstiner, C., Hélie, S., Turcotte, D., Weightman, P., Douglas, J., & Holroyd, J. (2010). *Canadian Incidence Study of Reported Child Abuse and Neglect—2008: Major Findings*. Ottawa: Public Health Agency of Canada.

Trocmé, N., MacLaurin, B., Fallon, B., Black, T., & Lajoie, J. (2005). *Child abuse and neglect investigations in Canada: Comparing 1998 and 2003 data*. CECW Information Sheet no. 26e. Montreal: School of Social Work, McGill University. Retrieved from: http://www.cec wcepb.ca/DocsEng/ciscomparisons26e.pdf.

Trocmé, N., MacLaurin, B., Fallon, B., Daciuk, J., Billingsley, D., Tourigny, M., Mayer, M., Wright, J., Barter, K., Burford, G., Hornick, J., Sullivan, R., & McKenzie, B. (2001). *Canadian Incidence Study of Reported Child Abuse and Neglect (CIS): Final report*. Ottawa: Minister of Public Works and Government Services Canada.

Trocmé, N., McPhee, D., Tam, K.K., & Hay, T. (1994). *Ontario incidence study of reported child abuse and neglect*. Toronto: Institute for the Prevention of Child Abuse.

US Department of Health and Human Services, Administration for Children and Families, Administration on Children, Youth, and Families, Children's Bureau. (2009). *Child maltreatment 2008*. Retrieved from: http://www.acf.hhs.gov/programs/cb/stats_research/index.htm#can.

US Department of Health and Human Services, Administration for Children and Families, Administration on Children, Youth and Families, Children's Bureau. (2010). *Child maltreatment 2008*. Retrieved from: http://www.acf.hhs.gov/programs/cb/stats_research/index.htm#can.

Ward, M.G.K., & Bennett, S. (2003). Studying child abuse and neglect in Canada: We are just at the beginning. (2003). *Canadian Medical Association Journal, 169*(9), 919–20.

Wolfe, D.A., Jaffe, P., Jette, J., & Poisson, S. (2001). *Child abuse in institutions and organizations: Improving public and professional understanding*. Ottawa: Law Commission of Canada.

Youth Leaving Care Hearings. (2012). *My REAL Life Book: Report from the Youth Leaving Care Hearings*. Toronto: Provincial Advocate for Children and Youth.

11

CHILDREN'S EXPOSURE TO DOMESTIC VIOLENCE INTEGRATING POLICY, RESEARCH, AND PRACTICE TO ADDRESS CHILDREN'S MENTAL HEALTH

ANGÉLIQUE JENNEY AND RAMONA ALAGGIA

INTRODUCTION

As our awareness of the complexity and harms inherent in family violence grows, so too does our understanding of how it negatively influences children who are exposed to that violence. As we begin to understand these effects, we can also identify how living in challenging life contexts is harmful to the mental health of children. Programs are in place to intervene and protect children while supporting the victimized parent. Such programs are based on a desire for a coherent intervention strategy that takes into consideration the needs of children exposed to violence within a cohesive family violence policy, research, and practice framework. The time has come for researchers and practitioners to work together to address more adequately the issues involved in working with children and families affected by domestic violence (DV). For years, agencies serving abused women and their children worked in isolation to identify, intervene, and attend to safety issues in the absence of empirically based literature. However, with more than twenty years of research exploring the effects of DV exposure on children, the time has come to develop and apply integrated responses and interventions.

This chapter reviews existing knowledge about the incidence and effects of children's exposure to domestic violence (EDV), including the limitations and gaps in this knowledge base. This review is prefaced by the recognition that children become aware of DV in multiple ways, including witnessing violent incidents, hearing conflict, feeling it in the emotional atmosphere, and seeing evidence of it in a parent's injuries after the fact, all of which constitute "exposure" (Holden, Geffner & Jouriles, 1998). "Exposure" is a more encompassing term favoured by clinicians and researchers over "witnessing" because it recognizes that "eye-witnessing" is not the only way children become aware of DV. The authors also describe the policy land-scape within which relevant systems operate, the issues that emerge from mandated child welfare involvement, and current approaches to interven-tion. In the final section of the chapter, the authors integrate theory into practice using clinical experience and illustrative vignettes.

A concerning number of children are exposed to domestic violence. Prevalence studies of community samples indicate that 24 percent of adults report EDV as children (Dong et al., 2004). The Canadian General Social Study (GSS) estimated that children in half a million households are exposed to domestic violence (Johnson & Dauvergne, 2001). Taylor-Butts (2005) found that almost half of all Canadians entering shelters were women with children, most of whom were fleeing from DV. Provin-cial and national studies of children reported to protection services show that between 24 percent and 34 percent of investigations involve children exposed to domestic violence (Alaggia, Gadalla & Shlonsky, 2010; Hazen et al., 2006). The Canadian Incidence Study of Child Abuse and Neglect of 2008 (CIS-2008) further found exposure to DV to be the most frequently substantiated form of child maltreatment in Canada, verified at the same rate as neglect (Trocmé et al., 2008). The estimated number of substantiated cases involving intimate partner violence increased dramatically between 1998 and 2003 and has stabilized between 2003 and 2008 (see Chapter 10 by Vine, Trocmé, MacLaurin, and Fallon in this volume).

THE EFFECTS ON CHILDREN

Although domestic violence is not a new social phenomenon, children who are exposed to it are the most recently acknowledged victims. Prior to the 1980s, research on domestic violence focused primarily on women victims of domestic violence and on other forms of child maltreatment, such as physical, sexual, or emotional abuse and neglect. A substantial body of research now shows that children exposed to violence may be more likely to experience greater difficulties than their peers (Evans, Davies & DiLillo, 2008; Holt, Buckley & Whelan, 2008; Kitzmann, Gaylord, Holt & Kenny,

2003; Onyskiw, 2003; Wolfe, Crooks, Lee, McIntyre-Smith & Jaffe, 2003). This research suggests EDV may negatively impact a child's social, psychological, and behavioural functioning. Children who experience EDV show greater depression, anxiety, social withdrawal, hyperactivity, aggression, lower social competence, diminished school performance and academic achievement, more post-traumatic stress symptoms, and more difficulties in regulating emotions than their non-exposed peers (Margolin & Vickerman, 2011; Moylan et al., 2010; Wolfe et al., 2003). These are serious impediments to healthy child development and are indicative of affect regulation problems: the inability to appropriately express and effectively deal with intense feelings that can arise from exposure to domestic violence. Immediate negative effects include excessive irritability, sleep disturbances, emotional distress, and other challenging behaviours that make parenting increasingly difficult (Bogat, DeJonghe, Levendosky, Davidson & von Eye, 2006; Zeanah, Danis, Hirschberg, Benoit & Heller, 1999).

An area of recent focus is that of infants and very young children exposed to DV because of new evidence suggesting that children under four years may be seriously affected by EDV (Bogat et al., 2006; McGuigan, Vuchinich & Pratt, 2000). Recent research has found that infants as young as one year of age have shown trauma symptoms from exposure to domestic violence (Bogat et al., 2006; Hunt, Martens & Belcher, 2011). This is concerning since infants, toddlers, and preschool children have less developmental capacity to manage feelings or effectively communicate distress, and limited ability to process threatening environmental information. As a result, they are among the most vulnerable not being identified, which may lead to an increased risk of psychological problems even if those will be exhibited only years later. Additional studies have shown that exposure to domestic violence at a young age can interfere with the development of trust and later exploratory behaviours that form the basis for child autonomy (Garbarino, Dubrow, Kostelny & Pardo, 1992; Leavitt & Fox, 1993; Osofsky & Fenichel, 1994). Given what is known about how caregiver experiences impact children (Levendosky, Leahy, Bogat, Davidson & von Eye, 2006; Osofsky & Fenichel, 1994), it is reasonable to expect that caregivers experiencing abuse may struggle with issues of sensitivity, responsiveness, emotional availability, and attunement, which, in turn, would then impact parent–child relations (Osofsky, 1997).

Such problematic parent–child interactions may be indicated by the occurrence of negative parental attributions toward the child. For example, McGuigan, Vuchinich, and Pratt (2000) found that when DV was present in the first year of a child's life, some parents developed significantly more negative views of their children. Studies with pregnant women who had experienced DV found that they "had significantly more negative representations of their infants and themselves as mothers and were significantly more likely to be classified as insecurely attached" (Huth-Bocks, Levendosky, Theran & Bogat, 2004, p. 79) than women who had not experienced domestic violence. Furthermore, women have reported being hit while holding infants in their arms and their children being injured while trying to intervene and stop the abuse (Edleson, 1999a, 1999b; McGee, 2000). Given that young children are disproportionately exposed to domestic violence due to their developmental stage and the increased proximity and dependency on their mothers, the magnitude of this problem is concerning (Bogat et al., 2006). Recent CIS-2008 data indicated that 25 percent of children investigated for direct exposure to intimate partner violence (IPV) were between one and three years of age, and 30 percent of exposed children were between the ages of four and seven, showing that cumulatively more than half of children exposed to DV are under the age of seven (see Table 11.1).

Children also get injured during a domestic assault, either as bystanders, through trying to intervene, or from an intentional act by the perpetrator who might harm a child to threaten his partner. Canadian research indicates that while co-occurrence of child maltreatment and domestic violence is high, relatively few children are physically injured as a result of being caught in the middle of a violent act between parents: physical injuries requiring medical attention were documented in less than 1 percent of such cases (Trocmé et al., 2001). Less common are incidents in which severe injury or death of the child is one of the outcomes of living with domestic violence. However, one has only to turn to the media to hear of tragic cases in which

Table 11.1 **Child Age in Substantiated Exposure to Intimate Partner Violence Investigations in Canada in 2008 (n = 20,970)**

	Direct Witness to Physical Violence		Indirect Exposure to Physical Violence	
	Frequency	Percent	Frequency	Percent
Child Age				
<1 year	1,341	10%	817	12%
1–3 years	3,538	25%	1,925	27%
4–7 years	4,167	30%	1,854	26%
8–11 years	3,036	22%	1,241	18%
12–15 years	1,818	13%	1,233	17%

Note: This table was produced using data from the CIS-2008 by Jennifer Ma (research associate, CIS-2008) at the request of the authors and under the direction of Barbara Fallon (co-investigator, CIS-2008).

children's lives have been taken by a parent in suicide-homicide occurrences (see Chapter 13 by Birnbaum in this volume).

Jaffe, Wolfe, & Wilson (1990) characterize children in violent homes as having minimal or no understanding of the dynamics of violence. For many children who are frequently exposed to domestic violence, such behaviour becomes the norm. A chronic pattern of violence can lead to long-term consequences with adverse effects on intrapersonal thoughts, emotional health, social skills, learning, and physical health (Hughes & Graham-Bermann, 1998; Kairys, Johnson & Committee, 2002). A common consequence is a combination of limited tolerance for frustration and poor impulse control, which manifests itself in both internalized and externalized anger (Edleson, 1999a; Fantuzzo et al., 1991; Hughes & Graham-Bermann, 1998; McGee, 2000). Studies of school-age children have demonstrated the negative effects of exposure to domestic violence in overall child functioning, attitudes, social competence, and school performance (Garbarino et al., 1992; Leavitt & Fox, 1993), problems that continue to manifest into adolescence.

Much of the research on the impact of DV on children is inconclusive and even contradictory. Kitzmann and colleagues (2003) point out that while children's functioning may be seriously disrupted in the short term, some children show no negative effects in the long term, and not all children are affected in the same ways to the same degree. Thus, taking "the context" into account is an important consideration when assessing impact (Overlien, 2010).

RISK, PROTECTIVE FACTORS, AND RESILIENCE

The effects of DV on children are mediated by a number of risk and protective factors, including the severity and intensity of the violence, the child's age and developmental level, as well as the child's gender and access to social supports. Level and duration of conflict is certainly one of the key factors. Sales, Manber, and Rohman (1992) found that as levels of interparental conflict increased, so did the difficulties experienced by children. The impact of domestic violence is also affected by the extent to which the violence is directed at the child (O'Keefe, 1995, 1996; Rossman, 1998). In addition to concerns about the emotional effects of EDV, there is also concern about the physical safety of children in families with domestic violence. Domestic violence threatens the child's feelings of safety about his or her immediate environment and can render parents, particularly the parent victims, less available to meet the child's physical and emotional needs due to their own distress (Margolin & Gordis, 2000).

A number of other studies have identified gender differences in the effects of exposure on children. In their review, Suderman and Jaffe (1999) found that girls were more likely to internalize their emotions and become depressed and withdrawn, while boys had a greater tendency to external- ize their reactions through increased aggressive behaviour toward others. Increased aggression by boys was also found in Jouriles and Norwood's (1995) study of forty-eight families who experienced domestic violence: boys exhibited greater levels of externalizing behaviour problems than girls. O'Keefe's (1994) study of 120 women living in shelters with their children found that the amount of violence the child was exposed to was a better predictor of behaviour problems for boys, whereas the amount of violence children were exposed to, combined with the amount of mother–child aggression, better predicted behaviour problems for girls. While most stud- ies have determined differences in the effects of exposure to domestic vio- lence, Kilpatrick and Williams's (1997) sample of elementary school children found no gender difference in levels of psychological distress. A more recent study found that while gender was a factor, the severity of violence was more strongly related to psychological distress than were either gender or ethnicity (McGruder-Johnson, Davidson, Gleaves, Stock & Finch, 2000).

Age and level of cognitive development influence the way in which children cope with conflict (Cummings, 1998). Hughes (1998) found that preschool children were more likely than older children to have problems. While the majority of research centres on children up to age eleven, there are increasing numbers of studies demonstrating the negative impact of exposure on older children (Cummings, 1998). Some studies have also shown differences in how children are affected over time. For example, in response to adult conflict, girls in early to middle childhood are likely to react with sadness. In later childhood, their reaction changes to one of anger (Cummings, Peplar & Moore, 1999).

Resilience theory has emerged as a framework for understanding the seemingly differential outcomes found among children living in adverse conditions such as being exposed to violence in the home (Edleson, 2004). In one of the few studies of the resilience of children exposed to DV, Howell and colleagues (2010) found that better parenting performance, fewer maternal mental health problems, and less severe violence exposure all predicted better emotion regulation and pro-social skill scores, which, in turn, were negatively correlated with maladaptive child behaviours. Masten (2011) has recently recommended a "fourth wave" of resilience research intended to "promote resilience well enough to understand it" (p. 503). Such an approach calls for collaborations of basic and applied researchers and policy-makers to increase knowledge on resilience processes alongside interventions attempting to promote competence in the face of adversity.

The theoretical literature also points to intergenerational transmission theory (IGTT) as a dominant explanatory framework for understanding DV and the effects of exposure. IGTT is based on the premise that adult behaviour modelled to children at formative developmental ages teaches them how to deal with conflict. When this modelling includes abusive behaviour, children do not learn healthy, non-violent ways of resolving conflict, and they may instead mimic dysfunctional behaviours (Bandura, 1977; Margolin, Gordis, Medina & Oliver, 2003; Renner & Slack, 2006; Stith et al., 2000). Although this theory is widely accepted in practice, preliminary research has found only a weak to moderate connection between EDV during childhood, and perpetrating or experiencing violence in an adult relationship (Stith et al., 2000). Nevertheless, the cycle of abuse and intergenerational transmission of violence remain the dominant theoretical constructs for understanding DV and for program development.

Before we proceed with a discussion of intervention approaches, it is essential to understand the legislative and policy backdrops for the interventions currently practised in Canada. Legal and child welfare policies and practices are important because they directly influence the identification of children being exposed to domestic violence as well as subsequent referrals to intervention services. The issues surrounding mandatory child welfare intervention will be examined closely.

CURRENT LEGISLATION, POLICIES, AND INITIATIVES

The Canadian criminal justice system has been addressing domestic violence in relation to adult victims through mandatory arrest policies, provincial domestic violence acts, and specialized domestic violence courts. Children's exposure to domestic violence as a form of child maltreatment falls under the mandate of child welfare legislation within individual provinces and territories, and thus is dealt with through completely different mechanisms. Based on the research on effects of domestic violence on children, and despite mixed findings regarding these effects (Johnson & Sullivan, 2008), policies that bring families into child welfare systems for investigation for harm and risk of harm to children have been strengthened and vigorously enforced. Child welfare policy reforms have contributed to an enormous increase in child protection cases across North America (Alaggia, Jenney, Mazucca & Redmond, 2007; Edleson, Gassman-Pines & Hill, 2006; Trocmé, Fallon, MacLaurin & Neves, 2005). In Canada, Alberta, Newfoundland, New Brunswick, Nova Scotia, Prince Edward Island, and Saskatchewan have incorporated children's exposure to domestic violence as a form of child maltreatment into their child welfare legislation.

Even with these changes, however, the legislation is open to broad interpretation because of the lack of consistent definitions. While all child welfare legislation defines a child in need of protection, the wording in relation to domestic violence varies from "severe domestic disharmony," "severe domestic violence," and "domestic violence." Nova Scotia defines cause for intervention as "harm caused by being exposed to repeated domestic violence" and includes a statement about the child in need of protective services if "the child's parent or guardian fails or refuses to obtain services or intervention to remedy or alleviate the violence."[1] The language used to describe this is problematic as it can be interpreted to hold both abuser and parent victim responsible for the child's exposure to the violence. Furthermore, the child protection system is designed to intervene mainly with the child's main caregiver, which in cases of DV is often the parent victim. This has led to tensions between child protection services and the violence against women sector because of concerns that children's rights were being prioritized over women's rights. However, the reality is that in these cases, women and children's safety cannot be reasonably separated.

To add to the difficulties, in Canada, domestic violence is considered a criminal act, so women become involved in two systems: the criminal justice system with her abusive partner, and the child welfare system with her children. The fragmented nature of the legal system in Canada means the criminal court and family court are two separate systems that often do not share information with one another. This leads to confusion and frustration, with women often being perplexed by ongoing court issues and child welfare procedures. For example, a woman may go to court accompanied by child welfare workers and be told that in order for her children to remain in the home, the abusive partner cannot return. This could then be followed by a decision in criminal court where the charges against her partner are dropped, thus allowing the partner to return home. Contradictions like this can lead to serious misunderstandings and place women and children at further risk of victimization by an abusive partner, as well as by the system itself. However, novel approaches to integrating criminal and family court cases in this regard have been implemented in New York (Aldrich & Kluger, 2010) and a similar model is currently being piloted in Toronto, Ontario (Integrated Domestic Violence Court Project).

To alleviate historical tensions among the various service sectors, and to improve outcomes for children and mothers, a number of initiatives have evolved to foster collaboration. Inter-agency training between child welfare authorities and domestic violence service providers is now an essential component of worker education in many child welfare jurisdictions across Canada and the United States (Aron & Olson, 1997). Several child welfare agencies in the United States have taken further steps toward increased collaboration by employing domestic violence specialists to help child welfare workers effectively assist clients who are victims of domestic violence (Aron & Olson, 1997). In Ontario, some of these initiatives have taken the form of community collaborations (e.g., the Children's Aid Society/Violence against Women collaboration protocol across the province); the establishment of domestic violence specialists within child protection organizations (e.g., domestic violence liaison workers, designated domestic violence intake teams); the institution of cross-sectoral trainings with both child protection and violence against women workers; the development of innovative fathering programs for men who expose children to domestic violence (e.g., Caring Dads program) (Edleson & Williams, 2006; Scott & Crooks, 2004); and the introduction of differential response models in child protection, which have all shown promise (Alaggia, Jenney, Mazzuca & Redmond, 2007; Edleson et al., 2006) in finding more productive ways for child protection services to engage with abused women. Similar to other areas of child protection work, however, many of these initiatives are limited by lack of structural support in the form of funding and other resources necessary for successful implementation. There is also the risk "that families not deemed 'high risk' are denied early intervention which might've promoted the welfare of the children concerned" (Gregory & Holloway, 2005, p. 48).

These "high needs" cases are challenging ones for child welfare workers whose caseloads are already demanding. Children from these families are at risk for re-exposure to violence in their families when they do not receive the attention they need and deserve. Using the expertise of domestic violence specialists provides one way to support mothers as they work with child welfare authorities, and can keep child welfare workers apprised of the myriad issues faced by victims of domestic violence (Aron & Olson, 1997). Workers also require the skills to engage with the perpetrators of DV in the name of child and mother safety. The Ontario Association of Children's Aid Societies (OACAS) is currently providing a new training curriculum[2] to address this need. This is a promising development intended to provide strategies for holding perpetrators accountable when, in practice, it has been a serious challenge.

While these are important steps toward increased collaboration, there is still a lack of documented initiatives between national child welfare systems and other agencies. This stems from the reality that much of the collaborative work remains in the early stages. The majority of service providers offer services for children exposed to domestic violence outside of child welfare involvement, with the exception of cases referred directly by a Children's Aid Society (CAS). Services for children have grown out of the programs and resources developed to respond to women who were victims of domestic violence and currently involve both mothers and children in the intervention process.

An integrated systems response to domestic violence and its impact on children, developed through joint relationships with community-based services, requires long-term planning to increase its potential for long-term success. This requires a shift in perspective among all service providers in focusing beyond the traditional perception of child welfare as a protection model compromising the interests of the non-offending parent. It is likely that collaboration between women's shelters and related agencies, Children's Aid Societies, and other community-based services could result in developing a system and legal response to domestic violence that helps to address the best interests and well-being of both the parent victim and her child together, not in isolation from each other (Callahan, 1993; Jenney, 2011).

THE INVOLVEMENT OF CHILD WELFARE AUTHORITIES

A discussion about intervening with families where domestic violence has occurred is not complete without acknowledging the necessary involvement of child welfare services. Initial debates on this topic were concerned with whether exposure to domestic violence should be explicitly defined as a form of child maltreatment and thus become subject to legal intervention by child welfare authorities, as suggested by Edleson (2004). In his review of the literature, Edleson (1999a) makes the critical point that studies of children who have been exposed to domestic violence show associations between exposure and negative outcomes on child development and functioning, but do not demonstrate direct cause–effect relationships. Based on this, Edleson (2004) has tackled the thorny issue of whether childhood exposure to adult domestic violence should be defined as child maltreatment under the law and recommends differential response as the most appropriate approach. Differential response involves customizing the service approach for each family on the basis of their unique needs. In particular, this approach embraces more community-based interventions, which emphasize both new and existing informal support systems for families (Waldfogel, 2008). His conclusion is based on extant data indicating that the degree of harm for exposed children depends on individual resiliency and context, and that assessments need to take these factors into account. Edleson (2004) views only some cases as appropriate for child welfare interventions, and recommends that the other cases be dealt with through voluntary, community-based services.

Methodological issues are also relevant here because studies often rely solely on clinical and shelter samples and on mothers as the sole source of data on children. There is also a lack of qualitative studies to help understand contextual factors (Overlien, 2010). So far there has been little focus in the research on understanding mediating and moderating influences on children's responses, or enough consideration given to contextual factors, particularly for factors supporting resilience (Kitzmann et al., 2003). In the few studies conducted with adults exposed to DV as children, participants identified abilities to overcome negative effects and develop adaptive coping strategies, but these have not been fully explored (Anderson & Danis, 2006; Humphreys, 2001). Poly-victimization and the presence of other forms of maltreatment for many children studied (i.e., physical abuse, neglect) is another confounding feature, and its effects often cannot be teased out from the effects of DV exposure alone (Dong et al., 2004; Hamby, Finkelhor, Turner & Ormrod, 2010). Despite the often-cited limitations of this research, the helping field and policy-makers in particular have embraced these preliminary findings and incorporated them in their efforts to serve the best interests of children by including "exposure to domestic abuse" and "failure to protect" as forms of child maltreatment (Strega et al., 2008)

Reporting child maltreatment in the context of domestic violence highlights a number of concerns. There is ample evidence that children exposed to domestic violence are at risk and may benefit from child welfare interventions, but viewing the child as a victim of maltreatment also raises complex and conflicting issues. For example, while the assaultive parent is certainly a perpetrator from a child maltreatment perspective, the parent victim may also be seen as a perpetrator as a result of her or his "failure to protect" the child from exposure to the domestic violence. The failure-to-protect concept stems from the premise that parents have an obligation to protect their children from avoidable harm. Filing a failure-to-protect report against an abused mother essentially blames the mother for failing to remove herself and her children from the abusive situation. This position fails to acknowledge that victims of domestic violence often have very limited choices, and that some stay in a violent situation because they may believe that leaving would put them and their children at increased risk of harm (Carter, Weithorn & Behrman, 1999; Hilton, 1992). Experience tells us that women are intensely concerned about the involvement of child welfare authorities. Furthermore, it is not uncommon for an abusive partner to threaten to "have the children taken away" by claiming that the woman is an unfit mother.

There is also a risk that a child maltreatment approach may focus too narrowly on the immediate protection of the child at the expense of assessing the longer-term needs of both the child and the parent victim. In addition, the specific inclusion of exposure to domestic violence in child welfare legislation imposes a duty to report all suspected cases, limiting the discretion of other community service providers to determine the extent to which a situation may or may not require child welfare intervention (Carter et al., 1999; Lemon, 1999).

The subject of state involvement in these cases evokes strong feelings from all parties involved in the treatment of children exposed to abuse. The debates centre on how existing systems can establish and maintain collaborative efforts to develop effective protocols and assessment and intervention programs that are both in the best interests of children as well as their victimized parents. Proponents of mandated involvement of child welfare authorities argue that: (1) the inclusion of EDV as a child protection issue serves as a clear mandate for child welfare intervention (Echlin & Marshall, 1995); and (2) this legislation provides an avenue for the perpetrators of the violence to be held accountable for both the domestic violence and its negative impact on the child (Carter et al., 1999). Opponents to such legislative changes argue that: (1) treating exposure to domestic violence as a child welfare matter may further victimize the parent victim of violence; (2) mandatory reporting laws could deter abused parents who are afraid of losing their children from seeking help; and (3) the already overloaded child welfare system does not have the capacity to adequately address the complex needs of these victimized families (*Developing a dialogue: A preliminary discussion paper on child protection issues in cases involving violence against women and children*, 2000; Edleson et al., 2006; Magen, 1999).

There are three core issues in the debate on mandated involvement:

1. How can the protection of the parent victim remain a central concern if the mother's safety and her ability to protect her children become undermined by interventions that focus only on the child and also potentially blame her for the exposure?
2. What is the best way to intervene with children during this process, knowing that exposure to domestic violence can have a negative impact on them, and that their relationship with the caregiver can often be the most reparative factor in resilience and recovery?
3. How can perpetrators of violence be held accountable as part of the approach to child protection involvement?

THE "DUTY TO REPORT" AND THE IMPACT ON INTERVENTION

Complicating the debate around these interventions are the "Duty to Report" guidelines. There are two primary reasons that child welfare might be involved in these cases: (1) if children are exposed to domestic violence; and (2) when they are or might be at risk of abuse or neglect. Such guidelines can be difficult to comply with when working with mothers and children to improve parenting techniques, such as behaviour management. For example, mothers are aware that they are not supposed to physically discipline their children and thus frequently avoid admitting this to child welfare workers, therapists, or other helpers, despite their own anxiety about using such parenting methods.

One woman in a group program reported that although she wanted to stop using physical punishment, she felt there was not enough education on non-violent ways of disciplining children. She was deeply ashamed and frightened about letting others know that she was hitting her children. In cases like this, children may also disclose the information to the therapist, who in turn risks jeopardizing the therapeutic alliance when child welfare is subsequently contacted. Unfortunately, this can make many practitioners ambivalent about reporting such incidents.

In other cases where the mother reunites with her abusive partner, the knowledge that the children are now potentially being re-exposed to violence puts the worker in the position of having to report. Workers from treatment agencies and child welfare services need to work co-operatively in order to preserve important therapeutic alliances for the benefit of clients, both children and parents. However, the reality remains that when reports to child welfare are made early in the intervention process, there is always the risk that the family will withdraw from services, often without adequate involvement with child welfare to fill the gap. Child welfare authorities currently lack the system capacity to address adequately the complex needs of these families. There is a growing concern about the number of cases referred to child welfare agencies that may be closed at intake without referral to appropriate follow-up services.

The complexity inherent in intervening in such situations requires the development of a child welfare response tailored to the needs of the children *and* the victimized parent. Regardless of whether or not their involvement is mandated, it is still critical for child welfare authorities to increase collaborative efforts with other service providers to establish the most effective means of meeting the needs of both the victimized parent and her child. Child welfare could potentially assist in the improvement of circumstances for the child and family with effective assessment procedures and services to address domestic violence.

The involvement of child welfare workers skilled in detecting and investigating family violence, and awareness of the need not to exacerbate already perilous situations by potentially revictimizing women, are critical. Skilled workers also resist pathologizing mothers or penalizing them, so that the best interests of the children are truly kept at the heart of their interventions. Unfortunately, due to a lack of resources for training and support in the child welfare sector, not all workers possess the knowledge necessary to intervene effectively with these families. Failure to understand the dynamics of woman abuse, coupled with belief in common myths and negative stereotypes about domestic violence, may cause some workers to respond in less than optimal ways. Mothers and children report having negative experiences with child welfare authorities, which causes them to fear such authorities and avoid any further involvement (Jenney, 2011).

On the other hand, women often credit workers skilled in this area for providing the necessary supports that make leaving the violent relationship, and remaining out of it, possible (Jenney, 2011). An illuminating example of the positive role that child welfare workers can play is illustrated in the following case:

One of our program clients said that her Children's Aid worker "saved her life." This worker validated her experience, found her space in a woman's shelter, and went so far as to pick her and her children up at her house to take them to the shelter. This worker then effectively mobilized services that provided support to this woman and her children, which helped her to maintain independence. In a subsequent incident, when the client was afraid to limit her husband's access to the children for fear of his reprisals, the worker advocated for her client, represented the client in discussions with the woman's husband, and sought out the requisite legal assistance required to ensure that child access for the father was supervised. When the mother and children were faced with financial difficulty after the separation, the Children's Aid worker accessed resources available within her organization to provide clothing allowances and other assistance to the family. This even included providing referrals to a sponsored summer camp for the children and finding money for special activities. This case illustrates how child welfare involvement can be supportive and helpful rather than intrusive or punitive.

Positive outcomes for the child and victimized parent are compromised when current child welfare intervention is delivered only in the form of investigating child maltreatment. If child welfare is seen as working toward enhancing the safety of parent victims as well as their children, rather than as an intrusive intervention, an effective response to domestic violence could develop out of a joint collaboration between child welfare and community-based services. Interventions should first and foremost focus on supporting the victimized parent's efforts to find a safe environment for herself and her children. Once safety is ensured, child welfare service providers can play a supportive role in helping children understand and come to terms with their experiences of violence. If a child is removed from the home, the child welfare system should offer consistent support to the mother so she can leave her situation safely with the goal of reuniting with her child. Supports should extend beyond the immediate physical needs of the parent victim to include assistance with new housing, employment, financial support, resources to enhance parenting skills, as well as emotional support as the parent adjusts to leaving a violent relationship and prepares to reunite with her child (Carter et al., 1999).

Supports that can be implemented by the child welfare system and other agencies that would not require intervention by child welfare on the basis of a child protection issue are more likely to generate a positive response not only from the parent victim but also from community resources and advocates (Carter et al., 1999; Rimer, 2001). Early detection of domestic violence and intervention by the child welfare system has the potential to deter future violence and ensure the necessary supports are in place to help women and their children. It is important to maintain individual consideration of a wide range of circumstances that may require multiple, community-based responses, but not necessarily legal or child welfare inter-ventions (Carter et al., 1999).

INTERVENTION APPROACHES: THE INTEGRATION OF THEORY INTO PRACTICE

In this section, the authors will highlight both familiar and emerging issues related to assessment, intervention, and ultimately the importance of pro-gram evaluation. Research efforts continue to identify relevant theoretical frameworks for understanding and addressing how children respond to exposure to violence, and this knowledge must be taken into account when attempting to provide intervention. The literature supports the experi-ence of practitioners in a number of ways and helps make sense of the various behaviours and coping mechanisms that children exhibit, such as aggression, hypervigilance, and parentification. Further problems with attachment, affect regulation, and difficulties with learning and social skill development that can arise from EDV pose a variety of challenges for these children as they attempt to navigate their way in the world. A broad range of interventions has been developed to meet the needs of children exposed to domestic violence, including community-based programs, educational initiatives for professionals, and therapeutic interventions with an individ-ual, group, or family focus (e.g., crisis intervention, support group, clinical assessment). Intervention goals for parent victims, for example, include the elimination of self-blame, an increase in levels of self-confidence and self-esteem, support in identifying and accessing resources (e.g., housing and financial assistance), understanding domestic violence and its negative impact on children, and strengthening appropriate parenting strategies (Humphreys, Mullender, Thiara & Skamballis, 2006; Lieberman & Van Horn, 2005; Rivett, Howarth & Harold, 2006; Suderman & Jaffe, 1999; Sul-livan, Egan & Gooch, 2004). Drawing on the past decade of practice experi-ence in providing services for children exposed to domestic violence and their mothers through the Family Violence Services unit at Child Develop-ment Institute in Toronto, the authors will provide practical considerations for intervention, highlighted with relevant clinical examples.

ASSESSING THE IMPACT

While families seek out services to address a range of issues, it is typically the acting-out behaviour of one child, often a male, who presents with problems of aggression or poor school performance that is identified as the reason for seeking help. More difficult to detect, but just as serious, are the internalized symptoms commonly observed in female children. Self-harming, eating disorders, risk of being victimized, and suicidal ideation are some of the more serious concerns that seem to manifest in these children, particularly over the long term. Only by considering a constellation of familial and social issues that typically accompany exposure to violence can issues specific to any one family member be identified and addressed.

In families where children are categorized as "good" or "bad," favoured or not favoured by either parent, interventions need to respond to all of the children, regardless of how they are labelled by the family. Moreover, it is not uncommon to hear women compare children to the abusive partner. This is further exacerbated when a child manifests aggressive, externalizing behaviour as a result of being exposed to family violence.

In order to determine the most appropriate form of intervention, it is important to determine the impact that the exposure to violence has had on a family. Besides gender, some of the factors that influence impact are developmental, including age and level of cognitive development. These are issues that determine how individuals make sense of their experiences through developing meaningful narratives. In addition, relationships with key family members also influence that experience, including the child's relationship to the abuser (whether or not the abuser is a biological parent, for example, or whether the child has a special relationship with that person). This can also impact on the relationship between siblings in families of mixed biological parentage where one child's father is the abuser, for example, and the other child has the "good" non-abusive father. This may be further complicated in some cases where the abusive father favours his biological child, thus contributing to disturbances within the sibling relationship system. The relationship that the child has with the parent victim (usually the mother) is a critical factor, since a positive relationship with the caregiver may be the most ameliorative factor in determining positive outcomes for children exposed to domestic violence. For example, in a valuable study by McGee (2000), one protective factor identified is the ability of mothers and their children to talk about the violence together. This supports one of the main goals of intervention, namely, breaking the silence and confirming the children's reality about their experiences. The children's relationships with their mothers are often a strong indicator for clinicians about the potential effectiveness of counselling. It is clear that children require a supportive parent in order for the process of intervention to be seen as helpful. This is not to suggest that merely talking about the event is enough to solve a family's problems, but it does become a point for initiating change. The theory related to "breaking the secret" contends that this enables members to verbalize the trauma. This is often the first goal of any family violence intervention program. Being able to talk openly about, or at least to acknowledge, the existence of the problems in the family can begin to help children sort out their feelings and confusion about what they have been experiencing.

The type and intensity of the violence and the proximity of the child to it when it occurs have also been found to make a difference in how children experience domestic violence. This can be a particularly challenging aspect of assessment since the majority of parents believe they have shielded their children from the violence, which makes ascertaining the amount of exposure problematic. Practice experience tells us that many caregivers are unaware of the extent to which their children have been exposed to the violence. Not surprisingly, often some of the most violent incidents are the ones in which women are the least likely to be aware that their children were present, when the mothers are caught up in the affective intensity of trying to protect themselves from harm.

In working with one woman who had been beaten to unconsciousness in the presence of her children, we found that when she subsequently brought her children to the program, she did not initially connect their problematic behaviour to this traumatic event. In the intake interview, she expressed her certainty that her children had not witnessed this particularly violent incident even though she knew that she had lost consciousness during the assault and couldn't have known the whereabouts of her children. Not surprisingly, both children continuously alluded to this event in their respective intervention groups. One of the children began to repeatedly draw a picture of his mother lying bloody on the floor with his father standing over her, weapon in hand. When we were able to help the children let their mother know that they had indeed been present for the assault, many of their previous problematic behaviours began to recede. It may have been the strain of pretending not to know about the incident that was perhaps most traumatizing to the children.

As stated earlier, the availability of a responsive caregiver in these moments of distress is the key to determining impact; even the presence of another relative or sibling who can provide comfort to the child can make an important contribution to lessening the impact. Furthermore, it may be more important to clarify the scope of impact than to classify the type of abuse. Even though emphasis is often put on the detrimental effects of physical violence, mothers and children appear to experience longer term effects from the emotional aspects of violence. Therefore, understanding how children interpret the violence they have been exposed to as part of their individual meaning-making, such as the way they "story" their own experience, is important to guide intervention. In other words, in the assessment phase, it is important to gather information that provides the narrative material for the "story" of the violence that has been experienced. To this end, asking mothers about developmental history and how they experienced their child from pregnancy to delivery to the early years of parenting helps to inform the clinician about the environment in which the child has developed. The child's developmental stages can provide much needed information about attachment processes and any developmental delays that might be important to consider when designing an optimal treatment plan.

Although there are parts of assessment that should be done with women individually, it is important for clinicians to be able to see mothers and their children interacting together. From this, one can observe relational patterns (playing together, or comforting a child in distress) and get the perspectives of child and mother together about their shared experiences of violence (making no assumptions about impact).

Part of any strong assessment is the attention paid to both risk and protective factors for both the family as a whole and the individuals within it. Risk factors are issues that impact on both emotional and physical safety of women and their children, such as ongoing contact with abusive partners. We know from practice that children continue to cope with the effects of *repeated* exposure "after the fact," as they have contact with their father after the family has been separated. This exposure can take the form of continued emotional, psychological, or financial abuse of their mother, and other control tactics, which persist in having an impact on the children. These difficulties are particularly apparent in children who, although undergoing counselling, continue to show signs of deterioration after each visit with the abusive parent. Fathers harbouring anger employ a range of tactics, often using the children to retaliate against the mother. In a significant number of cases we have seen fathers deny support payments, attend access visits sporadically, criticize the child's mother, and attempt to solicit knowledge of the mother's whereabouts or activities, all of which can be destructive for children's emotional well-being.

Protective factors for both mothers and children include available social supports, internal locus of control, and the ability to create physical and mental escapes (activities outside of the home or fantasy). Part of having a sense of control for children is for them to attempt to understand or make sense of what is going on in their family, in particular trying to predict, explain, prevent, or control the behaviour of the abuser or victim. They might develop their own strategies for staying safe, "running interference" for the victim, protecting or comforting the parent victim or their siblings. Finally, participating in therapeutic interventions can provide opportunities to further develop and strengthen resilience and protective factors in children's environments.

CONSIDERATIONS FOR EFFECTIVE INTERVENTIONS

Following the first step of assessment and determining the potential impact of EDV, the next step is designing the most appropriate intervention. In the programs offered at the Child Development Institute, we focus on the most common issues for children: breaking the secret, identifying forms of abuse, normalizing/validating experiences, addressing safety (both within the program and planning for it outside of the program), developing self-esteem, emotion regulation, and conflict resolution skills. In addition, attending to issues of grief and loss, reducing anxiety by teaching stress management skills, and strengthening family and community supports are all ways in which interventions can provide opportunities for personal growth and healing. To address these issues, we provide targeted interventions that begin with an introduction to the work, which helps families understand the process of intervention and what they can expect from their visits to the program. Providing concrete information about the structure of the program and the process of intervention can alleviate anxiety for families by allowing them to prepare for the weeks ahead, knowing what they can expect and what might be expected of them. The next session is to introduce the concepts of understanding and coping with a variety of feelings, as well as providing skills in stress management. This is done very early in the process so that when distressing material comes up, children and their mothers have already been given some tools to manage uncomfortable emotions as they arise throughout the program. We also build components of stress management techniques and positive self-esteem/self-care aspects into each week since these are powerful facilitators of resilience.

An important component of any intervention program is addressing safety issues. Although it is often assumed that, given their life experiences, children of abused women would know more about how to manage unsafe situations, the very opposite may be true. The issues around safety for children and their mothers are complex, commonly leaving children ill-equipped to deal with their everyday environments and contributing to their feeling frightened and out of control. McGee (2000) found that these feelings contributed to trauma in children and made their situations worse. Therefore, it may be that teaching safety planning to children will allow them to feel they have more control in a situation or at least better enable them to protect themselves (McGee, 2000). Teaching mothers and their children how to create safety plans for themselves will also bring the issue of safety to the fore, to be openly talked about and managed (Cooley & Frazer, 2006; Hardesty & Campbell, 2004).

Many children experience improvement simply by being removed from the violent environment. Frequently women recount their children's immediate improvement in sleeping, eating, school performance, etc., upon entering a shelter or other safe environment. Although it is not a solution for all issues, the value of a safe environment needs to be continually reinforced. Mothers often describe their children as happier or more relaxed once the perpetrator of violence is no longer continuously present in their lives. However, there is also the risk that when children begin to experience safety, the resulting newfound emotional freedom can sometimes result in children manifesting new acting-out behaviours that mothers often misinterpret as a parenting failure on their part. Some women return to a violent partner if they perceive their children to be difficult to manage, believing them to be angry about leaving or increasingly unhappy when this may not actually be the case. It can be surmised that children who find themselves in a new, often safer environment will allow themselves to express their needs or act in a more childlike manner. This can be a disconcerting experience as both mother and child try to renegotiate their relationship with one another.

Interventions that provide education around child development, sensitivity, and attunement are additional ways to improve mother's feelings of competence and comfort about parenting their children and managing challenging behaviours. Abused mothers are at an increased risk of being overly permissive in their attempts to assuage their feelings of guilt for exposing their children to the violence and "taking them away" from their father (Bilinkoff, 1995). Some women begin to perceive any attempts at discipline as mechanisms of power and control, behaviours they want to shy away from (Bilinkoff, 1995). However, the opposite can also operate where some women are overly punitive, both physically and emotionally, in an attempt to manage their children's behaviours. These overly harsh parenting behaviours can stem from multiple sources, among them the stress of being an impoverished single parent. It is imperative in any supportive counselling environment to encourage non-violent means of behaviour management and healthy discipline.

All too common in cases of domestic violence are those situations in which women are not available to meet the needs of their children because they are themselves emotionally consumed by the effects of abuse and trauma. In such cases, children may take on parentified roles by looking after themselves and their siblings in order to minimize their demands on their mother, or to care for her. They may also take on similar "adult" roles when having access contact with their father. They sometimes resort to overachieving, over-functioning, and masking their unhappy feelings. These behaviours are reinforced when the children are positively responded to for their "adult-like" behaviour. Intervention then needs to focus on conveying the importance of clear boundaries between parent and child in order to ensure future healthy relationships with others.

In another example, young children show a variety of attachment issues and an inability to self-soothe that is manifested in anxious, clingy behaviour, difficulty separating, and being difficult to hold or comfort. These children, often perceived as "difficult," may make it even harder for a mother to parent effectively when she is already struggling with a variety of issues. The importance of working with the mother and her child in order to facilitate greater understanding and "tuning in" to the child's needs is paramount in intervention. It is also important to underscore that a lack of parenting skills, combined with stress, can contribute to a mother's use of physical or emotional punishment, which, in turn, leads to even more difficulties and escalation of behaviour problems. Lack of proper information and parenting support, as well as stressors such as social isolation and financial hardship, intensify these problems.

The social isolation that can accompany domestic violence is of particular concern for the child who does not have access to support outside of the violent environment (Graham-Bermann, 1998). With social isolation comes an increased risk that abused women will use their children as emotional supports or confidants (Bilinkoff, 1995). In addition, poverty has also been found to be associated with amplifying the negative impact of exposure to domestic violence (Fantuzzo & Mohr, 1999; Kairys et al., 2002; Osofsky, 1999). For many victims of domestic violence, poverty (or the threat of poverty) may present a significant barrier to the safety of the woman and her children. Previous research into the experiences of low-income women reveals past and current physical abuse by a domestic partner (Correia & Ciorba VonDeLinde, 2002). Traditionally, the general response to serving the needs of abused women and their children was to provide immediate safety and possibly information on and referrals to subsidized housing programs. With policy changes and shrinking resources, the availability of these social supports may not be sufficient for a woman and her children to live above the poverty line. Many women in violent relationships are financially dependent on their abuser, and one of their greatest fears is not being able to financially support themselves and their children and obtain access to affordable permanent housing. Partnerships between the domestic violence community and anti-poverty groups to provide skills training and economic development are necessary to ensure the long-term ability of victims of domestic violence to become financially independent and secure. These are even more reasons for linking social justice initiatives with family violence services.

Sessions that address gender stereotypes and aspects of prevention, such as violence, power, and control, are included to help families understand how violence happens in a larger social context. One of the most pivotal sessions is the one that addresses violence in families, and this is a topic that is best approached after several weeks of engagement with a family. Following that, sessions that address worries and fears, anger, responsibility, loss and sadness, and family changes complete the curriculum of dominant concerns for most families. Family changes are particularly relevant when the person who once held the power in the family hierarchy—the perpetrator of the violence—is no longer present as there is an anxiety that plays itself out in the family dynamics when reorganization begins to occur. Sometimes children living in a violent environment may perceive their mother as a sibling or other powerless member of the family. Power struggles may ensue between mother and children to determine if she is now in charge. After witnessing their mother being berated and physically assaulted, many children question her ability to care for them. They may test to see if she can create safety, security, and structure, elements essential for effective family functioning. In some instances, children may openly blame their mother for the violence, blame her for the dissolution of the family, or even assume the role of abuser. A family systems intervention approach, as suggested by Bilinkoff (1995), for example, can focus on the hierarchical restructuring of the family and support the mother to set limits and create boundaries with her children to help them feel safe and cared for.

Service provision strategies are important aspects of intervention. For example, it is important for agencies delivering programming for children exposed to violence to employ both male and female group facilitators as a means of providing positive role models for children to experience positive interactions between men and women. Clinicians also need to be particularly aware of the language used when discussing family violence issues. It is important never to make assumptions about who the abuser is in a family by using language that refers only to fathers or male perpetrators. Violence between intimate partners is present in every form of relationship, from dating to common-law and same-sex unions. Using language based on heterosexist, white, middle-class assumptions may inadvertently exclude people and families from receiving appropriate screening, assessment, and interventions. That said, all of the clinical practice examples offered in this chapter refer to the experiences of children and mothers participating in group intervention where the mother's male partner, often the children's father, has been identified as the abuser.

Language used by the children and mothers to describe their experiences is also a valuable source of clinical information and indicates areas for focus and intervention. For example, sometimes language itself can become a trigger for trauma. This was the case when we worked with a young boy participating in our program who came from a Spanish-speaking family. This boy insisted that he did not know how to speak Spanish despite evidence that English was clearly not his first language. What eventually unfolded was that the family had spoken only Spanish when they lived with the perpetrator and only English when the mother fled to a shelter with her children. This boy truly believed that if they spoke only English, the violence would not return to their lives and they could live in a safe environment.

Although not widely available, programs that offer language-specific services to families are the preferred method of intervention for two important reasons. First, there are obvious benefits of receiving culturally sensitive services in one's own language for engagement purposes and overall comprehension. Second, often the traumatic events and their effects are encoded in the language in which these experiences occur, and resolution of these issues is best achieved within that language (Marian & Neisser, 2000; Schrauf, 2000).

INTERVENTION MODALITIES

There are several options when it comes to offering services for children exposed to domestic violence and their families, and the type of service may depend on agency resources, family dynamics, and child development. There are three main approaches: individual, group, and family work.

Individual Intervention

Individual therapy for children exposed to domestic violence varies according to individual age, level of development and functioning, and the specific needs of the child. Different approaches include crisis intervention, play therapy, and art therapy. Interventions involving play and/or expressive arts are aimed at helping children manage their feelings and relationships with their parents and siblings. Individual intervention is preferred when children are not appropriate for group work for any number of reasons (they are too young, too aggressive, or they have special needs, a serious lack of social skills, or inhibitions in a group environment). Individual intervention may also be provided for children who are still living in an unsafe environment; it provides children with a means to express their feelings and develop appropriate coping skills.

Group Intervention

Using a group model, based on concurrent involvement of mothers in parallel groups with their children, is hypothesized to be an effective means of breaking the intergenerational transmission of family violence (Sullivan et al., 2004). A group format can help to reduce a child's feeling of isolation and belief that he or she is the only one who has experienced exposure to domestic violence. In a group it is common for children to express relief at finding others who have had similar experiences. When asked, children often explain that they believed that the violence happened only in their family. Group interventions can also be effective in helping decrease children's feelings of being stigmatized and feeling unsafe. Common positive features of group therapy include providing a safe environment where children can feel secure in disclosing their fears and thoughts; developing skills to feel empowered and more self-confident; developing safety plans; developing alternative, non-violent strategies to resolve disputes, including alternative behaviours to express feelings of anger in a non-aggressive manner; and identifying forms of abuse (Gewirtz & Edleson, 2007; Graham-Bermann, Howell, Lilly & DeVoe, 2011; Graham-Bermann, Lynch, Banyard, DeVoe & Halabu, 2007; Suderman & Jaffe, 1999; Sullivan et al., 2004). Children are also afforded the opportunity to improve social skills and make friends in a safe environment. It is not uncommon for children to lack pro-social skills and to have problems with social relationships, and they might find themselves disliked at school or in their neighbourhoods because of these difficulties.

Dyadic or Family Intervention

Given the strong relationship between the adjustment of the child and adjustment of the primary caregiver, it is essential that supports and resources for the parent victim be an integral component of any form of intervention with children who are exposed to domestic violence (Appleyard & Osofsky, 2003; Buchbinder, 2004; Holden et al., 1998; Jaffe & Crooks, 2005; Levendosky & Graham-Bermann, 2001; Radford & Hester, 2006; Suderman & Jaffe, 1999). The involvement of the parent victim in children's treatment is essential. Some programs offer concurrent groups for both mother and child, while other programs include groups of mother–child pairings (Graham-Bermann & Hughes, 2003; Peled & Davis, 1995; Suderman & Jaffe, 1999; Sullivan et al., 2004).

Thus, intervening with families can occur on a dyadic basis, such as parent–child work, or with the family as a whole. A combination of the two approaches is preferable as the group environment allows members to deal with issues as a family, while dyadic work provides the opportunity to work out complex personal dynamics in specific relationships within the family makeup (Jenney, 1999). An innovative program developed and offered in Toronto combines both of these methods of intervention in a group program for mothers with abuse histories and their young children. The Mothers in Mind Program (Sura-Liddell & Jenney, 2012) is an attachment-informed, relationship-based model of group intervention with psycho-educational components for mothers with children between birth and four years of age. The ten-week format is designed to enhance parenting skills, strengthen parent–child relationships, and reduce parenting stress. Mothers learn child development and appropriate expectations, sensitivity and attunement, specific parenting techniques, as well as opportunities to practice reflective and relaxation skills as a form of stress management. Mothers and their children attend group together and participate in various age-appropriate activities.

EVALUATING PROGRAM EFFECTIVENESS

Regardless of the types of interventions being implemented, all domestic violence intervention programs should include an ongoing evaluation component to provide continual feedback about the effectiveness of approaches and to signal any changes needed to better meet the needs of the target population (Osofsky, 1999; Rivett et al., 2006). The process of conducting research with this population comes with a host of unique challenges, not the least of which is funding and other material resources. Engaging traumatized populations in the process of research is also very difficult, and conducting research with culturally and linguistically diverse clients is challenging. Ethical issues abound, and it is important to always consider the needs of the families themselves when designing methods of inquiry. Despite such difficulties, it is critical to recognize the importance of conducting both quantitative and qualitative research.

Clinical recordings need to be recognized and used as a valuable tool for evaluation. For example, narratives documenting children's experiences provide important information that may not otherwise be tracked with quantitative indicators: the boy who graduated from the program and never received another suspension from school again; the child with apparent learning disabilities who started achieving academically; the girl who never had any friends and was finally invited to a birthday party; the continuous reports from parents and children of improved parent–child relationships are only a few of the many successes. These are the very real experiences that families report; they can be used by both families and practitioners as testimonials regarding the effectiveness of treatment.

These programs designed to intervene with both mothers and children who have experienced domestic violence have undergone preliminary evaluations and both show promising outcomes. Over the course of several years, both quantitative and qualitative research designs, along with clinical observations of changes, have provided opportunities to use client experiences and outcome data to directly influence program changes in design and delivery (Jenney & Alaggia, 2003; Jenney & Root, 2010).

CONCLUSION

A growing body of literature on EDV and its treatment has pushed the topic from darkness into light. As research and reflective practice creates greater understanding of this complex issue, the potential to design more effective, longer-lasting, and systemic change initiatives will grow. The field of domestic violence research and practice has evolved from a distant adjunct in social work to a central focus for children's and women's health and mental health across disciplines. Advances in research within these disciplines have and will continue to support the advancement of EDV treatment, prevention, and policy work, even if questions persist. For example, despite the wealth of knowledge we have, there is much that remains unknown and unexplored. After twenty years of progress, there is still limited knowledge of what works best for children and their caregivers in both short- and long-term approaches. In particular, work needs to be done to develop the most effective means of keeping children safe while maintaining a central concern about the safety of their caregivers. Finally, fathers need to be part of the dialogue of intervention in order for them to be held accountable for the impact of their behaviour on their children.

Research gaps include relatively little knowledge of the contextual factors influencing EDV outcomes. For example, research examining samples of children exposed to domestic violence and not residing in a shelter might demonstrate different outcomes than those living within shelters. While it is unlikely that a sample would consist of children who remain in the home with continued violence, this group should also be given consideration when attempting to draw conclusions on the outcomes for children who are exposed to domestic violence.

On the clinical and intervention side, determining how best to respond to the issue of children's exposure to domestic violence requires systematic documentation of the numbers of children who are actually exposed to domestic violence. It also requires examining short-term and long-term individual experiences in context rather than generalized to and from others. Consideration should be given to the mechanisms underlying the impact of exposure to domestic violence on the process of healthy child development. Extant research and clinical experiences have documented the variety of behavioural, emotional, and cognitive functioning problems that face the increasing numbers of children who are being exposed to domestic violence. While current research and initiatives have begun to address the knowledge gaps and diverse needs of this special population, the central challenge continues to be providing services that can strike the right balance between the needs of victimized parents and the needs of their children.

As illustrated throughout this text, violence in families impacts multiple systems, from the parent victim and the exposed child to the broader social system, including societal attitudes toward violence in families and the role of external systems in addressing this serious problem. This is a systems issue and therefore future research and practice may wish to consider more ways to bring systems thinking into the discussion of EDV causes, consequences, and its treatment. By viewing the subject matter as interconnected and complex, clinical service providers and policy-makers are better able to design and implement response options that take into account this complexity, rather than treating it overly simplistically. Without integrating knowledge and approaches, the risk is that we will continue to separate experiences of women from children, of families from services, and populations from the communities where they live. Bringing these together holistically offers hope that we can build on the advances made in research and clinical practice to make the lives of women, children, and abusers better as we work toward eliminating domestic violence and its harmful sequelae for good.

NOTES

1 Nova Scotia Children and Family Services Act, 1990, c. 5, s. 1, 22(2)(i).
2 *Where Woman Abuse and Child Safety Intersect: Best Practice Interventions for Keeping Children and Women Safe* (Toronto: OACAS, 2010).

REFERENCES

Alaggia, R., Gadalla, T., & Shlonsky, A. (2010). *Differential response in cases of domestic violence in the child welfare system*. Toronto: Ontario Ministry of Children and Youth Services.

Alaggia, R., Jenney, A., Mazucca, J., & Redmond, M. (2007). In whose best interest? A Canadian case study of the impact of child welfare policies in cases of domestic violence. *Journal of Brief Therapy and Crisis Intervention, 7*(4), 275–90.

Aldrich, L., & Kluger, J.H. (2010). New York's one judge-one family response to family violence. *Juvenile and Family Court Journal, 60*(4), 77–86.

Anderson, K., & Danis, F. (2006). Adult daughters of battered women: Resistance and resilience in the face of danger. *AFFILIA, 21*(4), 419–32.

Appleyard, K., & Osofsky, J. D. (2003). Parenting after trauma: Supporting parents and caregivers in the treatment of children impacted by violence. *Infant Mental Health Journal, 24*(2), 111–25.

Aron, L., & Olson, K. (1997). Efforts by child welfare agencies to address domestic violence. *Public Welfare, 55*(3), 4–13.

Bandura, A. (1977). *Social learning theory.* Englewood Cliffs, NJ: Prentice-Hall.

Bilinkoff, J. (1995). Empowering battered women as mothers. In E. Peled, P.G. Jaffe & J.L. Edleson (Eds.), *Ending the cycle of violence: Community responses to battered women* (pp. 97–105). Thousand Oaks, CA: Sage.

Bogat, G.A., DeJonghe, E., Levendosky, A.A., Davidson, W.S., & von Eye, A. (2006). Trauma symptoms among infants exposed to intimate partner violence. *Child Abuse & Neglect, 30,* 109–25.

Buchbinder, E. (2004). Motherhood of battered women: The struggle for repairing the past. *Clinical Social Work Journal, 32*(3), 307–26.

Callahan, M. (1993). Feminist approaches: Women recreate child welfare. In B. Wharf (Ed.), *Rethinking child welfare in Canada* (pp. 172–209). Toronto: Oxford University Press.

Carter, L.S., Weithorn, L.A., & Behrman, R.E. (1999). Domestic violence and children: Analysis and recommendations. *The Future of Children, 9*(3), 4–20.

Cooley, B., & Frazer, C. (2006). Children and domestic violence: A system of safety in clinical practice. *Australian Social Work, 59*(4), 462–73.

Correia, A., & Ciorba VonDeLinde, K. (2002). *Integrating anti-poverty work into domestic violence advocacy: Iowa's experience.* Harrisburg, PA: National Resource Center on Domestic Violence.

Cummings, E.M. (1998). Children exposed to marital conflict and violence: Conceptual and theoretical directions. In G.W. Holden, R.A. Geffner & E.N. Jouriles (Eds.), *Children exposed to marital violence: Theory, research, and applied issues* (pp. 55–93). Washington, DC: American Psychological Association.

Cummings, J.G., Peplar, D.J., & Moore, T.E. (1999). Behavior problems in children exposed to wife abuse: Gender differences. *Journal of Family Violence, 14*(2), 133–56.

Developing a dialogue: A preliminary discussion paper on child protection issues in cases involving violence against women and children. (2000). Vancouver: Association of Specialized Victim Assistance & Counselling Programs, BC Institute Against Family Violence, BC Women's Hospital Sexual Assault Service Program.

Dong, M., Anda, R., Felitti, V., Dube, S., Williamson, D., & Thompson, T. (2004). The interrelatedness of mutliple forms of childhood abuse, neglect, and household dysfunction. *Child Abuse & Neglect, 28,* 771–84.

Echlin, C., & Marshall, L. (1995). Child protection services for children of battered women: Practice and controversy. In E. Peled, P.G. Jaffe & J.L. Edleson (Eds.), *Ending the cycle of violence: Community responses to children of battered women* (pp. 170–85). Thousand Oaks, CA: Sage.

Edleson, J.L. (1999a). Children's witnessing of adult domestic violence. *Journal of Interpersonal Violence, 14*(8), 839–70.

Edleson, J.L. (1999b). The overlap between child maltreatment and woman battering. *Violence against Women, 5*(2), 134–54.

Edleson, J.L. (2004). Should childhood exposure to adult domestic violence be defined as child maltreatment under the law? In P.G. Jaffe, L.L. Baker & A.J. Cunningham (Eds.), *Protecting children from domestic violence* (pp. 8–29). New York: Guilford.

Edleson, J.L., Gassman-Pines, J., & Hill, M.B. (2006). Defining child exposure to domestic violence as neglect: Minnesota's difficult experience. *Social Work, 51*(2), 167–74.

Edleson, J.L., & Williams, O.J. (Eds.). (2006). *Parenting by men who batter: New directions for assessment and intervention.* New York: Oxford University Press.

Evans, S.E., Davies, C., & DiLillo, D. (2008). Exposure to domestic violence: A meta-analysis of child and adolescent outcomes. *Aggression and Violent Behaviour, 13*, 131–40.

Fantuzzo, J.W., DePaola, L.M., Lambert, L., Martino, T., Anderson, G., & Sutton, S. (1991). Effects of interparental violence on the psychological adjustment and competencies of young children. *Journal of Consulting and Clinical Psychology, 59,* 258–65.

Fantuzzo, J.W., & Mohr, W.K. (1999). Prevalence and effects of child exposure to domestic violence. *The Future of Children, 9*(3), 21–32.

Garbarino, J., Dubrow, N., Kostelny, K., & Pardo, C. (1992). *Children in danger: Coping with the consequences of community violence.* San Francisco: Jossey-Bass.

Gewirtz, A.H., & Edleson, J.L. (2007). Young children's exposure to intimate partner violence: Towards a developmental risk and resilience framework for research and intervention. *Journal of Family Violence, 22*, 151–63.

Graham-Bermann, S.A. (1998). The impact of woman abuse on children's social development: Research and theoretical perspectives. In G.W. Holden, R.A. Geffner & E.N. Jouriles (Eds.), *Children exposed to marital violence: Theory, research, and applied issues* (pp. 21–54). Washington, DC: American Psychological Association.

Graham-Bermann, S.A., Howell, K.H., Lilly, M., & DeVoe, E.R. (2011). Mediators and moderators of change in adjustment following intervention for children exposed to intimate partner violence. *Journal of Interpersonal Violence, 26*(9), 1815–33.

Graham-Bermann, S.A., & Hughes, H.M. (2003). Intervention for children exposed to interpersonal violence (IPV): Assessment of needs and research priorities. *Clinical Child and Family Psychology Review, 6*(3), 189–204.

Graham-Bermann, S.A., Lynch, S.M., Banyard, V.L., DeVoe, E.R., & Halabu, H. (2007). Community-based intervention for children exposed to intimate partner violence: An efficacy trial. *Journal of Consulting and Clinical Psychology, 75*(2), 199–209.

Gregory, M., & Holloway, M. (2005). Language and the shaping of social work. *British Journal of Social Work, 35,* 37–53.

Hamby, S., Finkelhor, D., Turner, H., & Ormrod, R. (2010). The overlap of witnessing partner violence with child maltreatment and other victimizations in a nationally representative survey of youth. *Child Abuse & Neglect, 34*(10), 734–41.

Hardesty, J.L., & Campbell, J.C. (2004). Safety planning for abused women and their children. In P.G. Jaffe, L.L. Baker & A.J. Cunningham (Eds.), *Protecting children from domestic violence: Strategies for community intervention* (pp. 89–100). New York: Guilford Press.

Hazen, A.L., Connelly, C.D., Edleson, J.L., Kelleher, K.J., Landverk, J.A., Coben, J.H., et al. (2006). Assessment of intimate partner violence by child welfare services. *Children and Youth Services Review, 29,* 490–500.

Hilton, Z.N. (1992). Battered women's concerns about their children witnessing wife assault. *Journal of Interpersonal Violence, 7*(1), 77–86.

Holden, G.W., Geffner, R.A., & Jouriles, E.N. (1998). *Children exposed to marital violence: Theory, research, and applied issues.* Washington, DC: American Psychological Association.

Holt, S., Buckley, H., & Whelan, S. (2008). The impact of exposure to domestic violence on children and young people: A review of the literature. *Child Abuse & Neglect, 32,* 797–810.

Howell, K.H., Graham-Bermann, S.A., Czyz, E., & Lilly, M. (2010). Assessing resilience in preschool children exposed to intimate partner violence. *Violence and Victims, 25*(2), 150–64.

Hughes, H.M. (1998). Psychological and behavioral correlates of family violence in child witness and victims. *American Journal of Orthopsychiatry, 58,* 77–90.

Hughes, H.M., & Graham-Bermann, S.A. (1998). Children of battered women: Impact of emotional abuse on development and adjustment. *Journal of Emotional Abuse, 1,* 23–50.

Humphreys, C. (2001). The impact of domestic violence on children. In S. Tucker, J. Roche & P. Foley (Eds.), *Children in society: Contemporary theory, policy, and practice* (pp. 142–50). Houndmills, UK: Palgrave.

Humphreys, C., Mullender, A., Thiara, R., & Skamballis, A. (2006). "Talking to my mum": Developing communication between mothers and children in the aftermath of domestic violence. *Journal of Social Work, 6*(1), 53–63.

Hunt, K.L., Martens, P.M., & Belcher, H.M.E. (2011). Risky business: Trauma exposure and rate of posttraumatic stress disorder in African American children and adolescents. *Journal of Traumatic Stress, 24*(3), 365–69.

Huth-Bocks, A.C., Levendosky, A.A., Theran, S.A., & Bogat, G.A. (2004). The impact of domestic violence on mothers' prenatal representations of their infants. *Infant Mental Health Journal, 25*(2), 79–98.

Jaffe, P.G., & Crooks, C.V. (2005). *Understanding women's experiences parenting in the context of domestic violence: Implications for community and court-related service providers.* Retrieved from: Violence against Women Online

Resources: http://www.vaw.umn.edu/documents/commissioned/parentingindv.html.

Jaffe, P.G., Wolfe, D.A., & Wilson, S.K. (1990). *Children of battered women.* Newbury Park: Sage.

Jenney, A. (1999). Treating the effects of intergenerational trauma: A case study. *Imprint, 26,* 1–4.

Jenney, A. (2011). *Doing the right thing: Negotiating risk and safety in child protection work with domestic violence cases.* Toronto: Universty of Toronto Press.

Jenney, A., & Alaggia, R. (2003). *Here to help: How does it help? A qualitative report based on the questionnaire feedback from mothers' and dhildren's narrative responses.* Toronto: Child Development Institute.

Jenney, A., & Root, J. (2010). *Mother's in mind: A relationship-based intervention program for abused women involved with child protection services and their young children.* Paper presented at the OACAS Critical Connections Symposium, Toronto, Ontario, Canada.

Johnson, H., & Dauvergne, M. (2001). Children witnessing family violence. *Juristat: Canadian Centre for Justice Statistics, 21*(6), 1–13.

Johnson, S.P., & Sullivan, C.M. (2008). How child protection workers support or further victimize battered mothers. *Affilia, 23*(3), 242–58.

Jouriles, E.N., & Norwood, W.D. (1995). Physical aggression toward boys and girls in families characterized by the battering of women. *Journal of Family Psychology, 9,* 69–78.

Kairys, S., Johnson, C., & Committee. (2002). The psychological maltreatment of children: Technical report. *Pediatrics, 109*(4), 1–3.

Kilpatrick, K.L., & Williams, L.M. (1997). Post-traumatic stress disorder in child witnesses to domestic violence. *American Journal of Orthopsychiatry, 67,* 639–44.

Kitzmann, K.M., Gaylord, N.K., Holt, A.R., & Kenny, E.D. (2003). Child witnesses to domestic violence: A meta-analytic review. *Journal of Consulting and Clinical Psychology, 71*(2), 339–52.

Leavitt, L., & Fox, N. (1993). *The psychological effects of war and violence on children.* Hillsdale, NJ: Lawrence Erlbaum.

Lemon, N.K. (1999). The legal system's response to children exposed to domestic violence. *The Future of Children, 9*(3), 67–83.

Levendosky, A.A., & Graham-Bermann, S.A. (2001). Parenting in battered women: The effects of domestic violence on women and their children. *Journal of Family Violence, 16*(2), 171–92.

Levendosky, A.A., Leahy, K.L., Bogat, G.A., Davidson, W.S., & von Eye, A. (2006). Domestic violence, maternal parenting, maternal mental health, and infant externalizing behavior. *Journal of Family Psychology, 20*(4), 544–52.

Lieberman, A.F., & Van Horn, P. (2005). *Don't hit my mommy: A manual for child-parent psychotherapy with young witnesses of family violence.* Washington, DC: Zero to Three Press.

Magen, R. (1999). In the best interests of battered women: Reconceptualizing allegations of failure to protect. *Child Maltreatment, 4*(2), 127–35.

Margolin, G., & Gordis, E.B. (2000). The effects of family and community violence on children. *Annual Review of Psychology, 51*, 445–79.

Margolin, G., Gordis, E.B., Medina, A.M., & Oliver, P.H. (2003). The co-occurrence of husband-to-wife aggression, family of origin aggression, and child abuse potential in a community sample: Implications for parenting. *Journal of Interpersonal Violence, 18*(4), 413–40.

Margolin, G., & Vickerman, K.A. (2011). Post-traumatic stress in children and adolescents exposed to family violence: I. Overview and issues. *Couple and Family Psychology: Research and Practice, I*(S), 63–73.

Marian, V., & Neisser, U. (2000). Language-dependent recall of autobiographical memories. *Journal of Experimental Psychology: General, 129*(3), 361–68.

Masten, A.S. (2011). Resilience in children threatened by extreme adversity: Frameworks for research, practice, and translational synergy. *Development and Psychopathology, 23*(2), 493–506.

McGee, C. (2000). *Childhood experiences of domestic violence.* Philadelphia: Jessica Kingsley Publishers.

McGruder-Johnson, A.K., Davidson, E.S., Gleaves, D.H., Stock, W., & Finch, J.F. (2000). Interpersonal violence and post-traumatic symptomatology: The effects of ethnicity, gender, and exposure to violent events. *Journal of Interpersonal Violence, 15*(2), 205–21.

McGuigan, W.M., Vuchinich, S., & Pratt, C.C. (2000). Domestic violence, parents' view of their infant, and risk for child abuse. *Journal of Family Psychology, 14*(4), 613–24.

Moylan, C.A., Herrenkohl, T.I., Sousa, C., Tajima, E.A., Herrenkohl, R.C., & Russon, M.J. (2010). The effects of child abuse and exposure to domestic violence on adolescent internalizing and externalizing behavior problems. *Journal of Family Violence, 25*, 53–63.

O'Keefe, M. (1994). Linking marital violence, mother–child/father–child aggression, and child behavior problems. *Journal of Family Violence 9*, 63–78.

O'Keefe, M. (1995). Predictors of child abuse in martially violent families. *Journal of Interpersonal Violence, 10*, 3–25.

O'Keefe, M. (1996). The differential effects of family violence on adolescent adjustment. *Child and Adolescent Social Work Journal, 13*, 51–68.

Onyskiw, J.E. (2003). Domestic violence and children's adjustment: A review of the research. *Journal of Emotional Abuse, 3*(1/2), 11–45.

Osofsky, J.D. (1997). *Children in a violent society.* New York: Guilford Press.

Osofsky, J.D. (1999). The impact of violence on children. *The Future of Children, 9*(3), 33–49.

Osofsky, J.D., & Fenichel, E. (1994). Caring for infants and toddlers in violent environments: Hurt, healing, and hope. *Zero to Three, 14*, 1–48.

Overlien, C. (2010). Children exposed to domestic violence: Conclusions from the literature and challenges ahead. *Journal of Social Work, 10*(1), 80–97.

Peled, E., & Davis, D. (1995). *Groupwork with children of battered women.* Thousand Oaks, CA: Sage.

Radford, L., & Hester, M. (2006). *Mothering through domestic violence*. London: Jessica Kingsley Publishers.

Renner, L., & Slack, K.S. (2006). Intimate partner violence and child maltreatment: Understanding intra- and intergenerational connections. *Child Abuse & Neglect, 30*, 599–617.

Rimer, P. (2001). *Children exposed to family violence: Guidelines for community service providers*. Toronto: Toronto Child Abuse Centre.

Rivett, M., Howarth, E., & Harold, G. (2006). "Watching from the stairs": Towards an evidence-based practice in work with child witnesses of domestic violence. *Clinical Child Psychology and Psychiatry, 11*(1), 103.

Rossman, B.B.R. (1998). Descartes' error and posttraumatic stress disorder: Cognition and emotion in children who are exposed to parental violence. In G.W. Holden, R. Geffner & E.N. Jouriles (Eds.), *Children exposed to marital violence: Theory, research, and applied issues* (pp. 223–56). Washington, DC: American Psychological Association.

Sales, B., Manber, R., & Rohman, L. (1992). Social science research and child-custody decision-making. *Applied & Preventative Psychology, 1*(1), 23–40.

Schrauf, R.W. (2000). Bilingual autobiographical memory: Experimental studies and clinical cases. *Culture & Psychology, 6*(4), 387–417.

Scott, K.L., & Crooks, C.V. (2004). Effecting change in maltreating fathers: Critical principles for intervention planning. *Clinical Psychology: Science and Practice, 11*, 95–111.

Stith, S.M., Rosen, K.H., Middleton, K.A., Busch, A.L., Lundeberg, K., & Carlton, R.P. (2000). The intergenerational transmission of spouse abuse: A meta-analysis. *Journal of Family and Marriage, 62*(3), 640–54.

Strega, S., Fleet, C., Brown, L., Dominelli, L., Callahan, M., & Walmsley, C. (2008). Connecting father absence and mother blame in child welfare policies and practice. *Children and Youth Services Review, 30*, 705–16.

Suderman, M., & Jaffe, P.G. (1999). *A handbook for health and social service providers and educators on children exposed to woman abuse/family violence*. National Clearing House on Family Violence, Ottawa.

Sullivan, M., Egan, M., & Gooch, M. (2004). Conjoint interventions for adult victims and children of domestic violence: A program evaluation. *Research on Social Work Practice, 14*(3), 163–70.

Sura-Liddell, L., & Jenney, A. (2012). *Mothers in mind: A relationship-based group intervention program*. Toronto: Child Development Institute.

Taylor-Butts, A. (2005). Shelter for abused women. *Juristat: Canadian Centre for Justice Statistics, 25*(3). Catalogue no. 85-002.

Trocmé, N., Fallon, B., MacLaurin, B., & Neves, T. (2005). What is driving increasing child welfare caseloads in Ontario? Analysis of the 1993 and 1998 Ontario Incidence Studies. *Child Welfare, 84*(3), 341–62.

Trocmé, N., Fallon, B., MacLaurin, B., Sinha, V., Black, T., Fast, E., et al. (2008). Characteristics of substantiated maltreatment. *Canadian Incidence Study of Reported Child Abuse and Neglect: Major findings* (Chapter 4). Retrieved from: http://www.phac-aspc.gc.ca/cm-vee/public-eng.php.

Trocmé, N., MacLaurin, B., Fallon, B., Daciuk, J., Billingsley, D., & Tourigny, M. (2001). *Canadian incidence study of reported child abuse and neglect: Final report.* Ottawa: Minister of Public Works and Government Services.

Waldfogel, J. (2008). The future of child protection revisited. In D. Lindsay & A. Shlonsky (Eds.), *Child welfare research: Advances for practice and policy* (pp. 235–41). New York: Oxford University Press.

Wolfe, D.A., Crooks, C.V., Lee, V., McIntyre-Smith, A., & Jaffe, P. (2003). The effects of children's exposure to domestic violence: A meta-analysis and critique. *Clinical Child and Family Psychology Review, 6*(3), 171–87.

Zeanah, C.H., Danis, B., Hirschberg, L., Benoit, D., & Heller, S.S. (1999). Disorganized attachment associated with partner violence: A research note. *Infant Mental Health Journal, 20*(1), 77–86.

12

WHOSE FAILURE TO PROTECT?
CHILD WELFARE INTERVENTIONS WHEN MEN ABUSE MOTHERS

SUSAN STREGA

He would say that if I left him he would call social services and the kids would be taken away from me. That was such a fright, so I would just put up with his violence...he would not leave. He would not get out of here and this is my place.... After last winter when he did the break in here I had no choice. The ministry thought we were all unsafe. They took me and the kids out of here and they put us in the transition house for about three weeks. From then on they put conditions on me that he can't be around the kids...they didn't put any conditions on him. They've told me directly that if I get back with him they're taking my kids. But he breaks the no contact order all the time and nothing happens...the police arrive like four hours later to take a report. I asked the social worker, "Why do I have all these conditions on me and my ex doesn't have to do anything?" He told me I shouldn't be worried about that...he said to me, "What is it with you women, why do you put up with it, just get the heck out." I would just look at him...it isn't that easy.

—"Mary,"[1] quoted in Strega (2004)

INTRODUCTION

As concern has increased about children being affected by their exposure to violence inflicted on their mothers, stories like Mary's have become commonplace in Canada. According to the most recent incidence data (CIS-2008), exposure to intimate partner violence represents 34 percent of all substantiated child welfare investigations in Canada, the single largest maltreatment category (Trocmé et al., 2010). Although there are exceptions, these investigations usually focus on whether or not the "non-offending" caregiver is willing and able to protect the child from exposure. Although the notion of "failure to protect" is theoretically gender-neutral, it is consistently applied in gender-specific ways, in that the responsibility for children's exposure or witnessing is placed on the woman being assaulted rather than on the man abusing her, even when he is the father or father figure. Research invariably demonstrates that workers are preoccupied with the reactions and behaviours of mothers and not the violence of perpetrators (Bourassa, Lavergne, Damant, Lessard & Turcotte, 2006; Hughes, Chau & Poff, 2011; Johnson & Sullivan, 2008; Profitt, 2008; Strega, Fleet, Brown, Dominelli, Callahan & Walmsley, 2008). My discussion focuses on female victims and male perpetrators as this is overwhelmingly the most common type of intimate partner violence situation. From 1991 to 2003, 97 percent of Canadian spousal homicides involved a male perpetrator and a female victim (Li & Danvergne, 2006). In her review of Canadian child welfare incidence data, Black (2010) notes that fathers (73 percent) and stepfathers or common-law male partners (14.9 percent) are the perpetrators in most substantiated incidents of partner violence.

Concern about children being "exposed" to intimate partner violence has spread rapidly since its first mention in the child welfare literature in the mid-1980s. Canadian theorists were leading contributors in raising this concern. An article by Jaffe, Wilson, and Wolfe (1988) charts a shift from children being seen as "unintended or indirect victims of wife assault" (p. 157) to children being positioned as directly victimized as a consequence of exposure to their mothers being beaten. The nature of children's victimization is alleged to be twofold: immediate serious emotional or psychological disturbance and long-term intergenerational transmission of the perpetration or acceptance of abuse (Øverlien, 2010). Emerging in tandem with the reification of "children witnessing" is the corollary concept that mothers are "failing to protect" their children from witnessing this violence, and thus are guilty of child abuse or neglect. Recent dramatic increases in reports to child welfare authorities are significantly related to these concerns (OAITH, 2003; Swift & Callahan, 2003).

"Children witnessing" and mothers "failing to protect" are powerful and hegemonic concepts in child welfare that shape child protection practice and policy in ways that not only fail to address violence in the home effectively, but maintain and may even increase violence against women and danger to children. The mother-blaming and father-exculpating rhetoric and actions engendered by these concepts are injurious to women and children when mothers lose or are threatened with the loss of their children and children are threatened with the loss of their homes, families, and community connections. They are also collectively harmful in that they contribute to a continuing failure to hold responsible—or even notice—men who perpetrate violence against women and children. In this chapter I explain how child welfare has arrived at this situation, how those involved are positioned, and the policy, practice, and attitude changes that will move us from punishing and threatening victimized mothers to engaging purposefully with violent men in order to more effectively protect children. I start with a brief sketch of recent developments and their impact on child welfare.

CONTEXTUAL FACTORS

Social work and child welfare in particular are being influenced by several interrelated developments. Recent years have seen a move toward "scientific managerialism" in human service organizations (Leonard, 2001) with the attendant introduction of the concept of "risk" as a fundamental organizing principle in child welfare (Swift & Callahan, 2003). The shredding of the social safety net has been accompanied by the introduction of a discourse of "personal responsibility" as a feature of social policy legislation (Swift & Callahan, 2009). These two important shifts have coincided to further complicate an already challenging area of practice. Under the influence of neo-liberal ideologies, governments have over the last decade consistently reduced and withdrawn funds for support and prevention programs in child welfare. Faced with overwhelming demands, the criteria for using these programs have changed so that only families and children with the most severe problems have access. In child welfare legislation, policy, and discourse, "the best interests of the child" are separated from commitments to support and resource families (Swift & Callahan, 2003). Across Canada, the gap between the rich and the poor has increased significantly, leaving poor families with few resources: in the last twenty-five years, earnings fell more than 20 percent for the bottom 20 percent of wage earners, while at the same time rising substantially for the top 20 percent (Statistics Canada, 2008). The poorest of the poor are women, especially lone mothers (Statistics Canada, 2011).

In the wake of high-profile child death inquiries, Anglo-American child welfare systems became dominated by a preoccupation with risk, and child protection practice in most jurisdictions is constructed around the use of various risk assessment measures and procedures. These systems are "Anglo-American" in that they are common to Canada, the US, Australia,

New Zealand, and distinct from both the European family services approach seen in countries like Belgium, Sweden, and Germany (where child welfare is part of a universal and preventative approach) and the community caring systems preferred by indigenous peoples (where child welfare is a collaborative community concern that involves the extended family). Child death inquiries contribute to the obsession with risk, entangling workers in what Douglas (1992, cited in Rose, 1998, p. 192) calls a "'blaming system' in which every misfortune is turned into a risk which is potentially preventable" and for which someone, usually a social worker, can be held accountable. As a result, there is increased scrutiny and surveillance of both workers and mothers, and practice is conducted in a general atmosphere of assigning blame when things "go wrong" (Swift & Callahan, 2003). In such a climate, as Scourfield and Welsh (2003) note, "it is not the right decision that is important, but the defensible one" (p. 400). Practice is weighed down by mandatory forms and assessments, as well as by layers of scrutiny and review designed to avoid liability or service plausible deniability. Because supports and services can usually only be offered if there is a demonstrated child protection concern, judgment becomes an inevitable corollary to support.

This is the landscape in which workers must make extremely difficult decisions: there are few resources and supports available to support clients, large caseloads, little supportive supervision, and the likelihood of being held individually responsible in cases of child death or injury. Given these conditions, it is not surprising that the two-year turnover rate in child welfare ranges from 46 percent to 90 percent (Regehr, Leslie, Howe & Chau, 2000; Tham, 2007), meaning not only that many workers bring little experience to intervening in challenging situations, but that there may also be little experience to draw on in the workplace. In their discussion of risk, Hollis and Howe graphically describe the contemporary child protection situation (1987, cited in MacDonald & MacDonald, 1999):

> Think of her [the worker] as deciding in which of two categories the child belongs. Category A comprises children so much at risk that they should all be removed to a place of safety; Category B comprises those who will be safe if left at home. The child's death proves that it belongs in Category A. Must she not have been incompetent in assigning it to Category B? (p. 23)

Social workers are thus caught between the fear that they will be seen as intervening too little in situations in which children are later injured or die, or intervening too much, and thus be accused of interfering in the private sphere of the family.

While newer assessment techniques, such as "Signs of Safety" and "structured decision-making," purport to be a progressive departure from the focus on risk, they still mandate risk measurement as a routine assessment task (Gillingham & Humphreys, 2010). Measuring risk and assigning cases to categories decontextualizes people's lives and obscures their material circumstances and social identities. Thus, little consideration can be given to the significant role that class, race, and gender inequalities play in who comes to the attention of child protection authorities—and who does not—even though disproportionality in child welfare has been extensively documented. For example, in 2003, indigenous children comprised approximately 18 percent of children reported to Canadian child protection authorities, but only 5 percent of the child population (Lavergne, Dufour, Trocmé & Larrivee, 2008). Black children represent 65 percent of Toronto children in care, but only 8 percent of the population of Toronto is black (Child Welfare Anti-Oppression Roundtable, 2009, p. 8). Racial discrimination in child and family assessment processes has been highlighted in recent Canadian research (Lavergne et al., 2008). Poverty is also significantly implicated in who comes under the gaze of child welfare, and single poor mothers are especially likely to be targeted (Courtney, Dworsky & Zinn 2007; Cross 2008; Trocmé, MacLaurin, Fallon, Daciuk, Billingsley & Tourigny, 2001). It is essential to note that research does not document disproportionality in child maltreatment. Two studies, conducted ten years apart, indicated no significant differences in the incidence of child maltreatment among different American racial groups (Sedlak & Broadhurst, 1996; Sedlak & Schultz, 2005). After controlling for factors like income and family structure, the most recent American national incidence survey found significantly higher rates of maltreatment in white families than in non-white families (Sedlak & Schultz, 2005). Like all child maltreatment processes, "failure-to-protect" interventions are disproportionately enacted on indigenous, racialized, poor, and otherwise marginalized women. The next section describes child welfare policies and practices when men assault mothers and children are exposed to or witness the violence.

FAILURE-TO-PROTECT POLICIES AND THEIR IMPACT

Currently in Canada the legislation of seven provinces and one territory (Alberta, Saskatchewan, New Brunswick, Nova Scotia, Prince Edward Island, Quebec, Northwest Territories, and Newfoundland/Labrador) includes exposure or witnessing or living in a situation where there is violence as a specific form of child maltreatment. In other jurisdictions, the failure of the non-offending parent to protect children from exposure or witnessing is considered to be evidence of psychological or emotional abuse that could result in such a finding. Notably, child protection policies and statutes direct attention to the non-offending parent, almost always the mother, and away from the perpetrator, frequently the biological father or father figure and almost always a man (Alaggia, Jenney, Mazzuca & Redmond, 2007; Nixon, Tutty, Weaver-Dunlop & Walsh, 2007). The implication of "failure to protect," whether it is explicitly or implicitly constituted, is that victims of violence are neglectful or even abusive because their actions or inactions in response to violence either directly harmed their children or placed them at risk for harm (Bragg, 2003).

Workers are frequently directed by policy to assess whether the non-offending parent is "able and willing" to protect her children with no corollary requirement to assess whether the originator of the violence is able and willing to modify his behaviour. Policy makes no provision for taking into account the many ways that men's violence interferes with women's mothering (Bancroft & Silverman, 2004; Lapierre, 2010). As Terrance, Plumm, and Little (2008) point out, it is only by neglecting to consider the context of violence within which assaulted women live that they can be held responsible under "failure-to-protect" statutes. In the absence of policy direction or, indeed, space on assessment forms to consider contextual factors, workers are left to evaluate a woman's ability or willingness to protect on the basis of her individual actions without reference to significant contributing factors such as poverty, disability, or the cumulative effects of living with violence. The disproportionate focus on the allegedly inadequate, inappropriate, or pathological mothering of individual women is confirmed by Black's (2010) analysis. Her investigation of the unusually high substantiation rate for Canadian child welfare investigations of exposure or witnessing notes that risk factors attributed to non-offending mothers, but not those related to perpetrators, were significant in the decision to substantiate.

Conceptualizing harmful circumstances as a woman's failure to protect rather than a perpetrator's violence has been called an attribution error (Kaufman Kantor & Little, 2003, p. 350)—that is, overvaluing the explanatory power of individual psychological characteristics and undervaluing contextual and situational explanations. This type of attribution error is commonplace in child welfare, given that it is historically and presently a mother-blaming and father-absenting enterprise (Risley-Curtiss & Heffernan, 2003; Scourfield, 2003; Strega et al., 2008; Swift, 1995a). Widespread interest in the role of fathers in child development (Tamis-Lemonda, 2004) has little impact in child welfare, where gender inequitable practice is routine (Scourfield, 2003). For example, Coohey and Zang (2006) and Mayer, Dufour, Lavergne, Girard, and Trocmé (2003) note that even when children have two parents, neglect investigations focus primarily on mothers. Child protection workers routinely engage with mothers and ignore fathers and father figures even when fathers are the identified source of a family's difficulties (Scourfield, 2003; Strega et al., 2008). While mothers are particularly likely to be held responsible when men assault them (Coohey, 2007; Landsman & Copps Hartley, 2007), in physical or sexual abuse cases, mothers are routinely held to be at fault even when the assailant is the father or father figure (Krane, 2003; Radhakrishna, Bou-Saada, Hunter, Catellier & Kotch, 2001). Child protection focuses on the availability of mothers and their parenting skills while "assailants and fathers of the children have been virtually ignored" (Sullivan, Juras, Bybee, Nguyen & Allen, 2000, p. 590). Fathers who attempt to insert themselves into child protection proceedings are usually told to seek legal advice (Strega et al., 2008). This responsibilities/rights division lies at the heart of child welfare: mothers have responsibilities to physically and emotionally care for and protect children, while fathers have rights to access, visitation, and possibly to custody—even when they have been violent toward a child and/or the child's primary caregiver (Smart & Neale, 1999).

Although a woman may be acting in ways that she understands to be effectively protective of her children, child welfare often requires her to produce different and frequently confounding behaviours. For example, in order to be seen as acting protectively, women are routinely expected to monitor and manage the behaviour of violent men in very specific ways and to be solely responsible for ameliorating the consequences of violence (Hughes et al., 2011; Hughes, 2010; Scourfield, 2003). To encourage women to comply with their directives about adequate protective measures, workers sometimes use the possible apprehension of children as a threat or incitement (Hughes, 2011; Lessard & Chamberland, 2003). These threats are daunting, given that although children who are exposed to violence are less likely to be removed than children subjected to other types of maltreatment, children are very likely to be removed when exposure to partner violence coexists with any other form of maltreatment (Black, Trocmé, Fallon & MacLaurin, 2008). Child welfare workers routinely insist that women leave abusive partners in order to increase safety (Hughes, 2011; Strega, 2004), and women who choose to remain with violent partners, especially in the face of multiple violent incidents, are frequently considered on that evidence alone to be unwilling or unable to protect their children (Devoe & Smith 2003; Kaufman Kantor & Little, 2003; Lapierre, 2010). But research confirms what women themselves may know or sense: leaving increases risk; both lethal and non-lethal violence increase, sometimes markedly, post-separation (Beattie, 2005; Brownridge, 2006). Dobash, Dobash, and Medina-Ariza (2000) found that men who killed an intimate partner were ten times more likely to have been recently divorced or separated than those who committed non-lethal violence against an intimate partner. Men who abuse their partners or children continue this behaviour during post-separation visits and also use these visits as an opportunity to abuse the children's mothers (Peled, 2000). The vast majority of fathers and stepfathers who kill their children do so post-separation (Li & Danvergne, 2006).

When workers decide that remaining in a relationship with a domestically violent man is in and of itself evidence that a woman is unable or unwilling to protect her children, they ignore research about mothering in the context of violence documenting that mothers routinely take actions to safeguard their children (see, for example, Cavanagh, 2003; Hollander, 2002; Lapierre, 2010; Levendosky, Lynch & Graham-Bermann, 2000; Peled & Gil, 2011). Evaluations of a woman's "ability" or "willingness" to protect her children also fail to take account of direct attacks on her mothering by an abusive partner, who might denigrate her in front of her children and encourage the children to participate; demean her parenting abilities; and directly interfere in her mothering (Bancroft & Silverman, 2002; Jaffe, Johnston, Crooks & Bala, 2008; Lapierre, 2011). Despite these difficulties, most women with children engage in cautious, deliberate, and well-planned actions to reduce or escape violence (Lapierre, 2010; Moe, 2009).

That it is impossible for one adult to control the behaviour of another adult seems obvious, especially if that other adult has a demonstrated propensity for violence. But Bala et al. (2007) and Neilson (2001) document several Canadian cases in which mothers permanently lost custody of their children to child welfare authorities for "allowing" fathers to have contact with their children or for failing to terminate a relationship in which they were being assaulted. Although supervision orders that require a woman to control an abuser's behaviour and access to children or face temporary or permanent loss of her children are common, they rest on dangerous assumptions:

- that a woman can control her partner's violence
- that she will receive swift and supportive response from the criminal justice system should she choose to report
- that reporting the violence or leaving the perpetrator will reduce violence

As Kaufman Kantor and Little (2003, p. 340) point out, defining exposure to violence as a problem in its own right or as emotional abuse or neglect is an example of confounding cause with effect. Although workers maintain that it is the "best interests" of children that drive such decisions (Devoe & Smith, 2003), research suggests that there is little to be gained and a great deal to be lost for children when they are removed from the care of a non-abusive mother (Ewen, 2007).

The well-being of children is rarely independent of the well-being of their mother, especially when she is the primary caregiver (O'Hagan & Dillenburger, 1995). Conjoint work with children and mothers is noticeably effective in reducing trauma symptoms in children exposed to intimate partner violence (Sullivan, Egan & Gooch, 2004). Judging a woman's parenting abilities without offering opportunities and resources to support her in a difficult situation perpetuates, rather than ameliorates, the effects of abuse on both women and children (Humphreys, Mullender, Thiara & Skamballis, 2006). Workers tend to keep intimate partner violence cases open for lengthy periods, meaning that women are likely to face prolonged scrutiny and experience ongoing anxiety (Beeman, Hagemeister & Edleson, 2001; Black, 2010). Participants in Alaggia et al.'s (2007) Canadian research report that intimate partner violence investigations often set off a period of intensive child welfare scrutiny. Whatever prompts child welfare involvement, parents commonly experience ongoing uncertainty about exactly what child protection workers are looking for in terms of behaviour change (Brown, 2006; Dumbrill, 2006) and this seems to be especially true for victims of intimate partner violence (Hughes et al., 2011).

Woman-blaming responses are not particular to child welfare; they are congruent with dominant and widely circulated discourses about women's culpability when men are violent (Flood & Pease, 2006; Howe, 2008). For example, participants (undergraduate psychology students) in a study conducted by Terrance et al. (2008) were exposed to two physical child abuse by father scenarios: one in which the father had previously assaulted the mother and one in which he had not. Participants held assaulted mothers more responsible for the father's abuse toward the child than mothers who had not been abused. In Doherty's (2002) Canadian survey, more participants (54 percent) were concerned about negative psychological effects from witnessing family violence than about negative psychological effects from actually experiencing it (44 percent). Child welfare interventions in intimate partner violence are in line with these attitudes.

In some jurisdictions, such as British Columbia and Manitoba, statutes and policies mandate workers to connect directly with perpetrators, and some existing statutes allow workers to request a protective intervention order barring a dangerous or violent individual from contact with specific children. While workers sometimes use these and other tools to engage with perpetrators, whether or not statutes and policies direct or encourage such engagement, father-engaging practices are rare (Strega et al., 2008). Research findings indicate that even when law and policy direct them to do otherwise, workers intervene with women while ignoring men, whether the men involved are biological or social fathers or connected to children primarily through their involvement with the children's mother (Hughes et al., 2011; Navid, 2009; Profitt, 2008; Strega et al., 2008). These routine practices transform victims into child abusers while exculpating and absenting perpetrators of violence. The failure to engage directly with men's violence suggests that workers disregard the significant overlap between woman abuse and physical child abuse by male partners (Casanueva, Martin, Runyan, Barth, & Bradley, 2008; Letourneau, Fedick & Willms 2007; Salisbury, Henning & Holdford, 2009), thus increasing rather than reducing danger to children.

"Failure to protect" implies that it is the duty of individual mothers to protect their children, and that doing so is a relatively easy and straightforward task. In addition to increasing danger for both women and children, structural inequalities and individualized interpretations of risk render the protective measures that child welfare insists on not only complex but often impossible to achieve. In the next section, I elaborate on the difficulties women with children face when men abuse or assault them.

MOTHERS: CAUGHT IN THE CROSSHAIRS

While exceptions exist, what little ground feminism gained for women in both the public sphere (in relation to pay inequities and the gendering of jobs, for example) and the private sphere (in relation to the division of child care and housework responsibilities, for example) has eroded over the last few decades. Feminist attempts to instantiate a political and social analysis of violence against women and children have been muted by the de-gendering and depoliticization of men's violence, as reflected in the almost universally accepted descriptions of it as "domestic" or "family" violence. The depoliticization of violence against women has also been accomplished by locating attempts to change or ameliorate it within the private sphere of individual therapeutic treatments for all participants rather than in the public sphere of gender relations (Profitt, 2000; Whalen, 1996). It has been de-gendered through skewed and highly selective constructions and interpretations of surveys about violence in the family (Johnson, 2011). As feminist political activity has diminished, men's activism around their rights as fathers has expanded and influenced judicial interpretations of a child's "best interests" in cases of marital breakdown (Mann, 2003; Flood, 2010).

While concern about children's exposure to their mothers being abused has resulted in changes in child protection legislation and practice and the proliferation of "children who witness" programs, resources for women who are victimized have been reduced (OAITH, 2003; BC Institute against

Family Violence, 2003). Thus, the preoccupation with whether or not women are behaving protectively is concurrent with an absence of supports and resources that might help them do so. When we acknowledge these developments in concert with current child welfare approaches, we can begin to see just how tricky it is for victimized mothers to manoeuvre successfully. Fields (2008) and Hester (2011) contend that it is as if women must simultaneously live on three different planets, each with its own separate and often contradictory rules, expectations, and enforcement mechanisms. Using Field's metaphor of the planets and having detailed the challenges of the child welfare planet, let us briefly consider the others.

Embedded in the "failure to protect" is the notion that the criminal justice system serves assaulted women well. The criminal justice planet is solely concerned with adult behaviour, and women are encouraged to report assaults so that they can be protected and assailants can face consequences. In practice, the situation is rarely so straightforward, although it should be noted that when children are exposed to intimate partner violence, their mothers more often contact the police than do women without children (Akers & Kaukinen, 2009; Bonomi et al., 2006; Statistics Canada, 2006). But women may reasonably doubt that the criminal justice system will protect them. Barrett, St. Pierre, and Vaillancourt (2011) note that police only occasionally (27.3 percent of the time) remove perpetrators from the home. Although the official position of the criminal justice system is that it takes male violence against women seriously, few men are charged and fewer are convicted. Beckstead (2006), in her study of three British Columbia jurisdictions, found that "stay of proceedings" was the most frequent disposition for intimate partner violence cases. Assaulted women may also fear being arrested as "dual charging" has become routine across Canada (YWCA Canada, 2007). This practice of arresting both parties without regard for who initiated the violence, perpetrated most of it, or inflicted the most severe violence has become more common, especially in jurisdictions such as Manitoba, which has introduced zero-tolerance policies for intimate partner violence (Comack & Balfour, 2004).

Other remedies ostensibly available through the criminal justice system also fail to support women and protect children. Adams (2009) describes the restraining order process in British Columbia as complicated and challenging, noting that orders are often difficult to obtain. Tutty, Koshan, Jesso, and Nixon (2005) report that 20–25 percent of men breach their peace-bond conditions, often within a few days of the order being issued. More recent research notes that although official reports (such as those from police and Crown counsel) indicate a 20–25 percent violation rate, more detailed analysis, which included interviews with victims and offenders, suggests that about half of all peace bonds and restraining orders are violated (Fleury-Steiner, Fleury-Steiner & Miller, 2011). As Neilson (2001) documents, women sometimes voluntarily give up custody of their children to child protection authorities because they fear for their own and their children's safety, and do not believe that the criminal justice system will effectively protect them. The very real consequences of justice system ineffectiveness are routinely evident to anyone who reads newspapers or listens to the news: children, women, and sometimes both are murdered by current or former intimate partners, who are out on bail or under restraining orders or peace bonds.

. On the child custody and access planet, the violence that in child welfare is constructed as so harmful or potentially harmful that mothers can and do lose custody of their children is suddenly rendered invisible or irrelevant. In family court proceedings, violence toward a child's mother suddenly poses no real risk to children; violent men are routinely granted access, visitation, or even custody orders with which mothers must comply or face sanctions if they do not comply (Kernic, Monary-Ernsdorff, Koepsell & Holt, 2005). Although women applying for restraining orders are encouraged to emphasize their concern about their children's safety (Adams, 2009), on the custody and access planet, mothers must be wary of even mentioning their experiences of violence, lest they be accused of making false allegations. Fathers' rights advocates claim that mothers routinely make false allegations of abuse and these claims have an impact on custody and access determinations, frequently in favour of fathers (Mann, 2008). However, research documents a different reality. Looking specifically at custody or access dispute cases, Trocmé and Bala (2005) note a relatively small percentage (12 percent) of intentionally false allegations. Most significant are their findings that neglect, rather than violence or abuse, is the most common false allegation and that it is non-custodial parents (usually fathers) who most frequently make intentionally false reports.

It is difficult, if not impossible, to ensure children's safety without acknowledging the nature or source of threats to their safety, yet that is what many mothers are required to do lest they be accused of alienating children from their fathers. Although the notion of parental alienation rests on shaky theoretical grounds with little reliable evidence supporting it, "parental alienation syndrome" (PAS) has considerable currency in family court and is routinely relied on to dispute mothers' testimony about violence and abuse. While PAS is made to sound scientific, it relies on descriptive and anecdotal accounts and its many critics point out the absence of rigorous research validating its existence (Adams, 2006; Blank & Ney, 2006; Bruch, 2002). Mothers know that at any moment their attempts to be appropriately protective in child welfare eyes can be read as implacably hostile in family court (Harrison, 2008). Rather than supporting women in resolving these conundrums, Hughes et al. (2011) found that when violent former partners receive court-ordered visitation rights, child welfare placed the onus on mothers to ensure their children's safety under threat of having their children removed.

On the child welfare planet, a mother who is assaulted is quickly transformed from victim to child abuser. Although she may seek support from the criminal justice system to protect herself and her children, that support may be difficult to mobilize or may not exist at all. On the custody and access planet, a mother's attempts to protect herself and her children can be recast as efforts to alienate children from their father. For poor, indigenous, or otherwise racialized women, these challenges multiply exponentially.

Poor women, especially those receiving social assistance, may hesitate to separate from partners who provide covert material support, given that welfare payments in Canada are inadequate for even subsistence living (National Council of Welfare, 2010). Immigrant women, especially those whose sponsor is also their assailant, justifiably fear that separating from a violent partner may result in deportation (Alaggia, Regehr & Rishchynski, 2009). Indigenous women may be reluctant to report violence, knowing that domestically violent indigenous men are more likely to be charged, convicted, and receive custodial sentences than non-indigenous men (Comack & Balfour, 2004). Indigenous and otherwise racialized women may be reluctant to engage with any state system given the likelihood of receiving racist or culturalist responses. Several writers (see, for example, Jeffery, 2009; Maiter, 2009) have written about the persistent misapplication of white, middle-class values in evaluating the behaviours and attitudes of racialized, poor, and otherwise marginalized families. Of equal concern is the use of cultural competency practices that essentialize cultures (Maiter, 2009; Parada, 2009) and mistakenly attribute the origins of violence to culture. The predominance of young middle-class white women in front-line child protection positions (Fallon et al., 2003) increases the possibility of these attribution errors and the likelihood that contextual factors that frequently accompany violence will be disregarded.

The routine requirement that women must act swiftly and decisively, in ways prescribed by child welfare, or face the loss of their children, takes little account of the realities that victimized women face:

- an uncertain response from the criminal justice system
- the negative consequences of raising violence in custody and access disputes
- the particular challenges faced by poor, indigenous, immigrant, or racialized women

Living with intimate partner violence should never be characterized as a benign situation for children. But given the profoundly negative consequences of "failure-to-protect" interventions for a mother (who is usually the primary caregiver), we must assess whether these interventions actually help children, or whether they increase risk and cause further harm.

CHILDREN: FRONT AND CENTRE AS "WITNESSES"

It is beyond dispute that a significant proportion of children are regularly and frequently exposed to men abusing their mothers. In their large-scale retrospective study of a non-clinical population, Dong et al. (2004) found that almost one in four adults (24 percent) reported exposure to intimate partner violence as children. Hazen, Connelly, Kelleher, Landsverk, and Barth (2004) note that intimate partner violence was reported to occur in 29 percent of a national (US) child protection sample. In Canada, exposure to intimate partner violence represents the largest category of primary child maltreatment substantiated in child welfare investigations and more than half of these cases (56 percent) involved multiple incidents (Trocmé et al., 2010). About half of all women entering women's shelters in Canada have children with them (Taylor-Butts, 2007).

These statistics should be of no surprise to anyone, given that the nature and extent of violence toward women, many of whom are mothers, is well documented. Indeed, children have attained a hyper-visibility in the field of intimate partner violence. Yet the substantial research concerning the effects of exposing children to intimate partner violence, which seems to grow almost daily, remains confounding. Because most children exposed to a man assaulting their mother also experience other types of victimization, it is impossible, as Finkelhor, Ormrod, and Turner (2007) note, to make any direct causal link between children's exposure and negative short- or long-term consequences. Kitzmann, Gaylord, Holt, and Kenny (2003), in their meta-analysis, conclude that while children's functioning may be disrupted, especially in the short term, not all children seem to be affected. Further, they acknowledge the lack of understanding of mediating and moderating influences on children's responses.

Indeed, there is such wide variation in the functioning and responses of children exposed to intimate partner violence that Edleson (2004) argues it should not exist as a child protection intervention category. Wolfe, Crooks, Lee, McIntyre-Smith, and Jaffe (2003) critique the research and its use as a basis for intervention. Many studies of the effects of exposure draw from shelter or clinical populations, but researchers fail to consider how the multiple advantages faced by these populations may be affecting their measurements. The primarily psychological explanations that are offered for children's disturbed behaviour or failure to meet developmental milestones ignore contextual factors that deeply affect children's well-being, such as racism, poverty, and inadequate housing, and in this way contrive to hold individual women responsible for structural inequalities. Variability in children's response to exposure is also related to characteristics particular to children themselves (Holt, Buckley, and Whelan, 2008; Margolin et al., 2003). Retrospective research with adults who were exposed to partner violence as children documents children's ability to resist negative sequelae and implement positive and adaptive coping strategies (Anderson & Danis, 2006; Humphreys, 2001). Magen (1999) notes that many children, including children who witness television violence and children who live in violent communities, show the same "symptoms" as children exposed to intimate partner violence. Although concerns about these other forms of violence surface from time to time, it is notable that they have failed to attract the research interest or public policy intervention that has been elicited by children's exposure to intimate partner violence. This suggests that "failure-to-protect" interventions are inextricably linked to particular ideological readings of intimate partner violence, for example, that women are at least partially to blame when men are violent toward them.

We are also encouraged to be concerned about children's exposure because of the supposed likelihood that children exposed to violence will grow up to perpetrate violence against their own partners (if they are boys) or be victimized as adults (if they are girls). The notion that abuse or neglect is transmitted intergenerationally, an idea that can be traced to Freudian theory, has a long history and hegemony in child welfare; writing in 1983, Breines and Gordon note that "the great majority of child abuse experts believe that there is a 'cycle of abuse'" (p. 494). Chen (2005), Strega et al. (2002), and Swift (1995b), among others, document the use of cycle theory to support and rationalize child welfare intrusion into certain families beginning in the early 1900s, so that children of drunken or immoral parents did not themselves grow up to be drunken or immoral. Although the language of science has superseded the language of morality, a similar argument provides one of the main contemporary rationales for child welfare intervention in intimate partner violence.

But while intergenerational transmission of violence is often presented as fact, the evidence is equivocal. The overall results of a meta-analysis on the relationship between exposure to intimate partner violence during childhood and perpetrating or experiencing violence in an adult relationship found only a weak to moderate relationship (Stith, Rosen, Middleton, Busch, Lundeberg & Carlton, 2000). Renner and Slack's (2006) analysis found only a weak link between exposure and perpetrating or experiencing intimate partner violence as an adult and demonstrated only weak to moderate intergenerational associations between various forms of violence. These findings are in line with those demonstrated by past meta-analyses, such as those conducted by Kaufman and Zigler (1987) and Oliver (1993), which report "transmission rates" between 25 percent and 35 percent. While these rates may have some statistical significance, they do not represent either a causal or a co-relational relationship, and it is curious that there has been little effort to investigate why such significant proportions of children do not perpetrate or experience violence as adults.

Rather than focusing on short- and long-term child development and psychological impairments (see Chapter 11 for further discussion), we might better turn our attention to more obvious and concrete concerns, such as those documented by a number of sources and summarized by Cunningham and Baker (2007). For example, when a man is violent toward a child's mother, the attachment relationship between the child and the mother is almost certain to be damaged and that harm is exacerbated by the tendency of violent men to also be demeaning, belittling, verbally abusive, and undermining of a woman's mothering (Bancroft & Silverman, 2002). Child welfare policies and practices reflect a stereotypical view of exposure to partner violence: a child seeing and/or hearing a male (father, father figure, mother's boyfriend) assaulting her or his mother. But, as several researchers note (Bancroft & Silverman, 2004; Kaufman Kantor & Little, 2003; Thomison, 2000), exposure is rarely so straightforward and may not, in itself, be the primary source of a child's difficulties. A child may not be directly exposed to the violence, but still directly experience events related to the violence, such as seeing the mother's injuries, hearing post-incident conversations about the violence, participating in police or child protection interviews, or accompanying the mother to the hospital. Given that children's relationships with their mothers influence whether or not exposed children experience behaviour and developmental problems, these ancillary events have significant impacts. Children who are able to maintain positive perceptions of their mothers fare better than children who cannot (Toth, Cicchetti & Kim, 2002), as do children who are able to maintain a strong relationship with their mothers or another caring adult (Holt et al., 2008). These observations suggest that removing or threatening to remove children from their homes and their mothers is likely to result in negative outcomes for children.

When the assailant is a father or plays a fathering role, that attachment relationship will also be impaired. Perpetrators may elicit children's participation in violence, for example, by engaging the child in spying on her or his mother or encouraging the child to participate in verbally abusing or denigrating her or his mother (Bancroft & Silverman, 2004; Thomison, 2000). This might and too often does include children hearing police officers sympathize with the abuser and/or agree when he displaces the responsibility for his violence onto their mother. Police and courts may also be slow or entirely fail to enforce restraining orders or peace bonds, contributing to children's anxiety and fearfulness. Similarly, there has been little attention to the effects on children of the behaviours and attitudes of the perpetrator of violence, for example, the extent to which an assailant takes responsibility for his violence and whether or not he actively and visibly engages in change efforts. Bancroft and Silverman (2002) report that many violent men are coercive and emotionally abusive in interactions with their children. Because abusive men often isolate their victims and because family members may be instructed or understand that they must be secretive about abuse, children may be isolated from sources of support and from adults who might provide better role models and more positive and constructive caring. Frequently children's social relationships and childhood activities are disrupted as they will be reluctant to invite friends home or participate in recreational activities. We should also keep in mind that there is considerable overlap between exposure to partner violence and negative contextual factors. Focusing on single types of victimization directs attention to individual family factors rather than important contributing factors such as poverty or other structural inequalities and bullying, gang activity, and other forms of community violence (Cox et al., 2003). For example, Dixon, Browne, and Hamilton-Giachritsis (2009) note that financial resources and social supports serve as protective factors for stopping child maltreatment. As many researchers have noted (see, for example, Bedi & Goddard, 2007; English et al., 2005; Fantuzzo, Fusco, Mohr & Perry, 2007), it is complicated and perhaps impossible to distinguish any unique sequelae of children's exposure to partner violence.

Alarmingly, child welfare has been reluctant to engage with the most clear and present danger when men assault mothers: the likelihood that perpetrators of intimate partner violence will inflict other forms of child maltreatment. In 1999 Edleson provided a "best guess" estimate that intimate partner violence and child physical abuse co-occurred 30–60 percent of the time. More recent research confirms his assertion. Children in families that are characterized by intimate violence against their mother are more likely than children in non-violent families to experience other forms of victimization, with physical abuse being the most prevalent form of maltreatment (Terrance et al., 2008). Cox et al. (2003) report that after a reported incident of child witnessing, the odds of another form of child maltreatment occurring doubled to almost 30 percent within the subsequent two years. In their large-scale retrospective study, Dong, Anda, Dube, Giles, and Felitti (2003) found that 60 percent of their respondents had experienced multiple forms of childhood abuse. Renner and Slack (2006) report a co-occurrence rate of 40 percent. Holt et al.'s meta-analysis (2008) confirms that children exposed to intimate partner violence are likely to also experience physical, sexual, or emotional abuse. Kaufman Kantor and Little (2003) found that intimate partner abuse and physical child abuse co-occurred in 30–60 percent of cases. Rothman, Mandel, and Silverman's (2007) meta-analysis of co-occurrence studies concluded that between 30 percent and 70 percent of children exposed to partner violence are also physically or sexually abused by the batterer. Black et al. (2008), in reviewing Canadian incidence data, found a co-occurrence rate of 43 percent. Peled (2000) notes the findings of several studies that abusive men more often than abused women also maltreated their children. May-Chahal's (2006) comprehensive review of gender and violence in the family notes that, while men and women physically abuse children at roughly at equivalent rates, 90 percent of child sexual abuse is by men, one-third of those assaults occur within the family, and assaults by men are more likely to involve violence and force.

Too often, the violence inflicted on children by domestically violent men will be lethal. Intimate partner violence by men was a commonly recurring feature in case reviews of child deaths in the UK (Jenkins & Dunne, 2007). In Canada, between 1991 and 2003, fathers (66 percent) and stepfathers (2 percent) committed more than two-thirds of all family homicides involving child or youth victims (Li & Danvergne, 2006). Similarly, Cavanagh, Dobash, and Dobash (2007) note that intimate partner violence was a precursor to twenty-six murders of children by fathers, although most of the offenders in their study were stepfathers. In other words, a man who assaults a mother is at an elevated and perhaps extremely elevated risk of also harming her children. If the primary task in child welfare is to protect children, these facts should provide a compelling argument for child protection authorities to actively engage violent men who have access to children in order to do so. As the next section explains, this is rarely the case.

MEN: MISSING IN ACTION

The invisibility of men who assault mothers, at all levels of child welfare—whether practice, policy, or discourse—is so thorough and so profound that it seems like a conjuring trick. Language, power, and institutional practices construct violence against mothers as not only a victimless crime, as the mother is decentred in favour of her witnessing children, but also a crime without a perpetrator. When we describe situations in which men assault mothers as "domestic" or "family" violence, our attention is directed to where the violence takes place and drawn away from who is perpetrating and who is being victimized. I would suggest that one reason for our failure to engage with perpetrators is the continuing use of language that suggests or implies a mutuality of participation and responsibility, and descriptions that minimize or obscure the nature and extent of the violent acts.

In questioning language use, I am not meaning or implying that women are not sometimes also violent, and that there may, therefore, be some good reasons for a lack of specificity in discussions of intimate partner violence. While most violence in the home is that of men directed at women, women are also violent, occasionally to their male partners and sometimes to their children. Further, there are instances of same-sex violence in gay and lesbian relationships. The essentialism of many feminist discussions of violence against women has been justifiably criticized for rendering invisible important matters of class and race that make violence and how it is taken up deeply complex. Putting these considerations aside for the moment, I am suggesting that we use obscure language for the simplest of reasons: we are (sometimes justifiably) afraid of the consequences if we do not follow the existing policy of non-attribution. Howe (2008, p. 1) documents the vilification and demonization that follow on attempts to notice or name men's responsibility for violence, and the difficulties inherent in doing so, pointing out that "remarkably, it is still also unclear whether after decades of exposure, it is now culturally permissible in Western societies to hold men (and not their mothers, wives or girlfriends) responsible for their own violence."

Men are "absent" or "invisible" throughout child welfare (Risley-Curtiss & Heffernan, 2003; Scourfield, 2003; Strega et al., 2008). Child welfare file reviews note that violence is often sanitized and underplayed, and women are often held equally to blame for intimate partner violence (Mullender, 1996; Strega et al., 2008). When men are violent, they may be pathologized, yet at the same time are allowed to abdicate responsibility for their violence (Milner, 2004; Scourfield, 2003). The tendency to dichotomize men as perpetrators or fathers has serious policy and practice consequences, as Featherstone and Peckover (2007) note. While there is considerable focus on parenting by victimized women, little attention has been paid to parenting by men who perpetrate violence in the family. The twenty domestically violent fathers in Harne's (2002, cited in Fish, McKenzie & MacDonald, 2009) study were regularly involved in caring for their children and some of them reported to Harne that they were emotionally and sometimes physically abusive to them.

When workers instruct mothers, rather than male perpetrators, to end relationships, they are taking little account of the likelihood that these men are likely to remain in their children's lives and may also go on to establish new relationships in which they are abusive. In Salisbury et al.'s (2009) large-scale study of men convicted of intimate partner assault, 77.6 percent had a fathering role with a child or children less than eighteen years of age prior to and, in most cases, following their arrests. More than half expected to continue these family relationships after their release. Notably, the men in their study were not particularly concerned about the effects of their violence on the children with whom they were involved. Alternatively, Rothman et al. (2007) found that about half of violent fathers they surveyed (including both biological and social fathers) were concerned about the effects of their violence on their children. Almost two-thirds of participants stated they would stop their violence if they knew that they harmed their children by assaulting the children's mother. Even though these sentiments may reflect aspirations rather than actions, such findings suggest that the failure to engage directly with violent men because policies and interventions are directed solely at mothers represents a missed opportunity to stop violence.

Aiming interventions solely at mothers suggests an odd conceptualization of fatherhood because it renders a man's violence toward a child's mother irrelevant or of little import in his relationship with the child. But it is more curious that men, given the extensive documentation of their violence, are not grappled with as risks. Scourfield (2003) relates this to a gendered child welfare discourse, in which women are constructed as responsible for protecting children from the abusive behaviour of men, while men are variously constructed as a threat, of no use, irrelevant, or absent. But as Bancroft and Silverman (2002) point out, ignoring abusers significantly contributes to the devastating impact they have in the home. Practitioners can and should engage with abusers whether or not they are fathers as most domestically violent men play significant roles in the lives of the children whose mother they have assaulted.

It is essential that men be encouraged to acknowledge sole responsibility for violent behaviours and be held accountable for ameliorating the effects of it. Men need to be informed about and reflect on the impact of their actions on children and the home. Abusers should first be encouraged to take voluntary actions: leaving the home until they can ensure safe conduct within it; enrolling in an anti-violence program; seeking out and attending programs specific to violent fathers; voluntarily agreeing to a no-contact order. But workers must also be prepared to explain, and to use, in consultation with mothers, criminal justice or child welfare statutory sanctions such as no-contact, protective intervention, or supervision orders.

Some authors suggest that a man who batters a child's mother has, by definition, already committed an abusive act toward the child. For example, Peled (2000) defines all partner abusive men as psychologically abusive to children because they are usually assaulting the child's primary caregiver. Given the evidence, it seems essential that child protection workers accurately assess the risk men pose to both children and children's mothers, for example, by gathering all available information on the perpetrator's history of criminal activity and violence. Interviewing the abuser is an essential part of this process. Workers must be prepared to actively pursue domestically violent men, eliciting the support of the police or other systems when necessary.

When the child protection gaze shifts to include fathers, it must include fathers in all their complexity. The process of becoming a father involved with child welfare is not linear or singular, especially for men marginalized by race and class (Brown et al., 2009; Strega et al., 2009). Assessing the risk or danger that a particular father poses in the moment, or posed in the past, must always be accompanied by support for change efforts (Scott & Crooks, 2004; Perel & Peled, 2008). As Featherstone, Rivett, and Scourfield (2007, p. 3) contend, "We should not approach work with men on the assumption that we are dealing with men as a risk or a resource, a perpetrator or a victim. Either/or should be replaced with both/and." Some jurisdictions are providing specific advice to workers about how to engage fathers (Minnesota Fathers and Families Network, 2011). Relatively new practices in Anglo-American child welfare systems, such as family group conferencing and family development response, support the both/and approach.

Unfortunately, seeing fathers (and mothers) wholly in terms of dangers and deficits continues to be reinforced by current child protection assessment procedures and processes (Swift & Callahan, 2009). Positive, engaged fathering in child welfare can best be supported by shifting away from the individualized and investigatory paradigm toward indigenous and other holistic approaches grounded in the paradigm of community caring that are essential to transforming child welfare (Cameron et al., 2007). Many researchers (see, for example, Brown et al., 2009; Featherstone et al., 2007; Ferguson & Hogan, 2004; Strega et al., 2009) demonstrate how engaging fathers, including vulnerable and/or marginalized men, can strengthen families.

A WAY FORWARD

So long as concern about children's exposure to intimate partner violence is riveted on effects rather than responses, workers will inevitably fail to notice the actions that women take to resist violence and protect themselves and their children. Similarly, they will fail to notice that men have considerable control over when, and to whom, they are violent. Within existing child protection frameworks, good mothers are those who leave (and manage to avoid further violence or death), bad mothers are those who stay, and fathering by domestically violent men remains irrelevant. Women's mothering is hyper-visible while men's fathering is largely unnoticed. Such dichotomous and gender-essentialist readings fail to allow for other possibilities: that domestically violent men can, with commitment and effort, become protective and effective parents; that some women are ambivalent about mothering and may want to choose their abusive partner over their children.

It may be that in a time of diminished resources and a protective rather than preventive focus in child welfare, workers resort to a threatening posture toward mothers because they feel that they have little to offer in the way of support. In a time of scarce resources, workers may be defining children as in need of protection because that allows them to mobilize resources. Also, as child protection has increasingly become a technical skill focused on procedures, relationship disappears in favour of forcing clients to comply with bureaucratic requirements. Applying risk assessment, risk reduction, and risk management measures may provide workers with some insurance against being blamed should matters later go awry. But research about child welfare practice demonstrates that some workers make anti-oppressive interventions even when practice is compromised in these ways (Dumbrill, 2006). As Mullender (1996) points out, "the success of some social workers in offering the right kind of help means that practitioners are wrong if they feel there is little they can do" (p. 71).

Although statutory and policy changes that would more explicitly require child welfare engagement with perpetrators as well as victims of violence might support practice changes, instantiated traditions of mother-blaming and father invisibility are difficult to challenge. For example, the workers in Navid's (2009) research believed they were operating under an explicit "failure-to-protect" statute when none existed in their jurisdiction. Education and subsequent training about intervening with domestically violent men and supporting, rather than blaming, women are crucial pieces of the puzzle. A few jurisdictions, such as Massachusetts, mandate this approach to practice (Mederos, 2004).

We must also think carefully about which interventions are successful with men who are violent, and how men's participation in these interventions, and as fathers or father figures, can be assured without endangering mothers or children. Child welfare interventions with violent men will be successful only if they are supported by more effective actions in the criminal justice system and an ideological shift in conceptions of fathers' rights and mothers' responsibilities. But the most significant shift that not only child welfare workers but all of us must make is to abandon the rhetoric of exculpation that allows domestically violent men to avoid responsibility and accountability. Mothers who are being beaten require protection, resources, and support, while the men who beat them must become the primary focus of our interventions. If we transform child welfare in this way, we will lessen the dilemmas abused women face; more effectively protect children; and make men, and their responsibilities for safety and care giving, finally visible.

NOTE

1 "Mary" was a participant in the research for my dissertation, *The case of the missing perpetrator: A cross-national investigation of child welfare policy, practice, and discourse in cases where men beat mothers* (University of Southampton, 2004). All names and identifying circumstances of participants have been altered to protect their identities.

REFERENCES

Adams, J. (2009). The civil restraining order application process: Textually mediated institutional case management. *Ethnography, 10*(2), 185–211.

Adams, M. (2006). Framing contests in child custody disputes: Parental alienation syndrome, child abuse, gender, and fathers' rights. *Family Law Quarterly, 40*(2), 315–38.

Akers, C., & Kaukinen, C. (2009). The police reporting behavior of intimate partner violence victims. *Journal of Family Violence 24*, 159–71.

Alaggia, R., Jenney, A., Mazucca, J., & Redmond, M. (2007). In whose best interest? A Canadian case study of the impact of child welfare policies in cases of domestic violence, *Journal of Brief Therapy and Crisis Intervention*, 1–16.

Alaggia, R., Regehr, C., & Rishchvnski, G. (2009). Intimate partner violence and immigration laws in Canada: How far have we come? *International Journal of Law and Psychiatry 32*(6), 335–41.

Anderson, K., & Danis, F. (2006). Adult daughters of battered women: Resistance and resilience in the face of danger. Affilia: Journal of Women and Social Work, 21(4), 419–32.

Bala, N., Jaffe, P., & Crooks, C. (2007). Spousal violence and child-related cases: Challenging cases requiring differentiated responses. *Canadian Family Law Quarterly, 27*(1), 1–113.

Bancroft, L., & Silverman, J. (2002). *The batterer as parent.* Thousand Oaks, CA: Sage.

Bancroft, L., & Silverman, J. (2004). Assessing abusers' risk to children. In P.G. Jaffe, L.L. Baker & A.J. Cunningham (Eds.), *Protecting children from domestic violence: Strategies for community interventions* (pp. 101–19). New York: Guilford.

Barrett, B.J., St. Pierre, M., & Vaillancourt, N. (2011): Police response to intimate partner violence in Canada: Do victim characteristics matter? *Women & Criminal Justice, 21*(1), 38–62.

BC Institute against Family Violence. (2003). Newsletter. Retrieved from: http://bcifv.org/resources/newsletter/2003/spring /cuts.shtml.

Beattie, K. (2005). Spousal homicides. In K. AuCoin (Ed.), *Family violence in Canada: A statistical profile 2005* (pp. 48–51). Ottawa: Minister of Industry.

Beckstead, L. (2006). *Violence, policy, and the law: An exploratory analysis of Crown counsel's domestic violence policy in British Columbia* (Unpublished master's thesis). Simon Fraser University, Burnaby, BC.

Bedi, G., & Goddard, C. (2007). Intimate partner violence: What are the impacts on children? *Australian Psychologist, 42*(1), 66–77.

Beeman, S., Hagemeister, A., & Edleson, J. (2001). Case assessment and service receipt in families experiencing both child maltreatment and woman battering. *Journal of Interpersonal Violence, 16*, 437–58.

Black, T. (2010). *Children's exposure to intimate partner violence (IPV): Challenging assumptions about child protection practices* (Unpublished doctoral dissertation). University of Toronto, Toronto.

Black, T., Trocmé, N., Fallon, B., & MacLaurin, B. (2008). The Canadian child welfare system response to exposure in domestic violence investigations. *Child Abuse & Neglect, 32*(3), 393–404.

Blank, G., & Ney, T. *(2006).* The (de)construction of conflict in divorce litigation: A discursive critique of "parental alienation syndrome" and "the alienated child." *Family Court Review, 44(1),* 135–48.

Bonomi, A.E., Holt, V.L., Martin, D.P., & Thompson, R.S. (2006). Severity of intimate partner violence and occurrence and frequency of police calls. *Journal of Interpersonal Violence, 21*, 1354–64.

Bourassa, C., Lavergne, C., Damant, D., Lessard, G., & Turcotte, P. (2006). Awareness and detection of the co-occurrence of interparental violence and child abuse: Child welfare worker's perspective. *Children and Youth Services Review, 28*, 1321–28.

Bragg, H. (2003). *Child protection in families experiencing domestic violence.* Washington, DC: US Dept. of Health and Human Services, Administration for Children and Families, Administration on Children, Youth, and Families, Children's Bureau, Office on Child Abuse and Neglect.

Breines, W., & Gordon, L. (1983). The new scholarship on family violence. *Signs, 8*(3), 490–531.

Brown, D. (2006). Working the system: Re-thinking the institutionally organized role of mothers and the reduction of "risk" in child protection work. *Social Problems, 53*(3), 352–70.

Brown, L., Strega, S., Callahan, M., Dominelli, L., & Walmsley, C. (2009). Manufacturing ghost fathers: The paradox of father presence and absence in child welfare. Child and Family Social Work, 14, 25–34.

Brownridge, D. (2006). Violence against women post-separation. *Aggression and Violent Behavior, 11*, 514–30.

Bruch, C. (2002). Parental alienation syndrome and alienated children: Getting it wrong in child custody cases. *Child and Family Law Quarterly 381*, 393–96.

Cameron, G., Freymond, N., Cornfield, D., & Palmer, S. (2007). Positive possibilities for child and family welfare: Expanding the Anglo-American child protection paradigm. In G. Cameron, N. Coady & G. Adams (Eds.), *Moving toward positive systems of child and family welfare* (pp. 1–78). Waterloo: Wilfrid Laurier University Press.

Casanueva, C., Martin, S., Runyan, D., Barth, R., & Bradley, R. (2008). Quality of maternal parenting among intimate-partner violence victims involved with the child welfare system. *Journal of Family Violence, 23*(6), 413–27.

Cavanagh, K. (2003). Understanding women's responses to domestic violence. Qualitative Social Work, *2*, 229–49.

Cavanagh, K., Dobash, R.E., & Dobash, R.P. (2007). The murder of children by fathers in the context of child abuse. *Child Abuse and Neglect, 31*, 731–46.

Chen, X. (2005). *Tending the gardens of citizenship: Child saving in Toronto 1880s–1920s.* Toronto: University of Toronto Press.

Child Welfare Anti-Oppression Roundtable. (2009). Anti-oppression and child welfare: Laying the foundations for change. *OACAS Journal, 53*(1), 1–8.

Comack, E., & Balfour, G. (2004). *The power to criminalize: Violence, inequality, and the law.* Halifax: Fernwood Publishing.

Coohey, C. (2007). The relationship between mothers' social networks and severe domestic violence: A test of the social isolation hypothesis. *Violence and Victims, 22*(4), 503–12.

Coohey, C., & Zhang, Y. (2006). The role of men in chronic supervisory neglect. *Child Maltreatment, 11*(1), 27–33.

Courtney, M., Dworsky, A., & Zinn, A. (2007). Child, parent, and family predictors of child welfare services involvement among TANF applicant families. *Children and Youth Services Review, 29*(6), 802–20.

Cox, C.E., Kotch, J.B., & Everson, M.D. (2003). A longitudinal study of modifying influences in the relationship between domestic violence and child maltreatment. *Journal of Family Violence, 18*, 5–17.

Cross, T. (2008). Disproportionality in child welfare. *Child Welfare, 87*(2), 11–20.

Cunningham, A., & Baker, L. (2007). *Little eyes, little ears: How violence against a mother shapes children as they grow.* London, ON: Centre for Children and Families in the Justice System.

Danvergne, M., & Li, G. (2006). Homicide in Canada. *Juristat, 26*, 5.

Devoe, E., & Smith, E. (2003). Don't take my kids: Barriers to service delivery for battered mothers and their young children. *Journal of Emotional Abuse, 3*, 277–94.

Dixon, L., Browne, K., & Hamilton-Giachritsis, C. (2009). Patterns of risk and protective factors in the intergenerational cycle of maltreatment. *Journal of Family Violence, 24*(2), 111–22.

Dobash, R.P., Dobash, R.E., & Medina-Ariza, J. (2000). Lethal and non-lethal violence against an intimate partner: Risks, needs, and programs. Manchester: Economic and Social Research Council.

Doherty, D. (2002). *Health effects of family violence.* Ottawa: National Clearinghouse on Family Violence.

Dong, M., Anda, R., Dube, S., Giles, W., & Felitti, V. (2003). The relationship of exposure to childhood sexual abuse to other forms of abuse, neglect, and household dysfunction during childhood. *Child Abuse and Neglect, 27*(6), 625–39.

Dong, M., Anda, R., Felitti, V., Dube, S., Williamson, D., Thompson, T., et al. (2004). The interrelatedness of multiple forms of childhood abuse, neglect, and household dysfunction. *Child Abuse & Neglect, 28,* 771–84.

Dumbrill, G. (2006). Parental experience of child welfare intervention: A qualitative study. *Child Abuse and Neglect, 30*(1), 27–37.

Edleson, J. (1999). The overlap between child maltreatment and woman battering. *Violence against Women, 5,* 134–54.

Edleson, J. (2004). Should childhood exposure to adult domestic violence be defined as child maltreatment under the law? In P. Jaffe, L. Baker & A. Cunningham (Eds.), *Protecting children from domestic violence: Strategies for community intervention* (pp. 8–29). New York: Guilford.

Edleson, J., & Williams, O. (2007). Introduction: Involving men who batter in their children's lives. In J. Edleson & O. Williams (Eds.), *Parenting by men who batter: New directions for assessment and intervention* (pp. 3–18). Oxford: Oxford University Press.

English, D.J., Upadhyaya, M., Litrownik, A.J., Marshall, J.M., Runyan, D.K., Graham, J.C., et al. (2005). Maltreatment's wake: The relationship of maltreatment dimensions to child outcomes. *Child Abuse & Neglect, 29,* 597–619.

Ewen, B.M. (2007). Failure to protect laws: Protecting children or punishing mothers? *Journal of Forensic Nursing, 3*(2), 84–86.

Fallon, B., MacLaurin, B., Trocmé, N., & Felstiner, C. (2003). A national profile of child protection workers. In K. Kufeldt & B. McKenzie (Eds.), *Child welfare: Connecting research, policy, and practice* (pp. 41–52). Waterloo, ON: Wilfrid Laurier University Press.

Fantuzzo, J., Fusco, R., Mohr, W., & Perry, M. (2007). Domestic violence and children's presence: A population-based study of law enforcement surveillance of domestic violence. *Journal of Family Violence, 22,* 331–40.

Featherstone, B., & Peckover, S. (2007). Letting them get away with it: Fathers, domestic violence, and child welfare. *Critical Social Policy, 27,* 181–202.

Featherstone, B., Rivett, M., & Scourfield, J. (2007). *Working with men: Theory and* practice in health and social welfare, London: Sage.

Ferguson, H., & Hogan, F. (2004). *Strengthening families through fathers: Developing policy and practice in relation to vulnerable fathers and their families.* Waterford: Waterford Institute of Technology. Centre for Social and Family Research.

Findlater, J., & Kelly, S. (1999). Child protective services and domestic violence. *The Future of Children, 9*(3), 84–96.

Fields, M. (2008). Getting beyond "What did she do to provoke him?" *Violence against Women, 14*(1), 93–99.

Finkelhor, D., Ormrod, R., & Turner, H. (2007). Poly-victimization: A neglected component in child victimization. *Child Abuse and Neglect, 31,* 7–26.

Fish, E., McKenzie, M., & MacDonald, H. (2009). *"Bad mothers and invisible fathers": Parenting in the context of domestic violence.* Victoria, AU: Domestic Violence Resource Centre.

Fleury-Steiner, R., Fleury-Steiner, B., & Miller, S. (2011). More than a piece of paper? Protection orders as a resource for battered women. *Sociology Compass, 5*(7), 512–24.

Flood, M. (2010). "Fathers' rights" and the defense of paternal authority in Australia. *Violence against Women, 16*(3), 328–47.

Flood, M., & Pease, B. (2006). *The factors influencing community attitudes in relation to violence against women: A critical review of the literature.* Melbourne: Victorian Health Promotion Foundation.

Fox, G.L., Sayers, J., & Bruce, C. (2001). Beyond bravado: Redemption and rehabilitation in the fathering accounts of men who batter. *Marriage and Family Review, 32,* 137–63.

Fugate, J. (2001). Who's failing whom? A critical look at failure-to-protect laws. *New York University Law Review, 76,* 272–308.

Gillingham, P., & Humphreys, C. (2010). Child protection practitioners and decision-making tools: Observations and reflections from the front line. *British Journal of Social Work, 40,* 2598–2616.

Groves, B.M., Van Horne, P., & Lieberman, A.F. (2007) Deciding on fathers' involvement in their children's treatment after domestic violence. *In* J.L. Edleson & O.J. Williams (Eds.), *Parenting by men who batter: New directions for assessment and intervention* (pp. 65–84). *New York: Oxford University Press.*

Harrison, C. (2008). Implacably hostile or appropriately protective? Women managing child contact in the context of domestic violence. *Violence against Women, 14,* 381–405.

Hazen, A.L., Connelly, C.D., Kelleher, K., Landsverk, J., & Barth, R.P. (2004). Intimate partner violence among female caregivers of children reported for child maltreatment. *Child Abuse and Neglect, 28,* 301–19.

Henderson, B. (2008). *The managerial structure of child welfare: Perspectives from frontline workers.* Open Access Dissertations and Theses, Paper 480. Retrieved from: http://digitalcommons.mcmaster.ca/opendissertations/4807.

Hester, M. (2011). The three planet model: Towards an understanding of contradictions in approaches to women and children's safety in contexts of domestic violence. *British Journal of Social Work, 41*(5), 837–53.

Hollander, J. (2002). Resisting vulnerability: The social construction of gender in interaction. *Social Problems, 49,* 474–96.

Holt, S., Buckley, H., & Whelan, S. (2008). The impact of exposure to domestic violence on children and young people: A review of the literature. *Child Abuse and Neglect, 32,* 797–810.

Howe, A. (2008). *Sex, violence, and crime.* New York: Routledge-Cavendish.

Hughes, J. (2010). Putting the pieces together: How public health nurses in rural and remote Canadian communities respond to intimate partner violence. *Online*

Journal of Rural Nursing and Health Care, 10(1). Retrieved from: http://www
.rno.org/journal/index.php/online-journal/article/viewFile/219/266.

Hughes, J., Chau, S., & Poff, D. (2011). "They're not my favourite people": What mothers who have experienced intimate partner violence say about involvement in the child protection system. *Children and Youth Services Review, 33*(7), 1084–89.

Humphreys, C. (2001). The impact of domestic violence on children. In S. Tucker, J. Roche & P. Foley (Eds.), *Children in society: Contemporary theory, policy, and practice* (pp. 142–50). Houndmills, UK: Palgrave.

Humphreys, C., Mullender, A., Thiara, R., & Skamballis, A. (2006). "Talking to my Mum": Developing communication between mothers and children in the aftermath of domestic violence. *Journal of Social Work, 6*(1), 53–63.

Jaffe P., Johnston J., Crooks C., & Bala, N. (2008). Custody disputes involving allegations of domestic violence: Toward a differentiated approach to parenting plans. *Family Court Review, 46*(3), 500–22.

Jaffe, P., Wilson, S., & Wolfe, D. (1988). Specific assessment and intervention strategies for children exposed to wife battering: Preliminary empirical investigations. *Canadian Journal of Community Mental Health, 7*(2), 157–63.

Jeffery, D. (2009). Meeting here and now: Reflections on racial and cultural difference in social work encounters. In S. Strega & J. Carriere (Eds.), *Walking this path together: Anti-racist and anti-oppressive child welfare practice* (pp. 45–61). Halifax: Fernwood Publishing.

Jenkins, T., & Dunne, J. (2007). *Domestic abuse: The facts. A secondary research report.* London, UK: Equal Opportunities Commission.

Johnson, M. (2011). Gender and types of intimate partner violence: A response to an anti-feminist literature review. *Aggression and Violent Behavior, 16,* 289–96.

Johnson, S., & Sullivan, C. (2008). How child protection workers support or further victimize battered mothers. *Journal of Women and Social Work, 23*(3), 242–58.

Kaufman, J., & Zigler, E. (1987). Do abused children become abusive parents? *American Journal of Orthopsychiatry, 57*(2), 186–92.

Kaufman Kantor, G., & Little, L. (2003). Defining the boundaries of child neglect: When does domestic violence equate with parental failure to protect? *Journal of Interpersonal Violence, 18*(4), 338–55.

Kernic, M.A., Monary-Ernsdorff, D.J., Koepsell, J.K., & Holt, V.L. (2005) Children in the crossfire: Child custody determinations among couples with a history of intimate partner violence. *Violence against Women, 11,* 991–1021.

Kernic, M.A., Wolf, M.E., Holt, V.L., McKnight, B., Huebner, C.E., & Rivara, F.P. (2003). Behavioral problems among children whose mothers are abused by an intimate partner. *Child Abuse and Neglect, 27*(11), 1231–46.

Kitzmann, K., Gaylord, N., Holt, A., & Kenny, D. (2003). Child witnesses to domestic violence: A meta-analytic review. *Journal of Consulting and Clinical Psychology, 71*(2), 339–52.

Krane, J. (2003). *What's mother got to do with it? Protecting children from sexual abuse.* Toronto: University of Toronto Press.

Krane, J., & Davies, L. (2000). Mothering and child protection: Rethinking risk assessment. *Child and Family Social Work, 5*(1), 35–45.

Landsman, M., & Copps Hartley, C. (2007). Attributing responsibility for child maltreatment when domestic violence is present. *Child Abuse and Neglect, 31,* 445–61.

Lapierre, S. (2010). More responsibilities, less control: Understanding the challenges and difficulties involved in mothering in the context of domestic violence. *British Journal of Social Work, 40,* 1434–51.

Lapierre, S. (2011). Are abused women "neglectful" mothers? A critical reflection based on women's experiences. In B. Featherstone, C. Hooper, J. Scourfield & J. Taylor (Eds.), *Gender and child welfare in society.* Chichester, UK: John Wiley and Sons.

Lavergne, C., Chamberland, C., Laporte, L., & Baraldi, R. (2003). *Domestic violence: Protecting children by involving fathers and helping mothers.* CECW Information Sheet no. 6E. Montreal: Institut de recherche pour le développement social des jeunes and Université de Montréal.

Lavergne, C., Dufour, S., Trocmé, N., & Larrivée, M.-C. (2008). Visible minority, Aboriginal, and Caucasian children investigated by Canadian protective services. *Child Welfare, 87*(2), 59–76.

Leonard, P. (2001). The future of critical social work in uncertain conditions. *Critical Social Work, 2*(1). Retrieved from: http://www.criticalsocialwork.com.

Lessard, G. & Chamberland, C. (2003). Agir auprès des familles où il y a de la violence conjugale et de la violence parentale. In C. Chamberland (Ed.), *Violence parentale et violence conjugale. Des réalités plurielles, multidimensionnelles et interreliées* (pp. 277–320). Sainte-Foy: Presses de l'Université du Québec.

Letourneau, N., Fedick, C., & Willms, J. (2007). Mothering and domestic violence: A longitudinal analysis. *Journal of Family Violence, 22*(8), 649–59.

Levendosky, A., Lynch, S., & Graham-Bermann S. (2000). Mothers' perceptions of the impact of woman abuse on their parenting. *Violence against Women, 6*(3), 247–71.

Li, G., & Danvergne, M. (2006). Homicide in Canada 2005. *Juristat 26*(6). Catalogue no. 85-002XIE. Ottawa: Statistics Canada. Retrieved from: http://www.statcan.ca/english/freepub/85-002-XIE/85-002-XIE2006006.pdf.

Lothian, L. (2002). *Mapping contested terrain: The doctrine of failure to protect in Canadian criminal law* (Unpublished LLM thesis). Faculty of Law, University of British Columbia, Vancouver.

Macdonald, K., & Macdonald, G. (1999). Empowerment: A critical view. In W. Shera & L.M. Wells (Eds.), *Empowerment practice in social work: Developing richer conceptual foundations* (pp. 2–13). Toronto: Canadian Scholars' Press.

Magen, R. (1999). In the best interests of battered women: Reconceptualizing allegations of failure to protect. *Child Maltreatment, 4*(2), 127–35.

Magen, R., Conroy, K., & Del Tufo, A. (2000). Domestic violence in child welfare preventative services: Results from an intake screening questionnaire. *Children and Youth Services Review, 22*(3/4), 251–74.

Maiter, S. (2009). Race matters: Social justice not assimilation or cultural competence. In S. Strega & J. Carriere (Eds.), *Walking this path together: Anti-racist and anti-oppressive child welfare practice* (pp. 62–77). Halifax: Fernwood Publishing.

Mann, R. (2003). Violence against women or family violence? In L. Samuelson & W. Antony (Eds.), *Power and resistance: Critical thinking about Canadian social issues* (pp. 41–64). Halifax: Fernwood.

Mann, R. (2008). Men's rights and feminist advocacy in Canadian domestic policy arenas: Contexts, dynamics, and outcomes of antifeminist backlash. *Feminist Criminology, 3*(1), 44–75.

Margolin, G., Gordis, E.B., Medina, A.M., & Oliver, P.H. (2003). The co-occurrence of husband-to-wife aggression, family-of-origin aggression, and child abuse potential in a community sample. *Journal of Interpersonal Violence, 18*, 413–40.

May-Chahal, C. (2006). Gender and child maltreatment: The evidence base. *Social Work and Society, 4*(1), 53–68.

Mayer, M., Dufour, S., Lavergne, C., Girard, M., & Trocmé, N. (2003). *Comparing parental characteristics regarding child neglect: An analysis of cases retained by child protection services in Quebec.* Montreal: Centre of Excellence for Child Welfare.

Mederos, F. (2004). *Accountability and connection with abusive men: A new child protection response to increasing family safety.* Boston: Family Violence Prevention Fund.

Milner, J. (2004). From "disappearing" to "demonizing": The effects on men and women of professional interventions based on challenging men who are violent. *Critical Social Policy 1*, 79–101.

Ministry for Child and Family Development (MCFD). (2010). *Best practice approaches in child protection and violence against women.* Retrieved from: http://www.mcf .gov.bc.ca/child_protection/pdf/best_practice_approaches_nov2010.pdf.

Minnesota Fathers and Families Network. (2011). *Linking fathers.* Saint Paul, MN: Author.

Moe, A. (2009). Battered women, children, and the end of abusive relationships. *Affilia: Journal of Women and Social Work, 24*(3), 244–56.

Mullender, A. (1996). *Rethinking domestic violence: The social work and probation response.* London, UK: Routledge.

National Council of Welfare. (2011). *Welfare incomes 2009: Update as of March 2011.* Retrieved from: http://www.ncw.gc.ca/l.3bd.2t.1ils@-eng.jsp?lid=386.

Navid, C. (2009). *Fathers in the frame: Protecting children by including men in cases of violence against women* (Unpublished master's thesis). University of Manitoba, Winnipeg.

Neilson, L. (2001). *Spousal abuse, children, and the legal system: Final report for Canadian Bar Association.* Fredericton, NB: Muriel McQueen Fergusson Centre for Family Violence Research, University of New Brunswick. Retrieved from: http://www.unbf.ca /arts/cfvr/documents/spousal_abuse.pdf.

Nixon, K.L., Tutty, L.M., Weaver-Dunlop, G., & Walsh, C.A. (2007). Do good intentions beget good policy? A review of child protection policies to address intimate partner violence. *Children and Youth Services Review, 29,* 1469–86.

Northern Ireland Department of Health and Social Services. (1995). *Tackling domestic violence: A policy for Northern Ireland.* Belfast: Author.

O'Hagan, K., & Dillenburger, K. (1995). *The abuse of women within childcare work.* Buckingham, UK: Open University Press.

Oliver, J. (1993). Intergenerational transmission of child abuse: Rates, research, and clinical implications. *American Journal of Psychiatry, 150*(9), 1315–24.

Ontario Association of Interval and Transition Houses (OAITH). (2003). *In the best interests of children and mothers: A proposed child welfare response to violence against women.* Toronto: Author.

Øverlien, C. (2010). Children exposed to domestic violence: Conclusions from the literature and challenges ahead. *Journal of Social Work, 10,* 80–97.

Parada, H. (2009). Reconstructing neglect and emotional maltreatment from an anti-oppressive perspective. In S. Strega & J. Carriere (Eds.), *Walking this path together: Anti-racist and anti-oppressive child welfare practice* (pp. 173–86). Halifax: Fernwood Publishing.

Peled, E. (2000). Parenting by men who abuse women: Issues and dilemmas. *British Journal of Social Work, 30*(1), 25–36.

Peled, E., & Barak Gil, I. (2011). The mothering perceptions of women abused by their partner. *Violence against Women, 17*(4), 457–79.

Perel, G., & Peled, E. (2008). The fathering of violent men: Construction and yearning. *Violence against Women, 14,* 457–82.

Profitt, N. (2000). *Women survivors, psychological trauma, and the politics of resistance.* New York: Haworth Press.

Profitt, N. (2008). *In the best interests of women and children: Exploring the issue of "failure to protect" in the Acadian Peninsula.* Fredericton: Department of Social Work, St. Thomas University.

Radhakrishna, A., Bou-Saada, I.E., Hunter, W.M., Catellier, D.J., & Kotch, J.B. (2001). Are father surrogates a risk factor for child maltreatment? *Child Maltreatment, 6*(4), 281–89.

Regehr, C., Leslie, B., Howe, P., & Chau, S. (2000). *Stressors in child welfare practice.* Toronto: University of Toronto. Retrieved from: http://www.cecw-cepb .ca/files/file/en/Stressors.pdf.

Renner, L., & Slack, K.S. (2006). Intimate partner violence and child maltreatment: Understanding intra- and intergenerational connections. *Child Abuse & Neglect, 30,* 599–617.

Risley-Curtiss, C., & Heffernan, K. (2003). Gender biases in child welfare. *Affilia 18*(4), 395–410.

Rivett, M. (2010). Working with violent male carers (fathers and stepfathers). *In* B. Featherstone, C. Hopper, J. Scourfield & J. Taylor (Eds.), *Gender and child welfare in society* (pp. 195–222). Chichester: Wiley-Blackwell.

Rose, N. (1998). Governing risky individuals: The role of psychiatry in new regimes of social control. *Psychiatry, Psychology, and the Law, 5*(2), 177–95.

Rossman, B., & Rosenberg, M. (1997). Psychological maltreatment: A needs analysis and application for children in violent families. *Journal of Aggression, Maltreatment, and Trauma, 1*(1), 245–62.

Rothman, E., Mandel, D., & Silverman, J. (2007). Abusers' perceptions of the effect of their intimate partner violence on children. *Violence against Women, 13*(11), 1179–91.

Ryan, M. (2000). *Working with fathers. Oxford: Radcliffe Medical Press.*

Salisbury, E., Henning, K., & Holdford, R. (2009). Fathering by partner abusive men. *Child Maltreatment, 14*(3), 232–42.

Scott, K., & Crooks, C. (2006). Intervention for abusive fathers: Promising practices in court and community responses. *Juvenile and Family Court Journal, 57*(3), 29–44.

Scourfield, J. (2003). *Gender and child protection.* Basingstoke, UK: Palgrave Macmillan.

Scourfield, J., & Welsh, I. (2003). Risk, reflexivity, and social control in child protection: New times or same old story? *Critical Social Policy, 23*(3), 398–420.

Sedlak, A., & Broadhurst, D. (1996). *Third national incidence study of child abuse and neglect.* Washington, DC: US Department of Health and Human Services, National Clearinghouse on Child Abuse and Neglect Information.

Sedlak, A., & Schultz, D. (2005). Racial differences in child protective services investigation of abused and neglected children. In D. Derezotes, J. Poertner & M.E. Testa (Eds.), *Race matters in child welfare: The overrepresentation of African American children in the system* (pp. 97–118). Washington, DC: CWLA Press.

Silva, E., & Smart, C. (1999). The "new" practices and politics of family life. In E. Silva & C. Smart (Eds.), *The "new" family?* (pp. 1–12). London: Sage Publications.

Smart, C., & Neale, B. (1999). *Family fragments?* Cambridge: Polity Press.

Statistics Canada. (2006). *Family violence in Canada: A statistical profile 2006.* Ottawa: Minister of Industry.

Statistics Canada. (2008). *Earnings and incomes of Canadians over the past quarter century, 2006 Census.* Catalogue no. 97-563-X. Ottawa: Author.

Statistics Canada. (2011). *Women in Canada: A gender-based statistical report 2010–2011.* Catalogue no. 89-503-XWE. Ottawa: Author.

Stith, S.M., Rosen, K.H., Middleton, K.A., Busch, A.L., Lundeberg, K., & Carlton, R.P. (2000). The intergenerational transmission of spouse abuse: A meta-analysis. *Journal of Marriage and the Family, 62*(3), 640–54.

Strega, S. (2004). *The case of the missing perpetrator: A cross-national study of child welfare policy, practice, and discourse when men beat mothers* (Unpublished doctoral dissertation). University of Southampton, UK.

Strega, S., Brown, L., Callahan, M., Dominelli, L., & Walmsley, C. (2009). Working with me, working at me: Fathers' narratives of child welfare. *Journal of Progressive Human Services, 20,* 72–91.

Strega, S., Callahan, M., Rutman, D., & Dominelli, L. (2002). Undeserving mothers: Social policy and disadvantaged mothers. *Canadian Review of Social Policy, 49–50,* 175–98.

Strega, S., Fleet, C., Brown, L., Dominelli, L., Callahan, M., & Walmsley, C. (2008). Connecting father absence and mother blame in child welfare policies and practice. *Children and Youth Services Review, 30*(7), 705–16.

Sullivan, M., Egan, M., & Gooch M. (2004). Conjoint interventions for adult victims and children of domestic violence: A program evaluation. *Research on Social Work Practice, 14*, 163–70.

Sullivan, C., Juras, J., Bybee, D., Nguyen, H., & Allen, N. (2000) How children's adjustment is affected by their relationships to their mothers' abusers. *Journal of Interpersonal Violence, 15*(6), 587–602.

Swift, K. (1995a). *Manufacturing "bad mothers": A critical perspective on child neglect.* Toronto: University of Toronto Press.

Swift, K. (1995b). An outrage to common decency: Historical perspectives on child neglect. *Child Welfare, 74*(1), 71–91.

Swift, K. (2001). The case for opposition: An examination of contemporary child welfare policy directions. *Canadian Review of Social Policy, 47*, 59–76.

Swift, K., & Callahan, M. (2003). *Problems and potential of Canadian child welfare.* Waterloo, ON: Partnerships for Children and Families Project, Wilfrid Laurier University.

Swift, K., & Callahan, M. (2009). *At risk: Social justice in child welfare and other human services.* Toronto: University of Toronto Press.

Tamis-LeMonda, C. (2004). Playmates and more: Fathers' role in child development. *Human Development, 47*(4), 220–27.

Taylor-Butts, A. (2007). *Canada's shelters for abused women, 2005/2006.* Catalogue no. 85-002. Ottawa: Statistics Canada.

Terrance, C., Plumm, K., & Little, B. (2008). Maternal blame: Battered women and abused children. *Violence against Women, 14*(8), 870–85.

Tham, P. (2007). Why are they leaving? Factors affecting intention to leave among social workers in child welfare. *British Journal of Social Work, 37*, 1225–46.

Thomison, A.M. (2000). *Exploring family violence: Links between child maltreatment and domestic violence.* Issues in child abuse prevention, paper no. 13. Melbourne: Australian Institute of Family Studies.

Toth, S.L., Cicchetti, D., & Kim, J. (2002). Relations among children's perceptions of maternal behavior, attributional styles, and behavioral symptomatology in maltreated children. *Journal of Abnormal Psychology, 30*(5), 487–501.

Trocmé, N., & Bala, N. (2005). False allegations of abuse and neglect when parents separate. *Child Abuse and Neglect, 29*, 1333–45.

Trocmé, N., Fallon, B., MacLaurin, B., Sinha, V., Black, T., Fast, E., Felstiner, C., Hélie, S., Turcotte, D., Weightman, P., Douglas, J., & Holroyd, J. (2010). *Canadian Incidence Study of Reported Child Abuse and Neglect – 2008: Major findings.* Ottawa: Public Health Agency of Canada.

Trocmé, N., Knoke, D., Fallon, B., & MacLaurin, B. (2009). Differentiating between substantiated, suspected, and unsubstantiated maltreatment in Canada. *Child Maltreatment, 14*(1), 4–16.

Trocmé, N., MacLaurin, B., Fallon, B., Daciuk, J., Billingsley, D., Tourigny, M., et al. (2001). *Canadian Incidence Study of Reported Child Abuse and Neglect: Final report.* Ottawa: Minister of Public Works and Government Services.

Tutty, L., Koshan, J., Jesso, D., & Nixon, K. (2005). *Alberta's protection against Family Violence Act: A summative evaluation.* Calgary: RESOLVE Alberta.

Walmsley, C., Strega, S., Brown, L., Dominelli, L., & Callahan, M. (2009). More than a playmate, less than a co-parent: Fathers in the Canadian BSW curriculum. *Canadian Social Work Review, 26*(1), 73–96.

Whalen, M. (1996). *Counselling to end violence against women: A subversive model.* Thousand Oaks, CA: Sage Publications.

Wolfe, D.A., Crooks, C.V., Lee, V., McIntyre-Smith, A., & Jaffe, P.G. (2003). The effects of children's exposure to domestic violence: A meta-analysis and critique. *Clinical Child and Family Psychological Review, 6*(3), 171–87.

YWCA Canada. (2007). *Beyond shelter walls: No more running in circles.* Toronto: Author.

13

RENDERING CHILDREN INVISIBLE
THE FORCES AT PLAY DURING SEPARATION
AND DIVORCE IN THE CONTEXT OF FAMILY
VIOLENCE

RACHEL BIRNBAUM

INTRODUCTION

In 2005, this chapter began with several media stories about children being murdered and/or abducted by one of their parents as a result of a custody and access dispute. In 2011, little, if anything, has changed as separated families continue to pour into the family court system, seeking custody of and access to their children. Nowhere is the problem more pronounced than when family violence is involved.

The media tell their stories in 2011:

> A child custody dispute may have been the factor in a Whitby shooting in which a young man was killed and 13-month old baby girl injured.... A family friend said the injured baby's mother and father had been involved in a custody dispute and that the father had been issued a restraining order to stay away from the house.[1]

> Elaine Campione Trial: CAS raised fears about children, court told.... Ms. Campione drowned three-year-old Serena and 19-month-old Sophia in the family bathtub.[2]

Dr. Turcotte stabbed Anne-Sophie, 3 and Oliver, 5, on Feb. 20, 2009 after the messy breakup of his marriage.[3]

While family law initiatives have been recently introduced in Ontario[4] as well as in other jurisdictions across Canada[5], the current family court process remains the traditional adversarial system, an approach that continues to inflame the emotions of parents who are in the midst of separation and/or divorce.

The family law system, while focused on the "best interests of children" in law, more often than not in practice focuses on the rights of parents. Many academic scholars have written about "children's voices" being muted in the family court process even though their rights have been enshrined since Canada ratified the United Nations Convention on the Rights of the Child in 1991 (Birnbaum, 2009, Birnbaum & Bala, 2010; Birnbaum, Bala & Cyr, 2011; Breger, 2010; Cashmore, 2003; Smart, Neale & Wade, 2001). Cashmore (2003) and Kelly (2002) have argued that children want and will benefit from participating in the decision-making process during their parents' separation, and want to talk about their experiences. Justice Donna Martinson, of the Yukon Supreme Court, expressed strong views about the voice of the child[6] when she stated that there is no ambiguity in the language of the Convention, and that all children have legal rights to be heard. She emphasized that there is no exception for family cases involved in high-conflict divorces[7] or when a child is alienated from one parent or another—decision makers have no discretion to disregard children's legal rights contained in the Convention (Epstein, 2010).

This chapter continues to focus on the unintended victims of parental separation—children. No matter what the reasons for the family breakdown, several significant forces conspire to make children invisible throughout this process. Nowhere is the problem more pronounced than when family violence is involved. The preceding news reports all refer to the most tragic casualties where children have been killed by a "feuding" parent. In these situations, children are not the intended objects of a parent's anger and rage. Rather, they become victims in an adult "dispute"; the example the abuser attempts to make to his partner; the "weapons of choice" for achieving power and control in a relationship. Even the language often used to describe the nature of the couple's relationship or the behaviour of one of the partners—"feuding," "high-conflict," "disputing families," "revenge seeking," "chronically litigating divorcing parents who share mutual distrust of one another, fear and projection of blame"—masks those instances when children are being used as yet another tactic of violence by one partner against another.

It is the restructuring of familial relationships rather than their termination that is the central objective of the family justice system[8] as well as changing parental attitudes and behaviours that are often essential if good outcomes for children, in particular, are to be achieved. This is even more so when high-conflict families engage "to do battle" over their children (Bala, Birnbaum & Martinson, 2011). Regrettably, the trauma does not end with the parents' separation and/or divorce, but often continues under the guise of custody and access disputes (Bancroft & Silverman, 2002; Fidler, Bala, Birnbaum & Kavassalis, 2008; Geffner, Jaffe & Suderman, 2000; Jaffe & Geffner, 1998; Jaffe, Lemon & Poisson, 2003; Johnston, 2006).

Researchers and mental health practitioners have consistently demonstrated the array of difficulties that children face emotionally, academically, physically, and behaviourally as a result of being exposed to family violence and conflict post-separation and/or divorce (Jaffe, Baker & Cunningham, 2004; Jaffe, Johnston, Crooks & Bala, 2008; Johnston, 1994; Lemon, 1999; McIntosh, 2003a; Thompson & Amato, 1999; Wolfe & Jaffe, 1999).[9] Less clear, however, is how the social, political, and legal context in Canada both promotes and exacerbates children's well-being during these times.

The chapter focuses on the complex relationship between the principle of the best interests of the child and the social, political, and legal forces that give rise to children's invisibility during times of separation and/or divorce, particularly in the context of family violence.

Berkman, Casey, Berkowitz, and Maraŋs (2004) and Fantuzzo, Mohr, and Noone (2000) have used the term "invisible" to describe children who have been present at scenes of domestic violence where the focus is on the prosecution of the adult offender. The term also aptly describes children in custody and access disputes during separation and/or divorce and how they become pawns in the legal system under the guise of the "best interests of the child" principle. Their voices are silent in the process while those around them (lawyers, judges, mental health professionals, and child custody assessors) purport to know what is in their best interests. Throughout this discussion this latter theme—the invisibility of children—will be highlighted over and over again, particularly in the context of family violence.

Part 1 will explore the historical roots and development of Canada's legal responses in the courts with respect to decision making about the "best interests of children." What will become apparent is how decisions about children were based on societal values of the time and focused on adult behaviour, such as the adultery of one or both parents, not what was best for the child or children. In this section the legislation that governs custody and access of children, violence, and inadequate parenting across Canada will be discussed while highlighting the current context. Finally, this section will also emphasize the knowledge required by each professional discipline (mental health professionals, lawyers, and judges), the importance of collaboration, co-operation, and communication among and between the professionals, and the importance of allowing children to have a voice in decision making about their lives.

Part 2 will outline the different legislative provisions regarding custody and access matters following separation and/or divorce in other countries. The purpose of this discussion is to understand and learn from what has happened in other countries about the "interests of children" after separation and/or divorce, given the similarities to this debate in Canada. In this section it will also become apparent how politicized the language has become when decision making is involved regarding children's parenting relationships post-separation and/or divorce where once again, children are rendered invisible.

Part 3 will explore a blueprint for social and legal reform that addresses the need for an integrated holistic family law system that takes into account the voices of children in order to meet their needs during and after separation and/or divorce. This blueprint asserts that the needs of children will become *visible* only when we use a holistic, integrated approach, grounded in a clear philosophy and practice of intervention that is consistent and inclusive of the social, legal, and political nature of children's needs after separation and/or divorce. Only then will children's voices be heard and rendered visible during times of separation and/or divorce.

PART 1: ORIGINS OF CHILD CUSTODY DECISION MAKING

To appreciate the sweeping changes that have taken place in the status of child custody legislation, it is important to understand the historical evolution of the arrival of the best interests standard that dominates Canada's present-day legislation.

Bala and Clarke (1981) and McDonald (1986) identified three themes that illustrate how the enshrinement of custodial rights throughout history has paralleled the development of divorce legislation. These are: (1) the presumption of paternal superiority; (2) the moral conduct of the parents; and (3) the tender years doctrine.

The first theme, the presumption of paternal superiority, originates in the perception of the child as property with no relevant rights or feelings. Dating as far back as the Dark Ages, paternal power (*patria potestas*), regardless of the age of the child, was equated with absolute control over the child. During this time, infanticide and child slavery were not uncommon (Bala & Clarke, 1981; Franklin & Hibbs, 1980; McDonald, 1986) (see Chapter 4 by McGillivray and Durrant in this volume).

In England, it was not until 1839 in Talfourd's Act[10] that the court had the authority to give mothers access to their children and award custody to a mother (Kelly, 1994). However, a proviso stipulated that at the age of seven, the child would automatically return to the father. In 1855, the Custody of Infants Act, enacted in Upper Canada, gave mothers the right to seek custody and access to their children under the age of twelve. Once again, there was a proviso in this statute that stipulated mothers were prohibited from obtaining custody or access if they were guilty of adultery. There was no similar restriction based on adultery committed by fathers (Backhouse, 1981).

Children's rights were not addressed, let alone recognized, until the end of the nineteenth century, when laws were enacted to protect a child's physical and emotional well-being. For example, in Canada, the Factory Act (1887) regulated and limited the employment of children in factories, and the first Children's Aid Society was founded in the early 1890s to protect the welfare of minor children (Bala, 1999; Bala & Clarke, 1981; McDonald, 1986).

The second theme examined the moral conduct of parents. The court determined custody of children based on the behaviour and moral conduct of one or both parents. In other words, the issue of adultery could be raised against one parent or the other. In the Ontario Supreme Court of Appeal decision, *Young* v. *Young*, Justices Robertson, Laidlaw, and Roach wrote, "it would be positively against [the children's] interests and detrimental to their welfare to permit [their father] to associate or visit with them. He committed adultery and, after wrecking his marriage and the home life of his wife and children by his immoral conduct, he chose deliberately to continue his wickedness after the Court adjudged him guilty."[11]

Over time, with the increasing concern for the welfare of children and the impact on changing social attitudes to pre- and extramarital sexual relations, moral conduct soon became replaced with an examination of the parenting abilities of each parent (Bala & Clarke, 1981; Kelly, 1994; McDonald, 1986).

The third theme influencing the determination of custody rested on the awareness that early childhood was strongly influenced by the emotional bond between the mother and child. The courts accepted the principle known as the "tender years doctrine," advanced by an English judge, Thomas Noon Talfourd (Kelly, 1994). This principle held that children under the age of seven were better off in the care of their mother. In a 1933 Ontario Court of Appeal decision, *Re Orr* [1933] 2 D.L.R. 77, the court stated at 80–81: "In the case of a father and mother living apart and each claiming the custody of a child, the general rule is that the mother, other things being equal, is entitled to the custody and care of a child during what is called the period of nurture, namely, until *it* attains about seven years of age, the time during which it needs the care of the mother more than of the father" [emphasis added].

These three themes—paternal superiority, the moral conduct of parents, and maternal presumption (tender years doctrine)—share a common pattern of paternal dominance. The first pattern of paternal dominance refers to the ownership of children, in which they were viewed as chattels of a male property owner (Bala, 1999; Folberg, 1984). In fact, inheritance rights and property were only passed on through establishing paternity at the first instance, thereby allowing control of women and illegitimate children (Boyd, 2003). In the second pattern of paternal dominance, moral conduct is evaluated by a male-dominated judiciary. In *Re Leigh* (1871) a male judge told a mother who alleged physical abuse against her husband and was seeking custody of her four-year-old daughter that she (the mother) had not satisfied the court (the judge) that she had an excuse for leaving her husband's home and her duties as a wife,[12] once again demonstrating the theme of paternal superiority and dominance, and, more importantly for this discussion, not the interests of children. Finally, the shift to maternal presumption gave rise to a double-edged sword for mothers (Boyd, 1987, 2003). The role of the mother was relegated to child care, child nurturing, and the "tender years doctrine."[13] Boyd (2003) argues that judicial concern centred on the sanctity of the marriage, which women were responsible for, as well as the care and nurturance of the child, which continued to rest with the traditional view of motherhood. This was exemplified in *Bell* v. *Bell* (1955), where the trial judge awarded custody to the father because the mother had left him. The court of appeal overturned the trial judge's decision, stating that the child was a girl of tender years who needed the emotional support that only mothers could provide:

> This infant is a little girl of very tender years. No father, no matter how well intentioned or how solicitous for the welfare of such a child, can take the full place of the mother. Instinctively, a little child, particularly a little girl, turns to her mother in her troubles, her doubts and her fears. In that respect nature seems to assert itself. The feminine touch means so much to a little girl; the frills and the flounces and the ribbons in the matter of dress; the whispered consultations and confidences on matters which to the child's mind should only be discussed with Mother; the tender care, the soothing voice; all these things have a tremendous effect on the emotions of the child. This is nothing new; it is as old as human nature and has been recognized time after time in the decisions of our courts. (1955 O.W.N. 341 at 344)

The principle of the tender years doctrine was criticized on the grounds that it did not serve the best interests of the child and that it discriminated against fathers (Cochran, 1985; Drakich, 1989). Elster (1987) addressed the discriminatory and gender biased doctrine in the following manner:

> The maternal preference rule contained the seeds of its own destruction. By resting exclusively on considerations of the child's best interest, it invited lawmakers to turn that interest into explicit criterion for custody adjudication in each and every case. Why rest content with the rule of thumb that the interest of the child is always best served by maternal custody? Why not judge each case on its merits? (p. 9)

During the late 1970s and early 1980s another period of profound change occurred with respect to family law matters in Canada. The divorce rate was rising, attitudes regarding the role and status of women in both the family and labour market changed, social science literature expanded by focusing on children's growth and development, thereby differentiating children as separate entities apart from their parents (Bala, 1999; Cohen & Gershbain, 2001).[14] These changes also gave rise to the recognition of non-marital unions and gave women, in particular, new property rights upon divorce and placed a greater emphasis on each party becoming more self-sufficient following marriage breakdown.[15] Moreover, no-fault divorce was introduced, thereby eliminating blame by one party or the other. Of particular importance with respect to children was the adoption of the "best interest of the child" principle. This new federal legislative change was premised on a more gender-neutral perspective. However, there was no mention of issues with respect to children who may be involved in the context of family violence during separation and/or divorce. Unless mental health professionals, child custody assessors, lawyers, and the court understand the scope and severity of family violence in the context of custody and access disputes, children will continue to remain invisible during times of separation and/or divorce.[16] This theme is exemplified by Shaffer (2004) and Shaffer and Bala (2004) in their study of forty-two Canadian cases in which they argue for legal reform in family law that specifically acknowledges the significant impact of family violence on children during separation and/or divorce.

Socio-economic and Political Context

It is important to note that the shift in the legal discourse of child custody law paralleled the changing socio-economic and political attitudes of the times. There was a shift from an agrarian economy to an industrial economy in which the family unit became a reproductive and consumption unit and women became the primary child-care providers (Clingempeel & Reppucci, 1982; Ursel, 1992). Historically, legislation concerning custody of children advanced from a patriarchal notion in English and Canadian common law that only fathers could have custody of children to the presumption that infants of tender years should remain in the care of their mothers unless it was demonstrated otherwise, to the present-day adoption of the best interests of the child principle, which presumably offers no preference to maternal or paternal custody (Schnall, 1999).

Custody decision making reflects values about society, policies, and how children are to be parented after separation and/or divorce. The evolution of these same social, economic, and political forces continues to shape and influence child custody decision making with respect to custody of and access to children.[17] Yet the child's voice remains largely silent during this "adult" process. The famous quote by Lord Denning aptly demonstrates the rights of each parent and the invisibility of children:

> To be a good mother involves not only looking after the children, but making and keeping a home for them with their father.... In so far as she herself by her conduct broke up that home, she is not a good mother.
>
> It seems to me that a mother must realize that if she leaves and breaks up her home in this way, she cannot as of right demand to take the children from the father. If the mother in this case were to be entitled to the children, it would follow that every guilty mother (who was otherwise a good mother) would always be entitled to them, for no stronger case for the father could be found. He has a good home for the children. He is ready to forgive his wife and have her back. All that he wishes is for her to return. It is a matter of simple justice between them that he should have the care and control. Whilst the welfare of the children is the first and paramount consideration, the claims of justice cannot be overlooked.[18]
> —Lord Denning ([1962] 3All E.R. 1, 3, 4)

Current Context

In 1997, the Parliamentary Special Joint Committee on Child Custody and Access held hearings across Canada regarding children's interests following separation and/or divorce. The focus of the hearings, among others, was the notion that maximum contact between children and both parents should prevail following divorce. In 1998, the committee released its report, *For the Sake of the Children*, recommending reforms to the current legislation

(Report of the Special Joint Committee on Child Custody and Access, 1998).

In May 1999, the Government of Canada released its response, *Strategy for Reform*, acknowledging that there was a need for reform.[19] In December 1999, the federal government directed the Family Law Committee (representatives from each province and territory) to report on a comprehensive plan for changes to custody and access of children.

In early December 2002, the minister of justice and the attorney general of Canada introduced Bill C-22, a comprehensive document about custody of and access to children, in the House of Commons. The most significant change focused on eliminating the words "custody" and "access" under the Divorce Act, and replacing them with a model referred to as "parental responsibilities." The amendments would mean that both parents would be responsible for the well-being of their children after separation and/or divorce.

In 2003, Bill C-22 died when Parliament was prorogued and an election was called. It wasn't until many years later, after a majority government was formed in 2011, that the silence was broken with "talk" about making changes to the divorce legislation (Schmitz, 2011).[20]

The federal government did, in fact, provide the promised funding to the provinces and territories to promote the development and maintenance of court-related services (e.g., mediation, parent information programs, alternative dispute resolution, and duty/advice counsel) for families involved in the court system. With this increase in funding and attention to additional resources, it was anticipated that separation and/or divorce would become less adversarial and promote children's interests after separation. However, there has been virtually no empirical research anywhere across Canada that demonstrates whether in fact these "alternative services" have made any difference in the lives of children and families and, most notably, when family violence is the subject of concern (Birnbaum, Bala & Martinson, 2011).[21]

Legislation: Best Interests Principle

In Canada there is a shared responsibility between the federal government and the provinces and territories with respect to family law matters. The federal government is responsible for divorce, child and spousal support, as well as the resolution of child-related issues (e.g., visitation issues) when married couples are applying for a divorce. The provincial and territorial governments are responsible for property matters and all matters between parents who do not marry. In addition, the provinces and territories have responsibility for the enforcement of child and spousal support. There is considerable overlap in jurisdictions between governments and how they intervene in the lives of children and families with respect to children's interests after separation and/or divorce.

As stated, the current standard for matters concerning custody of and access to children is the "best interests of the child." The best interests test can be defined as a myriad of factors related to the interests of the child (the parents' conduct, maximum contact with each parent, statutory factors).

The Divorce Act, R.S.C. 1985.c.3 (2nd Supp.), as amended, sets out the federal legislation under Section 16:

1. A court of competent jurisdiction may, on application by either or both spouses or by any other person, make an order respecting the custody of or access to, any or all children of the marriage.
2. In making an order under this section, the court shall take into consideration only the best interests of the child of the marriage as determined by reference to the condition, means, needs and other circumstances of the child.
3. In making an order under this section, the court shall not take into consideration the past conduct of any person unless the conduct is relevant to the ability of that person to act as a parent of a child.
4. In making an order under this section, the court shall give effect to the principle that a child of the marriage should have as much contact with each spouse as is consistent with the best interests of the child and, for that purpose, shall take into consideration the willingness of the person for whom custody is sought to facilitate such contact.

In many provinces, there is specific provision in the legislation that recognizes domestic violence as a factor when determining child custody and access of children (Fidler, Bala, Birnbaum & Kavassalis, 2008). However, without the passing of Bill C-22, which would have provided some equality for children across Canada, now only *some* children are given that "privilege." Despite the changes, both legislative and the judge-made common law, there remains inconsistency in the way different judges assess the seriousness of family violence in the context of child custody decision making (Fidler, Bala, Birnbaum & Kavassalis, 2008). Moreover, the federal legislation that does exist continues to place the onus of providing evidence to the court to prove that custody and/or access may not be in the child's or children's best interest at that time is left to the abused parent (who is usually the mother). The custodial parent (usually the mother) is again left with proving on a balance of probabilities that violence occurred, which leaves children invisible at the most vulnerable time of family breakdown.

For example, in a 2008 Ontario case, *Donley* v. *Donley*,[22] the mother moved out of the home with her two children without telling the father where they were going. Each parent then went to court to obtain an interim custody order with allegations on both sides. The father denied all the allegations of abuse toward the mother, particularly in the presence of his children. The judge subsequently awarded interim custody to the father, concluding that the mother's allegations were not *proven* (emphasis added):

> On the evidence before me, it appears that Mrs. Donley was reacting to the response of counsellors and other professionals who encouraged her to move out of the home with the children based on one-sided information that was provided by her and her alone. When Mr. Donley came home on January 15, 2008, he saw that many of the contents of the home were removed and that his children were gone, with only a note left by his wife that stated that the children were safe and she was doing what the OPP and the Children's Aid had advised her to do. I find that the fact that Mrs. Donley had already withdrawn the children from the only school that they have ever known is further evidence that Mrs. Donley was creating an illusion of a dangerous situation for the children in order for her to accomplish the move that she did and attempt to get the subsequent sanction of the court.
>
> There is no reason that Mrs. Donley could not have contacted her lawyer and attempted to negotiate on notice a proper resolve to the custody issue. I also find that Mrs. Donley could have, and should have, come to court first on proper notice to Mr. Donley in order to get a court order prior to uprooting the children in the dramatic way that she did.[23]

The decision demonstrates how difficult it is to prove being a victim of domestic violence and then be able to establish that abuse even occurred. This is despite the large body of social science literature with respect to family violence demonstrating the silent nature of this type of abuse, which occurs behind closed doors and is often not reported by the abused parent (Jaffe et al., 2004; Geffner et al., 2000; Lemon, 1999; Neilson, 2004b). That is, the psychological abuse of threats; fantasies of homicide or suicidal ideation; the availability of weapons; obsessive, controlling, or possessive behaviours by the perpetrator that goes on behind closed doors. In turn, the victim, usually the mother, presents as a hysterical parent who is attempting to minimize the parent–child relationship rather than reacting to a controlling, coercive abuser.

As stated, many judges attend educational programs on family violence in the context of custody and access disputes among other topics related to family law. However, there still remains much more work to be done. For example, in a 2004 Nova Scotia case of *Walker* v. *Walker*,[24] the mother left the home with the two children four days after the husband allegedly assaulted her. She went to a shelter initially and then to live with relatives without informing the father about where they were going. Smith J. (the judge) wrote:

> There are few allegations more serious in a child custody case than abuse.... I have carefully considered the evidence presented concerning the allegations of abuse. The evidence does not satisfy me, on the balance of probabilities, that [the husband] has been abusive to either [the wife] or children. I conclude that the evidence of abuse is exaggerated...or incomplete ("I don't remember").
>
> In this case [the mother's] memory concerning a number of events that she now classifies as abusive is poor. Her conduct after the abuse is alleged to have occurred (including her willingness to leave the children in the care of [the father] despite the suggestion that he is an abuser) calls her allegations of abuse into question. Whether someone has been verbally or emotionally abusive towards another is open to subjective interpretation.... Controlling or jealous behaviour may be considered to be emotionally abusive by some and inappropriate behaviour by others.[25]

Similarly, lawyers also need to understand the impact of family violence in custody and access disputes. During a recent survey of family law lawyers in Ontario on access to justice issues, lawyers were asked whether litigants who were not represented by a lawyer were adequately protected in the courts when issues of family violence arose. Of those who responded, 70 percent believed that adequate protection is afforded to victims (women). The comments reflect both a belief that victims of family violence who do not have a lawyer may be more likely to be protected if they have a court hearing, and also recognition that this is not always the case:

> The judge often doesn't take the victim's allegations seriously enough and puts it down to a marital dispute—judges often do not consider the emotional abuse endured by the victim and do not seem to have an understanding of the effect upon a victim and their ability to stand up for their rights even with a lawyer representing them. Judges often hold the victim to a higher level of evidence even though the other party provides no evidence but just denies the allegations. It is difficult to prove many of the allegations that go on behind closed doors without any witnesses.[26]

One or both parents not having lawyers can also contribute to children being invisible in the process: information that the court needs to determine a child's best interest remains largely absent since parents are not always familiar with what evidence the court needs. As well, parents make allegations about one another and forget that it is the children whom the court wants to hear about and not the adult dispute.

The tension that exists between the Divorce Act on maximizing contact with both parents while minimizing conflict for children must be appropriately balanced to protect children in the face of family violence. If the justice system is truly predicated on the "best interests of the child," then the system must focus on children and their rights above those of the abuser and the abused. The silence of the legislation on this issue alone may result in some parents and professionals failing to appreciate and understand the social, emotional, and legal consequences of family violence on children. Only by recognizing and acknowledging that family violence in the context of custody and access disputes does exist and must be treated with a differentiated legal and mental health response, then and only then will the best interests of children be made visible in the process (Jaffe, Crooks & Bala, 2005; Johnston, 2006; Neilson, 2001).

Assessing the best interests of the child requires an understanding of individual and family dynamics, children's developmental ages and stages, family violence, and all aspects of family law. The balancing of these factors can be highly subjective and difficult, if not impossible, to evaluate during child custody disputes.

In *MacGyver* v. *Richards*, Abella J.A. stated:

Clearly, there is an inherent indeterminacy and elasticity to the "best interests" test which makes it more useful as legal aspiration than as legal analysis. It can be no more than an informed opinion made at a moment in the life of a child about what seems likely to prove to be in that child's best interests. Deciding what is in a child's best interests means deciding what, objectively appears most likely in the circumstances to be conducive to the kind of environment in which a particular child has the best opportunity for receiving the needed care and attention. Because there are stages to childhood, what is in a child's best interest may vary from child to child, from year to year, and possibly from month to month. This unavoidable fluidity makes it important to attempt to minimize the prospects for stress and instability.[27]

The difficulties are compounded when concerns arise about family violence in custody and access disputes. For example, it is not uncommon for
an abusive partner (often the father) to resort to threats of seeking custody
of their child or children to keep his partner in the relationship and continue abusing that partner (Bancroft & Silverman, 2002; Jaffe, Crooks &
Bala, 2005). As one judge commented of the relationship between family
violence and custody and access:

> An understanding of the theory of violence in domestic relation-
> ships and the impact of the violence on the abused spouse [*partner/
> child/children*] is essential to an understanding of the dynamics of
> the relationship between the batterer and the battered spouse [part-
> ner/child/children]. This in turn informs the understanding of the
> added complexities of a custody and access case involving a battered
> or abused spouse [*partner/child/children*]. (Schnall, 1999, p. 125;
> emphasis added)

This suggests to mental health professionals, child custody assessors,
lawyers, and judges that there is neither a single child custody and access
arrangement that works for all children, nor is there a definitive criterion
upon which to base custody and access arrangements as each child and
his or her family constellation is variable and complex (Birnbaum, Fidler
& Kavassalis, 2008). The need to understand and assess the level of risk to
children or lethality involved as a result of family violence during separation and/or divorce requires a differentiated and comprehensive assessment
(direct and indirect effects) of the family (including a cultural and social
context), as well as an understanding of family violence and its implications
for children (physical, sexual, and psychological) (Fidler, Bala, Birnbaum
& Kavassalis, 2008).

Johnston and Campbell (1993) were the first to provide a typology for
understanding the different patterns of family violence in custody disputes.
Since then, an important gathering of many different professionals from
across North America took place in 2007—the Wingspread Custody and
Domestic Violence conference. Five typologies were articulated for further
discussion. These were: (1) ongoing/episodic male battering (most closely
resembles cycle of violence); (2) female-initiated violence (women's use of
violence not in the context of self-defence); (3) male controlling interactive
violence (also known as mutual violence); (4) separation/divorce trauma (at
the time of separation); and (5) psychotic/paranoid (severe mental health
concerns) (Jaffe, Crooks & Bala, 2005). Others, such as Johnson (1995),

LaViolette (2005), and Frederick and Tilley (2001), have also attempted to differentiate the types of violence. While typologies are useful in helping to understand and respond to the complexity of violence, there are risks. Of significance is the lack of sensitive, reliable, and effective screening mechanisms to identify these various typologies. Moreover, there is also a serious risk in false negatives (failure to identify serious lethal violence) and false positives (identifying violence when in fact it may not be there) (Fidler, Bala, Birnbaum & Kavassalis, 2008). In addition, there is an expectation of different social and legal interventions accompanying these different typologies. Jaffe et al. (2008) have proposed five priorities to examine when child custody assessors are providing their input on parenting plans when family violence is present in child custody disputes. These are:

- *Priority 1:* Protect the child from violent, abusive, and neglectful parenting environments.
- *Priority 2:* Protect the safety and support the well-being of parent victims so that they will be better able to protect their children.
- *Priority 3:* Respect and empower parents to direct their own lives and make their own decisions in the interests of their child.
- *Priority 4:* Hold perpetrators of domestic violence accountable for past and future actions.
- *Priority 5:* Allow and promote the least restrictive parent–child contact and parenting plan that benefits the child.

The lower priorities should be addressed only after all higher priorities are satisfied, placing the safety of the child as the most important priority. Figure 13.1 provides a schema that summarizes the approach of Jaffe and his colleagues, linking the nature and degree of the parental conflict and domestic violence, the resources and interventions available, and the stage of the process to the various options for parenting arrangements, including both residential schedules and child-related decision making.

As noted above, each province has its own custody and access legislation, but uses similar factors when making determinations about custody of and access to children.[28] Bala (1999) and Cossman (2001) both argue that in practice there is no real difference between the federal and provincial legislation with respect to determining custody and access of children.

It is important to note that little of the provincial legislation across Canada contains a specific reference to spousal violence (emotional, physical, sexual, and/or verbal) as a factor to be considered during custody and access determinations. The only reference to this issue refers to past conduct of

Figure 13.1   Parenting Arrangements after Violence[a]

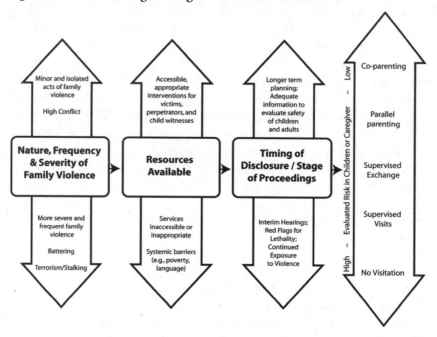

a Figure 13.1 and a discussion of parenting arrangements in cases of domestic violence can also be found on the Department of Justice website at: justice.gc.ca/en/pas/pad/reports/2005-FCY-3/chap3.html.

the parties. Newfoundland's Children's Law Reform Act, Nunavut's Children's Law Act, the Northwest Territories' Children's Law Act, and Ontario's Children's Law Reform Act are the only exceptions that specifically refer to domestic violence in relation to a parent's conduct, providing that:

> s.31(3) In assessing a person's ability to act as a parent, the court shall consider whether the person has ever acted in a violent manner towards
>
> a) his or her spouse or child;
> b) his or her child's parent; or
> c) another member of the household;
>
> otherwise a person's past conduct shall only be considered if the court thinks that it is relevant to the person's ability to act as a parent (Newfoundland). [Children's Law Act, R.S.N.L. 1990, chapter c-13, as amended.]

s.17(3) Court shall consider evidence that a person seeking custody or access has at any time committed an act of violence against his or her spouse, former spouse, child, child's parent or any other member of the person's household or family and any effect that such conduct had, is having, or may have on the child.

s.17(4) Subject to (3) a person's past conduct may be considered in respect of custody or access to a child only where the court is satisfied that it is relevant to the person's ability to act as a parent. (Children's Law Act [Nunavut] S.N.W.T. 1997 c. 14 as amended by S.N.W.T. 1998, C.17, S.N.W.T. 1999, C.5, and statutes enacted under Nunavut Acts. 76.05; Northwest Territories Children's Law Act, S.N.W.T. 1997, c. 14.)

An amendment to *Ontario's Children's Law Reform Act* came into force in 2006.

Sec. 24(4). In assessing a person's ability to act as a parent, the court shall consider whether the person has at any time committed violence or abuse against, (a) his or her spouse; (b) a parent or child to whom the application relates; (c) a member of the person's household; or (d) any child.

Critics have pointed out that the reference to violence does not clearly address how violence should be taken into account, and judicial approaches with respect to family violence continue to be inconsistent throughout the country (Fidler, Bala, Birnbaum & Kavassalis, 2008). In *Haider* v. *Malach*[29] the court stated that when considering the effects of domestic violence in the determination of custody and access matters, the court should explore: (1) the effect of the incidents of violence on the perpetrator's parenting skills; (2) the effect of the same incidents on the victim's parenting skills; and (3) the effect on the child. However, in another court, the trial judge made an order for joint custody with primary care and control to the mother even though the father admitted to having physically assaulted the mother and violently killing a pet. The trial judge found that the children were not shown to be at risk on access, but were at risk if the father were awarded sole custody.[30] In a New Brunswick court, the judge found that even though the father's undesirable personality traits, including an uncontrollable temper and abusive conduct toward women with whom he had relationships, had existed prior to the making of an original custody order in the father's favour, they had no substantial negative impact on the child, and the mother's application for custody was dismissed.[31]

The committee's report (Government of Canada's Response to the Report of the Special Joint Committee on Child Custody and Access: Strategy for Reform, 1999) clearly states, "a requirement for proof of conviction would be a very high standard for family law, especially in spousal abuse cases, where the abusive conduct often occurs in private and where the victims, for a variety of reasons, tend to hide or deny the abuse." It is now ten years later and not much has changed with respect to the silent and insidious nature of family violence and more so when children are involved.

In practice, most courts provide for access between a child and the non-custodial parent unless documented and *physical* evidence can be produced to the contrary. The courts and some mental health professionals continue to believe that contact between a child and non-custodial parent is import-ant. Moreover, the courts, in particular, have demonstrated a reluctance to suspend or terminate access solely on the basis of alleged family vio-lence even though a body of research knowledge questions this assumption (Birnbaum & Chipeur, 2010; Neilson, 2004b). The late law professor, James McLeod, noted in *Savidant* v. *MacLeod*:

> Clearly, courts continue to regard access as a parent- and child-cen-tred right. A parent should not be disentitled to access unless the child would suffer some harm. Supervision will often be seen as a solution to any "harm" or protection problems. If counsel intend to rely on emotional harm or psychological effects of conduct that may not be readily apparent, evidence on the point must be led. Counsel may not be entitled to raise literature in argument that is crucial to the finding of the "best interests of the child."[32]

Once again, children are rendered invisible during this process, as the focus is on the adults, not children. Children continue to have no voice in this process.

Under the federal Divorce Act, there are provisions that require the court to consider the willingness of one parent to facilitate a relationship between the child and the other parent and to consider the parent's past conduct only if it is relevant to the ability of that person to act as a parent of a child:

> 16(8) In making an order under this section, the court shall take into consideration only the best interests of the child of the marriage as determined by reference to the condition, means, needs and other circumstances of the child.
>
> (9) In making an order under this section, the court will not con-sider past conduct unless it is relevant to the ability of the person to act as a parent to the child.
>
> (10) In making an order under this section, the court shall give effect to the principle that a child of the marriage should have as much contact with each spouse as is consistent with the best interests of the

child, and for that purpose, shall take into consideration the willingness of the person for whom custody is sought to facilitate such contact.[33]

Section 16(10) presumes that access between a child and the non-custodial parent is an important factor. Lawyers have often used this section to aid in their arguments when acting for an abusive parent. The "friendly parent" provision of subsection (10) can effectively transfer custody from mothers who have been the primary caregivers of the child or children to an abusive partner. A compounding problem is that judges who ultimately make custody and access decisions, in practice, may not have the time or understanding to look beyond why parents are taking certain positions in the dispute. Zorza (1996) found that:

> Few courts even ask a mother why she may be discouraging the father's access to the children. Even if she manages to explain that she believes that she or her children are at risk, she will probably be disbelieved or her concerns ignored.... Friendly parent provisions punish her and the children if she raises concerns about his fitness or parenting ability because her very concern can be used as a weapon against her to deny her custody. (p. 1122)

Birnbaum and Bala (in press), in their survey of family law lawyers, inquired if the unrepresented get fair treatment in court by a judge when it comes to issues about family violence. One lawyer commented that the courts may be insufficiently skeptical of those claiming to be victims of family violence, observing that "in my experience, 'victims of violence' is more imagery than reality. It is unfortunate that the legal system virtually push[es] people into defining themselves as victims when in most cases they are not. The concept is overused to posture in front of the Court, mostly by psychologically disturbed women" (p. 16).

Humphreys (1993) argues that promoting the friendly parent provision, by which neither parent can dissuade or disparage the other, has the unintended consequence of leaving children: (1) invisible and vulnerable during this process; (2) keeping the abuse hidden; (3) not holding the abuser accountable for his actions; and, (4) further victimizing the abused parent and child. Children's wishes in the context of custody and access disputes and family violence can be problematic as they may be under the influence of the abuser and easily manipulated. However, allowing children a voice during a judicial interview may provide one avenue for children to express their concerns, if any, during the separation and/or divorce process about matters that so profoundly affect them after separation (Birnbaum & Bala, 2010; Birnbaum, Bala & Cyr, 2011; Cashmore & Parkinson, 2007, 2008).

The research literature overwhelmingly supports the need for ongoing education and training of all professionals involved in custody and access matters (Birnbaum, Fidler & Kavassalis, 2008; Gould, 1998, 2006; Jaffe, Crooks & Bala, 2005).

The Need for Interdisciplinary Training and Collaboration

When child custody disputes enter the legal system, mental health professionals who have expertise in understanding children's development and family dynamics are often called upon to assist the court in their decision making by conducting child custody evaluations (Birnbaum, Fidler & Kavassalis, 2008; Fidler & Birnbaum, 2006; Gould, 1998, 2006; Stahl, 1999). These evaluations are carried out by mental health professionals (social workers, psychologists, and psychiatrists) in both the privately and publicly funded sectors.

Each province has a provincially designated department that carries out child custody and access evaluations/investigations. Ontario is the only province that has both legal and clinical investigators, the Office of the Children's Lawyer, which focuses exclusively on children's interests before the court.[34]

In Ontario there are two pieces of legislation that guide the determination of when and who should conduct the child custody evaluation. These two pieces of legislation are Section 30 of the Children's Law Reform Act[35] and Section 112 of the Courts of Justice Act.[36] While each piece of legislation is different in its scope and mandate, the mental health professional (often a social worker) produces a comprehensive document that outlines the custodial and access responsibilities of each parent after thorough interviews with all those involved in the child or children's lives (Birnbaum, Fidler & Kavassalis, 2008; Fidler & Birnbaum, 2006).

Decision making about children's best interests is intended to provide a parenting plan after separation that best meets the emotional and physical needs of the child. By definition, decision making about children's future well-being is future oriented (Bala, 1996a). The recommendations made by these professionals can carry a significant amount of weight in court (Bala, 1996a; Birnbaum & Radovanovic, 1999).

Birnbaum, McCarty, and McTavish (2001) report that there are multiple guidelines[37] and few, if any, mandatory standards for child custody assessors across Canada to follow.[38] At present, there is only one online distance course that exists through the Justice Institute of British Columbia (Corrections and Community Justice Division, JIBC) that provides education to mental health professionals about carrying out child custody and access evaluations. This is the only online distance course that offers a hands-on approach for educating mental health professionals about the process and functions of conducting a child custody evaluation.[39] Since then, one course on how to conduct child custody assessments has been offered in continuing education in Ontario.[40]

There are numerous textbooks written by mental health professionals to guide the custody and access assessor in the process and methodology of conducting a custody and access assessment (Birnbaum, Fidler & Kavassalis, 2008; Gould, 1998, 2006; Leonoff & Montague, 1996; Melton, Petrila, Poythress & Slobogin, 2007; Stahl, 1994, 1999). While there has been more focus on assessing family violence in the last decade, training across disciplines continues to be inconsistent or absent when it comes to guiding the work of assessors, in particular, when dealing with family violence or any other significant practice issue that is raised in custody and access disputes (Austin, 2000; Drozd, Kuehnle & Walker, 2004; Birnbaum et al., 2001).[41] This is supported in the research by Shaffer and Bala (2004) in which they found that assessors were woefully lacking in an understanding of wife abuse and its impact on children. Clearly, there is a need for education, training, and policy development in this area to make children and their interests, in particular, visible.

Given the types of practice issues that can and often do arise during child custody disputes (e.g., a child being alienated from one parent or the other, same-sex child custody disputes, children being raised in different religious faiths, and concerns about family violence and the effects on children), it is imperative that mental health professionals called upon in this area receive comprehensive education and training in all facets of family law-related matters.

Child custody evaluators require specialized training in and knowledge of family development, child development, family violence, in addition to having knowledge and understanding of how the particular province's family law system intersects with family law child custody decision making. It also means that mental health professionals, child custody assessors, and lawyers must work collaboratively to assist children and families upon family dissolution. Communication and co-operation is essential between these disciplines. The consequences of a lack of experience, knowledge, training, and skill in this area can be, at best, harmful and, at worst, deadly to children.

Decision making about children and their future relationships with their parents after separation and/or divorce is one of the most important roles any mental health professional, child custody assessor, lawyer, and judge will have with respect to the life of a child.

Children's Voices

Conventional child development theory (Piagetian and attachment theory) influenced current thinking that children need to be protected during family breakdown. However, more recent approaches, such as the sociology of childhood, views children as gradually coming to know the world through their own learning experiences where they engage in reciprocal relationships with others. Sociology of childhood focuses more on a child's right to citizenship and being accorded the rights that come with it (Taylor, Smith, & Tapp, 1999). Nowhere is this more salient than when their parents dispute about custody and access.

There are many different ways the child's voice can be heard in custody and access disputes. In the context of family breakdown and children's decision making, their involvement is highly varied, both within and between jurisdictions (Birnbaum, 2009). In contested custody and access disputes, children's voices are ascertained by: (1) direct evidence from the child either as a witness in court or in an interview in the judge's chambers;[42] (2) indirect evidence related by a parent or other witness through hearsay (including a videotape or audiotape); (3) the evidence of a mental health professional who has conducted a custody and access assessment for the court; (4) written statements from a child in the form of a letter or affidavit; and (5) child legal representation (Birnbaum & Bala, 2010; Birnbaum, Bala & Cyr, 2011). For purposes of this chapter, child legal representation will be highlighted.

Child legal representation

Court orders and separation agreements bear the names of children, with whom they reside, and how often they will visit with their non-custodial parent. Yet, what part do children really play in the process and do they really have a "voice" about the decisions that are made in their "best interests"?

Legal representation of children in custody and access matters is an evolving concept. Historically, children had few rights and have only recently begun to be perceived as people with independent rights and interests. The United Nations adopted the Convention on the Rights of the Child in 1989.[43]

Child legal representation was one of forty-eight recommendations made by the Special Joint Committee of the Senate and the House of Commons (Special Joint Committee of the Senate and the House of Commons on Custody and Access, 1998). Ontario is the only province in Canada that has a formalized child legal representation program in custody and access disputes (Office of the Children's Lawyer).[44] Each province has a different model regarding the role of child's counsel.[45] For example:

1. the traditional lawyer advocate for the child (lawyer takes an instructional advocate role);
2. a *guardian ad litem* (this person may be a lawyer, a volunteer layperson, or a mental health professional) who may or may not have legal and/or mental health training in the area of child custody; the *guardian ad litem* acts as the child's counsel and guardian of his/her best interests; or

3. an *amicus curiae* (a neutral person who is appointed by the court to advise and inform both the child and the court about the facts of the case); this person is responsible to the court and not to the child (Birnbaum & Bala, 2011; Birnbaum & Moyal, 2002; Birnbaum, Bala & Cyr, 2011)

In Ontario, the lawyer for the child provides for a combination of all three models and represents the child's interest. The role of the lawyer is defined by a solicitor–client relationship in assisting the adult parties in resolving the dispute before the court. The lawyer acts as a broker for the child and advocates the child's interests so that they may be understood and communicated not only to the parents but to the court as well. Children do not "instruct" their lawyer. Rather, the lawyer conveys the child's wishes and views by providing context to those wishes and views to the family and the court. It is the context that allows the child's lawyer to present all the information that has been gathered through interviews with parents, significant caregivers, relatives, and other professional sources, as well as the child's views and wishes.

The strength of this program lies in the collaboration of clinicians and lawyers working together in custody and access disputes. Each discipline learns from the other and provides a strong voice for the child, who would not otherwise be heard through child legal representation and/or a clinical investigation alone (Birnbaum & Moyal, 2003). However, one of the limitations is that lawyers and clinicians more often than not speak on behalf of children by providing the "context" to their wishes. In turn, children can be silenced in this process as others speak *for* them instead of enabling *them* to speak for themselves, for example, to a judge (Birnbaum & Bala, 2010; Birnbaum, Bala & Cyr, 2011; Morag, Rivkin & Sorek, 2012; Smith, Taylor & Tapp, 2003).

Child legal representation alone without an accompanying context for those wishes can prove problematic. For example, Bala (1996b) found that:

Children's wishes can be very problematic in spousal abuse situations because the abused parent may be seen as weak and "ineffectual" and children may wish to align themselves with the "stronger," more powerful, abusive parent. An abusive spouse can be very manipulative and the denigration of the other parent may influence a child's relationship with the victim of abuse. (p. 257)

The allocation of weight that is given to children's wishes in family violence cases supports the view that there is no one single "correct" solution to a complex set of factors. In fact, Johnston and Roseby (1997) argue that:

there is no simple policy recommendation, nor procedural method, nor one treatment intervention that is suited for all domestic violence families. Differential assessments of domestic violence are necessary when helping parents make post-divorce plans for the custody of their children. Parent-child relationships are likely to vary with the different patterns of violence, and children of different ages and gender are affected differently. (p. 60)

Summary

Part 1 explored the historical roots of child custody legislation leading to the present-day adoption of the "best interest of the child" principle. It is clear that there are multiple systems involved in the decision making about the well-being of children after separation and/or divorce. Without legislation that specifically addresses family violence consistently across Canada, children are dealt with by a patchwork of legislative regimes and individual judicial determinations, leaving children's voices silent in the process. What is clear is that providing services and resources for children and families after separation and/or divorce requires a comprehensive, coordinated strategy to make children visible during these difficult times. That is, children need not only a voice to render them visible during their parent's separation and/or divorce, but also clearly defined policies and procedures—encompassing a coordinated effort by all those involved in the justice system—to meet their best interests.

PART 2: CUSTODY AND ACCESS AND THE NEVER-ENDING SEARCH FOR ALTERNATIVE LANGUAGE

In Part 2, the focus will be on describing and understanding the different definitions of parenting arrangements for children after separation and/or divorce in other jurisdictions. These varying definitions highlight the social, economic, and politicized nature of the tension inherent in family law reform that can and often does make children invisible in the process.

There is no shortage of social science literature that both supports and critiques the need for an ongoing relationship between children and their non-custodial parent following separation and/or divorce (Kelly, 1993, 2007, 2012; Kelly & Lamb, 2000; Thompson & Amato, 1999). Equally, there is no shortage of opinions offered by mothers, fathers, child custody assessors, and policy-makers about what the parenting arrangements should look like following separation and/or divorce. However, the one theme that is central to all those involved is the reduction of conflict for children after separation and/or divorce. Questions remain: What do we do to avoid the next headline shouting that a child has been victimized as a result of a custody and access dispute? How does the present-day adversarial system exacerbate and maintain the conflict and render children invisible in the process? Is it realistic or naive to assume that the laws and rules governing family law matters will affect a positive outcome for children who are caught between battling parents?

Similar reforms taking place in Canada to change the words "custody" and "access" also occurred in the United Kingdom,[46] Australia,[47] and many states throughout the US.[48] The reasons are varied. Historically, child custody and access have been associated with the traditional adversarial approach as whoever gets custody is the "winner" and the other parent becomes the "loser." Irrespective of the history, the focus remains on the adult perspective and not that of the child or children.

In Washington state, parents design a parenting plan without using the words "custody" and/or "access," but with concepts such as "parenting plans" and "parental functions." In the United Kingdom, custody and access is similarly replaced with "parental responsibility," "residence," and "contact." In Australia, the court orders shared parenting in which responsibilities are allocated between the parents according to the best interests of the child. Parkinson (2010) and Rhoades (2006) conclude that fathers' groups had a large role to play in the amendments of the Australian legislation.

Research into the long-term effects on children governed by these changes across the globe indicates that the Washington State Parenting Act (1986), the Children Act (1989) in the United Kingdom, and the Australian Family Law (Shared Parental Responsibility) Act (2006) all share similar problems in interpretation and implementation of the new language used to replace custody and access. That is, parents continue to face more litigation and more conflict about their children regarding post-separation parenting plans (Final Federal-Provincial-Territorial Report on Custody and Access to Child Support, 2002; Fehlberg, Smyth, Maclean & Roberts, 2011). The reasons vary. One argument put forward is that there is an inherent difficulty for parents to be co-operative while using the court system to settle their disputes. Another argument is that the language continues to be vague and has different meanings among lawyers, mental health practitioners, the courts, and the parents themselves (Rhoades, 2002). Gould (1998) argues that parenting plans are only hypotheses. He asserts that "parenting plans are experiments in social engineering guided by little, if any, empirical research. They are works in progress, needing to be continually reassessed for their usefulness with a particular family" (p. 247). Yet, countries have embraced this language and approach as the new messiah without regard for the impact on a child or children in situations of family violence through empirical investigation.

Other terms suggested are "shared parenting"[49] (parents are encouraged to jointly form parenting responsibilities upon separation and/or divorce), the "primary caretaker presumption"[50] (the parent who has been the primary caregiver to the child or children remains the primary caregiver), and the "approximation principle"[51] (parenting arrangements should approximate the arrangements prior to separation and/or divorce) have all found their way into the discourse on child custody decision making. These terms are an attempt to more accurately reflect the reality of parenting. However, they, too, have been found to be equally emotionally laden, with each parent taking opposite sides. More importantly, like parenting plans, these terms do not address how family violence is to be evaluated.

It would seem that more is required than changing the language. As a result, new and additional challenges in understanding children's needs in custody and access disputes arise. Children and families require clear definitions and expectations before and after family breakdown. Another question remains: How can all the systems that are involved with children work collaboratively to make family violence in custody and access disputes more visible and, hence, children more visible during these tumultuous times?

Summary

If the goal of our society is to provide a less adversarial approach to family law matters, it would seem that children's interests must be addressed in an integrated holistic manner before, during, and after family breakdown. Changing language alone does not change underlying attitudes and beliefs in practice about children and their needs upon family breakdown. Fundamental family law reform is difficult to achieve as it involves social, economic, and political reform as well.

Chief Justice Warren K. Winkler, in his opening remarks to the County of Carleton Law Association, Annual Institute of Family Law (2011) in Ottawa, stated the problem as such:

> I question the effectiveness of the "slow-and-steady" approach of fine-tuning and rationalizing the present system. Rather than incremental change, perhaps it is time to consider a more dramatic and pragmatic revision of the manner in which family law services is delivered across Ontario. In expressing concerns about the state of our family justice system, my hope was to raise the profile of this issue and begin a dialogue about what tangible steps we can take to make real changes that result in real results for clients. Thankfully, since I raised these issues they have begun to receive greater attention, with an increased sense of urgency. In the last 6 months there have been

several print and broadcast stories on the current crisis in family law. Just two weeks ago, the *Globe and Mail* ran three stories on this subject in their Saturday Focus section. My hope is that this dialogue will in fact lead to change. Decisions about children post separation and/ or divorce are policy decisions requiring a substantial investment in time, money, and research. The consequences of not providing these tools are to continue leaving children invisible during the separation and/or divorce process.[52]

Sadly, news stories last a few days and people forget. The consequence of "slow and steady" still silences children.

PART 3: A BLUEPRINT FOR SOCIAL, LEGAL, AND POLITICAL REFORM

Family law is unique in every aspect because it not only deals with child and spousal support as well as property issues, but, more importantly, with the emotional, behavioural, and physical arrangements of children's lives during and after separation and/or divorce. Their well-being is inextricably linked to the parental relationship. Children do not live in isolation from the family.

Family law reform remains a complex intertwining relationship between various systems and power relations (social, legal, and political). The laws and policies affecting children and their families pre-, during-, and post-separation and/or divorce are profound (socially, economically, and politically). Therefore, the solutions must be equally as profound and significant. The system needs to be changed from the inside out. Policy change is required at both the federal and provincial level as no one piece of legislation can change current practice across Canada.

National policies that make children visible in the separation and/or divorce process can offer a framework to guide mental health practitioners, lawyers, and the courts in their work together. Johnston and Roseby (1997) and Johnston, Roseby, and Kuehnle (2010) cogently argued for building multidisciplinary partnerships to advance family law reform in the interests of children more than ten years ago.

They proposed a dispute resolution continuum that would involve the court, lawyers, mental health professionals, and child custody assessors, all working together with divorcing families. Each level that a family goes through has a corresponding set of programs made available to assist them in the separation and/or divorce process. Movement has been "slow and steady."

While many provinces across Canada are presently offering services along the lines of a dispute resolution continuum, few, if any, are being empirically evaluated to understand what works and what does not for

Box 13.1   Integrated Services

The elements of each component would involve the following:

1. Public education services beginning in elementary school, where children are educated about family violence and family law issues
2. Public health services beginning in elementary school, where parenting education programs, family violence programs, substance abuse programs (testing, monitoring, and treatment), and counselling services are made available
3. Family law services that are collaborative in nature provided by both lawyers and mental health practitioners who have expertise and knowledge about children and families; included in this component would be services that provide therapeutic supervised access and parent coordinators to monitor and provide follow-up with children and parents
4. Child welfare services that focus on children's best interests and are integrated (humanly and technologically) with the other elements
5. Mental health services beginning in elementary school to offer children counselling and therapy as early as possible
6. Police services (including criminal justice) that provide specialized family violence services to children and families involved in all family law-related matters

children. In addition, it has been argued that another limitation to the dispute resolution continuum is that it often focuses on families who are already in conflict before the court. The services are typically offered only after family breakdown has occurred. More fundamental and structural change is required before, during, and after family breakdown.

The blueprint for a multidisciplinary partnership with the federal, provincial, and territorial governments involves systemic change at the social, legal, and political levels. This theme has been echoed throughout the literature to make children's interests centre stage, thereby rendering them visible during times of separation and/or divorce (Jaffe et al., 2004; Jaffe et al., 2003). This entails change not just on a human level, but, more importantly, on a technological and institutional level, where all services are coordinated and integrated in the interests of children (see Box 13.1). This partnership would require developing protocols and policies, providing training, education and mentoring, building collaborative networks, coordinating, and providing funding for capacity building to meet the needs for a social, legal, and political change in all the areas related to children.

Finally, only through program evaluation and rigorous empirical research will we know what is required. All too often evaluation and research components are add-ons rather than built into the design and implementation of programs. Critics cite that they are too expensive and unnecessary (Royce, Thyer & Padgett, 2010). However, it is imperative to know whether children's needs are being met by policy reform. We do not know how children are doing under the present set of policies and programs that are available, nor if the programs are being monitored for unintended consequences.

Governments would argue that this blueprint for change is unrealistic, expensive, and difficult, if not impossible, to achieve, given the breadth and scope of the systems involved. True family law reform will depend on what society as a whole really wants for its children and how much society is prepared to spend (financially and emotionally). The alternative is reading another headline about a child who has been abducted or killed, all in the name of the "best interests of the child."

CONCLUSION

Serious policy reform calls for leadership and vision. To the extent that society already has the necessary tools, specialization, and knowledge at its disposal, it is a unique moment in time to integrate and harness the expertise of all those involved. All too often "we" professionals operate in separate silos and the services provided tend to divide the problems of children and their families into rigid and distinct categories (civil and criminal), are uncoordinated and lack functional communication between the private and public sectors, take a one-size-fits-all approach, and fail to craft comprehensive solutions while addressing the interests of children (Bruner & Parachini, 1997). Better integration is necessary and must be achieved if children are to be visible during separation and/or divorce and family violence. The blueprint for change is specifically intended to make children visible and heard.

If the goal of our society is to be less adversarial when it comes to separation and/or divorce, then fundamental structural change needs to occur as early as possible and at all provincial, territorial, and federal policy levels; changes in language alone do not produce changes in behaviour or changes in attitudes and beliefs about children and their relationships upon family breakdown. Children need to be the central focus in this area.

The chapter began with real-life examples of the ultimate price children can and do pay during times of parental separation and/or divorce and family violence. The following quotation—taken from Fathers for Equality in Divorce—clearly illustrates the emphasis on the "rights" of parents and not children:

> How much longer must we so often read in our Monday newspapers of some desperate and distraught man, forced out of his home, denied access to his children, badly hurt by his former best friend and her lawyer, massacring his children, his estranged or former wife, and killing himself in a mind-numbing act? Who is responsible for pushing an otherwise decent man into such a hopeless position? Where was the caring, unbiased judge? Why was the lawyer let loose to take so much from him, and why did he not have access to a government-funded support group for men that could have given him some hope for fighting for his inalienable rights as a parent? ... Men must not be persecuted like this again. (quoted in Boyd, 2003, p. 109)

In contrast, it is salient to close with the voice of one of the children, the most vulnerable of the victims of family violence:

> You are the only one I can talk to about this. My father broke into our house and started to break things. He chased my mother down the hall, and knocked her down and started to choke her. I told him to stop hurting my mother and he did. I fixed it. If I were a scientist I'd create a time machine and take us all back in time so that none of this happened and we could be a happy family.[53]

NOTES

1 Retrieved from: http://www.thestar.com/news/article/1020150--child-custody-dispute-in-fatal-whitby-shooting.

2 C. Blatchford, *Globe and Mail*, October 14, 2010, A7.

3 S. Montgomery, *National Post*, June 21, 2011, A11.

4 See the attorney general of Ontario, who describes the "Four Pillars" for family law reform. See, e.g., C. Bentley, *Access to justice for Ontarians*, September 29, 2010 (podcast). Retrieved from: www.attorneygeneral.jus.gov.on.ca/english/AG_podcasts/Transcripts/20100929_access_justice_transcript.asp. See also: Ontario Ministry of the Attorney General, News Release, *Family law reform in Ontario*, December 9, 2010. Retrieved from: http://news.ontario.ca/mag/en/2010/12/family-law-reform-in-ontario.html.

5 Every province and territory has introduced two- to four-hour information sessions about separation and/or divorce. Many of these programs are mandatory for the litigants before they can proceed in court. These programs typically provide basic information about the legal process and different methods of

dispute resolution, with some emphasis on the value of settlement and non-adversarial dispute resolution, as well as some information about the emotional effects of separation on children. The information programs can serve a number of important objectives, including promoting the use of alternative dispute resolution and reducing children's exposure to parental conflict. For a review of programs in Alberta, see J.J. Paetsch et al., *High conflict intervention programs in Alberta: A review and recommendations* (Calgary: Canadian Research Institute for Law and the Family, Alberta Justice, 2007). Many provinces, such as Alberta and Saskatchewan, have a six-hour course on parenting education programs focused on high-conflict families.

6   *G. (B.J.) v. G. (D.L.)*, 2010 Carswell Yukon 108 (Y.T.S.C.).

7   This term was first coined in the early 1990s by well-known scholar and sociologist Janet Johnston. She described high-conflict families as litigious, exhibiting negative communication patterns, having difficulties in making workable parenting plans for their children, and, in some cases, by family violence.

8   For many of the same reasons, criminal prosecutions arising from violence in familial relationships are also different from other types of criminal cases, and special courts—the domestic violence courts—have been established. However, many have argued that having two separate courts to deal with domestic violence creates further problems for the victim, and there are many advantages to having both the criminal and family aspects of cases involving domestic violence dealt with by one judge. There is similar value to having judicial continuity and a judicial role in changing behaviour for domestic violence cases in the criminal courts, as is the practice in some locales. An integrated domestic violence court pilot project has begun in Toronto in which judges with specialized knowledge about domestic violence will be in a position to try to change behaviours and attitudes. The pilot project is based on a "one family–one judge" approach used in several states in the United States. The family and criminal proceedings are not combined, but they appear before the single judge in sequence. If the case is not resolved, trials will be heard by other judges; thus, the legal integrity of each process is maintained:

> The cases are not combined but they do appear before the single judge in sequence. The appropriate law, standard of proof, rules of procedure and rules of evidence will apply in each case as they would in any court. All Crown policies will apply to the case as in any domestic violence court. Generally, both cases will be dealt with on the same day, sequentially. The judge will proceed through the process to plea and sentence in the criminal case and through the case management process to resolution in the family case. If a trial is required in either proceeding, it will be heard by a different judge. (Justice G. Waldman, *Managing the domestic violence family law case* (Quebec City, November 17–19, 2010).

This is an important initiative that needs to be studied and, if successful, replicated. See also: Aldrich & Harris-Kluger (2010).

9 Researchers at Harvard University provide an excellent summary of the toxic effects of stress on children's development: http://developingchild.harvard.edu/index.php/activities/council/. When child custody disputes and family violence meet, the deleterious effects on children are compounded exponentially. McIntosh (2003) also provides an excellent review of the literature regarding short-term and long-term consequences for children witnessing family violence and the limitations inherent in the research (Agar, 2004).

10 This Act was a result of a custody and access dispute involving the famous literary artist, Caroline Norton. Her three children resided with their father, who refused to allow any contact or communication between the children and their mother.

11 *Young v. Young*, [1948], O.J. No. 343 (QL) (Ont. S.C., C.A.).

12 Leigh [1871], 5 Practice Reports 402 (U.C.).

13 With exceptions, under traditional Aboriginal traditions and laws, child custody was awarded mainly to mothers (Backhouse, 1981). A less property-oriented view was taken toward Aboriginal children in that their well-being was a collective concern.

14 For a detailed analysis of the waves of change in legislation regarding children throughout history, see Bala (1999) and McDonald (1986). See also Boyd (2003), who offers a feminist perspective on the discourse and impact of legal reforms on women and children through history.

15 See Boyd (2003) for a feminist analysis of the shifting discourses for women in the family and labour market.

16 The National Judicial Institute of Canada provides educational programs for judges across Canada. Mental health professionals and academics present on issues related to separation and divorce. The NJI has had several programs focused on domestic violence and, in particular, in custody and access disputes. A national benchbook has been published for judges. See Neilson (2009).

17 For example, before May 1997, fathers could deduct their child support for income tax purposes and mothers would have to include the amount of money for their taxes. Since May 1997, fathers do not deduct monies for taxes and mothers do not report the child support as income. Bala (1999) argues that to secure passage of the Federal Child Support Guidelines in 1997, the government promised to hold hearings across Canada on family law reform with respect to custody and access laws.

18 [1962] 3 All E.R. 1, at 3,4.

19 For a detailed critique of the Committee hearings and report see Bala (1999).

20 An Act to amend the Divorce Act, the Family Orders and Agreements Enforcement Assistance Act, the Garnishment, Attachment, and Pension Diversion Act, and the Judges Act and to amend other Acts in consequence, Bill C-22. Introduced to the House of Commons for First Reading on December 10, 2002. Second Reading on February 25, 2003. Bill C-22, the Bill amending the Divorce Act, died with the prorogation of Parliament. While many "rights" groups

continue to argue for shared parenting decision making following separation, the empirical research has been less than positive on the outcomes for children in Australia (Fehlberg, Smyth, Maclean & Roberts, 2011).

21 See Hunt and Roberts (2005). Family Policy Briefing no. 4 for outcome evaluations done conducted on some of these programs across the globe.

22 *Donley v. Donley*, 2008 CarswellOnt 596, 51 R.F.L. (6th) 164 (Ont. S.C.J.).

23 Ibid., at para 96–98.

24 *Walker v. Walker*, 2004 CarswellNS 167, 2004 NSSF 40, 223 N.S.R. (2d) 357, 705 A.P.R. 357 (N.S.S.C.).

25 Ibid., at para. 24–28.

26 Birnbaum and Bala (in press, p. 16).

27 (1995), 11 R.F.L. (4th) 432, 22 O.R. (3d) 481, 123 D.L.R. (4th) 562 (Ont.C.A.).

28 See the Government of Canada website for all federal legislation pertaining to custody and access: http://laws.justice.gc.ca/eng/. See each Ministry of Attorney General website for provincial legislation. In Alberta, 2006, the Protection against Family Violence Act and in Manitoba, the Domestic Violence and Stalking Act added stalking to the definition of family violence and provided a better definition of what constitutes family violence.

29 (1999), 48 R.F.L. (4th) 314 (Sask. C.A.) 44 R.F.L. 1, [1999] 1 S.C.R. 420 (S.C.C.).

30 *Manaigre v. Manaigre* (June 11, 1999), 89 A.C.W.S. (3d) 289 (Man.Q.B.).

31 *Humes v. St. Croix* [1991], W.D.F.L. 371 (N.B.Q.B., Feb. 8, 1991).

32 *Savidant v. MacLeod* (1992), 40 R.F.L. at 444.

33 Divorce Act, R.S.C. 1985, c.3 (2nd Supp.), s. 16(8)(9)(10).

34 An independent law office within Ontario's Ministry of the Attorney General. The office represents the interests of children before the court in custody and access disputes, child welfare proceedings, and civil litigation and estate matters.

35 The Children's Law Reform Act, R.S.O. 1990, c. C.12 (1). The court before which an application is brought in respect of custody of or access to a child, by order, may appoint a person who has the technical or professional skill to assess and report to the court on the needs of the child and the ability and willingness of the parties or any of them to satisfy the needs of the child.

36 Courts of Justice Act, R.S.O. 1990 c.C.43 (1). In a proceeding under the Divorce Act (Canada) or the Children's Law Reform Act in which a question concerning custody of or access to a child is before the court, the children's lawyer may cause an investigation to be made and may report and make recommendations to the court on all matters concerning custody of or access to the child and the child's support and education.

37 In Ontario there are three independent professional bodies. The Ontario College of Social Workers and Social Service Workers, the Ontario College of Psychologists, and the Ontario Interdisciplinary Association of Custody/Access Assessors.

38 The Canadian Association of Social Workers (CASW) does not have any mandatory practice guidelines for social workers involved in custody and

access matters before the court. In Ontario, the only mandatory practice guidelines are for psychologists only; the other two colleges remain as practice guidelines only.

39 C. McKnight (personal communication, January 12, 2011). It was offered as a pilot course in early November 2002, funded by the Department of Justice, Canada. The course continues to be offered on a fee basis as a long-distance Internet-based course from the Justice Institute of British Columbia.

40 See Factor-Inwentash Faculty of Social Work, University of Toronto, 2011–12 course calendar.

41 The Office of the Children's Lawyer in Ontario has and continues to provide training for clinical investigators, lawyers, and panel agents engaged in custody and access matters. This is the only interdisciplinary training that is offered in North America.

42 Section 64 of the Children's Law Reform Act provides for a judicial interview. Quebec is the only province in Canada where children are more inclined to speak to a judge than anywhere else in Canada as a result of Article 34 of the Quebec Civil Code, which creates a presumption that children will be directly heard by the court. See also Birnbaum and Bala (2010) and Birnbaum, Bala, and Cyr (2011) for empirical research on judicial interviews with children and what children have to say about speaking to mental health professionals and their lawyers in the context of family disputes.

43 Article 3 of the Convention provides that: "In all actions concerning children, whether undertaken by public or private social welfare institutions, courts of law, administrative authorities or legislative bodies, the best interests of the child shall be a primary consideration."

Article 9 of the Convention provides that "where the parents are living separately and a decision must be made as to the child's place of residence," the determination shall be made in "accordance with applicable law for the best interests of the child."

Article 9(3) specifies that governments "shall respect the right of the child who is separated from one or both parents to maintain personal relationships and direct contact with both parents on a regular basis, except if it is contrary to a child's best interests."

Article 12 provides that children have the right to express their views freely in matters concerning them. [1992] C.T.S. 3.

See also: Special Joint Committee on Child Custody and Access (1998), Recommendations 3; 22.4.

44 In Ontario, the Children's Law Reform Act explicitly sets out that judges must consider "the views and preferences of the child when such views and preferences can be reasonably ascertained" (s.24 [2]).

45 See Birnbaum and Bala (2011) on the controversy of the role of child's counsel in Ontario and Alberta.

46 The Children Act (England and Wales), 1989.

47 The Family Law (Shared Parental Responsibility) Act, 2006.

48 The Washington Parenting Act, 1986.

49 The concept of shared parenting provides a dangerous context for those children involved in family violence. The federal government moved away from a joint custody presumption advocated mostly by fathers' groups during the committee hearings in 1997 to a shared parenting concept. However, the talk seems to have started all over again (Schmitz, 2011).

50 In the United States, West Virginia applies the presumption in favour of the primary caregiver. In Louisiana, the statute refers to a consideration of the "responsibility for the care and rearing of the child/ren previously exercised by each party." In New Jersey, the statute refers to a consideration of the "extent and quality of time spent with the child/ren prior to or subsequent to the separation." In Virginia, the statute requires consideration of "the role each parent has played and will play in the future in the upbringing and care of the child." In Minnesota, the statute provides that the court should take into account, when determining the best interests of the child, the child's primary caretaker, but that it ought not to operate as a presumption. The Washington Parenting Act requires that the court, when determining the child's residential schedule, give greatest weight to the "relative strength, nature, and stability of the child's relationship with each parent, including whether a parent has taken greater responsibility for performing caretaking functions relating to the daily needs of the child."

51 This term was first coined by Scott (1992). The American Law Institute has recommended adoption of this principle.

52 County of Carleton Law Association, Annual Institute of Family Law in Ottawa, Ontario, April 8, 2011.

53 This is a custody dispute about two boys, ages eight and five. The eight-year-old boy shares this with the social worker. The five-year-old had been so traumatized by the violence that he has stopped talking and has an involuntary twitch in his left eye.

REFERENCES

Agar, S. (2004). *Interventions for children who witness intimate partner violence: A literature review.* Vancouver: British Columbia Institute against Family Violence.

Aldrich, L., & Harris Kluger, J. (2010). New York's one judge-one family response to family Violence. *Juvenile and Family Court Journal, 61*(4), 77–86.

Austin, W.G. (2000). Assessing credibility in allegations of marital violence in the high-conflict child custody case. *Family and Conciliation Courts Review, 38*(4), 462–77.

Backhouse, C. (1981). Shifting patterns in nineteenth-century Canadian custody law. In D. Flaherty (Ed.), *Essays in the history of Canadian law* (pp. 189–212). Toronto: University of Toronto Press.

Bala, N. (1996a). Mental health professionals in child-related proceedings: Understanding the ambivalence of the judiciary. *Canadian Journal of Family Law, 13*(2), 261–312.

Bala, N. (1996b). Spousal abuse and children of divorce: A differentiated approach. *Canadian Journal of Family Law, 13*(2), 215–85.

Bala, N. (1999). A report from Canada's "gender war zone": Reforming the child-related provisions of the Divorce Act. *Canadian Journal of Family Law, 16*(2), 163–227.

Bala, N., Birnbaum, R., & Martinson, D. (2011). One judge for one family: Differentiated case management for families in continuing conflict. *Canadian Journal of Family Law, 26*(2), 395–450.

Bala, N., & Clarke, K. (1981). *The child and the law.* Toronto: McGraw-Hill Ryerson.

Bancroft, L., & Silverman, J.G. (2002). *The batterer as parent: Addressing the impact of domestic violence on family dynamics.* Thousand Oaks, CA: Sage.

Berkman, M., Casey, R.L., Berkowitz, S.J., & Marans, S. (2004). Police in the lives of children exposed to domestic violence. In G.P. Jaffe, L.L. Baker & A.J. Cunningham (Eds.), *Protecting children from domestic violence: Strategies for community intervention* (pp. 153–70). New York: Guilford Press.

Birnbaum, R. (2009). *The voice of the child in separation/divorce mediation and other alternative* dispute resolution processes: A literature review. Family, Children, and Youth Section, Department of Justice, Canada. Retrieved from: http://www.justice.gc.ca/eng/pi/fcy-fea/lib-bib/rep-rap/2009/vcsdm-pvem/pdf/vcsdm-pvem.pdf.

Birnbaum, R., & Bala, N. (2010). Judicial interviewing with children in custody and access cases: Comparing experiences in Ontario and Ohio. *International Journal of Law, Policy, and the Family, 24*(3), 300–37.

Birnbaum, R., & Bala, N. (2011, November). Lawyers and the vulnerable very young. *Lawyers Weekly*, vol. 31, 26, 14. Carswell Publications.

Birnbaum, R., & Bala, N. (In press). Views of Ontario lawyers on family litigants withoutrepresentation. *University of New Brunswick Law Journal.*

Birnbaum, R., Bala, N., & Cyr, F. (2011). Children's experiences with family justice professionals and judges in Ontario and Ohio. *International Journal of Law, Policy, and the Family, 25*(3), 398–422.

Birnbaum, R., & Chipeur, S. (2010). Supervised visitation in custody and access disputes: Finding legal solutions for complex family problems. *Canadian Family Law Quarterly, 29*, 79–94.

Birnbaum, R., Fidler, B.J., & Kavassalis, K. (2008). *Child custody and access assessments: A* resource guide for legal and mental health professionals. Toronto: Thomson Carswell Publishing.

Birnbaum, R., McCarty, E., & McTavish, W. (2001). *Haider* v. *Malach*: Child custody guidelines gone awry. *Canadian Family Law Quarterly, 9*(3), 357–72.

Birnbaum, R., & Moyal, D. (2002). Visitation-based disputes arising on separation and divorce: Focused child legal representation. *Canadian Family Law Quarterly, 20*(3), 37–51.

Birnbaum, R., & Moyal, D. (2003). How social workers and lawyers collaborate to promote resolution in the interests of children: The interface between law in theory and law in action. *Canadian Family Law Quarterly, 21*(3), 379–95.

Birnbaum, R., & Radovanovic, H. (1999). Brief intervention model for access-based post-separation disputes: Family and court outcomes. *Family and Conciliation Courts Review, 37*(4), 504–13.

Boyd, S. (1987). *Child custody and working mothers. The impact of judicial bias on family law: Equality and judicial neutrality.* Toronto: Carswell.

Boyd, S. (2000). *Gendering the best interests principle: Custody, access, and relocation in a* mobile society. Special Lecture 2000: Family Law: A colloquium on the best interests of the child. New perspectives on the resolution of custody disputes. Conference 2000. Toronto: Law Society of Upper Canada.

Boyd, S. (2003). *Child custody, law, and women's work.* Oxford: Oxford University Press.

Breger, M.L. (2010). Against the dilution of a child's voice in court. Retrieved from: http://papers.ssrn.com/sol3/papers.cfm?abstract_id=1756948.

Bruner, C., & Parachini, L. (1997). *Building community: Exploring new relationships among service systems reform, community organizing, and community economic development.* Washington, DC: Together We Can Initiative, Institute for Educational Leadership.

Cashmore, J. (2003). Children's participation in family law matters. In C. Hallett & A. Prout (Eds.), *Hearing the voices of children: Social policy for a new century* (pp. 158–57). London: Bodmin Routledge: Falmer Press.

Cashmore, J., & Parkinson, P. (2007). What responsibility do courts have to hear children's voices? *International Journal of Children's Rights, 15,* 43–60.

Cashmore, J., & Parkinson, P. (2008). Children's and parents' perceptions on children's participation in decision making after parental separation and divorce. *Family Court Review, 46*(1), 91–104.

Clingempeel, W., & Reppucci, N. (1982). Joint custody after divorce: Major issues and goals for research. *Psychological Bulletin, 91,* 102–27.

Cochran, R. (1985). The search for guidance in determining the best interests of the child at divorce: Reconciling the primary caretaker and joint custody preferences. *University of Richmond Law Review, 20,* 1–65.

Cohen, J., & Gershbain, N. (2001). For the sake of the fathers? Child custody reform and the perils of maximum contact. *Canadian Family Law Quarterly, 19*(1), 121–83.

Cossman, B. (2001). *An analysis of options for changes in the legal regulation of child custody and access* (2001-fcy-2e). Ottawa: Department of Justice Canada, Family, Children, and Youth Section. Retrieved from: http://canada.justice.gc.ca/en/ps/cca/reports/2001-fcy-2e.pdf.

Drakich, J. (1989). In search of the better parent: The social construction of ideologies of fatherhood. *Canadian Journal of Women and the Law, 3*(1), 69–87.

Drozd, L., Kuehnle, K., & Walker, L. (2004). Safety first: A model for understanding domestic violence in child custody and access disputes. *Journal of Child Custody, 1*(2), 75–103.

Elster, J. (1987). Solomonic judgements: Against the best interest of the child. *University of Chicago Law Review, 54*(1), 1–45.

Epstein, P. (2010, November, 23). *This week in family news.* Family Law Newsletter.

Fantuzzo, J.W., Mohr, W.K., & Noone, M.J. (2000). Making the invisible victims of violence against women visible through university/community partnerships. *Journal of Agression, Maltreatment, and Trauma, 3*(1), 9–23.

Fehlberg, B., Smyth, B., Maclean, M., & Roberts, C. (2011). *Caring for children after parental* separation: Would legislation for shared parenting time help children? Family Policy Briefing no. 7. Oxford: University of Oxford, Department of Social Policy and Intervention.

Fidler, B.J., Bala, N., Birnbaum, R., & Kavassalis, K. (2008). *Challenging issues in child custody* disputes: A resource guide for legal and mental health professionals. Toronto: Carswell Thomson Reuters Publishing.

Fidler, B.J., & Birnbaum, R. (2006). Child custody disputes: Public and private assessments. *Canadian Family Law Quarterly, 25*(2), 137–67.

Final Federal-Provincial-Territorial Report on Custody and Access to Child Support. (2002). Retrieved from: http://www.justice.gc.ca/eng/pi/fcy-fea/lib-bib/rep-rap/2002/flc2002/pdf/flc2002.pdf.

Folberg, J. (1984). Custody overview. In J. Folberg (Ed.), *Joint custody and shared parenting* (pp. 3–10). Washington, DC/New York: Bureau of National Affairs/Guilford Press.

Franklin, R., & Hibbs, B. (1980). Child custody in transition. *Journal of Marriage and Family Therapy, 3,* 285–91.

Frederick, L., & Tilley, J. (2001). *Effective intervention in domestic violence cases: Context is* everything. Minneapolis: Battered Women's Justice Project.

Geffner, R.A., Jaffe, P.G., & Suderman, M. (Eds.). (2000). *Children exposed to domestic violence: Current issues in research, intervention, prevention, and policy development.* Binghamton, NY: Haworth Maltreatment & Trauma Press.

Gould, J.W. (1998). *Conducting scientifically crafted child custody evaluations.* Thousand Oaks, CA: Sage.

Gould, J.W. (2006). *Conducting scientifically crafted child custody evaluations* (2nd ed.). Sarasota, FL: Professional Resource Exchange.

Government of Canada's Response to the Report of the Special Joint Committee on Child Custody and Access. (1999). *Strategy for Reform.* Ottawa: Department of Justice Canada.

House of Commons Canada, The Divorce Act, R.S.C., 1985.c.3, 2002, 16.2(1), p. 1.

Humphreys, J. (1993). Children of battered women. In J. Campbell & J. Humphreys (Eds.), *Nursing care of survivors of family violence* (pp. 107–19). St. Louis: Mosby.

Hunt, J., & Roberts, C. (2005). *Intervening in litigated contact: Ideas from other jurisdictions.* Family Policy Briefing no. 4. Oxford: University of Oxford, Department of Social Policy and Social Work.

Jaffe, P.G., Baker, L.L., & Cunningham, A.J. (Eds.). (2004). *Protecting children from domestic violence: Strategies for community intervention.* New York: Guilford Press.

Jaffe, P.G., Crooks, C.V., & Bala, N. (2005). *Making appropriate parenting arrangements in* family violence cases: Applying the literature to identify promising practices. Ottawa: Department of Justice, Family, Children, and Youth Section, Justice, Canada.

Jaffe, P.G., & Geffner, R. (1998). Child custody disputes and domestic violence: Critical issues for mental health, social service, and legal professionals. In G. Holden, R. Geffner & E.N. Jouriles (Eds.), *Children exposed to marital violence: Research and applied issues* (pp. 371–408). Washington, DC: American Psychological Association.

Jaffe, P.G., Johnston, J.R., Crooks, C.V., & Bala, N. (2008). Custody disputes involving allegations of domestic violence: The need for differentiated approaches to parenting plans. *Family Court Review, 46*(3), 500–22.

Jaffe, P.G., Lemon, K.D., & Poisson, S.E. (2003). *Child custody and domestic violence: A call* for safety and accountability. Thousand Oaks, CA: Sage.

Johnson, M.P. (1995). Patriarchal terrorism and common couple violence: Two forms of violence against women. *Journal of Marriage and the Family, 57*(2), 283–94.

Johnston, J.R. (1994). High-conflict divorce. In The David and Lucille Packard Foundation (Eds.), *The future of children: Children and divorce* (pp. 165–82). Los Altos, CA: Packard Foundation.

Johnston, J.R. (1995). Research update: Children's adjustment in sole custody compared to joint custody families and principles for custody decision-making. *Family and Conciliation Courts Review, 31,* 282–89.

Johnston, J.R. (2006). A child-centred approach to high conflict and domestic violence families: Differential assessment and interventions. *Journal of Family Issues, 12*(1), 15–36.

Johnston, J.R., & Campbell, L. (1993). Parent–child relations in domestic violence families disputing custody. *Family and Conciliation Courts Review, 31,* 282–89.

Johnston, J.R., & Roseby, V. (1997). *In the name of the child: A developmental approach to understanding and helping children of conflicted and violent divorce.* New York: Free Press.

Johnston, J.R., Roseby, V., & Kuehnle, K. (2010) *In the name of the child: A developmental approach to understanding and helping children of conflicted and violent divorce* (2nd ed.). New York: Springer Publishers.

Kelly, J.B. (1993). Current research on children's adjustment: No simple answers. *Family and Conciliation Courts Review, 31*(1), 29–49.

Kelly, J.B. (1994). The determination of child custody. In The David and Lucille Packard Foundation (Eds.), *The future of children: Children and divorce* (pp. 121–42). Los Altos, CA: Packard Foundation.

Kelly, J.B. (2002). Psychological and legal interventions for parents and children in custody and access disputes: Current research and practice. *Virginia Journal of Social Policy & the Law, 10,* 129–63.

Kelly, J.B. (2007). Children's living arrangements following divorce: Risk and resilience perspectives. *Family Relations, 52,* 352–62.

Kelly, J.B. (2012). Risk and protective factors associated with child and adolescent adjustment following separation and divorce: Social science applications. In K. Kuehnle & L. Drozd (Eds.), *Parenting plan evaluations: Applied research for the family court* (pp. 49–84). New York: Oxford University Press.

Kelly, J.B., & Lamb, M.E. (2000). Using child development research to make appropriate custody and access decisions for young children. *Family and Conciliation Courts Review, 38,* 297–311.

Kerr, G., & Jaffe, P.G. (1999). Legal and clinical issues in child custody disputes involving domestic violence. *Canadian Family Law Quarterly, 17*(1), 1–37.

LaViolette, A. (2005). *Assessing dangerousness in domestic violence cases.* San Jose, CA: California Statewide Dispute Resolution Institute.

Lemon, N.K.D. (1999). The legal system's response to children exposed to domestic violence. In The David and Lucille Packard Foundation (Eds.), *The future of children: Children and divorce* (pp. 67–83). Los Altos, CA: Packard Foundation.

Leonoff, A., & Montague, R. (1996). *Guide to child custody assessments.* Scarborough, ON: Carswell.

McDonald, J. (1986). Historical perspectives of custody and access disputes: A lawyer's view. In R. Parry, E. Broder, E. Schmitt, E. Saunders & E. Hood (Eds.), *Custody disputes: Evaluation and intervention* (pp. 9–22). Lanham, MD: Lexington.

McIntosh, J.E. (2003). Children living with domestic violence: Research foundations for early intervention. *Journal of Family Studies, 9*(2), 219–34.

Melton, G., Petrila, J., Poythress, N., & Slobogin, C. (2007). *Psychological evaluations for the courts: A handbook for mental health professionals and lawyers.* New York: Guilford Press.

Morag, T., Rivkin, D., & Sorek, Y. (2012). Child participation in the family courts—Lessons from the Israeli pilot project. *International Journal of Law, Policy, and the Family, 26*(1), 1–30.

Neilson, L.C. (2001). *Spousal abuse, children, and the legal system: Final report for Canadian* Bar Association, Law for the Future Fund. Muriel McQueen Fergusson Center for Family Violence Research, University of New Brunswick. Retrieved from: http://www.unb.ca/fredericton/arts/centres/mmfc/_resources/pdfs/team2001.pdf.

Neilson, L.C. (2004a). Assessing mutual partner-abuse claims in child custody and access cases. *Family Court Review, 42*(3), 411–38.

Neilson, L.C. (2004b). Children and family violence in the New Brunswick law: How responsibilities get lost in rights. In M.L. Stirling, C.A. Cameron, N. Nason-Clark & B. Miedema (Eds.), *Understanding abuse: Partnering for change* (pp. 135–53). Toronto: University of Toronto Press.

Neilson, L.C. (2009). *Domestic violence and family law in Canada: A handbook for* judges with introductory comments by Justice John F. McGarry, Superior Court, Ontario. Ottawa: National Judicial Institute, EBB. In electronic format, this book is identified as Domestic Violence Family Law.

Parkinson, P. (2010). Changing policies regarding separated fathers in Australia. In M. Lamb (Ed.), *The role of the father in child development* (5th ed.), (pp. 518–614). Wiley and Sons.

Report of the Special Joint Committee on Child Custody and Access: Strategy for Reform. (1999, May). Retrieved from: http://www.justice.gc.ca/eng/pi/fcy-fea/lib-bib/rep-rap/1999/sjcarp02/pdf/sjcarp02.pdf.

Rhoades, H. (2002). The rise and rise of shared parenting laws: A critical reflection. *Canadian Journal of Family Law, 19,* 75–113.

Rhoades, H. (2006). Yearning for law: Fathers' groups and family law reform in Australia. In R. Collier & S. Sheldon (Ed.), *Fathers' rights activism and law reform in comparative perspective* (pp. 125–46). Oxford: Hart Publications.

Royce, D., Thyer, B.A., & Padgett, D.K. (2010). *Program evaluation: An introduction.* Belmont, CA: Wadsworth Publishing.

Schmitz, C. (2011, July 15). Divorce Act reforms could be coming down the pipe. *Lawyers Weekly,* vol. 31, 11, 13.

Schnall, E.M. (1999). Custody and access and the impact of domestic violence. *Canadian Family Law Quarterly, 18,* 99–221.

Scott, E. (1992). Pluralism, parental preference, and child custody. *California Law Review, 80,* 615.

Shaffer, M. (2004). The impact of wife abuse on child custody and access decisions. *Canadian Family Law Quarterly, 22*(1), 85–148.

Shaffer, M., & Bala, N. (2004). The role of family courts in domestic violence: The Canadian experience. In G.P. Jaffe, L.L. Baker & A.J. Cunningham (Eds.), *Protecting children from domestic violence: Strategies for community intervention* (pp. 171–87). New York: Guilford Press.

Smart, C., Neale, B., & Wade, A. (2001). *The changing experience of childhood: Families and divorce.* Oxford, UK: Polity Press.

Smith, A.B., Taylor, N.J., & Tapp, P. (2003). Rethinking children's involvement in decision-making after parental separation. *Childhood, 10*(2), 201–16.

Special Joint Committee of the Senate and the House of Commons on Custody and Access. (1998). *For the sake of the children.* Ottawa: Parliament of Canada.

Stahl, P.M. (1994). *Conducting child custody evaluations: A comprehensive guide.* Thousand Oaks, CA: Sage.

Stahl, P.M. (1999). *Complex issues in child custody evaluations.* Thousand Oaks, CA: Sage.

Taylor, N.J., Smith, A.B., & Tapp, P. (1999). *Children, family law, and family conflict: Subdued voices.* Retrieved from: http://www.lawyers.org.nz/conference/pdf%20files/S13%20papers.pdf.

Thompson, R.A., & Amato, P.R. (1999). (Eds.). *The post divorce family: Children, parenting, and society.* Thousand Oaks, CA: Sage.

UNGA Resolution. (1989, November 20). UN Doc a/res/44/25. The United Nations adopted the Convention on the Rights of the Child in 1989.

Ursel, J. (1992). *Private lives, public policy: 100 years of state intervention in the family.* Toronto: Women's Press.

Wolfe, D.A., & Jaffe, P.G. (1999). Domestic violence and children. In The David and Lucille Packard Foundation (Eds.), *The future of children: Children and divorce* (pp. 133–44). Los Altos, CA: Packard Foundation.

Zorza, J. (1996). Protecting the children in custody disputes when one parent abuses the other. *Clearinghouse Review, 29*(12), 1113–27.

14

VIOLENCE AGAINST WOMEN
A STRUCTURAL PERSPECTIVE

COLLEEN LUNDY

INTRODUCTION

Gender-based violence against women, although it is a serious human rights abuse worldwide, has yet to be fully addressed. In its 1993 declaration, the United Nations defined violence against women "as any act of gender-based violence that results in physical, sexual or psychological harm or suffering to women, including threats of such acts, coercion, or arbitrary deprivations of liberty, whether occurring in public or private life" (p. 444). Such violence takes a number of forms, including physical and sexual assault, stalking, sexual harassment, dowry-related violence, and genital mutilation. This chapter focuses primarily on physical, sexual, and emotional abuse in intimate heterosexual relationships.

Forty years ago, men's coercive control and brutalization of women was not an issue within the women's movement, let alone the larger society.[1] In these four decades, the women's movement mounted an organized resistance to and mobilization against violence, and demanded that the government respond to address the problem. These efforts heightened public awareness of the severity of the problem and prompted the state to reform the criminal justice system and establish a network of shelters and other services for women and their children, as well as programs for men who have been abusive. These developments have taken place in the context of the broader women's movement and the struggle for women's equality. While much has been accomplished, women still remain subordinate to men in economic and social terms, and the violence against them has continued unabated. This inequality is all the more pervasive and harmful when interlocked with relations of racism, colonialism, and class exploitation. Women are particularly vulnerable in the current global capitalist economic restructuring and financial crisis and the subsequent erosion of the welfare state and increasing economic, social, and political instability.

In the first section of this chapter, I outline the prevalence and nature of gender-based violence in Canada and include some international comparisons, as well as a critical analysis of violence surveys and measures. In the next section, I discuss theoretical explanations for understanding the dynamics of male violence against women and explore the connection between violence and social and economic conditions. I then critically examine the organizing efforts of the anti-violence movement and the response of the state. Finally, I offer some thoughts on the challenges facing the struggle to end violence against women.

PREVALENCE AND NATURE OF GENDER-BASED VIOLENCE

In Canada, there is now ample research that documents the incidence and nature of gendered violence. However, statistics often underestimate the degree and severity of violence that women endure. Brian Vallée, an award-winning journalist and author, alarmed at the number of women murdered by their male partners, identified the violence as the "War on Women." Yet, unlike the casualties of other wars, women remain invisible. Vallée makes a revealing comparison:

> In the same seven year period when 4,588 U.S. soldiers and policemen were killed by hostiles or by accident, more than 8,000 women— nearly twice as many—were shot, stabbed, strangled, or beaten to death by intimate males in their lives. In Canada, compared to the 101 Canadian soldiers and police officers killed, more than 500 women— nearly *five times* as many—met the same fate. (Vallée, 2007, p. 29; emphasis in the original)

In 2009, in Canada sixty-eight women were murdered by a current or former partner or boyfriend—one approximately every five days (Beattie & Cotter, 2010).

Victimization statistics are generally understood as underreporting woman abuse since fewer than one-quarter of partner assaults are reported to the police (Brennan, 2011). As in previous General Social Surveys (GSS), although the findings report comparable rates of violence experienced by men (6.0 percent) and women (6.4 percent), the risks and consequences of violence were significantly more severe for women (Brennan, 2011). These figures are in stark contrast to who actually uses services, given the number of women who enter shelters to escape violence. There are currently 593 shelters for abused women in Canada and between April 1, 2009, and March 31, 2010, there were over 64,500 admissions, representing a 5.0 percent increase from 2007/2008 (Burczycka & Cotter, 2011).

A number of researchers have thoroughly critiqued the gender symmetry that was found by the GSS researchers (Jiwani, 2002; Johnson & Dawson, 2011; DeKeseredy 2011). Methods of studying violence against women are varied and "the measurement tools one employs will determine the outcome of the study" (Johnson & Dawson, 2011, p. 37). Jiwani (2002) convincingly argues that "at a superficial level, the findings suggest that women and men are equally violent, thus feeding the backlash against the experiences and observations of front line workers, academics, and policy-makers who have long argued about the widespread prevalence of male violence" (p. 63). She concludes that the GSS does not have the sensitivity of the 1993 Violence against Women Survey (VAWS) and, as such, underestimates the gendered nature of violence.

The 1993 VAWS, the first national, federally funded survey of its kind in the world, provided comprehensive and disturbing data on the extent of violence against women in Canada based on a nationally representative probability sample. The VAWS methodology was groundbreaking in its design as a sensitive tool for measuring woman abuse. Until this survey was developed, the standard measure used to understand violence in intimate relationships was Murray Straus's Conflict Tactics Scale (CTS), which was largely concerned with all the small-scale arguments and fights in relationships (Straus, 1979). The VAWS was concerned with serious violence, and considered the full spectrum of coercive behaviours, including physical, emotional, and sexual abuse (Mann, 2003). The VAWS researchers randomly selected 12,300 women from across the ten provinces who were interviewed by telephone, in either French or English, regarding their adult experiences of sexual and physical assault by marital partners, dates, boyfriends, and strangers, as well as sexual harassment and their fear of urban violence.

The findings of the VAWS raised public awareness regarding the alarming prevalence of violence against women in Canada. One-half (51 percent) of all surveyed women had experienced at least one incident of sexual or physical assault since age sixteen. Sexual assault (39 percent of women) was even more common than physical assault (34 percent of women). Of the women who had ever lived with a male partner, 29 percent had been physically or sexually assaulted by him at some time in the relationship. Among women with disabilities or a disabling health concern, this increased to

39 percent. A weapon was used in 44 percent of these cases, and 45 percent of the women assaulted were physically injured. Despite the frequency and seriousness of the violence and the fact that 34 percent of the women feared for their lives, 22 percent of the women did not mention the violent incidents to anyone (Rogers, 1994).

Violence is also found in dating relationships. One-quarter (25 percent) of all women who were attending school at the time reported sexual or physical assault by a male date or boyfriend. With regard to violence outside of intimate relationships, 87 percent of women reported sexual harassment and of these, 51 percent of women reported sexual harassment by someone they knew. Young women, eighteen to twenty-four (14 percent), had three times the national average (4 percent) rate of violence perpetrated by a stranger (Rogers, 1994). In O'Sullivan, Byers, and Finkelman's (1998) research with Canadian college students, 18.5 percent of men and 42.5 percent of women reported sexual coercion from a partner of the opposite sex.

In addition to such national surveys, many researchers have focused on the diversity of women's experience with woman abuse. A number of studies suggest that immigrant women are particularly vulnerable to domestic violence, principally if their immigration status is undocumented or non-permanent through a sponsorship program (Fong, 2010; Orloff, 2000). A report by the Canadian Council on Social Development focuses on victimization rates among immigrant and visible minority women surveyed in the 1999 GSS and observed that 10.5 percent of immigrant women experienced emotional or financial abuse (compared to 14 percent of other women), while 4.2 percent disclosed that they suffered from physical or sexual abuse (compared to 6.2 percent of other women). Only 10 percent of immigrant and visible minority women and 14 percent of other women reported the abuse to police. It is important to note that these findings do not include women who do not speak either official language, excluding a significant number of immigrant women and thereby underrepresent immigrant women's experience of violence (Smith, 2004).

Immigrant and refugee women who are experiencing violence by a partner face additional obstacles that place them at risk. For women who do not have permanent resident status, disclosing violence and leaving an abuser may have an impact on their immigration status. The immigration experience can also increase women's vulnerability because it tends to isolate them from family and friends (Bauer, Rodriguez, Quiroga & Flores-Ortiz, 2000). To make matters worse, women who are recent immigrants may not know about the support programs that are available for them and face language barriers when accessing these programs (Raj & Silverman, 2002). At times, norms and expectations of a woman's culture of origin can also increase her risk of violence and her reluctance to disclose abuse; these norms can include gender role ideology, a sense that domestic violence is a family issue, and the acceptability of male violence (Raj & Silverman, 2002). Smith (2004) reminds us that "Unique to the problems faced by immigrant and visible minority women is the fact that they are not only leaving their partners, they may also have to leave their cultural community, extended family and faith communities as well" (p. 26). Women who are recent immigrants may also lack awareness that in Canada, woman abuse is a crime and are reluctant to leave because of fear of deportation (Dutton, Orloff & Hass, 2000). All of these factors are exacerbated in Canadian society, which views many immigrant cultures with a degree of hostility and distrust. In these circumstances a woman's disclosure of abuse threatens to reinforce dominant racist views of non-Canadian cultures and may inhibit disclosure (Raj & Silverman, 2002; Razack, 1999).

Aboriginal women also experience high rates of violence in their intimate relationships. Although underrepresented in national surveys, a number of Aboriginal researchers/writers state that family violence among Aboriginal peoples has reached epidemic proportions (Brownbridge, 2003; Proulx & Perrault, 2000; McGillivray & Comaskey, 1999). Prompted by the urgency of the situation, in 2011 the Standing Committee on the Status of Women produced the report *Call into the night: An overview of violence against Aboriginal women* (Fry, 2011). The report indicates that the rate of intimate violence for Aboriginal women (24 percent) continues to be more than three times higher than the rate for non-Aboriginal women (7 percent) and represents the most severe forms of violence. Equally alarming is that Aboriginal women are seven times more likely to be murdered than their non-Aboriginal sisters (Fry, 2011). In the last thirty years alone, more than 520 Aboriginal women have been reported missing or have been murdered (Amnesty International, 2009).

In understanding violence in the lives of Aboriginal women, the discussion necessarily begins with an examination of the historical context of colonization and residential schools (Proulx & Perrault, 2000; Razack, 1999; Fry, 2011). It is believed that some Aboriginal men have internalized white devaluation of women and themselves. As a way of easing the feelings of self-devaluation, some Aboriginal men seek to gain power over their partners (Brownbridge, 2003). "The colonization process and the Indian Act have dispossessed Aboriginal women of their inherent role as leaders in their own nation and have created a serious imbalance in Aboriginal society that accords Aboriginal men greater political, social and economic influence and opportunity than Aboriginal women" (Canadian Panel on Violence against Women, 1993, p. 148). In Nunavut, the role of men was changed more dramatically than for women by the introduction of Euro-centric values, and men are thought to be "lost between two cultures," contributing to male violence against women (Fry, 2011). Aboriginal status or background alone is one of fourteen social determinants that shape physical and mental health (Mikkonen & Raphael, 2011). The current reality of racial discrimination and marginalization, compounded by abject poverty, are all contributing factors in the continuing violence that Aboriginal women experience in Canada today.

In addition to understanding the experiences of diverse groups of women, researchers have also attempted to understand various types of woman abuse. The most detailed information on sexual assault is available from the 1993 VAWS in which researchers found that 39 percent of the Canadian women who were surveyed reported having had at least one experience of sexual assault since the age of sixteen. The definition of sexual assault used in this survey conformed to the Criminal Code definitions by asking about unwanted sexual touching and violent sexual attacks. In the VAWS, sexual assaults against women were twice as likely to involve familiar men as they were strangers, indeed 21 percent of all reported sexual assaults in 1993 were perpetrated by women's partners. Reported sexual assault increased by 152 percent between 1983 and 1993: in 1983, 11,932 incidents of sexual assault (forty-eight per 100,000 people) were reported to the police, while in 1993 there were 34,764 incidents reported (121 incidents per 100,000 population). Similarly, non-sexual assault reported to the police increased by 62 percent in the same period from 498 to 805 per 100,000. Johnson (2002) suggests that these increases can be explained, in part by legislative changes and legal reforms that may have increased awareness and publicity of violence against women, and women's increased confidence in the criminal justice system. She also suggests that changes in the attitudes of police could have increased their willingness to apprehend alleged perpetrators. However, Johnson (2002) points out that these reforms exist in a social context that included the changing status of women (social, economic, and political), the development of special investigation units in police stations, the growth of sexual assault centres, and the establishment of sexual assault/domestic violence centres within the hospitals. Thus, the increase in reported violence may not represent a change in the frequency of acts of violence or changes in legislation, but may be a reflection of how society perceives sexual assault and how we, as a society, respond to violence.

Financial abuse tends to exacerbate the negative effects of all types of abuse and is often overlooked by support people and professionals. Almost inevitably, domestic violence decreases a survivor's access to resources that might help her to cope with or leave the relationship. Financially abusive partners may prevent women from working outside the home, control all the major financial decisions, demand that women account for all of their spending, force women to hand over their paycheques, and/or prevent women from having any personal financial resources. Women have been found to be four times more likely than men to be denied access to family incomes and are twice as likely to have their possessions destroyed (Jiwani, 2002). Financial abuse is also a significant concern for people who are older. The GSS reported that 6 percent of older women experience financial abuse (Besserer, Brzozowski, Hendrick, Ogg & Trainer, 2001). By contrast, having their own income tends to improve women's ability to develop social contacts outside the home and to access social supports. This, in turn, often allows women to avoid returning to their abusive partners or at least to stay away longer to recuperate from abuse (Waldrop & Roesick, 2004).

In considering the aforementioned statistics, it is important to keep in mind that surveys such as the GSS and VAWS, because of their inherent limitations, tend to underreport the prevalence of violence against women. In the case of telephone sampling, a number of women are automatically excluded from participation. These include women without telephones, women who are not proficient in either official language or who have hearing or speech difficulties, and women who are in institutional settings.

Family Violence vs. Woman Abuse

A structural analysis of woman abuse also offers a framework for entering a central debate within the literature on woman abuse. This debate has been about the accuracy, sensitivity, and appropriateness of various tools to measure violence against women and the wide array of findings that result from the use of different tools. Researchers in the field of intimate violence have tended to organize on one of two sides of the debate. In the first camp are feminist researchers who utilize both qualitative and quantitative methods and have drawn largely on samples from shelters, emergency rooms, and women-centred surveys, and have used well-developed questionnaires that attend to the context, consequences, and varied nature of violence against women (Dobash & Dobash, 1979, 1992; Johnson, 1995). In the opposing camp are family violence researchers who are "rooted in a sociological paradigm that privileges quantitative methodologies" (Mann, 2003, p. 44). The increase in family violence research has been largely state driven, but also reflects a backlash against the women's movement (DeKeseredy & Schwartz, 2003). Family violence research is traditionally carried out through broad population surveys and focuses on incidents of abuse between couples using the Conflict Tactics Survey (CTS) (Straus, 1979; Archer, 1999, 2000; McFarlane, Wilson, Malecha & Lemmey, 2000).

Although I have overstated the division between these two "camps," the findings of each group of researchers have significant political implications. Feminist researchers have found that intimate violence is largely perpetrated by men against women, whereas family violence researchers have found the rates to be relatively evenly distributed among men and women. For example, Statistics Canada uses an adapted CTS in the GSS and reported that in 2004, 7 percent of women and 6 percent of men reported at least one incident of partner violence between 1999 and 2004 (Milhorean, 2005).

In recent years a number of researchers have tried to create a useful middle ground to understand the different findings between those carrying out family violence research and woman abuse research (Anderson, 1997; Johnson, 1995; Johnson & Pottie Bunge, 2001; Mann, 2003; Johnson, 2006). However, this shift did not occur until a great deal of work was done to challenge the CTS and what it failed to account for in its measurement of violence. The CTS comprises eighteen items designed to measure interpersonal conflict in family relations. Notably, it omits sexual violence and ignores the inequality in gendered relationships and the motives, intentions, and consequences of violence (DeKeseredy, 2011; Kimmel, 2002; Dobash & Dobash, 1992; Wilson & Daly, 1992). CTS statistics also obscure the disparity in the injuries that are incurred as a result of intimate violence or the economic inequalities experienced by women, which often leave women with no other choice than to use a shelter. In addition, rates of sexual assault and femicide show clear gender imbalances, supporting the argument that there is no gender symmetry in the consequences of intimate violence (Dobash & Dobash, 1992). The CTS counts acts of violence outside of a context that explores the motivation, circumstances, and impact of the violence (Kimmel, 2002). Consequently, when using this measure, it is difficult to know who initiated the violence and whether or not the woman was responding in self-defence or anger toward an abusive partner. Because women are, on average, smaller and less strong than men, a punch from a man will most likely cause more injuries than a punch from a woman. These critiques have resulted in a number of adaptations to the CTS, including the feminist-modified version that was used in the 1993 VAWS.

The VAWS was a significant step in trying to combine a feminist method with a quantitative scale. The research methods used in this study showed a greater sensitivity to the concerns of women who might be in unsafe conditions than any previous survey tools. Methods were developed in consultation with survivors of violence, academics, and people in the community. Such a collaborative approach ensured the development of indicators that would provide more accurate information about woman abuse. Interviewers were trained to understand the dynamics of violence and to recognize if a woman was feeling threatened when talking on the phone. They were also prepared to provide guidance on safety planning and referrals to support services in the event that the woman was currently being abused. Women were given a toll-free number in case they wanted to call back at some point or wanted to confirm the legitimacy of the survey. As explored in the opening of this chapter, this refined technique revealed dramatic rates of woman abuse, far in excess of what had been found with earlier statistical surveys.

Another important turning point in the debate happened in 1995 when Michael Johnson tried to unpack different "types" of violence. He is the first to acknowledge that his work built on earlier research, which had attempted such classifications (Johnson, 1995). That said, Johnson's research has been used extensively to make sense of different statistical findings from CTS-based and woman abuse research (Anderson, 1997; Kimmel, 2002; Mann, 2003). Specifically, he identified two types of violence against women. The first, "common couple violence," describes those acts of physical aggression that did not seem part of a general pattern of control, but arose as a result of "a specific argument in which one or both of the partners lash out physically" (Johnson & Ferraro, 2000, p. 949). The second type of violence, "patriarchal terrorism," is one tactic in a more general pattern of control. The violence is motivated by a wish to exert general control over one's partner (Johnson, 1995). Johnson argues that general population surveys, using tools like CTS, often captured rates of common couple violence. However, in surveys of women in emergency rooms and shelters, feminist researchers were measuring patriarchal terrorism. Thus, he argued that while there is some gender symmetry in common couple violence, the asymmetry occurs with patriarchal terrorism (Johnson, 1995). Johnson later revised and expanded his typology to include four types of partner violence (Kelly & Johnson, 2008; Johnson, 2006).

> In intimate terrorism, the individual is violent and controlling, the partner is not. In violent resistance, the individual is violent but not controlling; the partner is the violent and controlling one. In situational couple violence, although the individual is violent, neither the individual nor the partner is violent and controlling. In mutual violent control, the individual and the partner are violent and controlling. (Johnson, 2006, p. 1003)

While Johnson shifts the focus from the incident-specific definition of violence, Evan Stark comments that his "categories need to be flushed out empirically, theoretically elaborated, and refined" (Stark, 2006, p. 1019). It is unfortunate that Johnson uses gender-neutral language and his typology is likely to reinforce the myth that women are as abusive as men. Stark challenges Johnson's reference to mutual violence and argues that women

"typically lack the social facility to impose comprehensive levels of deprivation, exploitation and dominance found in CC [coercive control]," and adds
that he has "never encountered a case of CC with a female perpetrator and
male victim" (Stark, 2006, p. 1024).

Research has found that in the majority of cases, women use violence as a
means for retaliation or defence against their male partner's abuse. This is in
contrast to male violence, which, in the majority of cases, is aimed at maintaining or asserting control (Anderson & Umberson, 2001). Broader social
structures ensure that women cannot isolate or economically disadvantage
their male partners to the same degree that men can (Swan & Snow, 2002).
In both family violence and feminist studies, women are consistently the
party whose injuries are more severe and frequent, resulting in a consensus that women's violence and men's violence are both quantitatively and
qualitatively different (Mann, 2003).

When one explores statistics on violence in this manner, there are some
themes that continue to emerge: first, woman abuse is not an isolated problem of a few bad men and bad relationships, but rather represents a significant place on a continuum of violence that is exacerbated by and linked to
structural relations of sexism, racism, colonialism, class exploitation, and
globalization. Thus, while individual men may choose whether or not to
be violent in their relationships, these choices are shaped by broader social
relations and represent broader social tensions and struggles rather than
individual pathologies. Similar dynamics shape whether women are violent
in their relationships, both in terms of how they resist men's violence and/
or coercion, and in terms of whether they are aggressors in their relationships (Swan & Snow, 2002). Attending to the ways in which patriarchal
terrorism (woman abuse) and common couple violence differ, while also
understanding how they are both intersections of structural oppression,
helps us understand the complex ways violence in our society is one practice
through which gender difference and inequality are created and regulated
(Mann, 2003). Justification for such a perspective is highlighted in the lower
rates of abuse that we see in societies that rely less on patriarchal inequality and more on gender equality (Levinson, 1989). Similarly, we see higher
rates of woman abuse in communities that have been severely impacted by
the effects of globalization (Davis, 2000; Hall, 2002), by disaster (Enarson,
1999), and by war (Cockburn, 1998; Sajor, 1998).

Prevalence and Incidence of Woman Abuse in an International Context
While many countries have gathered statistics on the prevalence of violence against women, international comparisons have been difficult to carry
out. This is largely due to different methodological procedures (telephone

interviews, postal surveys, personal interviews, personally administered questionnaires), as well as variations in legal definitions of violence and the forms of abuse. The International Violence against Women Survey (IVAWS) was a Canadian initiative and involved comparative study with twenty-two participating countries around the world, including countries with low incomes and countries in transition (Ollus, 2001). The survey was built by Statistics Canada VAWS, and Holly Johnson, the lead researcher in the VAWS study and former chief of research at the Canadian Centre for Justice Statistics, was an active member of the team. This study had the potential to provide direct comparisons of woman abuse rates, but it was stalled (for fiscal reasons) and has never been implemented. Despite the limitations of existing data, an exploration of international statistics draws attention to the global dynamics of violence against women.

In 2000, the National Violence against Women Survey (NVAWS), a study of domestic violence, was conducted in the United States. Unlike the VAWS, the NVAWS interviewed both women and men, and identified those who were in same-sex relationships. Not surprisingly, women experience more intimate partner violence than men: 24.8 percent of women versus 7.6 percent of men reported being physically assaulted and/or raped by a partner at some time in their life. The survey also offers an interesting comparison of intimate violence rates among women in same-sex and opposite-sex relationships and suggests that women in heterosexual relationships were almost twice as likely to report being assaulted by a partner than were women in same-sex relationships: 20.3 percent versus 11.4 percent. However, in the case of same-sex–partnered men, 15.4 percent reported rape, physical assault, or stalking by a male partner, while 7.7 percent of men in opposite-sex relationships did so. The findings suggest that men are much more likely than women to be violent in intimate relationships (Tjaden & Thoennes, 2000). Such findings have led researchers to consider the links between masculinity and violence, which will be reviewed later in this chapter.

In 2002, the World Health Organization (WHO) drew on forty-eight population-based studies from around the world to conclude that 10–64 percent of women (depending on the study) reported being physically assaulted by a male partner (2002). The WHO found that most victims endured multiple acts of violence and varying types of abuse (sexual, emotional, psychological) over extended periods of time. The same review of international research revealed that between 40 percent and 70 percent of female murder victims were killed by their husband or boyfriend.

Throughout the world, factors associated with a man's risk of assaulting his female partner include youthfulness, having a low income and low academic achievement, witnessing abuse against women in his home of origin, excessive alcohol use, and/or being involved in aggressive or delinquent behaviour as an adolescent. While violence is a reality for women regardless of ethnicity, race, social class, educational achievement level, and age, there are factors that place women at risk. Researchers have found that women are most vulnerable in societies where "there are marked inequalities between men and women, rigid gender roles, cultural norms that support a man's right to inflict violence on his intimate partner and weak sanctions against such behaviour" (WHO, 2002, p. 16). Human Rights Watch (2000) paints a grim picture in their update five years after the United Nations World Conference on Women in Beijing, China. Their report on six countries—Jordan, Pakistan, Peru, Russia, South Africa, and the United States—show that rates of violence against women are not only high, but are "fueled all too often by the indifference of state officials and the failure to seriously investigate and prosecute cases of violence" (p. 1). Observers reported that women in all six countries surveyed continue to face overwhelming challenges when trying to secure adequate responses from police, health care providers, and legal systems after an incident of domestic, community, and/or sexual violence.

While violence against women is pervasive, it is not universal. Anthropologist David Levinson (1989) conducted the first international comparison of wife assault and established cross-cultural difference in the degree, frequency, context, and responses to violence. In his study of 120 cultural groups from sixty distinct cultural and geographic regions around the world, Levinson found sixteen societies to be free of family violence (wife assault, sibling violence, and child abuse). One such social group is the Central Thai, approximately 10 million people who speak the central Thai dialect and are predominantly Buddhist, who live in central and southern Thailand, primarily in rural communities. He was surprised that there was no division of labour by sex—both men and women plough fields, tend to children, participate in boat races, share property equally, and conduct business deals. Levinson concludes that violence will be more common in societies where it is considered acceptable to control conflicts through violence and where women experience economic inequality, male control over their lives, divorce restrictions, and have the prime responsibility for child-rearing.

COSTS AND CONSEQUENCES OF WOMAN ABUSE

The individual and social costs of woman abuse are extensive. The World Health Organization (2002) reports that, around the world, woman abuse has been linked to physical injuries and death, gastrointestinal disorders, chronic pain syndrome, depression, suicidal behaviour, gynecological disorders, unwanted pregnancy, premature labour and birth, as well as sexually transmitted diseases and HIV/AIDS. They also suggest that woman abuse makes it harder for women to perform well at work, increases the days they are absent, and makes it more difficult to maintain employment. In sum, woman abuse severely limits women's participation in society as a whole.

In Canada, researchers involved with the VAWS found that 40 percent of the abused women reported requiring medical attention as a result of the abuse. They reported that 45 percent of the assaults resulted in injuries, including bruises, cuts, scratches, or burns, and broken bones (Rogers, 1994). Researchers have found that, on average, 40 percent of women in emergency rooms are victims of woman abuse, and 10 percent of women are repeatedly seen by emergency room physicians because of recurring assaults by a partner (Stark & Flitcraft, 1988). Significantly more women (3 percent) than men (0.4 percent) have been found to report needing medical attention as a result of their injuries (Straus & Gelles, 1990). Women were much more likely than men to report being fearful for themselves and their children, and to have depression, anxiety attacks, sleeping problems, and lowered self-esteem as a result of abuse (Johnson & Pottie Bunge, 2001).

In the VAWS, 39 percent of the women surveyed reported that their children witnessed the violence against them. Child witnessing can take on any number of forms, including seeing, hearing, or being directly involved in the violence. In addition, many children are witnesses to the aftermath of violence, which can be equally as traumatic (Edleson, 1999). Recently, researchers have found that this exposure to violence against women and its aftermath can have negative long-term effects on children's emotional, cognitive, and behavioural functioning (Jaffe, Suderman & Geffner, 2000; Edleson, 1999; Smith, Berthelsen & O'Connor, 1997; James, 1994). These effects can exhibit themselves in behaviours that include acting out (i.e., temper tantrums, aggression, cruelty to animals, bullying) and internalizing behaviours (i.e., headaches, anxiety, sleep disturbances, social withdrawal, and depression) (Pepler, Catallo & Moore, 2000). In the long term, witnessing violence may increase a child's risk of becoming violent or being subject to another's violence (Dutton, 2000).

In Canada, government officials have drawn on a number of studies to conclude that woman abuse exerts a cumulative cost of $4.2 billion per year in terms of social services, criminal justice, labour, employment, medical costs, and education (Health Canada, 2002). In the health system alone, costs are estimated to be more than $1.5 billion per year, which includes lost time at work, acute medical and dental services, and treatment in hospitals, transition homes, etc. (Day, 1995). Thus, while the most significant consequences of woman abuse are borne by the individual women and children living in these violent situations, the continued existence of violence against women exacts a social and economic cost on us all. The outcome of violence in a relationship can, of course, be fatal for some women.

While newspaper headlines may create the image of a plague of stranger violence, statistics suggest an alternative reality. In a study of crime in Winnipeg, the Canadian Centre for Policy Alternatives (2000) found that 78 percent of crime reports involved people who knew one another. What is interesting is that despite the clear preponderance of intimate violence over stranger violence, women in general remain more afraid of strangers than their partners. A majority (60 percent) of Canadian women are fearful of walking alone after dark in their neighbourhoods. Urban victimization surveys in Canada and the United States have found that women are far more afraid than men to be outside in their own neighbourhoods at night (Gordon & Riger, 1989). This brings to light the complex ways in which patriarchy (a social system based upon male dominance) works to discipline women's lives (Koskela, 1997). While the fear of violence is sustained through dramatic reports of the stranger that all women should be afraid of, domestic violence is constructed as something women can control by avoiding abusive men. As such, women's public activities are severely curtailed, and attention is drawn away from the private violence that many women face in silence.

This is not to say that stranger violence is not a tragic reality for Canadian women. The VAWS found that 23 percent of women aged eighteen and over were physically assaulted by a stranger, and 19 percent were sexually assaulted (Johnson, 1996). For Aboriginal women and women working in the sex trade, violence remains a pervasive risk, as stories from Robert Picton's farm in British Columbia highlight. Women in the sex trade tend to be those who have also faced other forms of victimization—child sexual abuse, child physical abuse (Nixon, Tutty, Downe, Gorkoff & Ursel, 2002). As workers, they also face significant levels of violence from pimps, customers, police, professionals, and members of the general public (Farley & Kelly, 2000; Nixon et al., 2002; Raphael & Shapiro, 2004). Significantly, women have stated that violence prevented them from leaving the sex trade (Nixon et al., 2002).

Amnesty International joined forces with the Native Women's Association of Canada (NWAC) to support their Sisters in Spirit campaign by documenting the experiences of indigenous families who have lost loved ones to violence against women (Amnesty International, 2009). Yet government, the media, and Canadian society remain silent. The ways in which stranger violence against Aboriginal women is undervalued by the judicial system is well documented in Sherene Razack's (2002) study of the murder of Pamela George. Razack's analysis of the legal process that responded to the murder of Ms. George gives further evidence to support the claims by Amnesty International Canada and the NWAC that Canadian society continues to undervalue the lives of Aboriginal women, particularly if they are poor and/or working in the sex trade.

Of course, it is not only sex trade workers and Aboriginal women who are at risk of stranger violence, though they bear a disproportionate amount of the risk. Middle-class white women also face the risk of stranger violence, as the death of Ardeth Wood demonstrates. Ardeth Wood was cycling on a well-used public trail during daylight, only to be brutally murdered. Her story and the stories of other public murders of women serve as a warning to all women not to inhabit the public spaces of their communities. Whatever the identity of the woman killed by random violence, these incidents remain as an even more powerful warning because they seldom result in the charge and incarceration of the random perpetrator.

UNDERSTANDING VIOLENCE AGAINST WOMAN

Theoretical Frameworks

I argue for a structural approach as a theoretical framework to guide analysis, practice, and policy responses in the area of gender violence. Through this approach, the problem of violence against women is rooted in broad social, economic, and political conditions and institutions. Weldon (2002) takes such a structural approach in the study of public policy in response to gender violence and examines the impact of social structures on the policy process. She states that a structural approach is the only way of explaining the dynamic interaction between social movements and political institutions. By using a structural framework for thinking through woman abuse, we can attend to the various social conditions that engender violence and create appropriate policy responses that do not blame victims or rely upon pathologization.

Central to an analysis of male violence, according to Susan Schechter (1982), is an understanding that "violence is individually willed yet socially constructed" (p. 238). Women and men internalize the sexism, classism, racism, and heterosexism that are embedded in social policies, attitudes, and laws. It is therefore important to examine individual and interpersonal factors within a political, economic, and social context and in view of the institutional and ideological structures that contribute to and support violence against women.

Patriarchy, Social Class, and Woman Abuse

Patriarchy, and the gender inequality it creates, has often been linked to violence against women (Dobash & Dobash, 1979). Hunnicutt (2009) argues that the "concept of patriarchy holds promise for theorizing violence against women because it keeps the theoretical focus on dominance, gender and power" (p. 553). In patriarchal societies, social structures and ideology support the dominance of men over women and rigidly defined gender roles. Families remain as a key institution within patriarchal society and women still take primary responsibility for the care of children and other family members, while men's primary responsibility is to their paid employment outside the home. Not only does this result in women's unequal economic power and economic dependence, but it also increases their isolation within the family. These types of social relationships increase women's vulnerability to financial abuse, emotional abuse, and physical and sexual violence.

Sociologist Robert Connell (1995a) sees violence against women as a broader problem than simply the social roles given to men and women. He suggests that we need to attend to how issues of power, violence, or material inequality shape gender inequality. By using the notion of "hegemonic masculinity," Connell (1995b) makes visible the ways in which masculinity is culturally produced as an ideology and an institution that achieves dominance over women and, at times, subordinates men. Messerschmidt (1993) concretizes this definition by understanding hegemonic masculinity as constituted "through work in the paid labour force, the subordination of women, heterosexism, and the driven and uncontrollable sexuality of men" (p. 82). Because there is not just one such configuration in any society's gender order, Connell, like Messerschmidt, also speaks in terms of masculinities. Gender is not fixed but ever transforming. Masculinity is also not a fixed entity and is "constructed and reconstructed in everyday interactions with others.... The masculinities of the labourer, the middle-class college student, and the middle manager are all constructed with different resources and different forms of violence is the result" (Johnson, 1996, p. 25). While there is a continual reconstitution and diversity of masculinity, there are dominant forms that significantly shape the choices men have regarding how they behave in society.

Interestingly, Connell (1995b) argues that while acts of violence are perpetrated by a relatively small number of men (who are statistically more likely to be economically marginalized), all men in all class positions benefit from these behaviours. Hall and Connell also understand individual acts of violence as grouped within larger, structural relations through which male dominance is maintained, including the gap between the wealth of men and women in most societies. Thus, patriarchy is secured on multiple fronts. Hall builds on Connell's work to show that the problem of male violence against other men in public and women in private is not only a function of patriarchy but is shaped by changes in the labour market. He posits that current economic relations have resulted in further marginal-izing traditional working-class men and women (Hall, 2002). Other writers have also noted that patriarchal privilege is not shared equally among all men, and in fact working-class men may more often resort to violence than either black or white men in higher social classes because there are few other resources available to achieve control over their intimate partners (Staples, 1982). Lynn Segal (1990) identifies class as a factor in understanding vio-lence against women by noting that "power in the home is often the only prerogative experienced by men daily overworked, humiliated by poverty, facing arbitrary discipline, degrading working conditions or perhaps racist abuse and the threat of violence from other men" (p. 28).

Since masculinity is often connected to men's roles as workers and income earners, unemployment can be devastating. As an unemployed twenty-four-year-old man stated: "I hate to be unemployed...a man with-out a job is a dead man to me...and every man needs a job...you need to be productive in some kind of way" (Kost, 1997, p. 103). The Violence against Women survey registered higher rates of violence against women in homes where there was unemployment, low family income, and low occu-pational status. Where joint incomes were less than $15,000, unemployed men had rates of violence twice as high as those in more affluent families and employed men. Messerschmidt (1993) holds that working-class men who have limited power in the workplace develop an emotional dependency on the household (partner), demanding nurturance, service, and comfort. This is not to suggest that men who have access to more secure incomes and social resources are never abusive. It is clear that it is not class identity per se that correlates with increased rates of domestic violence; rather, economic insecurity puts extra stress on the family and creates greater potential for disagreements and for those disagreements to escalate into violence.

Early research into domestic violence by Gelles (1972) and Straus, Gel-les, and Steinmetz (1980) found that the rate of violence is twice as high in blue-collar families as in white-collar families, suggesting that the stressors experienced by those living with economic insecurity have been affecting families for decades. McKendy's (1997) review of literature up to the late 1990s supports this finding. Smith (2004), in a representative sample in Toronto, found that unemployed husbands were twice as likely as fully employed husbands to have attacked their wives during the survey year. Summarizing US research studies, Richmond (2001) adds support to the premise that domestic violence is more prevalent among the poor and argues for the importance of welfare reform policy. In her review of the research, she found that 15–30 percent of welfare recipients are current victims of partner abuse, and 50–60 percent experienced domestic violence at some point in their adult lives. It is important to offer one cautionary note when reading such statistics. It is clear that the gaze of law enforcement and academic researchers is often disproportionately focused on people in lower income brackets, particularly those living in poverty. In addition, people living in poverty endure more police surveillance and live in housing structures that afford much less privacy than those living in wealthier neighbourhoods. Such inequalities are likely to result in a distorted representation of the ways domestic violence affects working-class families.

Richmond (2001) concludes that redistributing social resources to decrease social inequality will subsequently reduce violence against women. However, these material changes are not sufficient on their own and must also be accompanied by broad ideological changes. Paulo Freire (1990) acknowledged the power of ideology in shaping attitudes and views and spoke of his own efforts to unlearn sexism. Although he was fully committed to women's equality, he understood that his struggle as a Latin American male was influenced by a sexist culture and, that while he could be progressive in discourse, his actions could be reactionary. He concluded that his attempts to be non-sexist and to lessen the difference between what he said and what he did would require a "lifetime obsession." Freire's reflection on integrating gender analysis into his broader liberation project resonates with the solutions feminists pose to ending violence against women. Clatterbaugh (1997) argues that in order for sexism to be eliminated and violence against women stopped, material change must occur—changes in the relations of production. "The power relations that teach men to be masculine make for good workers and authoritarian managers. And sexism survives in part because it benefits men and facilitates capitalist production" (p. 135). These thinkers suggest that the path to challenging the inequities that sustain violence against women involves a dramatic change wherein relations of equality are society's sustaining force. This requires an economic and social transformation.

Uncertainty in the Context of Neo-liberalism and Globalization

Global capitalism is in crisis; the economic recession that began in 2008 in the United States and quickly spread to Europe is now noted as the worst economic downturn since 1929 and the Great Depression. This situation is compounded by neo-liberalism and the transformation of social structures, institutional arrangements, and economic policies and practices along market lines. This involves deregulation, privatization, spending cuts, wage controls, and the elimination of trade barriers. Unemployment, part-time jobs, limited contracts, and casual jobs are now a reality for many. The current recession has resulted in closed businesses, job losses, the foreclosure of homes, and devastating stress in the lives of individuals and their families.

Women continue to earn less than men; are overrepresented among the poor and unemployed; are absent from positions of decision making, whether in government, business, or organizations; and endure severe forms of violence in their communities, workplaces, and homes. The nature of women's inequality can be understood by examining women's role in the labour force and in the home—women's underpaid and unpaid work.

In 2008, 82 percent of women between twenty-five and forty-four, the child-bearing years, were in the paid workforce. However, women who work full-time and year round earn only seventy-one cents for every dollar a man takes home. For women in the overall job market, it is sixty-three cents. Women are more likely to find themselves in precarious forms of work; they are 60 percent of those making minimum wage, and over four times as many women as men are in permanent part-time jobs and three times as many are in temporary part-time jobs. When they are unemployed, only 39 percent receive Employment Insurance benefits compared to 45 percent of their male counterparts (Townson, 2009).

Federal and provincial governments have abandoned their commitments to social and health programs, and have dramatically reduced the responsiveness of hospitals, the availability of affordable and safe housing, and the accessibility of education systems and community services. As a result, social needs are less often met by the state and more often constituted as the responsibility of the market and the family (McKeen & Porter, 2003). Overburdened public services are increasingly unable and unwilling to alleviate the inequalities that place women at risk of violence, and thereby force women to stay in abusive relationships. Such a restructuring has exacerbated the tensions from which violence in relationships occurs and places women, particularly women in poverty, women with disabilities, Aboriginal women, and women of colour, at increased risk for violence. In the first instance, the effects of neo-liberal globalization—namely, increased poverty, decreased social safety nets, and increasing labour instability—place added stress on families, increasing the risk of violence (Davis, 2000).

The rise of neo-liberalism and the resulting social and economic changes have been embodied by women who have increased their domestic labour while also being allocated to more "marginal and fragile positions within the labour market as the juggling of jobs, daycare, and other responsibilities becomes more difficult" (McKeen & Porter, 2003, p. 122). While women are increasingly picking up the slack of decreased home care services, hospital services, etc., issues such as accessible, affordable daycare are not even on the national agenda. Meanwhile, it is clear that programs such as universal daycare are instrumental in creating gender equality and alleviating some of the stress of poverty, which is an influential risk factor for violence against women.

There is also a punitive, regulatory tone to neo-liberal social policy changes that has resulted in many feminist interventions in the area of woman abuse being cut and/or co-opted into existing institutional structures, further regulating and marginalizing women. Mandatory charging is now being used to incarcerate women who have been violent as a means of self-defence (McMahon & Pence, 2003). In response to concerns about the impact that witnessing abuse has on children, Children's Aid Societies have the mandate to remove a woman's children if she is found to be unable to protect them from witnessing her partner's abusive behaviour (Kaufman Kantor & Little, 2003; Ontario Ministry of Community and Social Services, 2000). While this response recognizes the vulnerability of children who live in violent homes, it is an individualized assessment that does not account for the issues of poverty, etc., which may limit a woman's ability to protect her children. As a result, women who are victimized by their partners are sometimes further punished by the state, which assesses them as "bad" mothers. This punitive approach was highlighted in a recent report by Mosher et al. (2004), who conclude that "women who flee abusive relationships and turn to welfare seeking refuge and support find neither" (p. 79). At the very same time, the welfare system is: "readily exploitable by abusive men and enables rather than disables, their power and control. Their power and control is shored up when women return to, or can't leave, the relationship because they are unable to adequately provide for themselves and their children" (Mosher et al., 2004, p. 79).

These are often impossible choices for women: the system that demands she leave an abuser (who is more than likely the breadwinner) is unable to secure the resources that the breadwinner provides for the family. Put bluntly, women may be forced to choose between the emotional/physical abuse of a partner and the structural abuse of the state, represented by a life with inadequate shelter, income, and food (Health Canada, 1996; Sokoloff & Dupont, 2005). Not only this, but we find increasing restrictions on the opportunity for women to access education if they live on social assistance, which also obliges women to rely even further on the family, and possibly remain in a violent relationship (Fine & Weis, 2000). Labour instability in many Canadian communities increases women's vulnerability to violence. For example, when the fishery closed in the province of Newfoundland and Labrador, fishing communities faced unemployment and economic hardship. Barbara Parsons, conducting a report for the Fisherman, Food, and Allied Workers Union, visited twenty-seven communities and found that violence against women was a concern in the aftermath of the shutdown (Consultations with Women in the Newfoundland Fishery, 1994). Davis (2000) found similar experiences in her longitudinal study of a small southwest-coast fishing village in Newfoundland.

Individual and Interpersonal Factors Shaping Woman Abuse

While the social and political context that I have just described is central to the problem of woman abuse, there are many other factors that come into play in relationships where there is violence. There have been a number of theorists who study the way in which behaviour is learned from those who are influential in our lives. Research suggests that men who have experienced violence in their families of origin (witnessed or victimized) are more likely to be violent themselves (Straus, 1983; Straus et al., 1980). The VAWS found that men who witnessed their mothers being abused were three times as likely to be violent against their own wives as men who grew up in non-violent homes (Rogers, 1994). Also, women who observed violence against their mothers were more likely to be in abusive relationships, suggesting that we tend to replicate the behaviours that are most familiar. This is of concern since 39 percent of the cases of assault reported in the VAWS were witnessed by children. However, the fact that not all men who experience violence as boys are violent later, or that not all men who are violent have experienced violence as a child, suggests that there are many factors that shape our choices around using violence.

In addition to social learning, it has been shown that drugs and alcohol reduce people's inhibitions and are often a contributing factor to violent situations. The VAWS researchers found that in half of violent incidents, women reported the perpetrator was drinking, and these men were more likely than non-drinkers (65 percent vs. 40 percent) to engage in serious acts of violence. Women who live with male partners who are regular drinkers—at least four times a week—are three times more likely to be assaulted than women whose partners never drank (Rogers, 1994). In their study of the links between the use of alcohol, illicit drugs, and violence, Willson et al. (2000) found that daily drunkenness and/or illicit drug use dramatically increased a perpetrator's stalking behaviour and threats of abuse.

Learned behaviour and illicit drug and alcohol use are only a few of the myriad individual factors that shape how we respond to stressful situations, and thus our risks of violence. There are not one or even a few explanations of why intimate violence continues to pervade our society. The causal factors are many, as are the types of violence used and the experiences of people in violent relationships. In this section we have explored how the structures of society have an impact on our personal lives and have noted personal factors that also determine one's risk of violence and experience when living in or trying to leave a violent relationship. To develop effective responses to woman abuse, we need to have a complex, flexible, and context-specific understanding of violence in intimate relationships.

THE WOMEN'S MOVEMENT AND THE STATE

Canada has been lauded as a leader in responding to woman abuse. In her cross-national comparison of violence against women in thirty-six stable democracies, Laurel Weldon found that Canada and Australia moved most comprehensively and quickly in response to the problem of violence against women, Canada being the first and only country to take action in 1974 (Weldon, 2002). Weldon attributes this to the fact that, in Canada, there was both an autonomous and powerful women's movement that pressured for changes and a receptive and responsive government. Women advocates and activists connect male brutality against women with their subordinate position in society. To address this, they have consistently advocated for a comprehensive response to violence against women that includes adequate and stable funding for shelters and support services for women, a more responsive policing and criminal justice system, enhanced social programs and housing, and changes in women's employment opportunities and working conditions. The government response has been to engage women's organizations in a "consult and study" process and has provided minimal funding to a network of women's organizations while choosing to emphasize legal and policy changes. Increasingly over the years, the response to violence against women has become depoliticized, personalized, and largely situated within a criminal justice framework.

Insider-Outsider Partnerships

Weldon (2002) argues that, in Canada, "the women's movement was responsible for articulating the issue of violence against women, but the presence of a women's policy machinery made it possible for femocrats inside government to push for inclusion of violence against women on the decision agenda" (pp. 154–55). This multifaceted approach to social change was also identified by Sandra Preston (1999) in her review of Canadian policy interventions for the prevention of woman abuse. Preston sees the results of such an approach as both laudable and problematic as each group of women steered certain aspects of the violence against women agenda, leaving the state with significant room to create a system that meets their needs, at times to the detriment of women living in or leaving violent relationships.

A number of national organizations have been particularly visible within the women's anti-violence movement. In 1972, the National Action Committee on the Status of Women (NAC) was founded and quickly became the largest coalition of feminist organization in Canada and the most influential "outsider" representing the women's movement. Shelters and transition houses organized as an active and vocal movement to advocate for women's safety and equality. Since 1976 the Canadian Research Institute on the

Advancement of Women (CRIAW) has supported research on issues facing women. Later in 1985, the National Organization of Immigrant and Visible Minority Women of Canada (NOIVMWC) was established to advance equality for visible minority women, and in 1985 the DisAbled Women's Network Canada was organized to address issues of violence, accessibility, and employment for women with disabilities.

One of the primary insiders was the Canadian Advisory Council on the Status of Women (CACSW), formed by the federal government on the recommendation of the Royal Commission on the Status of Women.[2] Independent of government, the CACSW provided an "insider" voice for the women's movement to advise the government on women's issues and reported recommendations to Parliament through a minister. Provincial advisory councils were established and served to fund research projects and to advance the position of women across the country.

Regrettably, in the early 1990s, the government, citing a priority of reducing government spending, retracted its commitment to women's concerns and withdrew funding support for national organizations that were effectively lobbying for gender equality. In the case of the NAC, grants from the Secretary of State women's program, totalling $600,000 in the late 1980s, were reduced to $270,000 in 1993–94 and totally eliminated in 1998 (Hard times, 1994). Similarly, in 1993, the DisAbled Women's Network received only one-third of their expected funding from the Secretary of State and was forced to close its main office (Chouinard, 1999). Then in 1995 the Liberal government dismantled the CACSW as an independent council and placed its functions under Status of Women Canada.

Adamson, Briskin, and McPhail (1988), in their discussion of feminist organizing strategies, emphasize the importance of maintaining a tension between two key politics of change: "disengagement (desire to create alternative structures and ideologies based on a critique of the system and a standpoint outside of it) and mainstreaming (desire to reach out to the majority of the population with popular and practical feminist solutions to particular issues)" (p. 23). They argue that these two political practices often rely on each other with ambivalent effects:

> The funding practices of the state, on which so many women's organizations depend; the establishment of advisory commissions and women's councils that demonstrate change through bureaucracy; and the language of legislation, which often limits the actual benefits accruing to women, have all molded and to some extent undermined the struggle of women to make change. (pp. 153–54)

These developments reflect the contradictory actions of the state and the vulnerability of women's organizations and services that are supported by the state. Preston (1999) describes the problematic results of state intervention as most acute when the movement began to rely on state funding, which encouraged a problem management approach to violence against women, and later a fragmentation of services. A closer examination of state responses in regard to violence against women highlights this dilemma.

State Responses

Weldon qualifies her findings by stating that the responsiveness of a state does not automatically imply effectiveness of the actions. For example, while the Canadian government launched initiatives to study the problem and engage in consultation with women's groups, decisions were also made to drastically reduce funding to the very groups that provide front-line support and services to women.

The first national study of violence against women was initiated by the Canadian Advisory Council on the Status of Women, and the findings of the study conducted by Linda MacLeod were published in *Wife battering in Canada: The vicious circle,* in 1980. MacLeod reported that approximately one in ten married women was battered in Canada each year. In 1987, MacLeod published an update—Battered but not beaten—again supported by the Advisory Council on the Status of Women. Both reports were instrumental in placing violence against women on the public agenda.

However, it was the events of December 6, 1989, that turned the country's attention to the urgency of addressing gender violence. On that day Marc Lepine shot and killed fourteen women engineering students at École Polytechnique in Montreal because he saw them as feminists who had entered a traditionally male profession. This tragedy, now marked by a national day of mourning, jolted the government to respond. In 1988, the government had announced a four-year, $40 million family violence initiative that was set up to advise the government in its development of a national strategy on family violence. In the years that followed, the state has become particularly active and visible in its response to such violence.

As part of the strategy, the federal Conservative government invited four hundred researchers, practitioners, and policy-makers in the areas of child abuse, elder abuse, and wife assault to attend a four-day national consultation called Working together: National forum on family violence. The intention was to provide guidance on the strategy; however, there was no commitment of funding to implement a national strategy, without which making an adequate response to violence against women was unlikely. In fact, the 1989–90 federal budget severely cut funding to women's organizations, revealing the Progressive Conservative government's true level of non-commitment to ending violence. The already weakened Women's Program of the Secretary of State was targeted for a series of cutbacks that would include cuts in funding to women's publications, rape crisis centres, battered women's shelters, and eighty women's centres across the country.[3] In light of these facts, the post–Montreal Massacre response appears to lack any substance.

The Standing Committee on Health and Welfare, Social Affairs, Seniors, and the Status of Women was asked to study the problem, and in June 1991 they released the report *The war against women,* based on testimonies from abused women and their advocates. Although the report strongly recommended immediate action on a number of fronts, including a Royal Commission on Violence against Women, the Progressive Conservative government's only response was to appoint a panel to further study the problem and to develop a national action plan. The $10 million Canadian Panel on Violence against Women was formed in 1991 and two years later released its report, entitled *Changing the landscape: Ending violence—achieving equality.* The report, based on submissions from across Canada, clearly outlines and provides an initial analysis of the extent and nature of violence against women. However, the 497 recommendations were presented without timelines, a budget, or a process for implementation.

Support and Social Services
Since the 1970s there has been a proliferation of social welfare services specifically for survivors and perpetrators of violence. The first women's shelters in Canada are believed to be the Vancouver Transition House and Interval House in Toronto, both of which opened in 1973 (Gilman, 1988). Shortly after, shelters sprang up across the country, primarily funded by the provinces and territories. In 2001–2, 482 refuges across Canada sheltered 101,248 women and their children (Code, 2001/2002). Initially set up with a feminist vision of working in solidarity with women to change social conditions, these shelters have slowly shifted to a more professional model (Kendrick, 1998). This change has created greater distance between shelter workers and women coming for help, and there is concern that abused women are more likely to be subjects of study and program clients than sisters in struggle (Morgan, 1981; Walker, 1990). Although shelters were initially organized at the grassroots level and often had collective structures, more and more shelters have become organized with the hierarchical structures found in most service agencies. There has also been a shift from volunteer/grassroots workers to workers who are university educated and, in most cases, unionized. According to Andrea Currie (1989), the state's

involvement in funding shelters has come with a high price since it has meant "the dilution of the feminist vision of transition houses as part of a social movement, and the growth of a 'professional' model of transition houses as social service agencies" (p. 22). State funding demands more bureaucratic agency structures rather than the collective ones originally set up in many shelters. Sev'er (2002) points out how shelters "are caught in an uncomfortable dance to fulfill the rigid requirements for sustaining funding without totally sacrificing their raison d'être: ideological purity, feminist goals, and social activism" (p. 315).

In the late 1970s, the reality that most women returned to live with the men that abused them prompted attempts to work with men. Between 1979 and 1983, sixteen programs for abusive men were established, another sixty-three between 1984 and 1988, and forty-three between 1989 and 1993 (Health Canada, 1993, p. 2). Of these programs, two were designed for Aboriginal men, and one program has been set up explicitly for Indo-Canadian men. By 1999, there were 205 programs for men. The move to mandatory charging in the early 1980s was partly responsible for the rapid growth of men's programs. As a result of the development of domestic violence courts and a pro-arrest policy in recent years, programs for abusive men have been allocated increased funding to meet the greater demands. While the majority of such programs have been separated from services for women, several are attached to and managed by shelters. Also, private practitioners are "specializing" in the treatment of abusive men by offering individual and group counselling. However, men's programs are most effective when there are adequate services for women and a responsive criminal justice system.

Criminal Justice Response

Women's groups pressured the government for more effective policing, laws to protect women, and for harsher sentencing for perpetrators. Legislative victories include: assault of a partner as a criminal offence and mandatory charging of the perpetrator in domestic violence (1982 in Ontario), acknowledging rape of women in relationships as a criminal offence (1983), a broadening of the sexual assault law with regard to what is required for a woman to consent to sex (1992), and a new anti-harassment law that deals with stalking (1993).

Mandatory charging laws have been important in shifting violence against women into the public sphere. The move to pro-charging policies across Canada was to increase reporting of spousal violence and the number of charges laid, while removing responsibility from the victim to lay charges. Unfortunately, more reliance on the police and the criminal justice system has not always been positive for working-class, Aboriginal men and women, and members of visible minorities, who often experience serious negative repercussions when men are arrested for assault. Rozena Maart (1993), in her submission to the Canadian Panel on Violence against Women, speaks to this dilemma for minority women: "Black women and other racial minorities have long perceived elements in the police forces and social service agencies as dangerous to their communities. They know that by calling the police they risk getting their men maimed, psychologically humiliated and often times killed" (p. 81). Along with overt police racism against both men and women from minority groups, the legal process can be very costly and places additional stress on families struggling financially. Since women are acutely aware of the economic, emotional, and social consequences of their partner being charged, automatic charging keeps some women from seeking help. In the VAWS it was revealed that police were called in only a quarter of the violent incidents that women disclosed, and of these, only 28 percent resulted in criminal charges (Statistics Canada, 1993).

Once the legal process is set in motion, women have little control over what follows and they often experience revictimization by the criminal justice process. Women are placed in difficult and dangerous situations by long waiting periods between the time when a charge is laid and the court date. During this time, men often pressure women to drop charges or threaten them so they will not provide accurate testimony in court. Since the Crown attorney represents the state, the woman is considered only a witness for the prosecution and has no direct representation in the court. If the man chooses not to have a lawyer and to represent himself, the woman may find herself being cross-examined by the man who assaulted her. Recent initiatives, such as the domestic violence courts, have been set up across Canada to alleviate some of these concerns. Women are given clear and consistent information about the charges and the court procedures and available support and advocacy services to guide her.

As a result of pro-arrest policies and police who are "incident driven," dual arrests/charges and arrests of women have dramatically increased (Miller, 2001; Pollack et al., 2005). Miller (2001) points out how these charges are made without considering the context in which women chose violence as a response. She argues that women "often act in self-defense, they may have long histories of victimization, and they may use a weapon to equalize the force or threat used by their partners who are bigger and stronger than they are" (p. 134). In her research on immigrant and visible minority women, Smith (2004) reports that the practice of dual charging was a particular concern. A front-line worker explains the situation:

Often, the woman has experienced violence many times before she calls the police. She has gone through it so often, and finally, she might pick up a coffee cup, for example, and she gets charged with assault with a weapon. He just used his fists, so he gets a lesser charge of common assault. But these women need help, not charges. (p. x)

Martha McMahon and Ellen Pence (2003) argue that such arrests of women demonstrate a lack of understanding regarding the context of the relationship and the gendered nature of intimate violence. In Duluth, Minnesota, the anti-violence movement has responded to the practice of arresting battered women by encouraging police officers to assess if the violence is in self-defence and to apply the concept of primary aggressor. They have also approached defence lawyers to rigorously defend women charged with attacking their abusers. A number of jurisdictions in Canada have adopted a primary aggressor rule where the police officer determines who struck the first blow, the relative size and strength of the parties, the seriousness of the injuries, and prior history of abuse.

Many communities have adopted the view that it takes a whole community working together in order to adequately and effectively respond to violence against women. In Duluth, Minnesota, one of the leading cities in this regard, the Domestic Abuse Intervention Project (DAIP) has spearheaded "the Duluth model," which has guided communities around the world in the development of a coordinated community response (Shepherd & Pence, 1999). According to Shepherd and Pence (1999), coordinating institutional responses to woman abuse involves a philosophical approach that highlights victim safety, effective policies, and practice protocols for all agencies that are involved in an integrated response, enhanced communication among service providers, a monitoring and tracking system, community services and programs for women and men, and ongoing evaluation.

THE CHALLENGE AHEAD: A STALLED REVOLUTION

The context for women's organizing and work in the anti-violence movement has changed dramatically. Since coming into power in 2006, the Conservative government has dismantled programs and jeopardized the achievement of women's equality: the withdrawal of Status of Women's mandate to promote women's equality and research funding to provide documentation; the abolishment of the Law Commission of Canada and the Court Challenges Program, which supported women in taking legal action to advocate for their rights; the closure of the Canadian Labour and Business Centre; and the withdrawal of funding to the National Association of Women and the Law, resulting in its closure. Added to this list is the retraction of a signed agreement with the provinces to establish a national system of learning and child care (Townson, 2009). Accompanying the cuts to women's groups and services were changes to the funding criteria, prohibiting them from engaging in advocacy. There is no doubt that the women's movement has been severely weakened.

Evan Stark, an author and advocate for abused women for thirty years, reflects on the movement to end violence against women: "In the 1970s, we reached into the shadows to retrieve physical abuse from the canon of 'just life.' Now it appears that we did not reach nearly far enough" (Stark, 2007, p. 16). Stark (2007) holds that, while tremendous gains were made, current strategies are no longer effective and the revolution is stalled. There has been little impact on "coercive control, the most widespread and dev-astating strategy men use to dominate women in personal life" (Stark, 2007, p. 8). The limited progress on ending woman abuse is undoubtedly related to the overall social position of women, which has not been significantly transformed relative to that of men. While some gains have been made in equalizing gender relations in the public sphere—workplace, universities, and Parliament—little has changed in the private sphere. Moreover, it is clear that class and racial/ethnic inequalities buttress gender inequality. One way of elaborating this connection is to consider the ongoing economic crisis in Western industrialized countries and its implications for women. Achieving full equality for women, over half of the population, will not occur without a radically transformed political and economic order.

There is no question that women's organizing efforts are instrumental in the development of support services for abused women and the legal, social, and economic changes that benefit women. The energies that went into building a movement have been redirected to the provision of and professionalization of programs for women (Lehrner & Allen, 2009).

It is disheartening to realize that for women, the violence has been unabated and that long fought for gains are being taken away. There appears to be a trend toward mainstreaming women's organizing around violence, with the consequent dangers of co-optation and institutionalization. The effect of this, according to Gillian Walker (1990), is that "the sites of our struggles are dispersed, disconnected and depoliticized" (p. 63). While this may, in the end, limit our achievements, the multiplicity and fragmentation of the movement is consistent with many other contemporary movements (such as the anti-globalization movement), which have found that such an organizing style offers flexibility, spontaneity, and moments of striking col-lective action (Klein, 2003). Jane Ursel (1994) also sees the possibility of a convergence of state interests and women's interests, and suggests that "The policy implications of this alternative approach are to approach the state strategically, to select issues in which potential for convergence of interests does exist, and then to involve the state as much as possible in working toward those changes" (p. 91). Her position is supported by an historical and statistical overview of the changes to the criminal justice system in Manitoba, which resulted in increased options and support services for battered women.

However, the current political context is one in which our direct influence on the state has been diminished by cutbacks and an ideological hostility that signifies the disjuncture between neo-liberalism and feminism. Barbara Epstein (2001) provides a vivid description of the context in which women's groups must continue to work:

> The mass diffusion of feminist consciousness, the bureaucratization of leading women's organizations, and the high visibility of academic feminism are all consequences of the acceptance of feminism by major sectors of society. But these changes have not necessarily been good for the movement. Feminism has simultaneously become institutionalized and marginalized. It has been rhetorically accepted, but the wind has gone out of its sails. (p. 5)

Judy Rebick (2000) provides some useful strategies on how we can continue to get our issues on the agenda. She argues that women's groups influence the state and ensure a compromise from elites "when they can mobilize public opinion, attract media attention or disrupt politics" (p. 12). Returning to the work of Adamson, Briskin, and McPhail (1988), the task facing women's organizing against violence is to ensure a tension between the "politics of disengagement" and the "politics of mainstreaming"—that is, to develop and maintain a critique of existing economic and social structures while at the same time developing new strategies for social action, and mobilizing an extensive network of women's groups. This will require an organized resistance against neo-liberalism and its subsequent cutbacks to social welfare programs and services. The challenge is not unlike the one that feminists organized against four decades ago.

NOTES

1 For example, in 1969, although among the leading advocates for women's equality, Betty Friedan gave public presentations with a blackened eye carefully covered with makeup and did not place violence against women on the agenda of the women's movement (see Cohen, 1988). Also, violence was not addressed in the *Report* of the Royal Commission on the Status of Women in Canada (1970), nor was violence mentioned in the first Canadian anthology of women's issues: Anne Mclean, Gwen Hauser & Lynn Lang (Eds.), *Women Unite!* (Toronto: Canadian Women's Educational Press, 1972).

2 The Royal Commission on the Status of Women was established in 1967 in response to pressure from the women's movement and was the first Canadian commission to be chaired by a woman, Florence Bird. The 488-page report, based on hearings across the country, contained 167 recommendations to improve the condition of women. Surprising, violence against women was not mentioned.

3 Women's groups mounted a resistance across the country. In the spring of 1990 women in St. John's, Halifax, and Vancouver occupied the Secretary of State offices to protest the elimination of operational funding to women's centres. While police removed women in Halifax and Vancouver within a few hours, the occupation in St. John's lasted five days. The resistance resulted in the reinstatement of funding to all women's centres, at least temporarily.

REFERENCES

Adamson, N., Briskin, L., & McPhail, M. (1988). *Feminist organizing for change: The contemporary women's movement in Canada.* Toronto: Oxford University Press.

Amnesty International. (2009). *No more stolen sisters: The need for a comprehensive response to discrimination and violence against indigenous women in Canada* (pp. 1–27). Retrieved from: http://www.amnesty.org.

Anderson, K. (1997). Gender, status, and domestic violence: An integration of feminist and family violence approaches. *Journal of Marriage and the Family, 59*(3), 655–69.

Anderson, K., & Umberson, D. (2001). Gendering violence: Masculinity and power in men's accounts of domestic violence. *Gender & Society, 15*(3), 358–80.

Archer, J. (1999). Assessment of the reliability of the conflict tactics scales: A meta-analytic review. *Journal of Interpersonal Violence, 14*(12), 1263–89.

Archer, J. (2000). Sex differences in aggression between heterosexual partners: A meta-analytic review. *Psychological Bulletin, 126*(5), 651–80.

Bauer, H., Rodriguez, M., Quiroga, S., & Flores-Ortiz, Y. (2000). Barriers to health care for abused Latina and Asian immigrant women. *Journal of Health Care for the Poor and Underserved, 11*(1), 33–44.

Beattie, S., & Cotter, A. (2010). Homicide in Canada. *Juristat, 30*(3), 1–27.

Besserer, S., Brzozowski, J., Hendrick, D., Ogg, S., & Trainer, C. (2001). *A profile of criminal victimization: Results of the 1999 general social survey.* Ottawa: Statistics Canada.

Brennan, S. (2011). Violent victimization of Aboriginal women in the Canadian provinces. *Juristat* (May), 3–21.

Brodie, J. (1996). *Women and Canadian public policy.* Toronto: Harcourt Brace.

Brownbridge, D. (2003). Male partner violence against Aboriginal women in Canada. *Journal of Interpersonal Violence, 18*(1), 65–83.

Burczycka, M., & Cotter, A. (2011). Shelters for abused women in Canada 2010. *Juristat* (June 27), 1–25.

Canadian Centre for Policy Alternatives—MB. (2000). *Fast facts.* Winnipeg: CCPA—MB.

Canadian Panel on Violence against Women. (1993). *Changing the landscape: Ending violence—achieving equality.* Ottawa: Author.

Chouinard, V. (1999). Body politics: Disabled women's activism in Canada and beyond. In R. Butler & H. Parr (Eds.), *Mind and body spaces: Geographies of illness, impairment, and disability* (pp. 269–94). London: Routledge.

Clatterbaugh, K. (1997). *Contemporary perspectives on masculinity.* Boulder, CO: Westview.

Cockburn, C. (1998). *The space between us: Negotiating gender and national identities in conflict.* London: Zed.

Code, R. (2001/2002). *Canada's shelters for abused women. Juristat, 23*(4), 1–14. Ottawa: Canadian Centre for Justice Statistics, Statistics Canada.

Cohen, M. (1988). *The sisterhood.* New York: Ballantine.

Connell, R.W. (1995a). Politics of changing me. *Socialist Review, 25*(1), 135–59.

Connell, R.W. (1995b). *Masculinities.* Oxford: Blackwell.

Consultations with Women in the Newfoundland Fishery. (1994). *A report by the Women's Committee of Fisherman, Food, and Allied Workers Union* (FFAW/ CAW), submitted to the Secretary of State, April 11.

Currie, A. (1989). A roof is not enough: Feminism, transition houses, and the battle against abuse. *New Maritimes, 8*(1), 16–29.

Davis, D. (2000). Gendered cultures of conflict and discontent: Living "the crisis" in a Newfoundland community. *Women's Studies International Forum, 23*(3), 343–54.

Day, T. (1995). *The health-related costs of violence against women in Canada: The tip of the iceberg.* London, ON: Centre for Research on Violence against Women and Children.

DeKeseredy, W. (2011). *Violence against women: Myths, facts, controversies.* Toronto: University of Toronto Press.

DeKeseredy, W., & Schwartz, M. (1998). *Woman abuse on campus: Results from the Canadian national survey.* Thousand Oaks, CA: Sage.

DeKeseredy, W., & Schwartz, M. (2003). Backlash and whiplash: A critique of Statistics Canada's 1999 general social survey on victimization. *Journal of Justice Studies, 1,* 1–14. Retrieved from: http://ojjs.icaap.org/issues/1.1/dekeseredy -schwartz.html.

Dobash, R.E., & Dobash, R.P. (1979). *Violence against wives: A case against patriarchy.* New York: Free Press.

Dobash, R.E., & Dobash, R.P. (1992). *Women, violence, and social change.* New York: Routledge.

Dobash, R.E., Dobash, R.P., Wilson, M., & Daly, M. (1992). The myth of sexual symmetry in marital violence. *Social Problems, 39,* 71–91.

Dutton, D. (2000). Witnessing parental violence as a traumatic experience shaping the abusive personality. In P. Jaffe, M. Suderman & R. Geffner (Eds.), *Children exposed to domestic violence: Current issues in research, intervention, prevention, and policy development* (pp. 59–67). New York: Haworth.

Dutton, M., Orloff, L.E., & Hass, G.A. (2000). Characteristics of help-seeking behaviours, resources, and service needs of battered immigrant Latinas:

Legal and policy implications. *Georgetown Journal on Poverty Law and Policy, 7,* 245–305.

Edleson, J. (1999). Children's witnessing of adult domestic violence. *Journal of Interpersonal Violence, 14*(8), 839–70.

Eliasson, M., & Lundy, C. (1999). Organizing to stop violence against women in Canada and Sweden. In L. Brisken & M. Eliasson (Eds.), *Women's organizing and public policy in Canada and Sweden* (pp. 280–309). Montreal: McGill-Queen's University Press.

Enarson, E. (1999). Violence against women in disasters. *Violence against Women, 5*(7), 742–68.

Epstein, B. (2001). What happened to the women's movement? *Monthly Review: An Independent Socialist Magazine, 53,* 1–13.

Farley, M., & Kelly, V. (2000). Prostitution: A critical review of the medical and social sciences literature. *Women and Criminal Justice, 11,* 29–63.

Federal-Provincial-Territorial Ministers Responsible for the Status of Women. (2002). *Assessing violence against women: A statistical profile.* Ottawa: Status of Women Canada.

Fine, M., & Weis, L. (2000). Disappearing acts: The state and violence against women in the twentieth century. *Signs: Journal of Women in Culture and Society 25*(4), 1139–46.

Freire, P. (1990). A critical understanding of social work. *Journal of Progressive Human Services, 1*(1), 3–9.

Fong, J. 2010. *Out of the shadows: Woman abuse in ethnic, immigrant, and Aboriginal communities.* Toronto: Women's Press.

Fry, H. (2011). *Call into the night: An overview of violence against Aboriginal women.* Report of the Standing Committee on the Status of Women. Ottawa: House of Commons, Canada.

Gelles, R. (1972). *The violent home: A study of physical aggression between husbands and wives.* Beverly Hills, CA: Sage.

Gilman, S. (1988). A history of the sheltering movement for battered women in Canada. *Canadian Journal of Community Mental Health, 7*(2), 9–21.

Gordon, M., & Riger, S. (1989). *The female fear: The social cost of rape.* Urbana: University of Illinois Press.

Graham-Kevan, N., & Archer, J. (2003). Intimate terrorism and common couple violence: A test of Johnson's predictions in four British samples. *Journal of Interpersonal Violence, 18*(11), 1247–70.

Greaves, L., & Hankivsk, O. (1995). *Selected estimates of the costs of violence against women.* London, ON: Centre for Research on Violence against Women and Children.

Hall, S. (2002). Daubing the drudges of fury: Men, violence, and the piety of the "hegemonic masculinity" thesis. *Theoretical Criminology, 6*(1), 35–61.

Hall, S., & Winlow, S. (2003). Rehabilitating the Leviathan: Reflections on the state, economic regulation, and violence reduction. *Theoretical Criminology, 7*(2), 139–62.

Hard times put women's lobby deeper in the hole. (1994, June 13). *Ottawa Citizen*, A4.

Health Canada. (1993). *Canada's treatment programs for men who abuse their partners.* Ottawa: Author.

Health Canada. (1996). *Breaking the links between poverty and violence against women: A resource guide.* Ottawa: Author.

Health Canada. (1998). *Abuse in lesbian relationships: Information and resources.* Ottawa: Minister of Public Works and Government Services Canada.

Health Canada. (2002). *Woman abuse.* Ottawa: National Clearing House on Family Violence.

Human Rights Watch. (2000). *What will it take? Stopping violence against women: A challenge to governments.* Retrieved from: http://www.hrw.org/backgrounder/wrd/ fireplus.htm.

Hunnicutt, G. (2009). Varieties of patriarchy and violence against women: Resurrecting "patriarchy" as a theoretical tool. *Violence against Women. 15*(5), 553–73.

Jaffe, P.G., Suderman, M., & Geffner, R. (2000). *Children exposed to domestic violence.* New York: Haworth Press.

James, M. (1994). *Domestic violence as a form of child abuse: Identification and prevention.* Issues in Child Abuse Prevention 2. Melbourne: National Child Protection Clearing House.

Jiwani, Y. (2002). The 1999 general social survey on spousal violence: An analysis. In J. Larkin & M.J. McKenna (Eds.), *Violence against women: Canadian perspectives* (pp. 63–72). Toronto: Inanna.

Johnson, H. (1993). *Violence against women survey.* Ottawa: Statistics Canada.

Johnson, H. (1996). *Dangerous domains: Violence against women in Canada.* Toronto: Nelson.

Johnson, H. (2002). Methods of measurement. In K.M.J. McKenna & J. Larkin (Eds.), *Violence against women: New Canadian perspectives* (pp. 21–54). Toronto: Inanna.

Johnson, H., & Au Coin, K. (2003). *Family violence in Canada: A statistical profile.* Ottawa: Canadian Centre for Justice Statistics, Statistics Canada.

Johnson, H., & Dawson, M. (2011). *Violence against women in Canada: Research and policy perspectives.* Toronto: Oxford University Press.

Johnson, H., & Pottie Bunge, V. (2001). Prevalence and consequences of spousal assault in Canada. *Canadian Journal of Criminology, 43*(1), 27–45.

Johnson, M. (1995). Patriarchal terrorism and common couple violence: Two forms of violence against women. *Journal of Marriage and the Family, 57*(2), 283–94.

Johnson, M. (2006). Conflict and control: Gender symmetry and asymmetry in domestic violence. *Violence against Women, 12*(11), 1003–18.

Johnson, M., & Ferraro, K. (2000). Research on domestic violence in the 1990s: Making distinctions. *Journal of Marriage and the Family, 62*, 948–63.

Kaufman Kantor, G., & Little, L. (2003). Defining the boundaries of child neglect. *Journal of Interpersonal Violence, 18*(4), 338–55.

Kelly, J.B., & Johnson, M.P. (2008). Differentiation among types of intimate partner violence: Research update and implications for interventions. *Family Court Review, 46*(3), 476–99.

Kendrick, K. (1998). Producing the battered woman: Shelter politics and the power of the feminist voice. In N. Naples (Ed.), *Community activism and feminist politics: Organizing across race, class, and gender* (pp. 151–73). New York: Routledge.

Kimmel, M.S. (2002). Gender symmetry in domestic violence: A substantive and methodological review. *Violence against Women, 8*(11), 1332–63.

Klein, N. (2002). What's next? The movement against global corporatism doesn't need to sign a ten-point plan to be effective. In N. Klein (Ed.), *Fences and windows: Dispatches from the front lines of the globalization debate* (pp. 14–28). Toronto: Vintage.

Koskela, H. (1997). "Bold walk and breakings": Women's spatial confidence versus fear of violence. *Gender, Place, and Culture, 4*(3) 301–19.

Kost, K.A. (1997). A man without a job is a dead man: The meaning of work in the lives of young men. *Journal of Sociology and Social Welfare, 24*(3), 91–111.

Lehrner, A., & Allen, N. (2009). Still a movement after all these years? Current tensions in the domestic violence movement. *Violence against Women, 15*(6), 656–77.

Leventhal, B., & Lundy, S. (1999). *Same-sex domestic violence: Strategies for change.* Thousand Oaks, CA: Sage.

Levinson, D. (1989). *Family violence in cross-cultural perspective.* Newbury Park, CA: Sage.

Lupri, E., Grandin, E., & Brinkerhoff, M. (1994). Socioeconomic status and male violence in the Canadian home: A re-examination. *Canadian Journal of Sociology, 19*(1), 47–73.

Maart, R. (1993). *Violence against women of colour.* Ottawa: Canadian Panel of Violence against Women.

MacLeod, L. (1980). *Wife battering in Canada: The vicious circle.* Ottawa: Canadian Advisory Council on the Status of Women.

MacLeod, L. (1987). *Battered but not beaten.* Ottawa: Canadian Advisory Council on the Status of Women.

Mann, R. (2003). Violence against women or family violence? The "problem" of female perpetration in domestic violence. In L. Samuelson & W. Antony (Eds.), *Power and resistance: Critical thinking about Canadian social issues* (3rd ed., pp. 41–63). Halifax: Fernwood.

McFarlane, J., Wilson, P., Malecha, A., & Lemmey, D., (2000). Intimate partner violence: A gender comparison. *Journal of Interpersonal Violence, 15*(2), 158–69.

McGillivray, A., & Comaskey, B. (1999). *Black eyes all the time: Intimate violence, Aboriginal women, and the justice system.* Toronto: University of Toronto Press.

McKeen, W., & Porter, A. (2003). Politics and transformation: Welfare state restructuring in Canada. In W. Clement & L. Vosko (Eds.), *Changing*

Canada: Political economy as transformation (pp. 109–34). Montreal: McGill-Queen's University Press.

McKendy, J. (1997). Class politics of domestic violence. *Journal of Sociology and Social Welfare, 14*(3), 135–55.

McMahon, M., & Pence, E. (2003). Making social change: Reflections on individual and institutional advocacy with women arrested for domestic violence. *Violence against Women, 9*(1), 47–74.

Messerchmidt, J.W. (1993). *Masculinities and crime: Critique and reconceptualization of theory.* Lanham, MD: Rowman and Littlefield.

Mikkonen, J., & Raphael, D. (2011). *Social determinants of health: The Canadian facts,* 1–62. Retrieved from: http://www.thecanadianfacts.org/.

Milhorean K. (2005). Trends in self-reported spousal violence. *Family violence in Canada: A statistical profile* (pp. 13–22). Ottawa: Statistics Canada.

Miller, A. (1990). *For your own good: Hidden cruelty in child-rearing and the roots of violence.* New York: Noonday.

Miller, S.L. (2001). The paradox of woman arrested for domestic violence. *Violence against Women, 7*(12), 1339–76.

Ministry of the Attorney General. (2003, June). *Partner response (par) program standards.* Ottawa: Author.

Morgan, P. (1981). From battered wife to program client: The state's shaping of social problems. *Kapitalistate, 9,* 17–39.

Mosher, J., Evans, P., Little, M., Morrow, E., Boulding, J., & Vanderplaats, N. (2004). *Walking on eggshells: Abused women's experience of Ontario's welfare system.* Toronto: York University.

Native Women's Association of Canada (NWAC). Retrieved from: http://www.sistersinspirit.ca/enghome.htm.

Nixon, K., Tutty, L., Downe, P., Gorkoff, K., & Ursel, J. (2002). The everyday occurrence: Violence in the lives of girls exploited through prostitution. *Violence against Women, 8,* 1016–43.

Ollus, N. (2001). The international violence against women survey. *European Institute for Crime Prevention and Control, 36,* 214–20.

Ontario Association for Interval and Transition Houses (OAITH). (1996). *Home truth: Exposing the false facts of equality and safety rights for abused women in Canada.* Submission to the UN Rapporteur on Violence against Women.

Ontario Ministry of Community and Social Services. (2000). *Woman abuse: Increasing safety for abused women and their children.* CAS/VAW Joint Training—Participant Manual. Toronto: Author.

Orloff, L.E. (2000). *Statement of now legal defense and education fund in support of HR 3083, The battered immigrant women's protection act of 1999.* Retrieved from: http://judiciary.house.gov/legacy/orlo0720.htm.

O'Sullivan, L.F., Byers, E.S., & Finkelman, L. (1998). A comparison of male and female college students' experience of sexual coercion. *Psychology of Women Quarterly, 22,* 177–95.

Pepler, D., Catallo, R., & Moore, T. (2000). Consider the children: Research informing interventions for children exposed to domestic violence. In

P. Jaffe, M. Suderman & R. Geffner (Eds.), *Children exposed to domestic violence: Current issues in research, intervention, prevention, and policy development* (pp. 37–57). New York: Haworth.

Pollack, S., Green, V., & Allspach, A. (2005). *Women charged with domestic violence in Toronto: The unintended consequences of mandatory charge policies.* Toronto: Woman Abuse Council of Toronto.

Pottie Bunge, V., & Locke, D. (Eds.). (2000). *Family violence in Canada: A statistical profile 2000.* Ottawa: Statistics Canada.

Preston, S. (1999). The glass half full: Responses to woman abuse by the federal and Ontario governments, 1980–1995. *Canadian Review of Social Policy, 44,* 41–56.

Proulx, J., & Perrault, S. (2000). *No place for violence: Canadian Aboriginal alternatives.* Halifax: Fernwood.

Raj, A., & Silverman, J. (2002). Violence against immigrant women: The roles of culture, context, and legal immigrant status on intimate partner violence. *Violence against Women, 8*(3), 367–98.

Raphael, J., & Shapiro, D. (2004). Violence in indoor and outdoor prostitution venues. *Violence against Women, 10*(2), 126–39.

Razack, S. (1999). *Looking white people in the eye: Gender, race, and culture in courtrooms and classrooms.* Toronto: University of Toronto Press.

Razack, S. (2002). *Race, space, and the law: Unmapping a white settler society.* Toronto: Between the Lines.

Rebick, J. (2000). *Imagine democracy.* Toronto: Stoddart.

Richmond, E.M. (2001). The interface of poverty and violence against women: How federal and state welfare reform can best respond. *New England Law Review, 35*(2), 569–603.

Rogers, K. (1994). *Wife assault: The findings of a national survey. Juristat, 14*(9), 1–22. Ottawa: Canadian Centre for Justice Statistics, Statistics Canada.

Royal Commission on the Status of Women in Canada. (1970). Retrieved from: http://epe.lac-bac.gc.ca/100/200/301/pco-bcp/commissions-ef/bird1970-eng/bird1970-eng.htm.

Ruddick, S. (1996). Constructing difference in public spaces: Race, class, and gender as interlocking systems. *Urban Geography, 17,* 132–51.

Sajor, I.L. (1998). *Common grounds: Violence against women in war and armed conflict situations.* Quezon City, Philippines: Asian Centre for Women's Human Rights.

Schecter, S. (1982). *Women and male violence: The visions and struggles of the battered women's movement.* Cambridge, MA: South End.

Segal, L. (1990). *Slow motion: Changing Masculinities changing men.* Piscataway, NJ: Rutgers University Press.

Sev'er, A. (2002). A feminist analysis of flight of abused women, plight of Canadian shelters: Another road to homelessness. *Journal of Social Distress and the Homeless, 11*(4), 307–24.

Shephard, M.F., & Pence, E.L. (Eds.). (1999). *Co-ordinating community responses to domestic violence: Lessons from Duluth and beyond.* Thousand Oaks, CA: Sage.

Smith, E. (2004). *Nowhere to turn? Responding to partner violence against immigrant and visible minority women.* Ottawa: Canadian Council on Social Development.

Smith, J., Berthelsen, D., & O'Connor, I. (1997). Child adjustment in high-conflict families. *Child Care, Health, and Development, 23*(2), 113–33.

Sokoloff, N., & Dupont, I. (2005). Domestic violence at the intersections of race, class, and gender: Challenges and contributions to understanding violence against marginalized women in diverse communities. *Violence against Women, 11*(1), 38–64.

Standing Committee on Health and Welfare, Social Affairs, Seniors, and the Status of Women. (1991, June). *The war against women.* Ottawa: Author.

Staples, R. (1982). *Black masculinity: The black male's role in American society.* San Francisco: Black Scholars Press.

Stark, E. (2006). Commentary on Johnson's conflict and control: Gender symmetry and asymmetry in domestic violence. *Violence against Women, 12,* 1019–25.

Stark, E. (2007). *Coercive control: How men entrap women in personal life.* New York: Oxford University Press.

Stark, E., & Flitcraft, A. (1988). Violence among intimates: An epidemiological review. In V.B. Van Hasselt, R.L. Morrisson, A.S. Bellack & M. Herson (Eds.), *Handbook of family violence* (pp. 22–43). New York: Plenum.

Statistics Canada. (1993). The violence against women survey. *The Daily,* November 18. Ottawa: Statistics Canada.

Statistics Canada. (2011, January). *Family violence in Canada: A statistical profile.*

Straus, M. (1979). Measuring intrafamily conflict and violence: The conflict tactics scale. *Journal of Marriage and the Family, 41,* 75–88.

Straus, M. (1983). Corporal punishment, child abuse, and wife-beating: What do they have in common?" In D. Finkelhor, R. Gelles, G. Hotaling & M. Straus (Eds.), *The dark side of families: Current family violence research* (pp. 213–34). Beverley Hills, CA: Sage.

Straus, M., & Gelles, R. (1990). *Physical violence in American families: Risk factors and adaptations to violence in 8,145 families.* New Brunswick, NJ: Transaction.

Straus, M., Gelles, R., & Steinmetz, S. (1980). *Behind closed doors: Violence in the American family.* Garden City, NY: Anchor/Doubleday.

Swan, S., & Snow, D. (2002). A typology of women's use of violence in intimate relationships. *Violence against Women, 8*(3), 286–319.

Thomas Gilman, S. (1988). A history of the sheltering movement for battered women in Canada. *Canadian Journal of Community Mental Health, 7*(2), 9–21.

Tjaden, P., & Thoennes, N. (2000). *Full report of the prevalence, incidence, and consequences of violence against women: Findings from the National Violence against Women survey.* Washington, DC: National Institute of Justice and the Centre for Disease Control and Prevention.

Townson, M. (2009). *Women's poverty and the recession.* Ottawa: CCPA.

Trainor, C., & Mihorean, K. (2001). *Family violence in Canada: A statistical profile 2001.* Ottawa: Canadian Centre for Justice Statistics.

United Nations (UN). (1993, December 20). *Declaration on the elimination of violence against women, A/Res/48/104.* 85th Plenary Meeting, Geneva.

Ursel, J. (1994). Eliminating violence against women: Reform or co-optation in state institutions. In L. Samuelson (Ed.), *Power and resistance* (pp. 71–92). Halifax: Fernwood.

Vallée, B. (2007). *The war on women: Elly Armour, Jane Hurshman, and criminal violence in Canadian homes.* Toronto: Key Porter Books.

Waldrop, A., & Roesick, P. (2004). Coping among adult female victims of domestic violence. *Journal of Family Violence, 19*(5), 291–303.

Walker, G. (1990). *Family violence and the women's movement: The conceptual politics of struggle.* Toronto: University of Toronto Press.

Weedon, C. (1987). *Feminist practice and poststructuralist theory.* Oxford: Blackwell.

Weldon, L. (2002). *Protest, policy, and the problem of violence against women: A cross-national comparison.* Pittsburgh: University of Pittsburgh Press.

Willson, P., McFarlane, J., Malecha, A., Watson, K., Lemmey, D., Schultz, P., Gist, J., & Fredland, N. (2000). Severity of violence against women by intimate partners and associated use of alcohol and/or illicit drugs by the perpetrator. *Journal of Interpersonal Violence, 15*(9), 996–1008.

Wilson, M.I., & Daly, M. (1992). Who kills whom in spouse killings: On the exceptional sex ratio of spousal homicides in the United States. *Criminology, 30,* 189–215.

World Health Organization (WHO). (2002). *World report on violence and health.* Geneva: WHO.

15

IDENTIFYING, ASSESSING, AND TREATING MEN WHO ABUSE AND WOMEN ABUSED BY INTIMATE PARTNERS

LESLIE M. TUTTY

INTRODUCTION

The dawning reality that many individuals, couples, and families who seek clinical intervention are currently experiencing intimate partner violence, primarily abuse by men against women, represents a major paradigm shift for clinicians. Until two decades ago, social workers, psychologists, nurses, and doctors considered such abuse as rare, for the most part. Growing research and clinical literature have raised the awareness of many helpers that it is critical to assess for and address violence within families.

Nevertheless, many of us received little to no professional training in how to raise such sensitive topics and what to offer in the way of treatment (Tilden et al., 1994). Indeed, professionals have been soundly criticized for dealing ineffectively with women who have been victimized by their intimate partners (Eisikovits & Buchbinder, 1996). Chang et al. (2005) asked women abused by intimate partners what they wanted from the health care system. The women did not appreciate simply being told to "go to a shelter" without a more in-depth discussion of their personal circumstances or needs, and they were clear about not wanting the abuse reported to the police. What they most wanted was an intervention that took into consideration both the complexities of their lives and the fact that they were at different stages in their readiness to address the abuse. The women emphasized assistance that provided safety, autonomy, and privacy, all of which should be seen as underlying principles for intervention in this chapter.

Although much of the literature addresses abuse in heterosexual couples, violence among lesbian and male–male relationships occurs relatively often, according to the recent US National Violence against Women Survey (Tjaden, Thoennes & Allison, 1999). The serious nature and possible risk of harm in living with an abusive partner, and the long-term negative consequences of all forms of violence, suggest that every individual, couple (whether heterosexual or homosexual), and family seeking counselling should be assessed for current or historical abuse.

This chapter provides practical, clinical guidelines for assessing and treating perpetrators (mostly men) who abuse their intimate partners and the abused partners (mostly women). It provides a number of principles that underlie clinical practice in intimate partner violence, suggests how to raise the sensitive issue with couples, what to assess if violence is identified, and what clinical interventions have proven effective. The citations include a mix of publications from both early writers who remain relevant and more recently published clinicians. When possible, the work of Canadian clinicians has been highlighted.

PRINCIPLES WITH RESPECT TO INTIMATE PARTNER VIOLENCE
A number of principles underlie the suggestions for clinicians for assessing and treating intimate partner violence offered in the next section.

Violent Behaviour Is the Sole Responsibility of the Perpetrator
The first principle is the belief that violent behaviour is the sole responsibility of the perpetrator. As such, clinical assessment and intervention must first be directed to helping perpetrators gain and maintain control of their abusive behaviours, as well as assuring safety for victims.

Violent Behaviour May Be Part of a Larger Pattern of Abuse
A second principle is that if one form of abuse is occurring in a family, other forms of abuse may be as well. Although Finkelhor's (1983) writing on violence identified common features in families in which child abuse and spouse abuse coexist, until recently, these commonalities and the interconnectedness of various forms of violence have not been sufficiently highlighted. Psychological or emotional abuse is always an aspect of physical violence. Degrading slurs or threats to kill or commit suicide are powerful control mechanisms, even if physical assaults rarely occur. The extent to which men who abuse women partners also physically abuse their children has been obscured until recently (Adams, 2006; Tutty, 1999). This is partly

because researchers have tended to focus on one specific aspect of domestic violence, so that, for example, statistics on child abuse and marital rape are often not considered in discussions of women abused by their partners. Clearly, forms of abusive behaviour are not distinct entities in themselves, but represent patterns of the abuse of power in families, to a large extent by men toward women and children.

Safety Is Paramount

Addressing and supporting the safety of the victims of domestic violence is essential. This entails the clinician being ever aware of the potential negative effect of raising questions about violence without taking precautions (more on this below). Even if the interview takes place in a secure setting, and family members are reassured of the confidentiality of the interview, individuals may face serious consequences for disclosing family secrets. If child abuse is disclosed, for example, we are required to support the family in reporting the abuse to the appropriate authorities or, failing that, make the report ourselves. Finally, knowing how to assist clients in developing a safety plan is crucial (Davies, Lyon & Monti-Catania, 1998).

Recognize the Ongoing Impact of Childhood Abuse

Another principle is that a history of childhood abuse can have long-standing effects on adult relationships. The consequences of childhood sexual abuse, as one example, often have an impact on current marital dynamics for both women and men (Follette & Pistorello, 1995; Gill & Tutty, 1999) and parenting (Voth & Tutty, 1999). Similarly, in reviews of articles about the intergenerational transmission of partner abuse (Hotaling & Sugarman, 1986; Tutty, 1999), the majority of studies found that boys who witnessed their fathers abusing their mothers are at higher risk of abusing their own intimate partners, although girls exposed to marital conflict are not more likely to become victims. As such, clinicians should assess not only current abuse, but past history.

Abuse Is Typically Denied or Minimized

A further common occurrence is that partners deny or minimize abuse in their relationship. Given the now well-publicized societal concern about women abused by their partners, both men and women commonly under-report or deny intimate partner violence. However, men do so more often (Szinovacz & Egley, 1995). These authors also note that in studies with data from both members of couples who admit violent acts, typically only one spouse makes the claim, while the other denies the use of such tactics. Another common couple dynamic is that each accuses the other of being abusive. "Common couple violence" occurs more often than serious violence (Kelly & Johnson, 2008) and comprises primarily "low level" behaviours such as pushing and shoving. While any violent act is of concern and could cause serious injury, women tend to more readily admit when they have behaved violently and take responsibility for it sooner than men. Sometimes intimate partner violence is in self-defence or is pre-emptive, in anticipation of future violence. Identifying the primary aggressor is challenging and will be addressed in the next section on assessment because "intimate terrorism," the typical experience of women who seek the safety of shelters, can be addressed differently than common couple violence (Johnson & Leone, 2005).

Traditional Approaches Are Inadequate, Even Dangerous

In the 1980s, traditional family therapy approaches interpreted violence, including sexual abuse, as symptoms of dysfunction within the family. Since many family systems theorists see problems as a result of the development of homeostatic patterns that serve to keep the family together, when issues of abuse do arise, they tend to be viewed simply as further evidence of dysfunctional relationships and may not be directly addressed at all (Nichols & Schwartz, 2001). The victims are seen as part of the cycle of abuse in the family, whereby they are identified as part of the problem. A number of feminist writers expressed concerns about applying family systems theory to women abused by their partners (Hansen & Goldenberg, 1993). Bograd (1984) criticized a systems approach as not only potentially dangerous to the woman, but also, by looking for circular patterns within the relationship, subtly blames a woman for her partner's aggressive acts. Bograd also criticizes the principle of therapist neutrality, whereby therapists do not confront abusive behaviour nor assign responsibility for assaultive behaviour. As such, violence tends to be ignored and the focus shifts from the perpetrator's abusive behaviour to improving the interactions between partners. This leaves a woman vulnerable to escalating abuse after therapy sessions in which she is encouraged to talk about her partner's abusive behaviour, information that her husband could find inflammatory. A key clinical assumption of this chapter is that family therapy or traditional couples therapy per se are not appropriate interventions to address intimate partner violence, although some newer couples approaches that take the dynamics of partner abuse into consideration will be described (Greene & Bogo, 2002).

Need to Understand the Presence and Role of Trauma

A further principle is the utility of the trauma perspective in understanding both the immediate and the long-term effects of interpersonal violence.

Living in a chronically abusive relationship negatively affects the belief systems, behaviour, and self-esteem of victims. If trauma results, it should become a focus of clinical intervention. Abused women often report feeling depressed, suicidal, panicky, and may be drawn to abusing substances (Hegarty, 2011; Tutty, 1998; Zubretsky, 2002), each of which could suggest the need for psychiatric intervention. Importantly, though, diagnosing the abused individual ignores the context of living in an abusive relationship (Tutty & Goard, 2002).

Rather than looking at various symptoms in isolation, these are more helpfully conceptualized as trauma, similar to that experienced by other victims of violent crimes such as rape, robbery, and physical assault. The cluster of symptoms (anxiety, fears, recurrent nightmares, sleep and eating disorders, numbed affect, flashbacks, hypervigilance, and increased startle responses) are congruent with post-traumatic stress disorder (PTSD), a condition that was added to the DSM-IV (Tutty, 1998). An advantage of recognizing these symptoms as PTSD is that, by definition, trauma is seen as "normal responses to abnormal occurrences in the lives of these victims" (Gleason, 1993, p. 62). The major trauma reactions—numbing, avoidance, and hypervigilance—interfere with one's ability to focus on issues and problem-solving, the key processes of clinical intervention, thus providing a further rationale for attending to it.

Evidence for the trauma perspective is persuasive. Researchers have reported that high numbers of women seeking assistance for domestic abuse have clinical levels of PTSD (Woods et al., 2005; Tutty, 2006). More serious PTSD symptoms are associated with more severe abuse, greater threat, and more forced sex (Kemp, Green, Hovanitz & Rawlings, 1995).

Nevertheless, there is room for caution in utilizing any psychiatric diagnosis, even one that puts the relationship dynamics into context, because abused women could be further stigmatized by a medical diagnosis. Walker (1991) usefully commented that "it is important to remember that not all battered women develop PTSD and even when they do, they may not need more than a support group with others in similar situations" (p. 28).

Anger Management Is Not a Cure for Violence

A final principle is that male violence against women partners is not "caused" by anger or loss of control, but by beliefs that give men permission to control their "wives" and children by deliberately behaving in ways that isolate, intimidate, or punish them. These include a husband's "right" to physically chastise or beat his wife for such infractions as "not obeying her husband, talking back, not having food ready on time... refusing him sex or expressing suspicions of infidelity" (Heise, Ellsberg & Gottemoeller,

1999). This perspective has important implications for clinical intervention. A focus on individual reactions such as anger, as is offered in "anger-management" treatment, is unlikely to address the more profound societal and family belief systems that support using violence and controlling tactics.

ASSESSING INTIMATE PARTNER VIOLENCE

Men, unless mandated to programs, and women involved in abusive relationships typically present to counselling agencies asking for marital counselling without identifying violence as an issue, whether because of shame or denial that the problem is important (Robbie Babins-Wagner, personal communication, November 2011). While many clinicians understand the serious nature of domestic abuse, they may not know how to introduce the topic or feel comfortable addressing it. The following section provides suggestions with respect to introducing the possibility of abuse during assessment and what else to include in the assessment if violence is occurring.

Identifying Abuse and Violence

A key recommendation is to assess all individuals, couples, and families for a history of current abuse and/or past abuse whether or not this is their presenting problem. As was suggested by the earlier discussion about the prevalence of different forms of abuse within the same family, if one form of abuse is presented or discovered, clinicians would be well advised to find out if anyone else is being hurt.

It is essential to assess violence in ways that protect all family members. Family violence is a secret. The secret is kept, in part, by the social isolation common in families where woman and child abuse are perpetrated (Finkelhor, 1983). This secrecy is sanctioned in our society by the view that what happens within families is private. Once a clinician breaches this rule of privacy, family members can be at risk of escalated levels of violence. This is why it is important not to simply intervene by treating the violence as if it were any other symptom of family dysfunction, but to take special precautions to safeguard the victims.

Sometimes intimate partner violence is not assessed because clinicians assume that few families who come for help experience abuse or are abusive. In other cases, clinicians assume that families will volunteer information about abuse within the family. This supposition ignores the fact that denial and minimization, both on the part of victims and of perpetrators, may be a functional response that keeps the family together. Other clinicians ignore cues or ask questions that avoid dealing with the fact that abuse occurs within the family. Selective attention may occur in clinical settings, particularly when parents' discipline methods border on being abusive and clinicians would prefer not to report them to child protection authorities, although they are mandated to do so.

Initial Interviews

Joint initial interviews with family members are the norm in many agencies and remain a useful first assessment strategy. Some clinicians, particularly proponents of family therapy, may not address issues of abuse because their major focus is on the problem that the family presents for help. This is especially true in forms of brief family intervention such as solution-focused therapy or other models that accept the family's presenting problem without further assessment (Nichols & Schwartz, 2001). This is problematic in cases of women abused by their partners because violence is rarely raised as the problem that the family would like to address in counselling. Insisting that all family members attend all sessions, a trademark of other family therapy approaches, also mitigates against an open discussion of abuse within families. The view advocated in this chapter and by the majority of those who work closely with the victims and the perpetrators of intimate partner violence is that abusive behaviours are the sole responsibility of the perpetrator and not the result of family pathology. The abuse needs to be the major focus for clinical intervention, especially given the risk of lethality.

Introducing the Issue

The clinical literature provides relatively few guidelines about how best to assess violence, especially when abuse is not the presenting problem. In conjoint sessions, clinicians can ask individual family members how they deal with conflict and whether anyone gets hurt (Geffner & Rosenbaum, 1990). One can also utilize the McMaster Model of Family Functioning, which assesses roles and affect within the marital relationship (Epstein, Bishop & Baldwin, 1982) and includes questions about how family members deal with each other when one gets angry. Brekke (1987) recommends using a process called "funnelling," whereby the general discussion is directed toward conflict and how this is handled. Conflict is normalized by acknowledging that all families have problems to resolve. The question then becomes "So how do you deal with conflict in your relationship?"

While these procedures introduce a discussion of violence in family or couple sessions, the clinician must remain ever vigilant about the atmosphere in the room and be prepared to redirect the discussion quickly if tension becomes apparent. Asking an abused woman to disclose marital violence in sessions with her husband likely puts her at risk after the session is over. Tension may indicate that, not only is abuse an issue, but that retaliation is possible if the discussion continues. In cases such as these, the discussion of violence should be terminated and reintroduced in separate interviews, either at that point or at a later date. These can be set up without disclosing that abuse will be the major focus of discussion.

Over twenty years ago, Rosenbaum and O'Leary (1986) suggested interviewing each adult partner separately to inquire about any current abusive behaviour in the relationship or a history of other forms of abuse. The easiest way to do this is to let families know at the start of the session that you routinely reserve the option of seeing family members individually, if not at the end of the first interview, then at another point in time.

Guidelines for Questioning

When questioning women and/or men individually about relationship abuse, we should lead into the issue sensitively, but at the same time be prepared to be direct. Universal screening questions have been introduced by nurses or doctors in recent years. Starting with a general question is a good way to introduce the topic. The following question was developed for use in emergency departments in hospitals in the city of Calgary (Thurston et al., 2008), but can also be adapted for counselling agencies:

> We know that domestic violence and the threat of violence in the home is a problem for many people and can directly affect their health. Abuse can take many forms: physical, emotional, sexual, financial or neglect. We routinely ask all clients/patients about domestic abuse or violence in their lives. Is this or has this been a problem for you or your child(ren) in any way? (p. 519)

Asking questions about "domestic violence," "wife assault," or "partner abuse" should generally be avoided. Many abuse victims do not identify as "abused," but, if asked, will identify specific acts such as being hit or punched, threatened, restricted from or coerced into certain activities.

Guidelines and assessment questions from the gay and lesbian community that step away from gender as the key feature in identifying the "perpetrator" and the "victim" are useful for this task (Senseman, 2002). Veinot (1999) notes that some people describe any behaviour that they dislike as "abuse." She suggests asking for specifics about what happened before labelling any behaviour as "abuse"—in the context of the situation the other individual could be setting quite appropriate boundaries. Alternatively, one can ask who told them that the behaviour was "abusive." Veinot also provides the following assessment questions:

- Is this a pattern of behaviour? Does the accuser claim that the partner has committed one or more of these acts more than once?
- Who seems to be more in control of the other person? Who seems to make most of the decisions? Who gets their way most of the time?
- Has one partner changed jobs, friends, socialization patterns, ideas, and activities in response to the other person's requirements?
- Who is afraid of whom? Without prompting, has the client indicated fear of the partner? Is the client afraid to stay in the home with the partner, or afraid to fight or disagree with the partner?
- What have been the consequences of disagreements or if the authority of the accused is challenged?
- How do clients describe the impact of the abuse on them? How do they feel about themselves, their ability/need to please their partner?
- Does either partner admit to abuse/violence against the partner and how does he or she explain it? Is there blame or responsibility taken? Who initiated the violent incident? (It is important to remember that although someone may strike the first blow, the person may have done so because a past pattern of abuse alerted him or her to imminent violence.)

However, even with such guidelines, assessing whether the violence is one-sided or mutual is challenging in both heterosexual and same-sex couples (Pitt & Dolan Soto, 2001). Fear and chronicity are the trademarks of abuse, transforming marital conflict into issues of power and control.

If individuals disclose being in an abusive relationship, further assessment about the nature, the severity of the abuse, and the willingness of the perpetrator to accept responsibility for his or her actions is critical, but, once again, in individual rather than conjoint meetings. Men who are abusive can be assessed for the extent to which they are willing to take responsibility for their abusive behaviours (Jenkins, 1990). Women who have been victimized should be assessed for trauma, their current risk of danger, and whether they have developed safety plans.

It would be naive to assume that women necessarily conceptualize their partner's behaviour as abusive and, even if they do, that they will leave the relationship. Carlson (1997) identified a number of coping strategies and stages in women's perceptions of the abuse. In the first stage, "It's My Fault," women typically blame themselves for the abuse, a process that is often reinforced by their partner's criticisms. She is likely to cope by trying to be a better wife and mother. In the second stage, "It's Not My Fault, but I'll Help You," she attempts to change his behaviours, for example, his abuse of substances. If this is unsuccessful, she may enter the third stage, "It's Your

Fault and I Hope You'll Change." With this comes the recognition that she cannot change him, which can leave her feeling powerless and depressed. If he resists assistance and intervention, she may enter the last stage, "Despair," in which leaving the relationship becomes her only option.

Formal Assessment Measures

Carlson suggests using two short scales by Mary Ann Dutton (1992)—the Attribution Questionnaire and Appraisal of Violence Situation—to assess which stage the women are in because this clearly has clinical implications. However, some of the other risk assessment scales mentioned below may replace the latter measure. The key is alerting a woman to the patterns common to violent men and, when appropriate, validating her fears that she is living in a dangerous situation. Measures that assess PTSD, such as the Impact of Events Scales—Revised[1] (Weiss & Marmar, 1996) and the Trauma Symptom Checklist (Briere, 1996) can also inform the focus of clinical intervention for women.

Formal assessment measures that ask victims to document the type and frequency of abusive behaviours are useful adjuncts (Jackson, Petretic-Jackson & Witte, 2002).[2] Examples include the Hudson's Spouse Abuse Scales for both Physical and Psychological Abuse (Hudson, 1992), the Revised Conflict Tactics Scales (Straus, Hamby, Boney-McCoy & Sugarman, 1996), or the Psychological Maltreatment of Women Scale (Tolman, 1989). Recently, Hegarty, Sheehan, and Schonfeld (1999) took items from each of these four scales and factor analyzed them. They identified four major themes: severe combined abuse, psychological abuse, physical abuse, and harassment, and created an eighty-item scale that has since been reduced to thirty items (Hegarty, Bush & Sheehan, 2005). Adding a sub-scale on harassment was an important contribution to assessing domestic abuse. Nevertheless, these measures do not provide clinical cut-off scores to determine more precisely whether a woman can be considered abused or not. The standardized measures of abuse behaviours should complement the assessment interview rather than being the sole method of identifying intimate partner violence. In addition to documenting abusive behaviours, clinicians need to confirm to what extent victims fear injury and/or have been injured by their partner (Heyman, Feldbau-Kohn, Ehrensaft, Langhinrichsen-Rohling & O'Leary, 2001).

If abuse is occurring, safeguards should include an in-depth assessment of the frequency and severity of the battering, including the existence of weapons. If the woman admits to being abused, one could administer Campbell's Danger Assessment[3] (2001), which assesses the potential for lethality (homicide) in abusive relationships. Campbell suggests first providing a calendar of the past year and asking women to mark approximately when each violent episode occurred and, from a list of five forms of violence ranging from slapping to using a weapon, what happened. This both assists the woman to see patterns and helps to dilute the typical minimization of the abuse. The woman is then asked to note the presence or absence of fifteen risk factors for violence, including increases in severity over the past year, drug use, control of daily activities, and violence outside the home. This two-step process often assists victims in realizing the risk to themselves and their children (Campbell, 2004).

Alternatively, one could use the Spousal Assault Risk Assessment Guide (SARA) (Whittemore & Kropp, 2002) to assess the risk of re-assault rather than lethality. The victim documents the presence or absence of twenty risk factors linked to spousal violence. The existence of the factors can be determined by the clinician in consultation with either the partner or the perpetrator and includes both general violence risk factors and factors specific to spousal assault.

Women who disclose that they have been assaulted need to create a safety plan and be provided with information regarding the cycle of violence, the location of the closest emergency shelters, legal protection, and government financial support (Davies, Lyon & Monti-Catania, 1998; Dutton, 1992). The plan should fit with the woman's wishes to leave her marriage, or to leave should violence reoccur. A woman can be encouraged to identify a friend or neighbour to go to in an emergency, to save as much money as she can, and make an extra set of car keys. If a woman chooses to stay in the relationship at this time, she can be connected with community services such as emergency shelters, crisis phone lines, or agencies that provide support groups for abused women. If a clinician becomes aware that a batterer is seriously contemplating harm to his partner, she or he has the responsibility to warn the woman immediately (Hart, 1988) and assist the woman in determining the need to contact police services.

With respect to assessment tools for the perpetrators of violence, especially men, a relatively new scale for abusive men, the Propensity for Abusiveness Scale[4] (Dutton, Landolt, Starzomski & Bodnarchuk, 2001) shows promise. Originally developed using reports from abused women and psychological profiles of abusive men, the items do not ask men to directly self-report their abusive behaviour, yet they significantly differentiate abusive from non-abusive men. As such, the responses from perpetrators are more reliable than the more direct measures of abusive relationships mentioned previously, where social desirability and denial typically result in minimizing the abuse.

If the perpetrator of the violence is willing to consider abuse-specific intervention, a useful tool is the University of Rhode Island Change Assessment

(URICA-DV), specifically developed to assess readiness for such treatment (Levesque, Gelles & Velicer, 2000). Using the Transtheoretical Model of Change (Prochaska, 1995), men who are in pre-contemplation (denying that the violence is a problem) would not be considered ready for group treatment. Rather, they would need individual sessions that assist them to move to the contemplation stage in which they begin to recognize the negative consequences of their abusive behaviours to both their spousal relationship and to their parenting. Once they begin to take responsibility, they would be considered ready for group treatment.

Obviously, when we are recommending that the first focus of the clinical work be on the abuse, this feedback to the couple needs to be handled sensitively. In recommending separate gender group treatment, for example, rather than marital therapy (as suggested in the following section), we may well be entreated to reconsider. Stating that the agency/therapist has found this approach to be the most successful and that, if marital issues arise during group, joint interviews with the primary therapist could be considered, can also help to allay fears (Babins-Wagner, personal communication, November 2011).

CLINICAL INTERVENTIONS FOR INTIMATE PARTNER VIOLENCE
Having uncovered family violence issues in the assessment phase, how, then, should clinicians intervene? There are now fairly well-established methods of treating intimate partner abuse. A feminist perspective is integral across the recommended interventions for men, women, or children (Petretic-Jackson, Witte, & Jackson, 2002).

Group Work
Even when couples wish to remain together, current clinical wisdom suggests that both men who are abusive and women who have been victimized fare better in separate gender groups than in conjoint therapy. Support groups for assaulted women are an integral part of many shelters and community programs (Abel, 2000; Tutty & Rothery, 2002), and groups for men who batter are the mainstay of the attempt to change abusive behaviour, especially when the criminal justice system is involved (Gondolf, 2002; Ursel, Tutty & LeMaistre, 2008). Although there are certainly circumstances that would support individual or conjoint sessions, little research has validated those approaches.

The fact that such treatments are offered in groups rather than individually or with couples has significance beyond the practical matter of offering services to a larger number of individuals at one time. Group work allows members to deal with one characteristic of family violence that is pervasive across different forms of abuse: social isolation. Participating in groups allows victims to understand that the problems they are experiencing are common reactions to being in an unnatural situation, thus alleviating guilt. The process results in both victims and perpetrators seeing the problem as having societal roots rather than simply being the result of individual faults. Research evidence suggests the societal permission that allows aggression toward women and children is central to the occurrence of family violence (Heise et al., 1999) and groups are a powerful medium in which to address this.

Another important aspect of group work is that, as with other problems characterized by denial, confrontation by a fellow group member is often more readily accepted than confrontation by a group leader. Fellow members are also more intimately aware of the ways that individuals avoid or ignore such confrontation, so they may provide helpful insights about resisting change. Group members can also be important role models for each other in deciding to make changes and providing feedback about the impact of behaving with partners in non-abusive ways.

Group Treatment for Perpetrators

The major therapeutic interventions to address women abused by their partners have centred on group treatment for men who batter. Common models include educational approaches such as the Duluth model (Pence & Paymar, 1993), narrative therapy models (Augusta-Scott & Dankwort, 2002; Jenkins, 1990; McGregor, Tutty, Babins-Wagner & Gill, 2002), strength-based groups (Lehmann & Simmons, 2009), and therapy groups that address family of origin issues (Pressman & Sheps, 1994). Newer models address the need to connect with the men, not simply lecturing or challenging their gender role stereotypes.

Anger management groups have been criticized because they ignore North American cultural beliefs that support men to behave abusively with women. It is argued that a focus on anger alone is simplistic and misguided since many men who hit their wives are perfectly able to deal with anger outside their homes (Gondolf, 2002). However, while most group models teach the use of anger-management behavioural techniques such as "time-outs" and "anger-logs," conceptualizing intimate partner violence as primarily a problem with anger has been strongly criticized as ignoring societal sanctions for men to treat women abusively (Gondolf, 2002) and perpetuating the myth that violence stems from individual problems of "managing anger" and being "out of control." Rather, feminist-informed groups challenge the beliefs that give men permission to treat women abusively (Russell, 1995).

The common interventions in feminist-informed groups include finding ways for men to accept responsibility for their abusive behaviours rather than adopting the "Well, she did it too" or the "She was more abusive to me than I was to her" approach to which men often revert at the beginning of group treatment. Changing patriarchal beliefs that men have the right to control women's behaviours is key. Changing behaviours, such as anticipating events that might lead the men to be violent and planning ways to avoid such abuse, are also common group activities. Some group approaches also teach the men to identify their feelings before they feel overwhelmed and behave violently, and to develop empathy for their women partners (Gondolf, 2002).

Batterer intervention groups are commonly led by mixed-gender leadership teams who provide strong role modelling for respecting and treating women as equal partners. However, if the woman co-leader is being ignored or subtly (or not so subtly) discounted, the male co-leader has a valuable opportunity to identify and challenge the discounting and to model responding to her as an equal and valued individual. Notably, though, group process can be vulnerable to members with sociopathic tendencies who can effectively derail the group focus: clinical wisdom suggests screening out men with personality disorders.

In spite of their perceived clinical value, male perpetrator groups remain controversial for several reasons. Firstly, concern has been expressed that offering groups for men takes resources away from emergency shelters for women, which are chronically short of beds and underfunded. This concern can be countered by the fact that the treatment for men is important to protect other women with whom they may subsequently form relationships, and that funding for such groups may not necessarily deprive shelters of funding.

A second key concern is whether men's groups are effective (Edelson & Tolman, 1992; Tutty, 2002). A considerable number of evaluations have been conducted on such groups. Canadian studies include Augusta-Scott and Dankwort (2002) in Nova Scotia; Barrera, Palmer, Brown, and Kalaher (1994), Scott and Wolfe (2000), and Tutty, Bidgood, Rothery, and Bidgood (2001) in Ontario; and McGregor, Tutty, Babins-Wagner, and Gill (2002) in Alberta.

Men who assault their partners present challenges in research because, in addition to the typical methodological difficulties encountered in evaluating treatment of any form, battering is characterized by denial. Further, there is the possibility of triggering legal action if men are honest about their offending behaviour. Given the well-accepted clinical theory of the cycle of violence (Walker, 1979), it is difficult to interpret a reduction of violence over shorter periods of time as conclusive proof that aggression has ceased. It is rare to find research that documents the long-term effectiveness of the groups beyond six months. Two exceptions are Edelson and Syers (1991), who reassessed men at eighteen months, and Gondolf (2002), who conducted a fifteen-month follow-up of four batterer intervention groups and concluded that not only were program completers significantly less likely to re-assault than the dropouts, even the shorter programs were effective for completers.

However, Gondolf (2002) also identified a subgroup of about 20 percent of men mandated to intervention programs who were identified as dangerous and who continued to assault their partners despite intervention. Such offenders need a different treatment approach; however, they are difficult to identify. Further, Gondolf (2002) recommends screening for severe substance abuse and psychological problems that are associated with dropping out of programs.

Despite the mixed results on the efficacy of batterer intervention programs, generally domestic violence researchers agree that batterer intervention programs have some impact on reducing re-abuse (Babcock et al., 2004; Feder & Wilson, 2006; Feder et al., 2008; Lohr et al., 2006; Stuart et al., 2007).

A final concern is that, while the physical violence may cease, emotional abuse may continue or even increase, leaving victims still living in abusive partnerships (Pressman, 1989; Pressman & Sheps, 1994). Women's advocates remain concerned that the groups can teach men to be more effective manipulators using their knowledge to control their partners even more skilfully (Gondolf, 2002; Tutty, 2002). Only with research engaging the women partners to provide feedback about how their partner responded can we gauge the extent to which, and for whom, group intervention may be contraindicated.

Group Intervention for Abused Women

While groups for women remain the major therapeutic intervention, if women present with symptoms of PTSD, then individual clinical sessions are recommended to address initially. Cognitive therapy is one of the most commonly utilized strategies for PTSD (Olavson Rothbaum & Foa, 1996) and some models have been developed specifically for abused women (Kubany & Watson, 2002).

Groups—whether support, psycho-educational, or therapeutic—can be a powerful medium for women abused by intimate partners. The benefits of offering support to women in groups include the fact that groups reduce social isolation, one of the significant effects of being in an abusive relationship. Members of support groups provide encouragement to each other, allowing women to see that their experiences with and reactions to the abuse are not unique (Abel, 2000; Tutty & Rothery, 2002).

Group members are often at different stages in their acknowledgement of having been abused and willingness to decide what to do about it. Some may come to the group suspecting something is not right, but not fully recognizing the seriousness of their situation. Others may have left their partners, or may be in the process of deciding whether to do so or not. The opportunity to learn from others' experiences is clearly present and is seen as a prime benefit of the group process. A feminist perspective is key (Rinfret-Raynor & Cantin, 1997).

In 1994, Pressman and Sheps suggested guidelines for intervention that remain appropriate in abused women's groups today. First, the safety of the woman is critical and, if she has not already made one, the group should assist in developing safety plans in the event of further violence (see Davies, Lyon & Monti-Catania, 1998). Denying or minimizing the abuse may need to be confronted in a supportive way, or through education about the dynamics of intimate partner violence. The women may need to explore their reasons for having stayed in the abusive relationship in an effort to reduce their sense of self-blame. Assisting them to identify ways that they have resisted the abuse or acted to protect themselves and their children can help with this goal—and may have a positive impact on women's self-esteem and sense of efficacy.

Research evidence for the usefulness of women's support groups for intimate partner abuse is available. Several (Rinfret-Raynor & Cantin, 1997; Tutty, Bidgood & Rothery, 1993) reported statistically significant pre-test/post-test improvements in areas such as self-esteem, anger levels, attitudes toward marriage and the family, and depression. The results of two qualitative studies (Moldon, 2002; Tutty & Rothery, 2002) further support the utility of women's groups.

Moldon (2002) interviewed eight women who attended a support group known as the "Safe Journey" program, developing a framework to describe how the group provides an environment in which abused women move from the "lost self" to the "reclaimed self." She entitled the process "Reclaiming Stories" and views it as a spiral that incorporates both the content and process of attending group.

The group members developed a sense of safety both from building trust with the other members and the leaders, and being willing to disclose some details of the abuse in their intimate partner relationships. They began to realize how much of themselves they had forsaken to cope with the relationship, and developed bonds with each other as they identified the common experiences of being in abusive partnerships. The group members utilized information about the cycle of violence and the common experiences of women in abusive partner relationships to consider reclaiming their lives and making new decisions, either about how they will behave differently in their current relationships or whether they will separate and start anew.

This model provides a useful overview for conceptualizing the interaction of group content and process and is congruent with other descriptions of the benefits of groups for abused women (Pressman, 1989).

Other Clinical Interventions

While the use of family therapy for parents who physically abuse their children is widely accepted, as noted previously, its use with women abused by their partners is controversial. However, although traditional family and couples therapy have been strongly criticized for the manner in which they failed to address issues of wife assault (Pressman, 1989), it may be a mistake to entirely reject couples intervention as a form of intervention. The fact that so many women return home to abusive partners suggests that feminist-informed couples intervention for women who insist that they wish to remain in their relationships might be appropriate at some point (Brannen & Rubin, 1996; McCollum & Stith, 2008; Vetere & Cooper, 2001), likely after each has participated in gender-specific groups (Geffner & Rosenbaum, 1990; O'Leary, 1996). Family work with mothers and their children to deal with the impacts of the abuse has been suggested by Rabenstein and Lehmann (2000).

Unlike in traditional couples interventions, feminist-informed therapists accept the premise that the perpetrator is responsible for his actions, whatever the "provocation," and advocate that violence is not acceptable. They integrate this stance into a family systems approach in a way that allows the therapeutic intervention without implying that the victim is a part of the abuse (Magill, 1989). As ever, the safety needs of the women remain a major concern. Despite the suggestions offered regarding addressing safety, much skepticism remains about treating a couple together (Gondolf, 2002).

A recent evaluation of two couples groups, offered only after each member had participated in gender-specific groups for a year (Johannson & Tutty, 1998), showed significant increases in problem-solving and communication skills with violence levels approaching zero for those who completed the group work. The group was developed when previous gender-specific groups' members commented that they were able to use the communication and problem-solving skills that they had learned in groups with neighbours, bosses, and co-workers; however, they still found it difficult to change their behaviours with their intimate partners. The groups were offered for two hours a week over a period of twelve weeks. The group facilitators were a male/female social work team with experience in counselling, group work, and family violence. The educational focus was minimal, with treatment materials briefly reviewed, so that the major emphasis was on practising the skills. The facilitators served as guides in the couples' communication process to intervene and provide corrective direction in the couples' efforts to integrate skills. The group members provided support. Nevertheless, only a little more than half of the couples finished and several incidents of serious abusive behaviour occurred during the group sessions, including the kidnapping of children and the resurgence of violence.

Further research on couples approaches is essential. A recent article by O'Leary (2001) proposes that couples therapy could be one of a series of multiple interventions in complex cases. Nevertheless, the available evidence suggests caution in using systems interventions, especially as the sole mode of treatment.

If the couple has children, they, too, will likely have been exposed to the marital violence and could suffer such reactions as aggression and withdrawal (Jaffe, Wolfe & Wilson, 1990; Lehmann & Rubenstein, 2002), especially if they have been abused themselves (Hughes, 1988). Recently, some authors have conceptualized children exposed to martial violence as also at risk for PTSD. The co-occurrence of child abuse and partner abuse within the same family warrants clinical assessment and intervention (O'Leary, Smith Slep & O'Leary, 2000). Group interventions for children remain the norm, and evaluations commonly report improvements (Peled & Davis, 1995; Wagar & Rodway, 1995).

What if the assessment identifies the less typical, yet still concerning, pattern of the woman being the primary aggressor and the man the victim? While less commonly available, group treatment models have been developed to assist aggressive women (Hamberger & Potente, 1996; Tutty, Babins-Wagner & Rothery, 2009). Clinicians have noted that women seem more willing to admit their abusive behaviours with partners or children and more willing to seek assistance. However, we have yet to identify the most appropriate clinical strategy. Simply borrowing and applying the group approaches that work for abusive men seems inappropriate.

Even less common, understandably, are approaches to assist male victims of intimate partner violence (Tutty, 1999). A recent group format, developed by Calgary Counselling and offered to five cohorts of men who were primarily psychologically abused by women partners, shows promise (Tutty & Babins-Wagner, 2002).

CONCLUSION

There are certainly other methods by which clinicians can adapt their practice to be more sensitive to issues of family violence. Responding to intimate partner violence solely with clinical interventions is obviously not sufficient. Problems of resources—such as poverty, unemployment, substance abuse, and lack of adequate housing—are embedded in the problems experienced by these families and must be addressed in addition to focusing on the emotional distress created by living in a violent household (Tutty & Goard, 2002). Perhaps, ironically, while cautioning against utilizing family therapy as an intervention in intimate partner violence, we advocate assessing not only the family system but also the larger environment through an ecological framework. To date, parallel groups for victims, perpetrators, and children exposed to marital violence in a coordinated community approach have become the standard (Shepard & Pence, 1999), thus confirming that when violence occurs between any two family members, all are affected.

In the past, clinicians have largely ignored violence and inadvertently helped families to maintain their secret. Acknowledging the distress of the victims of family violence is the first step in becoming aware of the many ways that we can help families with violent members. The second step is recognizing that, unless we address the abuse directly, we remain another link in the system that keeps victims trapped in violent relationships.

NOTES

1 Contact: Daniel Weiss, Ph.D., Department of Psychiatry, University of California—San Francisco, Box f–0984, San Francisco, CA, 94143–0984.
2 Most measures must be purchased. Exceptions will be noted.
3 The 2001 version is available at: http://www.dangerassessment.org/Web Application1/.
4 Available at www.psych.ubc.ca/~ddutton/psychology430/Abuse/tsld051.htm.

REFERENCES

Abel, E.M. (2000). Psychosocial treatments for battered women: A review of the empirical research. *Research on Social Work Practice, 10*(1), 55–77.

Adams, C.M. (2006). The consequences of witnessing family violence on children and implications for family counsellors. *The Family Journal: Counselling and Therapy for Couples and Families, 14*, 334–41.

Augusta-Scott, T., & Dankwort, J. (2002). Partner abuse group intervention: Lessons from education and narrative therapy approaches. *Journal of Interpersonal Violence, 17*(7), 783–805.

Babcock, J.C., Green, C., & Robie, C. (2004). Does batterers' treatment work? A meta-analytic review of domestic violence treatment. *Clinical Psychology Review, 23*, 1023–53.

Barrera, M., Palmer, S., Brown, R., & Kalaher, S. (1994). Characteristics of court-involved men and non-court-involved men who abuse their wives. *Journal of Family Violence, 9*, 333–45.

Bograd, M. (1984). Family systems approaches to wife battering: A feminist critique. *American Journal of Orthopsychiatry, 54*(4), 558–68.

Brannen, S.J., & Rubin, A. (1996). Comparing the effectiveness of gender-specific and couples groups in a court-mandated spouse abuse program. *Research on Social Work Practice, 6*, 405–524.

Brekke, J. (1987). Detecting wife and child abuse in clinical settings. *Social Case-work: The Journal of Contemporary Social Work, 68,* 332–38.

Briere, J. (1996). Psychometric review of the Trauma Symptom Inventory (TSI). In B.H. Stamm (Ed.), *Measurement of stress, trauma, and adaptation* (pp. 381–83). Lutherville, MD: Sidran Press.

Campbell, J.C. (2001). Safety planning based on lethality assessment for partners of batterers in intervention programs. *Journal of Aggression, Maltreatment & Trauma, 5*(2), 129–43.

Campbell, J.C. (2004). Helping women understand their risk in situations of intimate partner violence. *Journal of Interpersonal Violence, 19*(12), 1464–77.

Carlson, B. (1997). A stress and coping approach to intervention with abused women. *Family Relations, 46,* 291–98.

Chang, J.C., Cluss, P.A., Ranieri, L., Hawker, L., Buranosky, R., Dado, D., McNeil, M., & Scholle, S.H. (2005). Health care interventions for intimate partner violence: What women want. *Women's Health Issues, 15,* 21–31.

Davies, J., Lyon, E., & Monti-Catania, D. (1998). *Safety planning with battered women: Complex lives/difficult choices.* Thousand Oaks, CA: Sage.

Dutton, D.G., Landolt, M.A., Starzomski, A., & Bodnarchuk, M. (2001). Validation of the Propensity for Abusiveness Scale in diverse male populations. *Journal of Family Violence, 16*(1), 59–73.

Dutton, M. (1992). *Empowering and healing the battered woman.* New York: Springer.

Edelson, J., & Syers, M. (1991). The effects of group treatment for men who batter: An 18-month follow-up study. *Research on Social Work Practice, 1*(3), 227–43.

Edelson, J.L., & Tolman, R.M. (1992). *Intervention for men who batter: An ecological approach.* Newbury Park, CA: Sage.

Eisikovits, Z., & Buchbinder, E. (1996). Pathways to disenchantment: Battered women's views of their social workers. *Journal of Interpersonal Violence, 11*(3), 425–40.

Epstein, N.B., Bishop, D.S., & Baldwin, L.M. (1982). McMaster Model of Family Functioning: A view of the normal family. In F. Walsh (Ed.), *Normal family processes* (pp. 115–41). New York: Guilford.

Feder, L., & Dugan, L. (2004). *Testing a court-mandated treatment program for domestic violence offenders: The Broward experiment.* NCJ Document no. 199729. Retrieved from: http://www.ncjrs.gov/pdffiles1/nij/199729.pdf.

Feder, L., & Wilson, D.B. (2006). Mandated batterer intervention programs to reduce domestic violence. In B.C. Welsh & D.P. Farrington (Eds.), *Preventing crime: What works for children, offenders, victims, and places* (pp. 131–45). London: Springer.

Finkelhor, D. (1983). Common features of family abuse. In D. Finkelhor, R. Gelles, G. Hotaling & M. Straus (Eds.), *The dark side of families* (pp. 119–30). Beverly Hills: Sage.

Follette, V.M., & Pistorello, J. (1995). Couples therapy. In C. Classen, (Ed.), *Treating women molested in childhood* (pp. 129–61). San Francisco: Jossey-Bass.

Geffner, R., & Rosenbaum, A. (1990). Characteristics and treatment of batterers. *Behavioural Sciences and the Law, 8,* 131–40.

Gleason, W. (1993). Mental disorders in battered women: An empirical study. *Violence and Victims, 8*(1), 53–68.

Gill, M., & Tutty, L. (1999). Male survivors of childhood sexual abuse: A qualitative study and issues for clinical consideration. *Journal of Child Sexual Abuse 7*(3), 19–33.

Gondolf, E.W. (2002). *Batterer intervention systems: Issues, outcomes, and recommendations.* Thousand Oaks, CA: Sage.

Greene, K., & Bogo, M. (2002). The different faces of intimate violence: Implications for assessment and treatment. *Journal of Marital and Family Therapy, 28*(4), 455–66.

Hamberger, L.K., & Potente, T. (1996). Counselling heterosexual women arrested for domestic violence: Implications for theory and practice. In L.K. Hamberger & C. Renzetti (Eds.), *Domestic partner abuse* (pp. 53–75). New York: Springer.

Hansen, M., & Goldenberg, I. (1993). Conjoint therapy with violent couples: Some valid considerations. In M. Hansen & M. Harway (Eds.), *Battering and family therapy: A feminist perspective* (pp. 82–92). Newbury Park, CA: Sage.

Hart, B. (1988). Beyond the "duty to warn": A therapist's "duty to protect" battered women and children. In K. Yllo & M. Bograd (Eds.), *Feminist perspectives on wife abuse* (pp. 234–48). Newbury Park, CA: Sage.

Hegarty, K. (2011). Domestic violence: The hidden epidemic associated with mental illness. *British Journal of Psychiatry, 198*(3), 169–70.

Hegarty, K., Bush, K., & Sheehan, M. (2005). The Composite Abuse Scale: Further development and assessment of reliability and validity of a multidimensional partner abuse measure. *Violence & Victims, 20*(5), 529–47.

Hegarty, K.L., Sheehan, M., & Schonfeld, C. (1999). A multidimensional definition of partner abuse: Development and preliminary validation of the Composite Abuse Scale. *Journal of Family Violence, 14*(4), 399–414.

Heise, L., Ellsberg, M., & Gottemoeller, M. (1999). *Ending violence against women.* Population Reports, Series L, no. 11. Baltimore: Johns Hopkins University School of Public Health, Population Information Program.

Heyman, R.E., Feldbau-Kohn, S.R., Ehrensaft, M.K., Langhinrichsen-Rohling, J., & O'Leary, K.D. (2001). Can questionnaire reports correctly classify relationship distress and partner physical abuse? *Journal of Family Psychology, 15*(2), 334–46.

Hotaling, G., & Sugarman, D. (1986). An analysis of risk markers in husband to wife violence: The current state of knowledge. *Violence and Victims, 1,* 101–24.

Hudson, W.W. (1992). The WALMYR *assessment scales scoring manual.* Tempe, AZ: WALMYR.

Hughes, H. (1988). Psychological and behavioural correlates of family violence in child witnesses and victims. *American Journal of Orthopsychiatry, 58*(1), 77–90.

Jackson, T.L., Petretic-Jackson, P.A., & Witte, T.H. (2002). Mental health assessment tools and techniques for working with battered women. In A.L. Roberts (Ed.), *Handbook of domestic violence intervention strategies: Policies, programs, and legal remedies* (pp. 278–97). New York: Oxford University Press.

Jaffe, P., Wolfe, D., & Wilson, S. (1990). *Children of battered women.* Newbury Park, CA: Sage.

Jenkins, A. (1990). *Invitations to responsibility: The therapeutic engagement of men who are violent and abusive.* Adelaide, AU: Dulwich Centre.

Johannson, M., & Tutty, L. (1998). An evaluation of after-treatment couple's groups for wife abuse. *Family Relations, 47*(1), 27–35.

Johnson, M.P., & Leone, J.M. (2005). The differential effects of intimate terrorism and situational couple violence. *Journal of Family Issues, 26,* 322–49.

Kelly, J.B., & Johnson, M.P. (2008). Differentiation among types of intimate partner violence: Research update and implications for interventions. *Family Court Review, 46*(3), 476–99.

Kemp, A., Green, B., Hovanitz, C., & Rawlings, E. (1995). Incidence and correlates of posttraumatic stress disorder in battered women. *Journal of Interpersonal Violence, 10*(1), 43–55.

Kubany, E.S., & Watson, S.B. (2002). Cognitive trauma therapy for formerly battered women with PTSD: Conceptual bases and treatment outcomes. *Cognitive and Behavioural Practice, 9,* 111–27.

Lehmann, P., & Rubenstein, S. (2002). Children exposed to domestic violence: The role of impact assessment & treatment. In A.R. Roberts (Ed.), *Handbook of domestic violence intervention strategies: Policies, programs, and legal remedies* (pp. 343–64). New York: Oxford University Press.

Lehmann, P., & Simmons, C.A. (2009). Strengths-based batterer intervention: A new paradigm in ending family violence. New York: Springer.

Levesque, D.A., Gelles, R.J., & Velicer, W.F. (2000). Development and validation of a stages of change measure for men in batterer treatment. *Cognitive Therapy and Research, 24*(2), 175–99.

Lohr, J.M., Hamberger, L.K., White, T.H., & Parker, L.M. (2006). Scientific evidence for domestic violence treatment. In J.E. Fisher & W.T. O'Donahue (Eds.), *Practitioners' guide to evidence-based psychotherapy* (pp. 258–65). New York: Springer.

Magill, J. (1989). Family therapy: An approach to the treatment of wife assault. In B. Pressman, G. Cameron & M. Rothery (Eds.), *Intervening with assaulted women: Current research, theory, and practice* (pp. 47–55). Hillsdale, NJ: Lawrence Erlbaum.

McCollum, E.E., & Stith, S.M. (2008). Couples treatment for interpersonal violence: A review of outcome research literature and current clinical practices. *Violence and Victims, 23*(2), 187–201.

McGregor, M., Tutty, L., Babins-Wagner, R., & Gill, M. (2002). The long-term impact of group treatment for partner abuse. *Canadian Journal of Community Mental Health, 21,* 67–84.

Moldon, J. (2002). Rewriting stories: Women's responses to the Safe Journey Group. In L. Tutty & C. Goard (Eds.), *Reclaiming self: Issues and resources for women abused by intimate partners* (pp. 81–97). Halifax: Fernwood.

Nichols, M., & Schwartz, R. (2001). *Family therapy: Concepts and methods* (5th ed.). Boston: Allyn and Bacon.

Olavson Rothbaum, B., & Foa, E. (1996). Cognitive-behavioural therapy for posttraumatic stress disorder. In B.A. van der Kolk, A.C. McFarlane & L. Weisaeth (Eds.), *Traumatic stress: The effects of overwhelming experience on mind, body, and society* (pp. 491–509). New York: Guilford.

O'Leary, K.D. (1996). Physical aggression within intimate couples can be treated within a marital context under some circumstances. *Journal of Interpersonal Violence, 11*(3), 450–52.

O'Leary, K.D. (2001). Conjoint therapy for partner who engage in physically aggressive behaviour: Rationale and research. *Journal of Aggression, Maltreatment & Trauma, 5*(2), 145–64.

O'Leary, K.D., Smith Slep, A.M., & O'Leary, S.G. (2000). Co-occurrence of partner and parent aggression: Research and treatment implications. *Behaviour Therapy, 31*(4), 631–48.

Peled, E., & Davis, D. (1995). *Groupwork with children of battered women: A practitioner's manual.* Thousand Oaks, CA: Sage.

Pence, E., & Paymar, M. (1993). *Education groups for men who batter: The Duluth model.* New York: Springer.

Petretic-Jackson, P.A., Witte, T.H., & Jackson, T.L. (2002). Battered women: Treatment goals and treatment planning. In A.L. Roberts (Ed.), *Handbook of domestic violence intervention strategies: Policies, programs, and legal remedies* (pp. 298–320). New York: Oxford University Press.

Pitt, E., & Dolan Soto, D. (2001). Clinical considerations in working with victims of same-sex domestic violence. *Journal of Gay and Lesbian Medical Association, 5*(4), 163–69.

Pressman, B. (1989). Treatment of wife-abuse: The case for feminist therapy. In B. Pressman, G. Cameron & M. Rothery (Eds.), *Intervening with assaulted women: Current theory, research, and practice* (pp. 21–45). Hillsdale, NJ: Lawrence Erlbaum.

Pressman, B., & Sheps, A. (1994). Treating wife abuse: An integrated model. *International Journal of Group Psychotherapy, 44,* 477–97.

Prochaska, J. (1995). An eclectic and integrative approach: Transtheoretical therapy. In A. Gurman & S. Messer (Eds.), *Essential psychotherapies: Theory and practice* (pp. 403–40). New York: Guilford.

Rabenstein, S., & Lehmann, P. (2000). Mothers and children together: A family group treatment. *Journal of Aggression, Maltreatment & Trauma, 3,* 185–205.

Rinfret-Raynor, M., & Cantin, S. (1997). Feminist therapy for battered women: An assessment. In G. Kaufman Kantor & J.L. Jasinski (Eds.), *Out of the darkness: Contemporary perspectives on family violence* (pp. 219–34). Thousand Oaks, CA: Sage.

Rosenbaum, A., & O'Leary, K.D. (1986). The treatment of marital violence. In N. Jacobson & A. Gurman (Eds.), *Clinical handbook of marital therapy* (pp. 385–405). New York: Guilford.

Russell, M.N. (1995). *Confronting abusive beliefs: Group treatments for abusive men.* Thousand Oaks, CA: Sage.

Scott, K.L. & Wolfe, D.A. (2000). Change among batterers: Examining men's stories. *Journal of Interpersonal Violence, 15*(8), 827–42.

Senseman, R.L. (2002). Screening for intimate partner violence among gay and lesbian patients in primary care. *Clinical Excellence for Nurse Practitioners, 6*(4), 27–32.

Shepard, M.F., & Pence, E.L. (1999). *Coordinating community responses to domestic violence: Lessons from Duluth and beyond.* Thousand Oaks, CA: Sage.

Straus, M.A., Hamby, S.L., Boney-McCoy, S., & Sugarman, D.B. (1996). The Revised Conflict Tactics Scales (CTS2): Development and preliminary psychometric data. *Journal of Family Issues, 17*(3), 283–316.

Stuart, G.L., Temple, J.R., Moore, T.M. (2007). Improving batterer intervention programs through theory-based research. *Journal of the American Medical Association, 298*(5), 560–62.

Szinovacz, M.E., & Egley, L.C. (1995). Comparing one-partner and couple data on sensitive marital behaviours: The case of marital violence. *Journal of Marriage and the Family, 57,* 995–1010.

Thurston, W.E., Tutty, L.M., Eisener, A., Lalonde, L., Belenky, C., & Osborne, B. (2008). Implementation of universal screening for domestic violence in an urgent care community health centre. *Health Promotion Practice, 9*(2), 517–26.

Tilden, V.P., Schmidt, T.A., Limandri, B.J., Chiodo, G.T., Garland, M.J., & Loveless, P.A. (1994). Factors that influence clinicians' assessment and management of family violence. *American Journal of Public Health, 84*(4), 628–33.

Tjaden, P., Thoennes, N., & Allison, C.J. (1999). Comparing violence over the life span in samples of same-sex and opposite-sex cohabitants. *Violence and Victims, 14*(4), 413–25.

Tolman, R.M. (1989). The development of a measure of psychological maltreatment of women by their male partners. *Violence and Victims, 4*(3), 159–77.

Tutty, L. (1998). Mental health issues of abused women: The perceptions of shelter workers. *Canadian Journal of Community Mental Health, 17*(1), 79–102.

Tutty, L. (1999). Considering emotional abuse in the link between spouse and child abuse. *Journal of Emotional Abuse, 1*(4), 53–79.

Tutty, L. (2002). Groups for men who abuse intimate partners: Cause for scepticism or cautious optimism? *Social Work Today, 2*(17), 13–15.

Tutty, L. (2006). *Effective practices in sheltering women leaving violence in intimate relationships: Phase II.* Final report to the YWCA Canada. Retrieved from: http://www.ywca.ca/public_eng/advocacy/Shelter/YWCA_Shelter Report_EN.pdf.

Tutty, L., & Babins-Wagner, R. (2002, September). *A turn for the better: A group model for men abused by intimate partners.* Paper presented at the 7th International Conference on Family Violence, San Diego, CA.

Tutty, L.M., Babins-Wagner, R., & Rothery, M. (2009). A comparison of women who were mandated and non-mandated to the Responsible Choices for Women Group. *Journal of Aggression, Maltreatment & Trauma, 18*(7), 770–93.

Tutty, L., Bidgood, B., & Rothery, M. (1993). Support groups for battered women: Research on their efficacy. *Journal of Family Violence, 8*(4), 325–43.

Tutty, L., Bidgood, B., Rothery, M., & Bidgood, P. (2001). An evaluation of men's batterer treatment groups: A component of a co-ordinated community response. *Research on Social Work Practice, 11*(6), 645–70.

Tutty, L., & Goard, C. (2002). Woman abuse in Canada. In L. Tutty & C. Goard (Eds.), *Reclaiming self: Issues and resources for women abused by intimate partners* (pp. 10–24). Halifax: Fernwood.

Tutty, L., & Rothery, M. (2002). Beyond shelters: Support groups and community-based advocacy for abused women. In A.L. Roberts (Ed.), *Handbook of domestic violence intervention strategies: Policies, programs, and legal remedies* (pp. 396–418). New York: Oxford University Press.

Ursel, J., Tutty, L., & LeMaistre, J. (2008). The justice system response to domestic violence: Debates, discussions, and dialogues. In J. Ursel, L. Tutty & J. LeMaistre (Eds.), *What's law got to do with it? The law, specialized courts, and domestic violence in Canada* (pp. 1–17). Toronto: Cormorant Press.

Veinot, T. (1999). Who is the abuser? A screening challenge. *Education Wife Assault, 9*(2), 6–10.

Vetere, A., & Cooper, J. (2001). Working systemically with family violence: Risk, responsibility, and collaboration. *Journal of Family Therapy, 23*, 378–96.

Voth, P., & Tutty, L. (1999). Daughter's perceptions of being mothered by an incest survivor: A phenomenological study. *Journal of Child Sexual Abuse, 8*(3), 25–43.

Wagar, J., & Rodway, M. (1995). An evaluation of a group treatment approach for children who have witnessed wife abuse. *Journal of Family Violence, 10*(3), 295–306.

Walker, L. (1991). Post-traumatic stress disorder in women: Diagnosis and treatment of battered woman syndrome. *Psychotherapy, 28*(1), 21–29.

Walker, L.E. (1979). *The battered woman.* New York: Harper and Row.

Weiss, D., & Marmar, C.R. (1996). The Impact of Event Scale—Revised. In K. Wilson & T.M. Keane (Eds.), *Assessing psychological trauma and PTSD* (pp. 399–411). New York: Guilford.

Whittemore, K.E., & Kropp, P.R. (2002). Spousal assault risk assessment: A guide for clinicians. *Journal of Forensic Psychology Practice, 2*(2), 53–64.

Woods, A.B., Page, G.G., O'Campo, P. Pugh, L.C., Ford, D., & Campbell, J.C. (2005). The mediation effect of posttraumatic stress disorder symptoms on the relationship of intimate partner violence and IFN-γ levels. *American Journal of Community Psychology, 36*(1/2), 159–75.

Zubretsky, T.M. (2002). Promising directions for helping chemically involved battered women get safe and sober. In A.L. Roberts (Ed.), *Handbook of domestic violence intervention strategies: Policies, programs, and legal remedies* (pp. 321–40). New York: Oxford University Press.

16

ELDER ABUSE AND NEGLECT IN CANADA
AN OVERVIEW

LYNN MCDONALD, JULIE DERGAL, AND APRIL COLLINS

INTRODUCTION

Elder abuse has been a growing concern over the last twenty years. While it has emerged as a significant health and social problem worldwide, advances in the field have been slow (Lowenstein, 2009). In 1989, the landmark national survey revealed that 4 percent of older Canadians living in private dwellings experienced some form of abuse and neglect (Podnieks, Pillemer, Nicholson, Shillington & Frizzel, 1990). It was the publication of this study that successfully brought the problem of elder abuse and neglect to the forefront of research and practice for Canadian academics and clinicians.

The 1990s introduced a new generation of researchers who began to design studies that could be used to guide practice, formulate policy, and, to a lesser extent, reform legislation (e.g., Beaulieu, 1992). More recent efforts in the field include an improved awareness of the problem, specifically in Canada through the New Horizons for Seniors funding initiative (HRSDC, 2011), an undertaking of more rigorous prevalence studies (Cooper, Selwood & Livingston, 2008), and the implementation of community development initiatives (Ontario Government, 2002; WHO, 2002). Nevertheless, much knowledge is still needed about elder abuse in both the community and in institutions, especially in Canada.

This chapter will describe our current state of knowledge in the field of elder abuse and neglect, particularly in Canada. An overview of some of the challenges associated with the varying definitions of elder abuse and neglect used in research and practice, along with the current estimates of the incidence and prevalence of abuse in the community and institutions will be discussed. Theories of abuse and neglect will be presented, as well as the existing evidence related to the risk factors for abuse and neglect. Current Canadian legislative approaches, advances in protocols for detection and intervention, as well as innovations in programs are also reviewed. The chapter concludes with an examination of the preventative approaches that have been implemented in Canada, along with future directions for research, policy, and practice.

DEFINING ELDER ABUSE AND NEGLECT

The lack of a generally accepted definition of elder abuse and neglect has resulted in a plethora of descriptions that continue to generate controversy and debate in the literature (Bennett, 1990; Chappell, Gee, McDonald & Stones, 2003; Council of Europe, 1992; Decalmer & Glendenning, 1993; Kozma & Stones, 1995; Sanchez, 1996; Wallace, 1996). Nevertheless, most scholars agree on three basic categories of elder abuse: (1) domestic elder abuse, (2) institutional abuse, and (3) self-abuse. In addition, most would support the notion that the major types of abuse include physical, psychological, and financial abuse. Notably, however, there is little agreement beyond this broad classification scheme (Decalmer & Glendenning, 1993; Hudson, 1994; Wolf, 1992). In this chapter, the definitions of abuse will be based on those used by the National Center on Elder Abuse (NCEA) in the United States because there is some consensus about their utility.[1]

Domestic elder abuse refers to any of several forms of maltreatment of an older person by someone who has a special relationship with the older adult, such as a spouse, sibling, child, friend, or caregiver in the older person's own home or in the caregiver's home (NCEA, 2011). The abuse is called domestic abuse because it occurs in the community as opposed to an institutional setting. The abusive behaviour has the potential to cause physical, psychological, and/or material injury to the older person, which in turn results in distress and suffering (Hudson, 1991; McDonald, 1996).

Physical abuse is defined as the use of physical force that may result in bodily injury, physical pain, or impairment. Physical abuse may include, but is not limited to: striking (with or without an object), hitting, beating, pushing, shoving, shaking, slapping, kicking, pinching, and burning (NCEA, 2011; Stones, 1995; Wolf & Pillemer, 1989). Maltreatment such as the inappropriate use of drugs, physical restraints, and force-feeding are also examples of physical abuse (NCEA, 2011).

Sexual abuse, which is sometimes subsumed under physical abuse (McDonald, 1996), is defined as non-consensual sexual contact of any kind with an older adult. Sexual contact with any person incapable of giving consent is also considered sexual abuse. It includes, but is not limited to: unwanted touching, all types of sexual assault or battery, rape, sodomy, coerced nudity, and sexually explicit photographing (NCEA, 2011).

Psychological or emotional abuse is defined as the infliction of anguish, pain, or distress through verbal or non-verbal acts. This type of abuse is perhaps the most difficult to assess. It includes, but is not limited to: verbal assaults, insults, threats, intimidation, humiliation, and harassment. Other examples of emotional abuse include treating an older person like an infant; isolating the person from his or her family, friends, or regular activities; giving the older person the "silent treatment" and enforced social isolation (NCEA, 2011).

Material abuse, often referred to as *financial abuse*, involves the illegal or improper exploitation of the older person's funds, property, or assets. Examples include, but are not limited to: cashing an elderly person's cheques without authorization, forging an older person's signature, misusing or stealing an older person's money or possessions, coercing or deceiving an older person into signing any document (e.g., a will), and the improper use of guardianship or power of attorney (Gordon, 1992; Health and Welfare Canada, 1993; McDonald, 1996; NCEA, 2011).

Neglect is intentional or unintentional behaviour on the part of an informal or formal caregiver in whom the older person has placed his or her trust, which is harmful (McDonald, 1996). Neglect typically means the refusal or failure to provide an older person with the necessities of life such as water, food, clothing, shelter, personal hygiene, medicine, comfort, personal safety, and other essentials (NCEA, 2011). Neglect can be difficult to identify because the symptoms can easily be confused with illness (Filinson & Ingman, 1989).

Self-neglect is characterized as behaviour that threatens an older person's own health and safety. Self-neglect usually means that the older adult refuses or fails to provide himself or herself with the necessities of life. This definition excludes the situation in which a mentally competent older person knowingly makes a voluntary decision to engage in acts that threaten his or her safety (NCEA, 2011). However, some researchers argue that self-infliction of abuse is a case of not looking after one's self due to dementia or other disabilities and is therefore a failure of the caregiving system, not a case of neglect (McDonald, 2011).

DEFINITIONAL CHALLENGES
Many elder abuse professionals are weary of the continuing search for definitions of elder abuse and neglect. However, this is an important issue as the definition used determines who is identified as abused, what the legislation covers, and who is eligible for services. The definition will also determine

the type of treatment offered and, ultimately, the effectiveness of the intervention. Therefore, accurate definitions of abuse and neglect are essential.

The variation in the definitions of elder abuse makes it difficult to compare or pool data collected across the different Canadian provinces and/or from different social agencies and makes international comparisons difficult. The "definitional disarray" noted by Pillemer and Finkelhor (1988, p. 52) can be attributed to a number of factors, not the least of which is that the definitions have been developed by different stakeholders with different perspectives—the abused older person, the caregiver, the health professional, the lawyer, the police, the social worker, and the policy-maker. Thus, the move toward embracing and listening to the diversity of perspectives in some ways has slowed the move toward consensus seeking. This, in turn, has perpetuated the problem of definitional imprecision.

A look at the earlier literature on elder abuse suggests that there was a tendency among researchers and practitioners to develop either taxonomies or typologies of elder abuse and neglect (Block & Sinnot, 1979; Chen, Bell, Dolinsky, Doyle & Dunn, 1981; Hickey & Douglass, 1981; Lau & Kosberg, 1979; McDonald, Hornick, Robertson & Wallace, 1991; Pillemer & Finkelhor, 1988; Rathbone-McCuan & Voyles, 1982; Sengstock & Hwalek, 1987; Sengstock & Liang, 1983; Steinmetz, 1990) or to establish broad, all-encompassing conceptual definitions to capture its multi-dimensional nature (Filinson, 1989; Fulmer & O'Malley, 1987; Hudson, 1988; Johnson, 1986, 1991; O'Malley, Everett, O'Malley & Campion, 1983; O'Malley, Segal & Perez, 1979; Podnieks, 1985; Rathbone-McCuan, 1980; WHO, 2002; Wolf, 1988). The problem with descriptive lists is that there is no uniformity among the categories or within the categories themselves. As well, the categories contain such a wide range of abuses that they tend to become ineffectual in application because every act has the potential of being construed as abusive or neglectful. The conceptual definitions also suffer from problems, with some focusing on causal factors, while others refer to the means and the outcome of abuse (Johnson, 1991; Stones, 1995). The unevenness of the conceptual definitions and their imprecise nature cause confusion for researchers and health care professionals alike.

Even though the terminology remains in a state of flux, there was a concerted effort in the 1990s to address the lack of consensus regarding definitions of abuse and neglect. Stones (1995), for example, helped to clarify that there are three basic approaches to the meaning and definitions of elder abuse and neglect in the professional literature. There are connotative definitions that emphasize the consequences of abuse; there are definitions based on structural criteria that indicate the contravention of acknowledged standards such as those specified in law; and finally, there are denotative definitions, which are the same as the descriptive lists noted above.

Even as the weaknesses of existing definitions are being tackled, new issues are emerging that complicate this matter. For example, the globalization of activities related to abuse and neglect has resulted in important contributions from authors around the world. This globalization has pushed local experts to address issues related to diversity within Canada and the United States (Bent, 2009; Spencer & Gutman, 2008). Currently, the results of a few Canadian studies have described abuse and neglect in different ethnocultural contexts (Aboriginal Nurses Association of Canada, 1992; Bent, 2009; Bergin, 1995; Spencer, 1996). However, our knowledge about this important issue is, at best, rudimentary.

Thus, the challenge before academics and clinicians alike will be to find the balance between honouring stakeholder perspectives and reaching consensus regarding what should be included in our definitions of elder abuse and neglect (McDonald, Hornick, Robertson & Wallace, 1991).

ELDER ABUSE AND NEGLECT IN THE COMMUNITY

One of the more recent developments is the increase in prevalence studies worldwide. Several systematic reviews have been conducted in the last several years (Cooper et al., 2008; McDonald, 2011). For example, a systematic review was conducted to measure the prevalence of elder abuse or neglect as reported by older people themselves, or family and professional caregivers, or in studies using objective measures conducted before 2006 (Cooper et al., 2008). The authors concluded that one in four older adults are at risk of abuse, and many of these cases go undetected.

A more recent review found thirteen community abuse prevalence studies that met the inclusion criteria of random sampling, clear inclusion factors, standardization of method, and standardized measurement instruments (McDonald, 2011). The community prevalence research included two studies from Canada (Podnieks, 1993; Pottie Bunge, 2000); three from the United States (Acierno et al., 2010; Laumann, Leitsch & Waite, 2008; Pillemer & Finkelhor, 1988); one from India (Chokkanathan & Lee, 2005); six from Europe (Comijs, Smit, Pot, Bouter & Jonker, 1998; Garre-Olmo et al., 2009; Iborra, 2005; Naughton et al., 2010; O'Keeffe et al., 2007; Soares et al., 2010); and one from Israel (Lowenstein, Eisikovits, Band-Winterstein & Enosh, 2009). As would be expected, the overall prevalence rates vary widely between countries (2.6 percent in the UK, 11.4 percent in the US, 29.3 percent in Spain) and within countries, as is the case for the United States—11.4 percent in Acierno and colleagues' (2010) study and 3.2 percent in Pillemer and Finkelhor's (1988) study. This comes as no surprise because the age for inclusion in the studies vary, as do the prevalence periods, the types of abuses addressed, the mechanisms for data collection, and the measures used. As well, abuse is a hidden problem that older adults sometimes feel uncomfortable reporting (McDonald et al., 1991), and since they are rarely in the public eye, the cases reported probably represent only "the tip of the iceberg." (See Chapter 17 for further discussion regarding the perspectives of older adults.)

The two studies carried out in Canada are somewhat outdated, but they are the only prevalence studies available today. The first study, a national telephone survey in Canada, was carried out in 1989 with 2,008 randomly selected older adults. The study found that about 4 percent of the sample reported some type of abuse (Podnieks et al., 1990), with approximately 2.5 percent of the sample experiencing financial abuse, 1.4 percent experiencing chronic verbal aggression, .5 percent suffering from physical abuse, and approximately .4 percent reported neglect. Spouses tended to perpetrate physical abuse and chronic verbal aggression, whereas financial abuse tended to be perpetrated by both relatives and non-relatives. Men and women were equally likely to be abused (Podnieks et al., 1990).

The second Canadian prevalence study, the 1999 General Social Survey on Victimization, conducted phone interviews with 4,324 randomly selected older adults sixty-five years of age and over. Only 1 percent of this population indicated physical or sexual abuse by a spouse, adult child, or caregiver in the five years prior to the survey (Pottie Bunge, 2000). According to Pottie Bunge (2000), of this group, 7 percent experienced psychological abuse and 1 percent financial abuse. However, the two studies are not comparable because the prevalence periods are different (i.e., five years versus one year), the abuse categories are different (i.e., sexual abuse was not measured in the Podnieks study), and different measures of financial abuse were used. As a result, little can be said about an increase, decrease, or constancy in abuse rates from 1989 to 1999 because of the significant differences between the studies.

Incidence rates (new cases in a given time frame) for elder abuse are still virtually unknown in most countries, including Canada. There is one incidence study of police-reported cases in 1999, from 164 police forces in seven provinces that participated in this incident-based Uniform Crime Reporting (UCR2) Survey, representing 46 percent of the national volume of reported crime. Adults sixty-five and over represented 2 percent of all victims of violent offences reported to a sample of police agencies in Canada. This incidence study identified that there were 802 cases of violence against older adults by family members. Among those who were mistreated by a family member, older adults were most likely to be abused by adult children (43 percent) and spouses (28 percent). While women were likely to be victimized by both adult children (37 percent) and spouses (34 percent), men were more often abused by an adult child (53 percent). Fifty-four percent of the older adults were the victims of common assault, 22 percent by uttering threats and 13 percent assault with a weapon or causing bodily harm, whether or not the victim was female or male (Pottie Bunge, 2000, p. 30).

There are two studies from the United States that provide data on the number of new cases of abuse that appear each year. The results from the National Elder Abuse Incidence Study in the United States provide some insight into this issue. In a 1996 survey, the NCEA found that approximately 450,000 people sixty years of age and older, in domestic settings, had been abused and/or neglected (Administration on Aging, 1998). It is noteworthy that of this total, only 16 percent (70,942) had been reported to and substantiated by Adults Protection Services (APS). Of the incidents of substantiated reports (70,942), nearly one-half (48.7 percent) involved neglect, while slightly more than one-third (35.4 percent) involved emotional or psychological abuse. Financial abuse accounted for slightly less than one-third (30.2 percent) of all substantiated reports, while one-quarter involved physical abuse (25.6 percent). Rates of abandonment (3.6 percent), sexual abuse (.3 percent), and other forms of maltreatment (1.4 percent), while important, had wide confidence bands so results should be interpreted cautiously (Administration on Aging, 1998).

More recently, a secondary analysis of national-level elder abuse data was conducted using the incident reports (N = 87,422) from the National Incident-Based Reporting System (NIBRS) in the United States, from 2000 to 2005 (Krienert, Walsh & Turner, 2009). This study improved upon previous work by using a national sample and employed a legal definition of elder abuse that alleviated some of the definitional concerns expressed in the literature. The measure used official incident reports that were derived from cases of victims aged sixty or older reported to law enforcement. These incident reports were then linked to data describing the characteristics of the victim and the offender. The results suggested that females were more frequently abused than males, and that males were more likely to be offenders. Older males were more likely to experience aggravated assaults, whereas females were more likely to experience both simple assaults and intimidation, with females more often reporting no injury from an event. The authors suggest that the abuse older women experience may be more difficult to identify because it may be psychological in nature.

In Canada, we have no way of knowing whether the problem is getting better or worse because we have only outdated prevalence data—a quick snapshot in 1989 and a family violence study in 1999—and only one police incidence study that likely taps only the most severe cases. As we prepare for the future, it would be helpful to know the actual dimensions of the problem so that we can ensure that our intervention and educational strategies are calibrated to meet current needs. A new incidence study of community-dwelling older adults would produce more accurate prevention and intervention programs. Likewise, an incidence study, comparable to the National Incidence Study of Child Abuse conducted by Health Canada, would help us plan for the future.

ELDER ABUSE AND NEGLECT IN INSTITUTIONS

Canadians have been relatively slow to investigate elder abuse and neglect in institutional settings, despite the fact that concern was expressed about this type of abuse in the early 1980s (Podnieks, 1985). The term "institution" typically refers to a wide range of settings such as hospitals and long-term care facilities, which include nursing homes and homes for the aged (McDonald, 1996). In 1994–95 the federal government, in partnership with a national advisory group of elder abuse professionals, produced three publications on abuse and neglect of older adults in institutional settings (Beaulieu & Tremblay, 1995; Spencer, 1994; Spencer & Beaulieu, 1994). Recognizing that institutional abuse is a "slippery concept," according to these reports, abuse and neglect in the institution "refers to any act or omission directed at a resident of an institution that causes harm, or wrongfully deprives that person of his or her independence" (Spencer, 1994, p. 19). By expanding this definition, the author adds a new dimension not contained in most other definitions—namely, an abuser in an institution could now also be considered another person in a position of trust, just like a family member or a friend. A recent review by McDonald and colleagues (2008) for the federal government provides an overview of the latest studies of institutional abuse worldwide.

Elder abuse and neglect in institutions fall into the same categories as those used to describe domestic abuse, but the victims are likely to be more vulnerable to abuse because they require the protective environment of a facility (Beaulieu & Belanger, 1995; McDonald et al., 2008). Some researchers have added violations of civil or basic rights to the list of abuses that can occur in institutions, as well as a specific category of medical abuse which entails, "any medical procedure or treatment that is done without the permission of the older person or his or her legally recognized proxy" (Spencer, 1994, p. 20). Abuse or neglect in institutional settings can take several forms, such as "a single act in complete opposition to society's sense of proper conduct" (e.g., punching a resident), or "a repeated pattern of any types of abuse or neglect" (Spencer, 1994, p. 20). Institutions may also be the scene of systemic abuse and neglect, which refer to harmful situations created, permitted, or facilitated by the procedures within the institution, which are supposedly designed to provide care (Spencer, 1994, p. 24). There is also little agreement about the definitions of abuse and neglect in the institution for many of the same reasons as in domestic abuse: differing professional perspectives; personal values and beliefs; cultural differences; and differing perspectives between the caregiver and the abused (Bennett & Kingston, 1993; Spencer, 1994). Despite this lack of consensus, an increasingly comprehensive and complex grasp of institutional abuse seems to be developing (Beaulieu, 1992).

THE INCIDENCE AND PREVALENCE OF ELDER ABUSE AND NEGLECT IN INSTITUTIONS

Institutional abuse is likely to become a more pressing issue in the immediate future in Canada for several important reasons. First, the proportion of people aged sixty-five or older living in institutions has remained stable at 7 percent since 1981 (Ramage-Morin, 2005); however, the actual number living in health care institutions rose from 173,000 to more than 263,000 residents in 2005 (Ramage-Morin, 2005). As a result, even though the latest government policies support "aging in place" (Szikita Clark, 2008), there will still be a substantial number of older adults who require institutional care (Kozak & Lukawiecki, 2001; Ramage-Morin, 2005). If the same level of institutionalization is maintained, it has been projected that over 565,000 Canadians will require long-term care by 2031 (Trottier, Martel & Houle, 2000), and the quality of care—including the prevention of abuse and neglect of residents—will become increasingly significant.

The second issue about institutionalization in Canada is that those eighty-five years and older constitute the largest age group in long-term care settings and are frailer, have more complex needs, and are more likely to have some degree of cognitive impairment, such as dementia or physical disabilities compared to their community-residing counterparts (Spector, Fleishman, Pezzin & Spillman, 2001). Only about 12–13 percent of residents are married, and many others lack a close family member who lives within an hour of the facility (Hawes, 2002). Without an advocate, older adults in institutions are more dependent on others to provide care, which heightens their vulnerability to abuse and neglect. Within this context, a study of institutional mistreatment in Canada would seem reasonable.

There have been some recent studies conducted on abuse in institutions that provide some insight into this issue, albeit there are no studies in Canada. One of the better institutional studies, however, was a multi-method study carried out on a random sample in Germany following a pilot study. Following on his pilot, Göergen (2004) used a multi-method approach to examine abuse and neglect in German institutions using 251 in-depth interviews, and a survey of 361 nursing home staff in twenty-seven nursing homes randomly selected in one area of Germany. The multi-stage sample first randomly drew nursing homes from a sampling frame for the area and from within the homes chosen, wards were randomly selected. As in the pilot study, the abusive or neglectful behaviour of staff was captured in their responses to a list of forty-six acts and omissions of care. These measurements of abuse were based on the Conflict Tactics Scale (Straus, 1979) commonly used in studies of family violence and the scales developed by Pillemer and Moore (1989).

In the survey, over 70 percent of staff reported that they had behaved in an abusive or neglectful way toward residents at least once over a one-year period. Psychological abuse and neglect were the most common forms of abuse reported by over 50 percent of the sample. Sexual abuse was not reported at all. As well, more than 70 percent of staff reported they had observed at least one incident of abuse or neglect by their co-workers during the same period. The second component of the study was in-depth qualitative interviews with eighty-one nursing home staff from eight of the nursing homes. In these interviews, 70 percent of nursing staff reported that they had engaged in at least one incident of abusive or neglectful behaviour, whereas slightly more staff (77 percent) had witnessed one or more incidents of abuse or neglect. Interestingly enough, qualified nurses made up 63 percent of the sample, which the researcher considered to be an overrepresentation of qualified personnel, which is different from other studies (Pillemer & Moore, 1989). The fact that there was no correlation between the ratio of residents to staff but a correlation between the ratio of residents to the ratio of registered nurses for observed incidents ($r = .35$, $p > .001$) suggests that it is not the number of the staff that may help prevent abuse, but the quality of the staff. Although one of the stronger studies, it is important to note the response rate was only 36 percent and, as a result, no prevalence or incidence rates could be reported.

A study conducted in 2005 in Michigan estimated the incidence of elder neglect in nursing homes using a random-digit dialing survey among family members who had a relative in a nursing home ($n = 414$) (Zhang et al., 2011). Results of this study suggested that approximately 21 percent of nursing home residents were neglected on more than one occasion within the last twelve months. Both functional impairment and behavioural problems of the resident were shown to increase the odds of neglect. Another national study was identified in the United States that focused only on sexual abuse in institutions and investigated 124 adults aged sixty and over who had allegedly reported abuse to authorities in five states over a six-month period. Of these, thirty-two cases were substantiated (Ramsey-Klawsnik, Teaster, Mendiondo, Marcum, & Abner, 2008). Another recent large-scale study was conducted among sixteen Norwegian nursing homes, using clustered random sampling, and found that 91 percent of nursing home staff (n = 616) reported observing at least one act of inadequate care (Malmedal, Ingebrigtsen & Saveman, 2009).

In Canada, there have been no national prevalence or incidence studies of abuse and neglect in institutions. A study from Ontario provides a rudimentary picture of the nature and extent of institutional abuse. A random telephone survey of 804 registered nurses and registered nursing assistants in Ontario was conducted to determine the extent, circumstances, and type of abuses they had witnessed or heard about in their work (College of Nurses of Ontario, 1993). Nearly one-half of the respondents witnessed one or more incidents of abuse, with verbal abuse being the most common type (37 percent of respondents), followed by physical abuse (32 percent of respondents). Less than half of the reported cases were followed up (College of Nurses of Ontario, 1993). It is important to note that the survey reports only alleged incidents of abuse and the incidents were not restricted to any specific time period.

A THEORETICAL UNDERSTANDING OF ELDER ABUSE AND NEGLECT

At the outset, it is important to note that much of the literature on elder abuse does not make the essential distinction between theoretical explanations and the individual risk factors related to abuse (McDonald, 1996; McDonald et al., 1991). Typically, a theory provides a general, systematic explanation for how some part of the world works. In the elder abuse literature, a particular risk factor, such as stress, is often treated as the theoretical explanation, even though stress is only one factor and could be subsumed under a number of different theories. The relationships between the various risk factors and elder abuse should, in fact, form the crucial scaffolding upon which theories are built.

In the short history of elder abuse, different accounts of the relationships among the risk factors have led to at least four distinct theoretical perspectives, all of which have been "borrowed" from other disciplines and fields of study with few modifications being made in the transfer to the field of elder abuse. While the usefulness of these theories has been called into question, there has been very little work to advance the theories on elder abuse (Harbison et al., 2008). McDonald (2011) has recently proposed the use of the life course perspective, in which the existing or new theories could be embedded and would allow abuse to be examined over a lifetime and on multiple levels. The theories to date include the following, even though they tend to be outdated.

THE SITUATIONAL MODEL

The first and most widely accepted perspective on the cause of elder abuse is the situational model, which has its roots in the mainstream perspectives on child abuse and family violence (McDonald et al., 1991; Phillips, 1986). A well-known premise of the situational model is that stressful situations cause the caregiver to abuse the older person, who is usually viewed as the source of the stress because of some type of physical or mental impairment. This approach implies that mistreatment is a rational response to stressful situations. The situational variables that this theory associates with abuse include factors related to the caregiver and the older person, as well as the social and economic conditions of both parties (McDonald, 1996). For example, an unemployed caregiver who has an alcohol problem may abuse an older parent who is financially secure, but mentally impaired. Interventions grounded in this perspective attempt to reduce the stress of the caregiver through the provision of more support services and support groups (Scogin et al., 1992). One major flaw of this perspective is that it fails to account for the fact that some caregivers who experience the same stresses as abusers do not abuse older people. The perspective has also been criticized for being dangerously close to blaming the victim because it identifies the older person as the source of the stress. Studies have found little to modest evidence to support this model (Pillemer, 1993; Pittaway & Westhues, 1993).

SOCIAL EXCHANGE THEORY

Social Exchange Theory is founded on the assumptions "that social interaction involves an exchange of rewards and punishments between at least two people, and that all people seek to maximize rewards and minimize punishments" (Glendenning, 1993, p. 25). In the social exchange perspective, it is argued that as people age, they become more powerless, vulnerable, and dependent on their caregivers, and it is these characteristics that place them at risk for abuse (Phillips, 1986). In essence, the older adult remains in the abusive relationship only as long as the satisfaction of his or her needs exceed the costs of the maltreatment. There are many difficulties with this perspective, one of which is its ageist assumption: people do not automatically become dependent and powerless as they age. Indeed, several researchers have argued and subsequently shown that the dependency may lie elsewhere (Pillemer & Wolf, 1986). Specifically, a number of investigations have found the abuser to be dependent on the older person. Thus, it is the abuser's sense of powerlessness that leads to maltreatment, not the older person's dependency (Homer & Gilleard, 1990; Pillemer & Suitor, 1992; Pillemer & Wolf, 1986, 1991). Interventions prompted by a social exchange analysis would seek to identify the dependent person and provide services designed to increase independence.

THE SYMBOLIC INTERACTION APPROACH

The Symbolic Interaction approach has been adopted from the family violence literature and focuses on the interactive processes between the older adult and the caregiver. This perspective emphasizes not only the behaviours of the older person and the caregiver, but also both people's symbolic interpretations of such behaviour. This analysis of elder abuse centres on the different meanings that people attribute to violence and the consequences these meanings have in certain situations (McDonald, 1996). Social learning, or modelling, is part of this perspective. The theory posits that abusers learn how to be violent from witnessing or suffering from violence, and the victims, in suffering abuse, learn to be more accepting of it. Treatment based on this approach would focus on changing family values and norms regarding abuse and would attempt to change the interpretations of the situation. The difficulty with this approach is that it does not consider the social or economic factors that might influence the abusive process and does not explain the finding that not all caregivers who were abused as children abuse older adults.

FEMINIST MODELS

Current prevalence studies indicate that spouse abuse is a significant dimension of elder abuse (Pillemer & Finkelhor, 1988; Podnieks, 1992). Despite these results, elder abuse experts have not shifted their perspective from the situational model. As a result, only limited theoretical advances have been made to explain this type of abuse (Aronson, Thornwell & Williams, 1995; McDonald, Pittaway & Nahmiash, 1995). Most scholars have assumed that spouse abuse is a form of wife abuse "grown old." It has been explained by a handful of feminist scholars as one consequence of family patriarchy, which is identified as one of the main sources of violence against women in society (Jack, 1994; Pittaway & Gallagher, 1995b; Vinton, 1991). Some scholars have belatedly questioned whether spouse abuse is ever first-time abuse in old age (Eckley & Vilakazi, 1995; Knight, 1994; McDonald et al., 1995; Neysmith, 1995). Feminist interventions generally include consciousness-raising and mutual problem solving within a caring and equal relationship. The shortcoming of this approach is that, to date, there is little empirical evidence to support the claims of the theory and it is, at best, a partial account of elder abuse since older men are just as likely as older women to be abused (Podnieks, 1993).

THE LIFE COURSE PERSPECTIVE

The complexity of elder abuse and neglect necessitates a longitudinal perspective that integrates the multiple levels that affect individual characteristics—contextual factors like institutional or community contexts and structural indicators such as policies. A possibility from social gerontology theory is the life course perspective, which can be either incorporated into existing theories like the "situation model" or utilized as a shell-like framework of the life course, which can host other theories and concepts about abuse and neglect at different levels of analysis (George, 2003). Most life course scholars focus on several of five paradigmatic principles that provide a concise, conceptual map of the life course: (1) development and aging as lifelong processes, (2) lives in historical time and place, (3) social timing, (4) linked lives, and (5) human agency (Elder & Pellerin, 1998). According to the principles of this framework, abuse and neglect can be treated as major turning points in a person's life. The benefits of using this perspective include the inclusion of systemic factors in abuse such as those found in institutions or policies; recognition that the abused older adult is embedded in relationships with others that incorporate professional and informal caregivers; the inclusion of period and cohort effects to show how abuse and neglect may be influenced by the historical times and the cohort with whom the person has travelled through life; and the appreciation that older adults are their own agents who are capable of making their own decisions (McDonald, 2011).

Few compelling theories have been proposed to explain the abuse of older adults in institutions. Several North American scholars have identified a number of factors that may contribute to the abuse of older residents by institutional staff. These include the lack of comprehensive and consistent policies with respect to institutionalized older people; the long-term care system, which has built-in financial incentives that contribute to poor quality care; the poor enforcement of nursing home standards; the culture and organization of institutions; the lack of highly qualified and well-trained staff; work-related stress and professional burnout; the powerlessness and vulnerability of the older residents; the personality traits of the staff; and the tendency of staff to avenge patient aggression (Beaulieu & Tremblay, 1995; Braun, Suzuki, Cusick & Howard-Carhart, 1997; Brennan & Moos, 1990; Cassell, 1989; Chappell & Novack, 1992; Feldt & Ryden, 1992; Gilleard, 1994; Kingdom, 1992; Meddaugh, 1993; Pillemer & Bachman-Prehn, 1991; Spencer, 1994; Stilwell, 1991; Whall, Gillis, Yankou, Booth & Beel-Bates, 1992). McDonald and colleagues (2008) have recently proposed institutional organization theory as one alternative to examining elder abuse in institutions, which considers the institutional logistics and the institutional context that affect the care provided. In addition, Schiamberg and colleagues (2011) have proposed an ecological model that focuses on the interaction between the characteristics of the nursing home resident and the nursing home staff. This proposed framework for examining risk factors is helpful because it considers the resident and the staff person as a dyad, incorporates the myriad of existing risk factors, and also considers the interaction between the resident and the staff that may lead to abuse. Further research is needed to support this framework.

RISK FACTORS FOR ABUSE IN THE COMMUNITY

Little research has been done on the risk factors associated with elder abuse, and yet an emphasis on risk factors undoubtedly follows from the demand for protocols to screen those at risk, to assess the nature of the abuse and neglect, and to choose appropriate interventions (McDonald et al., 1991). However, the limited research on risk factors suffers from a number of methodological difficulties, such as the definition of elder abuse used, which results in associations with different risk factors (Biggs, Manthorpe, Tinker, Doyle & Erens, 2009). The principal factors that have been associated with abuse include the personality traits of the abuser, the characteristics of the older adult, the intergenerational transfer of violence, dependency, stress, and social structural factors, such as ageism. Notably, all of these risk factors can be subsumed under any and all of the four theories previously described.

Following the National Research Council framework, which is extensively used in the research on abuse (Biggs et al., 2009), risk factors can be divided into three categories. There are factors validated by substantial evidence for which there is unanimous or near unanimous support from a number of studies; there are possible risk factors for which the evidence is mixed or limited; and there are contested risk factors for which the potential for increased risk has been hypothesized, but for which the evidence is lacking. Here we identify those factors that have been validated and those that have mixed evidence with some mention of the conflicting risk factors in institutions.

Seven factors clearly indicating risk include the following:

1. a shared living situation (Lachs, Williams, O'Brien, Hurst & Horwitz, 1997; Paveza et al., 1992; Pillemer & Finkelhor, 1988; Pillemer & Suitor, 1992)
2. social isolation and poor social networks (Compton, Flanagan & Gregg, 1997; Grafstrom, Nordberg & Winblad, 1993; Lachs, Berkman, Fulmer, & Horwitz, 1994; Phillips, 1983; Wolf & Pillemer, 1989)
3. the presence of dementia for physical abuse (Coyne, Reichman & Berbig, 1993; Homer & Gilleard, 1990; Paveza et al., 1992; Pillemer & Suitor, 1992; Tatara & Thomas, 1998)

4. mental illness of the perpetrator, mainly depression (Fulmer & Gurland, 1996; Homer & Gilleard, 1990; Pillemer & Finkelhor, 1989; Reay & Browne, 2001; Reis & Nahmiash, 1998; Williamson & Shaffer, 2001)
5. hostility of the perpetrator (Quayhagen et al., 1997)
6. alcohol abuse by the perpetrator (Anetzberger, Korbin & Austin, 1994; Bristowe & Collins, 1989; Greenberg, McKibben & Raymond, 1990; Homer & Gilleard, 1990; Reay & Browne, 2001; Wolf & Pillemer, 1989)
7. the perpetrator's dependency on the abused older adult (Anetzberger, 1987; Dyer, Pavlik, Murphy & Hyman, 2002; Greenberg et al., 1990; Pillemer & Finkelhor, 1989; Wolf, Strugnell, & Godkin, 1982)

The "possible" factors include gender (Tatara & Thomas, 1998; Wolf, 1997; Wolf & Pillemer, 1989); personality and behavioural characteristics of the victim (Comijs, Smit, Pot, Bouter & Jonker, 1998; Post et al., 2010); and race (Lachs et al., 1994; Lachs et al., 1997; Yan & Tang, 2004). The relationship between victim and perpetrator appears to be one in which the victims are more often abused by a spouse rather than by a child or any other family member (Bristowe & Collins, 1989; Pillemer & Finkelhor, 1988, 1989; Pillemer & Suitor, 1992). A contested and significant area for Canada is the area of ethnic diversity. There has been criticism of the elder abuse research for paying insufficient attention to diversity issues (Erlingsson, 2007). For example, despite the large proportion of immigrants in Canada, the relationship between ethnicity and elder abuse is not well understood. A report by the research study group on elder abuse (Chappell, 1993), which represented First Nations and Chinese communities, was one of the first to issue a strong statement about the need to examine abuse and neglect from a more culturally relevant perspective. This sentiment was further echoed in reports generated by two Canadian projects that also explored services across diverse communities (Bergin, 1995; Pittaway & Gallagher, 1995b).

There is some evidence confirming that violence against older people is a problem among many different ethnocultural groups. As such, two pressing questions regarding service delivery have emerged. First, are mainstream services appropriately addressing the needs of older people from diverse backgrounds? And if not, how should existing approaches be modified? Both the Bergin (1995) study and the Pittaway and Gallagher (1995b) project summarize the cultural issues that present challenges in providing services in cases of elder abuse. These challenges include the cultural differences in the definition of what constitutes abuse, which, in turn, influences help-seeking behaviour; the need for unbiased interpreters; the unavailability of translated pamphlets and other materials; the need for creative service delivery models that are culturally acceptable; the need to train service providers to be more culturally competent; and, finally, the need for stronger links between mainstream agencies serving older people and community resources directly affiliated with different ethnocultural communities.

Although there has been an increased focus to include diverse groups in the elder abuse literature, much work in this area is required. Walsh and colleagues (2011) conducted a literature review on oppression and elder abuse, and suggested there are several forms of oppression that influence elder abuse, including age, gender, disability, race and culture, sexual orientation, and poverty. While there is substantial literature to suggest that advanced age places adults at risk of abuse, there is inconsistent evidence regarding the link between gender and poverty and elder abuse. There is also a paucity of research among the gay, lesbian, bisexual, and transgendered (GLBT) community. The authors also discuss disability in terms of the physical and cognitive impairments of older adults, suggesting that as these impairments increase, such as in the case of dementia, older adults become more vulnerable to abuse. Walsh and colleagues (2011) also conducted a secondary data analysis of fifteen focus groups in Alberta and Ontario that was used to obtain the perspectives of both older adults of oppressed groups or their care providers. The study findings suggest increased vulnerability to elder abuse as a result of ageism, sexism, ableism/disability, racism, heterosexism/homophobia, and multiple intersecting types of oppression. While this research begins to bring these issues to the forefront by obtaining the perspectives of marginalized older adults, inclusion of diverse groups in future research is further warranted. Older adults with a developmental disability, such as an intellectual disability and cerebral palsy, are one group that has been virtually ignored in the research on elder abuse. Their omission from the existing literature on elder abuse may be due to the fact that growing old with a developmental disability is relatively new (Ansello & O'Neill, 2010). There is evidence however, that children with disabilities may be as high as five times more likely to experience abuse and neglect compared to children without disabilities (Sobsey, 1994; and see Chapter 7 for further discussion). In addition, sexual abuse is also more pervasive among those with disabilities, particularly for women, and underreported more frequently in this group. Although research in this area is lacking, it is likely that aging would only exacerbate the vulnerability of adults with developmental disabilities, placing them at a greater risk for elder abuse. Future studies would be needed to estimate the prevalence and incidence rates in this marginalized group. Researchers have put forth several areas that could be focused on to move this area forward, including: increased public awareness, support for caregivers of older adults with a developmental disability, training for older adults in self-care, self-advocacy and coping, improving data collection, improved coordination and collaboration across systems, and increased training for health professionals (Ansello & O'Neill, 2010). Clearly, there is a substantial amount of research required in this area.

RISK FACTORS FOR ABUSE IN INSTITUTIONS

Some scholars have identified a number of factors that they believe contribute to the abuse of older residents by staff in nursing homes, although the evidence is mainly contested. These include the following:

1. the lack of comprehensive and consistent policies with respect to the infirm elderly
2. the fact that the long-term care system is characterized by built-in financial incentives that contribute to poor-quality care
3. the poor enforcement of nursing home standards
4. the lack of highly qualified and well-trained staff
5. the powerlessness and vulnerability of the elderly residents, especially those with some type of dementia or memory loss
6. the tendency of staff to avenge patient aggression (Beaulieu & Tremblay, 1995; Braun et al., 1997; Brennan & Moos, 1990; Cassell, 1989; Chappell & Novack, 1992; Feldt & Ryden, 1992; Gilleard, 1994; Kingdom, 1992; McDonald et al., 2008; Meddaugh, 1993; Pillemer & Bachman-Prehn, 1991; Spencer, 1994; Stilwell, 1991; Whall et al., 1992).

Allen, Kellett, and Gruman (2003) conducted a retrospective case record review of complaints registered with the Connecticut long-term care Ombudsman's Office. They found that larger nursing homes, facilities with unionized staff, and the semi-private room rate were associated with higher rates of abuse and care complaints. Similarly, in his studies on employees in nursing homes in Germany, Göergen (2001) found that subtypes of elder abuse and neglect show differential correlation patterns with measures of work stress for nursing home staff. These stressors may be related to staff shortages or work overload and staffing patterns (Göergen, 2001, 2004).

It is important to note that there has been conflicting evidence about the relationship between cognitive and physical impairment as risk factors for elder abuse, with fairly consistent evidence demonstrating an association between behavioural problems and elder abuse (Ogioni et al., 2007). Achieving consensus in the field has been complicated by the fact that the identification of a risk factor may vary by subtype of abuse and depend upon how the data were collected (Shugarman, Fries, Wolf & Morris, 2003). Recently, a large-scale study contacted 36,676 households using random-digit dialing to identify family members who had a relative in long-term care, in order to identify the associations between behavioural problems, cognitive impairment, and physical impairment with elder abuse (Post et al., 2010). Of the 2,030 households identified, 816 family members who had an elderly relative aged older or older in long-term care participated in the study. Of these, one type of abuse was experienced by 14 percent, and one or more types of abuse were experienced by 29 percent. These findings suggest abuse rates higher than typically found in community-based studies. Behavioural problems were a significant risk factor for all types of abuse except financial, and were the most important risk factors of elder abuse among paid caregivers in the institution. In this study, physical impairment was a significant risk factor for emotional and verbal abuse as well as neglect, whereas cognitive impairment was not a significant risk factor. Given the mixed results on cognitive impairment, the authors suggested that family member proxies may not be able to easily identify the abuse of those cognitively impaired. However, they suggest that more research in this area is needed.

PROTOCOLS

Detection
The detection of elder abuse and neglect of older adults remains an extremely complex and notoriously difficult task, often complicated by the denial of the older person and his or her caregiver (Canadian Task Force on the Periodic Health Examination, 1994). Older adults who have been victimized often fail to report because of feelings of shame and stigma, the fear of retaliation, or of being placed in an institution (Fulmer, 1989; Mulligan, 1990). During the past two decades, tremendous energy has been invested in the development of instruments to identify older adults who are at risk for abuse or neglect. Many screening devices are currently available in the literature (Bloom, Ansell & Bloom, 1989; Fulmer & O'Malley, 1987; Johnson, 1991; Kosberg, 1988; Neale, Hwalek, Scott, Sengstok & Stahl, 1991; Pillemer, 1986; Quinn & Tomita, 1986; Reis, Nahmiash & Schrier, 1993; Sengstock & Hwalek, 1986). Most include items that direct investigation toward the characteristics of the older person, characteristics of the caregiver, and, depending on the theoretical stance of the author, characteristics of the family system (McDonald et al., 1991). These instruments usually rely heavily on the subjective impressions of health and social service staff and/or verbal reports from informants and abused older adults (Bloom et al., 1989; Kozma & Stones, 1995; Reis et al., 1993). Most fail to address issues related to the sensitivity and specificity of the measures.

Four of the better-known Canadian screening devices for risk include the QUALCARE Scale (Bravo, Girouard, Gosselin, Archambault & Dubois, 1995), the Brief Abuse Screen of the Elderly (BASE) (Reis, Nahmiash & Schrier, 1993), the Caregiver Abuse Screen (CASE) (Reis & Nahmiash, 1995a), and the Elder Abuse Suspicion Index (EASI) (Yaffe, Wolfson, Lithwick & Weiss, 2008).[2]

The original version of the QUALCARE Scale was developed by Phillips, Morrison, and Chae (1990) to evaluate the quality of care given by a caregiver to an older person. The instrument was designed to quantify the extent to which the caregiver satisfies the needs of the recipient. While Bravo and her colleagues (1995) found this measure to be a valid indicator of the risk of mistreatment, the reproducibility of this scale was not sufficient. Thus, while this work represents an important step forward, the findings must be interpreted cautiously.

Both the BASE and CASE were developed in Montreal in response to growing concern expressed by local service providers over a perceived increase in suspected abuse cases. The CASE serves as an effective complement to the screening provided by the BASE. Both the BASE and the CASE are screening instruments that have been the subject of psychometric scrutiny. The initial findings regarding the reliability and validity of these devices look promising. If these results can be replicated on a sufficiently representative sample of abuse and neglect victims, then both the BASE and CASE will be welcomed tools in the armamentarium of practitioners against abuse and neglect (Kozma & Stones, 1995; McDonald et al., 1995). Currently, there are a number of significant limitations to these screening tools. First, the indicators the tools rely upon have been derived from existing research on risk factors. As a whole, this literature is less than satisfactory. Many of the protocols, as a result, still favour the stereotype that older adults are abused only by their adult children and make no provision for spousal, sexual, or financial abuse. More recently, Reis and Nahmiash (1998) developed a screening tool, the Indicators of Abuse Screen (IOA), which can be used by practitioners to identify cases of abuse. The authors have demonstrated sufficient validity and reliability of the measure (Reis & Nahmiash, 1998). However, the IOA still focuses on abuse only by caregivers and fails to tap broader theoretical perspectives.

The EASI, also developed in Montreal, is a brief tool for physicians and other team members to use to indicate the presence or absence of elder abuse (Yaffe et al., 2008). The tool consists of only six items, can be completed very quickly, and has been subject to rigorous validation in several countries and is available in several languages.

With evidence-based tools as noted above, it is easier to understand and detect elder abuse and where or how to report possible abuse. The practitioner's knowledge helps reduce victims' hesitancy to acknowledge abuse, and encourages the practitioner to intervene, all of which will help improve practice (Giles, Brewer, Mosqueda, Huba & Melchior, 2010). A lack of coordination and integration of services has also presented a challenge for older adults to easily access appropriate services. Better working relationships are required between organizations to enable older adults to obtain the assistance that they need without having to navigate a complicated care delivery system.

Assessment

Assessment tools substantiate whether or not mistreatment has occurred or is occurring (Johnson, 1991) and assessments in general are the basis upon which intervention strategies are developed. Two government-sponsored surveys of programs for abuse of older Canadians (Health and Welfare Canada, 1992; Pittaway & Gallagher, 1995a) have noted a paucity of formal response protocols, policies, and procedures at the direct practice level. There are, however, a few notable exceptions.

A number of local initiatives have been carried out across Canada. These independently developed protocols range from unsystematic assessments, which rely on professional judgment rather than objective data (Rathbone-McCuan & Voyles, 1982) to checklists of risk indicators for abuse and/or neglect (Fulmer, 1989; Podnieks, 1988; Sengstock, Hwalek & Moshier, 1986). Such checklists may or may not include reviews of the victim's physical, psychological, medical, and social support (Glendenning & Decalmer, 1993; Johnson, 1991; Quinn & Tomita, 1986). The more detailed protocols, such as the Elder Abuse Diagnosis and Intervention model (Quinn & Tomita, 1986), the Staircase model (Breckman & Adelman, 1988), the SEVNA model (Smelters, 1993), the Victoria Elder Abuse Project (Gallagher, Anderson & Chamberlin, 1993), and the Project Care model (Reis & Nahmiash, 1995b), also outline intervention strategies and case management procedures.

Many of the assessment protocols that are currently being used are based on the assumptions found in the domestic violence literature, so they contain several weaknesses that originate in inadequate definitions, theory development, and research methodologies found in this field (McDonald et al., 1991; Phillipson, 1993). Like the screening instruments, many of these protocols utilize only one model (i.e., the situational model) and ignore the other factors that have been implicated. They also ignore the interactional aspects of abuse. Importantly, very few of these assessment instruments or protocols have been tested clinically. As a result, there is no evidence that they actually facilitate accurate identification or "case finding." Developing new screening and assessment instruments that are specific to the different types of abuse and neglect, or creating a multi-dimensional abuse scale would be useful. These instruments would be more sensitive to the construct of older abuse and neglect, potentially being able to detect cases more frequently and accurately.

Intervention

Decisions about how and when to intervene with victims of abuse and neglect are among the most difficult faced by service providers (Canadian Task Force on the Periodic Health Examination, 1994). Conceptually, two types of intervention protocols have developed in North America: agency-specific and community-based. The former define a particular agency's mandate and its procedures to respond to abuse and neglect, while the latter refer to approaches designed to coordinate and consolidate efforts between community and social service agencies (Health and Welfare Canada, 1997).

There have been a number of interesting and important developments at the community level across Canada, with a substantial shift toward establishing community protocols in an attempt to improve service delivery (Wolf, 1992). These include, but are not limited to: the Centres Locaux de Services Communautaires (CLSC), such as CLSC de NDG-Montreal West and CLSC René-Cassin in Montreal, the Advocacy Centre for the Elderly in Toronto, Elder Abuse Resource Centre in Winnipeg, the Kerby Centre in Calgary, and the North Shore Community Services in North Vancouver (McKenzie, Penny, Penny & Penny, 1995). A model intervention for elder abuse and dementia was developed in Cleveland, Ohio, which was the first initiative undertaken to address elder abuse and dementia as interfacing problems. It was a two-year collaborative project among five key organizations, which demonstrated success in increasing case identification, improving care planning and intervention, and promoting the prevention of abuse (Anetzberger et al., 2000).

Canada has clearly taken considerable initiative in the development of both local and community-based intervention protocols. For example, a study of 128 older adults identified as potential mistreatment cases in three community-based agencies in Quebec found that the type of mistreatment was associated with the type of perpetrator and circumstances related to mistreatment (Lithwick, Beaulieu, Gravel & Straka, 1999). Based on their results, the authors argued for the use of a harm-reduction model to address the complexity of mistreatment (Lithwick et al., 1999). However, because the efficacy of interventions has rarely been evaluated but rather has relied on anecdotal reports offered by practitioners, a word of caution is advised (Spencer, 1995). Many of the same limitations of the screening and assessment devices that are available are also subject to the same criticisms of current approaches to intervention. McDonald and colleagues (1991) offer three critical observations about the existing protocols. First, they assume a caregiver/situational model of abuse that still persists despite contradictory evidence emerging in the literature. Second, they fail to provide adequate definitions of the indicators of what strategies should be used, with whom, and under what circumstances. Third, they point to little or no evidence of the efficacy of treatments/interventions. Similar conclusions can be drawn from more recent studies. Stolee and Hillier (2008) reviewed the existing strategies for preventing, detecting, and responding to elder abuse, and concluded that there was minimal evidence to support their effectiveness. Likewise, Ploeg and colleagues (2009) conducted a systematic review of 1,253 existing interventions on elder abuse, which resulted in only eight of these met their inclusion criteria. Of these eight, all were conducted in the United States, except one in the United Kingdom, and none in Canada. There was no uniformity in the interventions used, which ranged from psycho-educational support groups, to legal and social services, to education and home visit training, to individual information and counselling sessions, and, lastly, advocacy coaching. The authors concluded that there was insufficient evidence to support the effectiveness of any particular intervention to target elder abuse (Ploeg et al., 2009). The interventions, programs, and services offered to abused older adults are greatly in need of being evaluated. Without an evaluation of existing services in place, it is unclear what is working and where future efforts and resources should be directed.

LEGISLATIVE APPROACHES

Unlike the United States, Canada does not follow a comprehensive elder abuse statute approach, but responds to different aspects of elder abuse within separate legislative responses to domestic violence, institutional abuse, and the adults who are incapable or unable to access assistance on their own. Canada responds to elder abuse using a group of laws that could apply to older adults, along with the Criminal Code of Canada, but these laws do not specifically fall under domestic violence, adult protection, human rights, and institutional abuse legislation (Hall, 2008). For example, in British Columbia, the abused older adult would receive rectification under the Adult Guardianship Act, RSBC 1996, c.6, while Nova Scotia and Prince Edward Island have Adult Protection Laws. Similarly, Article 48 of the Charte des Droits et Liberté de la Personne in Quebec and New Brunswick's Family Relations Act contain older adult-specific provisions (Hall, 2008). Most recently, the federal government announced that age would become an aggravating factor in the sentencing of convicted elder abuse perpetrators under a new amendment to the Criminal Code of Canada, which would result in harsher sentences (CBC, 2012).

The law does not often refer specifically to older adults, which may not be a problem if we do not want to marginalize older adults, and elder abuse and neglect may represent many problems that legislation could "mask" (Coughlan et al., 1995). The law is frequently directed only to those cases where it is perceived that the older adult is in need of protection. From a research perspective, there are few attempts to investigate the effectiveness of legislative provisions for adult protection on the resolution of the abuse and neglect of older adults (Harbison et al., 2008). In many cases, the legal enterprise highlights that legal involvement in older adult abuse issues may undermine the rights and autonomy of the individuals at hand by providing more intrusive solutions to problems that could have been handled by the health or social services systems (Harbison et al., 2008, p. 29; Harbison, Coughlan, Karabanow & VanderPlaat, 2005).

There is also debate over mandatory reporting of abuse and neglect, which currently varies across provinces in Canada (e.g., mandatory reporting in Alberta, Manitoba, and Ontario of institutional abuse and in the community in Nova Scotia and Newfoundland). It is still unknown whether elder abuse laws have had an impact on the detection or reporting of abuse in Canada or the United States (Rodriguez, Wallace, Woolf & Mangione, 2006). There is a lack of evidence with regard to mandatory reporting and its effectiveness in improving the treatment of elder abuse: previous research shows that voluntary or mandatory reporting is substantially less effective than public and professional education and awareness (Silva, 1992), but these data need to be updated and replicated. Research on the opinion of mandatory reporting of elder abuse has reported that younger adults had more support for mandatory reporting than older adults themselves, except when the older person was deemed incompetent and at risk (Roger & Ursel, 2009). Despite the small number of respondents (n = 167), this study's findings may reflect concerns among older adults about the consequences of reporting abuse. Watts and Sandhu (2006) compared the legal discourses and substantive laws between Canada and the United States in addressing elder abuse. It was concluded that Canada must "break the silence" and re-examine criminal justice issues regarding older adults, which may require legislative reform to better address issues of elder abuse and neglect (Watts & Sandhu, 2006).

PROGRAMS AND SERVICES

Four major kinds of programs have developed in response to elder abuse: (1) the statutory adult protection service programs; (2) programs based on the domestic violence model; (3) advocacy programs for older people; (4) and an integrated model.

Adult Protection Programs

Considerable controversy remains over adult protection legislation and programs. Proponents suggest that these interventions mean that the rights of the older adult are ultimately safeguarded and that attempts can be made to improve a person's level of functioning while protecting him or her from harm (McDonald et al., 1991). Those who oppose the enforcement-oriented approach argue, for example, that any system of care that is modelled on protectionist child welfare legislation will inevitably infantilize older adults and not respect their right to independence (ARA Consulting Group, 1991). Others have argued that the adult protection legislation is not useful because, in many instances, resources are insufficient to deal adequately with identified cases (ARA Consulting Group, 1991; Bond, Penner & Yellen, 1995). Without adequate services in place to support abused older adults, an adult protection services system cannot respond effectively to cases of abuse and neglect (ARA Consulting Group, 1991). Despite the fact that three models have been identified in Canada—the Atlantic provinces model, the Ontario model, and the British Columbia model (Gordon, 2001)—comprehensive evaluations of these models have not been conducted that provide sufficient evidence for identifying the most effective model for addressing elder abuse and neglect. While each presents various strengths and limitations (Gordon, 2001), with the exception of a review and recommendations for change (Poirier & Poirier, 1999), there are no data available to help policy-makers identify the best model.

Domestic Violence Programs

The domestic violence response to elder abuse and neglect has gained considerable momentum in North America because it does not violate people's civil rights or discriminate on the basis of age (Crystal, 1987; Finkelhor & Pillemer, 1984; McDonald et al., 1991). This response to elder abuse consists of a multi-pronged approach including: crisis intervention services; a strengthened role for police in the laying of charges; court orders for protection; the use of legal clinics; emergency and secondary sheltering; support groups for both the abused and the abuser; individual and family therapy; and the use of a range of health, social, and legal services (McDonald et al., 1991). An integral component of domestic violence services is public education, particularly education of the abused about their rights.

The domestic abuse model is not without its critics (Glendenning, 1999; McDonald et al., 1991; Phillipson, 1993). Problems with police response, restraining orders, poorly managed shelters, shortage of follow-up services, and failure to capture institutional abuse are but a few of the criticisms. Gerontologists have also cautioned against the singular use of crisis intervention because problems experienced by older people tend to be so complex, multiple, and interrelated that they may take a long time to sort out and need to be monitored closely (Hancock, 1990). The model also fails to apply in cases of neglect.

Advocacy Programs
Advocacy refers to the actions performed on behalf of an individual or group to ensure that their needs are met and their rights are respected. Like the domestic violence model, an advocacy approach acknowledges that the older person is potentially vulnerable and may be in a dangerous situation. Advocacy programs for the abused believe that the least restrictive and intrusive interventions should be applied to an older person's situation. There can be two types of advocates: informal and formal. Informal advocates are usually volunteers, such as friends or family, who do not take part in a structured program. Formal advocates are professionals and are paid for their services within the context of a structured program. In practice, advocates advise clients of their rights and the alternative services available to them in carrying out agreed-upon plans. The most important feature of advocacy is the advocate's independence of any formal delivery system; the distance allows the advocate to establish a positive relationship with the older person. Two well-known advocacy programs in Canada illustrate this independence: the Advocacy Centre for the Elderly in Toronto (Gordon, Verdun-Jones & MacDougall, 1986) and North Shore Community Services in North Vancouver (McKenzie et al., 1995).

The Integrated Model
An observable trend at the community level has been the development of multidisciplinary teams made up of workers from a broad array of agencies. These community-based teams provide consultations on atypical and difficult cases of abuse, help resolve agency disagreements, and provide services, such as legal and medical consultations not readily available in the community (Wolf, 1992). In situations involving elder abuse, researchers and policy-makers frequently advocate coordinating health care and social services in the detection and intervention process (Decalmer & Marriott, 1993; Health and Welfare Canada, 1993; Pittaway & Gallagher, 1995a). In Canada, Project Care (Reis & Nahmiash, 1995b) is an extension of this integrated

model. Project Care, funded by the Family Violence Prevention Division, Health Canada, was designed to develop a global intervention program through which professionals and volunteers could effectively intervene in instances of abuse and neglect (McDonald, 1996). The most successful and accepted interventions that have been reported using this approach include: nursing and other medical care and homemaking assistance; empowerment strategies, such as support groups; information about rights and resources; and buddies/advocates. For abusers who were caregivers, the most successful and accepted strategies include: individual supportive counselling to reduce anxiety, stress, and depression; and education and training (Nahmiash & Reis, 2000).

PREVENTION

Education and public awareness are fundamental to the prevention of elder abuse, and have been one of the main goals of the International Network for the Prevention of Elder Abuse (INPEA) (Lowenstein, 2009). Education is not just about learning new information. It is about changing attitudes, behaviours, and values. As such, education is a fundamental preventative strategy (Gallagher et al., 1993; Greene & Anderson, 1993; Podnieks & Baillie, 1995; Podnieks et al., 1990). Stones and Bedard (2002) describe a threshold model of attitudes toward elder abuse and neglect. Using a unifying theoretical framework, the model attempts to reconcile attitudinal differences about abuse. In their study, the Elder Abuse Survey Tool was used to compare older adults' and health professionals' views of abuse. The study found that when people were asked to evaluate abuse using a common frame of reference, different thresholds for abuse emerged. This suggests that perhaps a focus on attitudes regarding what constitutes abuse and neglect may be an important target for preventative efforts (Stones & Bedard, 2002). The importance of educating older adults about abuse and neglect, as well as providing information about where to turn for help, cannot be overstated (Podnieks & Baillie, 1995). Knowledge is power and can be used to help people help themselves. It allows victims (or potential victims) to protect themselves and their rights. This, in turn, contributes to feelings of increased control and self-efficacy (Reis & Nahmiash, 1995b). A recent systematic review evaluated the existing literature on the effectiveness of educational interventions to improve health professionals' recognition and reporting of elder abuse and neglect (Alt, Nguyen & Meurer, 2011). The study identified fourteen articles describing twenty-two programs. The authors determined that while these programs may result in increased awareness and improved detection, there is little detail provided to allow for replication and limited evaluations conducted on their effectiveness to inform future program planning.

In Canada, practitioners have grown to realize that information provided in isolation is not enough, and there has been a move in Canada to develop support and problem-solving interventions, which serve as adjuncts to educational programs. The assumption has been that these additional services not only offer protection against abuse, but also reduce isolation (British Columbia Seniors Advisory Council, 1992). The active involvement of older Canadians in addressing the issue of elder abuse is a welcome movement in the field. Increasingly, health and social service agencies are realizing that care needs to be client-centred and client-driven. Many of the well-established elder abuse programs in Canada have supported older adults to be active players in the development and day-to-day operation of their services (i.e., Elder Abuse Resource Centre in Winnipeg; CRNs in British Columbia; Project Care in Montreal).

EDUCATING PROFESSIONALS, CAREGIVERS, AND THE PUBLIC

It is especially important for professionals to be able to identify when older people are abused and intervene constructively and appropriately. An important first step lies in finding ways to teach clinicians to reflect on their own attitudes and beliefs about aging and violence in general (Johnson, 1995). Unfortunately, sources of bias and discrimination are often deeply hidden (Pittaway & Gallagher, 1995a, 1995b). It is imperative to provide opportunities for consciousness-raising so that individuals, agencies, and communities can critically reflect on their belief systems and examine how these influence their response to elder abuse. The National Initiative for the Care of the Elderly (NICE) is one organization in Canada that has taken the lead in disseminating information across Canada to health care professionals, older adults, and the general public about elder abuse (NICE, 2011). Introducing more gerontological content into the curricula of health professionals is also important as there has been some literature that documents attempts to educate health professionals with some evidence of effectiveness (HRSDC, 2011). Incorporating more systematic inclusion of violence content in curricula, particularly on elder abuse, is therefore essential.

Major strides have been made in increasing professional awareness in the broader community through training sessions and seminars on abuse. Elder abuse has also been on the agenda of most education and scientific meetings, conferences, and workshops in gerontology (Podnieks & Baillie, 1995), and as a result the field has grown across Canada with many examples of available training programs and resource kits (Hoff, 1994; McGregor, 1995; Pay, 1993). In addition, there is a wealth of information on government websites about elder abuse for both health professionals and the public. The Government of Canada has demonstrated its support for embracing a national effort to address elder abuse in Canada. This support is demonstrated by the New Horizons Initiative to fund projects related to elder abuse (National Seniors Council, 2007) and its identification of elder abuse as one of the initial priorities, for which the National Seniors Council was mandated to provide a report on in its inaugural year (Ekos Research Associates Inc., 2011). As a result of this report, the Government of Canada funded a three-year Federal Elder Abuse Initiative (FEAI) from April 2008 to March 2011. To assess the impact of this initiative on societal awareness of elder abuse, a seventeen-minute telephone survey with 3,012 participants was conducted across all provinces. Participants were randomly selected using random-digit dialing, and were eighteen years of age or older (Giles et al., 2010). Results from this survey suggest that 93 percent of participants were aware of elder abuse, which had increased more than 10 percent from the previous year, and were more knowledgeable than before about issues pertaining to abuse.

Assistance to family members through education and training programs for caregivers plays a vital role in prevention. Caregiver support groups have a long and distinguished history as a resource to assist in the care of the elderly, offering mutual support, stress reduction, and problem-solving strategies. The underlying assumption is that the combination of social support and education/training will work together to reduce the likelihood that anger, aggression, and conflict will emerge in the caregiving relationship (Podnieks & Baillie, 1995).

It is also essential to promote public awareness of elder abuse efforts in this area, which can be evidenced by the launch of a World Elder Abuse Awareness Day on June 15, initiated in 2006. It is everyone's responsibility to take action against this hidden crime and offer support to victims in a manner that encourages them to get help. Public education campaigns should be geared toward abused older adults and those in a position to recognize that abuse is occurring (Podnieks & Baillie, 1995). In Canada, many excellent public education tools, programs, and materials have been developed (Council on Aging, 1987; Podnieks & Baillie, 1995). There have also been recent attempts in many Canadian communities to develop preventive programs that teach children early in life to respect older adults and create opportunities for intergenerational relationships (Podnieks & Baillie, 1995).

SETTING PRIORITIES FOR FUTURE DIRECTIONS

In reviewing the developments of elder abuse and neglect in Canada, it is evident that some progress has been made, although more work remains. To make greater strides in tackling the problem of elder abuse and neglect in Canada, specific issues need to be targeted, which include: a national prevalence study of abuse, a prevalence study of abuse in institutions, case control studies to determine risk factors for abuse, and continued testing of screening and assessment instruments. Increased education and training of health professionals, as well as evaluations of practice, legislation, and prevention programs, are also required. In the United States, the Archstone Foundation in California has proposed Vision for 2020 for efforts worldwide to improve the response to elder abuse as a result of the lessons learned from twenty projects supported by their Elder Abuse and Neglect Initiative, which include: (1) increased public awareness and shifting public opinion; (2) improved identification and triage of cases; (3) increased integrated service models; (4) improved justice system response; and (5) utilizing untapped resources (e.g., technology and volunteers) to better address elder abuse issues. Older Canadians would also benefit from strides made in these areas. These goals outlined for the next decade, if attained, could make important contributions to the field of elder abuse and improve the lives of older adults. Canada could be among those who lead the way.

NOTES

1 The National Center on Elder Abuse is a comprehensive resource centre for practitioners and researchers in the United States. It is funded by the Administration on Aging and operated collaboratively by the American Public Human Services Association, the National Association of State Units on Aging, the University of Delaware's College of Human Resources, and the National Committee for the Prevention of Elder Abuse. These groups have managed to agree on official definitions of elder abuse, which they used in the national incidence study.

2 The BASE, CASE, IOA, and EASI can be downloaded from www.nicenet.ca.

REFERENCES

Aboriginal Nurses Association of Canada. (1992). *Annual general meeting report for 1992: Abuse of the elders in Aboriginal communities.* Fort Qu'Appelle, SK: Indian and Inuit Nurses of Canada.

Acierno, R., Hernandez, M.A., Amstadter, A.B., Resnick, H.S., Steve, K., Muzzy, W., & Kilpatrick, D.G. (2010). Prevalence and correlates of emotional, physical, sexual, and financial abuse and potential neglect in the United States: The National Elder Mistreatment Study. *American Journal of Public Health, 100*(2), 292–97.

Administration on Aging. (1998). *The national elder abuse incidence study: Final report, September 1998.* Washington, DC: Administration on Aging and National Center on Elder Abuse at the American Public Human Services Association.

Allen, P.D., Kellett, K., & Gruman, C. (2003). Elder abuse in Connecticut's nursing homes. *Journal of Elder Abuse & Neglect, 15*(1), 19–42.

Alt, K.L., Nguyen, A.L., & Meurer, L.N. (2011). The effectiveness of educational programs to improve recognition and reporting of elder abuse and neglect: A systematic review of the literature. *Journal of Elder Abuse & Neglect, 23*, 213–33.

Anetzberger, G.J. (1987). *The etiology of elder abuse by adult offspring.* Springfield, IL: Charles C. Thomas.

Anetzberger, G.J., Korbin, J.E., & Austin, C. (1994). Alcoholism and elder abuse. *Journal of Interpersonal Violence, 9*(2), 184–93.

Anetzberger, G.J., Palmisano, B.R., Sanders, M., Bass, D., Dayton, C., Eckert, S., & Schimer, M.R. (2000). A model intervention for elder abuse and dementia. *Gerontologist, 40*(4), 492–97.

Ansello, E.F., & O'Neill, P. (2010). Abuse, neglect, and exploitation: Considerations in aging with lifelong disabilities. *Journal of Elder Abuse & Neglect, 22*(1–2), 105–30.

ARA Consulting Group. (1991). *A review of community/program responses to elder abuse in Ontario.* Toronto: Ministry of Citizenship.

Aronson, J., Thornwell, C., & Williams, K. (1995). Wife assault in old age: Coming out of obscurity. *Canadian Journal on Aging, 14*(2), 72–88.

Beaulieu, M. (1992). La formation en milieu de travail: L'expression d'un besoin des cadres en ce qui concerne les abus à l'endroit des personnes agées en centre d'accueil. *Le Gérontophile, 14*(3), 3–7.

Beaulieu, M., & Belanger, L. (1995). Intervention in long-term care institutions with respect to elder mistreatment. In M. MacLean (Ed.), *Abuse and neglect of older Canadians* (pp. 27–40). Ottawa: Thompson Educational.

Beaulieu, M., & Tremblay, M.J. (1995). *Abuse and neglect of older adults in institutional settings: Discussion paper building from French language sources.* Ottawa: Health Canada, Mental Health Division.

Bennett, G. (1990). Action on elder abuse in the 1990's: New definitions will help. *Geriatric Medicine, 20*(4), 53–54.

Bennett, G., & Kingston, P. (1993). *Elder abuse: Concepts, theories, and interventions.* London, UK: Chapman and Hall.

Bent, K. (2009). *Literature review: Aboriginal senior abuse in Canada.* Ottawa: Native Women's Association of Canada.

Bergin, B. (1995). *Elder abuse in ethnocultural communities: An exploratory study with suggestions for intervention and prevention.* Ottawa: Canadian Association of Social Workers.

Biggs, S., Manthorpe, J., Tinker, A., Doyle, M., & Erens, B. (2009). Mistreatment of older people in the United Kingdom: Findings from the first National Prevalence Study. *Journal of Elder Abuse & Neglect, 21*(1), 1–14.

Block, M.R., & Sinnot, J.D. (1979). *The battered elder syndrome: An exploratory study.* College Park, MD: Center on Aging, University of Maryland.

Bloom, J.S., Ansell, P., & Bloom, M.N. (1989). Detecting elder abuse: A guide for physicians. *Geriatrics, 44*(6), 40–44, 56.

Bond, J.B., Penner, R., & Yellen, P. (1995). Perceived effectiveness of legislation concerning abuse of the elderly: A survey of professionals in Canada and the United States. *Canadian Journal on Aging, 14*(2), 118–34.

Braun, K.L., Suzuki, K.M., Cusick, C.E., & Howard-Carhart, K. (1997). Developing and testing training materials on elder abuse and neglect for nurse aides. *Journal of Elder Abuse & Neglect, 9*(1), 1–15.

Bravo, G., Girouard, D., Gosselin, S., Archambault, C., & Dubois, M. (1995). Further validation of the QUALCARE Scale. *Journal of Elder Abuse & Neglect, 7*(4), 29–47.

Breckman, R.S., & Adelman, R.D. (1988). *Strategies for helping victims of elder mistreatment.* Newbury Park, CA: Sage.

Brennan, P.L., & Moos, R.H. (1990). Physical design, social climate, and staff turnover in skilled nursing facilities. *Journal of Long-Term Care Administration, 18*(2), 22–27.

Bristowe, E., & Collins, J.B. (1989). Family mediated abuse of noninstitutionalized frail elderly men and women living in British Columbia. *Journal of Elder Abuse & Neglect, 1,* 45–64.

British Columbia Seniors Advisory Council. (1992). *A delicate balance: Assisting elderly victims of abuse and neglect.* Victoria: British Columbia Seniors Advisory Council.

Canadian Task Force on the Periodic Health Examination. (1994). Periodic health examination, 1994 update: 4. Secondary prevention of elder abuse and mistreatment. *Canadian Medical Association Journal, 151*(10), 1413–20.

Cassell, E.J. (1989). Abuse of the elderly: Misuses of power. *New York State Journal of Medicine, 89*(3), 159–62.

CBC (2012, March 15). *Elder abuse sentences to be toughened.* Retrieved from: http://www.cbc.ca/news/canada/toronto/story/2012/03/15/pol-elder-abuse-sentences.html.

Chappell, N.L. (1993). *Research study group on elder abuse: Final report.* Unpublished manuscript, Centre on Aging, University of Victoria.

Chappell, N.L., Gee, E.M., McDonald, L., & Stones, M. (2003). *Aging in contemporary Canada.* Toronto: Prentice Hall.

Chappell, N.L., & Novack, M. (1992). The role of support in alleviating stress among nursing assistants. *The Gerontologist, 32*(3), 351–59.

Chen, P.N., Bell, S.L., Dolinsky, D.L., Doyle, J., & Dunn, M. (1981). Elderly abuse in domestic settings: A pilot study. *Journal of Gerontological Social Work, 4,* 3–17.

Chokkanathan, S., & Lee, A.E. (2005). Elder mistreatment in urban India: A community-based study. *Journal of Elder Abuse & Neglect, 17*(2), 45–61.

College of Nurses of Ontario. (1993). *Abuse of clients by registered nurses and registered nursing assistants: Report to council on results of Canada Health Monitor Survey of Registrants.* Toronto, ON.

Comijs, H.C., Smit, J.H., Pot, A.M., Bouter, L.M., & Jonker, C. (1998). Risk indicators of elder mistreatment in the community. *Journal of Elder Abuse & Neglect, 9*(4), 67–76.

Compton, S.A., Flanagan, P., & Gregg, W. (1997). Elder abuse in people with dementia in Northern Ireland: Prevalence and predictors in cases referred to a psychiatry of old age service. *International Journal of Geriatric Psychiatry, 12*(6), 632–35.

Cooper, C., Selwood, A., & Livingston, G. (2008). The prevalence of elder abuse and neglect: A systematic review. *Age and Ageing, 37*(2), 151–60.

Coughlan, S., Downe-Wamboldt, B., Elgie, R., Harbison, J., Melanson, P., et al. (1995). *Mistreating elderly people: Questioning the response to elder abuse and neglect (Vol. 2), Legal responses to elder abuse and neglect*. Halifax: Dalhousie University Health Law Institute.

Council of Europe. (1992). *Violence against elderly people*. Strasbourg: Council of Europe Steering Committee on Social Policy.

Council on Aging. (1987). *Enhancing awareness of elder abuse: Three educational models*. Ottawa: Council on Aging of Ottawa-Carleton.

Coyne, A.C., Reichman, W.E., & Berbig, L.J. (1993). The relationship between dementia and elder abuse. *American Journal of Psychiatry, 150*(4), 643–46.

Crystal, S. (1987). Elder abuse: The latest "crisis." *Public Interest, 88*, 56–66.

Decalmer, P., & Glendenning, F. (Eds.). (1993). *The mistreatment of elderly people*. Newbury Park, CA: Sage.

Decalmer, P., & Marriott, A. (1993). The multidisciplinary assessment of clients and patients. In P. Decalmer & F. Glendenning (Eds.), *The mistreatment of elderly people* (pp. 117–35). Newbury Park, CA: Sage.

Dyer, C., Pavlik, D.B., Murphy, K., & Hyman, D.J. (2002). The high prevalence of depression and dementia in elder abuse and neglect. *Journal of the American Geriatrics Society, 48*, 205–58.

Eckley, S.C.A., & Vilakazi, P.A.C. (1995). Elder abuse in South Africa. In J.I. Kosberg & J.L. Garcia (Eds.), *Elder abuse: International and cross-cultural perspectives* (pp. 171–82). New York: Haworth.

Ekos Research Associates Inc. (2011). *Follow-up and Final Awareness and Perceptions of Elder Abuse Survey 2010*. Ottawa: Government of Canada.

Elder, G., & Pellerin, L. (1998). Linking history and human lives. In J. Giele & G. Elder (Eds.), *Methods of life course research: Quantitative and qualitative approaches*. Thousand Oaks, CA: Sage.

Erlingsson, C.L. (2007). Searching for elder abuse: A systematic review of database citations. *Journal of Elder Abuse & Neglect, 19*(3/4), 59–78.

Feldt, K.S., & Ryden, M.B. (1992). Aggressive behavior: Educating nursing assistants. *Journal of Gerontological Nursing, 18*(5), 3–12.

Filinson, R. (1989). Introduction. In R. Filinson & S.R. Ingman (Eds.), *Elder abuse: Practice and policy* (pp. 17–34). New York: Human Sciences Press.

Filinson, R., & Ingman, S.R. (Eds.). (1989). *Elder abuse: Practice and policy*. New York: Human Sciences Press.

Finkelhor, D., & Pillemer, K. (1984). *Elder abuse: Its relationship to other forms of domestic violence*. Paper presented at the 2nd National Conference on Family Violence Research, Durham, NH.

Fulmer, T.T. (1989). Mistreatment of elders: Assessment, diagnosis, and intervention. *Nursing Clinics of North America, 24*(3), 707–16.

Fulmer, T.T., & Gurland, B. (1996). Restriction as elder mistreatment: Differences between caregiver and elder perceptions. *Journal of Mental Health and Aging, 2*, 89–98.

Fulmer, T.T., & O'Malley, T.A. (1987). *Inadequate care of the elderly: A health care perspective on abuse and neglect*. New York: Springer.

Gallagher, E., Anderson, B., & Chamberlin, E. (1993). *Victoria Elder Abuse Project: Final report*. Victoria: Community Elder Abuse Committee.

Garre-Olmo, J., Planas-Pujol, X., Lopez-Pousa, S., Juvinya, D., Vila, A., & Vilalta-Franch, J. (2009). Prevalence and risk factors of suspected elder abuse subtypes in people aged 75 and older. *Journal of the American Geriatrics Society, 57*(5), 815–22.

George, L. (2003). Life course research: Achievements and potential. In J.T. Mortimer & M.J. Shanahan (Eds.), *Handbook of the life course* (pp. 671–80). New York: Kluwer Academic Publishers.

Giles, L., Brewer, E.T., Mosqueda, L., Huba, G.J., & Melchior, L.A. (2010). Vision for 2020. *Journal of Elder Abuse & Neglect, 22*(3–4), 375–86.

Gilleard, C. (1994). Physical abuse in homes and hospitals. In M. Eastman (Ed.), *Old age abuse: A new perspective* (2nd ed., pp. 93–112). London: Chapman and Hall.

Glendenning, F. (1993). What is elder abuse and neglect? In P. Decalmer & F. Glendenning (Eds.), *The mistreatment of elderly people* (pp. 1–34). London, UK: Sage.

Glendenning, F. (1999). Elder abuse and neglect in residential settings: The need for inclusiveness in elder abuse research. *Journal of Elder Abuse & Neglect, 10*(1–2), 1–11.

Glendenning, F., & Decalmer, P. (1993). Looking to the future. In P. Decalmer & F. Glendenning (Eds.), *The mistreatment of elderly people* (pp. 159–68). London, UK: Sage.

Göergen, T. (2001). Stress, conflict, elder abuse, and neglect in German nursing homes: A pilot study among professional caregivers. *Journal of Elder Abuse & Neglect, 13*(1), 1–26.

Göergen, T. (2004). A multi-method study on elder abuse and neglect in nursing homes. *Journal of Adult Protection, 6*(3), 15–25.

Gordon, R.M. (1992). Material abuse and powers of attorney in Canada: A preliminary examination. *Journal of Elder Abuse & Neglect, 4*(1/2), 173–93.

Gordon, R.M. (2001). Adult protection legislation in Canada: Models, issues, and problems. *International Journal of Law & Psychiatry, 24*(2–3), 117–34.

Gordon, R.M., Verdun-Jones, S.N., & MacDougall, D.J. (1986). *Standing in their shoes: Guardianship, trusteeship, and the elderly Canadian*. Burnaby, BC: Criminology Research Centre, Simon Fraser University.

Grafstrom, M., Nordberg, A., & Winblad, B. (1993). Abuse is in the eye of the beholder: Report by family members about abuse of demented persons in home care. A total population-based study. *Scandinavian Journal of Social Medicine, 21*(4), 247–55.

Greenberg, J.R., McKibben, M., & Raymond, J.A. (1990). Dependent adult children and elder abuse. *Journal of Elder Abuse & Neglect, 2*, 73–86.

Greene, B., & Anderson, E. (1993). *Breaking the silence on the abuse of older Canadians: Everyone's concern*. Ottawa: Standing Committee on Health, Welfare, Social Affairs, Seniors, and the Status of Women.

Hall, M. (2008). Constructing elder abuse: The Canadian legal framework, HRSDC Expert Roundtable on Elder Abuse, Ottawa.

Hancock, B.L. (1990). *Social work with older people* (2nd ed.). Englewood Cliffs, NJ: Prentice-Hall.

Harbison, J., Beaulieu, M., Coughlan, S., Karabanow, J., VanderPlaat, M., et al. (2008). *Conceptual frameworks: Understandings of "elder abuse and neglect" and their implications for policy and legislation.* Ottawa: Human Resources and Social Development Canada.

Harbison, J., Coughlan, S., Karabanow, J., & VanderPlaat, M. (2005). A clash of cultures: Rural values and service delivery to mistreated and neglected older people in Eastern Canada. *Practice—Social Work in Action, 17*(4), 229–46.

Hawes, C. (2002). Elder abuse in residential long-term care facilities: What is known about prevalence, causes, and prevention. Testimony given before the US Senate Committee on Finance, June 18.

Health and Welfare Canada. (1992). *A shared concern: An overview of Canadian programs addressing the abuse of seniors.* Ottawa: Family Violence Prevention Division, Supply and Services Canada.

Health and Welfare Canada. (1993). *Community awareness and response: Abuse and neglect of older adults.* Ottawa: Health and Welfare Canada.

Health and Welfare Canada. (1997). *Adults with vulnerability: Addressing abuse and neglect.* Toronto: Health and Welfare Canada.

Hickey, T., & Douglass, R.L. (1981). Mistreatment of the elderly in the domestic setting: An exploratory study. *American Journal of Public Health, 71*(5), 500–7.

Hoff, L.A. (1994). *Violence issues: An interdisciplinary curriculum for health professionals.* Ottawa: Mental Health Division, Health Services Directorate, Minister of Supply and Services, Health Canada.

Homer, A.C., & Gilleard, C. (1990). Abuse of elderly people by their carers. *British Medical Journal, 301*(6765), 1359–62.

HRSDC. (2011). *New Horizons for Seniors Program.* Retrieved from: http://www .hrsdc.gc.ca/eng/community_partnerships/seniors/index.shtml.

Hudson, J.E. (1988). Elder abuse: An overview. In B. Schlesinger & R. Schlesinger (Eds.), *Abuse of the elderly: Issues and annotated bibliography* (pp. 12–31). Toronto: University of Toronto Press.

Hudson, M.F. (1991). Elder mistreatment: A taxonomy with definitions by Delphi. *Journal of Elder Abuse and Neglect, 3*(2), 1–20.

Hudson, M.F. (1994). Elder abuse: Its meaning to middle-aged and older adults, part II: Pilot results. *Journal of Elder Abuse and Neglect, 6*(1), 55–82.

Iborra, I. (Ed.). (2005). *Violencia contra personas mayores.* Barcelona: Centro Reina Sofía para el Estudio de la Violencia.

Jack, R. (1994). Dependency or interdependency? Is the concept of "dependent-abuse" helpful? In M. Eastman (Ed.), *Old age abuse: A new perspective* (2nd ed., pp. 77–92). London, UK: Chapman and Hall.

Johnson, T.F. (1986). Critical issues in the definition of elder mistreatment. In K. Pillemer & R.S. Wolf (Eds.), *Elder abuse: Conflict in the family* (pp. 167–96). Dover, MA: Auburn House.

Johnson, T.F. (1991). *Elder mistreatment: Deciding who is at risk*. Westport, CT: Greenwood Press.

Johnson, T.F. (1995). Ethics and elder abuse mistreatment: Uniting protocol with practice. *Journal of Elder Abuse & Neglect, 7*(2/3), 1–18.

Kingdom, D. (1992). Preventing aggression. *Canadian Nursing Home, 3*(2), 14–16.

Knight, B. (1994). Homicide in elderly couples. In M. Eastman (Ed.), *Old age abuse: A new perspective* (2nd ed., pp. 51–66). London: Chapman and Hall.

Kosberg, J.I. (1988). Preventing elder abuse: Identification of high-risk factors prior to placement decisions. *Gerontologist, 28*(1), 43–50.

Kozak, J., & Lukawiecki, T. (2001). *Returning home: Fostering a supportive and respectful environment in the long-term care setting*. Ottawa: National Clearinghouse on Family Violence.

Kozma, A., & Stones, M.J. (1995). Issues in the measurement of elder abuse. In M. MacLean (Ed.), *Abuse and neglect of older Canadians: Strategies for change* (pp. 117–28). Toronto: Thompson.

Krienert, J.L., Walsh, J.A., & Turner, M. (2009). Elderly in America: A descriptive study of elder abuse examining National Incident-Based Reporting System (NIBRS) data, 2000–2005. *Journal of Elder Abuse & Neglect, 21*(4), 325–45.

Lachs, M.S., Berkman, L., Fulmer, T., & Horwitz, R.I. (1994). A prospective community-based pilot study of risk factors for the investigation of elder mistreatment. *Journal of the American Geriatrics Society, 42*(2), 169–73.

Lachs, M.S., Williams, C., O'Brien, S., Hurst, L., & Horwitz, R. (1997). Risk factors for reported elder abuse and neglect: A nine-year observational cohort study. *Gerontologist, 37*(4), 469–74.

Lau, E., & Kosberg, J.I. (1979). Abuse of the elderly by informal care providers. *Aging* (September/October), 10–15.

Laumann, E.O., Leitsch, S.A., & Waite, L.J. (2008). Elder mistreatment in the United States: Prevalence estimates from a nationally representative study. *Journals of Gerontology, 63*(4), S248–S254.

Lithwick, M., Beaulieu, M., Gravel, S., & Straka, M. (1999). The mistreatment of older adults: Perpetrator–victim relationships and interventions. *Journal of Elder Abuse & Neglect, 11*(4), 95–112.

Lowenstein, A. (2009). Elder abuse and neglect—old phenomenon: New directions for research, legislation, and service developments. *Journal of Elder Abuse & Neglect, 21*, 278–87.

Lowenstein, A., Eisikovits, Z., Band-Winterstein, T., & Enosh, G. (2009). Is elder abuse and neglect a social phenomenon? Data from the First National Prevalence Survey in Israel. *Journal of Elder Abuse & Neglect, 21*(3), 253–77.

Malmedal, W., Ingebrigtsen, O., & Saveman, B.I. (2009). Inadequate care in Norwegian nursing homes—as reported by nursing staff. *Scandinavian Journal of Caring Sciences, 23*(2), 231–42.

McDonald, L. (1996). Abuse and neglect of elders. In J.E. Birren (Ed.), *Encyclopedia of gerontology: Age, aging, and the aged* (Vol. 1). San Diego: Academic Press.

McDonald, L. (2011). Elder abuse and neglect in Canada: The glass is still half full. *Canadian Journal on Aging, 30*(3), 1–30.

McDonald, L., Beaulieu, M., Harbison, J., Hirst, S., Lowenstein, A., et al. (2008). *Institutional abuse of older adults: What we know, what we need to know.* Ottawa: Human Resources and Social Development Canada.

McDonald, L., Hornick, J.P., Robertson, G.B., & Wallace, J.E. (1991). *Elder abuse and neglect in Canada.* Toronto: Butterworths.

McDonald, L., Pittaway, E.D., & Nahmiash, D. (1995). Issues in practice with respect to mistreatment of older people. In M. MacLean (Ed.), *Abuse and neglect of older Canadians: Strategies for change* (pp. 5–16). Toronto: Thompson.

McGregor, A. (1995). *The abuse and neglect of older adult: An education module for community nurses.* Gloucester, ON: Victorian Order of Nurses, Ottawa–Carleton.

McKenzie, P., Penny, T., Penny, L., & Penny, Y. (1995). Community-based intervention strategies for cases of abuse and neglect of seniors: A comparison of models, philosophies, and practice issues. In M. MacLean (Ed.), *Abuse and neglect of older Canadians: Strategies for change* (pp. 17–26). Toronto: Thompson.

Meddaugh, D.I. (1993). Covert elder abuse in the nursing home. *Journal of Elder Abuse & Neglect, 5*(3), 21–37.

Mulligan, S. (1990). *A handbook for the prevention of family violence.* Ottawa: Health and Welfare Canada.

Nahmiash, D., & Reis, M. (2000). Most successful intervention strategies for abused older adults. *Journal of Elder Abuse & Neglect, 12*(3/4), 53–70.

National Seniors Council. (2007). *Report on the National Seniors Council on Elder Abuse.* Ottawa: Government of Canada.

Naughton, C., Drennan, J., Treacy, M.P., Lafferty, A., Lyons, I., Phelan, A.,...Delaney, L. (2010). *Abuse and neglect of older people in Ireland: Report on the National Study of Elder Abuse and Neglect.* Belfield, Dublin: University College Dublin.

NCEA. (2011). *Major types of elder abuse.* Retrieved from: http://www.ncea.aoa .gov/NCEAroot/Main_Site/FAQ/Basics/Types_Of_Abuse.aspx.

Neale, A.V., Hwalek, M., Scott, R., Sengstok, M.C., & Stahl, C. (1991). Validation of the Hwalek-Sengstock Elder Abuse Screening Test. *Journal of Applied Gerontology, 10*(4), 406–18.

Neysmith, S.M. (1995). Power in relationships of trust: A feminist analysis of elder abuse. In M. MacLean (Ed.), *Abuse and neglect of older Canadians: Strategies for change* (pp. 43–54). Toronto: Thompson.

NICE. (2011). *Elder abuse team: Knowledge to Action Project.* Retrieved from: http:// www.nicenet.ca/detail.aspx?menu=48&app=237&cat1=661&tp=2&lk=no.

Ogioni, L., Liperoti, R., Landi, F., Soldato, M., Bernabei, R., et al. (2007). Cross-sectional association between behavioral symptoms and potential elder abuse among subjects in home care in Italy: Results from the Silvernet Study. *American Journal of Geriatric Psychiatry, 15*(1), 70–78.

O'Keeffe, M., Hills, A., Doyle, M., McCreadie, C., Scholes, S., Constantine, R.,...Erens, B. (2007). *UK study of abuse and neglect of older people: Prevalence survey report.* London: National Centre for Social Research.

O'Malley, T.A., Segal, H.D., & Perez, R. (1979). *Elder abuse in Massachusetts: A survey of professionals and paraprofessionals.* Boston: Legal Research and Services for the Elderly.

Ontario Government. (2002). *Ontario government takes action on elder abuse.* Retrieved from: http://www.gov.on.ca/citizenship/english/about/n280302.htm.

Paveza, G.J., Cohen, D., Eisorfer, C., Freels, S., Semla, T., Ashford, W.J.,...Levy, P. (1992). Severe family violence and Alzheimer's disease: Prevalence and risk factors. *The Gerontologist, 32,* 493–97.

Pay, D. (1993). *Ask the question: A resource manual on elder abuse for health care personnel.* Vancouver: Institute on Family Violence.

Phillips, L.R. (1983). Abuse and neglect of the frail elderly at home: An exploration of theoretical relationships. *Journal of Advanced Nursing, 8*(5), 379–92.

Phillips, L.R. (1986). Theoretical explanations of elder abuse: Competing hypotheses and unresolved issues. In K. Pillemer & R.S. Wolf (Eds.), *Elder abuse: Conflict in the family* (pp. 197–217). Dover, MA: Auburn House.

Phillips, L.R., Morrison, E.F., & Chae, Y.M. (1990). The QUALCARE Scale: Testing of a measurement instrument for clinical practice. *International Journal of Nursing Studies, 27*(1), 77–91.

Phillipson, C. (1993). Abuse of older people: Sociological perspectives. In P. Decalmer & F. Glendenning (Eds.), *The mistreatment of elderly people* (pp. 76–87). London, UK: Sage.

Pillemer, K. (1986). Risk factors in elder abuse: Results from a case control study. In K. Pillemer & R.S. Wolf (Eds.), *Elder abuse: Conflict in the family* (pp. 239–63). Dover, MA: Auburn House.

Pillemer, K. (1993). The abused offspring are dependent: Abuse is caused by the deviance and dependence of abusive caregivers. In R.J. Gelles & D.R. Loseke (Eds.), *Current controversies on family violence* (pp. 237–49). Newbury Park: Sage.

Pillemer, K., & Bachman-Prehn, R. (1991). Helping and hurting: Prediction of maltreatment of patients in nursing homes. *Research on Aging, 13,* 74–95.

Pillemer, K., & Finkelhor, D. (1988). The prevalence of elder abuse: A random sample survey. *The Gerontologist, 28*(1), 51–57.

Pillemer, K., & Finkelhor, D. (1989). Causes of elder abuse: Caregiver stress versus problem relatives. *American Journal of Orthopsychiatry, 59*(2), 179–87.

Pillemer, K., & Moore, D.W. (1989). Abuse of patients in nursing homes: Findings from a survey of staff. *The Gerontologist, 29*(3), 314–20.

Pillemer, K., & Suitor, J.J. (1992). Violence and violent feelings: What causes them among family caregivers? *Journal of Gerontology, 47*(4), S165–S172.

Pillemer, K., & Wolf, R.S. (Eds.). (1986). *Elder abuse: Conflict in the family.* Dover, MA: Auburn House.

Pillemer, K., & Wolf, R.S. (1991). *Helping elderly victims: Results from the evaluation of four elder abuse model projects.* Paper presented at the Annual Meeting of the Gerontological Society of America, San Francisco.

Pittaway, E.D., & Gallagher, E. (1995a). *A guide to enhancing services for abused older Canadians.* Victoria: Office for Seniors.

Pittaway, E.D., & Gallagher, E. (1995b). *Services for abused older Canadians.* Victoria: Office for Seniors.

Pittaway, E.D., & Westhues, A. (1993). The prevalence of elder abuse and neglect of older adults who access health and social services in London, Ontario, Canada. *Journal of Elder Abuse & Neglect, 5*(4), 77–93.

Ploeg, J., Fear, J., Hutchison, B., MacMillan, H., & Bolan, G. (2009). A systematic review of interventions for elder abuse. *Journal of Elder Abuse & Neglect, 21*(3), 187–210.

Podnieks, E. (1985). Elder abuse: It's time we did something about it. *Canadian Nurse, 81*(11), 36–39.

Podnieks, E. (1988). Définitions, facteurs, et profils. *Vis-à-Vis, 6*(3), 4, 8.

Podnieks, E. (1992). Emerging themes from a follow-up study of Canadian victims of elder abuse. *Journal of Elder Abuse & Neglect, 4*(1/2), 59–111.

Podnieks, E. (1993). National Survey on Abuse of the Elderly in Canada. *Journal of Elder Abuse & Neglect, 4*(1/2), 5–58.

Podnieks, E., & Baillie, E. (1995). Education as the key to the prevention of elder abuse and neglect. In M. MacLean (Ed.), *Abuse and neglect of older Canadians* (pp. 81–94). Ottawa: Thompson Educational.

Podnieks, E., Pillemer, K., Nicholson, J., Shillington, T., & Frizzel, A. (1990). *National Survey on Abuse of the Elderly in Canada: Final report.* Toronto: Ryerson Polytechnical Institute.

Poirier, D., & Poirier, N. (1999). *Why is it so difficult to combat elder abuse and, in particular, financial exploitation of the elderly?* Final report. Moncton, NB: Law Commission of Canada.

Post, L.A., Page, C., Conner, T., Prokhorov, A., Fang, Y., et al. (2010). Elder abuse in long-term care: Types, patterns, and risk factors. *Research on Aging, 32*(3), 323–48.

Pottie Bunge, V. (2000). Abuse of older adults by family members. In V. Pottie Bunge & D. Locke (Eds.), *Family violence in Canada: A statistical profile* (pp. 27–30). Ottawa: Statistics Canada.

Quayhagen, M., Quayhagen, M.P., Patterson, T.L., Irwin, M., Hauger, R.L., et al. (1997). Coping with dementia: Family caregiver burnout and abuse. *Journal of Mental Health and Aging, 3*, 357–64.

Quinn, M.J., & Tomita, S. (1986). *Elder abuse and neglect: Causes, diagnosis, and intervention strategies.* New York: Springer.

Ramage-Morin, P.L. (2005). Successful aging in health care institutions. *Health Reports, 16*(Suppl.), 47–56.

Ramsey-Klawsnik, H., Teaster, P.B., Mendiondo, M.S., Marcum, J.L., & Abner, E.L. (2008). Sexual predators who target elders: Findings from the first national study of sexual abuse in care facilities. *Journal of Elder Abuse & Neglect, 20*(4), 353–76.

Rathbone-McCuan, E. (1980). Elderly victims of family violence and neglect. *Social Casework, 61*(5), 296–304.

Rathbone-McCuan, E., & Voyles, B. (1982). Case detection of abused elderly parents. *American Journal of Psychiatry, 139*(2), 189–92.

Reay, A.M., & Browne, K.D. (2001). Risk factor characteristics in carers who physically abuse or neglect their elderly dependants. *Aging & Mental Health, 5*(1), 56–62.

Reis, M., & Nahmiash, D. (1995a). Validation of the Caregiver Abuse Screen (CASE). *Canadian Journal on Aging, 14*(2), 45–60.

Reis, M., & Nahmiash, D. (1995b). *When seniors are abused: A guide to intervention.* North York, ON: Captus Press.

Reis, M., & Nahmiash, D. (1998). Validation of the indicators of abuse (IOA) screen. *Gerontologist, 38*(4), 471–80.

Reis, M., Nahmiash, D., & Schrier, R. (1993). *A Brief Abuse Screen for the Elderly (BASE): Its validity and use.* Paper presented at the 22nd Annual Scientific and Educational Meeting of the Canadian Association on Gerontology, Montreal.

Rodriguez, M.A., Wallace, S.P., Woolf, N.H., & Mangione, C.M. (2006). Mandatory reporting of elder abuse: Between a rock and a hard place. *Annals of Family Medicine, 4*(5), 403–8.

Roger, K., & Ursel, J. (2009). Public opinion on mandatory reporting of abuse and/or neglect of older adults in Manitoba, Canada. *Journal of Elder Abuse & Neglect, 21*, 115–40.

Sanchez, Y.M. (1996). Distinguishing cultural expectations in assessment of financial exploitation. *Journal of Elder Abuse & Neglect, 8*(2), 49–59.

Schiamberg, L.B., Barboza, G.G., Oehmke, J., Zhang, Z., Griffore, R.J., Weatherill, R.P., et al. (2011). Elder abuse in nursing homes: An ecological perspective. *Journal of Elder Abuse & Neglect, 23*(2), 190–211.

Scogin, F., Stephens, G., Bynum, J., Baumhover, A., Beall, C., et al. (1992). Emotional correlates of caregiving. *Journal of Elder Abuse & Neglect, 4*(4), 59–69.

Sengstock, M.C., & Hwalek, M. (1986). A critical analysis of measures for the identification of physical abuse and neglect in the elderly. *Home Health Care Quarterly, 6*(4), 27–39.

Sengstock, M.C., & Hwalek, M. (1987). A review and analysis of measures for the identification of elder abuse. *Journal of Gerontological Social Work, 10*(3/4), 21–36.

Sengstock, M.C., Hwalek, M., & Moshier, S. (1986). A comprehensive index for assessing abuse and neglect of the elderly. In M. Galbraith (Ed.), *Elder abuse: Perspectives on an emerging crisis* (Vol. 3, pp. 41–64). Kansas City: Mid-America Congress on Aging.

Sengstock, M.C., & Liang, J. (1983). Domestic abuse of the aged: Assessing some dimensions of the problem. *Interdisciplinary Topics in Gerontology, 17*, 58–68.

Shugarman, L.R., Fries, B.E., Wolf, R.S., & Morris, J.N. (2003). Identifying older people at risk of abuse during routine screening practices. *Journal of the American Geriatrics Society, 51*(1), 24–31.

Silva, T.W. (1992). Reporting elder abuse: Should it be mandatory or voluntary? *HealthSpan, 9*(4), 13–15.

Smelters, D. (1993). Addressing elder abuse: The SEVNA model. Saint Elizabeth Visiting Nurses Association. *Perspectives, 17*(1), 7–10.

Soares, J.F., Barros, H., Torres-Gonzales, F., Ioannidi-Kapolou, E., Lamura, G., Lindert, J., et al. (2010). *Abuse and health among elderly in Europe*. Kaunas, Lithuania: ABUEL. Retrieved from: http://www.age-platform.org/.

Sobsey, D. (Ed.). (1994). *Violence and abuse in the lives of people with disabilities: The end of silent acceptance*. Baltimore: Paul H. Brookes Publishing.

Spector, W.D., Fleishman, J.A., Pezzin, L.E., & Spillman, B.C. (2001). *Characteristics of long-term care users*. Rockville, MD: Agency for Healthcare Research and Quality.

Spencer, C. (1994). *Abuse and neglect of older adults in institutional settings: A discussion paper building from English language resources*. Ottawa: Health Canada.

Spencer, C. (1995). New directions for research on interventions with abused older adults. In M.J. Maclean (Ed.), *Abuse & neglect of older Canadians: Strategies for change* (pp. 143–55). Toronto: Thompson Educational Publishing.

Spencer, C. (1996). *Diminishing returns: An examination of financial responsibility, decision-making, and financial abuse among older adults*. Vancouver: Gerontology Research Centre, Simon Fraser Unversity.

Spencer, C., & Beaulieu, M. (1994). *Abuse and neglect of older adults in institutional settings: An annotated bibliography*. Ottawa: Health Canada.

Spencer, C., & Gutman, G.M. (2008). *Sharpening Canada's focus: Developing an empirical profile of abuse and neglect among older women and men in the community. Final report—Expert Roundtable on Elder Abuse in Canada*. Ottawa: Human Resources and Social Development Canada.

Steinmetz, S.K. (1990). *Duty bound: Elder abuse and family care*. Newbury Park, CA: Sage.

Stilwell, E.M. (1991). Nurses' education related to the use of restraints. *Journal of Gerontological Nursing, 17*(2), 23–26.

Stolee, P., & Hillier, L. (2008). *Best practices in dealing with elder abuse: Identifying, communicating, and adopting processes for prevention, detection, and response*. Ottawa: Human Resources and Social Development Canada.

Stones, M. (1995). Scope and definitions of elder abuse and neglect in Canada. In M. MacLean (Ed.), *Abuse and neglect of older Canadians* (pp. 111–16). Ottawa: Thompson Educational Publishing.

Stones, M., & Bedard, M. (2002). Higher thresholds for elder abuse with age and rural residence. *Canadian Journal on Aging, 21*(4), 577–86.

Straus, M.A. (1979). Measuring intra family conflict and violence: The Conflict Tactics Scale. *Journal of Marriage and Family, 41*, 75–88.

Szikita Clark, C. (2008). *Aging at home: Allowing seniors to live safely at home with dignity and independence*. Toronto: Faculty of Social Work, University of Toronto.

Tatara, T., & Thomas, C. (1998). *National Elder Abuse Incidence Study: Final report*. Washington, DC: National Center on Elder Abuse, American Public Human Services Association.

Trottier, H., Martel, L., & Houle, C. (2000). Living at home or in an institution: What makes the difference for seniors? *Health Reports, 11*(4), 49–61.

Vinton, L. (1991). Factors associated with refusing services among maltreated elderly. *Journal of Elder Abuse & Neglect, 3*(2), 89–103.

Wallace, H. (1996). *Family violence: Legal, medical, and social perspectives.* Boston: Allyn and Bacon.

Walsh, C.A., Olson, J.L., Ploeg, J., Lohfeld, L., & MacMillan, H.L. (2011). Elder abuse and oppression: Voices of marginalized elders. *Journal of Elder Abuse & Neglect, 23*(1), 17–42.

Watts, L., & Sandhu, L. (2006). The 51st state—the "state of denial": A comparative exploration of penal statutory responses to criminal "elder abuse." *Elder Law Journal, 14*(1), 207–11.

Whall, A.L., Gillis, G.L., Yankou, D., Booth, D.E., & Beel-Bates, C.A. (1992). Disruptive behavior in elderly nursing home residents: A survey of nursing staff. *Journal of Gerontological Nursing, 18*(10), 13–17.

WHO. (2002). *"Missing voices" older persons' views of elder abuse.* Geneva: World Health Organization.

Wolf, R.S. (1988). Elder abuse: Ten years later. *Journal of the American Geriatrics Society, 36*(8), 758–62.

Wolf, R.S. (1992). Victimization of the elderly: Elder abuse and neglect. *Reviews in Clinical Gerontology, 2*(3), 269–76.

Wolf, R.S. (1997). Elder abuse and neglect: An update. *Reviews in Clinical Gerontology, 7*, 177–82.

Wolf, R.S., & Pillemer, K.A. (1989). *Helping elderly victims: The reality of elder abuse.* Irvington, NY: Columbia University Press.

Wolf, R.S., Strugnell, C.P., & Godkin, M.A. (1982). *Preliminary findings from three model projects on elderly abuse.* Worcester, MA: Center on Aging, University of Massachusetts Medical Center.

Yaffe, M.J., Wolfson, C., Lithwick, M., & Weiss, D. (2008). Development and validation of a tool to improve physician identification of elder abuse: The Elder Abuse Suspicion Index (EASI). *Journal of Elder Abuse & Neglect, 20*(3), 276–300.

Yan, E.C.-W., & Tang, C.S.-K. (2004). Elder abuse by caregivers: A study of prevalence and risk factors in Hong Kong Chinese families. *Journal of Family Violence, 19*(5), 269–77.

Zhang, Z., Schiamberg, L.B., Oehmke, J., Barboza, G.E., Griffore, R.J., et al. (2011). Neglect of older adults in Michigan nursing homes. *Journal of Elder Abuse & Neglect, 23*(1), 58–74.

17

OLDER PEOPLE ARE SUBJECTS, NOT OBJECTS RECONSIDERING THEORY AND PRACTICE IN SITUATIONS OF ELDER ABUSE

JOAN HARBISON, PAM MCKINLEY, AND DONNA PETTIPAS

> Most of the professional literature on ageing is aimed at the know-how-oriented reader, whose interest is in information about the state of the elderly as an object. Only a smattering of research is dedicated to deciphering the world of old people as subjects, and even less of this work attempts to understand the ways in which knowledge about ageing is produced and reproduced. (Hazan, 1994, p. 3)

INTRODUCTION

Despite universal recognition and relatively high levels of professional and academic activity in the field, it is generally accepted that there are many gaps and inadequacies in our knowledge and understanding of the mistreatment and neglect of older people, and in our responses to it (Lowenstein, 2009; McDonald & Collins, 2000). As a consequence, both research and practice are governed by a pragmatism that responds to immediate needs for knowledge and intervention, but inhibits the growth of a solidly acceptable and scholarly knowledge base for practice (Biggs & Goergen, 2010; Biggs, Phillipson & Kingston, 1995; Ploeg et al., 2009).

This chapter begins by contextualizing some of these gaps and inadequacies through a discussion of the historical and continuing development of elder abuse and neglect during its career as a social problem. It comments on how the subject has been theorized and what structural factors are associated with these theorizations. It proposes an extension of the theoretical perspectives that are used to frame conceptualization and practice. In doing so, it refers to "four major competing constructions" of "elder abuse and neglect" and the "differing needs discourses" that they represent (Fraser, 1986; Harbison & Morrow, 1998). It then discusses how these "needs discourses" are in turn linked with the characteristics present in specific frameworks for intervention (Harbison, 1999a; Harbison & Morrow, 1998). Finally, relevant knowledge for practice with elder abuse is discussed.[1]

The second part of the chapter explicates how approaches to practice can be informed by the exploration referred to above. Situations based on actual cases that exemplify the challenges of working with mistreated and neglected older people living in the community are presented and analyzed. This analysis demonstrates how the knowledge and skills for helpful interventions can be linked to important theoretical concepts, available research, and practice wisdom.

THE PROMOTION OF "ELDER ABUSE AND NEGLECT" AS A SOCIAL PROBLEM

Theorists suggest that social problems have careers whose development through stages is subject to a variety of forces associated with their success or failure (Best, 1989; Blumer, 1971). According to Blumer, these stages include the emergence and legitimation of a social problem, followed by action, which leads to the implementation of official plans to address it (Blumer, 1971; Kingston & Penhale, 1995). Of considerable interest in understanding why "elder abuse" emerged in Canada and the ways in which it is perceived and addressed are the findings of Leroux and Petrunik (1990). Using Blumer's model, they concluded that elder abuse had been promoted primarily by policy-makers and providers rather than by older people themselves (see discussion in Harbison & Morrow, 1998). Similarly, Baumann (1989), in the United States, explored the "claims-making" activities of American researchers in the field of gerontology and found that they had facilitated the construction of mistreatment and neglect of older people as a social problem that needed to be addressed by "experts" (see also Anetzberger, 2005). And in the United Kingdom, support for legitimation and then action regarding elder abuse also came from professionals and academics (Kingston & Penhale, 1995).

From the beginning, then, elder abuse was predominantly the territory of "experts," whether academics or professional service providers. This universal lack of connection to older people's expression of needs (Bradshaw, 1972) and the fact that they were not central participants in the initial framing of the issue have crucially influenced the ways in which elder abuse has been defined and the responses to it (Harbison, 1999a, 1999b). Fraser (1986) has discussed how "expert needs discourses" promote the interests of the experts in power, status, and resources at the expense of the subjects of their assistance. Recently, postmodern theory has encouraged us to embrace uncertainty and focus our attention on how people experience their lives (Irving, 1999, p. 30). It is therefore important, first of all, to explore why, in contrast to younger women and the issue of "domestic abuse," older people have not laid claim to "elder abuse and neglect" for themselves.

"ELDER ABUSE AND NEGLECT" AND THE AGENCY OF OLDER PEOPLE

Any discussion of the behaviour or wishes of "older people" must take place with the acknowledgement of their heterogeneity along many dimensions. Older people have now been established as highly diverse relative to other age groups with regard to health, wealth, ethnicity, culture, and political affiliations (Calasanti, 1996; Markson, 2003). For example, often overlooked is the fact that those subsumed under the term "the elderly" can vary in age by up to forty years, and in physical and mental health from fit and symptom-free to frail and illness-ridden (Daatland & Biggs, 2006; McPherson & Wister, 2008). Yet although many older people are active as volunteers (Chappell, 1999), this does not necessarily translate into an activism that challenges the work of politicians, policy-makers, and "experts." Diversity in political ideologies apart, there may be other reasons why older people are not inclined toward radical politics. The following sections illustrate this point. We examine how older people were constructed as "dependent" during the second half of the twentieth century and how this intersected with the rise of gerontology, how this construction as dependent has evolved given economic and demographic change, and how some older people locate themselves within action to address elder abuse and neglect.

Old Age as "Structured Dependency"

The question of the relative lack of agency of older people in relation to their own mistreatment, while highly complex, may be answered in a variety of ways (Harbison, Coughlan, Karabanow & VanderPlaat, 2005; Harbison, 1999a; Harbison & Morrow, 1998; Gilleard & Higgs, 2000; for a discussion of the "controversial concept" of agency, see Neysmith & MacAdam, 1999). Acknowledgement of the mistreatment and neglect of older people came during a period when their valuation had been shaped by a number of forces. From the 1950s on, industrialized Western nations wanted to replace the older members of its workforce with younger people; older workers were pensioned off to what was, for many, enforced retirement, thus losing their role and status in society's economic productivity (Townsend, 1981). Echoing this economically structured dependency, retirement was constructed by some gerontologists, notably in Cumming and Henry's (1961) disengagement theory, as a period during which one would gradually relinquish one's social roles and responsibilities prior to exiting from life.

This socially influenced reduction in older people's social capacities, in their active contribution to markets and in their agency, was also associated with a much-anticipated deterioration in physical capacity (Hazan, 1994). Responses to the experiences of physiological aging treat them as symptoms requiring medical/professional interventions. In other words, "the needs of the elderly [were] defined and processed by the medical-industrial complex in ways that serve[d] to medicalize old age further and to exacerbate rather than alleviate the dependency of the elderly" (Estes, 2001, p. 12). Retirees took on a "master status" of old age, one that "[overrode] all other statuses and [had] the most priority in the characterization of the individual" (Leroux & Petrunik, 1990, p. 653).

So, we might conclude that these generations of elderly people, having been diminished in so many ways, would hardly be inclined to perceive themselves as having the capacity to address the mistreatment of their peers. Thus, the field was cleared for professional and academic "experts." These experts set relatively narrow parameters for understanding abuse, framing it as a matter of violence within the family, or as the problematic interactions of older people with substitutes for family caregiving in the home or in residential care (Biggs & Goergen, 2010; Phillipson, 1993).

The "Third Age"

Gilleard and Higgs (2000) argue that "structured dependency theory," in combination with "the political economy approach," no longer provides a satisfactory understanding of aging and old age because these theories focus on disadvantaged and marginalized minorities. Thus, they fail to take account of the increasing numbers of men and women who are better off in retirement than they were earlier in life. Older people's relative affluence, youth, and health (given higher incomes, better pensions, and earlier retirement) allow them to establish new and positive identities associated with the concept of a "third age" (Higgs, 1995, p. 539). However, these positive identities frequently focus on leisure, and in a world where work has now recaptured its pre-eminence for human valuation, such identities may not elicit positive regard in the rest of society (Riley, Kahn & Foner, 1994). In addition, Blaikie (1999) points out that these images fail to "[parallel] the egalitarian concerns of politically active lobbyists" acting on behalf of seniors (p. 22). Instead, they can further accusations that older people are getting more than they deserve (Gee & Gutman, 2000). But the worm has turned again and the concept of "successful aging," which first emerged as self-fulfillment (Baltes & Baltes, 1993; Friedan, 1993; Rowe & Kahn, 1998), has been superseded by the theory of "productive aging" where, in these financially uncertain times, older people are expected to take care of them-selves and one another both financially and physically, too often when they are ill-equipped to do so (Estes, 2001; Harbison, 2000).

Moreover, despite the advent of an extended "third age," a "fourth age"—reserved for the "frail elderly" as well as those marginalized by gender, race, and poverty—still looms (Whittaker, 1997). Evidence suggests that, not surprisingly, older people want to avoid it as long as possible. Given that this "fourth age" is the natural location for those suffering abuse and neglect, older people have even greater reason to dissociate themselves from it. In other words, "fourth age agendas remain agendas for 'the other' in contrast to the self-interest of third age ones which are personal" (Gilleard & Higgs, 2000, p. 198). Anecdotally, it is not unusual for older people to articulate this position: "It's too negative a view—I don't want to dwell on abuse and neglect" (personal communication from a very active senior).

Older People and Political Activism

As we discuss later, some third-age seniors in Canada do take up the cause of elder abuse and neglect, and do so through their own seniors-led organiza-tions. But elder abuse and neglect is usually one of many issues competing for attention in organizations with limited resources. And concerns about health care and pensions are higher on the agenda. For instance, in recent years Canadian seniors have twice successfully lobbied against federal gov-ernment pension reforms that were a threat to their incomes (Harbison, 2000). Yet despite a critical mass of older voters who could force govern-ments to pay attention if seniors were to take on special issues such as the mistreatment of older people, this has rarely happened. Seniors' overall lack of political agency, when combined with the diversity of their opin-ions, ensures this (Wilson, 2000). However, recently a reactivated Canadian Association of Retired Persons (CARP), which has traditionally spoken for those who have had professional careers, has begun to actively lobby govern-ment. While the focus remains on ensuring adequate pensions and health care, the organization has also drawn attention to issues of "elder abuse."

The failure of older people to address their oppression directly may also be seen as an issue of power relations related to gender (Calasanti & Slevin, 2001). For, reflecting age demographics, many older activists in the elder abuse field are women. And many do not choose confrontational politics, but instead support the inclusion of men in their efforts (Harbison, 1999b). Even where older women are political activists, they may not choose to address the mistreatment of older people, preferring instead to associate themselves with issues associated with younger age groups, such as child abuse, the environment, and peace. "Elder abuse," as one "Raging Granny" expressed it, is "too close to the bone" (Hall, 2005).

THEORIZING THE ISSUES

Theoretical Challenges and Debates

The failure of theory to evolve and develop, given that the career of elder abuse and neglect has been sustained, is both remarkable and remarked upon by authors in the field as McDonald et al. have discussed earlier in this volume. Yet this failure is hardly surprising given that the field, as we have seen, has been dominated by "expert" practitioners and researchers, most of whom operate within a medical-gerontological framework. It follows that they have tended to take a positivist-empirical approach to theory, research, and intervention—one that fosters "the classification of phenomena into increasingly refined and extensive categories...with, it must be said little advancement in the understanding of abuse itself" (Biggs et al., 2003, p. 1).

This approach also incorporates individualistic explanatory frameworks relating to aging as disease and decline—frameworks that are considered ageist by critical gerontologists and indeed have increasingly been challenged by the findings of scientific research (Markson, 2003). Nevertheless, those working within traditional medical-gerontological approaches (Estes, 2001) perceive the problems of theorizing the mistreatment and neglect of older people as confined mostly to the lack of success of positivistic-empirical methods of research in finding support for individualistic interpretations of "elder abuse" phenomena (Ploeg et al., 2009).

Other scholars embrace a theoretical pluralism as a temporary measure in addressing issues of theory (Phillipson & Biggs, 1995). Just what that pluralism should encompass is a matter of debate. Sprey, a family theorist, suggests a multidisciplinary approach, including psychology, social psychology, sociology, and anthropology. However, he does not accept the centrality of a critical analysis framework that addresses societal structures, issues of power, and human agency. Theorists who espouse a feminist political economy think differently. Whittaker (1997) challenges:

> "add-on" approaches to theorizing elder abuse [which] tend to focus on the difference that age or gender makes in relation to a particular area of study such as the family rather than recognizing that social

life is organized around age and gender as well as around other forms
of social division. (pp. 127–28)

This leads Whittaker to suggest an integration of political economy and
life course approaches. Yet while feminist perspectives on domestic violence might have been expected to strongly influence older women active
in addressing mistreatment and neglect, this has not often been the case:
"feminists are no different than other gerontological scholars and professionals...in their failure to engage with power and gender issues surrounding aging" (Harbison, 2008, p. 223). Further, although there is no clearly
defined chronological divide between those who are "old" and those who
are not, older women's feminism may be different from that of younger
women, and in particular more inclusive of men (Harbison, 1999b). So
older and younger women rarely unite to address the subject of domestic
abuse. In addition, "age relations carry with them an additional unique form
of oppression that intersects with gender, race, ethnicity, class and sexual
preference" (Calasanti & Slevin, 2001, p. 191).

Further, Whittaker's suggestion does not address a relatively new phenomenon, that is, the successful globalization of "elder abuse and neglect." For through the lobbying efforts of the International Network for
the Prevention of Elder Abuse (INPEA), the issue has been taken up by
the World Health Organization. There is little doubt that older people in
widely varying societies are mistreated and neglected. However, the relevance of theoretical frameworks, rooted in Western medical gerontology
for understanding and addressing mistreatment and neglect throughout the
world, needs further scrutiny. For instance, Truscott (1996) suggests that
the apparent consistency of elder abuse and neglect across cultures (Tatara,
1999) is another example of colonization through cultural hegemony.

So, despite expressions of interest on the part of many authors in
expanding theoretical approaches to the mistreatment and neglect of older
people (Biggs & Georgen, 2010; Lowenstein, 2009; Aitken & Griffin, 1996;
Harbison, 1999b; McDonald & Collins, 2000; Phillipson, 1993; Whittaker,
1997), Whittaker appears correct in saying that most of these do little to
foster theoretical development. And so expressions of frustration about
the state of theory on the part of academics in the field continue. Despite a
burgeoning critical social gerontology, which includes critical theory and
feminist perspectives (Bernard & Scharf, 2007; Estes, Biggs & Phillipson,
2003; Katz, 1996; Lynott & Lynott, 1996), notions of "elder abuse and neglect" remain rooted in medicalized expertise.

Finally, there are political-structural forces that influence those involved
in the field. For instance, the construction of social problems "in technical

and administrative terms" (Harbison & Morrow, 1998) has long been popular with governments (Manning, 1985). And the popularity of these technical approaches has increased with the rise of neo-liberalism, which identifies most social problems as emanating from the individual, and requiring technical-individualistic solutions (Biggs & Powell, 1999; Epstein, 1994). Governments in recent times have promoted "scientific management" (Morgan, 1997, pp. 22–23) in social service delivery systems, including those targeted at mistreatment and neglect. This includes "tools," such as those that make detailed assessments of numerous risk factors based on individual behaviours (Webb, 2006). Keeping the focus on matters such as risk factors allows problems like insufficient income, poor housing, and the profound societal ageism (which provides the context for many forms of abuse) to be sidestepped (Chappell, McDonald & Stones, 2008). Thus, in the present political climate, the direction for elder abuse theory and research is likely to continue in a state of highly flawed empiricism.

FRAMING RESPONSES TO ELDER ABUSE AND NEGLECT

Given the weakness of its theoretical base, it is important to find other ways of understanding existing responses to the mistreatment and neglect of older people. Harbison and Morrow (1998) examined the social construction of elder abuse and neglect in the Canadian context and identified "four major competing constructions reflecting four differing needs discourses...in legislation, programmes and services, and in the actions of individuals" (p. 691). These include the construction of older abused people as "'victims' of domestic violence" (p. 699), "persons subject to illegal acts" (p. 702), "adults in need of protection" (p. 697), and as "agents for their own lives" (p. 703).

"Victims" of Domestic Violence

Various explanations have been given for why elder abuse has not been included under the rubric "victims" of domestic violence. Chief among these is the fact that "elder abuse and neglect" was the creature of gerontology through which it was medicalized and depoliticized (Baumann, 1989). As a consequence, a structural analysis of "the power inequities within the family" was avoided, and instead a view of families "as the site of support and resources" was retained (Harbison & Morrow, 1998, p. 698). This means that, as discussed above, much elder abuse theory and intervention focuses on individualistic explanations that characterize elder abuse and neglect as predominantly a matter of intergenerational dysfunction in families (Biggs & Haapala, 2010; Harbison & Morrow, 1998; Kurrle, Sadler & Cameron, 1992). Services offered are likely to be "intended to alleviate or assist their escape from situations of abuse" (Harbison, 1999a, p. 7).

However, older people's values frequently mean that they turn down such offers, for research suggests that the retention of positive views of the family is of great importance to many older people, even those who are suffering abuse within them (Harbison et al., 2005; Podnieks, 1992).

People Subject to Illegal Acts

Older people's protectiveness of their family's image may also be an important reason why they, and those acting on their behalf, fail to construct them as individual people subject to illegal acts. Despite the considerable potential that exists to do so (Ogrodnik, 2007), little use is made of provisions under the Criminal Code to address situations of mistreatment and neglect. At the same time, both within families and within institutional care, research suggests that, as with younger victims of so-called domestic assaults, fears of a range of negative consequences for taking action may be justified. Physical abuse may be increased but hidden from view by further isolating the individual, visits from loved ones or contact with grandchildren may cease, and threats may be made of future punishment (Harbison & Morrow, 1998). Where exploitation is material, older people may choose to tolerate it for other reasons. For instance, they may not wish to experience the humiliation of being exposed as having fallen prey to one of various prevalent scams, such as those asking for money for worthless or never delivered goods and services, or they may fear that their mental and social competency will be questioned (Barer, 1997). The recent expansion and development of "Elder Law" following the aging of the population has so far chiefly represented the interests of individual older people. However, publicity given to high-profile cases, especially of fraud and financial exploitation, may encourage some older people of means to acknowledge and address their issues of mistreatment (see, for instance, the Advocacy Centre for the Elderly).

Adults in Need of Protection

Where older people suffering mistreatment or neglect are perceived as "adults in need of protection," responses are paternalistic, reflecting the "benign but ultimately controlling reach of the therapeutic state" (Gordon, 2001, p. 130). Gordon (2001) provides an overview and critical analysis of the diversity and complexity of the legislation targeted at elder abuse and neglect, which is increasingly in use throughout Canada (see also Harbison et al., 2008). Such legislation is too often based on ageist assumptions of older people's deficits—for instance, that they are dependent and incapable of making good decisions about their welfare. This is especially transparent in the provincial legislation that models itself on that used for child protection (Harbison, 1999a). Further, where legislation involves provision for mandatory reporting of suspected abuse, it can represent a well-meaning desire to impose "community standards" on older people (Coughlan et al., 1996; Gordon, 2001). Collingridge (1993) expresses his concerns about protective measures this way:

> In their haste to do something policy makers are overlooking important questions about the legal bases for intervention as well as side stepping more fundamental ethical questions about the general societal and individual obligations concerning care of the vulnerable, the limits of intervention and the balance between autonomy and protection. (p. 32)

Indeed, concerns about older people's rights under the Canadian Charter of Rights and Freedoms (1982) have led to policy guidelines regarding protection and guardianship legislation that emphasize "least intrusive" interventions—frequently those based on risk assessment tools (Harbison et al., 2008). However, protective investigations involve gathering "collateral" information—for instance, from family and neighbours, as well as professionals—and frequently includes several or more agencies. So these interventions also require scrutiny for their potential to override the rights and wishes of physically and mentally competent older people and to do harm (Poirier, 1992). The approach also sidesteps the issue of the needs for services, which are often greater than the issues of abuse and neglect, and the services are equally often unavailable (Harbison et al., 2005).

The discussion above indicates that legal remedies, whether through targeted adult protection legislation or based on the civil or criminal codes, are limited in providing effective responses to elder abuse and neglect that fully respect the autonomy and rights of older people. Nevertheless, when carefully constructed and sensitively implemented, legislation can offer positive assistance, and "the framing of abuse as a crime can point to the seriousness of the situation, and to society's willingness to recognize the issues as being of public [and not just a private] concern" (Harbison & Morrow, 1998, p. 703). As an alternative, Gordon (2001) raised the question of the potential of restorative justice to address issues of mistreatment. The approach has been historically associated with Canada's First Nations, but is now being employed in some jurisdictions to address the mistreatment of older people (Groh, 2003). It involves the diversion of cases brought before the courts to a process addressing the hurt suffered by the victim. This process includes ways in which the needs generated by that hurt can be addressed by those who have inflicted it. However, whether issues of power can be satisfactorily addressed through this means is in question (Wolhuter et al., 2009), and "Winterdyk and King argue that many issues need to be researched and addressed before the restorative approach has widespread implementation" (Harbison, 2011, p. 267; Matsuoka, Clarke & Murphy, 2010).

Agents for Their Own Lives

As we have seen, there appear to be several reasons why elder abuse and neglect remains the territory of expert professionals and academics, and one to which older people do not lay claim. Not only was it initially constructed as a medical-gerontological enterprise, but in an ageist society, older people have tended, where possible, to distance themselves from the negative identification of old age, which elder abuse represents (Hall, 2005). Finally, invitations issued by "experts" to participate in the field may be experienced as further marginalization, and tensions may arise between the "expert" and seniors' groups (Aronson, 1993; Harbison, 1999b). Nevertheless, older people have initiated or made major contributions to a number of highly innovative programs. For instance, the British Columbia Coalition to Eliminate Abuse of Seniors (BCCEAS, a seniors-led organization) had a well-established reputation for advocacy, peer counselling, and other innovative programs—for instance, securing funds to run a group for immigrant seniors suffering abuse (Ward-Hall, 2001). Notably, that program has now become a professionally led legal aid clinic. And seniors were at the forefront of designing and acquiring funds for the only purpose-built shelter for abused older men and women in Canada, in Calgary, Alberta (McKreight, 1999). And the St. Christopher House and the Portuguese Women Fifty-Five Plus Support Group of Ontario "joined forces in 1992 to address the issue of elder abuse" on a number of fronts. These included popular education based on the teachings of Paulo Freire through mimed theatrical presentations by seniors (Nascimento, Sestrem & the Christopher House Elder Abuse Prevention Group, 2000, p. 178).

Older people have also carried out extensive educational work throughout Canada, targeting both older people and the general public. In conjunction with lawyers, police, and banks, they have found ways to publicize older people's rights and to provide educational forums and packages in attempts both to prevent abuses and encourage the abused to seek assistance. For instance, Canadian Pensioners Concerned, Nova Scotia, produced a handbook on *The law and older Nova Scotians* (2001) and one offering information on "elder abuse" called *Battered and betrayed* (2003). More recently, older people were recruited as team members and regional disseminators for a project funded by a federal New Horizons grant conducted under the aegis of the Network Initiative for the Care of the Elderly (NICE) at the University of Toronto Centre for Life Course and Aging. The project identified or developed evidence-based tools for the identification of, and potential intervention into, cases of "elder abuse." The Canadian Network for the Prevention of Elder Abuse (CNPEA) consists mainly of "expert" professionals, representatives of government agencies, and academics, but representatives of "seniors" groups are included.

Seniors have also been active with individuals who are being mistreated or neglected through the provision of peer counselling services. This is one way of attempting to circumvent older people's reluctance to expose their families to scrutiny because the abused person perceives older peers as more closely allied to their values and wishes and therefore less likely than professionals to take unwanted action. However, an exploratory study of five peer counselling groups in five Canadian provinces suggested that professional expertise retains its influence over this work in several ways. On the one hand, senior peer counsellors were wary of the judgment of professionals: "I think there are professionals who just do not think that you have the ability to think once you retire"; on the other hand, they were grateful to have professionals to "fall back on" when situations were especially difficult. When seniors functioned most autonomously, they were found to be most creative in their roles. They were also more inclined toward advocacy: "I don't ever think I'm going to counsel somebody with depression or anything like that, but I sure as heck would do a lot of yelling and talking and being very bullish. If I feel there is a need to be there, I will be there. And I will talk to everybody" (Harbison, 2002, p. 18).

APPROACHING PRACTICE WITH MISTREATED AND NEGLECTED OLDER PEOPLE

Knowledge about Aging

As Hazan points out, most of the professional literature on aging continues to be based on observations of older people rather than on accounts of their experience. In addition, it is conceded that social and psychological theories, such as the disengagement theory discussed above, can be used to support "certain negative aspects of social policy and attitudes towards older people" (Coleman, 1993, p. 85).

> It [disengagement theory] provided a scientific rationale for the new twentieth-century practice of retirement from the labour force. It justified the rocking-chair lifestyle, and placement of housing schemes for older people on the periphery of towns and cities, away in the peace and quiet. It could even be seen to excuse custodial forms of treatment in institutional care. It was a particularly dangerous form of theory because of its potential of becoming a self-fulfilling prophecy.

> If we expect and demand less of people because they are old, they are
> likely to conform to this expectation. (Coleman, 1993, p. 85)

Moreover, we need to be alert to the sources of evidence on which theories
are based. For instance, it has been acknowledged that the laboratory conditions within which attempts to understand physiological and psychological
aspects of aging take place limit the interpretation of the research (Coleman,
1993, p. 63). Further, a recurring theme in the literature on aging is that,
even where mental or physical disease is present, these do not necessarily
limit the person's abilities for self-determination (Chappell et al., 2008;
Wilson, 2000).

We may conclude that in order to work effectively with older people,
we need to make ourselves familiar with the current state of knowledge
about aging. For instance, we must be able to understand how disease and
physiological or emotional stress and loss, as well as social conditions, might
affect a person's intellect, emotions, or behaviours. We also need to critically appraise that knowledge, the assumptions on which it is based, and
therefore its value in addressing the matter at hand in a manner consistent
with a social work value base (Mullaly, 2002; Neysmith & MacAdam, 1999).
For instance, have matters such as class, culture, race/ethnicity, and gender
been sufficiently attended to? And are racism, sexism/heterosexism, and
ageism linked to the situation and its interpretation?

These issues are just beginning to be addressed in the field of elder abuse.
The public face of elder abuse "experts" and senior volunteers tends not
only to be female and middle class, but also predominantly Caucasian.
This reflects the dominance of these groups both in the professions and in
leadership roles in mainstream seniors' organizations. However, the "career"
of elder abuse in Canada is now at a stage where diverse populations are
becoming involved (see, for instance, Cornwell, 2000, pp. 84–91; Hansell,
1999, p. 73; Matsuoka et al., 2010; Singh Sodhi & Joshi, 2000, p. 83; Tam &
Neysmith, 2006; Walsh, Ploeg, Lohfeld, Horne, MacMillan & Lai, 2007).

Knowledge about "Elder Abuse and Neglect"?

That there is a great deal of professional and academic activity in Canada
and elsewhere specific to the field of elder abuse is evident from the discussion above. We have also noted that much of the knowledge emanating
from this activity is acknowledged as highly flawed, even by its proponents. Nevertheless, professionals practising in the field should make themselves fully aware of mainstream knowledge about elder abuse, with all
its uncertainties. However, as with knowledge about aging, they need to
closely examine and assess this knowledge base through the lens of critical

gerontology (Harbison et al., 2012, in press; Harbison et al., 2008; Calasanti & Slevin, 2001; Katz, 1996; Laws, 1995; Neysmith & MacAdam, 1999).

Societal Ageism and Responses to "Elder Abuse and Neglect"

In the field of elder abuse and neglect, as in the general field of aging, much of the knowledge does lack validity, not just on the basis that it fails tests of empiricism, but because it treats "the elderly" as object rather than subject (Hazan, 1994). Indeed, older people experience the world so much as objects that it may be difficult for them to transcend that position. It follows that they themselves may have a tendency to perceive situations through the lens of professional "objectivity." For instance, a senior, well educated in professional and policy issues with regard to elder abuse, expressed his support for legislation that was proposed (and subsequently abandoned) in Ontario that would have allowed unwanted entry into older people's homes where abuse or neglect were suspected. However, when asked what he would do if someone entered his home under the legislation for that reason, he said, "I would go after them with a baseball bat" (personal communication).

There are also indications that older people may construct their responses to abusive situations differently than professional onlookers. Podnieks (1992) found that abused seniors perceived themselves as having a positive identity as "copers" rather than as victims. This may connect to an earlier period in their lives when coping skills were learned in dealing with the hardships of economic depression and war. More recent generations, with their focus on feminist perspectives and victims' rights, may take a different view of how individual suffering should be dealt with.

There is much support for the idea that within Western societies, there is a high degree of cognitive dissonance in how we view older people (Biggs, Phillipson & Kingston, 1995; Bytheway, 1995; Marriott, 1997). On the one hand, older people of most cultural origins are said to be highly valued, and in some instances this may be evidenced in how they are treated. On the other, they are devalued, marginalized, taken advantage of in material ways by both intimates and strangers, and turned into servants. In extreme situations, they become the objects of active physical and psychological abuse and neglect. It is suggested that the origins of this ageism lie in the anxiety and fear that younger people have about aging and death (Hazan, 1994).

> Ageism... allows younger people to see elders as different from themselves. They cease to identify with elders as human beings and thereby reduce their own fears of ageing. It also becomes a useful expedient whereby decision takers in society can promote viewpoints about

older people in order to relieve themselves of responsibility towards them. (Biggs, Phillipson & Kingston, 1995, p. 61)

In the political-economic arena, the negative viewpoints about older people in Canadian society are clear for all to see. They are frequently styled as freeloaders who are taking resources from younger people and children who need them more (Harbison, 1999b; Rozanova, Northcott & MacDaniel, 2006). Claims are also made by apocalyptic demographers that increases in the numbers of older people will overwhelm services and undermine economic growth (Gee & Gutman, 2000). Neither of these claims stands up under scrutiny. This is both because of the past and continuing contributions of older people to society, and because the figures and arguments used in calculating the "burden" that they place on society have been distorted (Gee & Gutman, 2000). Indeed, "demographic alarmism is very much an offspring of the contemporary [social] climate of anxiety and insecurity" (Furedi, 2002, p. xiv).

What all this means in terms of provision of services for older people is that where possible, they are being returned to families in communities, whether this is viable in terms of actual resources or not (Neysmith & Mac-Adam, 1999; Tester, 1996). In the case of elder abuse, which has chiefly been constructed as a problem of dysfunctional families, this must surely pose a problem since the maintenance of the psychological well-being of society as a whole depends on the state being seen to take action where such "aberrations" occur (Epstein, 1994). In many instances of responses to elder abuse, what this consists of is "surveillance" rather than assistance (Biggs & Powell, 1999), in other words, the establishment of policies, protocols, and procedures, which may lead to identification of, rather than solutions to, problems (Kozma & Stones, 1995; McDonald & Collins, 2000). However, achieving positive outcomes in the inevitably complex situations of mistreatment and neglect is, as we will see, a highly skilled, creative, and time-consuming endeavour. And even where such interventions are in place, the resources required are under considerable pressure. Specifically, this is because of the economically driven current preference for short-term technical solutions to individual social problems, where personnel are interchangeable units rather than autonomous professionals (Neysmith & MacAdam, 1999; Webb, 2006).

Social Work Responses in Situations of the Mistreatment and Neglect of Older People

It must be clear by now that there are no easy solutions to the phenomena that are subsumed under "elder abuse and neglect," for if we were to use a medical analogy, "it is more like a metastasized cancer of society than a simple [and discrete] medical condition" (Harbison, 1999a, p. 2). In addition, as we have seen, psychological accounts of the meaning of older people's behaviour, including those in situations of abuse and neglect, have come under question. First, this is because these accounts rarely include the viewpoint of older people themselves and, second, because much of the empirical research does not meet tests of reliability and validity (Ploeg et al., 2009). However, social work is uniquely positioned to provide helpful responses to situations of mistreatment and neglect. The difficult social nature of the issues that are intrinsic to the mistreatment and neglect of older people, combined with its complex interpersonal and psychodynamic dimensions, are familiar aspects of social work territory. Social work education and training introduces social workers to the broad socio-economic and political issues affecting social welfare, and through a critical lens, it explores how these may relate to the experiences of groups and individuals. Social work education also affords opportunities for the development of knowledge about various theories of the interpersonal and psychodynamics of human behaviour, as well as their critical appraisal. And social workers learn how to select from models of intervention in order to work in each unique practice situation. Such a generalist approach to practice not only supports the worker in considering a wide range of information and options, but also allows her or him to shift the focus of attention and to change interventive strategies as the need arises. These elements are essential to good practice where older people are suffering mistreatment and neglect.

What follows is a discussion of the practice issues raised by situations representing a variety of degrees and types of abuse or neglect. Possible ways of responding to them within the theoretical and conceptual frameworks presented above are suggested. Each case example refers to circumstances that are typical of the work and the challenges that it represents. The different scenarios illustrate issues relating to the interpersonal relationships and dynamics, service delivery systems, cultural diversity, and social structural issues. The situations also illustrate the inadequacy of narrow individualistic frameworks, or risk assessment models, in such very complex circumstances.[2]

The Issue of Self-Neglect
Statistics in some jurisdictions suggest that the largest numbers of cases dealt with by those addressing mistreatment and neglect in older people are those constituting self-neglect (Gordon, 2001). From the point of view of numbers alone, therefore, it is important to be knowledgeable about how to approach such situations. The first of the two situations, discussed under the heading of "self-neglect," is one where the client's degree of self-neglect is beginning to be of concern to the public health nurse, who then

shares this concern with a social worker with whom she has an ongoing collaborative relationship. The intervention to provide supports to address the neglect is both respectful of the client's wishes and modestly success- ful in outcome. The second situation described demonstrates many of the concerns discussed in the literature about the construction of "elder abuse and neglect" as a medical problem. Only the well-informed and assertive intervention of the social worker prevents the client from being unneces- sarily treated as an "adult in need of protection."

A Situation of Self-Neglect

A social worker, Ms. Matthews, working for a community-based agency in a large inner-city neighbourhood, received a telephone referral from a public health nurse. The nurse, Ms. Smith, has periodically visited Ms. Williams, a seventy- seven-year-old Afro-Caribbean woman, in her own home during the past year to dress a recurring ulcer on her leg. The request was based on the nurse's concern that Ms. Williams' personal hygiene, as well as the cleanliness of the home, were deteriorating to a point where they presented a further health hazard. As far as Ms. Smith was aware, Ms. Williams was quite alone in the world as there was no evidence that relatives or friends ever visited, and Ms. Williams appeared quite reclusive. However, her nursing assessment of Ms. Williams was as fairly mentally able for her years and though Ms. Williams' physical condition and that of the house was poor, from her previous professional experience, Ms. Smith knew that things were not at a stage where there were legal grounds to step in to protect Ms. Williams. Instead, the nurse thought that a home helper, and perhaps a volunteer from the seniors' home assistance program, run by Ms. Matthews' agency, might help out with laundry and house cleaning. In response to Ms. Matthews' query about whether Ms. Williams had initiated or agreed to the referral, the nurse said that when she had suggested to Ms. Williams that she "could use some help around the house," Ms. Williams had "not appeared to object."

Here is the first ethical and professional dilemma posed by the situation. Is Ms. Williams really in agreement with the referral or did she feel she had no choice? Is she going to view the advent of a social worker offering "help" as an intrusion and an assault on her independence, especially since Ms. Matthews was Caucasian and so not connected to Ms. Williams' ethno- racial origins? As an experienced social worker working mainly with older people from diverse cultures, Ms. Matthews was immediately alert to these issues. She also wondered what was behind the "deterioration." Was Ms. Williams merely physically incapacitated and unable to keep up her previous standards? Was she in the early stages of a dementia that caused her to be unaware of increasing deficiencies in her personal and domestic hygiene? Or was Ms. Williams' behaviour associated with the mild depression that afflicts some older people, especially those of African descent (Markson, 2003)? Did she really have no friends or relatives, or had they simply not been present at the time of Ms. Smith's visits? In other words, Ms. Matthews expanded the horizons of her beginning assessment of the situation well beyond that of practical assistance.

Ms. Matthews decided to drop in on Ms. Williams. By not telephoning to make an appointment, Ms. Matthews was taking a calculated risk. It was possible that Ms. Williams might be offended by this. On the other hand, Ms. Williams might not be any more comfortable with a telephone call, and it would be easier for her to say no to assistance. When Ms. Matthews arrived, she found that Ms. Williams lived in a very modest home that had seen much better days, and in a downtown neighbourhood that had once been predominantly Caribbean, but which was now increasingly Caucasian. There was no answer to her knock at the front door, so she went around to the back and knocked again. When she still received no reply, she eventually announced her presence through a partly open window. This brought Ms. Williams to the back door. She was wearing a stained housedress and smelled faintly of urine. The kitchen behind her looked extremely untidy and dirty. She demanded to know what Ms. Matthews was doing there and who had sent her. When told that it was her public health nurse, Ms. Smith, Ms. Williams said firmly, "If I had known that, I wouldn't have opened the door. I don't need any help, thank you very much," and turned to re-enter the house. Ms. Matthews' response was instantaneous and, though respectful, in the same firm tone: "But I am very glad that you did open the door. May I come in for a few minutes?" Seeing Ms. Williams, and in the light of the information that she had already, the social worker had concluded that Ms. Williams was indeed in some mental or emotional distress. She also concluded that leaving now would be walking away from the one opportunity to make a connection with her. She thought that her only chance to make progress was to be as equally firm as Ms. Williams.

Ms. Williams did agree to have a chat with Ms. Matthews, but she refused all of the potential services offered. These included a few hours a week of home help, voluntary assistance with the garden, which Ms. Matthews noted was neglected, and a lunch club at a community centre noted for its ethno-racial diversity. However, she did not raise objections to Ms. Matthews' comment that she would "drop round again to see how she was getting on." Two months later, on the social worker's third visit, Ms. Williams accepted the home help. As it turned out, she was in the early stages of a dementia-type illness and found it increasingly difficult to cope, even though she did not admit to this. In her relationship with Ms. Matthews, it emerged that Ms. Williams was a single, former white-collar government worker with a reasonable pension who had immigrated to Canada in her late twenties. Most of her relatives had returned to the Caribbean and friends had drifted away as the neighbourhood changed; the increasing insistence of local teenagers that Ms. Williams contribute to undocumented "charities" had made her feel exploited and increasingly anxious about social contact. Over the two years following Ms. Matthews' initial visit, she required an intensification of both voluntary and statutory services. Each increase was carefully broached by the social worker. Assistance is now given not only with care of the home but with personal care, such as bathing and laundry. Eventually Ms. Williams also agreed to be driven by a volunteer to the lunch club. While she tends to keep her distance from other members, she appears to enjoy it, and the volunteer driver from her country of origin has become a confidant. Plans are afoot for her to attend a nearby Afro-Caribbean church as she had done many years ago. In addition, coaxed by Ms. Matthews, she has recently agreed to purchase a new mattress to replace one that had become urine-soaked as her incontinence increased.

What this situation demonstrates is that successfully offering assistance in situations of self-neglect requires very well-considered interventions over time. Where people are experiencing fragility of mind, they may respond to someone who offers them both respect and at the same time the reassurance of a less fragile mind. Ms. Matthews demonstrated that by her initial firmness. In addition, it is important to offer a relationship, but one that allows the older people to gradually come to their own conclusions about their changing needs. When Ms. Williams initially refused any services, Ms. Matthews responded with what she describes as a strategy of "not quite going away." By saying simply that she *would* drop around again, she maintained the connection with Ms. Williams and kept open the possibility that she would eventually accept help. This does mean that the worker must have the flexibility to make herself or himself available at intervals over a long period of time, a circumstance increasingly rare in today's service delivery systems (Harbison, Coughlan, Karabanow & Vanderplaat, 2004).

On the surface, the above seems a relatively simple situation. But consider what might have happened had it been handled with less knowledge and skill. Had the public health nurse been more concerned about "covering herself" than with the outcome of an intervention, she might have made a referral to an agency operating under a legislative mandate to protect. This would have required a formal assessment. Since Ms. Williams was both unable to identify a need for assistance and very wary of its imposition, the mandatory assessment would likely have entrenched her position against accepting help. By any legislative guidelines, Ms. Williams would not have been considered legally "in need of protection." Perhaps a referral would have been made for services such as Ms. Matthews' agency provided, but it is very likely that Ms. Williams would have been so alienated by the process that she would have refused any services. The deterioration in her physical and mental condition, and that of her home, would then have continued without interruption. This would have made it all the more difficult to connect Ms. Williams with services at a later date, when she may have become a danger to herself.

It is also important to note that even when a person's state of self-neglect provides grounds for mandatory intervention, it can be very difficult to come to a successful resolution of a self-neglect case within the constraints of legislation. The individual's rights may override what others consider to be their "best interests" (Collingridge, 1993; Gordon, 2001). Moreover, even where a "rescue" is effected, it may not result in a positive outcome for the client. After a client, taken from a filthy home judged to be a health hazard, was unable to settle elsewhere and died within months, one worker reflected on the "rescue": "I liken the whole experience to picking a wildflower in the woods—you pick them and you take them out of their environment and they wilt and they die. And I really think that is what happened. And it bothers me" (Harbison et al., 2005, p. 237).

The Construction of an "Adult in Need of Protection"
As we have seen, a number of provinces in Canada have legislation that is specifically targeted at adults who are considered to be in need of protection. This is usually because of their perceived lack of ability to judge what might be harmful for them and/or take the actions necessary to protect themselves. In the case of older people, action under the legislation may be taken after professional assessment of mental and/or physical infirmity. The following is an account of a situation that illustrates how a well-intentioned medical/gerontological approach to an elderly client constructed the client's behaviour as evidence of his incompetence, and how a vigilant and assertive social worker defended him from this "charge" and protected the client's right to self-determination.

This account comes from Ms. Jones, a social work with responsibility for taking action under provincial legislation to protect vulnerable adults. She became involved with this situation when she received a referral from a care coordinator to assess one of the care coordinator's clients, Mr. Bates, as an adult in need of protection. In order to carry out her assessment, Ms. Jones pieced together the following information: Mr. Bates was a ninety-four-year-old man of English origin and a former army officer, living alone in a large old rented apartment, as he had done since his wife's death fourteen years previously. The couple was childless. However, throughout their lives, the Bates had had a large circle of friends of more than one generation. So, although many of Mr. Bates's friends had died, and others were institutionalized or housebound, he still had a number of social contacts.

Mr. Bates was described by his care worker as fiercely independent and determined not to end his life in institutional care. Threats to his independence, such as periodic minor illnesses, made him irritable and "hard to handle," but his regular workers accepted this. Mr. Bates managed all of his own domestic and financial affairs. In addition, he had made an arrangement with a younger and fitter friend to assist him by driving him to buy groceries and to necessary appointments. Mr. Bates had a number of health problems, including limited vision as a result of cataracts. In addition, he periodically required assistance from a Victorian Order of Nurses (VON) nurse because of recurring leg ulcers. Mr. Bates preferred to deal with these himself, but he would call the VON for assistance when he judged that he needed it. A care worker visited for one hour weekly to assist with meal preparation and housekeeping. During a periodic review of services, Mr. Bates angrily dismissed suggestions from a relief care coordinator that he would be eligible for an increase in the quantity of service and perhaps could benefit from it. Indeed, he threatened to cancel all of his services. However, when the care coordinator backed down and apologized, Mr. Bates agreed to continue with the existing services.

Mr. Bates's well-orchestrated independence came under threat when he fell while getting into his friend's vehicle during a regular shopping expedition. He had considerable pain in his chest area as well as lacerations on his face. As a consequence, he asked his friend to take him to the local hospital emergency department. At first he was quite pleasant in response to the emergency staff's questions for assessment purposes, but eventually Mr. Bates became quite agitated and left the department before the results of an X-ray were available. On his chart the emergency staff noted that he "was unable to tolerate questioning." Later he was contacted by telephone and told that he had fractured three of his ribs.

This incident seemed to have had a negative effect on Mr. Bates's self-confidence as well as his physical state. Over the next couple of days, Mr. Bates made two more visits to the emergency department, complaining of the pain and saying that he was afraid that he was dying. The emergency staff suggested that Mr. Bates attend an appointment at a geriatric clinic, where he could obtain a specialist's opinion of his injuries. Immediately following the appointment in the clinic, Mr. Bates called his regular care coordinator, who had just returned from vacation, and cancelled all his services. The female geriatrician also called the care coordinator. She said that Mr. Bates had declared his intention to refuse all services as he left the assessment interview. The geriatrician was convinced that Mr. Bates was attempting to mask mental incompetence and this was the reason he had walked out of the interview when the multidisciplinary assessment team was attempting to do a "mini-mental" examination to confirm this. The geriatrician and her team had reached the conclusion that Mr. Bates was an adult in need of protection and that most likely a nursing home placement was warranted. The team wanted an assessment under the protection of vulnerable adults legislation.

The care coordinator was concerned by this turn of events. She called Mr. Bates, hoping to persuade him to accept services again. Mr. Bates expressed his distress at recent events, but was easily calmed and agreed fairly readily to this. The care coordinator then called Ms. Jones, the social worker who was responsible for assessments under the protection of adults legislation. In conversation with the care coordinator, the above information emerged. It seemed to Ms. Jones that by walking out of the interview, Mr. Bates had responded to the threat to his independence in a manner that did indeed threaten his "best interests," as referred to in the legislation. However, this did not appear to be sufficient evidence of incompetence. Ms. Jones telephoned the geriatrician to obtain more information and to share with her the news that Mr. Bates had agreed to retain her services. The geriatrician noted that Mr. Bates had earlier refused an increase in services; further, she also appeared convinced that the volatility of Mr. Bates's behaviour could lead to serious physical health problems, for instance, should his leg ulcers be left unattended. The geriatrician said that the time had come for Mr. Bates to go to a nursing home. If Mr. Bates would not agree to the plan, then it was his family physician's professional responsibility or, if he refused, it would be her responsibility to declare him incompetent in order to bring this about.

When contacted by the social worker, Ms. Jones, the family physician expressed some surprise at the designation of incompetence, but said he "was no expert" and would leave it up to Ms. Jones and the geriatrician to sort out what was best. The social worker was very concerned that this elderly man, who in her opinion had, over a long period of time, demonstrated his mental competency by managing his limitations so well, might be forcibly admitted to a nursing home because of what the experts were convinced were his "best interests." As a social worker, Ms. Jones knew that she did not have the professional jurisdiction to assess mental competence, so she reframed the issue as one of functional competence; in other words, had Mr. Bates's behaviours so far ensured that he was adequately provided with health and social care? Ms. Jones asked for a meeting with the geriatric team. She listened carefully as the team made its case. However, she had done her homework well and was quietly able to counter their arguments as she gave a detailed historical account of the evidence of Mr. Bates's functional competence. She emphasized that Mr. Bates's recent erratic behaviour appeared to be a consequence of the psychological trauma, specifically, the threat to his highly prized independence, which resulted from the physical trauma of the fall. She pointed out that the mini-mental exam carried out in the geriatric assessment had convinced Mr. Bates that they were going to "label me crazy" and increased his agitation. The worker included information from the VON nurse, the care worker, and the care coordinator, all of whom had known him over a long period of time and were convinced of Mr. Bates's ability to remain in his own home. The social worker's report was accepted by the team. Thus, the further trauma of a court hearing under adult protection legislation was avoided.

Perhaps the most puzzling thing about this situation is why the geriatrician and her team pushed so hard to have Mr. Bates declared incompetent. They, of all professional groups, should be in a position to avoid ageist stereotypes based on advanced chronological age, and to make generous interpretations of behaviours that disrupted the health system but were intended by the patient to maintain his highly valued independence. Ms. Jones thought that the team's response might be in part an assumption that because of his advanced age, Mr. Bates's health would now rapidly deteriorate, and it was therefore an attempt to protect both him and the health system from wasteful visits to the emergency department. In addition, she wondered about their personal reaction to a somewhat arrogant and challenging patient, a man of very advanced years in the unusual circumstance of living on his own, who had not shown respect for their professional expertise. On the other hand, those professionals and caregivers who knew Mr. Bates well admired his independent spirit and tolerated the professional inconvenience sometimes associated with it. Bringing together their positive opinions and observations with her own innovative framing of the competency issue as "functional" won the day for Ms. Jones's client. At the same time, the social worker hoped that her handling of the situation— interpreting the situation through a normalizing, non-ageist lens, demonstrating the importance of gathering information from those who know the person best, and weighing up everyone's observations in her report—offered a constructive model for the future interaction of the geriatric team.

A Situation of Domestic Violence

The situation of domestic violence discussed below is not one involving a husband and wife, but one that is often described in the literature on elder abuse—that of a mother with an alcoholic child who is dependent on her. It raises ethical and professional questions about whether social workers should be willing to work with the perpetrators as well as the recipients of violence in a domestic situation. It also raises the issue of whether social workers should agree to work with clients who choose to remain in a domestic situation where they may continue to be the recipients of violence. In this case the social worker is one who, although operating from a position of feminism, has come to terms with her own reservations about working with perpetrators and victims together. At the same time, she carefully monitors the effect on the boundaries of the relationship and is vigilant with regard to any manifestations of violence.

> **Mrs. Crawford is seventy-three** years of age and owns a small home in a rural community. Her grandparents had immigrated to the area to farm in the late nineteenth century. Her forty-two-year-old son, James, has lived with her for the past ten years. James moved back into the family home when his relationship with his common-law wife broke up. This was shortly after the death of Mrs. Crawford's abusive and alcoholic husband, James's stepfather. At first, things went fairly well with James, partly because his job as a long-distance truck driver took him away from home a great deal. However, when he lost his job after being caught in charge of a truck while legally intoxicated, things began a downward spiral. James failed to get another job and when his unemployment benefits ran out, he began to "borrow" money from his mother that she could ill afford. He spent some of this on periodic binge drinking. When drunk, he raged at his mother, blaming her for his drinking and failure in life because his stepfather had focused his abuse on James, favouring Mrs. Crawford's other two children, who were fathered by him. James would occasionally also "push her around" after he had been drinking. Afterwards he would express considerable guilt and try to make it up to her, but the pattern would always recur.

Mrs. Crawford's own guilt about her husband's treatment of James was considerable, and the abuse was a familiar pattern from her marriage, so she told no one. Her other two sons didn't get along with James and lived at some distance, so they rarely visited. James was quite possessive and discouraged her from contact with friends, just as her husband had. The situation surfaced in the health care system when Mrs. Crawford fell to the floor after James pushed her, broke her arm, and she had to go to the hospital emergency room. While she was there, her family physician, who was concerned about her generally unhealthy appearance and noticed old bruising on her arms, asked directly if she was being beaten. Mrs. Crawford denied it. Not believing this and wanting to offer some help, the physician said that he thought that she needed "building up" and suggested she might join a health and nutrition club for older people at the local community centre. This centre, he knew, was run by a social worker who worked with older people, and who had had some success with another of his older patients who was in an abusive situation. When Mrs. Crawford hesitantly agreed, he arranged for Ms. Melanson, the social worker, to drop by with information about the club.

When Ms. Melanson arrived, Mrs. Crawford was at home on her own. Mrs. Crawford began to express doubts about going to the club as she didn't think James would like it because she needed to be there for him. However, the worker persuaded her that keeping up her health was important both for herself and in her role as a caring mother. When James arrived home, he demanded to know who Ms. Melanson was and what she was doing there. When she said that she was there to offer assistance to his mother, James said angrily that he could do with some help himself. He had just been at the local employment office and there were no decent jobs available—everything needed qualifications of some sort or another. Ms. Melanson seized the moment. She acknowledged his difficulty and offered to put him in touch with one of the centre's recently retired volunteers, who had spent a career in employment counselling. While he seemed surprised by the offer, James somewhat reluctantly agreed to it. In this way the worker was not only offering James something, but helping to assuage Mrs. Crawford's guilt and attempting to create some space for her to develop a life of her own.

Following this initial meeting, Ms. Melanson had occasional individual meetings with Mrs. Crawford to build a relationship with her through talking over how things were going and what she wanted for herself. Mrs. Crawford also developed a good relationship with her volunteer driver, enjoyed the activities of the club, and began to make friends. James enjoyed the individual and positive attention and assistance of the male volunteer for one of the few times in his life. He made progress in job search skills and eventually got an interview for a desk job with a transport company. However, when a temporary slowdown in the firm's business meant that the hiring would be postponed for six months, James responded by going on a drinking binge again. When he returned home, his abusive and threatening yelling at his mother distressed the new neighbours, who called the police. The police kept James in a cell overnight, but released him without charge as he had not physically attacked his mother and she would not agree to make any complaint against him. However, Mrs. Crawford had had enough. Based on earlier discussions with Ms. Melanson about what she wanted to do if the violence recurred, Mrs. Crawford called to ask her to arrange for a short-term admission to the local women's shelter. This was as much to protect her from changing her mind as to protect her from James. She then told James that though she loved him and wanted the best for him, she wanted him to make arrangements to live elsewhere. She gave him a week to get himself organized and do so. James complied, and after moving out, eventually got a job and a new relationship, and appeared to keep his drinking under control. Mrs. Crawford continued to build a life for herself.

One of the remarkable things about working with mistreated and neglected older people is encountering instances such as this. A woman who has lived in oppressive and violent relationships with men for most of her life is able to respond to support and assistance, and take action to change her situation. It suggests that despite a lifetime of abuse, some women retain a sufficiently positive sense of identity to be able to make a move when given the opportunity and support to make new choices. Podniek's (1992) research demonstrating the existence of the abused person's positive identity as "coper" provides a conceptual framework for this idea. What the social worker did here was to support the development of Mrs. Crawford's positive identity in a way that did not demand early on that she abandon her "caregiver as coper" role for James. At the same time, by providing an alternative source of support for James, she relieved Mrs. Crawford of the responsibility and guilt surrounding her relationship with James. This gave them both opportunities to grow.

Establishing the Rights of New Citizens
A number of programs have been developed in response to the concerns of representatives of new immigrants to Canada who are older adults from a variety of cultures. Discomfort with how they are being treated within their families arises from the observations of older people themselves or from leaders of immigrant communities. This demonstrates the importance of avoiding assumptions about the existence of universally good treatment for older people within traditional cultures. As we have noted above, workers in community centres, health clinics, or other services who become aware of instances of abuse, whether or not they are openly expressed by the abused, look for ways to assist these individuals and groups.

For new immigrants, there can be extra barriers to providing assistance beyond those encountered for more established members of communities. For instance, it is important to be able to offer two-way communication to inform seniors about their rights, and to offer accessible and helpful services when abuse is occurring. In this respect, language may be a barrier. A start has been made in breaking down this particular barrier. In most provinces, information about elder abuse is now translated into many different languages and widely distributed; however, getting messages to these new immigrants about their rights to good treatment can still be difficult.

Community and faith leaders often work to get the word out and to act as intermediaries in encouraging families to let their older members participate in community programs. In some instances the messages about abuse are delivered in a very direct way. As we have noted, at least one community centre providing services for multi-ethnic groups in a large city has worked with seniors to devise brief skits illustrating various types of abuse—for instance, financial exploitation or exploitation of their labour. These are presented on occasions such as open days in the centres, thus informing families in general about seniors' rights in Canadian society. The seniors mime the dramatic action so that any language barrier is overcome. Another strategy is that of offering group programs on apparently non-controversial matters, such as the health and nutrition group mentioned in the context of the domestic abuse case. Today, the term "health" can cover not only medical matters but also mental and emotional ones, allowing information to be given and questions to be raised about mistreatment and neglect from both seniors and those who are trying to assist them.

There can be some surprises in doing this work. One seniors' group received support from a fund for women's programs to run a group for immigrant women who identified themselves as abused. However, on the first occasion quite a number of those who came were men. Thinking that perhaps the men were there to oversee the women's participation, the group leader explained as tactfully as she could, through the interpreter, that the group was for women only. This caused consternation among both men and women. Further discussion revealed that the men were there because they also were experiencing abuse. The ultimate decision was to have two groups: one for men and the other for women. So while it is very important to take culture into account in working with new immigrants, sensitivity to cultural difference should not override the rights of new older Canadians to have equal treatment with those who are younger. Clearly, we should also avoid the assumption that these new Canadians want to retain norms of their cultures of origin that affect them negatively.

CONCLUSION

The complexity and uncertainty surrounding the state of knowledge about elder abuse and how to address it presents considerable challenges to the practitioner. Social workers working with older people in situations of mistreatment and neglect encounter unique demands. Their responses need to be rooted within a knowledge base that encompasses many aspects of how society constructs aging and older people, and how older people deal with those constructions in the ways they choose to live their lives. The examples given above illustrate the importance, within this context, of exploring how abuse or neglect is experienced by older people, as well as its significance and meaning for their lives. Social workers also need to be able to connect with these experiences in order to enter the mistreated or neglected older person's world in ways that are respectful, yet create opportunities for new choices that can offer a better life. As we have seen, such interventions require particular abilities: to make a connection that can lead to trust; to pursue reluctant clients in ways that will not further alienate them, but will engage them; and to be flexible and creative in seizing the moment to foster positive change.

At the same time, social workers do not do this work alone but in the context of a myriad other people offering assistance. These include friends, family, and volunteers offering "informal help," and other professionals providing assistance through the formal service delivery system (Harbison et al., 2004). Good practice involves fostering positive working relationships with these groups in order to provide assistance and find solutions to problems. In addition, it is important to recognize when to take leadership and when to acknowledge that others are likely to be more effective in reaching out to the older person in question. Finally, as practitioners, especially in rural and ethnocultural contexts where formal services are few, social workers must sometimes take the initiative in generating community responses to individual situations as well as for education and advocacy.

NOTES

1 The terms "elder abuse" and "elder abuse and neglect" are often used interchangeably in the literature, and may include "self-neglect," as they do here (Papadopoulous & La Fontaine, 2000). Both terms are understood as constructed meanings. Moreover, their use has long been questioned because the term "elder" has a very specific meaning in some traditional cultures, including among Canada's Aboriginal peoples. As a consequence, they are used within the chapter only where it is considered necessary to reference the construct. Where possible, the phrase "mistreatment and neglect of older people" is substituted.
2 The scenarios within this chapter are based on actual incidents of abuse and neglect known to the authors. However, the details have been changed considerably in order to disguise both the province in which they occurred and the people involved.

REFERENCES

Advocacy Centre for the Elderly (ACE). *The Advocacy Centre for the Elderly: A celebration of twenty years of operation, 1984–2004.* Toronto: Holly Street Advocacy Centre for the Elderly.

Aitken, L., & Griffin, G. (1996). *Gender issues in elder abuse.* London: Sage.

Annetzberger, G. (2005). (Ed.). *The clinical management of elder abuse.* New York: Haworth Press.

Aronson, J. (1992). Are we really listening? Beyond the official discourse on needs of older people. *Canadian Social Work Review, 9*(1), 73–87.

Aronson, J. (1993). Giving consumers as say in policy development: Influencing policy or just being heard? *Canadian Public Policy, 19*(4), 367–78.

Baltes, M.M. (1996). *The many faces of dependency in old age.* Cambridge, UK: Cambridge University Press.

Baltes, M., & Baltes, P. (1993). *Successful aging: Perspectives from the behavioural sciences.* New York: Cambridge University Press.

Barer, B.M. 1997. The secret shame of the very old: "I've never told this to anyone else." *Journal of Mental Health and Ageing 3*(3): 365–75.

Bartlett, R., & O'Connor, D. (2010). *Broadening the dementia debate: Towards social citizenship.* Bristol: Policy Press.

Baumann, G. (1989). Research rhetoric and the social construction of elder abuse. In J. Best (Ed.), *Images of issues: Typifying contemporary social problems.* New York: Aldine de Gruyter.

Beaulieu, M., Gordon, R., & Spencer, C. 2003. The abuse and neglect of older Canadians: Key legal and related issues. In A. Soden (Ed.), *Advising the older client* (pp. 197–233). Markham, ON: LexisNexis, Butterworths.

Bernard, M., & Scharf, T. (2007). (Eds.). *Critical perspectives on ageing societies.* Bristol: Policy Press.

Best, J. (Ed.). (1989). *Images of issues: Typifying contemporary social problems.* New York: Aldine de Gruyter.

Biggs, S., & Goergen, T. (2010). Theoretical development in elder abuse and neglect. *Ageing International, 35,* 167–70.

Biggs, S., & Haapala, I. (2010). Theoretical development and elder mistreatment: Spreading awareness and conceptual complexity in examining the management of socio-emotional boundaries. *Ageing International, 35,* 171–84.

Biggs, S., Lowenstein, A., & Hendricks, J. (2003). *The need for theory: Critical approaches to social gerontology.* Amityville, NY: Baywood.

Biggs, S., Phillipson, C., & Kingston, P. (1995). *Elder abuse in perspective.* Buckingham, UK: Open University Press.

Biggs, S., & Powell, J. (1999). Surveillance and elder abuse: The rationalities and technologies of community care. *Journal of Contemporary Health, 4*(1), 43–49.

Blaikie, A. (1999). *Ageing and popular culture.* Cambridge, UK: Cambridge University Press.

Blumer, H. (1971). Social problems as collective behaviour. *Social Problems, 18*(3), 298–306.

Bond, J., Coleman, P., & Peace, S. (1993). *Ageing in society: An introduction to social gerontology.* London: Sage.

Bradshaw, J. (1972). The concept of human need. *New Society, 30*(March), 640–43.

Bytheway, B. (1995). *Ageism.* Buckingham, UK: Open University Press.

Calasanti, T.M. (1996). Incorporating diversity: Meaning, levels of research, and implications for theory. *The Gerontologist, 36*(2), 147–56.

Calasanti, T.M., & Slevin, K.F. (2001). *Gender, social inequalities, and ageing.* Walnut Creek, CA: AltaMira Press.

Canadian Association of Retired Persons (CARP). Retrieved from: www.carp.ca/wp-content/uploads/2011/09/2010-Advocacy-Report.pdf.

Canadian Network for the Prevention of Elder Abuse (CNPEA). Retrieved from: www.cnpea.ca.

Canadian Pensioners Concerned, Nova Scotia. (2001). *The law and older Nova Scotians: A handbook of federal, Nova Scotia law, and other related issues* (2nd ed.). Halifax: Author.

Canadian Pensioners Concerned, Nova Scotia. (2003). *Battered and betrayed: Facing up to elder abuse in Nova Scotia.* Halifax: Author. (Original work published 1992.)

Chappell, N. (1999). *Older adults and volunteering.* Retrieved from: http://www
.volunteer.ca/volunteer/canada_adults_report_toc .htm.

Chappell, N., McDonald, L., & Stones, M. (2008). *Aging in contemporary Canada*
(2nd ed.). Toronto: Prentice-Hall.

Coleman, E. (1993). *The American health care system—betrayed by greed.* New
York: Vantage.

Collingridge, M. (1993). Protection of the elderly: Some legal and ethical issues.
Australian Journal on Ageing, 12(4), 32–36.

Cornwell, L. (2000). Nobody knows our sorrow: Working to eliminate elder
abuse affecting immigrant women from ethno-racial communities. In Institute of Human Development, Life Course and Aging (Ed.), *Proceedings of the
Ontario Elder Abuse Conference* (pp. 84–91). Toronto: Institute of Human
Development, Life Course and Aging.

Coughlan, S., Downe-Wamboldt, B., Elgie, R., Harbison, J., Melanson, P., &
Morrow, M. (1996). Mandatory reporting of suspected elder abuse and neglect:
A practical and ethical evaluation. *Dalhousie Law Journal, 19*(1), 45–70.

Cumming, E., & Henry, W.E. (1961). *Growing old: The process of disengagement.*
New York: Basic. de Beauvoir, S. (1972). *Old age.* London, UK: Andre Deutsch.

Decalmer, P., & Glendenning, F. (Eds.). (1997). *The mistreatment of elderly people*
(2nd ed.). London: Sage.

Epstein, L. (1994). The therapeutic idea in contemporary society. In A.S. Chambon & A. Irving (Eds.), *Essays in postmodernism and social work* (pp. 3–18).
Toronto: Canadian Scholars' Press.

Estes, C. (2001). *Social policy and ageing: A critical perspective.* Thousand Oaks,
CA: Sage.

Estes, C.L., Biggs, S., & Phillipson, C. (2003). Social theory, social policy, and
ageing: A critical introduction. Maidenhead, UK: Open University Press.

Fraser, N. (1986). *Unruly practices: Power discourse and gender in contemporary
social theory.* Oxford: Polity Press Blackwell.

Friedan, B. (1993). *The fountain of age.* New York: Simon and Schuster.

Furedi, F. (2002). *Culture of fear: Risk-taking and the morality of low expectation*
(rev. ed.). New York: Continuum.

Gee, E., & Gutman, G. (2000). *The overselling of population ageing: Apocalyptic
demography, intergenerational challenges, and social policy.* Toronto: Oxford
University Press.

Gilleard, G., & Higgs, P. (2000). *Cultures of ageing.* Harlow, UK: Pearson
Educational.

Gordon, R.M. (2001). Adult protection in Canada: Models, issues, and problems.
International Journal of Law and Psychiatry, 24(2–3), 117–34.

Griffin, L.W. (1994). Elder maltreatment among rural African-Americans. *Journal of Elder Abuse and Neglect, 6*(1), 1–27.

Groh, A. (2003). *A healing approach to elder abuse and mistreatment: The Restorative
Approaches to Elder Abuse Project.* Kitchener, ON: Community Care Access Centre of Waterloo Region. Retrieved from: www.mcmaster.ca/mjt/5-ib.htm.

Hall, F. (2005). *Old rage and the mistreatment and neglect of older people: Perspectives from the raging grannies* (Unpublished master's thesis). Dalhousie University, Halifax.

Hansell, E. (1999, November). Multicultural brochures on elder abuse. In Institute for Human Development, Life Course and Aging (Ed.), *Proceedings: Second National Conference on Elder Abuse* (pp. 73–79). Toronto: Institute for Human Development, Life Course and Aging, University of Toronto.

Harbison, J. (1999a). Models of intervention for "elder abuse and neglect": A Canadian perspective on ageism, participation, and empowerment. *Journal of Elder Abuse and Neglect, 10*(3/4), 1–17.

Harbison, J. (1999b). The changing career of "elder abuse and neglect" as a social problem in Canada: Learning from feminist frameworks. *Journal of Elder Abuse and Neglect, 11*(4), 59–80.

Harbison, J. (2000). The repudiated self: The failure of social welfare policy for older people. In U. McCluskey & C.A. Hooper (Eds.), *Psychodynamic perspectives on abuse: The cost of fear* (pp. 291–306). London: Jessica Kingsley.

Harbison, J. (2002). Rising to the challenge: Why seniors do elder abuse work. *A Shared Concern: Newsletter of the BC Coalition to Eliminate Abuse of Seniors, 10*(2), 17–19.

Harbison, J. (2008). Stoic heroines or collaborators: Ageism, feminism, and the provision of assistance to abused old women. *Journal of Social Work Practice 22*(2), 221–34.

Harbison, J. (2011). Older people crime and state intervention. In B. Perry (Ed.), *Diversity, crime, and justice in Canada* (pp. 253–76). Toronto: Oxford University Press.

Harbison, J., Beaulieu, M., Coughlan, S., Karabanow, J., VanderPlaat, M., & Wildeman, S (2008, August 31). *Conceptual frameworks: Understandings of "elder abuse and neglect" and their implications for policy and legislation.* Background paper for Human Resources and Social Development Canada Round Table on Elder Abuse (HRSDC).

Harbison, J., Coughlan, S., Beaulieu, M., Karabanow, J, VanderPlaat, M., Wildeman, S., & Wexler, E. (2012, in press). Understanding "elder abuse and neglect": A critique of the assumptions underpinning the responses to the mistreatment and neglect of older people. *Journal of Elder Abuse and Neglect, 24*(2).

Harbison, J., Coughlan, S., Karabanow, J., & VanderPlaat, M. (2004). Offering the "help" that's needed: Responses to the mistreatment and neglect of older people in a rural Canadian context. *Rural Social Work, 9*, 147–57.

Harbison, J., Coughlan, S., Karabanow, J., & VanderPlaat, M. (2005). A clash of cultures: Rural values and service delivery to mistreated and neglected older people in Eastern Canada. *Practice: A Journal of the British Association of Social Workers, 14*(4), 229–46.

Harbison, J., & Morrow, M. (1998). Re-examining the social construction of "elder abuse and neglect": A Canadian perspective. *Ageing and Society, 18*, 691–711.

Hazan, H. (1994). *Old age constructions and deconstructions.* Cambridge, UK: Cambridge University Press.

Higgs, P. (1995). Citizenship and old age: The end of the road? *Ageing and Society, 15,* 535–50.

Hightower, H. (2002). Senior citizen counsellors terminated. *A Shared Concern: Newsletter of the BC Coalition to Eliminate Abuse of Seniors, 10*(2), 1, 4–7.

Hummert, M.L., Wiemann, J.M., & Nussbaum, J.F. (1994). *Interpersonal communication in older adulthood.* Thousand Oaks, CA: Sage.

International Network for the Prevention of Elder Abuse. Retrieved from: http://www.inpea.net/.

Irving, A. (1999). Waiting for Foucault: Social work and the multitudinous truth(s) of life. In A.S. Chambon, A. Irving & L. Epstein, *Reading Foucault for social work* (pp. 27–50). New York: Columbia University Press.

Kappeler, S. (1995). *The will to violence: The politics of personal behaviour.* Cambridge, UK: Polity.

Katz, S. (1996). *Disciplining old age: The formation of gerontological knowledge.* Charlottesville, VA: University Press of Virginia.

Kingston, P., & Penhale, B. (1995). *Family violence and the caring professions.* Basingstoke, UK: Macmillan.

Kozma, A., & Stones, M. (1995). Issues in the measurement of elder abuse. In M. MacLean (Ed.), *Abuse and neglect of older Canadians: Strategies for change* (pp. 117–28). Toronto: Canadian Association on Gerontology, Thompson Educational.

Kurrle, S., & Sadler, P. (1994). *Assessing and managing abuse of older people.* Sydney, NS: NSW Office on Ageing.

Kurrle, S., Sadler, P., & Cameron, I. (1992). Patterns of elder abuse. *The Medical Journal of Australia, 157,* 673–76.

Laws, G. (1995). Understanding ageism: Lessons from feminism and postmodernism. *The Gerontologist, 35*(1), 112–18.

Leroux, T.G., & Petrunik, M. (1990). The construction of elder abuse as a social problem: A Canadian perspective. *International Journal of Health Services, 20*(4), 651–63.

Lowenstein, A. (2009). Elder abuse and neglect—"old phenomenon": New directions for research, legislation, and service developments. *Journal of Elder Abuse and Neglect, 21,* 278–87.

Lynott, R.J., & Lynott, P.P. (1996). Tracing the course of the theoretical development in the sociology of aging. *The Gerontologist, 36*(6), 749–60.

MacLean, M. (Ed.). (1995). *Abuse and neglect of older Canadians: Strategies for change.* Toronto: Canadian Association on Gerontology, Thompson Educational.

Manning, N. (1985). *Social problems and welfare ideology.* Aldershot, UK: Gower.

Markson, E.W. (2003). *Social gerontology today: An introduction.* Los Angeles: Roxbury.

Marriott, A. (1997). The psychology of elder abuse and neglect. In P. Decalmer & F. Glendenning (Eds.), *The mistreatment of elderly people* (2nd ed.). London, UK: Sage.

Matsuoka, A., Clarke, A., & Murphy, D. (2010). Restorative justice-based mediation for elder abuse among ethno-racial minority seniors. In D. Durst & M. MacLean (Eds.), *Diversity and aging among immigrant seniors in Canada: Changing faces and graying temples* (pp. 149–67). Calgary: Detselig Enterprises.

McDonald, L., & Collins, A. (2000). *Abuse and neglect of older adults: A discussion paper.* Ottawa: National Clearinghouse Family Violence, Health Canada, Ottawa. Retrieved from: http://www.hc-sc.gc.ca/hp pb/family violence/html/neglect/english.

McDonald, L., Collins, A., & Tergal, J. (2006). The abuse and neglect of older adults in Canada. In R. Alaggia & C. Vine (Eds.), *Cruel but not unusual: Violence in Canadian families* (pp. 425–66). Waterloo, ON: Wilfrid Laurier University Press.

McKreight, B. (1999). Kerby Rotary House. In Institute for Human Development, Life Course and Aging (Ed.), *Proceedings of the Second National Conference on Elder Abuse* (pp. 239–43). Toronto: Institute for Human Development, Life Course and Aging, University of Toronto.

McPherson, B.D., & Wister, A. (2008). *Aging as a social process: Canadian perspectives.* Toronto: Oxford University Press.

Morgan, G. (1997). Images of Organization (2nd ed.). Thousand Oaks, CA: Sage.

Morgan, K.S. (1994). *Medicine meets virtual reality: Global healthcare grid.* Washington, DC: IOS.

Mullaly, R.(2002). *Challenging oppression: A critical social work approach.* Toronto: Oxford University Press.

Nascimento, O., Sestrem, L., & the Christopher House Elder Abuse Prevention Group. (2000). Elder abuse prevention: Seniors acting out. In Institute of Human Development, Life Course and Aging (Ed.), *Proceedings of the Ontario Elder Abuse Conference* (pp. 178–80). Toronto: Institute of Human Development, Life Course and Aging, University of Toronto.

National Initiative for the Care of the Elderly (NICE). Retrieved from: http://www .nicenet.ca.

Neysmith, S. (1995). Power in relationships of trust: A feminist analysis. In M. MacLean (Ed.), *Abuse and neglect of older Canadians: Strategies for change* (pp. 43–54). Toronto: Canadian Association on Gerontology, Thompson Educational.

Neysmith, S., & MacAdam, M. (1999). Controversial concepts. In S. Neysmith (Ed.), *Critical issues for future social work practice with aging persons* (pp. 43–54). New York: Columbia University Press.

Ogrodnik, L. (2007). *Seniors as victims of crime.* Catalogue no. 85F0033MIE. Ottawa: Statistics Canada, Canadian Centre for Justice Statistics, Ministry of Industry. Retrieved from: www.statcan.ca.

Papadopoulos, A., & La Fontaine, J. (2000). *Elder abuse: Therapeutic perspectives in practice.* Chesterfield, UK: Winslow Press.

Penhale, B. (1999). Researching elder abuse: Lessons for practice. In P. Slater & M. Eastman (Eds.), *Elder abuse: Critical issues in policy and practice* (pp. 1–23). London, UK: Age Concern.

Phillipson, C. (1993). Abuse of older people: Sociological perspectives. In P. Decalmer & F. Glendenning (Eds.), *The mistreatment of elderly people* (pp. 76–87). London, UK: Sage.

Phillipson, C., & Biggs, S. (1995). Elder abuse. In P. Kingston & B. Penhale (Eds.), *Family violence and the caring professions.* London, UK: Macmillan.

Pillemer, K. (1993). *Methodological issues in the study of elder abuse.* Working paper no. 1. London: Action on Elder Abuse.

Ploeg, J., Hutchinson, B., MacMillan, H., & Bolan, G. (2009). A systematic review of interventions for elder abuse. *Journal of Elder Abuse and Neglect, 21,* 187–210.

Podnieks, E. (1992). Emerging themes from a follow-up study of Canadian victims of elder abuse. *Journal of Elder Abuse and Neglect, 4*(1/2), 59–111.

Poirier, D. (1992). The power of social workers in the creation and application of elder protection statutory norms in New Brunswick and Nova Scotia. *Journal of Elder Abuse and Neglect, 4*(1/2), 113–34.

Pritchard, J. (Ed.). (1996). *Elder abuse work: Best practice in Britain and Canada.* London, UK: Jessica Kingsley.

Quinn, M.J., & Tomita, S.K. (1997). *Elder abuse and neglect: Causes, diagnosis, and intervention strategies.* New York: Springer.

Riley, M.W., Kahn, R.L., Foner, A. (Eds.). (1994). *Age and structural lag: Society's failure to provide meaningful opportunities in work, family, and leisure.* New York: Wiley.

Rowe, J.W., & Kahn, R.L. (1998). *Successful aging.* New York: Pantheon.

Rozanova, J., Northcott, H.C., & MacDaniel, S.A. (2006). Seniors and portrayals of intra-generational and intergenerational inequality in the *Globe and Mail. Canadian Journal on Aging, 25*(4), 376–86.

Singh Sodi, L., & Joshi, A. (2000). "Saithi Mere," friend of mine. In Institute of Human Development, Life Course and Aging(Ed.), *Proceedings of the Ontario Elder Abuse Conference* (p. 83, abstract of film of the same name by Amadeus Media Productions). Toronto: Institute of Human Development, Life Course and Aging.

Sprey, J. (1990). *Fashioning family theory: New approaches.* Newbury Park, CA: Sage.

Tam, S., & Neysmith, S. (2006). Disrespect and isolation: Elder abuse in Chinese communities. *Canadian Journal on Aging, 25*(2), 141–51.

Tatara T. (Ed.). (1999). *Understanding elder abuse in minority populations.* Philadelphia: Taylor and Francis.

Tester, S. (1996). *Community care for older people: A comparative perspective.* New York: St. Martin's Press.

Townsend, P. (1981). The structured dependency of the elderly: The creation of social policy in the twentieth century. *Ageing and Society, 1*(1), 5–28.

Truscott, D. (1996). Cross-cultural perspectives: Toward an integrated theory of elder abuse. *Policy Studies, 17*(4), 287–98.

Walsh, C.A., Ploeg, J., Lohfeld, L., Horne, J., MacMillan, H., & Lai, D. (2007). Violence across the lifespan: Interconnections among forms of abuse as described by marginalized Canadian elders and their care-givers. *British Journal of Social Work, 37*(3), 491–514.

Ward-Hall, C. (2001, July). *Educating seniors and others about abuse: A decade of experience from a provincial organization.* Paper presented at the meeting of the 17th Congress of the International Association of Gerontology, Vancouver.

Way-Clark, R., & Pace, J. (1994). *Battered and betrayed: Facing up to abuse of the elderly in Nova Scotia.* Halifax: Canadian Pensioners Concerned, Nova Scotia.

Webb, S.A. (2006). *Social work in a risk society: Social and political perspectives.* Basingstoke, UK: Palgrave Macmillan.

Whittaker, T. (1997). Rethinking elder abuse: Towards an age and gender integrated theory of elder abuse. In P. Decalmer & F. Glendenning (Eds.), *The mistreatment of elderly people* (2nd ed., pp. 116–28). London: Sage.

Wilson, G. (2000). *Understanding old age: Critical and global perspectives.* London, UK: Sage.

Winterdyk, J.A., & King, D.E. (1999). *Diversity and justice in Canada.* Toronto: Canadian Scholars' Press.

Wolhuter, L., Olley, N., & Denham, D. (2009). *Victimology: Victimization and victims' rights.* London, UK: Routledge-Cavendish.

Conclusion

BUILDING THE FUTURE

RAMONA ALAGGIA AND CATHY VINE

There is no doubt that violence in Canadian families is an urgent social problem. The aim of this book was to bring distinctive areas of knowledge and practice together and shine an intense light on the vast and often hidden dimensions of violence. In doing so, we tried to expose readers to advances in knowledge and practice and, most importantly, to provide useful information to better serve individuals and groups personally affected by violence. In particular, there is a critical intersection where "private" ails require public action, and we hope that we have strengthened the case for intervention at multiple levels—individual, family, community, and policy—as a way to focus and mobilize change.

Indisputably, Canadians of all ages—from infants in arms to older adults—bear the cruel brunt of violence in their families. Equally disturbing is the persistent and pervasive character of this problem: violence in families and intimate relationships has existed for a very long time. Women and children in particular have been controlled through various forms of abuse and overt violence for centuries. History is replete with examples of child-rearing practices steeped in long traditions of physical punishment and other harsh practices. High rates of child poverty continue to contribute to child neglect, and whole communities trying to support families are plagued by systemic injustices. Aboriginal children, families, and communities were decimated by colonization. This legacy is painfully obvious in increased rates of violence across Aboriginal communities today. Similarly, children and adults with disabilities experience higher rates of abuse, and

questions persist about how violence and disability are inextricably connected. Lesbian, gay, bisexual, transgender, and queer community members
are caught in the bind of trying to draw attention to the partner violence
hidden within their communities, while at the same time fearing they will
fuel negative stereotyping by a homophobic society. Many of these groups
are disenfranchised and have been both similarly and uniquely oppressed.
The in-depth examination of the historical *and* current experiences and
issues faced by these and other groups makes it impossible to pretend that
relationship-based violence is a recent phenomenon or only the problem
of particular individuals and groups.

Throughout the book we used a range of perspectives to examine the
many faces of violence in intimate relationships and families. We attempted
to convey the common and unique experiences of violence experienced
by groups that have been marginalized. We used a developmental lens to
examine the experiences of children as they grow up with violence, or are
targets of abuse and neglect in their homes, or substitute family settings.
Clearly, numerous forms of child abuse occur commonly across Canada.
Physical punishment of children continues to be a legally sanctioned form
of assault, while similar acts committed against all other people are illegal.
Overwhelming research evidence points to negative short- and long-term
effects and yet as recently as 2004, the Supreme Court of Canada upheld
Section 43, despite the United Nations Committee calling for its repeal and
a legislative ban on "all forms of violence against children, however light."
Starting as early as infancy, new research helps uncover the neurobiological
effects of violence. However, research with infants in relation to family
violence continues to be a neglected area. Advances in trauma and resilience knowledge strengthen the understanding that practitioners bring to
working with individuals and groups affected by violence.

We probed the abuse of women in their intimate relationships by providing an analysis of the history, theory, and context along with offering current clinical practice approaches. Women are abused in their relationships
on a regular basis. The media headlines alone remind us that they continue
to die at the hands of their partners. While the deaths may continue to be
newsworthy, not one of the stories is new. Immigrant women are particularly vulnerable because of their status issues and the precarious position
they hold during the immigration-granting process. It is unclear how many
withhold disclosure of violence in their lives for fear of jeopardizing their
citizenship application and because of cultural prohibitions. What is more
astounding is how old the story really is for all women. With respect to the
experiences of older adults, we recognize that how we view older people and
the evolution of our thinking about "elder abuse" has taken a different path

than that travelled by theorists, researchers, and practitioners concerned with other forms of violence in the family. Again, older Canadians—both women *and* men—are abused on a regular basis in their homes and in the institutions established to care for them.

Common. Frequent. Regular. These terms permeate the literature. The rates of violence and abuse experienced by people, across the lifespan, in Canada, is significant. Do we have policies and legislation in place that recognize the scope of this problem? Do our practices support individuals to make real choices in dealing with the violence in their lives? No, not yet. The work presented in this book actively and directly connects the lives and experiences of adults and children and how their efforts to live with and/or escape violence are affected by policy, legislation, system intervention, and practice. Over the years, tremendous strides have been made; the work chronicled here alone is testament to this. However, the scope of the challenges—the work still to be done—has never been more apparent. The extensive material and analyses presented bring these challenges to the fore. Scatter-shot "prevention" programs look all the more ill conceived and futile when presented against the backdrop of these profound and long-standing problems. Nevertheless, "prevention" programs—programs designed to raise awareness and make people resistant to violence—do have a role to play: they may be the one time that a child or adult grasps some further understanding of what he or she may be experiencing at home. But what are we saying about ourselves as a society if "prevention" is limited to one-off, violence-inoculation activities?

The call to action continues. The need for legislative and policy reform is clear. Throughout the book, individual contributors make recommendations for significant change along policy, legislative, legal, theoretical, research, systems intervention, and practice lines. Some suggestions represent fresh thinking and fundamentally challenge the approaches taken thus far. Other recommendations echo the calls that have come long before— because they still have not yet been heard.

And the silence is resounding. With recent federal budget cuts, the risks have just *increased* for individuals and groups who depend on specific programs and services for support to manage, if not leave, intolerable situations. Broad public education programs concerning human development, intimate relationships, and parenting are critically needed. It feels impossible at times to imagine creating a public agenda focused on health and wellness, where our aspirations for child and family life are supported through strong public policy, when it is hard to even hold on to the gains that have been made.

As we reflect on the past, survey the present, and build the future, we hope that the material in the book encourages and challenges readers to:

- support all people—young and old—who live with violence;
- hold individuals and systems accountable for maintaining violence;
- educate colleagues and others to increase knowledge and awareness;
- advocate for individual, community-level, systemic, and structural changes to address violence; and
- inspire others to join us.

We dedicate our work to the people—young and old—who believe so strongly that no one else should be subjected to the abuse they have endured.

CONTRIBUTORS

Ramona Alaggia is associate professor of social work and the Factor-Inwentash chair in children's mental health at the University of Toronto, where she teaches social work practice with children and their families. Funded by the Social Sciences and Humanities Research Council of Canada, her studies examine disclosure processes of child sexual abuse and intimate partner violence survivors, the impact of various forms of justice on survivors of sexual violence, and help-seeking for survivors of intimate partner violence. The results of this research have culminated in Dr. Alaggia's most recent publication, *Risky business: An ecological analysis of intimate partner violence disclosure.* She currently acts as consultant to and evaluates programs delivering services to survivors and their children, and to fathers who expose their children to intimate partner violence.

Cyndy Baskin is an assistant professor in the School of Social Work at Ryerson University. Cyndy is of Mi'kmaq and Celtic descent, and has worked primarily within Toronto's Aboriginal community for the past twenty years in the areas of community development, culture-based programming, healing, and training. Her work focuses on family violence interventions, restorative justice, Aboriginal ways of helping, and anti-colonial research and writing. She has also authored two novels, *The invitation* (Toronto: Sister Vision, 1992) and *Sage* (Toronto: Sister Vision, 1999), and a text published in 2011 titled *Strong helpers' teachings: The value of indigenous knowledges in the helping professions* (Toronto: Canadian Scholars' Press).

Rachel Birnbaum is an associate professor, cross-appointed in childhood studies and social institutions and social work, King's University College, Western University. She teaches clinical practice and research with children, individuals, and families, as well as in ethics and the law, family mediation, and collaboration between law and social work. Her research focus is on evaluation and outcome interventions for children and families during times of separation and/or divorce. She has presented and published both nationally and internationally. She has over twenty years of clinical practice experience advocating for children's interests in separation and/or divorce matters before the court.

April A. Collins, M.S.W., R.S.W., is a researcher and practitioner at the Centre for Addiction and Mental Health. Her primary area of research and expertise is in the area of family intervention. Her research interests also include abuse of older people, models of service delivery for the seriously mentally ill and first-episode psychosis.

Julie Dergal works in the area of gerontology and health. Her specific research interests include caregiving for older people with dementia, quality of care in nursing homes, elder abuse, and homelessness among older adults.

Shaindl Diamond is a psychologist working in Toronto. She received her undergraduate degree from Trent University in women's studies and psychology, and her M.A. and Ph.D. from the Ontario Institute for Studies in Education/University of Toronto in counselling psychology. Her academic interests include lesbian/gay/bisexual/transgender/queer psychology, multicultural psychology, critical psychology, mad studies, and anti-oppressive approaches in psychotherapy.

Molly Dragiewicz is associate professor of criminology in the Faculty of Social Science and Humanities at the University of Ontario Institute of Technology. Her recent books include *Equality with a vengeance: Men's rights groups, battered women, and antifeminist backlash* (Boston: Northeastern University Press, 2011) and the *Routledge handbook of critical criminology* (New York: Routledge, 2012), co-edited with Walter DeKeseredy. She received the New Scholar Award from the American Society of Criminology Division on Women and Crime in 2009.

Joan E. Durrant is a child clinical psychologist and a professor of family social sciences at the University of Manitoba. For more than twenty years, her research has focused on the psychological and cultural factors that contribute to parental use of corporal punishment, and on the history and impact of law reform internationally. She was the lead author of the *Joint statement on physical punishment of children and youth* (Ottawa: Children's Hospital of Eastern Ontario, 2003), which has been endorsed by more than 450 Canadian organizations. She co-edited *Global pathways to abolishing physical punishment: Realizing children's rights* (New York: Routledge, 2011), an exploration of the process of law reform in nineteen nations.

Barbara Fallon has written extensively in the field of child welfare and is one of the collaborators on the Canadian Incidence Study of Reported Child Abuse and Neglect (CIS). Dr. Fallon was involved with the first cycle of the CIS in 1998 as a co-manager, and was the manager in 2003 for both the CIS-2003 and the Ontario Incidence Study of Reported Child Abuse and Neglect (OIS-2003). Currently, Dr. Fallon is the director and co-investigator for the CIS-2008 and the principal investigator for the OIS-2008. Dr. Fallon's specific research interests include child welfare workers, organizational behaviour, and service delivery effectiveness.

J. Roy Gillis is associate professor in the Department of Applied Psychology and Human Development at the Ontario Institute for Studies in Education at the University of Toronto. He is a past recipient of the Teaching and Education Award from Division 44, the Society for the Psychological Study of Lesbian, Gay, Bisexual, and Transgender Issues, of the American Psychological Association. His research includes developing models of the psychological impact of hate crime victimization and same-sex partner abuse. He has written extensively about the impact of homophobia on society, and conducts research on the teaching of sexual orientation diversity. Professor Gillis is also active in health promotion research, especially HIV-prevention research; the prevention of classroom bullying; international gay, lesbian, bisexual, and transgender issues; and serves as the representative of the Canadian Psychological Association for the International Network on Lesbian, Gay, Bisexual Concerns, and Transgender Issues in Psychology. He is also the founding editor of the open-access journal, the *Canadian Online Journal of Queer Studies in Education*.

Joan Harbison is an adjunct professor in the Faculty of Graduate Studies and the School of Social Work at Dalhousie University, Halifax. Her primary interests lie in the application of critical theory within the field of aging. Her current research focuses on the theorization of the mistreatment of older people. This is an area in which she has published widely in both national and international journals.

Angélique Jenney is the director of Family Violence Services for Child Development Institute, a multi-service child and family agency in Toronto. Dr. Jenney has over sixteen years of experience in engaging both victims and perpetrators of family violence in intervention and prevention services within the violence against women and children's mental health sectors. Dr. Jenney's research and program development has been devoted to understanding and responding to the impact of violence in families. Her current research and practice interests include family-based interventions for childhood trauma, child welfare responses to domestic violence cases, the experience of mothering in the context of trauma, and reflective approaches to teaching and training social work students. She regularly promotes knowledge translation and exchange through her international work, invited speaking engagements, community-based workshops, and conference presentations.

Colleen Lundy is a social work professor at Carleton University. Among her publications is a book on the history of social work in Canada (with Therese Jennissen), *One hundred years of social work: A history of the profession in English Canada 1900–2000* (Waterloo, ON: Wilfrid Laurier University Press, 2011), the first complete history of social work in Canada. A second edition of her book, *Social work, human rights, and social justice: A structural approach to practice* (Toronto: University of Toronto, 2011) makes an important contribution to the understanding of structural social work and a social justice/human rights perspective. The text has been revised throughout and includes four new chapters, including one on immigrant and refugee settlement. Her research on women, particularly gender violence, includes projects in Sweden, Russia, and Cuba. Her current research focuses on the history and current realities of social work in the Far North (Nunavut, Northwest Territories, and the Yukon).

Bruce MacLaurin is an assistant professor at the Faculty of Social Work, University of Calgary and a senior researcher at Wood's Homes. He has been a co-investigator on the three cycles of the Canadian Incidence Study of Reported Child Abuse and Neglect, as well as the principal investigator for provincial studies in British Columbia, Alberta, and Saskatchewan. His research and publishing has focused on child maltreatment, child welfare service delivery and outcomes, youth at risk, and street-involved youth. He has more than fifteen years of front-line and management experience in non-profit children's services in Alberta and Ontario.

Sarah Maiter, M.S.W., Ph.D., is associate professor in the School of Social Work at York University, Faculty of Liberal Arts and Professional Studies. Her research focuses on cross-cultural/racial issues and child maltreatment with the aim of improving interventions for minority families involved with the child welfare system. Dr. Maiter has served on the board of directors of the American Professional Society on the Abuse of Children, is working on several funded research projects relating to child maltreatment and to minority issues, and is a reviewer for a number of social work journals.

Lynn McDonald is the interim director of the Institute for Human Development, Life Course and Aging, and professor in the Faculty of Social Work at the University of Toronto. Her primary area of research and expertise is the older worker and retirement. Her research interests also include elder abuse, older homeless adults, and women and poverty.

Anne McGillivray is professor of law at the University of Manitoba and author of over fifty published works. Her research centres on children's rights, including the law and history of corporal punishment, sexual abuse, the child as witness, the Aboriginal child, childhood, and the child in literature. Her book, *Black eyes all of the time: Intimate violence, Aboriginal women, and the justice system* (Toronto: University of Toronto Press, 1999), investigates the experience of abuse and the role of law from childhood to adulthood. Her edited collection, *Governing childhood* (Aldershot, UK: Dartmouth, 1997), looks at state roles in the formation of childhood. She is presently investigating children's rights in the context of education and religion.

Pamela McKinley holds a Master of Social Work degree from Dalhousie University. For a number of years, Pamela's practice focused on working with older adults in situations of mistreatment and neglect. In particular she was involved in programs offering group and peer support to this population. Pamela is currently employed by the Nova Scotia Department of Health.

Ina Motoi is a professor of social work in the Département de développement humain et social de l'Université du Québec en Abitibi-Témiscamingue (UQAT) and has taught and conducted research there since 2003. She recently co-authored *La femme, sa sexualité, et son pouvoir sexuel* (Québec : Presses de L'Université de Québec, 2011). She has studied sexology, philosophy, and social work. She was the director of Réseau des femmes du Sud de l'Ontario and SOS femmes, a province-wide emergency phone line for francophone women in Ontario (1985–2003). In this role, she participated in founding French-speaking services for women in southern Ontario.

Bruce D. Perry is the senior fellow of the Child Trauma Academy, a not-for-profit organization based in Houston, and adjunct professor in the Department of Psychiatry and Behavioral Sciences at Northwestern University

School of Medicine in Chicago. Dr. Perry is the author, with Maia Szalavitz, of *The boy who was raised as a dog* (New York: Basic Books, 2007), a best-selling book based on his work with maltreated children, and *Born for love: Why empathy is essential and endangered* (New York: HarperCollins, 2010). Over the last thirty years, Dr. Perry has been an active teacher, clinician, and researcher in children's mental health and the neurosciences, holding a variety of academic positions.

Donna Pettipas holds a certificate in gerontology from Mount Saint Vincent University and a master's degree in social work from Dalhousie University. For many years Donna has worked in a variety of settings and circumstances that have given her experience in working with older citizens in situations of mistreatment or neglect. She is currently employed by the Nova Scotia Department of Community Services.

Deborah Sinclair is in the third year of her doctoral studies at the Factor-Inwentash Faculty of Social Work at the University of Toronto. Her research is funded by a CIHR fellowship through its IMPART program (Intersections of Mental Health Perspectives in Addictions Research Training) under the auspices of the BC Centre of Excellence for Women's Health. She was the YWCA 2010 Woman of Distinction for Social Justice. Over her thirty-five-year involvement in the social justice and feminist movements, Deborah has worked as a feminist social work activist, clinician, writer, public speaker, trainer, researcher, community organizer, and expert witness in order to contribute to the prevention of and recovery from domestic violence and trauma.

Sonia A. Sobon has a Ph.D. in educational psychology from the University of Alberta and is a registered psychologist in private practice in Alberta. She holds an associate faculty position at St. Stephen's College, University of Alberta campus, where she teaches lifespan psychology in their Master of Psychotherapy and Spirituality program. Sonia also teaches adult learning and development in the Faculty of Extension at the University of Alberta. Her research contributions include reanalysis of a national US database focused on reported cases of maltreatment of children with disabilities, and her doctoral research explored attachment of at-risk adolescents.

Richard Sobsey is a professor emeritus of educational psychology and associate director of the J.P. Das Developmental Disabilities Centre at the University of Alberta, where he also serves as an adjunct professor at the John Dossetor Health Ethics Centre. He has worked with children and adults with disabilities and their families since 1968. His primary research interests are understanding violence against people with disabilities, and healthy adjustments of families with children with severe disabilities.

Susan Strega is an associate professor in the School of Social Work, University of Victoria, where she is responsible for the Child Welfare Specialization. She has worked in most areas of social work, including child protection, and is a long-time feminist activist. She is the co-editor, with Leslie Brown, of *Research as resistance: Critical, indigenous, and anti-oppressive approaches* (Toronto: Canadian Scholars' Press, 2005); the co-editor, with Sohki Aski Esquao (Jeannine Carrière), of *Walking this path together: Anti-racist and anti-oppressive child welfare practice* (Black Point, NS: Fernwood, 2009); and the co-editor, with Julia Krane, Simon Lapierre, and Cathy Richardson, of *Failure to protect: Moving beyond gendered responses* (Black Point, NS: Fernwood, forthcoming).

Nico Trocmé is the Philip Fisher chair in social work and director of the Center for Research on Children and Families at McGill University, School of Social Work. Professor Trocmé's research focuses on the epidemiology of child maltreatment and on measuring child welfare service outcomes.

Leslie M. Tutty is a full professor with the Faculty of Social Work at the University of Calgary. Over the past twenty-five years, her research has focused on prevention programs and services for family violence, including a number of evaluations of shelter and post-shelter programs for abused women, support groups for abused women, treatment for adult and child victims of sexual abuse, and groups for men who abuse their partners. Recent research interests include homelessness. From 1999 to 2011, Leslie served as the academic research coordinator of RESOLVE Alberta, a tri-provincial research institute on family violence.

Michael Ungar is a social worker and marriage and family therapist who works with youth and families in child welfare, mental health, education, and corrections settings. A Killam professor of social work at Dalhousie University and co-director of the Resilience Research Centre, he leads a $5 million program of research involving researchers from more than a dozen countries. He has published over one hundred articles and book chapters on resilience and clinical practice, and is also the author of eleven books, including a novel, *The social worker* (Halifax: Pottersfield Press, 2011). Among his professional and trade non-fiction books are: *The social ecology of resilience: A handbook of theory and practice* (New York: Springer, 2012); *Counseling in challenging contexts: Working with individuals and* *families across clinical and community settings* (Belmont, CA: BrooksCole, 2011); *Too safe for their own good: How risk and responsibility help teens thrive* (Toronto: McClelland and Stewart); and *Strengths-based counseling with at-risk youth* (Thousand Oaks, CA: Corwin Press, 2006).

Cathy Vine engages in research, writing, and action projects to advance the well-being and rights of children and youth. Recently she worked with Ontario's Office of the Provincial Advocate for Children and Youth to support young people to hold the first-ever Youth Leaving Care Hearings at Queen's Park, home of the Ontario Legislature. Previously, Cathy oversaw publication of forty reports on children's issues, and worked extensively with children, youth, and adults affected by child abuse and intimate violence, conducting research and developing innovative support and clinical services. She taught part-time at the School of Social Work, Ryerson University. Publications include the recent co-authored report, *Resilience: Successful navigation through significant threat* (Toronto: Child and Family Partnership, 2010) and the co-authored book, *Gardens of shame: The tragedy of Martin Kruze & the sexual abuse at Maple Leaf Gardens* (Vancouver: Greystone Books, 2002).

INDEX